Cracknell's
Law Students' Companion

Conflict of Laws

Cracknell's
Law Students' Companion

Conflict of Laws

Second Edition

ROBERT M MACLEAN LLB, Dip LP, LLM, PhD
Solicitor

and

GWYN TOVEY LLB, PGCE
Senior Lecturer in Law, University of Glamorgan

Series Editor
D G Cracknell, LLB
of the Middle Temple, Barrister

OLD BAILEY PRESS

OLD BAILEY PRESS LIMITED
The Gatehouse, Ruck Lane, Horsmonden, Kent TN12 8EA

First published 1969
Second Edition 1996

© Old Bailey Press Ltd 1996

All Old Bailey Press publications enjoy copyright protection and the copyright belongs to the Old Bailey Press Ltd.

All rights reserved. No part of this publication may be reproduced or transmitted in any form or by any means, electronic, mechanical, photocopying, recording or otherwise, or stored in any retrieval system of any nature without either the written permission of the copyright holder, application for which should be made to the Old Bailey Press Ltd, or a licence permitting restricted copying in the United Kingdom issued by the Copyright Licensing Agency.

Any person who infringes the above in relation to this publication may be liable to criminal prosecution and civil claims for damages.

ISBN 1 85836 035 8

British Library Cataloguing-in-Publication.

A CIP Catalogue record for this book is available from the British Library.

Printed and bound in Great Britain.

Contents

Preface to the Second Edition	ix
Preface to the First Edition	xi
Cases	1
Statutes	185
Wills Act 1837 [536–541]	185–187
Bills of Exchange Act 1882 [542–545]	187–188
Foreign Marriage Act 1892 [546–551]	189–191
Evidence (Colonial Statutes) Act 1907 [552]	191–192
Perjury Act 1911 [553]	192
Maintenance Orders (Facilities for Enforcement) Act 1920 [554–558]	192–196
Administration of Justice Act 1920 [559–563]	197–199
Administration of Estates Act 1925 [564–566]	199–202
Evidence (Foreign, Dominion and Colonial Documents) Act 1933 [567]	202–203
Foreign Judgments (Reciprocal Enforcement) Act 1933 [568–578]	203–209
National Assistance Act 1948 [579–580]	209–210
Marriage Act 1949 [581–586]	210–213
Arbitration Act 1950 [587–629]	214–230
Marriage (Enabling) Act 1960 [630]	230
Oaths and Evidence (Overseas Authorities and Countries) Act 1963 [631–632]	230
Wills Act 1963 [633–638]	231–232
Diplomatic Privileges Act 1964 [639–646]	232–240
Carriage of Goods by Road Act 1965 [647–651]	240–241
Consular Relations Act 1968 [652–664]	241–257
International Organisations Act 1968 [665–678]	257–268
Family Law Reform Act 1969 [679]	268
Administration of Justice Act 1970 [680]	268

Administration of Estates Act 1971 [681–683]	268–270
Maintenance Orders (Reciprocal Enforcement) Act 1972 [684–716]	271–290
Civil Evidence Act 1972 [717]	290–291
European Communities Act 1972 [718–720]	291–293
Matrimonial Causes Act 1973 [721–728]	293–297
Domicile and Matrimonial Proceedings Act 1973 [729–731]	297–298
Arbitration Act 1975 [732–738]	298–300
Evidence (Proceedings in Other Jurisdictions) Act 1975 [739–744]	300–303
Legitimacy Act 1976 [745–751]	303–305
Adoption Act 1976 [752–770]	305–314
Unfair Contract Terms Act 1977 [771–772]	315
Employment Protection (Consolidation) Act 1978 [773–774]	316
Domestic Proceedings and Magistrates' Courts Act 1978 [775–778]	316–318
State Immunity Act 1978 [779–797]	319–326
Arbitration Act 1979 [798–803]	327–331
Protection of Trading Interests Act 1980 [804–811]	331–335
Magistrates' Courts Act 1980 [812–813]	336–338
Limitation Act 1980 [814–817]	339–340
Civil Jurisdiction and Judgments Act 1982 [818–869]	340–406
Foreign Limitation Periods Act 1984 [870–875]	406–408
County Courts Act 1984 [876]	408
Matrimonial and Family Proceedings Act 1984 [877–881]	408–410
Companies Act 1985 [882–894]	411–417
Child Abduction and Custody Act 1985 [895–923]	417–434
Family Law Act 1986 [924–961]	434–452
Recognition of Trusts Act 1987 [962–963]	452–455
Diplomatic and Consular Premises Act 1987 [964–967]	456–458
Family Law Reform Act 1987 [968–971]	458–460
Children Act 1989 [972–978]	460–464

Contracts (Applicable Law) Act 1990 [979–983]	464–472
Foreign Corporations Act 1991 [984]	472–473
Social Security Contributions and Benefits Act 1992 [985–986]	473
Maintenance Orders (Reciprocal Enforcement) Act 1992 [987]	473
European Communities (Amendment) Act 1993 [988–994]	474–475
Private International Law (Miscellaneous Provisions) Act 1995 [995–1008]	475–479
Rules of the Supreme Court 1965 [1009–1013]	479–483
Glossary	485
Index	499

Preface
to the Second Edition

When the first edition of Cracknell's Law Students' Companion on the Conflict of Laws was written, man had just set foot on the Moon and the United Kingdom had not joined its Western European neighbours in the Common Market. Much has changed since then, not least the content of the Conflict of Laws. Not all would agree that the changes have been beneficial. The criticisms of the Rome Convention, and its incorporation into English law via the Contracts (Applicable Law) Act 1990, have given rise to at least as many academic articles as one would expect to encounter following a controversial House of Lords' opinion on a matter of public importance. The debate over what is now the Private International Law (Miscellaneous Provisions) Act 1995 was just as polarised.

Nevertheless, the authors of this second edition are delighted to have been given the opportunity to summarise more than 500 of the most important cases in this fast-moving area of law. Developments up to 1 November 1995 have been taken into account, although the 1995 Act, which received the Royal Assent on 8 November 1995, has also been covered. Cases reported after 1875 are High Court decisions unless it is stated otherwise.

The pleasures and benefits to be reaped from studying this fascinating, all-pervading subject are enormous. It is hoped that the selection of cases, and the differing amount of detail in each, together with the statutes and glossary, will lead to this book fulfilling its objective of being a 'Law Students' Companion' and, as such, will promote beneficial study amongst undergraduates and postgraduates alike.

R M MACLEAN and G TOVEY

Preface to the First Edition

English Conflict of Laws is very largely dependent on case law. But it is of comparatively recent growth, and not too often the subject of litigation, so that the number of important reported cases has so far kept within reasonably manageable limits. In the light of these considerations, it is hoped that a book like the present one can fairly aspire to set out most of the rules of the subject while preserving the framework in which they were developed, ie that of the cases themselves. But, like its predecessors in the series, it is chiefly designed as a source-book for those who cannot see as much as they would like of the Law Reports, and as an aide-mémoire for those who have forgotten some or all of what they once saw in them.

In the case summaries, the aspect chiefly emphasised is the reasoning on which the ultimate decision rests, because in the Conflict of Laws this is always important and frequently complex. The cross-references between cases are a little more elaborate than in some of the earlier volumes in the series, but this is an inevitable result of the tendency of many of the leading cases to contain significant rulings upon two or more distinct issues. By contrast the facts of the cases are usually stated fairly shortly.

The author acknowledges with gratitude the helpful and courteous assistance which he has received from the General Editor, Mr D G Cracknell, and from the publishers.

M R CHESTERMAN
May 1969

Cases

A (a minor) (abduction), Re [1988] 1 FLR 365 **[1]**
(Court of Appeal)

The child of a marriage of Canadian citizens living in Canada was taken to England by his mother who did not intend to return to Canada and her husband. Within a year, the Supreme Court of British Columbia had ordered, by consent, that the parents be granted joint custody of the child. However, as the mother intended to keep the child in England, she sought an order making the child a ward of court with care committed to her. The father instituted proceedings under the Child Abduction and Custody Act 1985. It was not disputed that the child had been wrongfully detained in England under Article 3 of the Hague Convention on the Civil Aspects of International Child Abduction as enacted by the 1985 Act. Accordingly, under Article 12, the court was bound to 'order the return of the child forthwith' unless the mother could establish under Article 13(b) that returning him would lead to a 'grave risk' which 'would expose the child to physical or psychological harm or otherwise place the child in an intolerable situation ...'. EWBANK J ordered the return of the child after receiving assurances from the parents that the child would return to Canada in the mother's care and that this was acceptable to the father until such time that the British Columbia court ordered otherwise. The mother appealed contending that EWBANK J had impermissibly exercised discretion. *Held*, (1) the judge had not exercised discretion in concluding that any psychological harm which might result was not of sufficient degree to come within Article 13(b) of the Hague Convention: his judgment was correctly based on the facts of the case and the wording in Article 13(b). Accordingly, he had no power to refuse an order for the child's return; (2) the consequences of an order could not be ignored and evidence for this proposition could be found within Article 13. (See also *Re A and another (minors: abduction), Re A and another (minors)(abduction: acquiescence), Re G (a minor)(abduction)* and the consolidated appeal in *In re H (minors) (abduction: custody rights)*.)

A and another (minors: abduction), Re [1991] 2 FLR 241 **[2]**
(Court of Appeal)

In a quarrel which developed during a trans-Atlantic telephone conversation, an English-born woman on holiday in England with her two children told her American husband that their marriage was over and that she would not be returning to him. He agreed to the children remaining with their mother for a specific period after which he petitioned for a divorce and he sought an order for custody of the children in the Arizona court. Under the law of Arizona, where the children were habitually resident, the parents had joint custody rights. Six months after the quarrel he visited the children and stayed at his wife's home. During his visit, he informed his wife and members of her family that he did not intend to remove the children. However, shortly after arriving back in the USA, he obtained a decree of divorce and he succeeded with his application for custody of the children. Accordingly, he then instituted proceedings under the Child Abduction and Custody Act 1985 applying for the return of the children. The mother contested the application alleging the father had acquiesced in her retention of the children. If her contention was correct, then the case came within the exceptions in Article 13 of the Convention to the mandatory rule in Article 12 that children wrongfully retained should be returned. Her contention was rejected at first instance and she appealed citing the same ground of appeal. *Held*, dismissing the appeal, (1) the mother had breached the joint rights of custody of the parties on a date which was no later than the end of the period in which the father had consented to the children staying in England with their mother; (2) the fact that the father had not delayed in seeking a custody order in Arizona was inconsistent with the alleged acquiescence on his part; (3) the judge at first instance had concluded from evidence that, inter alia, the mother had not believed the father's remarks in relation to the non-removal of the children. Thus, there was no acquiescence on the father's part and the judge had made the correct decision. (See also *Re A (a minor)(abduction)*, *Re A and another (minors)(abduction: acquiescence)* and the consolidated appeal in *In re H (minors)(abduction: custody rights)*.)

A and another (minors) (abduction: acquiescence), Re [3]
[1992] 1 All ER 929 (Court of Appeal)

Shortly after the divorce in Australia of British subjects who were resident there, the woman returned to England with her two children. The Australian Family Court had not made any order relating to the children as it was satisfied with the arrangements made for their welfare which included residence with their mother and access by the father at weekends and at other times by consent. In an exchange of correspondence between the man and his ex-wife, the man noted that what she had done was illegal but, for the sake of the children, he would not make an issue of it and he requested that his letters and presents be passed on to them and that he should be kept informed of their progress. However, having obtained legal advice and having ascertained that his ex-wife was going to remain in England indefinitely, the man applied for the return of the children under the Hague Convention on the Civil Aspects of International Child Abduction. In proceedings in England, the mother conceded that removing the children was wrongful under the Convention but that the court should exercise its discretion under Article 13 of the convention and not order the children's return because of the father's acquiescence and/or that their return would place them in an 'intolerable situation' under Article 13(b) since the father no longer had remunerative employment and that he was dependent on state benefits, thus making him unable to provide for the children financially. *Held*, (1) the father's acceptance of what the mother had done constituted acquiescence; but (2) since the mother failed to establish her case under Article 13(b), as she and the children were dependent on state benefits in England, the case would be remitted to the High Court for consideration under Article 13 of whether the children should be returned to Australia. (See also *Re A and another (minors: abduction)* and *Re G (a minor) (child abduction: enforcement)*.)

A Co Ltd v Republic of X and Commission of the European Communities [1994] 1 Lloyd's Rep 111 [4]

A garnishee order nisi was made in respect of all debts due or accruing due by Barclays Bank plc to the Republic of X, including the amounts held to the credit of this State in a 'Special SIP [Sectoral Import Programme] Account' in a particular branch of the bank. The hard currency (money), in ECUs, was provided for the use of the State by the transfer of Community funds to the account in question. It was intended for the purchase and import into the State of machinery and equipment for use by agricultural producers in that country. The issue to be decided by the court was whether the order should be made absolute in respect of this debt. The Commission of the European Communities had obtained leave to intervene on the basis that the order interfered with its rights, was contrary to EC law and was a wrong exercise of the discretion given to the court. The judgment creditors of the Republic of X challenged the Commission's submissions. *Held*, (1) 'the money was supplied to and accepted by the State from the Communities for specific purposes, which did not include the discharge of judgment debts incurred by the State. ... [so] English law would treat the fund in question as subject to some trust or similar equitable right sufficient either to take it outside the meaning of 'debt' in [RSC] O.49 or at least to make it inappropriate to exercise my discretion under the Rule to make the order absolute' (*per* SAVILLE J); (2) the fact that the debt due from the bank to the State was an 'English debt' (ie governed by English law) did not establish that the relationship between the EC and the State which preceded and resulted in the English debt was also governed by English law; (3) such rights and obligations as were created existed as a matter of public international rather than English or indeed any other private law. The relevant relationship was one under a European treaty (the Third Lome Convention) which had its own disputes resolution provisions; (4) the indebtedness of the bank to the State could not be described as the property or assets of the EC; (5) the account was no more than a debt due to the State from the bank within the meaning of RSC O.49; (6) as there were no enforceable EC rights, and making the order absolute would place the garnishee (the bank) under no liability to the Republic of X, it was a proper exercise of the court's discretion to make the garnishee order absolute.

Abate v Abate (orse Cauvin) [1961] P 29 [5]

A man domiciled in Italy dissolved his marriage by obtaining a decree of nullity in Switzerland, the Swiss court's jurisdiction being based on the fact that the man had removed his name from a civil population register in an Italian town and placed it on a similar register in Switzerland. The decree was recognised in Italy. *Held*, it would also be recognised in England, on the ground that in the court of the spouses' domicile at the time when it was granted it would be treated as valid. (See also *Salvesen (or Von Lorang)* v *Administrator of Austrian Property*.)

Abidin Daver, The [1984] 1 AC 398 (House of Lords) [6]

Following a collision in the Bosphorus between two vessels, one owned by the Cuban plaintiffs and the other by Turkish defendants, the Cuban vessel was arrested in Turkish territorial waters at the suit of the defendants who then commenced proceedings in Turkey. Two months later, the plaintiffs brought an action in rem in the Admiralty Court against the defendants for damages consequent upon the collision, a writ having been served on a sister ship of the defendants' vessel. However, the defendants' application for a stay was granted by the judge at first instance (SHEEN J) who decided that the Turkish court was a forum in which justice could be done between the parties at substantially less inconvenience and expense and that since the defendants had undertaken to provide security for any cross-claim the plaintiffs might make in the Turkish action, the plaintiffs would not be deprived of a legitimate personal or juridical advantage. SHEEN J's decision was reversed by the Court of Appeal and the defendants appealed to the House of Lords. *Held*, by a unanimous decision, 'Where a suit about a particular subject matter between a plaintiff and a defendant is already pending in a foreign court which is a natural and appropriate forum for the resolution of the dispute between them, and the defendant in the foreign suit seeks to institute as plaintiff an action in England about the same matter to which the person who is plaintiff in the foreign suit is made defendant, then the additional inconvenience and expense which must result from allowing two sets of legal proceedings to be pursued concurrently in two different countries where the same facts will be in issue and the testimony of the same witnesses required can only be justified if the would-be plaintiff can establish objectively by cogent evidence that there is some personal or juridical advantage that would be available to him in the English action that is of such importance that it would cause injustice to him to deprive him of it' (*per* LORD DIPLOCK). SHEEN J had correctly exercised his discretion in staying the English proceedings. Moreover, 'the time is now ripe to acknowledge frankly [that] the field of law with which this appeal is concerned [is] indistinguishable from the Scottish legal doctrine of forum non conveniens' (*per* LORD DIPLOCK). (See also *Spiliada Maritime Corporation* v *Cansulex*.)

Abouloff v Oppenheimer & Co (1882) 10 QBD 295 [7]
(Court of Appeal)

In proceedings in a Russian court, the plaintiff obtained a judgment against the defendants for the return of certain goods or their value. When she sought to enforce it in England, the defendants pleaded that she had obtained it by fraudulently concealing the fact that throughout the proceedings she had had the goods in question in her possession. *Held*, this was a good defence, on the ground that an English court would not enforce a foreign judgment where the foreign court had misled into pronouncing it be fraud on the part of the successful party. (See also *Vadala* v *Lawes* and *Owens Bank* v *Bracco*; contrast *House of Spring Gardens* v *Waite*.)

Adams v Cape Industries [1990] Ch 433 (Court of Appeal) [8]

Cape Industries, a company incorporated in England, had been involved with the mining, in South Africa, and marketing of asbestos. Cape marketed asbestos in the USA through NAAC, one of its subsidiary companies, which was incorporated in Illinois. The marketing of asbestos for Cape had constituted only a minor part of NAAC's activities: much of its work was in conducting its own business within the USA. Capasco, another subsidiary company of Cape, had the responsibility for marketing asbestos throughout the rest of the world. The use of the asbestos in a Texas factory had led employees and ex-employees to institute claims for damages for personal injuries as a result of exposure to asbestos dust. The claims against, inter alia, Cape, Capasco and NAAC, were upheld in the Texan town of Tyler. This concluded 'the Tyler 1 actions'. A second group of plaintiffs then proceeded with their claims in Tyler ('the Tyler 2 actions'). However, NAAC had been lawfully liquidated and Cape and Capasco refused to have anything to do with the claims. Nevertheless, the actions proceeded and, eventually, a default judgment was given against them. The trial judge awarded a sum in excess of $15,000,000 and directed that plaintiffs' counsel should determine the bands of compensation and who should benefit by what amount, although neither Cape nor Capasco had assets anywhere in the USA. Accordingly, an attempt was made to enforce the judgments in England. *Held*, (1) neither Cape nor Capasco was present in Texas. SLADE LJ said that there was a difference between parent and subsidiary companies. Accordingly, the presence of NAAC in Illinois did not establish the presence of Cape or Capasco anywhere in the USA. In discussing whether a corporation was present in a foreign country, SLADE LJ expressed the view that: 'The English courts will be likely to treat a trading corporation incorporated under the law of one country ('an overseas corporation') as present within the jurisdiction of the courts of another country only if either (i) it has established and maintained ... a fixed place of business of its own in the other country and for more than a minimal period of time has carried on its own business at or from such premises by its servants or agents ... or (ii) a representative of the overseas corporation has for more than a minimal period of time been carrying on *the overseas corporation's* business in the other country at or from some fixed place of business ... [and where the overseas corporation has had a representative in the foreign country a] not exhaustive ... [or] necessarily conclusive [list of questions will need to be answered in order to determine whether the corporation was present in the foreign country. The list of questions includes] (a) whether or not the fixed place of business from which the representative operates was originally acquired for the purpose of enabling him to act for the overseas corporation; (b) whether the overseas corporation has directly reimbursed him ... for the cost of his accommodation ... [and] the cost of his staff; (c) what other contributions, if any, the overseas corporation makes to the financing of the business of the representative; (d) whether the representative is remunerated ... by commission, or by fixed regular payments ...; (e) what degree of control the overseas corporation exercises over the running of the business conducted by the representative; (f) whether the representative reserves ... part of his accommodation [or] part of his staff for conducting business relating to the overseas corporation; (g) whether the representative displays the overseas corporation's name at his premises or on his stationery, and if so, whether he does so in a way as to indicate that he is the representative over the overseas corporation; (h) what business, if any, the representative transacts as a principal exclusively on his own behalf; (i) whether the representative makes contracts with customers ... in the name of the overseas corporation ...; [and] (j) whether the representative requires specific authority in advance before binding the overseas corporation.' (2) The Tyler court was not competent to give judgment against Cape and Capasco as neither was present in Texas. (3) The decision of the trial judge in the Tyler court to permit counsel for the plaintiffs to determine which plaintiffs would receive a quantum of damages determined by counsel following a judicial guideline of an average of $75,000 per claimant was contrary to the requirements of substantial justice contained in English law. (4) Even though the defendants had not applied to have the default judgment set aside they would not be precluded from relying on breach of natural justice because they had not been informed of the unusual way in which the trial judge or the plaintiffs arrived at their decisions. (See also *Littauer Glove Corporation* v *F W Millington Ltd* and *Vogel* v *Kohnstamm*.)

Adams v National Bank of Greece SA [1961] AC 255 [9]
(House of Lords)

In 1956, soon after the first instance decision in *National Bank of Greece and Athens SA* v *Metliss*, the forerunner of this case, the Greek Government passed a decree amending the amalgamation decrees of 1953 retrospectively, so that the new bank was deemed to have been since 1953 the universal successor of its two predecessors except as regards certain liabilities including those arising under an old bank's guarantee of bonds. In 1958, various bondholders sued the new bank for principal and interest. *Held*, this new decree of 1956 did not relieve the new bank from liability under the guarantee. If treated as a law as to the discharge of contractual liabilities, it could not affect a liability arising from a contract governed by English law and clearly binding on the new bank between 1953 and 1956. If treated as a law as to succession, it was ineffective because English courts did not recognise foreign retrospective laws altering rights acquired under a succession. If treated as a law as to status, it would not be recognised because in omitting to transfer some of the liabilities it was unjust and contrary to the notion of a true amalgamation. (See also *National Bank of Greece and Athens SA* v *Metliss* and *Lynch* v *Provisional Government of Paraguay*.)

Addison v Brown [1954] 1 WLR 779 [10]

A man domiciled in California, USA, signed an agreement with his wife (who was living in England) whereby he promised to pay her a weekly sum for maintenance. The agreement stated that neither party should seek to vary its terms in divorce proceedings in 'any court' and that any variation ordered in such proceedings should be ineffective. The man later obtained a divorce in California, where the court adopted the agreement while reserving the right to vary it. *Held*, the wife could sue in England for arrears due under the agreement. An agreement purporting to oust the jurisdiction of a foreign court would not be treated as contrary to English public policy, even though the same agreement in relation to an English court would be so treated. (See also *Saxby* v *Fulton*; compare *Hope* v *Hope*.)

Agnew v Usher (1884) 51 LT 752; affd (1884) 51 LT 752 [11]

The plaintiffs issued a writ claiming rent due under a lease of English land and obtained leave under (what is now) RSC O.11, r.1(1)(h), to serve it on the defendant lessees, in Scotland, their place of residence. *Held*, service should be set aside, because an action for rent did not involve a 'contract, obligation or liability *affecting* land', as required in the rule.

Al Battani, The [1993] 2 Lloyd's Rep 219 [12]

The plaintiffs claimed that the value of their cargo of potatoes and citrus fruit shipped from Egypt to Germany on board the defendants' vessel fetched £200,000 less than anticipated because of its deterioration in transit. They claimed that this was caused by the defendants' breach of contract in delaying delivery by directing their vessel to berth in Cyprus to collect another cargo for delivery to the UK before proceeding to Germany to delver the plaintiffs' cargo. The plaintiffs maintained that the defendants had contracted for their vessel to proceed directly from Alexandria, Egypt, to Hamburg, Germany. The defendants denied there was such a contract and they relied on clause 3 of the bill of lading which provided that: 'Any dispute arising under this bill of lading shall be decided in the country where the carrier has his principal place of business and the law of that country shall apply except as provided elsewhere.' In response to the plaintiffs taking an action in rem against one of eight ships named in a writ, the defendants applied for a stay of action contending that the parties had agreed that disputes should be heard in a court in Egypt and that England was not the natural or appropriate forum: an Egyptian court was clearly and distinctly more appropriate for trial of the action. *Held*, that as the plaintiffs had founded jurisdiction in the English courts as of right then, applying *The Spiliada*, it was for the defendants to establish that England was not the natural or appropriate forum and to establish that Egypt was the more appropriate forum. Whereas SHEEN J believed that there were many factors in this case which led to the conclusion that an Egyptian court was the natural forum for trial of the action, despite many factors militating against trial in Egypt, he then went on to consider whether there were circumstances by reason of which justice required that a stay should not be granted. Having highlighted that, (1) there would be a delay in translating documents and survey reports from English to Arabic; (2) that an action in Egypt would take five years to come to judgment; and that (3) it was to the advantage of both parties to litigate in England, there was 'a strong cause for not granting a stay. Accordingly this motion is dismissed.' (See also *The El Amria* and *Spiliada Maritime Corporation* v *Cansulex*.)

Albeko Schuhmaschinen AG v Kamborian Shoe [13]
Machine Co Ltd (1961) 111 L Jo 519

The defendant, an English manufacturing company, posted a letter in England to the plaintiff, a Swiss company, offering to appoint the plaintiff as its distribution agent in Switzerland. The plaintiff alleged that it accepted this offer by a letter posted in Switzerland, but no such letter was received by the defendant. Under English law, the general rule is that the contract is complete on the posting of a letter of acceptance, but under Swiss law, this letter would have to reach the defendant. In an action by the plaintiff for breach of contract, *Held*, even if the letter of acceptance had been posted (which was not proved), there was still no completed contract. The proper law of the contract, if completed, would be Swiss law and under that law receipt of the letter of acceptance was essential to bring the contract into existence. (See also *Re Bonacina, Le Brasseur* v *Bonacina* and *Kelly* v *Cruise Catering Ltd and Kloster Cruise Ltd*.)

Alcock v Smith [1892] 1 Ch 238 (Court of Appeal) [14]

A bill of exchange, drawn and accepted by English firms and payable in England to bearer, was seized from the plaintiff, its holder, in Norway in the course of execution proceedings by a creditor, and was sold by public auction. This sale conferred good title on the purchaser under Norwegian law, but under English law the plaintiff was still entitled to it. The purchaser endorsed the bill to the defendant, who took in good faith. *Held*, the plaintiff could not impeach the defendant's title to the bill, because the effect of the public sale as between two parties claiming title was determined according to the law of Norway, the country where the sale took place. (See also *Cammell* v *Sewell* and *Embiricos* v *Anglo-Austrian Bank*.)

Ali v Ali [1968] P 564 [15]

Two Muslims domiciled in India were married there according to Muslim law, which permitted polygamy. In 1961, the husband acquired an English domicile. He later instituted divorce proceedings based on the wife's desertion in 1959, whereupon she filed a cross-petition alleging adultery in and since 1964. *Held*, the husband's acquisition of English domicile in 1961 converted the marriage from a potentially polygamous one into a monogamous one, because it precluded him from taking another wife. Thus the court had jurisdiction, but only as regards the adultery, this being the only matrimonial offence occurring since 1961. (See also *Ohochuku* v *Ohochuku*.)

Amin Rasheed v Kuwait Insurance Co [1984] 1 AC 50 [16]
(House of Lords)

The plaintiff was a Liberian shipping corporation carrying on business from Dubai. The plaintiff's cargo vessel, the *Al Wahab*, had been detained by Saudi Arabian authorities and its master and crew were imprisoned for the attempted smuggling of oil. The plaintiff, who denied the allegation, and who had insured the vessel with the Kuwait company, claimed for the total constructive loss of the vessel. The insurance policy was based on the standard Lloyd's policy and was written in English although it was expressed to be issued in Kuwait which was also the place where claims were payable. However, the policy contained no express statement of the law governing the contract and at the time of issuing the policy there was no indigenous law of marine insurance in Kuwait. At first instance, BINGHAM J had held that Kuwait law was the proper law of the contract and, accordingly, he had no discretion to serve notice of the writ out of the jurisdiction. In the alternative, if the plaintiff's claim did come within the scope of RSC O.11, he would exercise his discretion against allowing service out of the jurisdiction as the plaintiff had not discharged its onus of showing the case was a proper one for service out of the jurisdiction. However, with regard to the proper law of the contract, the House of Lords *Held*, (1) the proper law of the contract was English law since it was the law which the parties intended to apply. Since no intention was expressed, it was for the court to presume the proper law of the contract from the terms of the contract contained in the insurance policy and the relevant surrounding circumstances. (2) The plaintiff corporation had failed to discharge its onus under RSC O.11, r.4(2) of making it 'sufficiently to appear to the court that the case is a proper one for service out of the jurisdiction under this order'. Kuwait was the forum conveniens. (See also *Mackender* v *Feldia AG*.)

Andros, Re, Andros v Andros (1883) 24 Ch D 637 [17]

In an English will, residuary personalty was bequeathed to the sons of the testator's nephew. One of the nephew's sons was born out of wedlock, but the subsequent marriage of his parents legitimated him under the law of Guernsey, where his father was domiciled throughout. *Held*, the legitimation under Guernsey law would be recognised so as to entitle the son to inherit under the will. There was no reason to confine the bequest to sons legitimate under English domestic law only. (See now the Family Law Reform Act 1987 ss1, 18 and 19.)

Angelo v Angelo [1967] 3 All ER 314 [18]

A German woman married a domiciled Englishman in England, without changing her nationality. She later left him, returned to live in Germany and some five months later obtained a decree of divorce there. *Held*, the decree would be recognised in England because the wife had a 'real and substantial connection' with Germany, deriving from her habitual residence there and her nationality. (See also *Brown* v *Brown* [1968] 2 All ER 11.)

Anglo-Iranian Oil Co Ltd v Jaffrate, The Rose Mary [19]
[1953] 1 WLR 246 (Supreme Court of Aden)

The Government of Iran passed an oil nationalisation law which, although general in its terms, had the sole purpose and effect of expropriating without compensation an oil concession in Iran which it had granted some years earlier to an English company and promised not to annul. A year later, the company brought an action in detinue in respect of a cargo of crude oil which had been taken from the concession since its expropriation and was on board a ship lying in Aden. *Held*, the action would succeed. The validity of the nationalisation law could be brought into question because the company against which it operated was not a subject of Iran. It should be refused recognition because, on principles of international law, expropriation without compensation was invalid. (See also *Lecouturier* v *Rey* and *Luther* v *Sagor*; contrast *Williams and Humbert Ltd* v *W & H Trade Marks (Jersey) Ltd*.)

Anna H, The (1994) The Independent 8 September [20]
(Court of Appeal)

Owners of cargo lately laden on the *Anna H* brought an action in rem against the shipowners who applied to set aside the claim on the basis that they were domiciled in Germany and, in accordance with Article 2 of the Brussels Convention 1968, that is where they should be sued. *Held*, Article 57 of the

Brussels Convention provided that that Convention was subject to the provisions of other international Conventions. In this case, the International Convention Relating to the Arrest of Seagoing Ships 1952, which provided that 'a ship flying the flag of one of the Contracting States may be arrested in the jurisdiction of any of the Contracting States in respect of any maritime claim', took precedence. Moreover, since the Arrest Convention requires only that the legal effect of judicial detention of the ship is that it becomes security for a maritime claim, not that the plaintiff's commercial motive is solely to obtain security, the arrest constituted 'the detention of a ship by judicial process to secure a maritime claim' within the meaning of Article 1(2) of that Convention. (See also *The Po* and *The Tatry*.)

Annesley, Re, Davidson v Annesley [1926] Ch 692   [21]

An English testatrix whose domicile of origin was English lived in France for 56 years, then died leaving a will of movables. Under French law, her power to dispose of her property by will was limited, but a French court would refer the question of her succession by her lex nationalis because she had never taken the formal steps required by French law for obtaining a French domicile. *Held*, (1) her lex domicilii at death was French law because 'the question whether a person is or is not domiciled in a foreign country is to be determined in accordance with the requirements of English law as to domicile, irrespective of the question whether the person in question has or has not acquired a domicile in the foreign country in the eyes of that country' (*per* RUSSELL J); and (2) this law governed her dispositions of her movable property, but it referred the matter to English law, her lex nationalis; however, English law in turn referred it back to French law and this second reference or 'renvoi' was accepted by French law, with the final result that her power of testation was limited as in French law. (See also *Casdagli* v *Casdagli* and *Re Ross, Ross* v *Waterfield*.)

Anziani, Re, Herbert v Christopherson [1930] 1 Ch 407   [22]

By a document executed in Italy and expressed to operate as a conveyance inter vivos and as a will, a domiciled Italian woman purported to exercise a power of appointment conferred on her in her marriage settlement. The settlement was in English language and form, the trustees resided in England and the funds subject to the power were in England. The exercise of the power was valid under English law but void under Italian law, by virtue of a rule of public policy which made it a requirement of essential validity that such a document should be executed as a 'public document'. *Held*, even though the document exercising the power had been admitted to probate in England, it was none the less invalid, because its validity was a matter for Italian law, the lex domicilii of the appointer and the lex actus. (See also *Lee* v *Abdy*.)

Apt (orse Magnus) v Apt [1948] P 83 (Court of Appeal)   [23]

A woman domiciled and resident in England married a man domiciled and resident in Argentina by proxy, the ceremony being performed in Argentina in the presence of a representative appointed by the wife. Proxy marriages were valid under Argentinian law but not under English law. *Held*, the marriage was valid. The question whether consent could be given by proxy was a question of formalities and therefore governed by Argentinian law, the lex loci celebrationis. The recognition of proxy marriages celebrated abroad did not contravene English public policy. (See also *Hooper (orse Harrison)* v *Hooper*.)

Arab Monetary Fund v Hashim (No 3) [1991] 2 AC 114 [24]
(House of Lords)

The Arab Monetary Fund was established as a corporate body under an international agreement involving twenty Arab States and Palestine. It was accorded 'independent juridical capacity' in the United Arab Emirates and, in particular, in Abu Dhabi where the AMF had its headquarters. The AMF wished to bring an action in England against its former Director-General, Dr Hashim, claiming that he had stolen money from it. Dr Hashim put forward a defence based on the decision in *Rayner v DTI* [1989] Ch 72 (in which it was held that an international treaty had no effect in English law unless it was specifically incorporated under legislation), claiming that since the AMF had been established by treaty under international law it had no status under English law in the absence of English legislation and, accordingly, it could not sue. *Held*, the comity of nations required that the courts of the UK should recognise a corporate body created by the law of a foreign state (such as the UAE) recognised by the Crown. Since the UAE decree conferring corporate personality on the AMF was established not just under international law but under the law of the UAE, then it was entitled to sue in England. (See also *Bumper Development Corporation v Commissioner of Police of the Metropolis*.)

Arab Monetary Fund v Hashim (No 6) [25]
(1992) The Times 24 July

AMF sought an injunction to restrain Dr Hashim and his wife and son from continuing proceedings in California, USA, against a former employee of AMF's who had made an affirmation on behalf of AMF in their proceedings against Dr Hashim. Dr Hashim's action in California was based on the claim that the former employee's affirmation was false and malicious and part of a conspiracy to ruin himself (Dr Hashim) and his family. *Held*, an action to restrain proceedings in a foreign jurisdiction should normally be granted only in very narrowly restricted circumstances and that when the question was simply one of justice between the litigants, uninfluenced by differences of public policy, the normal assumption was that the English court had no superiority over a foreign tribunal in knowing what justice required. In this case, the question of whether the Californian proceedings should be stayed or should proceed did not raise any question which could not equally and more appropriately be decided in California. Accordingly, AMF's application would be dismissed. (See also *SNIA v Lee Kui Jak*; compare *Castanho v Brown & Root (UK) Ltd*.)

Arcado v Haviland (Case 9/87) [1988] ECR 1539 [26]
(European Court of Justice)

In proceedings relating to the wrongful termination of an agency agreement, the Cour d'Appel, Brussels, referred the following question to the ECJ: 'Are proceedings relating to the wrongful repudiation of an (independent) commercial agency agreement and the payment of commission due under such an agreement proceedings in matters relating to a contract within the meaning of Article 5(1) of the Brussels Convention ...?' *Held*, the answer was in the affirmative. 'Proceedings relating to the wrongful repudiation of an independent commercial agency agreement and the payment of commission due under such an agreement are proceedings in matters relating to a contract within the meaning of Article 5(1) ...'. (See also *Mulox IBC Ltd v Geels*.)

Armitage v Attorney-General; Gillig v Gillig [1906] P 135 [27]

A wife settled separately from her husband in South Dakota, USA, and obtained a divorce there on the ground of cruelty. The husband was domiciled in New York, where the divorce was recognised as valid. Neither English law nor New York law regarded cruelty as a ground for divorce. *Held*, the divorce was none the less entitled to recognition in England. English courts would recognise a divorce which, though not granted in the court of the spouses' domicile, would be recognised as valid by that court.

Askew, Re, Marjoribanks v Askew [1930] 2 Ch 259 [28]

An Englishman domiciled in Germany had a daughter by a woman other than his wife then later married this woman after having divorced his wife. Under German law, but not under English law, this legitimated the child. Because of the father's nationality, a German court would refer the daughter's status to English law. *Held*, the daughter was legitimate. A foreign legitimation per subsequens matrimonium was recognised in England if it was valid according to the father's lex domicilii at the time of the birth and of the marriage. In this case, the lex domicilii was German law, but a German court would refer the question to English law; however, English law would refer it back again to German law as the lex domicilii, whereupon (according to expert evidence) a German court would accept the 'renvoi' and apply German law. (See also *Re Wellington (Duke of), Glentanar v Wellington*; compare *Re Grove, Vaucher v Treasury Solicitor*.)

Assunzione, The [1954] P 150 (Court of Appeal) [29]

An Italian ship which flew the Italian flag and had an Italian captain was chartered from its owners, an Italian firm, by a French company, in order to carry wheat from France to Italy. The charterparty was signed in France after negotiations between brokers in France and Italy. It was in standard form in English, but with a supplement in French, and it provided for payment of freight and demurrage in an Italian port in Italian currency. Bills of lading for the cargo were issued in France in the French standard form and were indorsed to Italian consignees. Proceedings for damage to the cargo and short delivery were brought by the charterer against the owners. *Held*, the proper law of the contract of affreightment between them was Italian law. Having regard to all the surrounding and relevant circumstances known to them at the time, and in particular to the obligation to pay freight and demurrage in Italian currency in Italy, this was 'what just and reasonable persons ought to have intended if they had thought about the matter at the time when they made the contract' (*per* SINGLETON LJ). (See also *Chatenay* v *The Brazilian Submarine Telegraph Co* and Article 4(4) of the Rome Convention.)

Assurances Generales de France IART v The Chiyoda Fire & Marine Co (UK) [1992] 1 Lloyd's Rep 325 [30]

Under a reinsurance programme designed to cover Italian jewellers and Italian dealers in furs and antiques against loss and damage, retrocessionaires domiciled in London purported to avoid the policies of reinsurance on grounds of non-disclosure, misrepresentation and breach of duty of the utmost good faith. This led to the institution of four actions, of which three were in England and one in Italy, viz, actions 1, 3 and 4 in England and action number 2 in Italy. One of the issues to be decided was which court had become first seised of the dispute. *Held*, (1) an English court was first seised of the proceedings for the purposes of Articles 21 and 22 when the writ was served and not when it was issued: accordingly, with respect to the first action in which the English proceedings were served in March

1990 – three months prior to the serving of the Italian proceedings – the English court was first seised. (2) However, since AGF had sought leave to amend their writ, then, with regard to the proposed amendments, the question of seisin depended upon whether the first and second actions and the amendments were related proceedings; if they were, the English court was the court first seised by virtue of Article 22; if this was not the case, then the Italian courts were first seised by virtue of Article 21. The evidence was that the second action was invalid in so far as one defendant company had ceased to exist and this procedural defect was rectified only after the English court was seised of the third and fourth actions. (See also *Neste Chemicals* v *DK Line, The Sargasso*.)

Atlantic Emperor, The see Rich (Marc) & Co v Societa Italiana Impianti PA

Atlantic Emperor (No 2), The see Rich (Marc) & Co v Societa Italiana Impianti PA (No 2)

Atlantic Star, The [1974] AC 436 (House of Lords) [31]

The *Atlantic Star*, a Dutch container vessel, sank two barges, one Belgian and one Dutch, and two men were drowned when it collided with the barges whilst attempting in sudden dense fog and without having the help of tugs to enter a lock in Belgian river waters. Whereas the owners of the Belgian barge and its insurers began an action in the Belgian courts, the owner of the Dutch barge elected, initially, to take an action in rem in England. However, prior to the action being heard in England, he began an action in Belgium in order to preserve the Belgian time-limit if his English action was stayed, though he undertook to discontinue this if the English action was allowed to proceed. At that time, at least four other actions against the *Atlantic Star* were pending in Belgium. The owners of the *Atlantic Star* wished to stay the English proceedings in favour of litigation in Belgium. This was refused at first instance and in the Court of Appeal. *Held*, allowing the appeal, (1) where jurisdiction of the English courts was rightly founded, the traditional rule of staying proceedings only on the basis that they would be 'vexatious' or 'oppressive' to the defendant was subject to the court taking into account any advantage to the plaintiff and any disadvantage to the defendant; (2) Admiralty jurisdiction per se did not mean that a stay would be refused as an English court retained a residual right to decline its jurisdiction; (3) on the basis of the foregoing, the English action would be stayed. (See also *The Chaparral*.)

Attorney-General for Alberta v Cook [1926] AC 444 (Privy Council) [32]

A wife obtained a decree of judicial separation in Alberta, Canada, then presented a divorce petition in Alberta. She had lived continuously in Alberta since before the decree, but her husband had not lost his domicile of origin in Ontario. *Held*, the court in Alberta had no jurisdiction to hear the divorce petition, because jurisdiction in divorce depended on domicile and the wife's domicile was in Ontario. 'The contention that a wife judicially separated from her husband is given choice of a new domicile is contrary to the general principle on which the unity of domicile of the married pair depends' (*per* LORD MERRIVALE). (See now s1 of the Domicile and Matrimonial Proceedings Act 1973.)

Attorney-General of New Zealand v Ortiz [1984] AC 1 [33]
(House of Lords)

The A-G of New Zealand brought an action to restrain the sale in London of a Maori carving, an 'historic article', and asked the court to order that it should be returned to New Zealand. It had been illegally exported from New Zealand in violation of local legislation which provided for the forfeiture to the Crown of historic articles which were, or were sought to be, illegally exported from New Zealand. STAUGHTON J, at first instance, thought, inter alia, that the legislation was not penal and, accordingly, it would be enforceable in England. The Court of Appeal reversed this particular point which then was not contested on appeal to the House of Lords. *Held*, a true construction of the New Zealand statute was that the carving would only be forfeited to the Crown if seizure had taken place within New Zealand. As this was not the case, then the Crown was neither the owner nor entitled to possession of the carving. The House made no comment on the opinions expressed in the Court of Appeal, which were obiter, regarding the penal nature of the New Zealand statute. (See also *Bank voor Handel en Scheepvaart NV v Slatford*, *Williams and Humbert Ltd v W & H Trade Marks (Jersey) Ltd* and *Anglo-Iranian Oil Co Ltd v Jaffrate*.)

Attorney-General of the Republic of Ghana and Ghana National Petroleum Corporation v Texaco Overseas Tankships Ltd see Texaco Melbourne, The

B's Settlement, Re, B v B [1940] Ch 54 [34]

In the course of Belgian divorce proceedings between Belgian spouses, custody pendente lite of their nine-year-old son was awarded to the father. The mother, who had the son at a school in England, refused to deliver him to the father. Some two years later, the father sought an order for custody in England. *Held*, despite the Belgian order, the mother should retain custody for the time being at least, because it was best for the boy to leave him where he was. 'I ought to give due weight to any views formed by the courts of the country whereof the infant is a national. But ... this court is bound in every case, without exception, to treat the welfare of its ward as being the first and paramount consideration, whatever orders may have been made by the courts of any other country' (*per* MORTON J). (See also *McKee v McKee*.)

Babanaft International Co v Bassatne [1990] Ch 13 [35]
(Court of Appeal)

Having already secured a Mareva injunction covering the defendant's assets in England, the plaintiffs then sought and obtained a Mareva injunction to cover the defendant's assets outside the jurisdiction. The plaintiffs' solicitors notified more than 40 natural and juristic persons in various countries of the terms of this worldwide injunction. The defendant appealed. *Held*, in allowing the appeal in part: 'It would be improper for the court to grant, after judgment, an unqualified Mareva injunction extending to the defendant's assets outside the jurisdiction because such an injunction would amount to an exorbitant assertion of extraterritorial jurisdiction over third parties; that such post-judgment injunctions should be restricted so as to bind only the defendant personally and should contain a limiting provision to ensure that they did not purport to have an unintended extraterritorial operation and to make it clear that they did not affect third parties' (*per* KERR LJ). (See also *Republic of Haiti v Duvalier* and *Derby & Co Ltd v Weldon (No 1)*.)

Babcock v Jackson [1963] 2 Lloyd's Rep 286 [36]
(Court of Appeals, State of New York)

The plaintiff and the defendant were residents of New York, USA, and the defendant owned a car which was licensed, insured and garaged there. The defendant took the plaintiff on a week-end trip in the car from New York to Ontario, Canada, and while in Ontario injured her by negligently driving the car into a wall. In order to prevent fraudulent claims against insurers, an Ontario statute provided that a gratuitous passenger in a car could not sue the driver for injuries caused by his negligent driving. The plaintiff sued the defendant for damages in New York, where there was no such statute. *Held*, the defendant was liable. Although the Ontario statute formed part of the lex loci delicti commissi, its 'policy' clearly did not require it to be applied to actions by a New York passenger against a New York driver. 'The issue here ... is whether the plaintiff, because she was a guest in the defendant's automobile, is barred from recovering damages for a wrong concededly committed. As to that issue, it is New York, the place where the parties resided, where their guest-host relationship arose and where the trip began and was to end, rather than Ontario, the place of the fortuitous occurrence of the accident, which has the dominant contacts and the superior claim for application of its law' (*per* FULD J). (But see *Szalatnay-Stacho v Fink*.)

Baindail v Baindail [1946] P 122 (Court of Appeal) [37]

Two Hindus domiciled in India contracted a marriage which was potentially polygamous under Hindu law. Later, while the wife was still living, the husband went through a ceremony of marriage with a domiciled Englishwoman at an English registry office. *Held*, the second marriage was void, because the husband was a 'married man' according to his lex domicilii and this status, although not recognised in England for all purposes because of its polygamous aspect, was sufficient to debar him from contracting a second marriage in England. (See also *Srini Vasan v Srini Vasan* [1946] P 67 and *Hashimi v Hashimi* [1972] Fam 36.)

Balfour v Scott (1793) 6 Bro Parl Cas 550 (House of Lords) [38]

The heir of a man who died intestate and domiciled in England was entitled to a share in his movable estate through being also one of his next-of-kin. The estate included movables in England and immovables in Scotland, under whose law an heir of land could not share in movables as one of the next-of-kin unless he allowed the land to be combined with the movables in a common fund for division. *Held*, the heir was not affected by this rule because his right to share in the movables stemmed from English law, the deceased's lex domicilii, which had no equivalent rule. (See also *Re Ogilvie, Ogilvie v Ogilvie*.)

Bamgbose v Daniel [1955] AC 107 (Privy Council) [39]

The deceased, who had lawfully entered into nine polygamous marriages in Nigeria, died domiciled in Nigeria and intestate. Twelve respondents claimed to be legitimate children of the deceased and opposed the appellant who claimed as lawful nephew of the deceased to succeed to the whole estate. *Held*, subject to the respondents establishing their status of legitimacy, they would come within the class of persons entitled to succeed to the estate. Firstly, the succession to the deceased's estate was governed by the law of England which could not be limited in its local application to children who were the issue of monogamous marriages; and, secondly, the principle in *Re Goodman's Trusts* was applicable to children of polygamous marriages, ie, 'if a child is legitimate by the law of the country where at the time of its birth its parents were domiciled, the law of England, ...

recognises and acts on the status thus declared by the law of the domicile' (*per* COTTON LJ).

Banco, The, Monte Ulia (owners) v Banco and others (owners) [1971] P 137 (Court of Appeal) [40]

The plaintiffs' vessel, the *Monte Ulia* (*M*), and a jetty were both damaged when the vessel collided with the jetty following emergency evasive action due to the alleged negligent navigation of the *Banco*. The *M* ruptured an oil pipe-line and the plaintiffs were subject to large claims for fire damage consequent upon the rupture. The plaintiffs then brought an action in rem against the defendant owners of the *Banco*, serving a writ on the *Banco* and six sister ships. LANE J set aside service of the writ on the sister ships and also discharged the warrants of arrest on them. The plaintiffs appealed contending that the word 'or' in s3(4) of the Administration of Justice Act 1956, where reference is to the invocation of 'Admiralty jurisdiction ... by [way of] an action in rem against-(a) that ship ... ; *or* (b) any other ship ...' was to be interpreted as 'and/or' because 'There are examples in the Act of 1956 where "or" clearly means "and/or" including one example in section 3(4). Therefore "or" must mean "and/or" in those places where "or" alone is used.' Furthermore, 'The interpretation Act 1889, s1, states that words in the singular should include the plural unless the contrary intention appears.' Thus, they claimed, service of the writ on the sister ships should not have been set aside nor the warrants of arrest discharged. *Held*, rejecting the plaintiffs' contentions, Admiralty jurisdiction could be invoked either against the offending ship or against any other ship in the same ownership but not against more than one ship. LORD DENNING MR referred to the use of the word 'or' in s3(4) AJA 1956 and said: 'It is used to express an alternative as in the phrase "one *or* the other".' He cited with approval a dictum in *The St Elefterio* where WILLMER J said the purpose of the Act is to confer 'the right to arrest *either* ship in respect of which the action is alleged to have arisen *or* any other ship in the same ownership'. LORD DENNING concluded: 'That is clearly right. There is no doubt about it.' The provision of the Interpretation Act 1889 was inapplicable because the contrary intention was evident in the 1956 Act, viz, 'The jurisdiction may be invoked against *either* the offending ship *or* any other ship in the same ownership, but not more than one. ... The plaintiff is entitled, as soon as his cause of action arises, to issue his writ in rem against the offending ship and all other ships which at that time, that is, the date of issue of the writ, belong to the same owner. ... Then he can wait until he finds the *one* ship which he thinks most suitable to arrest. ... That having been done, he cannot go against the other ships and should strike them out of the writ.'

Banco Atlantico SA v The British Bank of the Middle East [1990] 2 Lloyd's Rep 504 (Court of Appeal) [41]

The defendant British Bank, incorporated in England, claimed that, as guarantor for a debt, it was prevented from making payments to the plaintiffs in Spain as it had been instructed not to do so by the Head of the Department of Ministry of Justice, Sharjah Civil Court, and to breach this order would be to invite serious criminal penalties for contempt. Nevertheless, the plaintiffs brought an action in England claiming damages. The defendants sought a stay contending that the appropriate forum was the courts of the United Arab Emirates. *Held*, refusing a stay: (1) the proper law of the contract was Spanish law, where the contract of guarantee was made, and that the Sharjah courts would not apply the proper law of the contract; (2) notwithstanding the defendants obligation under the guarantee had to be established, the plaintiffs had established English jurisdiction as of right; and (3) it would be unjust to require the plaintiffs to litigate in a jurisdiction where it would face summary dismissal of its claims. (See also *Spiliada Maritime Corporation* v *Cansulex*; contrast *Charm Maritime Inc* v *Kyriakou and Mathias*.)

Banco de Viscaya v Don Alfonso de Borbon y Austria [42]
[1935] 1 KB 140

The recently deposed King of Spain sued an English bank to recover securities which he had purchased with his own money and deposited with the bank to be held to the order of a Spanish bank as his agent. Decrees of the Spanish Republic had declared that the ex-King was a traitor and outlaw, that his property was forfeited to the Republic and that all bankers holding such property should hand it to the Republic. The Spanish bank intervened in the action to claim the securities on the Republic's behalf. *Held*, this claim failed, because the decrees were 'penal' in nature and would therefore not be enforced directly or indirectly in an English court. (But see *Luther* v *James Sagor* and *Huntington* v *Attrill*.)

Bank of Africa Ltd v Cohen [1909] 2 Ch 129 [43]
(Court of Appeal)

A wife domiciled in England executed a deed in England whereby she agreed to mortgage her land in South Africa to a South African bank as a guarantee for a loan to her husband. Under South African law, this guarantee was void unless she personally renounced the benefit of the protection conferred on married women by that law. She purported to do this by an agent, but this attempt was ineffective, with the result that the bank could not register the mortgage in South Africa. *Held*, the bank could not sue the wife in England for specific performance of the mortgage agreement. The agreement was void because capacity to enter into an agreement relating to land was governed by the lex situs of the land. (But see *British South Africa Co* v *De Beers Consolidated Mines Ltd* and *Charron* v *Montreal Trust Co*.)

Bank voor Handel en Scheepvaart NV v Slatford [44]
[1953] 1 QB 248

After the conquest of The Netherlands in 1940, the Dutch Government in exile passed a decree requisitioning all property belonging to Dutch residents with a view to preventing it falling into German hands. Gold deposited in London and belonging to the plaintiff, a Dutch bank, was subject to the decree, but it was taken over instead by the British Custodian of Enemy Property, who sold it. After the war, the Dutch Government made an order revesting the gold in the plaintiff, which then sued the Custodian for conversion. *Held*, the Custodian was not liable. The Dutch decree did not affect the gold, because the law governing the transfer of movables was the lex situs, and the court could not invent a new rule of public policy to the effect that decrees of an allied Power taking over property of its nationals so as to keep it out of the hands of a common enemy should be effective over property in England. (Compare *Jabbour* v *Custodian of Israeli Absentee Property*; see also *Attorney-General of New Zealand* v *Ortiz*.)

Bankes, In re, Reynolds v Ellis [1902] 2 Ch 333 [45]

Prior to their marriage, a domiciled Italian and a domiciled Englishwoman executed in Italy a marriage settlement in English form, whereby she settled funds invested in an English mortgage with a direction that, if realised, they should be reinvested in English investments. The settlement was valid under English law, but wholly void under Italian law because it was not executed before a notary and because it altered the Italian order of succession. *Held*, the settlement was valid because the English elements in it caused it to be governed by English law. 'The matrimonial domicile here was Italian, no doubt, so that prima facie this ought to be construed with reference to the law of the matrimonial domicile. But is there reason to the contrary? It seems to me, on the facts I have mentioned, there is reason to the contrary' (*per* BUCKLEY J). (See also *Re Fitzgerald, Surman* v *Fitzgerald*.)

Banque Paribas v Cargill International SA [46]
[1992] 2 Lloyd's Rep 19 (Court of Appeal)

In matters relating to a couple of contracts to be performed in The Netherlands, D owed B money. One of the contracts contained a 'no set-off' clause and the other provided for English choice of law and jurisdiction. B became insolvent and P were the alleged assignees of the moneys due under the contracts. D sought a declaration in Switzerland, where it had its main place of business, that the 'no set-off' clause was invalid as it wished to set off against any sums due under the contracts a sum representing the quantum of damages suffered as a result of repudiation by B of a third contract. All previous contracts between B and D were subject to English law and jurisdiction and payment by D was always to a bank in London. P sued in England and were granted leave to serve a writ out of the jurisdiction under RSC O.11. D applied to set aside the leave. *Held*, dismissing D's appeal, (1) D's failure to pay P in London was a breach within the jurisdiction under RSC O.11; (2) P had a good arguable defence that a set-off was not available; (3) there was a good arguable case that the contract which contained no express choice of law or jurisdiction clauses was subject to English law by virtue of a previous pattern of trading; and (4) all contractual terms and the interests of justice pointed to England being the appropriate forum in which to hear and decide the case. (See also *Kelly* v *Selwyn*.)

Barclays Bank of Swaziland v Hahn [1989] 1 WLR 506 [47]
(House of Lords)

The bank, via its agent, inserted a writ through the defendant's letter box in the belief that he was at home or that he would be at home later that day. In fact, he arrived at Heathrow airport from Geneva two hours later when he was warned of the delivery of the writ. Without going to his home he returned to Geneva the following day. *Held*, in the unanimous opinion of the House, the defendant's knowledge of the delivery of the writ when he was within the jurisdiction meant that under RSC O.10, r.1(3)(a) the writ had been duly served. (See also *Maharanee of Baroda* v *Wildenstein*.)

Baschet v London Illustrated Standard Co [48]
[1900] 1 Ch 73

The plaintiff, a French resident, was entitled to copyright under French law in certain photographs. In proceedings against the defendant for breach of the copyright in England, he claimed an injunction (a remedy unknown to French law) and penalties, as provided in English copyright law. Under the International Copyright Act 1886 he could not have any 'greater right' of copyright in England than in France, the country of first production of the photographs. *Held*, an injunction and penalties were the proper remedies, because the Act did not require the court to abandon its normal rule that remedies are granted according to the lex fori. It merely laid down the condition that some form of remedy under French law should be available on the facts against the defendant. (Compare *Phrantzes* v *Argenti*; see also *Boys* v *Chaplin*.)

Bata v Bata [1948] WN 366 (Court of Appeal) [49]

The plaintiff issued a writ against the defendant claiming damages for a libel contained in a circular letter which the defendant had composed in Switzerland and sent by post to various people in England. The writ was served in Switzerland pursuant to an order under (what is now) RSC O.11, r.1(1)(f), but the defendant applied to set aside service. *Held*, service should not be set aside. The tort was committed in England because the publication, which is of the 'very essence' of libel, took place in England. (Compare *Monro (George) Ltd v American Cyanamid and Chemical Corporation*; see also *Shevill v Presse Alliance*.)

Bater v Bater (orse Lowe) [1906] P 209 (Court of Appeal) [50]

A domiciled English couple were married in England, then they acquired a domicile in New York, USA, and the wife obtained a decree of divorce there. *Held*, the decree must be recognised in England even though it was given in respect of an English marriage between a couple domiciled in England at the time of the marriage. A decree of the court of the domicile operated as a judgment in rem throughout the world. (See also *Indyka v Indyka*.)

Beatty v Beatty [1924] 1 KB 807 (Court of Appeal) [51]

A wife obtained an order for weekly alimony payments against her husband in the course of divorce proceedings in New York, USA. Under New York law, she could apply to the court for the amount to be altered if her circumstances changed materially, but any alteration could not affect the amount of instalments already due. She brought an action in England claiming arrears due under the order. *Held*, her claim would succeed, because (1) the actual sum due to her could be ascertained by 'simple arithmetical calculation'; and (2) the order was 'final and conclusive' as to the arrears due, seeing that the New York court had no power to alter the amount thereof. (Compare *Colt Industries Inc v Sarlie (No 2)* and *Sadler v Robins*.)

Beaumont, In re [1893] 3 Ch 490 [52]

A domiciled Scotsman died leaving a widow and four children. The widow remarried and went with three of the children to live with her husband in England, where he acquired a domicile of choice. The fourth child, Catherine, stayed in Scotland with an aunt, but died there shortly after attaining the age of 21. *Held*, Catherine died domiciled in Scotland. The domicile of fatherless infants did not automatically change with that of the mother, but only 'as the result of the exercise by her of a power vested in her for the welfare of the infants, which in their interest she may abstain from exercising, even when she changes her own domicile' (*per* STIRLING J). The facts here indicated that this power had not been exercised. (See also *Potinger v Wightman*.)

Bell v Kennedy (1868) LR 1 Sc & Div 307 (House of Lords) [53]

A man left Jamaica, his domicile of origin, 'for good' and set sail for Scotland with a view to residing there permanently. When he arrived, he changed his mind and was uncertain whether to settle in Scotland or not. *Held*, in Scottish proceedings, his and his wife's domicile at this time was still his Jamaican domicile of origin. 'The domicile of origin adheres until a new domicile is acquired' (*per* LORD WESTBURY). But, 'if the intention of permanently residing in a place exists, a residence in pursuance of that intention, however short, will establish a domicile [of choice]' (*per* LORD CHELMSFORD). Here, actual residence in Scotland and an intention to reside there permanently never coincided in point of time, so a Scottish domicile had never been acquired. (See also *Udny* v *Udny*; but see *Winans* v *Attorney-General*.)

Benaim and Co v Debono [1924] AC 514 (Privy Council) [54]

Debono, the respondent buyer, who carried on business in Malta, had complained of the quality of anchovies he had received from the appellant sellers, Benaim and Co, who carried on business in Gibraltar; but it was only when his (Debono's) customers refused to accept them that he purported to rescind his contract with the sellers. *Held*, the place of performance of the contract was Gibraltar and under the law of Gibraltar an Ordinance of 1895, which was expressed in the same terms as a provision of the Sale of Goods Act 1893, the respondent had lost his right of rescission when he acted in a manner inconsistent with the ownership of the sellers. (See also *Chatenay* v *The Brazilian Submarine Telegraph Co.*)

Berchtold, Re, Berchtold v Capron [1923] 1 Ch 192 [55]

Under the will of his father, a domiciled Hungarian nobleman was entitled to the proceeds of sale of English freehold land vested in English trustees on trust for sale. While this land was still unsold, he died intestate. *Held*, his interest in the land should devolve as an immovable – ie, according to the lex situs – even though it was subject to the equitable doctrine of conversion. 'The doctrine of conversion is that real estate is treated as personal estate or personal estate is treated as real estate; not that immovables are turned into movables, or movables into immovables' (*per* RUSSELL J). (Contrast *Re Cutliffe's Will Trusts, Brewer* v *Cutliffe* and *Re Piercy, Whitwham* v *Piercy*.)

Berthiaume v Dastous [1930] AC 79 (Privy Council) [56]

A marriage between a couple domiciled in Quebec, Canada, was celebrated in a religious ceremony in France. However, the civil formalities which should have preceded the ceremony and which were necessary for validating the marriage under French and Quebec law, had not been complied with. Thirteen years later, the French courts declined to entertain the respondent's application for a divorce as she was unable to produce a civil certificate of marriage and to award civil effects in her favour as her husband had retained his Canadian (Quebec) domicil. In proceedings instituted in Quebec, *Held*, the marriage was void. 'If there is one question better settled than any other in international law, it is that as regards marriage – putting aside the question of capacity – locus regit actum' (ie the law of the place where the act takes place governs that act) (*per* VISCOUNT DUNEDIN). (See also *Starkowski* v *Attorney-General*; but see *Catterall* v *Catterall* and *Taczanowska (orse Roth)* v *Taczanowski*.)

Bethell, Re, Bethell v Hildyard (1887) 38 Ch D 220 [57]

While living among the Baralongs, a native tribe in Bechuanaland, a domiciled Englishman took one of the native women as his wife, the ceremony being conducted according to native rites. Under Baralong custom, she was his 'principal wife', but he was entitled to take other women as concubines. He died leaving a child of this union. *Held*, the child had no rights of inheritance because this union, though clearly a marriage as understood by the Baralongs, was not a union 'to the exclusion of all others' and therefore not a marriage in English eyes. (See also *Hyde* v *Hyde and Woodmansee*; but see *Baindail* v *Baindail*.)

Bier v Mines de Potasse d'Alsace SA (Case 21/76) [58]
[1978] 1 QB 708 (European Court of Justice)

The defendant, who was engaged in mining in France, was alleged to have discharged such large quantities of residuary salts into the Rhine in France that the ensuing pollution damaged the Dutch plaintiff's property (seed beds) in The Netherlands. The plaintiff appealed against a Dutch court of first instance decision that it had no jurisdiction because 'the place where the harmful event occurred' within the meaning of Article 5(3) of the Brussels Convention of 1968 was France. The Dutch appellate court requested a preliminary ruling from the ECJ. *Held*, both the French and Dutch courts had jurisdiction. 'Where the place of the happening of the event which may give rise to liability in tort, ... and the place where that event results in damage are not identical, the expression "place where the harmful event occurred", in Article 5(3) ... may be understood as being intended to cover both the place where the damage occurred and the place of the event giving rise to it. The result is that the defendant may be sued, at the option of the plaintiff, either in the courts for the place where the damage occurred or in the courts for the place of the event which gives rise to and is at the origin of that damage.' (See also *Minster Investments* v *Hyundai Precision & Industry Co Ltd* and *Metall und Robstoff AG* v *Donaldson Lufkin & Jenrette*.)

Bischoffsheim, Re, Cassel v Grant [1948] 1 Ch 79 [59]

A domiciled Englishwoman was married in New York, USA, to her deceased husband's brother, who was also domiciled in England. This marriage was valid under New York law but void for affinity under English law. The spouses later acquired a domicile in New York, then had a son. *Held*, the son, being legitimate under New York law, could inherit under an English will which bequeathed a mixed fund held on trust for sale to the 'child' of the wife. 'Where succession to personal property depends on the legitimacy of the claimant, the status of legitimacy conferred on him by his domicile of origin (ie, the domicile of his parents at birth) should not be entertained as a relevant subject for investigation' (*per* ROMER J). (See also *Seedat's Executors* v *The Master (Natal)*; but see *Shaw* v *Gould*.)

Black v Yates [1991] 3 WLR 90 [60]

Mr Black had been killed in Spain when riding as a pillion passenger on Mr Yates's motorcycle. That Mr Yates's negligence was responsible for Mr Black's death was not in issue. Accordingly, the Spanish criminal proceedings which ensued were largely confined to determining compensation for the deceased's wife and his children. The sum awarded was about £18,000. The English solicitor retained by the deceased's wife, the plaintiff, did not realise that it was necessary to reserve the right to bring civil proceedings in the course of the criminal proceedings: he merely informed the Spanish lawyer representing the plaintiff and her children that he wanted to establish the exclusive liability of the defendant for the accident so that the issue of quantum of damages could be determined in England where it was thought that a sum in the region of £75,000 would be an appropriate award. The plaintiff then commenced proceedings in England on behalf of herself and the two children as dependants. *Held*, (1) the plaintiff could not succeed on her own behalf because proceedings were brought on the same cause of action as that in respect of which the Spanish judgment had been given: that the Spanish judgment was enforceable in England meant that under s34 of the Civil Jurisdiction and Judgments Act 1982 'No proceedings may be brought ... on a cause of action in respect of which a judgment has been given ... in a court of an overseas country ...'; but (2) the claims brought on behalf of the children and the deceased's estate were successful because (i) the Spanish proceedings were contrary to the interests of the children and there was no evidence that they were able to consent to the power of attorney that led to their representation in the Spanish proceedings; that notwithstanding the provisions of s34 the court could repudiate the power of attorney and permit the claims of the children to proceed; and (ii) because the plaintiff had not purported to act on behalf of the deceased's estate in the Spanish proceedings the estate would not be bound by those proceedings. (See also *The Indian Grace, Republic of India* v *India Steamship Co.*)

Black-Clawson International v Papierwerke Waldhof-Aschaffenburg AG [1975] AC 591 (House of Lords) [61]

The plaintiffs, who became holders of bills of exchange, commenced proceedings just before expiry of the six-year period of limitation under English law. Proceedings were begun in Germany, where there was a three-year limitation period and in England where leave was obtained to serve the defendants out of the jurisdiction under RSC O.11. The proceedings in the German courts were dismissed on the ground that the limitation period had expired. The defendants then succeeded in convincing the Court of Appeal that a proper construction of s8(1) of the Foreign Judgments (Reciprocal Enforcement) Act 1933 revealed that the German judgment was 'conclusive' and binding on the English courts. *Held*, s8(1) of the Act only operated to make a foreign judgment conclusive to the matter adjudicated upon, viz, the period of limitation: the German judgment was not a decision on the merits of the case. Accordingly, the proceedings brought by the English company in the English courts were not barred. (See also *Harris and Adams* v *Quine*; see, now, s3 of the Foreign Limitation Periods Act 1984 and Article 10(1)(d) of the Rome Convention 1980.)

Blair v Blair [1969] 1 WLR 221 (Birmingham Assizes) [62]

A domiciled Englishman married a Norwegian woman in Norway and acquired a Norwegian domicile. However, whilst on a training course in England for the purpose of his work in Norway, his wife, who was living in the matrimonial home in Norway, informed him that she was pregnant by another man. The Englishman then decided to stay in England (thereby re-acquiring an English domicile) and immediately instructed solicitors to initiate divorce proceedings in Norway. *Held*, despite the husband's English domicile when the proceedings began, the ensuing Norwegian divorce should be recognised in England, because this was 'just and appropriate'. The husband had had a Norwegian domicile and a 'real and substantial connection' with Norway right up to the time when he instructed his solicitors to commence litigation. (See also *Mayfield* v *Mayfield* and *Indyka* v *Indyka*.)

Blanckaert & Willems v Trost (Case 139/80) [63]
[1981] ECR 819 (European Court of Justice)

The Belgian defendant's furniture was marketed in Germany by Bey, a German furniture agent acting as an independent commercial agent. Bey also represented other Belgian furniture manufacturers on similar terms. Bey then contracted with Mrs Trost, authorising her to 'represent the aforesaid undertaking' (Blanckaert) in a particular region of Germany but requiring her to send all orders to him (Bey). However, after discovering that Mrs Trost also represented other furniture manufacturers, Blanckaert terminated its contract with her and then with Bey. Mrs Trost sued the defendants in the German courts for, inter alia, outstanding commission. In response to the defendants contention that the court had no jurisdiction, Mrs Trost contended that it had jurisdiction under Article 5(5) of the Brussels Convention of 1968. Whereas the Regional Court decided that it had no jurisdiction, this point was reversed by the Higher Regional Court and then, because of a question of interpretation of European law was involved, the Bundesgerichtshof (Federal Court) referred to the ECJ a couple of questions, including: 'Is a commercial agent who is a business negotiator to be considered as an "agency" or "other establishment" within the meaning of Article 5(5) of the [Brussels Convention]?' *Held*, the answer was 'no'. 'An independent commercial agent who merely negotiates business inasmuch as his legal status leaves him basically free to arrange his own work and decide what proportion of his time to devote to the interests of the undertaking which he agrees to represent and whom that undertaking may not prevent from representing at the same time several firms competing in the same manufacturing or marketing sector, and who, moreover, merely transmits orders to the parent undertaking without being involved in either their terms or their execution, does not have the character of a branch, agency or other establishment within the meaning of Article 5(5) ...'. (See also *SAR Schotte GmbH v Parfums Rothschild SARL*.)

Blohn v Desser [1962] QB 116 [64]

The defendant, who resided in England, was a registered but inactive partner in a firm which was registered and carried on business in Austria through a resident managing partner. The plaintiff obtained a judgment by default in Austria against the firm. Under Austrian law, this did not operate against the individual partners, so that to make any one of them personally liable, the plaintiff would have to take further proceedings in which personal defences could be raised. The plaintiff sued to enforce the judgment against the defendant in England. *Held*, the Austrian court had jurisdiction over the defendant because by becoming a registered partner in a firm operating in Austria and appointing a managing partner who resided there to run the business as her agent, she had impliedly agreed to submit to the jurisdiction of the Austrian courts in respect of partnership transactions conducted in Austria by the agent. But the judgment was not enforceable against her in England, because (1) it was given against the firm, not against her personally, and (2) it was not a 'final' judgment on account of her right in Austrian law to raise further defences on her own behalf. (Compare *Copin v Adamson*; see also *Harrop v Harrop*.)

Bodley Head Ltd, The v Flegon [1972] 1 WLR 680 [65]

The Russian novelist Alexander Solzhenitsyn had signed a power of attorney which was to be governed by Swiss law permitting H, his Swiss lawyer, to deal, outside Russia, with his literary works. H sold publication rights of a novel which were acquired by the plaintiff paperback publisher and the serialisation rights to an English Sunday newspaper. However, at about the same time, F, the defendant, offered the publisher and the newspaper extracts from an English version of the same novel which he was preparing. His price was less than that sought by the authorised sellers of the rights. When the plaintiff publisher sought an injunction to restrain F from infringing their rights in the book, F contended that the plaintiff could not have any copyright in the work because, inter alia, it had first been published in Russia by 'samizdat', the clandestine circulation to educated people of duplicated copies and because, by Russian law, the author had lacked the capacity to contract with H. *Held*, finding no evidence of publication by samizdat, that, subject to the validity of the power of attorney, the plaintiff was entitled to copyright in the United Kingdom; and as the author's capacity to contract was to be governed by Swiss law, under which there was no evidence that the author's power of attorney was invalid, the plaintiff was entitled to the injunction sought. (See also *Male* v *Roberts*; *Charron* v *Montreal Trust Co* and *Campbell, Connelly and Co Ltd* v *Noble*.)

Boissevain v Weil [1950] AC 327 (House of Lords) [66]

In 1944, when Monaco was occupied by the Germans, the defendant, a British subject involuntarily resident there, borrowed a large sum in French francs from the plaintiff, a Dutchman also resident there. She promised to repay the loan in sterling after the war, as soon as English law permitted. At the time of the loan, it was illegal under the UK Defence Regulations for British subjects, wherever resident, to borrow foreign currency. *Held*, the plaintiff could not recover the loan after the war, whatever its proper law. The regulations forbade the very act of borrowing, so it could not be a 'source of civil rights' in an English court. (Compare *Dynamit A-G* v *Rio Tinto Co Ltd*)

Bonacina, Re, Le Brasseur v Bonacina [1912] 2 Ch 394 [67]
(Court of Appeal)

An Italian debtor, trading in England, signed in Italy an unsealed public document called a 'privata scrittura', whereby he promised to pay to an Italian creditor a debt which was not disclosed in bankruptcy proceedings. Moreover, the creditor had been unaware of the bankruptcy proceedings. Under Italian law, the signing of the document in Italian form created a legal obligation, but in English law the promise was unenforceable for lack of consideration. *Held*, the creditor could enforce the promise in England, because the proper law of the 'privata scrittura' was Italian law and under that law it operated as a binding contract even though consideration was lacking. (See also *Albeko Schuhmaschinen AG* v *Kamborian Shoe Machine Co Ltd*; compare *De Nicols* v *Curlier*.)

Bonython v Commonwealth of Australia [1951] AC 201 [68]
(Privy Council)

In 1895, when Queensland, Australia, used sterling currency, the Queensland Government issued debentures in Queensland as security for a large loan. They were repayable 50 years later in 'pounds sterling' in Brisbane, Sydney, Melbourne or London, at the holder's option. In 1931, the Australian pound was devalued in relation to sterling and in 1932 the debentures were surrendered in exchange for inscribed stock issued by the Commonwealth of Australia on the same terms. In subsequent proceedings in Australia, a holder of a quantity of stock claimed repayment in London in pounds sterling. *Held*, the Commonwealth was only bound to repay the stock in Australian pounds, whichever place of payment was chosen. Being part of 'the substance of the obligation', the amount payable was determined by the proper law, ie, 'the system of law by reference to which the contract was made or that with which the transaction has its closest and most real connection' (*per* LORD SIMONDS). The proper law was Queensland law, it being unlikely that the Queensland Government would raise a loan under a law other than its own. (See also *Whitworth Street Estates (Manchester) Ltd* v *James Miller & Partners Ltd*; but see *R* v *International Trustee for the Protection of Bondholders AG*; compare *Mount Albert Borough Council* v *Australian Temperance & General Mutual Life Assurance Society Ltd*.)

Bowie (or Ramsay) v Liverpool Royal Infirmary see Ramsay v Liverpool Royal Infirmary

Boyle v Sacker (1888) 39 Ch D 249

The plaintiffs were granted an ex parte order to serve a writ on the Russian defendant and substituted service was effected by serving it on his London solicitors. The defendant did not enter an appearance but he was represented by counsel who argued the case on its merits. *Held*, that by arguing the case on its merits the defendant had submitted to the jurisdiction of the court. (Contrast *Obikoya* v *Silvernorth*.)

Boys v Chaplin [1971] AC 356 (House of Lords)

The plaintiff and the defendant were English servicemen stationed in Malta. While riding as a pillion-passenger on a motor-cycle, the plaintiff was injured in a collision with a car driven negligently by the defendant. Both vehicles were insured in England. The plaintiff returned to England for treatment, then sued the defendant for damages in England. Under Maltese law, the plaintiff was entitled only to £53, which represented special damages and damages for financial loss, but under English law he would recover a further £2,250 for pain and suffering, making a total of £2,303. *Held*, the larger figure of £2,303 should be awarded. The ratio of *Boys* v *Chaplin* (which was identified in the later cases of *Church of Scientology of California* v *Commissioner of the Metropolitan Police* (1976) 120 SJ 690 and *Coupland* v *Arabian Gulf Oil Co*) is contained in the speech of LORD WILBERFORCE who said that the general rule was that to found liability the defendant's conduct must require 'actionability as a tort according to English law, subject to the condition that civil liability in respect of the relevant claim exists as between the actual parties under the law of the foreign country where the act was done'. What distinguished this from the rule in *M'Elroy* v *M'Allister* was the qualification of the double actionability rule by an element of flexibility which LORD WILBERFORCE thought was required in certain individual cases and which formed the crux of the present case. He opined: 'the necessary flexibility can be obtained ... through segregation of the relevant issue and consideration whether, in relation to that issue, the relevant foreign rule ought, as a matter of policy or ... of science, be applied. For this purpose it is necessary to identify the policy of the rule, to inquire to what situations, with what contacts, it was intended to apply; whether or not to apply it, in the circumstances of the instant case, would serve any interest which the rule was devised to meet. This technique appears well adapted to meet cases where the lex delicti either limits or excludes damages for personal injury: it appears even necessary and inevitable. No purely mechanical rule can properly do justice to the great variety of cases where persons come together in a foreign jurisdiction for different purposes with different pre-existing relationships, from the background of different legal systems. It will not be invoked in every case or even, probably, in many cases. The general rule must apply unless clear and satisfying grounds are shown why it should be departed from ...'. (See also *Szalatnay-Stacho* v *Fink*, *Johnson* v *Coventry Churchill* and *Red Sea Insurance Co Ltd* v *Bouygues SA and others*).

BP Exploration Co (Libya) Ltd v Hunt [1976] 1 Lloyd's Rep 471

In 1960, after being granted a concession by the Libyan Government for the search and exploration of oil in Libya, Mr Hunt entered into an agreement with BP for a joint exploration of the concession. BP were to pay Mr Hunt a substantial sum of money for this share of the concession. The agreement was made in London, though it was later amended in Texas, USA. In 1971, the Libyan Government nationalized BP's half share of the concession. Mr Hunt's half share was nationalized in 1973. BP applied under RSC O.11 to serve a writ on the defendant in Dallas, Texas, for a declaration that the contract had become frustrated and they claimed such sum as the court considered just in respect of benefits obtained by the defendant under the Law Reform (Frustrated Contracts) Act 1943. The defendant petitioned for a declaration in Texas that he was under no liability to BP. *Held*, inter alia, BP's claims came within O.11; they had a seriously arguable case; and the English courts were the forum conveniens. (See also *Metall und Rohstoff AG* v *Donaldson Lufkin & Jenrette*.)

Brailey v Rhodesia Consolidated Ltd [1910] 2 Ch 95 [72]

In a case involving the application of the law of (what then was) Southern Rhodesia to the affairs of a company incorporated there, evidence on this law was supplied by R W Lee, the Reader in Roman-Dutch law at the Council of Legal Education, London. He had never actually practised law in Southern Rhodesia, but he had made a special study of Roman-Dutch law as applicable there in order to teach it to students who intended to practise there. *Held*, he was a sufficiently qualified expert to give this evidence. (But see *Bristow* v *Sequeville*.)

Breen (orse Smith) v Breen [1964] P 144 [73]

After obtaining a divorce in England, a husband remarried in Ireland. At all material times, he and his second wife were domiciled in England. She petitioned for a nullity decree, alleging that a provision of the Irish Constitution prohibited any husband who had been divorced abroad from remarrying in Ireland while his first wife was still alive. *Held*, the provision was not to be so interpreted, but if it was, it would make the second marriage void even though the husband had capacity under English law, the law of his domicile, by virtue of an English divorce. (But see *Brook* v *Brook*.)

Brinkibon Ltd v Stahag Stahl [1983] 2 AC 34 (House of Lords) [74]

The culmination of negotiations for the purchase of mild steel by B, in London, England, from S, in Vienna, Austria, was an offer made by B contained in a telex sent to S. S's response was equivocal. Following S's withdrawal from the purported contract, B sought leave to sue S in England under RSC O.11, r.1(1)(d)(i). *Held*, the contract (if one was made) was made when and where the acceptance of the instantaneous communication was received. In this case, this was on 3 May 1979 in Vienna. 'The question whether a contract was made within the jurisdiction will often admit of a simple answer: if both parties are in England at the time of making it, or if it is contained in a single document signed by both parties in England, there is no difficulty. But in the case of contracts involving negotiations, where one party is abroad, the answer may be difficult to find. Since 1955 the use of telex communication has been greatly expanded, and there are many variants on it. The senders and recipients may not be the principals to the contemplated contract. They may be servants or agents with limited authority. The message may not reach, or be intended to reach, the designated recipient immediately: messages may be sent out of office hours, or at night, with the intention, or upon the assumption, that they will be read at a later time. There may be some error or default at the recipient's end which prevents receipt at the time contemplated and believed in by the sender. The message may have been sent and/or received through machines operated by third persons. And many other variations may occur. No universal rule can cover all such cases: they must be resolved by reference to the intentions of the parties, by sound business practice and in some cases by a judgment where the risks should lie' (*per* LORD WILBERFORCE). (See also *Entores* v *Miles Far East Corporation*.)

Bristow v Sequeville (1850) 5 Exch 275 [75]

In an action for the return of money which he had previously paid to the defendant, the plaintiff put in evidence certain unstamped receipts which the defendant had signed in Cologne. As an expert witness on the Code Napoleon (the law in force in Cologne), the defendant called the jurisconsult and legal adviser to the Prussian consul in England, who stated that he had studied the Code at a university and that in his view the receipts were inadmissible in evidence under the Code for the lack of a stamp. *Held*, the defence failed, because (1) a witness who had never practised a foreign law was incompetent to give evidence on it even though he had studied it at a university, and (2) an unstamped instrument which was merely inadmissible under its governing foreign law could be admitted in England, though not if through the lack of a stamp it was wholly void under the foreign law. (Contrast *Brailey* v *Rhodesia Consolidated Ltd*.)

British Aerospace v Dee Howard [1993] 1 Lloyd's Rep 368 [76]

The plaintiffs, British Aerospace, (BAe) had entered a Technical Assistance Agreement (TAA) with DHC, a company incorporated in and carrying on business in Texas, USA. A clause in the contract provided that: 'This agreement shall be governed by ... English law and the parties hereto agree that the courts of law in England shall have jurisdiction to entertain any action ...'. When DHC suspended the TAA it commenced proceedings in the Texan courts alleging that BAe had failed to carry out its obligations under the TAA. BAe commenced proceedings in the English courts where DHC sought to set aside leave granted to BAe to serve DHC out of the jurisdiction and to stay proceedings on the grounds that they (DHC) had commenced proceedings in Texas and that that court was the appropriate forum for the action. *Held*, whether the clause in the contract was an exclusive jurisdiction clause was a matter of construction; 'there is no real purpose ... in submitting disputes to the jurisdiction of the English court as well as choosing English law unless the intention is to make England exclusive.' [And in this case] 'the words ... "any action" clearly mean *all* actions. Thus in my view this clause under English law is an exclusive jurisdiction clause' (*per* WALLER J). Furthermore, the clause was one which the parties had freely negotiated and it was impermissible for DHC 'to rely before the English court on the factor that they have commenced proceedings in Texas and therefore that there will be two sets of proceedings unless the English court stops the English action.' This was a proper case for service out of the jurisdiction and England was the appropriate forum. (See also *Spiliada Maritime Corporation* v *Cansulex*.)

British Airways Board v Laker Airways Ltd [1985] 1 AC 58 [77]
(House of Lords)

Following the liquidation of Laker Airways in 1982, the British liquidator commenced proceedings in the USA under, inter-alia, the US Anti-Trust Laws, alleging that two British airlines (including British Airways) had conspired with other airlines and aircraft manufacturers to drive Sir Freddie Laker out of business. If the liquidator won the case he would be entitled to treble damages, ie the actual compensation trebled. Such an action could not have been brought in England, so the defendant airlines sought an injunction from the court restraining the liquidator from his action in the US on the basis that it would be unjust to them and against public policy. This was refused at first instance but then granted by the Court of

Appeal after the Secretary of State acted under the Protection of Trading Interests Act 1980 preventing British Airways from producing documents or information to the US courts. The Court of Appeal thought that this rendered a proper trial in the US impossible. Nevertheless, this decision was appealed to the House of Lords. *Held*, the injunction would be refused, ie the foreign proceedings would not be restrained. LORD DIPLOCK, speaking on behalf of a unanimous House of Lords, said that where a foreign court was the only forum which was of competent jurisdiction to determine the claim of a plaintiff who was amenable to the jurisdiction of the English courts, an English court would intervene to issue an injunction restraining the plaintiff from bringing his claim in the foreign court, but only if it would infringe a legal or equitable right of the defendant not to be sued in the foreign court, so that it would be an injustice if the defendant was not protected from the foreign claim. Since British Airways could not show that it would be unconscionable to allow Laker to proceed in the USA, the injunction would be refused. (Contrast *Midland Bank plc* v *Laker Airways Ltd*.)

British Linen Co v Drummond (1830) 10 B & C 903 [78]

By a written agreement executed in Scotland, the plaintiff, a company trading in Scotland, agreed to give credit to the defendant, who was resident and domiciled there. Under Scottish law, the plaintiff's right of action for repayment of the amount due was extinguished after 40 years, but under English law the period of limitation was only six years. An English action was brought more than six but less than 40 years after the amount became payable. *Held*, the action would fail because the English period of limitation applied. (Compare *Harris and Adams* v *Quine*; see now s3 of the Foreign Limitation Periods Act 1984.)

British South Africa Co v Companhia de Mocambique [79]
[1893] AC 602 (House of Lords)

The plaintiff, a Portuguese company, sued the defendant, an English company, for damages for trespass to its land in South Africa. The defendant disputed the plaintiff's right to possession of the land. *Held*, the court had no jurisdiction to hear the action. An English court would not assume jurisdiction in actions directly involving determination of the title to, or the right to possess, immovable property situated in a foreign country, nor would it assume jurisdiction in actions for damages for trespass to such property. (But see *St Pierre* v *South American Stores (Gath and Chaves) Ltd* and *Penn* v *Lord Baltimore*.)

British South Africa Co v De Beers Consolidated [80]
Mines Ltd [1910] 2 Ch 502 (Court of Appeal)

By a deed executed in London, the defendant, an English company, agreed to issue mortgage debentures secured on all its assets to the plaintiff, a South African company. The assets included mines in (what then was) Northern Rhodesia (which was governed by English law) and Southern Rhodesia (which was governed by Roman-Dutch law) and land in England. The agreement contained a grant of a licence to work the mines, which was valid under Roman-Dutch law but not under English law. *Held*, the plaintiff was not entitled to specific performance of the agreement to grant the licence, even in respect of the mines in Southern Rhodesia, because the proper law of the whole agreement was English law. 'Contracts relating to immovables are governed by their proper law as contracts, so far as the lex situs of the immovables does not prevent their being carried into execution' (*per* COZENS-HARDY MR). (But see *Bank of Africa Ltd* v *Cohen*.)

Brook v Brook (1861) 9 HL Cas 193 (House of Lords) [81]

A man married his deceased wife's sister in Denmark, this being permissible under Danish law, but prohibited on grounds of affinity under English law. Both parties to the marriage were British subjects domiciled in England. *Held*, the marriage was void. 'While the forms of entering into the contract of marriage are to be regulated by the lex loci contractus ... the essentials of the contract depend upon the lex domicilii, the law of the country in which the parties are domiciled at the time of the marriage and in which the matrimonial residence is contemplated' (*per* LORD CAMPBELL LC). (See also *Sottomayor* v *De Barros (No 1)*; compare *Schwebel* v *Ungar*.)

Brown v Gregson [1920] AC 860 (House of Lords) [82]

A testator dying domiciled in Scotland left six-sevenths of his residuary estate to be divided equally among six of his children and the remaining one-seventh share to his seventh child for life with remainder to her five children. The residue included land in Argentina, under whose law all trusts of land were forbidden on grounds of public policy and the seven children were entitled to inherit the land in equal shares. The five grandchildren claimed in Scottish proceedings that the children must elect, ie, must allow the gift to take effect according to its terms in relation to the Argentinian land if they wished to receive their full shares of the other property comprised in it. *Held*, the claim failed, because Argentinian law, the lex situs, did not merely treat the gift of land as invalid, but prohibited the children from making any other disposition of it which would have the same effect as the gift. Election was therefore impossible. (Compare *Re Piercy, Whitwham* v *Piercy*.)

Buchanan v Rucker (1808) 9 East 192 [83]

The plaintiff brought an action in England for enforcement of a judgment obtained in Tobago. He had succeeded in obtaining a judgment against the defendant by means of a substituted service of the writ on him, ie, service was effected by nailing a copy of the writ to the courthouse door. This was permitted under the law of Tobago and was held, by that law, to be effective even though the defendant had never been to Tobago. *Held*, enforcement of this judgment would be refused under English law. LORD ELLENBOROUGH asked: 'Can the island of Tobago pass a law to bind the rights of the whole world? Would the world submit to such an assumed jurisdiction? In essence, the answer to each question was "no".' (Contrast *Schibsby* v *Westenholz* and RSC O.11.)

Buckland v Buckland [1968] P 296 [84]

A Maltese man, apparently domiciled in Malta, was compelled to marry a Maltese girl by being threatened with a prosecution for seducing her, which was likely to succeed even though he was innocent. He never cohabited with her, but left Malta, acquired an English domicile and petitioned for a nullity decree. *Held*, the marriage was void for lack of real consent on the husband's part. (But see *Parojcic (orse Ivetic)* v *Parojcic*.)

Bumper Development Corporation v Commissioner of Police of the Metropolis [1991] 1 WLR 1362 (Court of Appeal) [85]

A dispute arose in London over a twelfth-century bronze idol representing the Hindu God Siva. The idol had been stolen from a derelict temple in the Indian State of Tamil Nadu, brought to England and then bought in good faith by the Bumper Development Corporation. When the identity of the new 'owners' was discovered a number of claims were served on them, including one from the representative of the temple. While the temple was entitled to sue under the law of Tamil Nadu, the question to be answered was: was it entitled to sue in England? *Held*, the question would be answered in the affirmative: since the temple was entitled to sue under the law of Tamil Nadu, it would not run counter to English public policy to permit the temple or, in this case, the duly authorised representative of the temple to sue in England. (See also *Arab Monetary Fund* v *Hashim (No 3)*.)

Cammell v Sewell (1860) 5 H & N 728 (Exchequer Chamber) [86]

A Russian firm sold a cargo of timber to an English purchaser and shipped it from Russia en route to England on board a Russian ship. The purchaser insured the cargo with the plaintiffs. The ship was wrecked off the coast of Norway, whereupon the cargo was sold in Norway by public auction to the British Vice-Consul, despite objections by the plaintiffs (to whom the original purchaser had abandoned its interest in the cargo). The auction sale was confirmed by a Norwegian court and under Norwegian law, though not English law, it conferred a good title on the Vice-Consul. He resold to the defendants and delivered the cargo to them in England. *Held*, the plaintiffs could not claim the cargo from the defendants even though it was now in England, because an English court would recognise the title acquired by the Vice-Consul under Norwegian law, the lex situs at the time of the auction. The Exchequer Chamber approved the dictum of POLLOCK CB in the court below where he said: 'If personal property is disposed of in a manner binding according to the law of the country where it is, that disposition is binding everywhere.' (See also *Winkworth* v *Christie, Manson and Woods Ltd*.)

Campbell, Connelly & Co Ltd v Noble [1963] 1 WLR 252 [87]

By an agreement governed by English law, the composer of a popular song (*The Very Thought of You*) assigned to the plaintiff all present and future rights of copyright in it for all countries of the world. The song later acquired copyright protection in the USA, where, in contrast to England, the law provided for a 'renewal period' of copyright for which the composer, if still alive, could apply on expiry of the initial period, and which he could assign in advance if he wished. The composer of the song obtained this 'renewal copyright' in the USA and sought to assign it to the defendant. *Held*, the plaintiff was entitled as against the defendant to the 'renewal copyright'. As it was created by US law, the same law determined whether and under what conditions it was assignable. However, under English law, the proper law of the first assignment, the terms thereof could be construed widely enough to include an assignment of this particular form of future copyright. (See also *Trendtex Trading Corporation* v *Credit Suisse*.)

Carl Zeiss Stiftung v Rayner and Keeler Ltd (No 2) [88]
[1967] 1 AC 853 (House of Lords)

The administration of a scientific and charitable foundation established in the late nineteenth century in what was East Germany was taken over in 1952 by a regional governing body called the Council of Gera. This Council brought passing-off proceedings on the foundation's behalf in West Germany, but the court held that it had no authority to sue on the foundation's behalf. At the Council's instigation, similar passing-off proceedings were instituted in England in the foundation's own name, whereupon a defendant, who had also been a defendant in the West German proceedings, contended that the West German decision deprived the Council of authority to act on the foundation's behalf. *Held*, the decision of a competent foreign court on a particular issue could raise issue estoppel preventing it being further litigated in England between the same parties, though the foreign action must be carefully scrutinised to determine what issue or issues it actually decided. But there was no issue estoppel here because (inter alia) there were different plaintiffs in the two sets of proceedings. Thus the Council's right to act as the foundation's governing body should be determined afresh according to (what then was) East German law, the law of the foundation's domicile. (See also *The Sennar (No 2)*.)

Carrick v Hancock (1895) 12 TLR 59

The defendant, an Englishman residing and trading in Norway, was sued by the plaintiff in a Swedish court for commission due on an agreement between them. The writ was served on him personally while he was paying a short visit to Sweden. The plaintiff recovered judgment and sought to enforce it in England. *Held*, he could do so. The Swedish court had jurisdiction over the defendant because of his presence in Sweden at the time of action. It was immaterial that he was not domiciled or resident there and that he was only present there for a short time. (See also *Colt Industries Inc v Sarlie (No 1)*; compare *Littauer Glove Corporation v F W Millington (1920) Ltd*.)

Casdagli v Casdagli [1919] AC 145 (House of Lords)

At one time, Egyptian law made special provision for Englishmen living in Egypt in that various specified aspects of their life, including personal status, were subject to the control of English consular courts in Cairo applying English law. In other respects they were governed by the normal rules of Egyptian law. A British subject whose domicile of origin was in England went to Cairo to live there permanently. *Held*, he thereby acquired a domicile of choice in Egypt. His right to have recourse to local English courts and English law in matters of personal status did not prevent this because this right stemmed from Egyptian law. Similarly, it was not necessary to show that he had intermingled with the Egyptian community and adopted their customs. (See also *Re Annesley, Davidson v Annesley*.)

Casthano v Brown & Root (UK) Ltd [1981] AC 557
(House of Lords)

P, who was Portuguese, was employed on the second defendant's Panamanian ship and suffered severe injuries on board, when the ship was in English waters. He started an action in England against the first defendants (a UK company) and the second defendants, for damages. He was then approached by American lawyers who had discovered that both defendants were members of a group of Texas companies and was persuaded to hand over the conduct of his case to them. An action was started in Texas where higher damages could be obtained. The second defendants had already admitted liability and made interim payments in respect thereof. Accordingly, an injunction to restrain continuance of the Texas proceedings was sought. P then gave notice to discontinue the English action, and start another one in Texas. It was sought to restrain this. *Held*, D had to show both that the English court was a forum to which it was amenable and in which justice could be done at less expense and inconvenience than in the Texas court and that the grant of an injunction to restrain P from suing in Texas would not deprive him of a legitimate personal or juridical advantage. The Texas court was, the House said, as much a natural forum (though not, it seems, *more natural*) than the English court. P could weight the scales in his favour by showing the advantage to himself of the higher damages obtainable in Texas. (See also *British Airways Board v Laker Airways Ltd*; contrast *South Carolina Insurance Co v Assurantie*.)

Castrique v Imrie (1870) LR 4 HL 414 (House of Lords) [92]

The owner of an English ship mortgaged it to the plaintiff, but when it arrived in a port in France, it was seized by the indorsee of a bill previously given by the captain to pay for repairs and provisions. The indorsee obtained from a French court a judgment in rem declaring him to have a 'privilege' on the ship as against the plaintiff and ordering the ship to be sold to satisfy the bill. The plaintiff, who had unsuccessfully argued in the French court that his rights under English law prevailed over those of the indorsee, then sued in England to recover the ship from the defendants, who had purchased it in the sale and brought to England. *Held*, this claim would fail. The French judgment, although not in conformity with English law, was binding as a judgment in rem because it was delivered by a court in the country of situs of the ship having authority under the lex situs to deliver such a judgment. (See also *Re Trepca Mines Ltd*.)

Catterall v Catterall (1847) 1 Rob Eccl 580 [93]

In a marriage ceremony performed by a Presbyterian minister in New South Wales, Australia, in 1835, the parties to the marriage expressed their consent to marry each other. *Held*, this was a valid marriage under the common law doctrine in the form in which this doctrine had been received in New South Wales law. In a colony, it would be inappropriate to insist on the rule in England and Ireland that the minister should have been episcopally ordained. (See also *Wolfenden v Wolfenden*.)

Century Credit Corporation v Richard (1962) 34 DLR (2d) 291 [94]
(Ontario Court of Appeal)

M sold a motor car in Quebec, Canada, to F, a resident of Quebec, under a conditional sales contract which provided that the car should remain the property of M until the price was fully paid. However, the car was then taken by F to Ontario without the knowledge or consent of M and sold there to R, a resident of Ontario, who had no knowledge of M's interest in the car. The law of Ontario required conditional sales contracts to be registered, the law of Quebec did not. *Held*, R's title prevailed; he could keep the car. The decision was based on s25(2) of the then Ontario Sale of Goods Act which provided that where 'a person having bought or agreed to buy goods obtains, with the consent of the seller, possession of the goods ... in good faith and without notice of any lien or other right of the original seller ... has the same effect as if the person making the delivery ... were a mercantile agent in possession of the goods ... with the consent of the owner'. (See also *Goetschius v Brightman*.)

Cesena Sulphur Co Ltd v Nicholson (1876) 1 Ex D 428 [95]

The Cesena company was incorporated in England under the Companies Acts 1862–1867, thereafter it was registered for all purposes in Italy. The company had been founded for the purpose of taking over and working sulphur mines in Cesena, Italy. However, the articles of association set up a board of directors in London having control of the 'sale, ... direction and management [of] the working of the company's mines, the mode of disposal thereof, and the general business of the company'. In the UK, the company held their meetings at the registered office in London. A delegation of the board, consisting of two or three members who were resident in Italy, had the responsibility for all the practical management of the company's property and affairs in Italy. *Held*, since virtually every managerial act, or central control, of the company was performed in London the company was resident in London and, accordingly, it was liable to pay income tax in

England upon the whole of its profits, wherever earned. (See also *De Beers Consolidated Mines* v *Howe* and *Egyptian Delta Land and Investment Co* v *Todd*.)

Chaney v Murphy [1948] WN 130 (Court of Appeal) [96]

The plaintiff was a member of the English bar who went to the Bahamas to take up the post of Attorney-General there. The following year he decided he wanted to practise privately as a barrister in the colony. However, on being refused permission, he resigned his appointment of Attorney-General and, again, announced his intention of practising privately in the Bahamas. This led to his being declared an 'undesirable person' and he was invited to leave the colony on or before 1 August 1947. On 31 July 1947 the plaintiff issued a writ in the Supreme Court of the Bahamas against the Government of that colony claiming various relief including a declaration that the Government was not entitled to declare the plaintiff to be an undesirable person, and damages. Five days later, however, an order was made directing the plaintiff to leave the colony within a week and not to return thereafter. On the same day, the plaintiff was also informed that the Government was seeking an order to set aside his writ for an irregularity which was that the Government of the colony was not a body capable of being sued. The order was, in fact, set aside the following week. Nevertheless, the plaintiff continued to take action on his arrival back in the UK. He issued a writ against members of the executive council of the Bahamas seeking a declaration that his deportation was unlawful and damages. Writs were served on two members of the council while in England on holiday. However, DENNING J refused the plaintiff permission to serve the other defendants in the Bahamas and he refused to stay the actions against the two defendants served in England. *Held*, the appeals would be dismissed since, inter alia, the plaintiff was challenging the very order, which by making it illegal for him to practise in the Bahamas at the time when he issued the writ, afforded a perfectly good reason why he should issue the writ here and not in the Bahamas. The refusal of permission to serve the other defendants out of the jurisdiction under (what is now) RSC O.11, r.1(1)(c) was based on noting that if the plaintiff succeeded in his claims against the two defendants already served he would be entitled as against all of them to the full amount of damages which he would be found to have suffered; and the risk of those defendants not being able to pay would not justify the court in taking the inconvenient course of allowing the other seven defendants to be served out of the jurisdiction. (See also *Multinational Gas and Petrochemical Co* v *Multinational Gas and Petrochemical Services Ltd* and *John Russell* v *Cayzer, Irvine and Co Ltd*.)

Chaparral, The, Zapata Off-Shore Co v The Bremen [97]
and Unterweser Reederei GmbH [1972] 2 Lloyd's Rep 315
(United States Supreme Court)

In breach of a 'forum selection clause', which had nominated the High Court of Justice in London, England, the plaintiffs sued the defendants in a US District Court after their drilling barge had been damaged whilst being towed by the defendants' tug from the USA to Italy. The defendants began proceedings in England but the plaintiffs secured an injunction in the US District Court preventing the defendants litigating further in the English courts. The defendants' appeal to the US Court of Appeals was dismissed and they further appealed to the US Supreme Court. *Held*, *per* BURGER CJ, (1) 'far too little weight was given to the forum [selection] clause in resolving this controversy;' (2) 'The correct approach would have been to enforce the forum clause specifically unless [the plaintiffs] could clearly show that enforcement would be unreasonable and unjust, or that the clause was invalid for such reasons as fraud ...'. (3) Since there was nothing to support a refusal to enforce the forum clause the appeal was allowed and the case was remitted to the District Court for reconsideration. (Compare *The Eleftheria*.)

Chapelle v Chapelle [1950] 1 All ER 236 [98]

A Roman Catholic Maltese domiciled in Malta married a domiciled Englishwoman in a civil ceremony in England. They lived together in Malta for some time until the wife returned to settle on her own in England. The husband then obtained a decree of nullity in Malta on the ground that religious formalities had not been observed at the marriage ceremony. *Held*, this decree would not be recognised in England. In declaring the marriage void ab initio, the court 'cut away the very ground on which its jurisdiction was based' (ie, the ground of common domicile) because, by freeing the wife's domicile retrospectively from dependence on that of her husband, it made her domicile English (*per* WILLMER LJ). (But see *Lepre v Lepre*.)

Chaplin v Boys see Boys v Chaplin

Charm Maritime Inc v Kyriakou and Mathias [99]
[1987] 1 Lloyd's Rep 433 (Court of Appeal)

The plaintiff Liberian corporation, Charm Maritime, instituted proceedings in England against Mr Kyriakou, who was a Greek ship owner and first defendant, and Mr Mathias who was the second defendant. Charm wished to secure delivery of share certificates from the first defendant who had been holding the shares in trust for the second defendant who, in turn, had assigned his title in the shares to Charm Maritime under an agreement which was subject to English law. Charm's action in Greece on the same issue had been dismissed on purely procedural grounds. The first defendant contended that it was an abuse of process for Charm to raise issues in the English courts which could and should have been raised in the Greek proceedings and that Greece was the appropriate forum for the resolution of the dispute between the parties. *Held*, this action might give rise to cause of action estoppel providing the foreign judgment was a final judgment on the merits. However, the evidence before the court did not establish that Charm was no longer further free to litigate its claim to the shares in Greece. Accordingly, there was no abuse of process. Moreover, and with reference to the decision in *The Spiliada,* SLADE LJ said that the issues of the appropriate forum and advantages to the plaintiff should be considered together and not as part of a two-stage process. On the evidence, Greece was not the more appropriate forum. Thus, the first defendant's appeal would be dismissed. (See also *Banco Atlantico SA v The British Bank of the Middle East*.)

Charron v Montreal Trust Co (1958) 15 DLR (2d) 240 [100]
(Court of Appeal, Ontario)

From the time of their marriage, a husband and wife lived together in Ontario for 12 years. They then executed in Ontario a separation and maintenance agreement, which they had capacity to do under Ontario law, but not under Quebec law, where the husband had his domicile of origin. The wife sued in Ontario for arrears of maintenance. *Held*, the parties had capacity to make the agreement. Apart from marriage settlements and the contract of marriage itself, capacity to enter into a contract was governed by the proper law, which in this case was clearly Ontario law. (But see *Male v Roberts*.)

Chartered Mercantile Bank of India v Netherlands India Steam Navigation Co Ltd (1883) 10 QBD 521 [101]
(Court of Appeal)

Two Dutch ships flying the Dutch flag and belonging to the defendant, an English company, collided on the high seas as a result of the negligence of both captains. Goods shipped on board one of them by the plaintiff bank were lost. The bill of lading provided for many exceptions, and loss by 'collision' was expressly excepted. *Held*, whereas no action could be maintained against the defendants for breach of contract created by the bill of lading, the plaintiff could, nevertheless, recover from the defendant in England damages in tort, because the law applicable to a tort committed on the high seas between two foreign ships was not the law of their flag, but the maritime law, which was 'part of the common law of England as administered in this country' (*per* BRETT LJ). (See also *The Esso Malaysia*.)

Chatenay v The Brazilian Submarine Telegraph Co [102]
[1891] 1 QB 79 (Court of Appeal)

A Brazilian subject residing in Brazil executed in that country in the Portuguese language a power of attorney empowering a London broker to buy and sell shares. In a dispute over the sale of some of the plaintiff's shares it fell to be determined whether Brazilian or English law was to govern the power of attorney. *Held*, if the power of attorney authorised the broker to act upon it in England, the extent of his authority in England should be ascertained according to English law. '... if a contract is made in one country to be carried out between the parties in another country, either in whole or in part, unless there appears something to the contrary, it is to be concluded that the parties must have intended that it would be carried out according to the law of that other country' (*per* LORD ESHER MR). (Compare *The Assunzione*.)

Chaudhary v Chaudhary [1985] Fam 19 (Court of Appeal) [103]

Four years after a Pakistani national had married and left his wife, W1, in Pakistan he went through a ceremony of marriage with another woman in a register office in England where he had acquired a domicile of choice. Subsequently he pronounced oral talaq in England and notified W1. He repeated this procedure in Pakistan where it was immediately effective under the law of Pakistan. However, the register office ceremony of marriage was declared void and bigamous 13 years after the ceremony and W1 petitioned for a divorce citing her husband's adultery with the other woman. The husband sought a declaration that his marriage to W1 had been lawfully dissolved prior to W1's petition either by the first talaq in England or the second in Pakistan. *Held*, at first instance, (1) the first talaq could not be recognised because, at the time it was pronounced, the husband had acquired a domicile of choice in England and under s16(1) of the Domicile and Matrimonial Proceedings Act 1973 no proceedings in the UK could validly dissolve a marriage unless instituted in a court of law; and (2) the later 'bare' talaq could not be regarded as 'judicial or other proceedings' within provisions of the Recognition of Divorces and Legal Separations Act 1971: this point was affirmed by the Court of Appeal. (Contrast *Quazi v Quazi*.)

Chaudhry v Chaudhry [1976] Fam 148 [104]

The parties to a marriage under Islamic law in Pakistan later moved to England although the husband retained his Pakistani domicile. After the husband had obtained a divorce by pronouncing a talaq in the Pakistani Embassy in London, the wife applied under s17 of the Married Women's Property Act 1882 for a declaration of her interest in the former matrimonial home. The husband contended that there was no jurisdiction to hear the wife's application on the basis that the words 'husband and wife' in the Act of 1882 were inapplicable to polygamous or potentially polygamous marriages. *Held*, the court had jurisdiction because 'the parties having been married according to the law of their domicile, the English court would regard them as husband and wife for the purpose of deciding any application by either of them under section 17 of the Married Women's Property Act 1882. Any other conclusion would ... be most impractical and an affront to common sense ...' (*per* DUNN J). (See also *Coleman v Shang* and, now, s52 of the Family Law Act 1986.)

Cheni (orse Rodriguez) v Cheni [1965] P 85 [105]

An uncle and his niece, being Sephardic Jews domiciled in Egypt and permitted to marry according to Jewish but not English law, married each other in Cairo. Their Jewish community permitted polygamy, providing no child was born within ten years of marriage. In this case, the birth of a child within two years of the marriage made the marriage monogamous. The wife later sought a decree of nullity in England on the ground of consanguinity. *Held*, (1) the court had jurisdiction because the marriage was irrevocably monogamous at the time of the proceedings, it being irrelevant that it was potentially polygamous at its inception; and (2) a decree should be refused because the marriage was valid according to the spouses' lex domicilii at the time of celebration and it was not so incestuous as to offend English public policy. (See also *Parkasho v Singh*; but see *Breen (orse Smith) v Breen*.)

Chesterman's Trusts, In re, Mott v Browning [106]
[1923] 2 Ch 466 (Court of Appeal)

Before World War I, two Germans mortgaged their interests under an English settlement to Dutch banks as security for loans totalling 64,000 German marks (then equivalent to some £3,150 sterling). The mortgages were expressly made subject to English law. The banks were at the date of the execution of the mortgages entitled in German law to insist on repayment in gold. However, in 1914 they lost this right under a German decree which made treasury notes legal tender for the payment of all debts. After the war the mark depreciated substantially, so much so that the sterling equivalent of 64,000 paper marks became less than five pounds. Proceedings were instituted to administer the settlement. *Held*, this was all that the banks were entitled to. They were obliged by the contracts of loan to accept repayment in whatever was legal tender at the time for the 64,000 marks which they had lent. This meant that they were bound by the German decree, even though the proper law of the contracts of loan was English law. (See also *Kahler v Midland Bank Ltd* and *Re Helbert Wagg & Co Ltd*.)

Chetti (Venugopal) v Chetti (Venugopal) [1909] P 67 [107]

A domiciled Englishwoman was married in England to a Hindu of Indian domicile. The husband subsequently brought nullity proceedings on the ground that Hindu law prohibited him from marrying outside his caste. *Held*, even assuming that the Indian courts would give effect to this prohibition, the marriage was still valid. A foreigner domiciled abroad who came to England and married a British subject of English domicile could not rely on a 'personal disqualification' under his lex domicilii as a ground for repudiating the marriage. (See also *Ogden v Ogden (orse Philip)*.)

Chiwell v Carlyon (1897) 14 SC 61 [108]
(Supreme Court of the Cape of Good Hope)

A husband and wife were married in the Cape of Good Hope without making any antenuptial contract or settlement, so that under the law of the Cape their property came under a community system whereby it was pooled and jointly owned between them. Shortly after the marriage, they made a joint will disposing of their joint estate. Later, while they were living in England, the husband acquired land in England. After both spouses had died, the Supreme Court in England was asked to determine whether this land was disposed of by the joint will, and it remitted two questions to the Supreme Court of the Cape to be answered according to the law of the Cape. *Held*, the answers were: (1) assuming that the spouses were domiciled in the Cape at the time of the marriage and during their joint lives, the land in England would fall within the community system; and (2) assuming that they were domiciled in the Cape at the marriage but acquired a domicile in England before the land was purchased, this change of domicile would have no effect on their respective rights in the land, because otherwise a husband could deprive his wife of her rights under the system by a simple change of domicile. (On receipt of these answers, the English court decided that the land was effectively disposed of in the will, even though the spouses might have acquired an English domicile before it was purchased). (But see *Lashley* v *Hog*.)

Cleveland Museum of Art v Capricorn Art International SA and another [1990] 2 Lloyd's Rep 166 [109]

Capricorn, a Panamanian registered company, were the owners of a very valuable reliquary, an important piece of Pakistan art, dating from the first century AD. They agreed to loan the reliquary to the Cleveland Museum of Art (CMA) for exhibition in Ohio and other US States. Prior to its collection and despatch to Ohio by Rogers, an English company, the reliquary had been stored for about a year at premises in Carlton Hill, London. On arrival in Ohio, it was discovered that part of the reliquary was missing. Where or how the part came to be missing was not discovered. Capricorn then commenced proceedings against CMA in Ohio for breach of the loan agreement by failing to return the missing part and failure to insure it; and they claimed jointly against CMA and Rogers as bailees and/or for negligence in handling the reliquary on the basis that CMA and Rogers were principal and agent in the shipping of the reliquary. However, CMA denied the allegations and claimed that Rogers were the agents of Capricorn and that Capricorn or Rogers were responsible for the loss. In pursuit of this, CMA obtained a stay of the Ohio proceedings and attempted to serve a writ by post on Capricorn at the Carlton Hill address. If this address constituted a place of business established by Capricorn as an overseas company then the service would be valid under s695(2) of the Companies Act 1985. Capricorn contended that the Carlton Hill address did not constitute a place of business thus invalidating service of the writ; or, in the alternative, if it did constitute a place of business, validating service of the writ, they sought a stay of English proceedings on the basis of lis alibi pendens in Ohio. *Held*, (1) the Carlton Hill address constituted a place of business: this could be deduced from the extensive storage by Capricorn of highly insured works of art on the premises and the fact that they permitted viewing works of art there; and (2) on applying *The Spiliada*, HIRST J concluded that Ohio was not only another available forum having competent jurisdiction but that 'there are a number of factors ... which in my judgment point very strongly indeed in favour of Ohio as the more appropriate forum for the trial of these disputes, viz: ... Capricorn have already expended $75,000 in legal costs in those proceedings ... The law of Ohio is the proper law of the loan agreement ... Ohio is the more convenient forum for the witnesses ... Issues arise about insurance in America which do not arise in the English proceedings. ... Taking all these considerations into account, I am satisfied and I hold that further pursuit of the English action would result in substantial additional expense, inconvenience and delay of the kind described by LORD DIPLOCK in *The Abidin Daver*.' Accordingly, Capricorn's application for a stay of the English action against them would be granted.

Cohen v Rothfield [1919] 1 KB 410 (Court of Appeal) [110]

The plaintiff, a moneylender, employed the defendant as his manager in businesses in Newcastle and Glasgow. He sued the defendant in England, claiming damages for having taken away some of the Glasgow customers by starting his own business and for secretly withholding some of the profits of the two businesses. The plaintiff alleged that the defendant's activities occurred whilst he (the plaintiff) was serving a term of imprisonment. However, the defendant cross-claimed and began an action in Scotland for remuneration due to him. The plaintiff sought an injunction in England to restrain the defendant from proceeding with his action in Scotland. *Held*, an injunction would be refused, because the plaintiff could not satisfy the court that the Scottish action was oppressive or vexatious. The fact that this action was in a British court did not give rise to a presumption in his favour, because often the procedures in British courts outside England (including Scottish ones) are different from English procedures. Moreover, the plaintiff in the foreign action was not plaintiff but defendant in the English action. (See also *St Pierre v South American Stores (Gath and Chaves) Ltd*.)

Cohn, Re [1945] 1 Ch 5 [111]

A mother and daughter, both domiciled Germans, were killed in an air raid in London and it was impossible to determine the order of their death. Under Article 20 of the German Civil Code, the two would be presumed in such a case to have died simultaneously, but under s184 of the English Law of Property Act 1925, the mother, being the elder, would be presumed to have died first. In determining a question of entitlement, under the mother's will, *Held*, the German presumption, ie, that of her lex domicilii, should be applied. Matters of evidence, including mode of proof, were procedural and governed by the lex fori, but proof here stopped short at the finding that it was impossible to discover the order of death. Thus, the two opposing presumptions, when classified in their respective contexts, were really rules of substantive law stating what should be the legal effect of such a finding and the presumption to be chosen was that of the lex causae, not the lex fori. (See also *Mahadervan v Mahadervan*.)

Coleman v Shang (alias Quartey) [1961] AC 481 (Privy Council) [112]

A domiciled Ghanaian married his first wife in Ghana according to a monogamous ceremony, then after her death contracted a second marriage in Ghana according to native custom, which permitted polygamy. On his death, the second wife and the daughter of the first marriage both applied to the Supreme Court of Ghana for letters of administration of his estate. The law of Ghana incorporated the English law of succession as it was in 1874, when a statute of Henry VII and the Statute of Distributions 1670 were in force to regulate grants of administration. *Held*, although these statutes spoke of grants to a deceased man's 'wife' or 'widow', they should here be interpreted to include wives under polygamous marriages which were valid according to the law of Ghana; consequently it was proper to grant letters of administration to the two applicants jointly. (See also *Chaudhry v Chaudhry*.)

Collens (deceased), Re, Royal Bank of Canada (London) Ltd v Krogh and others [1986] Ch 505 [113]

The deceased died intestate and domiciled in Trinidad and Tobago. His estate consisted of property in Trinidad and Tobago, Barbados and the UK. The value of the estate in Trinidad and Tobago was very substantial and the comparatively small estate in the UK consisted, in part, of immovable property. In a dispute over succession to the estate, the plaintiff's widow, his second wife, accepted $1 million in satisfaction of her rights over the Trinidad and Tobago estate. The widow also claimed that under s46 of the Administration of Estates Act 1925 she was entitled to a statutory legacy of £5,000 out of the deceased's English estate. *Held*, 's46 can only impose a charge for the statutory legacy on the proceeds of the English immovables. There is no way it can be made to impose a charge on assets not devolving under English law since such charge is part of the English law of succession. ... I can see no way in which the charge on the English immovable estate can be said to have been satisfied out of the overseas assets of the deceased. ... Therefore ... the charge on the English immovable property remains unsatisfied. [Accordingly] the widow is entitled to her statutory legacy out of the English assets' (*per* SIR NICHOLAS BROWNE-WILKINSON VC). (See also *Nelson* v *Bridport* and *Balfour* v *Scott*.)

Collier v Rivaz (1841) 2 Curt 855 [114]

An Englishman died domiciled in Belgium leaving a will and six codicils. Probate was sought in England, but was opposed as to four of the codicils on the ground that, though valid under English law, they did not satisfy the formal requirements of Belgian law. According to Belgian law, the deceased was not really domiciled in Belgium because he had not obtained royal authority to reside there, so all questions of his succession would be referred to his lex nationalis. *Held*, the will and all six codicils should be admitted to probate. The four opposed codicils would obtain probate in a Belgian court because that court would apply English law, and, as the testator died domiciled in Belgium, 'the court sitting here ... decides as it would if sitting in Belgium' (*per* SIR HERBERT JENNER). (See also *Re Annesley, Davidson* v *Annesley* and *Re Priest, Bellfield* v *Duncan*.)

Colonial Bank v Cady (1890) 15 App Cas 267 (House of Lords) [115]

A domiciled Englishman died owning shares in a company incorporated in New York, USA. His executors signed their names on the transfer form on the back of the share certificates, then sent them to a broker in London instructing him to have the shares transferred to the executors' names on the company's register in New York. The broker fraudulently deposited the certificates with two English banks as security for a loan to his firm. Under English law the banks did not thereby obtain title to the shares. *Held*, the executors could claim the shares as against the two banks. Although New York law determined what was necessary to transfer legal title to the shares and what rights were conferred on the legal holder of them, the question whether a binding sale or pledge had been affected was a matter for English law, the lex actus and the lex domicilii of the parties concerned. (See also *Guatemala (Republica de)* v *Nunez*.)

Colorado, The, Hills Dry Docks Engineering Co Ltd v Owners of the Colorado [1923] P 102 (Court of Appeal) [116]

In a dispute over priorities, the English court had to decide whether an English necessaries man had priority over a French bank claiming as mortgagees. Hills had repaired the *Colorado* and then had it arrested in order to obtain judgment for the amount due for the repairs. Hills obtained judgment in November 1921 and the French bank obtained judgment in May 1922. The Court of Appeal decided that whereas the question as to what rights were created by the mortgage deed was to be decided according to French law, the question of priorities was to be decided by English law, BANKES LJ approving the dictum of CHIEF JUSTICE MARSHALL in *Harrison* v *Sterry* ((1809) 5 Cranch 289). *Held,* in the absence of clear evidence to the contrary, the French claim was in the same class as a maritime lien or the right created by an English mortgage and this would rank higher than Hills' claim which was a mere right to proceed in rem: they had no possessory lien. Accordingly, Hills' contention, that they would have had priority under French law, would be dismissed. (See also *The Zigurds* and *The Halcyon Isle.*)

Colt Industries Inc v Sarlie [1966] 1 WLR 440 (Court of Appeal) [117]

The plaintiff, a New York, USA, company, obtained judgment in New York for a debt against the defendant, a Frenchman. It then issued a writ to enforce the judgment in England and served it on the defendant while he was staying for a short time in a hotel in England for reasons unconnected with the litigation. *Held,* the court had jurisdiction in the enforcement proceedings. A defendant's temporary presence in England though not even amounting to residence, was a sufficient basis for jurisdiction in personam, except only if he had been 'tricked' by the plaintiff into coming there so that proceedings could be instituted against him. (See also *Carrick* v *Hancock, Maharanee of Baroda* v *Wildenstein* and *Watkins* v *North American Land and Timber Co Ltd.*)

Colt Industries Inc v Sarlie (No 2) [1966] 1 WLR 1287 [118]

The defendant was sued to judgment by the plaintiff company in the Supreme Court of New York in the USA. His appeal to the Appellate Division failed, so he then filed a notice of motion for leave to appeal further to the New York Court of Appeals. *Held,* the plaintiff could none the less enforce the judgment against him in England. It was still a 'final and conclusive judgment' even though it might later be upset in the appeal, already pending, to a higher tribunal. (But see *Nouvion* v *Freeman.*)

Compagnie D'Armement Maritime SA v Compagnie Tunisienne de Navigation SA [1971] AC 572 (House of Lords) [119]

A contract between a Tunisian company and French shipowners for the carriage of crude oil from one Tunisian port to another contained a proviso in clause 13 that: 'This contract shall be governed by the laws of the flag of the vessel carrying the goods.' Clause 28 provided that 'Shipments [were] to be effected in tonnage owned, controlled or chartered' by the French shipowners 'of 16,000/25,000 tons at owner's option'. Apart from clause 18 providing that disputes were to be settled by arbitrators in London, the contract had no connection with England. When a dispute was referred to arbitration in London, and arguments were advanced to establish the proper law of the contract, the arbitrators found that whereas vessels owned by the French shipowners would be used 'at least primarily', shipments in the first four months of the contract had, in fact, been made in Norwegian, Swedish, French, Bulgarian and two Liberian ships. *Held,* although no clear ratio was expressed in relation to the choice of law, clause 13 read together with clause 28 sufficiently pointed to French law as the proper law of the contract. (See also *Vita Food Products Inc* v *Unus Shipping Co Ltd.*)

Compania Naviera Vascongada v Steamship Cristina and all Persons Claiming an Interest Therein, The Cristina [1938] AC 485 (House of Lords) [120]

A Spanish merchant ship which had berthed in dock in Cardiff in England and Wales (as the country is known for conflict of laws purposes, Wales not having a separate legal system) was requisitioned by the Spanish Government for use in the Spanish Civil War. The Spanish consul had gone aboard, claimed the ship on the Government's behalf and installed a new captain. The plaintiffs, a Spanish company who owned the *Cristina*, issued a writ in rem against the ship, claiming possession of it. *Held*, the Spanish Government was entitled to have the writ set aside, as a consequence of two established rules of international law which were 'engrafted' on to English law. 'The first is that the courts of a country will not implead a foreign sovereign. That is, they will not by their process, whether the sovereign is a party to the proceedings or not, seize or detain property which is his, or of which he is in possession or control' (*per* LORD ATKIN). But it was doubtful whether ships used by a foreign sovereign for private trading purposes were thus immune. (See also *Mighell* v *Sultan of Johore, Trendtex* v *Central Bank of Nigeria* and the State Immunity Act 1978.)

Connelly v RTZ Corporation plc and another [121]
(1995) The Times 20 October (Court of Appeal)

C had instituted proceedings in England against the defendants claiming damages for personal injuries, alleging that he had contacted cancer while working in a uranium mine in Namibia which was operated by a subsidiary of the first defendant's. In the English action, he accepted that Namibia was, prima facie, the jurisdiction with which the claim had the most real and substantial connection. However, he pursued his action in England on the basis that as he was wholly without means and that he would be unable to receive legal aid in Namibia, then, relying on *The Spilida,* he claimed that it would be possible for the English courts to be satisfied that the Namibian courts would be the forum 'in which the case may be tried more suitably to the interests of all parties and the ends of justice'. *Held*, WAITE LJ delivering the court's decision, the court had to ask itself: 'If proceedings that had only a tenuous connection with England were started here by a plaintiff who was impecunious but eligible for legal aid and there was a foreign jurisdiction with which the action had the most real and substantial connection but in which the impecunious plaintiff would be ineligible for assistance, was the English court bound, by reason alone of the plaintiff's eligibility for legal aid in the one jurisdiction and ineligibility in the other, to refuse a stay?' According to law, there were four reasons why the answer had to be 'no'. The reasons were: (1) the essence of the objective of reaching a broad consensus among major common law jurisdictions was that an action would be tried in the forum with which it had the most real and substantial connection. This would be disrupted if considerations of legal aid eligibility were allowed to interfere with it. (2) It would not be of benefit to the court to make value judgments between the many and varied forms of public assistance for litigation in different countries, especially when it was unlikely that more than an impressionistic survey of the competing features of the two regimes could be made. (3) The exclusion of considerations of legal aid in (2) did not extend to private resources, which remained a relevant consideration. (4) The exclusion of legal aid was consistent with provisions of the Legal Aid Act 1988. Accordingly, the English action would be stayed. (See also *Smith Kline & French Laboratories* v *Bloch*.)

Continental Bank NA v Aeokos Cia Naviera SA [122]
[1994] 2 All ER 540 (Court of Appeal)

A term of a loan agreement between the bank and a group of one-ship companies managed by a Greek shipping company in Athens was that the agreement was governed by English law and that each borrower and guarantor (collectively, the appellants) was to irrevocably submit to the jurisdiction of the English courts. However, when the borrowers defaulted on the loan repayments, they brought an action in the Greek courts claiming damages against the bank for exercising its rights under the loan agreement contrary to Greek law. In response, the bank commenced proceedings in England to restrain the appellants from continuing the Greek proceedings in breach of the exclusive jurisdiction agreement. The appellants sought to strike out or stay the English proceedings pending the outcome of the Greek proceedings. They sought to rely on Articles 21 ('same cause') and 22 ('related cause') of the Brussels Convention 1968. At first instance the judge granted an injunction in the bank's favour. *Held*, dismissing the appeal, a proper construction of the jurisdiction clause was that it bound the parties to submit all disputes relating to the loan facility, including the subject matter of the Greek proceedings, to the English courts. Article 17 then applied to deprive the courts of other Contracting States of jurisdiction. Thus, contentions under Articles 21 and 22 did not arise since the provisions of Article 17 took precedence over them: 'there is no discretionary power in the convention itself to override the conclusive effect of an exclusive jurisdiction agreement ...' (*per* STEYN LJ). (See also *Meeth* v *Glacetal Sarl* and *Kurz* v *Stella Musical Veranstaltungs GmbH*.)

Cooke's Trusts, Re (1887) 56 LT 737 [123]

While under 21 and domiciled in England, an English girl married a French nobleman who was domiciled in France. At the time of the marriage she executed a marriage contract in France. She later parted from him and, believing him to be dead, went through a ceremony of marriage with another man, with whom she settled in New South Wales for the rest of her life. Her first husband died shortly before she did. *Held*, (1) the marriage contract was void because her capacity to enter into it was governed by English law, the law of her ante-nuptial domicile; (2) she acquired a domicile of choice in New South Wales at the moment of her first husband's death, as this event rendered her immediately free to do so and she already had the necessary residence and intention. (See also *Cooper* v *Cooper*.)

Cooper v Cooper (1888) 13 App Cas 88 (House of Lords) [124]

Prior to marrying a domiciled Scotsman, an 18-year-old girl, domiciled in Ireland, executed a marriage contract in Ireland. She had the capacity to do this under Scottish law. The girl and her husband intended to settle in Scotland after the marriage and, in fact, did so. *Held*, in Scottish proceedings, that the contract was void, because the question of her capacity was determined by her lex domicilii at the time of execution or (possibly) the lex loci contractus – ie, on either alternative, Irish law – and not by the law of the intended matrimonial domicile. (See also *Viditz* v *O'Hagan* and *Re Cooke's Trusts*.)

Copin v Adamson (1875) LR 1 Ex D 17 (Court of Appeal) [125]

The constitution of a company incorporated in France provided that all disputes between members during liquidation should be submitted to the jurisdiction of a French court, that every member should elect a 'domicile' for service of process and that in default of election a member's domicile should be the company's office. The company went into liquidation. In an action in the French court the liquidator sued a member who was resident and domiciled in England for the amount unpaid on his shares, serving the writ at the office because no domicile had been elected. After obtaining a judgment by default, the liquidator sought to enforce it in England. *Held*, he could do so. By joining the company, the member in effect had agreed to submit to the jurisdiction of the French court and to the mode of service which was used. But such an agreement would not be implied simply from membership in a French company where there were not such express provisions in the constitution. (See also *The Tharsis Sulphur and Copper Co Ltd* v *La Socièté des Metaux*; but see *Blohn* v *Desser*.)

Cordova Land Co Ltd v Victor Bros Inc [1966] 1 WLR 793 [126]

A quantity of skins bought in the USA by the plaintiff, an English company, were carried from the USA to England on board two ships owned by the defendant, an American company. The captains of the ships issued bills of lading in Boston stating that the skins were in good condition on shipment, but on arrival they were found to be damaged. The plaintiff applied for leave under (what is now) RSC O.11, r.1(1)(f) to serve a writ claiming damages against the defendant for fraudulent misrepresentation by the captains. *Held*, the application should not be granted because the alleged tort did not take place in England. The 'substance' of it was the misrepresentation which took place in Boston, and it was not enough to show that it became 'complete' in England through the plaintiff's reading and acting upon the misrepresentation in England. (Compare *Kroch* v *Rossell et Cie*.)

Coupland v Arabian Gulf Oil Co [1983] 3 All ER 226 [127]
(Court of Appeal)

The plaintiff, P, who was living and domiciled in Scotland, was employed under a contract of employment made in London by a nationalised company in Libya which was registered in England as an overseas company. After P was seriously injured at work in Libya he instituted proceedings against the defendants in England for damages for personal injuries. The defendants claimed that the proper law of the contract and/or any other obligation owed by them to the plaintiff was Libyan law. *Held*, the contract was only relevant to the claim in tort in so far as it purported to exclude or restrict the claim in tort. In the absence of a term in the contract restricting the plaintiff's right to claim damages in tort, irrespective of whether the contract was governed by Libyan or English law, and given that the claim was actionable as a tort under Libyan law and English law, the trial could proceed on the ordinary principles of common law negligence in England. (See also *Johnson* v *Coventry Churchill*.)

Courtney, Re, ex parte Pollard (1840) Mont & Ch 239 [128]

Two partners, who resided in England, created an equitable mortgage in writing of land belonging to the partnership and deposited the title-deeds with the mortgagee. According to the law of Scotland, where the land was situated, this transaction did not confer any interest in the land on the creditor. The partners later went bankrupt in England. *Held*, the mortgagee could have a declaration as against the assignee in bankruptcy that he was entitled to an equitable mortgage of the land. As there was no positive rule of Scottish law, the *lex situs*, preventing enforcement of the written agreement, the English court had jurisdiction and would enforce it by a decree in personam granted according to English rules of equity. (See also *Ewing* v *Orr-Ewing*; compare *British South Africa Co* v *De Beers Consolidated Mines Ltd*.)

Cruse v Chittum (formerly Cruse) [1974] 2 All ER 940 [129]

After 11 years of marriage, W, in the company of a US serviceman, left H, her husband. Thereafter, H heard nothing from W for three years when she wrote from Mississippi informing him that, 'I have got a divorce so you are a free man now. ... it has been final for a year now. It is quite easy to obtain a divorce here.' H did nothing for a further seven years when he wished to remarry. His solicitors obtained from a Mississippi court two documents, viz, a 'Bill of Complaint for Divorce' and a 'Final Decree'. The latter included a statement that W was 'an actual bona fide resident citizen of Harrison County, Mississippi, and has been for more than one year next immediately preceding the filing of the bill'. H then sought a declaration that the Mississippi decree would be recognised in England. *Held*, 'habitual residence' was an indicator of the quality of residence rather than its duration: it was equivalent to the residence required to establish domicile without the element of animus necessary for the purpose of domicile. The finding of fact that W was 'habitually resident' in Mississippi when she instituted proceedings, there being no evidence to the contrary, would suffice for the decree to be recognised. (See also *Quazi* v *Quazi* and s46 of the Family Law Act 1986.)

Cuban Atlantic Sugar Sales Corporation v Compania [130]
de Vapores San Elefterio Limitada [1960] 1 QB 187
(Court of Appeal)

The defendant company agreed with the plaintiff company to ship the plaintiff's sugar from Cuba to 'one safe port United Kingdom at charterers' option, excluding Manchester and Dunston'. The discharge port was to be nominated by the plaintiff 120 hours prior to the vessels arrival off Land's End. The agreement (charterparty) was governed by American law. Before the nomination was made, however, the ship sank on the high seas. The plaintiff obtained leave under (what is now) RSC O.11, r.1(1)(e) to serve a writ claiming damages for breach of contract upon the defendant out of the jurisdiction. *Held*, service should be set aside because there was no breach of contract committed within the jurisdiction. The obligation of the defendant was to deliver at *one* safe port in the UK. Accordingly, there was not a breach at *every* such port. Moreover, the *one* safe port was not necessarily within the jurisdiction, since the plaintiff could have nominated a port in Scotland or Northern Ireland. (Contrast *Union Transport* v *Continental Lines SA*.)

Cunnington, In re, Healing v Webb [1924] 1 Ch 68 [131]

A testator died domiciled in France leaving a will in English form which he had executed in England. In his will, the testator had bequeathed his property to an English executor on trust to pay legacies to certain domestic servants in France and to divide the residue, which comprised movables in England, among ten English beneficiaries resident in England. However, that two of the beneficiaries predeceased the testator meant that under English law a partial intestacy arose. By contrast, under French law, the remaining eight took the whole residue. *Held*, the succession indicated by French law should apply, because prima facie the testator's lex domicilii at death regulated constructive intention on his part. (See also *Philipson-Stow* v *IRC*.)

Cutliffe's Will Trusts, Re, Brewer v Cutliffe [1940] Ch 565 [132]

In 1897, an intestate died domiciled in Ontario, Canada. At the time of his death, he was entitled to an interest in certain English investments which were the proceeds of a sale of land subject to the Settled Land Act (SLA) 1882. His next-of-kin by the law of Ontario claimed interest in a movable. It had to be decided under s22(5) SLA 1882 (subsequently re-enacted as s75(5) SLA 1925) whether the interest was movable or immovable. *Held*, since the statutory provision specifically provided that capital money was to be regarded as land 'for all purposes', the interest in the investments was an immovable. There appeared to be at least two grounds on which this decision could be justified: (1) regarding s75(5) SLA 1925 as an overriding statutory provision which applies irrespective of the choice of law process; and (2) regarding the lex situs as the appropriate legal system for determining how a particular asset is to be characterised. (Contrast *Re Berchtold*.)

D v D (1993) The Independent 13 October [133]

The petitioner and his wife were married in Ghana pursuant to Ghanaian custom in 1977. They came to live in England where the wife issued divorce proceedings in January 1990, the same month as the husband went back to Ghana where he applied to the customary arbitration tribunal for the dissolution of the marriage. Whereas the wife had no knowledge that the proceedings were taking place, it was reported that the wife's mother was the defendant and that she attended the proceedings. The husband's application was successful and he later asserted that the dissolution was entitled to recognition in the UK under s46 of the Family Law Act 1986. However, WALL J noted that two experts in Ghanaian law had clearly stated that both parties to the marriage must have voluntarily expressed their agreement to submit to arbitration. Here, the failure to inform the wife of the Ghanaian proceedings meant that she had neither voluntarily submitted to nor agreed to be bound by the proceedings. Moreover, the dissolution could only be arrived at after the tribunal had heard both sides in a judicial manner and its decision had to be 'effective under the law of the country in which it was obtained'. The judge accepted the evidence of the wife's expert that decree would not be upheld by the High Court of Ghana. *Held*, accordingly, the Ghanaian dissolution was not entitled to recognition under s46 of the Family Law Act 1986, though if he was wrong on that point then, under s51, the judge would exercise his discretion and refuse recognition because of the failure to take the steps which could and should have been taken to notify the wife of the Ghanaian proceedings. (See also *Quazi* v *Quazi* and *Chaudhary* v *Chaudhary*.)

D'Almeida Araujo Lda v Sir Frederick Becker & Co Ltd [134]
[1953] 2 QB 329

In a contract, governed by Portuguese law, for the purchase of palm oil from the plaintiff company, the defendant company promised to make payment by opening a credit in the plaintiff's favour in Lisbon. The plaintiff was buying the oil from a supplier in Lisbon, with whom it agreed to use the same method of payment and to pay an indemnity of £3,500 for any breach of contract. The defendant did not open a credit as promised, with the result that the plaintiff did not open one for the supplier and had to pay the £3,500 indemnity. In an action against the defendant for damages for breach of contract, the plaintiff sought to recover this £3,500 as part of its damages. It would be entitled to do so under English law but not Portuguese law. *Held*, the question of whether the plaintiff could recover from the defendant the £3,500 which it had paid to its supplier in Lisbon was one of remoteness of damage, which, being an issue of substance, was governed by Portuguese law, the proper law of the contract. By contrast, a mere issue of quantification of damage would be procedural, and determined according to the lex fori. (Compare *Boys* v *Chaplin*.)

De Beers Consolidated Mines Ltd v Howe [135]
[1906] AC 455 (House of Lords)

The appellant foreign corporation, De Beers Consolidated Mines Ltd, was incorporated in South Africa where all its profits were generated from the mining and sale of diamonds. However, the majority of the company's directors were resident in England and, for income tax purposes, it had to be decided if the company was resident in England. *Held*, the test for residence is 'to see where it really keeps house and does business ... the real business is carried on where the central management and control actually abide' (*per* LORD LOREBURN). Accordingly, the foreign corporation was resident in this country for income tax purposes. (Compare *Cesena Sulphur Co Ltd v Nicholson*.)

de Bloos v Bouyer (Case 14/76) [1976] ECR 1497 [136]
(European Court of Justice)

de Bloos, a Belgian firm, had been given the exclusive rights to distribute the products of the French firm, Bouyer, in certain countries, including Belgium. When a dispute arose between the firms, de Bloos sought redress from the Belgian courts. Bouyer contested the court's jurisdiction on the basis that they were not domiciled in Belgium. de Bloos sought to rely on Article 5(1) of the Brussels Convention 1968 which provides that: 'A person domiciled in a Contracting State may, in another Contracting State, be sued: (1) in matters relating to a contract in the courts for the place of performance of the obligation in question.' The point was referred to the ECJ for a preliminary ruling. *Held*, the obligation in question refers to 'the obligation forming the basis of the legal proceedings, namely the contractual obligation of the grantor which corresponds to the contractual right relied upon by the grantee in support of the application'. In other words, the defendant's non-performance in the place of performance of the obligation imposed on him by his contract with the plaintiff enables the latter to invoke the special jurisdiction provisions of Article 5(1) of the Brussels Convention. A further issue decided by the ECJ was that exclusive distribution, per se, did not lead to a secondary establishment of the manufacturer within the meaning of Article 5(5) of the Brussels Convention. (See also *Shenavai v Kreischer, Union Transport v Continental Lines SA* (Article 5(1)), *Somafer SA v Saar-Ferngas AG* Case 33/78 [1978] ECR 2183 and *SAR Schotte GmbH v Parfums Rothschild SARL* (Article 5(5)).)

de Cavel v de Cavel (Case 120/79) [1980] ECR 731 [137]
(European Court of Justice)

During the course of divorce proceedings, the husband was ordered by a French court to pay his wife, pending divorce, a maintenance allowance of FF3,000 per month. An application by the wife to have the award enforced in Germany was, at first, approved but then set aside on appeal to a German Higher Regional Court on the basis that the decision of the French court constituted an interim measure granted in the course of divorce proceedings and was accordingly concerned with litigation relating to the status of persons, which was outside the ambit of the Brussels Convention 1968. The wife appealed to the German Federal Court to restore the order. Meanwhile, the French court granted a divorce on the ground of the parties' mutual fault and awarded the wife an interim compensatory allowance of FF2,000 per month. The wife also appealed against that judgment. The German Federal Court then referred two questions to the ECJ. In essence, they were: (1) does the Brussels Convention apply to the enforcement of an interlocutory order made by a French judge in divorce proceedings; and (2) is the Convention applicable to the payment of interim compensation, on a monthly basis? In considering 'whether the Convention can apply to a maintenance order made in divorce proceedings?' the Advocate General in the ECJ expressed a very brief opinion 'that the answer was "yes" '. *Held*, accordingly, that 'The [Brussels] Convention ... is applicable, on the one hand, to the enforcement of an interlocutory order made by a French court in divorce proceedings whereby one of the parties to the proceedings is awarded a monthly maintenance allowance and, on the other hand, to an interim compensation payment, payable monthly, awarded to one of the parties by a French divorce judgment ...'. (Contrast *Reichert v Dresdner Bank (No 2)*.)

de Dampierre v de Dampierre [1988] 1 AC 92 (House of Lords) [138]

In divorce proceedings concerning French nationals who married in France and lived together in England for five years, the wife, who was now resident in New York, petitioned for a divorce in England. The husband commenced divorce proceedings in France and applied for a stay of the English proceedings under provisions of the Domicile and Matrimonial Proceedings Act 1973 (DMPA 1973). The application was refused at first instance and dismissed by the Court of Appeal. *Held*, allowing the husband's appeal by a unanimous decision, 'that judges of first instance should approach their task in cases under the statute [DMPA 1973] in the same way as they now do in cases of forum non conveniens where there is a lis alibi pendens. ... the court should not, as a general rule, be deterred from granting a stay of proceedings simply because the plaintiff in this country will be deprived of such [a legitimate personal or juridical] advantage, provided that the court is satisfied that substantial justice will be done in the appropriate forum overseas. ... and I find it impossible to conclude that, objectively speaking, justice would not be done if the wife was compelled to pursue her remedy for financial provision ... in the [French] courts ... which provide, most plainly, the natural forum for the resolution of this matrimonial dispute' (*per* LORD GOFF). (See also *Spiliada Maritime Corporation v Cansulex*.)

De Nicols v Curlier [1900] AC 21 (House of Lords) [139]

Two domiciled French subjects were married in France without having made a marriage contract. They therefore became subject to the French system of community property, whereby they were deemed to have agreed that each of them should have a half share in all property which either of them owned or afterwards acquired. Under French law, their rights under this system were not altered by a change of domicile. The couple acquired an English domicile and the husband died. *Held*, the wife was entitled by virtue of the community system to a half of their joint movable property, despite any attempt by the husband to dispose of it by will as his own. The implied contract created on their marriage by the law of their matrimonial domicile conferred upon her 'real property rights' which could not be obliterated merely by a change of domicile. (See also *Re De Nicols, De Nicols v Curlier*; compare *Re Egerton's Will Trusts, Lloyds Bank Ltd v Egerton*.)

De Reneville v De Reneville [1948] P 100 (Court of Appeal) [140]

A domiciled Englishwoman married a domiciled Frenchman in France and lived with him there for some years. She then returned to England and presented a nullity petition on the ground of wilful refusal to consummate. She failed to give evidence of French law on this topic. *Held*, the court had no jurisdiction because her residence in England was insufficient to confer it and she was not domiciled in England. Her domicile must be taken to be French because (1) the question whether wilful refusal made the marriage void or voidable was for French law, being the law of her husband's antenuptial domicile and of the intended matrimonial domicile; (2) in the absence of evidence of French law, it was presumed to be the same as English law; and (3) English law treated the marriage as voidable, ie, valid until annulled, which meant her domicile was dependant on the French domicile of her husband. (See also *Ramsay-Fairfax (orse Scott-Gibson) v Ramsay Fairfax*.)

de Wolf v Cox (Case 42/76) [1976] ECR 1759 [141]
(European Court of Justice)

de Wolf obtained judgment by default in Belgium against Harry Cox BV, an undertaking with a head office in The Netherlands. Since Cox failed to comply with the judgment, de Wolf applied to the Dutch courts for an order that Cox be made to pay the sums awarded. Initially, judgment was given in favour of this application, and the basis of the judgment was contained in Articles 26 and 31 of the Brussels Convention 1968. Article 26 provides that: 'A judgment given in a Contracting State shall be recognised in the other Contracting States without any special procedure being required'; and Article 31 provides that: 'A judgment given in a Contracting State and enforceable in that State shall be enforced in another Contracting State when, on the application of an interested party, the order for its enforcement has been issued there.' However, under the relevant Netherlands legislation, as the procedure for enforcement would cost more than bringing a second action concerning the same subject matter, the court decided that it was in the interests of the parties that the second course should be followed. The Attorney-General to the Dutch court objected to this on the basis that it infringed Article 31 of the Brussels Convention 1968: de Wolf's application for a fresh judgment should be declared inadmissible as the only course available to him consisted in his submitting an application for the enforcement of the original Belgian judgment. *Held*, in giving a preliminary ruling: 'The provisions of the [Brussels] Convention 1968 prevent a party who has obtained a judgment in his favour in a Contracting State, being a judgment for which an order for enforcement under Article 31 of the Convention may issue in another Contracting State, from making an application to a court in that other State for a judgment against the other party in the same terms as the judgment delivered in the first State.' (See also ss18(8) and 34 of the Civil Jurisdiction and Judgments Act 1982.)

Debaecker v Bouwman (Case 49/84) [1985] ECR 1779 [142]
(European Court of Justice)

In 1980, B, a Dutch national, leased business premises in Belgium from D for use as an art gallery. In 1981, he left without giving notice or leaving a forwarding address. D obtained leave to serve a writ at reduced notice (B being summoned to appear before the court one week later) which was served at an address which accorded with the requirements of the Belgian Judicial Code. B sent a registered letter to D's lawyer repudiating the lease, returning the keys and giving an address at which he could be reached. The letter reached D's lawyer only three days before B was summoned to appear before the cantonal judge in Belgium. D's lawyer took no action and B was left unaware of the service of the writ. Consequently, B did not appear in court and a judgment in default was given against him. Notice of the judgment was served in the same way as the writ. B was made aware of the judgment against him at about the same time as an application was made for his bank account in The Netherlands to be frozen and the enforcement of the judgment against him was authorised. B appealed to the Dutch courts, basing his appeal on, inter alia, Article 27(2) of the Brussels Convention (which provides reasons for not recognising a judgment) contending that the writ was not served 'in sufficient time to enable him to arrange for his defence'. B succeeded in his appeal and D appealed to the Supreme Court of The Netherlands who sought preliminary rulings from the ECJ. *Held*: (1) 'The requirement laid down in Article 27(2) of the [Brussels] Convention ... that service of the document which instituted the proceedings should have been effected in sufficient time is applicable where service was effected within a period prescribed by the court of the State in which judgment was given or where the defendant resided, exclusively or otherwise, within the jurisdiction of that court or the same country as that court. (2) In examining whether service was effected in sufficient time, the court in which enforcement is sought may take account of exceptional circumstances which arose after service was duly effected. (3) The fact that the plaintiff was apprised of the defendant's new address, after service was effected, and the fact that the defendant was responsible for the failure of the duly served document to reach him are matters which the court in which enforcement is sought may take into account in assessing whether service was effected in sufficient time.' (See also *Pendy Plastics* v *Pluspunkt* and *Noirholme* v *Walklate*.)

Derby & Co Ltd v Weldon [1989] 2 WLR 276 (Court of Appeal)

The plaintiff companies sought substantial damages for, inter alia, breach of contract, negligence and breach of fiduciary duty, against the defendants who were former directors of some of the plaintiff companies. In response to the plaintiffs' seeking Mareva injunctions within and outside the jurisdiction, the defendants denied that they had any or any valuable assets within the jurisdiction and they contested the court's jurisdiction to grant an extra-territorial Mareva injunction. At first instance, the plaintiffs succeeded in being granted a Mareva injunction in relation to assets within the jurisdiction but they failed to get one in relation to the assets outside the jurisdiction as this was said to be contrary to the court's practice. *Held*, (1) this was a case 'which cries out for a worldwide Mareva injunction even though it is being sought before judgment. The amount involved and the findings of the judge [at first instance] ... make this clear' (per MAY LJ); and (2) 'there is every justification for a worldwide Mareva, so long as, by undertaking or proviso or a combination of both, (a) oppression of the defendants by way of exposure to a multiplicity of proceedings is avoided, (b) the defendants are protected against the misuse of information gained from the ordinary order for disclosure in aid of the Mareva, and (c) the position of third parties is protected' (*per* PARKER LJ). (See also *Babanaft* v *Bassatne International Co* and *Republic of Haiti* v *Duvalier*.)

Derby & Co Ltd v Weldon (Nos 3 and 4) [1989] 2 WLR 412 (Court of Appeal)

Having obtained Mareva injunctions against the first two defendants, the plaintiffs sought Mareva injunctions against the third and fourth defendants, a Panamanian company and a Luxembourg company, respectively, and the appointment of receivers in furtherance of the injunctions as, allegedly, neither of the defendants had any assets within the jurisdiction. A Mareva injunction was granted in respect of the fourth defendant as it could be enforced under the Brussels Convention as scheduled to the Civil Jurisdiction and Judgments Act 1982, but refused with respect to the third defendant as there was no evidence that such an injunction could be enforced in Panama even if it had any assets there. The fourth defendant (the Luxembourg company) appealed and the plaintiffs cross appealed against the refusal to grant a Mareva injunction against the third (Panamanian company) defendant. *Held*, the existence of assets within the jurisdiction was not a pre-condition of granting a Mareva injunction and there was no need to make a distinction between the defendants when granting the injunction, which operated in personam, or appointing a receiver.

Deschamps v Miller [1908] 1 Ch 856 [145]

J and M, who were parties to a marriage in France and who were domiciled in France, agreed at the time of their marriage that their property should be governed by the French community system, whereby (inter alia) the wife (M) was entitled to claim a half share in any property subsequently acquired by the husband (J). The husband later married another woman (CT) bigamously in India and between 1865–1869 settled upon her some Indian land acquired by him since the first marriage. After J, M and CT had died, M's administrator claimed a half share in the Indian land from the trustees of the settlement, who resided in England. *Held,* the court had no jurisdiction in the action, by virtue of the rule in *British South Africa Co v Companhia de Mocambique*. The case did not fall within the exceptions to this rule, which all depended on 'the existence between the parties to the suit of some personal obligation arising out of contract or implied contract, fiduciary relationship or fraud, or other conduct which, in the view of a Court of Equity in this country, would be unconscionable' (*per* PARKER J). (See also *Penn v Lord Baltimore*.)

Despina R, The, Owners of MV Eleftherotria v Owners [146]
of MV Despina R [1979] AC 685 (House of Lords)

The object of the consolidated appeals, one in tort and the other in contract, was to determine the currency in which damages should be awarded. In the first appeal, agreement had been reached that the owners of the *Despina R* would pay to the owners of the *MV Eleftherotria* 85 per cent of the loss and damage suffered as a result of the collision between the two Greek ships off Shanghai. Expenses were incurred in renmibi yuan (or 'RMB', a Chinese currency), Japanese yen, US dollars and sterling. At first instance, whereas BRANDON J held that he had jurisdiction to award damages in a foreign currency, it had to be the currency of expenditure. This was reversed by the Court of Appeal which held that the appropriate currency was that which the plaintiff could prove was the one with which he conducted his business. *Held,* approving the Court of Appeal's approach, the principles to be applied in ascertaining the currency of the loss were those of restitutio integrum and reasonable foreseeability. Accordingly, where a plaintiff proved that he conducted his business in a specific currency and it was reasonably foreseeable that he would use that currency to purchase the necessary currency to meet the immediate and direct expenditure caused by the defendant's tort, then judgment should be expressed in the plaintiff's currency. Here, the appropriate currency was US dollars. In the second appeal, where a contract was governed by English law, the plaintiffs had settled a claim against them in Brazilian currency which they had purchased with French francs. In a claim for reimbursement from the defendants, arbitrators made their award in French francs – a decision reversed at first instance but restored by the Court of Appeal. *Held,* where the terms of a contract governed by English law did not expressly or by implication show that the parties had intended that payments arising from breach of contract were to be paid in the currency of account or other named currency, the court should give judgment in the currency that best expressed the party's loss. Here, that was French francs. LORD WILBERFORCE added a qualification, however, when he said that: 'I wish to make it clear that I would not approve of a hard and fast rule that in all cases where a plaintiff suffers a loss or damage in a foreign currency the right currency to take for the purpose of his claim is "the plaintiff's currency". I should ... emphasise that it does not suggest the use of a personal currency attached, like nationality, to a plaintiff, but a currency which he is able to show is that in which he normally conducts trading operations.' (See also *Miliangos* v *George Frank (Textiles) Ltd.*)

Diamond v Bank of London and Montreal Ltd [147]
[1979] 1 QB 333 (Court of Appeal)

The plaintiff, who began an action for damages against the defendant bank for negligent misrepresentation, applied under RSC O.11, r.3 for leave to serve a writ on the defendant out of the jurisdiction. However, the judge at first instance decided that either the court had no jurisdiction since the action begun by writ was not 'founded on a tort committed within the jurisdiction' under (what is now) RSC O.11, r.1(1)(f) or, if it did have jurisdiction, he would not exercise his discretion to grant leave because the plaintiff had not discharged his burden of proof as to financial loss. The plaintiff made no appeal against this decision; instead, he began a separate action for damages, citing substantially the same evidence as in the first action, alleging that fraud caused his losses and again he sought leave to serve out of the jurisdiction. For the second time, leave was refused because if fraud had been committed the substance of the tort had been committed outside the jurisdiction as was the case in the first action. *Held*, negligent or fraudulent misrepresentations which originated out of the jurisdiction but which were made by means of instantaneous communications, ie by telex or by telephone in this case, were made, and the substance of the tort committed, within the jurisdiction: accordingly, the court had jurisdiction to grant leave under (what is now) O.11, r.1(1)(f); but leave would not be granted because, on the facts of the case, the plaintiff did not have a good arguable case that he had suffered the losses he had claimed. (Contrast *Cordova Land Co Ltd* v *Victor Bros Inc.*)

Dimskal Shipping v International Transport Workers' [148]
Federation, The Evia Luck [1992] 2 AC 152 (House of Lords)

The International Transport Workers' Federation had threatened to 'black' Dimskal's vessel while it was in a Swedish port unless Dimskal entered into new contracts with the crew, and pay back-dated increased wages. Dimskal avoided the 'blacking' by agreeing to the demands and paying the money. The proper law of the contract was English law, under which a contract induced by duress is voidable by the innocent party. One form of duress is illegitimate economic pressure and this includes the 'blacking' of a ship. On this basis, Dimskal sued ITWF in London for a declaration that the contracts were void for duress and for return of the sums paid not under the void contracts. Economic pressure amounting to duress was not unlawful in Sweden. *Held*, Dimskal would succeed: the terms were invalid under the proper law. (Contrast *Trendtex Trading Corporation* v *Credit Suisse.*)

Distillers Co (Biochemicals) v Laura Anne Thompson [149]
[1971] AC 458 (Privy Council)

The drug distoval, which contained thalidomide obtained in bulk from German suppliers, was manufactured in England and marketed in, inter alia, New South Wales, Australia. Although thalidomide had led to congenital deformities in newborn babies when the mothers had taken the drug within the first three months of pregnancy, the English manufacturers had taken no steps to warn purchasers of the drug of its potentially harmful effects if it were taken by a pregnant woman. The plaintiff's mother took the drug whilst pregnant with the plaintiff who, subsequently, was born with defective eyesight and without arms. *Held*, the cause of action arose in New South Wales. In deciding that the tort consisted of a negligent failure to give an adequate warning of the drug's harmful propensities, it was said that: 'The right approach is, when the tort is complete, to look back over the series of events constituting it and ask the question, where in substance did this cause of action arise?' (*per* LORD PEARSON.) (See also *Metall und Rohstoff AG v Donaldson Lufkin & Jenrette.*)

Dresser UK v Falcongate Freight Management [150]
[1992] 1 QB 502 (Court of Appeal)

Proceedings relating to the loss of goods at sea were commenced in The Netherlands and in England. Proceedings began in England with the issue of a writ in July 1988 which was served in July 1989. However, in February 1989, the defendants had commenced proceedings in the Dutch courts for limitation of liability with respect to the lost cargo without admitting liability. The defendants applied for a stay of the English proceedings on the basis (1) that the plaintiffs were bound by an exclusive jurisdiction clause contained in the bill of lading which provided that the bill of lading was to be governed by Dutch law; and (2) since the English courts were not seised of the action until July 1989 the Dutch courts were first seised of a related action for the purposes of Article 22 of the Brussels Convention. At first instance, it was decided that the plaintiffs were not bound by the exclusive jurisdiction clause and that the English courts were first seised of the proceedings in July 1988. *Held*, inter alia, (1) the absence of an agreement between the cargo owners and the defendants (who were sub-contractors who had named the freight management company as consignees) meant the cargo owners were not bound by the exclusive jurisdiction clause; and (2) as a general, but not invariable rule, the English courts became seised of an action when a writ was served on the defendant not when it was issued. (Contrast point (2) with the decisions in *Kloeckner and Co AG v Gatoil Overseas Inc* and *Neste Chemicals SA v DK Line SA, The Sargasso.*)

Du Pont & Co v Agnew and others [1987] 2 Lloyd's Rep 585 [151]
(Court of Appeal)

A man who had been administered the plaintiffs anti-coagulant drug in an operation developed necrosis in both legs which had to be amputated below the knees. Subsequently, he was awarded US$26 million which included punitive damages of US $13 million. The plaintiffs, who were insured under several policies against product liability claims, then initiated proceedings in England, where the leading policy was issued, claiming indemnity from their insurers. This was resisted by the defendant insurers in proceedings begun in Illinois, USA, on the basis that they were not bound to indemnify the plaintiffs against an award of punitive damages and forum non conveniens. The defendants also sought an injunction to restrain the English proceedings. The defendants pursued their case to the Court of Appeal. *Held*, whereas none of the insurance policies contained an express choice of law, the proper law of the lead policy was English and, unless displaced, the inference that English law was intended to govern was overwhelming; applying *The Spiliada*, the defendants had not shown that Illinois was a clearly more appropriate forum but the plaintiffs had established that England was clearly the more appropriate forum; and as the plaintiffs had a strongly arguable case the defendants' appeals would be dismissed. (See also *Du Pont v Agnew (No 2).*)

Du Pont v Agnew (No 2) [1988] 2 Lloyd's Rep 240 [152]
(Court of Appeal)

Following the decision of the English Court of Appeal in *Du Pont* v *Agnew*, the Illinois court dismissed applications by the insurers and Du Pont for summary judgment in the Illinois proceedings. The court had earlier dismissed a motion by the insurers to restrain Du Pont from proceeding with the English proceedings and a motion by Du Pont to stay the Illinois proceedings pending the outcome of the English proceedings. By contrast with the Court of Appeal finding, however, the Illinois court believed that Illinois law governed the construction of the insurance policies. As it appeared that the Illinois proceedings would go to trial before the English proceedings, Du Pont applied to the English Commercial Court for one of two forms of injunction – essentially an injunction restraining the insurers from continuing with the Illinois proceedings – and one of two forms of declaration, particularly that the proper law of the policies was English; that the insurers were not entitled to rely on the Illinois judgment; and that the insurers were bound to indemnify Du Pont. *Held*, inter alia, (1) to grant an injunction preventing the insurers from continuing their action in Illinois 'would be to do precisely what Lord Goff said [in *The Spiliada*] is not right: the English court would be arrogating to itself the power to resolve the dispute between the English and Illinois Court as to which is the natural forum' (*per* DILLON LJ). Accordingly, it was not granted. (2) Since it was clear that prior to final judgment of the Illinois court there could be no application by the insurers to amend their pleadings in the English proceedings to rely on a final Illinois judgment as an estoppel, Du Pont's application for a declaration was premature and would not be granted.

Duke of Wellington, Re, Glentanar v Wellington see Wellington (Duke of), Re, Glentanar v Wellington

Dulles' Settlement (No 2), Re, Dulles v Vidler [153]
[1951] Ch 842 (Court of Appeal)

Proceedings begun on behalf of an infant against his father who was resident in the USA included a claim for the infant's maintenance. The father was legally represented in court and he contested the court's jurisdiction. Did this representation constitute submission to the jurisdiction? *Held*: 'I cannot see how anyone can fairly say that a man has voluntarily submitted to the jurisdiction of a court, when he has all the time been vigorously protesting that it had no jurisdiction. If he does nothing and lets judgment go against him in default of appearance, he clearly does not submit to the jurisdiction. What difference in principle does it make, if he does not merely do nothing, but actually goes to the court and protests that it has no jurisdiction? I can see no distinction at all' (*per* DENNING LJ). (See also *Williams & Glyn's Bank* v *Astro Dinamico*.)

Duncan v Lawson (1889) 41 Ch D 394 [154]

A testator who died domiciled in Scotland left various legacies and the ultimate residue of his estate to English and Scottish charities. The legacies were payable in part out of leasehold property in England, but under English law any testamentary gift of an interest in land to charity was void. *Held*, as the leasehold property was an immovable, English law, the lex situs, was applicable. English law then (1) rendered the legacies and residuary gift void so far as the leasehold was concerned; and (2) determined which of the next-of-kin should take on the resulting intestacy. (See also *Freke* v *Lord Carbery*.)

Dunlop Pneumatic Tyre Co Ltd v Achtiengesellschaft [155]
für Motor und Motorfahrzeugbau Vorm Cudell & Co
[1902] 1 KB 342 (Court of Appeal)

The defendant, a company incorporated in Germany as a manufacturer of motor-cars, hired a stand for nine days for its own exclusive use at an exhibition in Crystal Palace, London, where it displayed its products under its own name. The person in charge of the stand was an employee (who was neither a director nor the secretary) who was there to explain the working of the articles exhibited, to take orders and to endeavour to promote sales. The defendant company did not operate elsewhere in England. The plaintiff company issued a writ against it, alleging infringement of a patent, and served it on the employee at the stand during the exhibition. *Held*, the court had jurisdiction over the defendant and this was good service. As a 'substantial part' of the defendant's business was being carried on by its representative on its behalf at a fixed place in England and for a reasonable length of time, the defendant was 'resident' in England for the purposes of jurisdiction. (See also *Thames and Mersey Marine Insurance Co* v *Societa di Navigazione a Vapore del Lloyd Austriaco*.)

Dynamit Actien-Gesellschaft (Vor Mals Alfred Nobel [156]
Co) v Rio Tinto Co Ltd [1918] AC 260 (House of Lords)

Prior to the outbreak of World War I, Rio Tinto (RT), an English company, contracted to sell to a German company approximately two million tons of copper ore, to be extracted from mines in Spain, to be delivered over a period of four years. The contract contained a suspensory clause providing that if RT should be prevented from shipping or delivering the ore for a cause over which they had no control, including war, then the obligation to ship and deliver should be suspended during the course of the impediment and for a reasonable time afterwards. The contract provided for corresponding provisions in favour of the buyers. The contract was governed by German law. Litigation was commenced after the outbreak of the war, under the Legal Proceedings Against Enemies Act 1915. *Held*, inter alia, the parties' rights were not merely suspended by the war, they were terminated. Although the proper law of the contract was not English law, the suspensory clause was void in England because it contravened the overriding rule of public policy prohibiting British subjects from trading with the enemy in time of war. (Compare *Boissevain* v *Weil*.)

Effer v Kanter (Case 38/81) [1982] ECR 825 [157]
(European Court of Justice)

K, a German patent agent, claimed in the German courts for the payment of a fee, the amount of which was not disputed and for work carried out in Germany, from an Italian manufacturer of cranes who had sold its products in Germany through an undertaking which had become bankrupt. The crane manufacturer, Effer, disputed that K had been contracted by them, implying that he had been commissioned by the bankrupt firm, and in the absence of a contract between Effer and K, Effer contended that the German courts had no jurisdiction to decide the dispute. The German Federal Court then sought a preliminary ruling from the ECJ. *Held*, 'The plaintiff may invoke the jurisdiction of the place of performance in accordance with Article 5(1) of the [Brussels] Convention 1968 ... even when the existence of the contract on which the claim is based is in dispute between the parties.' (See also *Tesam Distribution Ltd* v *Schuh Mode Team GmbH and Commerzbank AG*.)

Egerton's Will Trusts, Re, Lloyds Bank Ltd v Egerton [158]
[1956] Ch 593

A domiciled English soldier married a domiciled Frenchwoman in England. At the time, they agreed that 'as soon as possible' they should establish a permanent home in France, but this did not in fact happen until more than two years later. On the husband's death, the wife claimed that his estate should be administered in community property according to French law. *Held*, this claim should be rejected. There was insufficient evidence to rebut the prima facie rule that, in the absence of a marriage contract or settlement, the spouses' marital property rights were governed by the law of 'matrimonial domicile', which meant in this context the husband's domicile at the marriage. A mere agreement to change that domicile to France 'as soon as possible' did not imply an agreement to adopt French marital property law. (Compare *De Nicols* v *Curlier*.)

Egyptian Delta Land and Investment Co Ltd v Todd [159]
[1929] AC 1 (House of Lords)

The appellant company was incorporated in England in 1904 under the Companies Acts with a nominal capital of £500,000. Its main objects were to acquire, hold, sell, let, or otherwise dispose of and deal in land situate in any district in Egypt served, or thereafter to be served, by railways belonging to the Egyptian Delta Light Railways Ltd. In 1907 the company's business was transferred to Cairo from where it was then controlled, managed, directed and carried on. To comply with the requirements of the Companies Acts there was a registered office of the company in London, at which the registers of members and directors and also a register of bearer warrants were kept. To meet those statutory requirements the company paid a fee to a man who carried on the business of secretary of public companies, and who provided them with a registered office at his address in London, where the name of the company, together with the names of five other companies, appeared on the door. The Crown claimed income tax in respect of interest accruing from mortgages and leases of land made in Egypt. *Held*, the company was not resident in England: it was resident only in Egypt. (But see *Cesena Sulphur Co* v *Nicholson* and *Swedish Central Railway Co Ltd* v *Thompson*.)

El Amria, The, Aratra Potato Co Ltd v Egyptian Navigation Co [160]
[1981] 2 Lloyd's Rep 119 (Court of Appeal)

In an action claiming damages for breach of contract and/or negligence in the stowage, custody and care of a cargo of potatoes on board the *El Amria*, the plaintiffs sought to invoke the jurisdiction of the English courts contrary to Clause 3 of the bill of lading providing, inter alia, that: 'Any dispute arising under this Bill of Lading shall be decided in the country where the carrier has his principal place of business, and the law of such country shall apply ...'. The defendants sought a stay on the basis that the dispute was to be decided by an Egyptian court. At first instance, SHEEN J decided that all the most significant features of the case were solely concerned with events which occurred in England and that as they had no direct connection with Egypt the disputes was most closely connected with England. Accordingly, he refused the stay. *Held*, the appeal would be dismissed. BRANDON LJ reiterated the principles he had expressed in *The Eleftheria*. The plaintiffs had established good cause why they should not be held to their agreement. (See also *Evans Marshall & Co Ltd* v *Bertola*.)

Elefanten Schuh GmbH v Jacqmain (Case 150/80) [161]
[1981] ECR 1671 (European Court of Justice)

J, a Belgian resident, was the sole sales agent in certain provinces of Belgium for the Belgian subsidiary of E, a company having its registered office in Germany. A dispute arose after J had been dismissed without notice on urgent grounds in December 1975. J brought proceedings before a Belgian Labour Tribunal against E and its Belgian subsidiary for damages for breach of the contract of employment but it appeared that his original contract of employment, which was drafted in German, contained a clause giving exclusive jurisdiction to a German court. E, accordingly, challenged the jurisdiction of the Belgian Labour Tribunal. However, a provision of the Belgian Judicial Code provided that no provision to the contrary could deprive the plaintiff of the right to bring his claim before that tribunal. On that basis, the tribunal rejected the plea as to jurisdiction and ordered the companies to pay most of the damages claimed. Furthermore, another Belgian law required J's contract of employment to be written in Dutch. Thus, the contract of employment, having been written in German, was null and void so that Article 17 of the Brussels Convention (on prorogation of jurisdiction) could not apply. Following challenges to these decisions, questions on the applicability of Articles 17 and 18 were referred to the ECJ for a preliminary ruling. *Held*, (1) 'Article 18 of the [Brussels] Convention 1968 ... [which gives jurisdiction to the court of a Contracting State before whom the defendant enters an appearance] applies even where the parties have by agreement designated a court which is to have jurisdiction within the meaning of Article 17 of that Convention.' (2) 'Article 18 ... must be interpreted as meaning that the rule on jurisdiction which that provision lays down does not apply where the defendant not only contests the court's jurisdiction but also makes submissions on the substance of the action, provided that, if the challenge to jurisdiction is not preliminary to any defence as to substance, it does not occur after the making of the submissions which under national procedural law are considered to be the first defence addressed to the court seised.' (3) 'Article 17 ... must be interpreted as meaning that the legislation of a Contracting State may not allow the validity of an agreement conferring jurisdiction to be called in question solely on the ground that the language used is not that prescribed by that legislation.' (See also *Rank Film Distributors* v *Lanterna Editrice SRL*.)

Eleftheria, The, Owners of Cargo Lately Laden on Board the Ship or Vessel Eleftheria v The Eleftheria (Owners) [162]
[1970] P 74

The plaintiffs, who were the owners of cargo lately laden on the *Eleftheria*, brought an action in rem against the Greek defendants, the owners of the vessel *Eleftheria*, for breach of contracts of carriage as contained in the bills of lading. A cargo of timber which was consigned to Hull had, in fact, been discharged in Rotterdam and the plaintiffs had arranged for the on-carriage at their own expense. The defendants sought to rely on the provisions of Clause 3 of the bill of lading and applied for a stay of action. Clause 3 provided that: 'Any dispute arising under this bill of lading shall be decided in the country where the carrier has his principal place of business, and the law of such country shall apply ...'. *Held*, per BRANDON J: 'The principles established by the authorities can, I think, be summarised as follows: (1) Where plaintiffs sue in England in breach of an agreement to refer disputes to a foreign court, and the defendants apply for a stay, the English court, assuming the claim to be otherwise within its jurisdiction, is not bound to grant a stay but has a discretion whether to do so or not. (2) The discretion should be exercised by granting a stay unless strong cause for not doing so is shown. (3) The burden of proving such strong cause is on the plaintiffs. (4)

In exercising its discretion the court should take into account all the circumstances of the particular case. (5) In particular, but without prejudice to (4), the following matters, where they arise, may properly be regarded: (a) In what country the evidence on the issues of the fact is situated, or more readily available, and the effect of that on the relative convenience and expense of trial as between the English and foreign courts. (b) Whether the law of the foreign court applies and, if so, whether it differs from English law in any material respects. (c) With what country either party is connected, and how closely. (d) Whether the defendants genuinely desire trial in the foreign country, or are only seeking procedural advantages. (e) Whether the plaintiffs would be prejudiced by having to sue in the foreign court because they would: (i) be deprived of security for their claim; (ii) be unable to enforce any judgment obtained; (iii) for political, racial, religious or other reasons be unlikely to get a fair trial.' As the plaintiffs had failed to establish good cause why they should not be held to their agreement, the action would be stayed. (See also *The El Amria* and *Evans Marshall & Co Ltd* v *Bertola*.)

Ellis v M'Henry (1871) LR 6 CP 228 [163]

A debtor executed a composition deed operating in England as a discharge in bankruptcy. Subsequently, he was sued to judgment in Upper Canada (then a British colony subject to English bankruptcy law) for a debt due under a contract governed by Canadian law. He did not attempt to set up the composition deed as a defence. The successful creditor then sued to recover the debt in England, specifying two counts: (1) the judgment, and (2), because in all places where English bankruptcy law was in force it operated as a discharge of all debts, whatever their proper law. *Held,* the action would succeed on count (1) because the judgment, being that of a competent court, was final and conclusive between the parties even though the deed, if pleaded, would have provided a good defence. (See also *Godard* v *Gray*.)

Emanuel v Symon [1908] 1 KB 302 (Court of Appeal) [164]

While residing in Western Australia, the defendant entered into a partnership formed to work a mine in Western Australia which the partnership owned. He later left Western Australia and settled in England. In the course of Western Australian proceedings for dissolution of the partnership, the plaintiffs, who were the other partners, obtained a default judgment against the defendant for his share of the partnership debts. They sought to enforce the judgment in England, arguing that the West Australian court had jurisdiction over the defendant by virtue of (1) his participation in the partnership or (2) his share in the partnership land, or both. *Held*, neither of these was a sufficient basis of jurisdiction to render the judgment enforceable in England. 'In actions in personam there are five cases in which the courts of this country will enforce a foreign judgment: (1) where the defendant is a subject of the foreign country in which the judgment has been obtained; (2) where he was resident in the foreign country when the action began; (3) where the defendant in the character of the plaintiff has selected the forum in which he is afterwards sued; (4) where he has voluntarily appeared; and (5) where he has contracted to submit himself to the forum in which the judgment was obtained' (*per* BUCKLEY LJ). (See also *Schibsby* v *Westenholz*.)

Embiricos v Anglo-Austrian Bank [1905] 1 KB 677 [165]
(Court of Appeal)

The plaintiffs, the payees under a cheque drawn in Romania on a London bank, indorsed it in Romania in favour of a London firm, from whom it was stolen by one of the London firm's employees. Bearing a forged indorsement by the London firm, it was later presented at an Austrian bank in Vienna and, by paying cash for it, the Austrian bank acquired good title to it according to Austrian law, though not according to English law. The bank indorsed the cheque to the defendant, a bank in England, which cashed it at the bank on which it was drawn and was then sued for conversion by the plaintiffs. *Held*, the action would fail because the bank in Vienna, through which the defendant claimed, had acquired a good title. 'The rule that the validity of the transfer of chattels must be governed by the law of the country in which the transfer takes place, applies to a bill or cheque' (*per* VAUGHAN WILLIAMS LJ). Section 72(2) of the Bills of Exchange Act 1882 also seemed to protect the defendant. (See also *Cammell* v *Sewell* and *Winkworth* v *Christie, Manson & Woods*.)

Emery's Investments Trusts, Re, Emery v Emery [166]
[1959] Ch 410

A husband living in South America bought American shares and registered them in his wife's name in New York in order to avoid a New York withholding tax to which he, but not his wife, would be liable. They intended to share any profit equally, but the husband's failure to disclose this fact to the authorities in New York was a breach of the taxing statute. The wife later sold the shares. *Held*, the husband could not recover his share of the proceeds of sale. To rebut the presumption of advancement in his wife's favour (arising from the purchase in her name), he would have to rely on the illegally concealed agreement, and the court would not lend its assistance to the carrying out of an agreement designed to breach the revenue laws of a friendly country. (See also *Foster* v *Driscoll*.)

EMI Records v Modern Music Karl-Ulrich Walterbach GmbH [1992] 1 QB 115 [167]

Modern Music had succeeded in obtaining an ex-parte injunction restraining EMI from reproducing and distributing recordings of a certain pop group. The injunction was granted without prior notice or service of documents on the defendant, EMI. The latter appealed against registration of the judgment. *Held*, allowing the appeal, the order of the German court was not a judgment within Article 27(2) of the Brussels Convention registrable under s4 of the Civil Jurisdiction and Judgments Act 1982. HOBHOUSE J noted that 'Article 27 provides that judgments shall not be recognised for a number of reasons of which the second is: "where it was given in default of appearance, if the defendant was not duly served with the document which instituted the proceedings or with an equivalent document in sufficient time to enable him to arrange for his defence".' Accordingly, the registration would be set aside. (Contrast *Noirholme* v *Walklate*.)

Entores v Miles Far East Corporation [1955] 2 QB 333 [168]
(Court of Appeal)

The plaintiffs, an English company with a registered office in London, contracted with the defendants' agents, who were based in The Netherlands, for the purchase of goods from the defendants who were an American corporation with headquarters in New York. The contract had been concluded by way of an exchange of telex messages, acceptance of the plaintiffs' offer being received by the plaintiffs on their telex machine in London. The plaintiffs subsequently alleged that the defendants had breached the contract and they sought leave under RSC O.11 to serve the defendants out of the jurisdiction. Service out of the jurisdiction under O.11 could properly be allowed if the contract had been made within the jurisdiction. The defendants claimed the contract was made in The Netherlands. *Held*, 'the rule about instantaneous communications between the parties is different from the rule about the post. The contract is only complete when the acceptance is received by the offeror; and the contract is made at the place where the acceptance is received' (*per* DENNING LJ). Thus, the contract was made in London and it was a proper case for service out of the jurisdiction under RSC O.11. (See also *Brinkibon Ltd* v *Stahag Stahl*.)

Esso Malaysia, The [1975] 1 QB 198 [169]

All 24 members of the crew of a Soviet vessel were drowned following a collision between a Panamanian vessel, the *Esso Honduras*, and the Soviet vessel, the master and crew of the Panamanian vessel being liable, in part, in negligence for the collision. The plaintiff, as administrator of the estates of the Russian seamen, brought an action in rem against the *Esso Malaysia*, a sister ship of the *Esso Honduras*, claiming damages under the Fatal Accidents Acts 1846–1959. *Held*, a differentiation was to be made between 'statutes which, on the one hand, create new rules of conduct, and those which, on the other hand, remove exceptions to common law liabilities, or attach new liabilities to the violation of existing rules of conduct. The Act of 1846 falls into the second part of the second category, being a statute which attached new liabilities to the violation of existing rules of conduct' (*per* BRANDON J). Accordingly, the plaintiff had a good cause of action for the recovery of damages in England from the owners of the Panamanian vessel under the aforementioned Fatal Accidents Acts. (Contrast *Sayers* v *International Drilling Co NV*.)

European Asian Bank AG v Punjab and Sind Bank [170]
[1982] 2 Lloyd's Rep 356 (Court of Appeal)

J, an Indian company based in New Delhi, contracted to buy goods for US$2,250,000 c & f, from B, a Singapore company, payment to be made 180 days from the bill of lading by irrevocable letter of credit. J asked the defendant bank to cause a letter of credit to be opened and the defendants instructed their correspondents in Singapore to advise B through the plaintiff bank of the opening of the letter of credit. The normal course of procedures were then followed until, in due course, in response to the plaintiffs' enquiry of the paying bank if the latter had been put in funds to honour the credit, the answer was that there was no record of that credit. J had been informed earlier that the vessel carrying their goods had sunk with total loss of the consignment and they had obtained an injunction restraining the defendants from paying under the letter of credit. When the confirming bank in Singapore also denied liability, the plaintiffs commenced an action in England for the $2,250,000 plus interest. J and the defendants sought a stay of action, contending that India or Singapore was the natural forum for the action, not England. Their applications were dismissed at first instance. *Held*, J's application would be dismissed on the basis that they had no locus standi as they could not show, inter alia, that it would be a fraud on J to allow the plaintiffs to proceed with an action in England; and the defendants' application was dismissed because neither India nor Singapore was the natural or clearly more appropriate forum for the trial of the action. Indeed: 'This country's Commercial Court is clearly a natural and appropriate court to try yet another claim on a letter of credit by the application of the classic principle that the contract created by the issue of a letter of credit is independent of any underlying contract between buyer and seller and must be performed by prompt payment against documents' (*per* STEPHENSON LJ). (See also *Spiliada Maritime Corporation* v *Cansulex*.)

Evans Marshall & Co Ltd v Bertola [1973] 1 WLR 349   **[171]**
(Court of Appeal)

An agreement was reached between the plaintiffs, Evans Marshall, an English company who were wholesale wine merchants, and a Spanish company, the first defendants, that produced and shipped sherry. The plaintiffs were to be the first defendants' sole agents for the sale of their sherry in England. In the event of any dispute, Clause 15 of their agreement provided that: 'If any law claim arises between the two parties it will be submitted to the Barcelona Court of Justice.' Later, the first defendants contended that the plaintiffs' activities under the agreement were unsatisfactory and they purported to appoint another company, the second defendants, as their sole agents in England. The plaintiffs then commenced actions against both defendants seeking, inter alia, damages from both defendants and an injunction against the first defendants restraining them from selling their sherry in the UK other than through the plaintiffs' agency. The plaintiffs also sought leave under RSC O.11 to serve the first defendants out of the jurisdiction. Leave was granted at first instance because of the special circumstances which included the fact that the substance of the case was exclusively concerned with England and that the dispute involved not only the parties to clause 15 but also the second defendants. The plaintiffs appealed against the refusal of the grant of the injunction and the first defendants appealed against the service under O.11. *Held*, leave under O.11 had been rightly given because the situation was in the scope of that order and it embraced exceptional circumstances: thus, the first defendants' appeal would be dismissed; and the plaintiffs' appeal would be allowed as it was important to maintain the status quo since damages were an inadequate remedy. (See also *The Eleftheria* and *The El Amria*.)

Ewing v Orr-Ewing (1883) 9 App Cas 34 (House of Lords)   **[172]**

A testator died domiciled in Scotland leaving immovable property in Scotland and movables in Scotland and England. In his will he appointed six persons as executors and trustees, of whom three resided in Scotland and three in England. A beneficiary instituted an administration action, serving the Scottish trustees under RSC O.11, but before the hearing the trustees removed all the English property to Scotland. *Held*, the English court had jurisdiction even though all the trust property, including land, was situated out of England. 'The English Courts of Equity are, and always have been, courts of conscience operating in personam and not in rem, and in the exercise of this personal jurisdiction they have always been accustomed to compel the performance of contracts and trusts as to subjects which were not either locally or ratione domicilii within their jurisdiction' (*per* LORD SELBOURNE LC).

Fatima, In re [1986] 1 AC 527 (House of Lords)   **[173]**

A Pakistani man resident in England purported to divorce his wife, who was resident in Pakistan, by pronouncing a talaq. He complied with the Pakistan Muslim Laws Ordinance 1961 in sending a written notice of his pronouncement of the talaq to his wife and to the chairman of his local union council in Pakistan. The Ordinance provided for the dissolution of his marriage 90 days after receipt of the notice by the chairman of the local union council. When the man's new fiancée arrived at Heathrow Airport from Pakistan, she was refused leave to enter the UK on the ground that the immigration officer was not persuaded that the intended marriage could take place within a reasonable time because he was of the opinion that the man's divorce would not be recognised in the UK. The fiancée's motion for judicial review of the immigration officer's decision was dismissed as was her appeal in the Court of Appeal. In the House of Lords, LORD

ACKNER said: 'The essential question for your Lordships' decision is whether the divorce ... is to be recognised as a valid overseas divorce under section 2 of the Recognition of Divorces and Legal Separations Act 1971 (the 'Recognition Act').' *Held*, dismissing the fiancée's appeal, that ss2 and 3(1) of the 'Recognition Act', 'when read together, make it clear that the "proceedings" in section 2(a) must be a single set of proceedings which have to be instituted in the same country as that in which the relevant divorce was ultimately obtained' (*per* LORD ACKNER). As the pronouncement of the talaq had taken place in England the requirements of s3(1) had not been complied with: accordingly, the immigration officer was correct in deciding that the proposed marriage could not take place within a reasonable time. (See now ss45 and 46 of the Family Law Act 1986.)

Fehmarn, The [1958] 1 WLR 159 (Court of Appeal) [174]

A Russian company shipped turpentine from Russia to the plaintiff, an English company, in London. The bill of lading stipulated that all disputes arising out of it should be adjudicated in Russia according to Russian law. The plaintiff, alleging that the turpentine was contaminated on arrival, brought proceedings in England for damages against the defendant, a German company which owned the ship and carried on business in England and Germany. The plaintiff alleged that it would be calling English witnesses and the defendant claimed to be intending to call Russian witnesses. *Held*, the defendant's application for a stay of proceedings should be refused, because the 'English element' in the case was far stronger than the Russian. 'A stipulation that all disputes should be judged by the tribunals of a particular country is not absolutely binding ... it is subject to the overriding principle that no one by his private stipulation can oust these courts of their jurisdiction in a matter that properly belongs to them' (*per* LORD DENNING). (See also *The Eleftheria*, *The El Amria*, and *Evans Marshall & Co Ltd* v *Bertola*; compare *Mackender* v *Feldia AG*.)

Felixstowe Dock & Railway Co v United States Lines Inc [175]
[1989] QB 360

English and European companies that were trade creditors of the defendant American company obtained ex parte Mareva injunctions restraining the defendants from removing their assets out of the jurisdiction. The defendants sought to set aside the injunctions on the basis that they were already subject to a restraining order made by the US bankruptcy court under chapter 11 of the United States Federal Bankruptcy Code. This is a procedure under which a financially distressed company undergoes a major programme of reorganisation and retrenchment under the supervision of a creditors' committee and the court, with all claims against the company being frozen during the currency of the order. *Held*, the restraining order made by the US court was an order in personam which did not have to be accorded recognition by the English courts. Indeed, the nature and degree of any co-operation between the English and US courts had to be governed by English bankruptcy practice which did not countenance an order under which an overseas company's English assets were removed entirely outside the control of the English courts. Moreover, 'it follows that, in view of the intended withdrawal of USL from Europe, there could be no possible benefit [to the plaintiffs] in seeing the Mareva funds repatriated to the USA and ploughed into USL's general funds ... to keep USL afloat as a going concern. ... So far as prejudice is concerned, I am satisfied that USL will suffer no material prejudice if the Mareva injunctions continue, since the assets will remain safely here, and there is no prospect of their being distributed without the intervention of ancillary winding-up proceedings' (*per* HIRST J). (See also *Re Trepca Mines Ltd*; contrast *Travers* v *Holley*.)

Fitzgerald, Re, Surman v Fitzgerald [1904] 1 Ch 573 [176]
(Court of Appeal)

Prior to marrying in Scotland, a domiciled Englishman and a domiciled Scotswoman executed a settlement in Scottish form whereby on her death he acquired a life-interest in a fund situated in Scotland, but only on condition that the income thereof could not be assigned nor executed against by creditors. This form of 'alimentary' restriction was substantially effective under Scottish law but was not recognised in English law. After the marriage, the couple were domiciled in England, as were the trustees of the settlement. After the wife had died, the husband executed various mortgages of his life-interest. *Held*, the mortgages should take effect only so far as Scottish law permitted. Although normally a marriage settlement was governed by the law of the matrimonial domicile, the circumstances here indicated that the parties had impliedly contracted with reference to Scottish law. (Compare *Marlborough (Duke) v Attorney-General* [1945] Ch 78.)

Flynn deceased, Re, Flynn v Flynn [1968] 1 WLR 103 [177]

The film actor Errol Flynn, whose domicile of origin was uncertain, though probably in an Australian State, acquired a domicile of choice in California, USA, but then left that State in 1952 without any intention of returning. He had relinquished all interest in his California home by 1956 and, later, when he regarded Jamaica as his permanent home, he developed a positive intention never to return to California, mainly for financial reasons. *Held*, he lost his domicile of choice in California some time between the time of his departure in 1952 and the development of the positive intention in 1956 never to return. A domicile of choice was lost by physical departure coupled with a lack of any intention to return. It was not necessary to prove a positive determination never to return to the place in question. Accordingly, his domicile of origin (whatever that was) revived in or after 1956 and that, in turn, was replaced by a new domicile of choice in Jamaica when he regarded that country, in which he had owned estates and a house for more than ten years, as his permanent home. (Contrast *In the Goods of Raffenel*.)

Fordyce v Bridges (1848) 2 Ph 497 [178]

An English testator bequeathed his residuary personalty on trust to be applied to the purchase of land in England or in Scotland and, in the latter case, according to the terms of a strict Scottish entail. Most of the personalty was invested in this way in Scottish land, but the estates tail thus created contravened the English rule against perpetuities. *Held*, they were none the less valid, because this rule did not apply to testamentary dispositions affecting land outside England, even when contained in an English will. (But see *Re Groos, Groos v Groos*.)

Forsikringsaktieselskapet Vesta v Butcher [179]
[1989] AC 852 (House of Lords)

The plaintiffs, FV, insured a Norwegian fish farm against, inter alia, loss of stock due to storms. They entered into a contract of reinsurance with the defendant, Butcher (B), in respect of 90 per cent of their liability under the original insurance contract. Both the original insurance contract and the reinsurance contract contained the same terms including a warranty that a 24-hour watch would be kept over the fish farm. A further term rendered the contracts null and void if the warranty was breached. The contracts contained a 'follow settlements' clause pursuant to which the defendant was bound to indemnify FV in respect of claims settled by FV and a 'claims control' clause giving B sole control of all negotiations with the insured. In September 1978 the fish farm sustained a substantial loss of stock as a result of a storm. FV settled the claim for (approximately) £250,000 and then claimed 90 per cent of that sum from B on the reinsurance contract. A 24-hour watch had not been kept over the fish farm. B claimed that as a result, the reinsurance contract was null and void. Under Norwegian law FV could not rely on the breach of warranty to avoid paying the insured unless the breach was causative of the loss sustained. However, in the present case it was not. At first instance B was found liable to FV. The judgment was upheld on appeal by the Court of Appeal. *Held*, dismissing B's appeal, in the absence of any express statement to the contrary in the reinsurance policy, a warranty must produce the same effect in both the insurance policy and the reinsurance policy; that under the reinsurance contract B had agreed to indemnify FV in respect of 90 per cent of the liability incurred by FV under the original contract of insurance. That being the intention of the parties, B could not rely upon the breach of warranty to avoid its liability under the original insurance contract. As the original insurance contract took effect in Norway and was subject to Norwegian law, B's liability under the reinsurance contract was governed by the liability imposed on FV by Norwegian law. (See now Articles 3 and 4 of the Rome Convention 1980 as enacted by the Contracts (Applicable Law) Act 1990.)

Forum Craftsman, The, Islamic Republic of Iran Shipping Lines v Ierax Shipping Co of Panama [180]
[1991] 1 Lloyd's Rep 81

On discharge at Bandar Abbas, Iran, of a cargo of sugar carried by the vessel *Forum Craftsman* from Foynes to Bandar Abbas, some of the cargo was found to have been wetted by sea water. The *Forum Craftsman* was shifted from berth to anchorage and it remained at anchor for the next 79 days. A dispute arose between the owners of the vessel and the charterers because the charterers objected to the inclusion of the 79 days in the period for which demurrage was payable. The charterers had accepted that when the *Forum Craftsman* was shifted from berth to anchorage it was already on demurrage and they further accepted the principle 'once on demurrage always on demurrage' but they sought to rely on two special reasons why they should not be liable for the period of 79 days, viz, (1) a letter from the Regional Health Department to the customs in Bandar Abbas 'instruct[ing] the unloading of the cargo to be stopped until necessary investigations are conducted'. The charterers contended that this meant they could rely on clause 28 providing for 'government interference' to exclude their liability; and (2) the admission of the owners of the vessel *Forum Craftsman* that they had been in breach of clause 42 of the charter-party which guaranteed the seaworthiness of the vessel. On referral of the dispute to arbitration, the arbitrators allowed seven days' demurrage arising from the owners' breach of clause 42 but decided that clause 28 provided no defence to a claim to further demurrage. The charterers appealed, contending that there was an error of law in the award. *Held*, HOBHOUSE J dismissing the appeal, inter alia, (1) 'The charterers had failed to discharge the burden of proof which lay upon them to establish the causal relationship between the owners' admitted breach of [clause 42] and the delay of 79 days save for about seven days of that period.' (2) The subject matter of clause 28 did not make it clear that it was intended to exclude a liability in demurrage. 'For a clause to have such a clear intention requires language that leaves one in no doubt that that is what the parties intended. Clause 28 falls short of demonstrating such an intention.' (3) Neither in relation to clause 28 or clause 42 had the arbitrators made an error of law. (See also *MacShannon v Rockware Glass*.)

Foster v Driscoll [1929] 1 KB 470 (Court of Appeal) [181]

A group of English residents made various agreements among themselves whereby they constituted themselves a partnership for the purpose of exporting whisky to the USA and selling it there in contravention of American prohibition laws then in force. The venture failed. *Held*, the agreements were unenforceable by the parties thereto because they were entered into for the express purpose of violating laws (which were not of a tax or revenue nature) of a foreign and friendly country. (See also *Regazzoni* v *K C Sethia (1944) Ltd.*)

Freke v Lord Carbery (1873) LR 16 Eq 461 [182]

A testator who died domiciled in Ireland bequeathed a mixed fund, which included the lease of a house in London, to be held on certain trusts in which the period of accumulation of income was permissable under Irish law but exceeded the limits allowed by English law. *Held*, so far as the lease was concerned, the period of accumulation must be reduced so as to comply with English law, the lex situs, because a lease of land, although personalty, was an immovable. 'Land, whether held for a chattel interest or held for a freehold interest, is in nature, as a matter of fact, immovable and not movable' (*per* LORD SELBOURNE LC). (See also *Re Wellington (Duke of)*, *Glentanar* v *Wellington*; *Re Hoyles*, *Row* v *Jagg*.)

Fuld, In the Estate of, (No 3) [1968] P 675 [183]

On the death of a testator domiciled in Germany, three codicils executed by him were challenged on the grounds, inter alia, that he lacked testamentary capacity on account of illness and that he did not 'know and approve' of their contents. *Held*, the question of his testamentary capacity, including incapacity from ill health as well as from immaturity of status, was governed by German law, his lex domicilii at death. But questions of burden of proof, a procedural matter, were governed by the lex fori; this meant that the court should apply the English rule that in cases of doubt the testator's 'knowledge and approval' of the contents of his will must be affirmatively shown. (Compare *Re Cohn*; see also *Re Groos*, *Groos* v *Groos*.)

Furse, Re [1980] 3 All ER 838 [184]

The home of an American for the last 39 years of his life was on a farm in England. Although he had declared an intention to return to the USA if ever he became unable to lead an active physical life on the farm, he remained there until his death, aged 80. *Held*, the contemplation of leading an inactive physical life was so vague that it did not prevent the acquisition of an English domicile of choice. (Contrast *Winans* v *Attorney-General* and *IRC* v *Bullock*.)

G (a minor) (abduction), Re [1989] 2 FLR 475 [185]
(Court of Appeal)

A woman left her matrimonial home and her husband in Australia and returned with their nine-year-old son to England where she intended to live with another man. Within two days of her departure, the husband had obtained an order from an Australian court giving him sole custody of the child. Subsequently, he made an application under the Child Abduction and Custody Act 1985 for the boy to be returned to him. In opposing the application, the boy's mother sought to rely on Article 13 of the Hague Convention, as enacted by the 1985 Act, contending that the boy's enforced return would entail the grave risk of psychological harm to him, and that his objection to his return should be taken into account. At first, the judge ruled against the mother on both accounts but then, on the intervention of the Attorney-General for Australia and the refusal of the boy's father to give certain undertakings required of him, the father's application was denied. However, following a change of view by the A-G for Australia, and an acceptance of undertakings by the father, the judge granted the father's application. The mother appealed, contending that undue reliance had been put on the mitigating factors of the father's undertakings and the expressed wishes of the boy not to return to Australia had not been taken into account. *Held*, dismissing her appeal, the court had an absolute obligation to return the boy unless there was some grave risk of his suffering psychological harm or the fact that he objected to returning brought him within the discretionary rules provided by Article 13. The undertakings given by the father would ensure that the boy's return to Australia would cause the boy no psychological harm; and the boy's wishes could best be investigated at an inter partes hearing in the Family Court of Australia. Thus, Article 13 was inapplicable. (See also *Re A and another (minors) (abduction: acquiescence)*.)

G (a minor) (child abduction: enforcement), Re [186]
[1990] 2 FLR 325

A separation agreement between Belgian nationals gave the parents' joint custody of their child, though if one parent left Belgium the child was to stay with the parent remaining there. In essence, the agreement was embodied in a divorce decree and executed when the mother left Belgium. Later, however, the mother changed her mind and she informed the father that she wanted sole custody of the child. The father began proceedings in Belgium to give himself sole custody and to prevent the mother taking the child out of Belgium without his consent, but an order to such effect was incorrectly addressed and the mother did not receive it. The mother took the child, with the father's consent, for a holiday to Italy but she then took the child to England where she said he was going to stay, contrary to the Belgian court order, of which she was unaware, and contrary to the agreement embodied in the divorce decree. On hearing of the Belgian order the mother applied to the Belgian court for custody but her application was dismissed. The father applied to the English court under the Child Abduction and Custody Act 1985 and for recognition and enforcement of both decisions of the Belgian courts. *Held*, the first Belgian order would be recognised and enforced because the mother had not availed herself of the opportunities to inform the Belgian court of her ignorance of its proceedings: it would be wrong for the English court to exercise its discretion to refuse recognition and enforcement on the ground of non-service; and recognition and enforcement of the first Belgian order would give effect to the agreement ratified in the divorce decree which was not incompatible with any fundamental principle of English law. The second Belgian order would not be recognised as it added nothing to the first order. (See also *Re A (a minor)(abduction)*.)

Gaetano and Maria, The (1882) 7 PD 137 (Court of Appeal) [187]

The defendant owners of cargo, who were domiciled in England, shipped goods from the USA to England on board an Italian ship in fulfilment of a charterparty executed in England. The ship had to be put into a port in the Azores for repairs, and to pay for these the captain gave a bottomry bond over the ship her cargo and freight. This was done without the captain communicating with the defendants. Whereas this was valid under Italian law, such a bond was invalid under English law for lack of authority unless the ship was in necessity and it was impossible to communicate with the owners. Without proving these additional facts, the plaintiffs, indorsees of the bond, sued the defendants on it in England. *Held*, the bond was valid, because, (1) the question of the captain's authority to give the bond was governed by Italian law, the law of the ship's flag, and (2) the question whether these additional facts had to be proved, as opposed to the mode of proving them, was a question of substance and therefore governed by the lex causae (Italian law) not the lex fori. (See also *Lloyd* v *Guibert*.)

Gascoine v Pyrah [1994] ILPr 82 (Court of Appeal)

Mr and Mrs Gascoine wanted to purchase a horse that would be suitable for show-jumping. They engaged Mr Pyrah, who was domiciled in England, to locate and purchase a horse and he, in turn, engaged the veterinary services of Dr Cronau, who was domiciled in Germany, to inspect the horse and produce a written report on it. Dr Cronau's report referred to a decalcified area in the horse's right front leg. However, in a subsequent telephone conversation, Mr Pyrah alleged that Dr Cronau informed him that this was not a serious problem. Accordingly, the horse was purchased for £75,000. The decalcified area proved to be far more serious, in fact, rendering the horse unsuitable for show-jumping and lowering its value to £3,000. When the Gascoine's knew of the telephone conversation between Pyrah and Dr Cronau they wished to take proceedings against both men in England. They relied on an exception in Article 6(1) to the general rule in Article 2 that a person could only be sued in the courts of his domicile. Article 6 provides that: 'A person domiciled in a Contracting State may also be sued: (1) where he is one of a number of defendants, in the courts for the place where any one of them is domiciled.' *Held*, Dr Cronau, as well as Mr Pyrah, could be sued in England. Article 6(1) applied where it was expedient to hear the related claims together so as to avoid the risk of irreconcilable judgments which might result from separate proceedings. Referring to the alleged telephone conversation between Dr Cronau and Mr Pyrah, HIRST LJ said: 'where a potential conflict on this vital issue of fact has been so clearly demonstrated ... there must be an option, which the plaintiffs are entitled to exercise under Article 6(1) to sue Dr Cronau as well as Mr Pyrah in this court'. (See also *Kalfelis* v *Bankhaus Schroder, Munchmeyer, Hengst & Co*.)

Godard v Gray (1870) LR 6 QB 139

The plaintiffs, French merchants, brought an action in France against the defendants, English shipowners, for breach of a charterparty governed by English law. The defendants entered a defence, but the court awarded damages against them. The record of the judgment showed that the court, in purporting to construe the charterparty according to English law, had made an error of English law which affected the amount of damages. *Held*, the plaintiffs could nevertheless enforce the judgment by action against the defendants in England. As the French court had jurisdiction in the case, its judgment created a binding obligation, which was not negatived merely by showing that it had made an error of law, even an error of English law appearing on the face of the record. (See also *Schibsby* v *Westenholz*; *Ellis* v *M'Henry*.)

Goetschius v Brightman (1927) 156 NE 660

A car was sold in California, USA, on terms that reserved title with the seller until it had been fully paid for, and until it was fully paid for it was not to be removed from California. Before it was paid for, however, the car was taken to New York without the seller's consent. There it was sold to a bona fide purchaser. By the law of New York, the bona fide purchaser acquired good title because such reservation of title clauses were void against subsequent purchasers in good faith, unless the contract was registered in a New York register. (In this case, the original California sale was not registered.) In contrast, the law of California provided that the original seller's title was good against even innocent subsequent purchasers. *Held*, (New York court) the New York statute that required registration was limited to domestic, ie, New York transactions. Thus the New York law did not prevent the recognition of the reservation of title in a Californian sale. Since the California purchaser did not acquire title under the law of California, the California seller's title would be recognised in New York. (See also *Century Credit Corporation* v *Richard*.)

Goodman's Trusts, Re (1881) 17 Ch D 266 (Court of Appeal) [191]

An Englishman domiciled and resident in The Netherlands had a daughter there by an Englishwoman, whom he afterwards married in The Netherlands. This legitimated the daughter in Dutch law, but not in English law. The father's sister subsequently died intestate, domiciled in England. *Held*, the daughter could share in her estate as one of her next-of-kin, because she was legitimate under the law of her parent's domicile at the time of her birth. 'Can it be possible that a Dutch father, stepping on board a steamer at Rotterdam with his dear and lawful child, should on arrival at the port of London find that the child had become a stranger in blood and in law, and a bastard, filius nullius?' (*per* JAMES LJ). (See also *Re Askew, Marjoribanks* v *Askew*; and compare s14 of the Family Law Reform Act 1969.)

Government of India v Taylor see India (Government of) v Taylor

Gray (otherwise Formosa) v Formosa [192]
[1963] P 259 (Court of Appeal)

A Roman Catholic Maltese domiciled in England married a domiciled Englishwoman in a civil ceremony in England. Later, he left her and returned to Malta where he re-acquired a Maltese domicile of choice. A Maltese court refused to enforce against him a maintenance order which the wife had obtained in England because it declared the marriage void on his petition on the ground that the canon law formalities prescribed for Roman Catholics under Maltese law had not been complied with. The wife then brought divorce proceedings for desertion. *Held*, the Maltese nullity decree should be refused recognition on the ground that it offended against English notions of substantial justice. It was 'flagrantly unjust' to treat the wife as a 'mere concubine' and her children as bastards when the marriage ceremony was valid under the lex loci celebrationis. Instead, the wife was granted a divorce on the grounds of the husband's desertion and his repudiation of the marriage. (See also *Lepre* v *Lepre*; compare *Scarpetta* v *Lowenfield*.)

Grey's Trusts, Re, Grey v Stamford [1892] 3 Ch 88 [193]

An English will contained a devise of English realty in remainder to the 'children' of the testator's son, H. After the testator's death, H, who was domiciled in the Cape of Good Hope, had a son by a woman whom he later married, thereby legitimating the son under the Roman-Dutch law of the Cape, though not under English law. *Held*, the son could share in the devise because his legitimation under the law of the Cape was entitled to recognition. Even though English land was involved, there was no need to confine the term 'children' to children legitimate under English domestic law only. (See also *Re Andros, Andros* v *Andros* and s15 of the Family Law Reform Act 1969.)

Groos, Re, Groos v Groos [1915] Ch 572 [194]

A married woman made a will in Dutch form, then married a domiciled Dutchman in The Netherlands. When she died, she was domiciled in England. Under English law, but not Dutch law, a subsequent marriage revoked a will. Under Dutch law, three-quarters of her estate would have been distributable amongst her children as their legitimate portion, the other quarter share going to her husband. *Held*, the testamentary capacity of the woman had been increased by her acquisition of an English domicile. As argued by counsel for the husband's executor, the effect of the change of her domicile was to enlarge the area of the property over which the will extended in favour of the husband. Accordingly, her husband became entitled to the whole of her estate. (Contrast *Re Annesley*.)

Grove, Re, Vaucher v Treasury Solicitor (1888) 40 Ch D 216 [195]
(Court of Appeal)

A Swiss national domiciled in Geneva had a daughter by a woman whom he later married in England, having changed his domicile to England. Under the law of Geneva, but not English law, the marriage legitimated the daughter. *Held*, the daughter was illegitimate, because a legitimation per subsequens matrimonium under a foreign law would only be recognised if the father was domiciled in the foreign country at the time of the birth *and* of the subsequent marriage. (See also *Re Luck's Settlement Trusts, Walker v Luck*.)

Guatemala (Republica de) v Nunez [1927] 1 KB 669 [196]
(Court of Appeal)

By a letter written in Guatemala, the President of Guatemala instructed a London bank with which he had deposited a sum of money to transfer it to his illegitimate son. This assignment was valid under English law, but under the law of Guatemala, where both parties were domiciled, it was void for two reasons: (1) that it had not been executed by both of them before a notary; and (2) that the son, being an infant, lacked capacity to receive under a voluntary assignment. *Held*, the assignment was void. The formalities of an assignment of a debt and the capacity of the assignee were governed, not by the lex situs, but by *either* the lex actus or the lex domicilii of the parties. No final choice was made between these two because on either view it was the law of Guatemala. (See also *Re Anziani, Herbert v Christopherson*; but see *Kelly v Selwyn*.)

H (infants), Re [1966] 1 WLR 381 (Court of Appeal) [197]

An American woman had custody of her two infant children by virtue of a New York court order which permitted access to the father and stipulated that the children should remain in New York State. She nevertheless removed them to England and ignored a New York order to take them back again. Some six months after their arrival in England, the father applied for an order that they be returned to New York. *Held*, on being satisfied that this would not harm the children, the court should act in support of the New York court by granting the application. As they had only been in England for a short time, it would be unwise to investigate fully what was best for them, because the delay might cause them to 'take root' in England. (See now the Child Abduction Act 1985.)

H (minors) (abduction: custody rights), In re; [198]
S (minors) (abduction: custody rights), In re
[1991] 2 AC 476 (House of Lords)

The consolidated appeals concerned the abduction and bringing to the UK of children prior to the Hague Convention on the Civil Aspects of International Child Abduction being given the force of law in the UK by the Child Abduction and Custody Act 1985. The English courts had claimed that under the Convention they had no jurisdiction over the wrongful removals of the children from the countries of their habitual residences (Canada and the USA) because the removals had taken place prior to the Convention coming into force in those countries. Nevertheless, the children were made wards of court and interim care and control of them was given to the mothers, with leave to take them out of the jurisdiction. The mothers appealed against the refusal of the courts to grant summary orders for return of the children under the 1985 Act. *Held*, dismissing the appeals, removal and retention of the children from the courts of their habitual residences were mutually exclusive concepts: they were single events occurring on a specific occasion, but removal was the removal of a child from the jurisdiction of the State of its habitual residence, and retention was the retention of a child lawfully removed for a limited period from the jurisdiction but not returned on the expiry of that period; and as the children in these consolidated appeals were removed rather than retained, with the removals taking place prior to implementation of the Convention in Canada and the USA, the courts had no jurisdiction to make summary orders for their return under the 1985 Act.

Hacker v Euro Relais (Case C-280/90) [1992] ILP 515 [199]
(European Court of Justice)

A provision in a contract between the plaintiff, domiciled in Germany, and a German-based firm of travel agents stipulated that she should have the use of a holiday home in The Netherlands and, for an additional payment, a reservation would be made for her travel to the holiday home, although she paid the fare direct to the shipping company. The accommodation proved unsatisfactory and the plaintiff sued for breach of contract claiming a reduction in the price paid and damages under various heads. In the light of a previous ECJ ruling (*Rosler* v *Rottwinkel*) that Article 16(1) of the (unamended) Brussels Convention applied to holiday lets, meaning that proceedings had to be taken in the courts of the Contracting State in which the immovable property was situated, it fell to be determined whether the plaintiff could sue in Germany. *Held*, Article 16(1) (prior to its amendment by the San Sebastian Convention) had to be interpreted 'as not applying to a contract concluded in a Contracting State whereby a professional travel organiser, which has its registered office in that State, undertakes to procure for a client domiciled in the same State the use for several weeks of holiday accommodation in another Contracting State which it does not own, and to book the travel'. Accordingly, Article 16(1) was inapplicable in this case, leaving the plaintiff free to sue in Germany. (See also *Lieber* v *Gobel*.)

Hagen, The [1908] P 189 (Court of Appeal) [200]

Two English ships and a German ship were involved in a collision on the River Elbe in Germany. The owner of one of the English ships issued proceedings in England against the owner of the other, then obtained leave under (what is now) RSC O.11, r.1(1)(c) to serve a writ out of the jurisdiction on the German shipowner, joining him as a defendant. The German shipowner had been preparing to sue in Germany and, after issuing his writ there, he applied to set aside service of the English writ on him. *Held*, although strictly the case fell under (what then was RSC O.11, r.1(g)) what has now been modified and re-numbered r.1(1)(e), the court should exercise its discretion to set aside service, so that the case could proceed in its natural forum, the German court. In cases under O.11, r.1, the court should observe three rules: (1) it should be 'exceedingly careful' before it allowed a writ to be served abroad on a foreign defendant; (2) any doubt as to the construction of the rule should be resolved in the defendant's favour; and (3) the plaintiff invoking the rule should make 'full and fair disclosure' (*per* FARWELL, LJ). (See also *Kroch* v *Rossell et Cie*; but see *Zapata Off-Shore Co* v *The Bremen and Unterweser Reederei GmbH, The Chaparral*.)

Haiti, Republic of, v Duvalier [1989] 2 WLR 261 [201]
(Court of Appeal)

The Republic of Haiti, as one of the plaintiffs, commenced proceedings in France contending that the defendants, who were resident in France, had embezzled US$120 million alleged to be the Republic's money. The plaintiffs then sought an order in England to restrain the defendants from disposing of certain of their assets and requiring them to disclose information relating to their assets. This was granted at first instance pursuant to s25(1) of the Civil Jurisdiction and Judgments Act 1982 (CJJA 1982), as was service of a writ out of the jurisdiction without leave on the defendants pursuant to RSC O.11, r.1(2). The defendants appealed. *Held*, dismissing the appeal, O.11, r.1(2) applied to a claim for interim relief under s25 CJJA 1982. Accordingly, 'I would construe Ord.11, r.1(2) as giving effect to the obligation of the United Kingdom in England and Wales to make available in aid of the courts of other Contracting States such provisional and protective measures as our domestic law would afford if our courts were seized of the substantive action' (*per* STAUGHTON LJ). (See also *Babanaft International Co* v *Bassatne* and *Derby & Co Ltd* v *Weldon (No 1)*.)

Halcyon Isle, The, Bankers Trust International [202]
v Todd Shipyards Corpn [1981] AC 221 (Privy Council)

A British-registered ship, the *Halcyon Isle*, had been repaired in New York. As the repair bill had remained unpaid, the ship was arrested in Singapore and sold there by court order. However, the proceeds were insufficient to satisfy the claims made by an English bank as mortgagees and by the ship's repairers and it was necessary to determine the order of priorities. US law gave the ship's repairers a maritime lien having a priority over mortgagees. *Held*, nevertheless, by a majority of 3-2, that the mortgagees had priority because, according to the majority view, the ship's repairers did not have a maritime lien. Whereas there was no disagreement in the Privy Council that procedural issues were to be determined by the lex fori – in this case Singapore law (which was the same as English law) – there was disagreement over how the claims to be ranked in order of priority were to be analysed. In giving the mortgagees priority, LORD DIPLOCK, for the majority, said this decision was consistent with the decision in *The Colorado*. For the minority, however, LORDS SALMON and SCARMAN, they issued a joint opinion in which they stated that: 'The question is – does English law, in circumstances such as these, recognise the maritime lien created by the law of the United States of America, ie the lex contractus where no such lien exists by its own internal law? In our view the balance of authorities, the comity of nations, private international law and natural justice all answer this question in the affirmative. If this be correct then English law (the lex fori) gives the maritime lien created by the lex loci contractus precedence over the mortgagees' mortgage. If it were otherwise, injustice would prevail. The ship repairers would be deprived of their maritime lien, valid as it appeared to be throughout the world, and without which they would obviously never have allowed the ship to sail away without paying a dollar for the important repairs.' (See also *The Colorado* and *The Zigurds*.)

Halley, The (1868) LR 2 PC 193 (Privy Council) [203]

A collision in Belgian territorial waters between the defendants' ship and the plaintiffs' ship was caused by the negligence of a compulsory pilot whom the defendants were compelled by Belgian law to employ. Under that law, but not under English law, the defendants were liable for the pilot's negligence. In Admiralty proceedings, *Held*, the plaintiffs could not recover damages from the defendants in respect of the collision. An English court would not enforce a foreign law so as to award damages in tort against a defendant where according to English law his act imposed no liability upon him. (See also *M'Elroy* v *M'Allister*.)

Hanbridge Services Ltd v Aerospace Communications Ltd [204]
[1994] 1 ILRM 39 (Supreme Court of Ireland)

The plaintiff company, which was registered and domiciled in Ireland, claimed that it had contracted with the defendant company, which was registered and domiciled in the UK, for the manufacture and sale to the defendant of 8,000 computer systems; and that since the performance of the obligation arising out of the contract was in Ireland, the plaintiff claimed that the Irish courts would have jurisdiction to hear and determine its claim under Article 5(1) of the Brussels Convention 1968. The defendant company claimed that no contract had been concluded and that it had no obligation to the plaintiff. *Held*, unanimously, in the case of a claim for a breach of contract it was for the plaintiff to prove that the claim came within the exception provided for in Article 5(1) of the Brussels Convention, and that the obligation in question in that claim was an obligation which had to be performed in Ireland. In this case the obligation in question was the obligation to place orders for specific quantities, at specific times, of the 8,000 computers; and as there was no evidence to justify a finding that this was an obligation which had to be performed in Ireland, the defendant was granted an order striking out the proceedings on the ground that they were not maintainable within the jurisdiction of the Irish courts. (See also *Effer* v *Kanter* and *Tesam Distribution Ltd* v *Schuh Mode Team GmbH and Commerzbank AG*.)

Haque v Haque (No 2) (1965) 114 CLR 98 [205]
(High Court of Australia)

The deceased, who had died domiciled in India, was, at the time of his death, the registered proprietor of land in Western Australia. He had contracted to sell this land but the purchase money had not been paid. The deceased had also been a member of two solvent partnerships, one of which was dissolved by his death. Amongst the assets of each partnership was land in Western Australia, some of which had also been contracted to be sold. It had already been decided that the deceased's movables had passed by succession in accordance with Muslim law. *Held*, (1) the land registered in the deceased's name and contracted to be sold, and the purchase moneys owing thereon, were movables, as were (2) the share in the partnership that was dissolved by his death and the money which the subsisting partnership agreement provided should be paid into his estate by the surviving partners in satisfaction of the deceased's share. (Contrast *Re Hoyles*.)

Harmattan, The [1975] 1 WLR 1485 [206]

The German plaintiffs had chartered their ship, the *Harmattan*, to Polish charterers for the carriage of goods from Poland to Pakistan. A provision of the charterparty was that the receivers of the cargo would be liable to the plaintiffs for demurrage in respect of time lost waiting at berth. The plaintiffs sought to recover demurrage for 67 days lost as a result of the *Harmattan* being bomb-damaged by Indian aircraft at Karachi. However, the consignees, a corporation established under a government ordinance, had been dissolved by the time the plaintiffs commenced their action and had been succeeded by a Department of the Pakistan Government. It was the latter which became the defendant to the plaintiffs' action and which claimed sovereign immunity. This defence succeeded at first instance. *Held*, dismissing the plaintiffs appeal, no exception to the principle that a sovereign cannot personally be impleaded had been established. 'I can see no reason at all for departing from rules which have been recognised by the commercial world now for nearly a hundred years.' per LAWTON LJ. (However, see now *Trendtex Trading Corporation* v *Central Bank of Nigeria* and the State Immunity Act 1978; see also *The Parlement Belge* and *Compania Naviera Vascongado* v *SS Cristina*.)

Harris and Adams v Quine (1869) LR 4 QB 653 [207]

The plaintiffs, Manx solicitors, sued the defendant in a Manx court for professional fees incurred in the Isle of Man, but failed on account of the Manx statute of limitations, which imposed a three-year limit for actions on a simple contract. They then sued in England, being within the six-year period prescribed in the corresponding English statute. *Held*, the Manx judgment did not bar the action, because the Manx statutory provision was purely procedural and did not extend to actions outside the Isle of Man. The result would be different if this provision had laid down a rule of substance, so as to extinguish the actual right conferred by the contract, and not merely the remedy. (Compare *Kohnke* v *Karger*; see also *Huber* v *Steiner* and *Black-Clawson International* v *Papierwerke Waldhof-Aschaffenburg AG*; but see now s3 of the Foreign Limitation Periods Act 1984.)

Harris v Taylor [1915] 2 KB 580 (Court of Appeal) [208]

The plaintiff sued the defendant in the Isle of Man for damages for loss of consortium and criminal conversion occurring in the Isle and in England. The writ was served on the defendant in England, whereupon he filed a conditional appearance, contending that the Manx court had no jurisdiction under its own rules because he was neither domiciled nor resident in the Isle. This objection to jurisdiction was dismissed. The defendant took no further part in the proceedings and the plaintiff, having obtained a judgment in default of defence, sought to enforce it in England. *Held*, he was entitled to do so, because the defendant must be taken to have submitted voluntarily to the jurisdiction of the Manx court. Having 'sought its protection' by taking steps to contest its jurisdiction, he was bound by its decision against him and debarred from contesting the matter of jurisdiction again. (But see *Re Dulles' Settlement (No 2), Dulles* v *Vidler* and *Williams & Glyn's Bank* v *Astro Dinamico*.)

Harrison v Harrison [1953] 1 WLR 865 [209]

A married couple were domiciled and resident in England at the birth of their son, but they emigrated to South Australia and acquired a domicile of choice there when he was 18. The son remained for a while in England and then went to New Zealand where he got married and where he and his wife intended to settle. He and his wife returned to England for a temporary purpose, but shortly after he turned 21 (which, at that time, was the age of majority, ie the age at which a person becomes sui juris), she instituted divorce proceedings in England. She argued that he had a domicile of dependence in South Australia between 18 and

21 (ie while he was still a minor), that on turning 21 his intention to acquire a domicile of choice in New Zealand caused the South Australian domicile to lapse but could not itself become effective because he was not in New Zealand, that his domicile of origin in England therefore revived and that this gave the court jurisdiction. *Held*, the contention was correct: the court had jurisdiction. Although he had the intention to make New Zealand his permanent home, there had been no factum of residence since he became sui juris. (See also *Henderson v Henderson*; compare *Re Scullard's Estate*, *Smith v Brock*.)

Harrods (Buenos Aires) Ltd, Re [1992] Ch 72 [210]
(Court of Appeal)

L, a Swiss-based minority shareholder in a company which was registered in England but did all its business in Argentina, where it had its central management and control, complained that the affairs of the company were being conducted in a manner which was unfairly prejudicial to L. Accordingly, L sought an order directing the majority shareholder, also Swiss-based, to purchase L's shares in the company or that the English company be wound up. A petition was served on the majority shareholder, Intercomfinanz, out of the jurisdiction. Intercomfinanz responded by requesting that service of the petition be set aside and for the petition to be stayed on the ground that Argentina was a more appropriate forum for the trial of the issues raised. However, as the company had its seat (domicile) in England, thus invoking application of the Brussels Convention 1968, a preliminary issue for determination was whether the court retained its discretion to grant a stay on the basis of forum non conveniens. *Held*, on the preliminary issue, s49 of the Civil Jurisdiction and Judgments Act 1982 preserved the power of the English court to stay or dismiss proceedings where to do so was not inconsistent with the Brussels convention 1968 which was scheduled to the Act, that is, where the case involved a conflict of jurisdiction between the courts of a Contracting State and the courts of a non-Contracting State; and that the court would stay the petition as Argentina was the more appropriate forum for trial of the issues. On the substantive appeal, although the Argentinian courts had no power to order the majority shareholder to purchase the shares of the minority shareholder, its powers to wind up the company and award damages for negligent or unlawful handling of the company's business were such that L could obtain substantial justice in Argentina. Accordingly, the proceedings would be stayed. (See also *Spiliada Maritime Corporation v Cansulex* and *de Dampierre v de Dampierre*.)

Harrop v Harrop [1920] 3 KB 386 [211]

A wife obtained a magistrate's order in Perak (Malaysia) for periodical maintenance payments from her husband. If the husband wilfully neglected to pay it, the wife was entitled under Perak law to apply to the magistrate for arrears to be levied out of the husband's assets, whereupon the magistrate could alter the amount of the payments, apparently even retrospectively, on proof of 'change of circumstances'. *Held*, the wife could not recover arrears due under the order in England. It was not a 'final and conclusive' order because (1) a further order had to be obtained to enforce it in Perak, and (2) it was liable to be abrogated or varied when the further order was applied for. (But see *Beatty v Beatty*.)

Heidberg, The, Partenreederei M/S Heidberg [212]
v Grosvenor Grain and Feed Co [1993] 2 Lloyd's Rep 324

Two French companies, UNAC and GroupAma were the second and third defendants, respectively, as shippers and insurers of cargo on the plaintiffs' vessel.

The ship was involved in a collision with a jetty in the river Gironde, near Bordeaux, France, and various claims were made for, inter alia, cargo loss, expenditure incurred as a result of the collision and contributions to general average loss. The plaintiffs sought a declaration that an arbitration clause was incorporated into the contract evidenced by the bill of lading and that the parties were bound to refer the dispute to arbitration. The defendants sought, inter alia, declarations that the plaintiffs were not entitled to proceed with arbitration and that the arbitrators had no jurisdiction. Discovery of documents was ordered to establish whether the French defendants had 'title to sue', ie whether they were parties to a contract with owners on terms of the bill of lading. However, they claimed that they were prohibited by French law from complying and they would commit a criminal offence in doing so. They sought to rely on a 1980 law which prohibited all persons from applying for, searching or communicating in writing, verbally or in any other form, documents or information to support foreign administrative or legal proceedings. However, that law was designed to prevent US-style anti-trust discovery and had not been used in ordinary commercial disputes. *Held*, dismissing the defendants' contentions, that (1) the evidence did not disclose that an offence would be committed, or that there was a risk of criminal prosecution as (a) there had been no English decision where it had been submitted that the court should not order discovery against a French defendant; (b) French companies had regularly given discovery, as plaintiffs or defendants, in English commercial disputes; and (c) there was no evidence of any person being prosecuted under the 1980 French law for giving discovery; (2) all matters of procedure are governed by the domestic law of the lex fori which, in England, includes discovery; and there is a distinction between RSC O.24 (which provides for discovery) and (say) the more extensive procedures available in many jurisdictions within the USA; and (3) the French defendants had not shown 'sufficient cause' within O.24, r.17 to revoke the order for discovery.

Helbert Wagg & Co Ltd, Re [1956] Ch 323 [213]

By an agreement governed by German law, a German company which did not carry on business in England borrowed a large sum from an English company, promising to repay it by instalments in sterling in London. Before the final instalment was due, Germany passed a moratorium law to the effect that all debts payable in foreign currencies should be discharged by payment of an equivalent sum in German marks into a government 'Konversionkasse'. The German company paid the balance due under the loan into the Konversionkasse. *Held*, the loan had been duly paid, for these reasons: (1) at the time of the moratorium law, discharge of the agreement was governed by its proper law, not the lex situs of the debt, because it was still a debt payable in the future; (2) in any event, German law was the lex situs as well as the proper law, because the debtor's only residence was in Germany and the stipulation for repayment in London had thus no effect on the debt's situs; and (3) the German moratorium law, being a genuine exchange control measure enacted bona fide to protect the German economy in a time of stress, should not be refused recognition on grounds of public policy, even though it confiscated private property (including property of foreigners) without providing compensation. (But see *Anglo Iranian Oil Co Ltd* v *Jaffrate, The Rose Mary*; see also *National Bank of Greece and Athens SA* v *Metliss* and *New York Life Insurance Co* v *Public Trustee*.)

Hellman's Will, Re (1866) LR 2 Eq 363 [214]

A testator dying domiciled in England bequeathed legacies to a girl of 18 and a boy of 17, both domiciled in Hamburg. Under Hamburg law, girls attained their majority at 18 and boys at 22. *Held*, the girl, being of age under her lex domicilii, should receive her legacy forthwith, but the boy's legacy should be dealt with as an infant's legacy until he attained his majority under either his lex domicilii or English law, whichever first happened.

Henderson v Henderson [1967] P 77 [215]

A man who had a Scottish domicile of origin and had a legitimate son while living in England, acquired a domicile of choice in England while the son was an infant. After the son reached the age of 21, he moved to Scotland for two years before moving to Canada and then returning to England. An issue arose in divorce proceedings. *Held*, the son thus had a Scottish domicile of origin and an English domicile of choice at the age of 21. Moreover, there was insufficient evidence to establish that he had intended to abandon his English domicile of choice (or 'quasi-choice') and resurrect his Scottish domicile of origin. (See also *Harrison v Harrison*.)

Hesperides Hotels v Muftizade [1979] AC 508 [216]
(House of Lords)

The plaintiff Cypriot companies owned hotels in the northern part of Cyprus which was occupied by Turkish troops in the invasion of 1974. The plaintiffs vacated the hotels and moved to another part of the island. Some time after the plaintiffs' evacuation they learnt that, in London, a travel agent and the Turkish Federated State of Cyprus (the unrecognised government of the northern part of the island), were advertising and organising holidays in their hotels. The plaintiffs initiated proceedings in the English courts against the travel agent and a London representative of the Turkish Federated State of Cyprus alleging trespass and conspiracy to trespass to the hotels. Later, they added a claim of trespass to the contents of the hotels. *Held*, following *British South Africa Co v Compania de Mocambique* and allowing the appeal in part, whereas no action could be maintained for trespass or conspiracy to trespass upon foreign land, 'There remains the appellants' claim as regards the chattel contents of the hotels. To this the Mocambique rule has no application. [Accordingly] I would allow the appellants' appeal so far as to permit the action as regards the chattels ...' (*per* LORD WILBERFORCE). (However, see now s30 of the Civil Jurisdiction and Judgments Act 1982 which provides for a statutory reversal of this decision).

Hewitson v Hewitson [1995] 1 All ER 472 [217]
(Court of Appeal)

Parties to a marriage, who were divorced in California in 1987, cohabited briefly both in the USA and in England before finally parting in 1992. A consent order made by a court of competent jurisdiction in California provided for spousal support for a limited period and capital payments: it was meant to be comprehensive and final, creating a 'clean break'. However, in proceedings before the English courts, the wife contended that in reliance on the husband's promise to maintain her for the rest of her life, she had been induced to take financial steps to her detriment and that as he now refused to maintain her she was entitled to apply for financial relief under Part III of the Matrimonial and Family Proceedings Act 1984. Her contention succeeded at first instance, WALL J believing that the husband had prima facie by his conduct incurred fresh obligations towards her. The husband appealed. *Held*, unanimously, as under s13 of the Act leave to make an application for financial relief would not be granted unless 'there is substantial ground for the making of an application for such an order', and as the instant case was not one contemplated by Parliament, 'there was no reason to give to those in the position of the wife a benefit which was not intended by the passing of the 1984 Act and was unavailable under the domestic matrimonial legislation. The 1984 Act was intended to mitigate disadvantage and not give extra advantages to a particular group of applicants. It would be wrong in principle and contrary to public policy to extend the narrow compass of an Act designed to meet limited objectives to cover a wider and unintended situation. ... The prospects of success of the application under section 13 were nil and thus there was no substantial ground for the making of the application' (*per* BUTLER-SLOSS LJ). (See also *Holmes* v *Holmes*.)

High Commissioner for India v Ghosh [1960] 1 QB 134 [218]
(Court of Appeal)

The Governments for India and West Bengal and the High Commissioner for India sued an Italian doctor for repayment of money lent to him to enable him to study in England. He responded by delivering a defence and also a counter-claim for damages for a libel by employees of the High Commissioner, which was alleged to have damaged his professional reputation at an Indian students' hostel in London. *Held*, the plaintiffs could plead immunity as regards the counter-claim. By instituting proceedings, they had waived their sovereign or diplomatic immunity to any defence, but not to a counter-claim which had no connection with the subject-matter of their action. (See also *Mighell* v *Sultan of Johore*.)

Hoffman v Krieg (Case 145/86) [1988] ECR 645 [219]
(European Court of Justice)

After more than 25 years of marriage between German nationals, the husband left the matrimonial home and settled in The Netherlands. The wife obtained an order from the local court in Germany requiring her husband to pay maintenance to her every month. Later, in default of appearance and on the application of German law, the husband was granted a decree of divorce in the Dutch courts. Apart from divorce not coming within the scope of the Brussels Convention 1968, a foreign divorce is recognised in Germany only after a decision of the Regional Administration of Justice, and then it is given retroactive effect. When the German courts dismissed the husband's application to discontinue the maintenance payments following the divorce, the Dutch court, being uncertain of the effects of the Dutch decree of divorce on the German maintenance order, which presupposed the continuing validity of the marriage, referred several questions to the ECJ. *Held*, '(1) A foreign judgment which has been recognised by virtue of Article 26 of the Convention must in principle have the same effects in the State in which enforcement is sought as it does in the State in which the judgment was given. (2) A foreign judgment whose enforcement has been ordered in a Contracting State pursuant to Article 31 of the Convention and which remains enforceable in the State in which it was given must not continue to be enforced in the State where enforcement is sought when, under the law of the latter State, it ceases to be enforceable for reasons which lie outside the scope of the Convention. (3) A foreign judgment ordering a person to make maintenance payments to his spouse by virtue of his conjugal obligations to support her is irreconcilable within the meaning of Article 27(3) of the Convention with a national judgment pronouncing the divorce of the spouses. (4) Article 36 of the Convention must be interpreted as meaning that a party who has not appealed against the enforcement order referred to in that provision is thereafter precluded, at the stage of the execution of the judgment, from relying on a valid ground which he could have pleaded in such an appeal against the enforcement order, and that that rule must be applied of their motion by the courts of the State in which enforcement is sought. However, that rule does not apply when it has the result of obliging the national court to make the effects of a national judgment which lies outside the scope of the Convention conditional on its recognition in the State in which the foreign judgment whose enforcement is at issue was given.'

Hollandia, The [1983] 1 AC 565 (House of Lords) [220]

A road-finishing machine shipped from Scotland to the Dutch West Indies aboard a Dutch vessel suffered extensive damage while it was being unloaded at the port of destination. The bill of lading had expressly provided for: 'Law of application and jurisdiction. The law of The Netherlands in which the Hague rules ... are incorporated ... shall apply to this contract. ... All actions under the present contract of carriage shall be brought before the Court of Amsterdam ...'. The bill of lading also provided that the maximum liability per package would amount to about £250. The shipper estimated the damage at about £22,000. The shipper commenced an action in rem in the High Court against the *Hollandia*, a sister ship of the carrying vessel. The carrier's application for a stay succeeded at first instance but the Court of Appeal allowed an appeal by the shipper. Held, LORD DIPLOCK, speaking on behalf of a unanimous House of Lords, dismissing the carrier's appeal, the Carriage of Goods by Sea Act 1971 which contained certain of the Hague Rules as amended by the Hague-Visby Rules 'are to be treated as if they were part of directly enacted statute law'. Accordingly, they rendered null and void the purported limitation of the carrier's liability and the purported choice of jurisdiction whose substantive law provided a lower maximum limit of the carrier's liability: and since 'the foreign court chosen as the exclusive forum would apply a domestic substantive law which would result in limiting the carrier's liability to a sum lower than that to which he would be entitled if ... the Hague-Visby Rules applied, then an English court is in my view commanded by the Act of 1971 to treat the choice of forum clause as of no effect'. As there were no other valid grounds for granting a stay, the shipper's action was allowed to proceed.

Holmes v Holmes [1989] Fam 47 (Court of Appeal) [221]

A couple who were married in England were each granted a divorce decree in New York, USA, where they had lived for eight years. The New York court made an order for the maintenance of the wife and child of the marriage, and also ordered that a property in New York in the husband's sole name and a cottage in England in joint names should be sold and that the proceeds should be divided equally between the parties. The wife returned to England with the child and lived in the cottage. The wife's attempt to buy the husband's interest in the cottage failed because she was unable to satisfy a New York judge that she could raise a loan. Accordingly, an order for the sale of the cottage was confirmed. Her application to the Family Division of the High Court for leave to apply for financial relief under s13 of the Matrimonial and Family Proceedings Act 1984 (MFPA 1984) was dismissed on the basis that questions of her financial provisions were a matter for the New York court. Held, there was no substantial ground for granting leave for her to apply for financial relief under s13(1) of the MFPA 1984. It was an issue that had already been examined by the judge in the natural forum, New York, and the judge at first instance in England had properly refused leave under s13(1) of the 1984 Act to apply for financial relief. (See also *Hewitson v Hewitson*.)

Hooper (orse Harrison) v Hooper [1959] 1 WLR 1021 [222]

A man and a woman who were British subjects, were married to each other in a church in Iraq. According to English law, the marriage was void because, as they were aware, no banns had been published. Under Iraqi law, the validity of the marriage depended on whether the forms and requirements of English law, the lex nationalis, had been complied with. *Held*, the marriage was formally invalid, because the court of the locus celebrationis, referring to English law, would so consider it. (Compare *Re Trufort, Trafford v Blanc*; see also *Berthiaume v Dastous*.)

Hope v Hope (1857) 8 De GM & G 731 [223]

A husband domiciled in France but living in England signed an agreement with his wife, who resided in France, whereby the wife was to retain custody of one of their children despite a prior contrary order of the Lord Chancellor in England and was to facilitate divorce proceedings already instituted by the husband in England. The wife later sued in England for specific performance of this agreement. *Held*, even if the agreement were governed by French law and valid under that law, it could not be enforced in an English court because, in so far as it contemplated disobedience of an English custody order and collusion in English divorce proceedings, it was 'contrary to the laws and policy' of England. (See also *Kaufman v Gerson*.)

Hoskins v Matthews (1855) 8 De GM & G 13 [224]

An Englishman who still retained his English domicile of origin purchased a villa in Italy and went to live there, because he had been advised that the climate would improve his poor health. He made only short visits to England, but he left his children there to be educated and he said that he would prefer to live there. He died in Italy. *Held*, he had acquired a domicile of choice in Italy. Although it was his ill health that induced him to live there, this did not mean that he could not acquire a domicile there, because 'he was exercising a preference, and not acting upon a necessity' (*per* TURNER LJ). (See also *Re Martin, Loustalan v Loustalan*.)

House of Spring Gardens v Waite [1991] 1 QB 241 [225]

The plaintiffs succeeded in obtaining judgment for a sum in excess of £3,000,000 in an action in Ireland against three defendants for the misuse of confidential information and the breach of copyright in relation to the design and construction of bullet-proof vests. Later, an appeal by two of the defendants that the judgment had been obtained by fraud was dismissed. When the plaintiffs tried to enforce the judgment in England, SIR PETER PAIN at first instance, held that in the absence of fresh evidence the defendants were estopped from again raising the defence of fraud. The third defendant appealed. *Held*, dismissing the appeal, the judgment was a judgment against the defendants jointly and severally and that even though he (the third defendant) had not been a party to the proceedings to set aside the Irish judgment, he was aware of them and privy to them. Accordingly, in the absence of fresh evidence he, too, would be estopped from raising the defence of fraud. In the alternative, if such a judgment did not create an estoppel it was an abuse of the process of the court and contrary to justice and public policy for the issue of fraud to be re litigated in the forum when the issue had been specifically tried and decided by the foreign court. (Contrast *Abouloff v Oppenheimer, Vadala v Lawes, Jet Holdings Inc v Patel, Owens Bank v Bracco* and *Syal v Heyward*.)

Howard v Shirlstar Container Transport [1990] 3 All ER 366 [226]
(Court of Appeal)

Two aircraft had been leased from Shirlstar for private use in Nigeria. When the hire instalments became overdue, Shirlstar was entitled to repossess the aircraft. They aimed to do this by engaging Howard, a qualified pilot, to recover them under contracts which provided, inter alia, for the payment of £25,000 to Howard 'for successfully removing [each] aircraft ... from Nigerian airspace'. (The contract provided for half the amount to be paid when the aircraft was removed from Nigerian air space and the other half on return of the aircraft to England). Howard went to Lagos, Nigeria, with a wireless operator (his fiancée) where he found one of the aircraft parked at the airport. They prepared it for take-off with the assistance of two British engineers who were there. Then, when Howard was warned that 'powerful people wished to prevent them taking the aircraft', and that his life and that of his wireless operator was in danger, he took-off in the aircraft without obtaining permission from air traffic control at the airport. The aircraft was flown to the Ivory Coast where it was seized by the Ivory Coast Government and subsequently returned to Nigeria. Howard and his wireless operator were allowed to return to England where he sued for the second instalment because Shirlstar refused to pay the full amount on the basis that the contract had been illegally performed in Nigeria, ie taking off without permission. *Held*, although the court would not normally enforce a contract which would enable a plaintiff to benefit from his criminal conduct, since to do so would be an affront to the public conscience, there were circumstances where it would be wrong to disqualify a plaintiff from recovery, even though his claim was derived from conduct which constituted a statutory offence. Here the conscience of the court would not be affronted by allowing the plaintiff to succeed since he had committed the illegal act to save his life and that of his wireless operator. Howard would succeed in his claim.

Hoyles, Re, Row v Jagg [1911] 1 Ch 179 (Court of Appeal) [227]

A testator who died domiciled in England left to charity a share of his residuary estate, which included his interest as mortgagee in five mortgages of land in Ontario. A testamentary gift of mortgages of land to charity was void under mortmain legislation in both England and Ontario. *Held*, (1) the mortgages should be classified under Ontario law, the lex situs; (2) classified under that law, as also under English law, they were immovable property for international law purposes, even though for certain domestic law purposes they might be treated as personalty; and (3) the gift therefore was governed by the lex situs and was struck down by that law. (See also *Freke v Lord Carbery*; contrast *Haque v Haque (No 2)*.)

Huber v Steiner (1835) 2 Bing NC 202 [228]

A promissory note given by the defendant to the plaintiff while they both resided in France, was dishonoured on presentation. The plaintiff brought action on the note in England more than 15 years later, this being within the English limitation period, but outside the five-year period stipulated by French law, after which such an action was 'prescribed'. *Held*, the action was not defeated by lapse of time, because the limitation period in the lex fori applied. 'Now, the question is, whether the defendant has made out ... that this prescription has the necessary force of extinguishing and annulling the contract upon the note ... for unless the prescription has this force, it operates on the remedy only; which ... will be governed by the lex fori, and not by the lex loci contractus. And ... we think the French law is not shown to have the force contended for by the defendant' (*per* TINDAL CJ). (Compare *British Linen Co v Drummond*.)

Huntington v Attrill [1893] AC 150 (Privy Council) [229]

The defendant, a director of a company incorporated and carrying on business in the State of New York, USA, signed a certificate which falsely stated that the company's shares were fully paid up. He thereby made himself personally liable under a New York statute for all the company's debts. Relying on the statute, the plaintiff obtained judgment against him in New York for a debt owed by the company, but in enforcement proceedings in Ontario the defendant pleaded that the statute was penal and therefore unenforceable outside New York. *Held*, the statute was not penal within the meaning of the relevant private international law rule, which must be interpreted and applied according to the forum's own views. It set up a private remedy, whereas 'a proceeding, in order to come within the scope of the rule, must be in the nature of a suit in favour of the State whose law has been infringed' (*per* LORD WATSON). (See also *Raulin* v *Fischer*; contrast the Court of Appeal's opinion in *Attorney-General of New Zealand* v *Ortiz*.)

Hussain (Aliya) v Hussain (Shahid) [1983] Fam 26 [230]
(Court of Appeal)

An English domiciled man married a Pakistani domiciled woman in Pakistan in 1979 in a ceremony which was valid according to Pakistani law. When the wife petitioned for a decree of judicial separation in England in 1981, the husband challenged the validity of the marriage on the ground that under s11(d) of the Matrimonial Causes Act 1973 the marriage was potentially polygamous. *Held*, since s11(d) referred to the capacities of the parties entering into the marriage, such a marriage could only be potentially polygamous if at least one of the parties had the capacity to marry another spouse during the subsistence of the marriage in question. That was not the case here: neither the woman under Pakistani law nor the man under English law had the capacity to marry another spouse. Accordingly, the marriage was valid under English law and the wife was entitled to the decree sought. (See also *Parkasho* v *Singh* and *Radwan* v *Radwan (No 2)*; contrast *Hyde* v *Hyde and Woodmansee*.)

Hyde v Hyde and Woodmansee (1866) LR 1 P & D 130 [231]

An Englishman joined the Mormon community in the American State of Utah and contracted a marriage which under Mormon doctrine and the law of Utah was potentially polygamous. He subsequently renounced the Mormon faith and, having resumed his English domicile, petitioned for divorce in England. *Held*, the court had no jurisdiction, because this union was not a 'marriage' as understood in the Divorce Court, where the relief granted was suitable for monogamous unions only. 'I conceive that marriage, as understood in Christendom, may for this purpose be defined as the voluntary union for life of one man and one woman, to the exclusion of all others' (*per* LORD PENZANCE). (See also *Re Bethell, Bethell* v *Hildyard*; but see *Hussain* v *Hussain*.)

Igra v Igra [1951] P 404 [232]

A German Jew domiciled in Germany but living in England as a wartime refugee was divorced by his wife in Germany. He never received actual notice of the proceedings, but he was represented in them by a curator whose appointment was to some extent advertised. *Held*, his lack of notice was not a ground for refusing to recognise the divorce in England seeing that English courts themselves often dispensed with personal service of process upon the respondent in divorce cases. (See also *Wood* v *Wood*.)

India (Government of) v Taylor [1955] AC 491 [233]
(House of Lords)

A company incorporated in England, but carrying on business in India, sold its assets and undertaking in India to the Indian Government, remitted the proceeds to England and went into voluntary liquidation in England. The Indian

Government submitted a proof of debt in the liquidation for unpaid income tax and capital gains tax. *Held*, the proof must be rejected, because English courts would not enforce the tax laws of a foreign country, even though it was a country within the British Commonwealth. (See also *Huntington* v *Attrill* and *Regazzoni* v *K C Sethia (1944) Ltd*.)

India, Republic of, and the Government of the Republic of India (Ministry of Defence) v India Steamship Co, The Indian Grace [1993] AC 410 (House of Lords) [234]

After fire had broken out in the hold of a ship carrying munitions from Sweden to India, some shells were jettisoned following an inspection in France and others were found to be damaged. The owners of the cargo obtained judgment in India for £9,000 on an action in personam for short delivery in respect of the shells jettisoned. However, before judgment was pronounced, they commenced proceedings in rem in England in respect of the loss of the cargo as a whole because of crushing and radiant heat damage. This claim was for a sum in excess of £2.5 million. The claim was struck out at first instance. The Court of Appeal dismissed the appeal, holding (1) in essence, the cause of action involved the same subject matter: accordingly, the doctrine of res judicata applied; (2) relitigation of the same cause of action was impermissible following enactment of s34 of the Civil Jurisdiction and Judgments Act 1982. *Held*, the judgment of the Court of Appeal would be reversed and the plaintiffs allowed to proceed with their claim. LORD GOFF accepted that the facts gave rise to only one cause of action. However, with regard to s34 of the CJJA 1982 which states that: 'No proceedings may be brought by a person in England ... on a cause of action in respect of which a judgment has been given in his favour in proceedings between the same parties, or their privies, in a court ... of an overseas country unless that judgment is not enforceable or entitled to recognition', LORD GOFF said that this meant that the provision operated to furnish the defendant with a defence to a second claim, but it was a defence which could be lost by estoppel, waiver or agreement: the question would be remitted as it was for the Admiralty judge to decide if the s34 defence was applicable. (See also *Black* v *Yates*.)

Indian Grace, The see previous case

Industrial Diamond Supplies v Riva (Case 43/77) [235]
[1977] ECR 2175 (European Court of Justice)

An Italian court had ordered Industrial Diamond Supplies (IDS), a partnership with limited liability having its registered office in Belgium, to pay Mr Riva, a commercial representative residing in Italy, a sum of money. In due course, a Belgian court granted Mr Riva's application for an order authorising the enforcement of the Italian court. However, IDS appealed against the decision to the Belgian court under Article 36 of the Brussels Convention 1968 and sought a stay of action under Articles 30 and 38. Article 30 provides that: 'A court of a Contracting State in which recognition is sought of a judgment given in another Contracting State may stay the proceedings if an ordinary appeal against the judgment has been lodged.' Article 38 provides that, inter alia: 'The court with which the appeal under the first paragraph of Article 37 is lodged may, on the application of the appellant, stay the proceedings if an ordinary appeal has been lodged against the judgment in the State in which that judgment was given or if the time for such an appeal has not yet expired; in the latter case, the court may specify the time within which such an appeal is to be lodged.' IDS lodged an appeal with the Supreme Court of Appeal in Italy which constituted an ordinary appeal within the meaning of Articles 30 and 38 of the Convention. The Belgian court then stayed the proceedings pending preliminary rulings from the ECJ on a couple of questions which included: 'to what judgments are Articles 30 and 38 of the [Brussels] Convention applicable?' *Held*, 'The expression 'ordinary appeal' within the meaning of Articles 30 and 38 of the [Brussels] Convention 1968 ... must be defined solely within the framework of the system of the Convention itself and not according to the law either of the State in which the judgment was given or of the State in which recognition of enforcement of that judgment is sought. (2) Within the meaning of Articles 30 and 38 of the Convention, any appeal which is such that it may result in the annulment or the amendment of the judgment which is the subject-matter of the procedure for recognition or enforcement under the Convention and the lodging of which is bound, in the State in which the judgment was given, to a period which is laid down by the law and starts to run by virtue of that same judgment constitutes an "ordinary appeal" which has been lodged or may be lodged against a foreign judgment.' (See also *Petereit* v *Babcock International Holdings Ltd.*)

Indyka v Indyka [1969] 1 AC 33 (House of Lords) [236]

In 1949, a Czechoslovakian wife who had always lived in Czechoslovakia obtained a divorce there, at a time when her husband, who was also a Czechoslovak, was domiciled in England. Shortly after the decree, statutory jurisdiction over divorce petitions presented by wives who had resided in England for three years or more was introduced for the first time into English law. *Held*, the divorce should be recognised in England, the following alternative grounds being put forward in the judgments of their Lordships: (1) that the reciprocity principle could be applied, even though the basis of jurisdiction being recognised (a petitioner wife's residence for three years) did not enter into English law itself until shortly after the decree; (2) that there was a 'real and substantial connection' between the petitioner and Czechoslovakia, seeing that it was the country of her residence throughout her life, her last common residence with her husband and her nationality; and (3) that the matrimonial home, in which the petitioner had remained up to the time of the proceedings, was in Czechoslovakia. (Compare *Travers* v *Holley.*)

Inglis v Robertson [1898] AC 616 (House of Lords) [237]

A London wine merchant stored a quantity of whisky in a Scottish warehouse, receiving delivery warrants in return. He purported to pledge the whisky to the plaintiff, another English merchant, by indorsing and delivering the warrants to him. This was apparently a valid pledge under English law, but it was ineffective under Scottish law because no notice was given to the warehouse-keeper. The defendants, Scottish creditors of the pledgor, arrested the whisky in order to found jurisdiction over the pledgor under Scottish law and to obtain security for their debt. Proceedings were instituted in Scotland. *Held*, the plaintiff could not maintain a proprietary interest in the whisky as against the defendants, because the validity of the pledge should be determined by Scottish law, the lex situs. (See also *Re Korvine's Trusts, Levashoff* v *Block.*)

Inland Revenue Commissioners v Bullock [238]
[1976] 1 WLR 1178 (Court of Appeal)

A man who was born in and had a domicile of origin in Nova Scotia, Canada, came to England in 1932 to join the RAF. He married an Englishwoman in England shortly after World War II, and remained in the RAF until he retired in 1959. He wanted to return to live in Canada on his retirement but did not do so because his wife disliked the idea. However, in a will made and executed in Nova Scotia in the 1960s, he declared that: 'my domicile is and continues to be the Province of Nova

Scotia, Dominion of Canada, where I was born and brought up, to which province I intend to return and remain permanently upon my wife's death'. In 1972, after he had lived in England for 40 years, the IRC had claimed that he had acquired a domicile of choice in England during the two previous tax years. His appeal was allowed by the special commissioners but reversed by BRIGHTMAN J on appeal by the Crown. He appealed against this decision. *Held*, unanimously, he had not acquired a domicile of choice in England. BUCKLEY LJ said: 'Undoubtedly the fact that a man establishes his matrimonial home in a new country is an important consideration in deciding whether he intends to make that country his permanent home ... but this is not a conclusive factor.' With regard to the contingency of the man surviving his wife, 'The question can perhaps be formulated in this way where the contingency is not itself of a doubtful or indefinite character: is there a sufficiently substantial possibility of the contingency happening to justify regarding the intention to return as a real determination to do so upon the contingency occurring rather than a vague hope or aspiration? In the present case in my opinion that question should be answered affirmatively.' Thus, the man had the factum but not the animus to acquire a domicile of choice in England. (See also *Winans* v *Attorney-General*; contrast *Re Furse* and *White* v *Tennant*.)

Inland Revenue Commissioners v Plummer see Plummer v Inland Revenue Commissioners

Interdesco SA v Nullifire Ltd [1992] 1 Lloyd's Rep 180 [239]

The defendants, Nullifire, had terminated a distribution agreement for Interdesco's paint after three years of the five-year agreement. They did so on the basis of the paint failing to satisfy particular standards and thus being unmarketable. Interdesco denied Nullifire's claims and they succeeded in gaining judgment in their favour when both parties brought proceedings in France. Interdesco then applied to have the judgment registered in England. However, Nullifire appealed to the Court d'Appel in France, seeking to set aside the French judgment on the ground that it was, inter alia, obtained by fraud. Furthermore, they applied to stay the English proceedings, basing their argument on Article 38 of the Brussels Convention which provides for the court to stay the proceedings 'if an ordinary appeal has been lodged against the judgment in the State in which that judgment was given ...'. *Held*, PHILLIPS J dismissing the appeal, that (1) where a court in another Contracting State had in its judgment already ruled on precisely the matters the defendant raises when challenging the judgment, Articles 29 and 34 of the Convention preclude the court in the forum from reviewing the judgment of the foreign court; (2) 'where registration of a Convention judgment is challenged on the ground that the foreign court has been fraudulently deceived, the English court should first consider whether a remedy lies in such a case in the foreign jurisdiction in question. If so it will normally be appropriate to leave the defendant to pursue his remedy in that jurisdiction'; (3) 'the English court should not normally entertain a challenge to a Convention judgment where it would not permit a challenge to an English judgment'; and (4) 'A defendant can institute [the French appeal] at any time after the judgment appealed against. It follows that it does not constitute "an ordinary appeal under the Convention ...".' (See also *SISRO* v *Ampersand Software BV*.)

IP Metal Ltd v Ruote OZ SpA [1993] 2 Lloyd's Rep 60 [240]

The plaintiff sellers of aluminium, IP Metal, entered into seven contracts of sale with the defendant buyers, Ruote, each sale being confirmed by a telex containing the clause 'law – English; competent forum – London' (punctuation supplied). The first six contracts became the subject of proceedings in England which were served on the defendants on 30 January 1992. The seventh contract was subject to proceedings issued by the defendants in Italy and served on IP Metal on 29 January 1992. It was common ground that the Italian proceedings were related within the meaning of Article 22 of the Brussels Convention and that for the purpose of Article 22 the Italian court was 'first seised'. However, for the purpose of Article 21, the proceedings were not based on the same cause of action. Accordingly, for the purpose of the plaintiffs' action in England, the English courts were 'first seised'. On the basis that under Article 2 a defendant must be sued in the jurisdiction of his domicile, and that under Article 17 there was no agreement depriving them of this jurisdiction, Ruote applied for a declaration that the English court had no jurisdiction and for a stay of the English proceedings. *Held* WALLER J, refusing the applications, (1) 'Article 21 is inapplicable and only Article 22 can apply. In Article 22 the language used is "may" and that article on any view makes it discretionary as to whether the English court will stay the proceedings or decline jurisdiction.' (2) '[W]hen the court is considering Article 17 ... where Article 22 also applies and where there is a risk that there could be irreconcilable judgments on jurisdiction or proper law and thus ultimately even on the merits ... the English court will ... want to be as clear as possible, and at least form the view that it is highly likely, that if the matter were tried out the plaintiff would succeed in his argument on the jurisdiction clause.' Since Article 17 is an exception to the general rule that a defendant must be sued in the jurisdiction of his domicile it must be strictly construed. (3) With reference to the confirmation of the terms of the contract in a telex and, in particular, the 'law English forum London', 'It is, or can be, contrary to good faith to deny the existence of a term ... which ... has been brought expressly to the attention of one of the parties.' (4) The court was satisfied that agreements were made and evidenced in writing in a form which accorded with the practices which the parties had established between themselves and that by choosing one jurisdiction the provisions of Article 17 gave the English court exclusive jurisdiction. (See also *Dresser UK v Falcongate Freight Management.*)

ISC Technologies Ltd v Guerin [1992] 2 Lloyd's Rep 430 [241]

The plaintiffs were English subsidiaries of an English company, ISC Group plc, which merged with Ferranti in 1987. The plaintiffs contended that the defendants had fraudulently represented the level of profits the ISC Group were making, thereby enabling the defendants to deceive Ferranti to agreeing to a merger on terms advantageous to the ISC Group. The plaintiffs had already secured judgment against seven of the first nine defendants when they applied for leave under RSC O.15, r.6(2)(b)(ii) to join the tenth defendant, Pindell, and 11 Panamanian companies; and for leave under RSC O.11 to serve them all out of the jurisdiction. *Held* HOFFMANN J, (1) the alleged fraud was committed in England and upon English companies. [Accordingly] 'England has been shown to be the appropriate forum for the proceedings against Mr Pindell'. (2) As England is the proper forum, 'I can see nothing unfair or contrary to the spirit of the rules in allowing the plaintiffs to litigate the whole of their case against Mr Pindell here' because Mr Pindell is a proper party to an action against the only party still defending: the case fell within RSC O.11, r.1(1)(c). (3) It was correct to grant leave to serve the defendants out of the jurisdiction. 'It has been customary to analyse the requirements for leave under RSC O.11 into three elements. First, the plaintiff must have a 'good arguable case'. Secondly, the claim must come within the 'letter and spirit' of the sub-paragraph relied upon. Thirdly, it must be shown that England is the 'forum in which the case can most suitably be tried in the interests of all the parties and for the ends of justice'. More recent cases show that the first and third requirements are interlinked. The more obviously England appears to be the natural forum for the action, the less the court need concern itself with examining the plaintiff's prospects of success. (See also *Metall und Rohstoff AG* v *Donaldson Lufkin & Jenrette*.)

Israel Discount Bank of New York v Hadjipateras [242]
[1984] 1 WLR 137 (Court of Appeal)

Having obtained default judgments in New York, USA, against the defendants, who were father and son, the bank sought to enforce them in England. The son resisted enforcement on the basis that he had only acted as a guarantor for the loans made to two Liberian companies under the undue influence of his father. However, he did not raise this defence in the New York court. *Held*, rejecting his defence, 'I do not doubt that an agreement obtained by undue influence, like an agreement obtained by duress or coercion, may be treated by our courts ... as contrary to the distinctive public policy of this country. [However] a defendant must take all available defences in a foreign court. ... It is impossible for the ... defendant, who is at fault in not raising this defence in the New York court, to impeach the court's judgment' (*per* STEPHENSON LJ). (See also *Ellis* v *M'Henry*.)

Ivenel v Schwab (Case 133/81) [1982] ECR 1891 [243]
(European Court of Justice)

Ivenel lived and worked in France. He worked as a traveller and commercial representative for Schwab who was based in Germany. Ivenel brought proceedings before a French court claiming payment for various sums and, in particular, commission which allegedly had not been paid to him since 1975 and various allowances by reason of the termination of the contract of employment. Schwab, on the other hand, contended that Ivenel was not an employee but an independent contractor, and that the court having jurisdiction over the dispute would be a German court, not a French court. The French courts had no doubt the Ivenel worked under a contract of employment but because of the uncertainty surrounding the interpretation of Article 5(1) of the Brussels Convention 1968, particularly in relation to the question of the place of the performance of the obligation, proceedings were stayed until the ECJ gave a preliminary ruling on this point. *Held*, 'The obligation to be taken into account for the purposes of the application of Article 5(1) of the [Brussels] Convention 1968 ... in the case of claims based on different obligations arising under contract of employment as a representative binding a worker to an undertaking is an obligation which characterises the contract.' (See also *Mulox IBC Ltd* v *Geels*.)

Jabbour v Custodian of Israeli Absentee Property [244]
[1954] 1 WLR 139

An English insurance company issued a policy covering property in Palestine through its agents there. After a claim had arisen under the policy, the property of the policy-holders was expropriated under a general degree of the Israeli Government (which had been established in Palestine) and vested in a Custodian. *Held*, the Custodian was entitled to the policy moneys as against the policy-holders. Palestine was a place of residence of the insurance company and, under an implied term of the policy or by virtue of 'the ordinary course of business and the inferred expectations of the parties', it was the 'primary' place of payment. It was thus the situs of the debt, and being a part of the lex situs, the Israeli decree was effective to transfer the debt to the Custodian. (But see *Re United Railways of Havana and Regla Warehouses Ltd* and *Re Helbert Wagg & Co Ltd*.)

Jacobs, Marcus & Co v Credit Lyonnais [245]
(1884) 12 QBD 589 (Court of Appeal)

The defendant, a London bank, agreed in London to buy esparto from the plaintiff, a London firm, to be collected and approved in Algeria, shipped to London on the plaintiff's ship and paid for in London. Owing to a rebellion in Algeria, the defendant was unable to provide the full quantity agreed upon. Under French law, the law prevailing in Algeria, but not under English law, the rebellion provided a defence of force majeure. *Held*, the plaintiff was entitled to damages for breach of contract. The proper law of the contract was English law, this being the natural inference even though certain obligations under it were to be performed in Algeria. Although French law might regulate the mode of performance of those obligations, it was for the proper law to determine the consequences of their non-fulfilment. (See also *Bonython* v *Commonwealth of Australia*.)

Jacobson v Frachon (1927) 44 TLR 103 (Court of Appeal) [246]

The defendant, a merchant in France, sued the plaintiff, a London merchant, in a French court, alleging breach of an agreement by the plaintiff to purchase silk goods. The court appointed an expert to inspect the silk in the plaintiff's possession, but the expert made only a perfunctory inspection and refused to hear any witnesses, and his report, later described as 'the uncandid production of a biased and prejudiced mind', was very prejudicial to the plaintiff. Despite objections by the plaintiff, it was none the less accepted by the court, which gave judgment for the defendant. In proceedings for breach of the same contract already commenced by the plaintiff in England, the defendant now pleaded that the plaintiff was estopped by the French judgment. *Held*, this was a good plea because, even allowing for the expert's bias, the French judgment did not infringe the principles of natural justice and must be recognised. It would be different if (1) the court had been bound by its own rules to accept the expert's report without letting the plaintiff raise objections to it, or (2) the expert had been nominated by the defendant in the knowledge that he would be biased and would mislead the court. (See also *Igra* v *Igra*; but see *Price* v *Dewhurst*.)

Jet Holdings Inc v Patel [1990] 1 QB 335 (Court of Appeal) [247]

The plaintiff succeeded in California, USA, in obtaining judgment by default against the defendant for misappropriating funds. When attempting to enforce the judgment in England, the plaintiff was met with the defence of fraud or that the judgment had been obtained in proceedings which offended against English views of substantial justice. The defendant claimed that he been subjected to extortion by the plaintiff's actual and threatened violence and that this led to his failure to secure legal representation because he could no longer pay his lawyers; moreover, he feared his life would be endangered if he went to Los Angeles to comply with a court order for a medical examination as ordered by the Californian court. *Held*, 'a foreign judgment cannot be enforced if it was obtained by fraud, even though the allegation of fraud was investigated and rejected by the foreign court. ... [and] the foreign court's views on fraud are neither conclusive nor relevant whether the fraud is said to be fraud going directly to the cause of action or collateral fraud ... [Accordingly, the decision at first instance must be reversed since] there is an issue to be tried in this case as to whether the defendant is entitled to resist enforcement, at any rate on the ground of fraud. Accordingly, this appeal should be allowed, and the judgment set aside' (*per* STAUGHTON LJ). (See also *Abouloff* v *Oppenheimer* and *Owens Bank* v *Bracco*; contrast *House of Spring Gardens* v *Waite*.)

John Russell v Cayzer, Irvine and Co Ltd see **Russell (John) v Cayzer, Irvine and Co Ltd**

Johnson v Coventry Churchill [1992] 3 All ER 14 [248]

The plaintiff was an English employee working as a joiner in Germany for an English company. He was injured on a building site when the plank on which he was crossing a trench collapsed. Whereas, under English law, such an accident would make the employer liable for failure to provide a safe system of work, no such liability would arise under German law unless there was a wilful, as opposed to negligent, breach. *Held*, since the parties were both English and the contract was expressed to be subject to English law, then the country with which the occurrence (ie the accident) and the parties had the most significant relationship was England. Accordingly, the plaintiff was allowed to sue in England even though his claim was not actionable under the lex loci delecti commissi – German law. As the defendant could have, and did, insure against liability under English law, they would not be disadvantaged by being sued in England. (Contrast *Sayers v International Drilling Co NV.*)

Johnson v Taylor Bros & Co Ltd [1920] AC 144 [249]
(House of Lords)

The appellant, a Swedish subject domiciled in Sweden, had supplied under contract for eight years, pig iron to Taylor Bros in England. When he refused to make further deliveries, the English respondents sought leave to serve a writ out of the jurisdiction on him for breach of contract under RSC O.11, contending that, inter alia, the appellant had, in breach of contract, failed and neglected to tender any shipping documents to the respondents for any instalments of pig-iron in 1916. Leave was obtained at first instance and service effected. The appellant applied to set aside the writ and its service on the ground that the breach on which the action was founded was not committed within the jurisdiction. However, the first instance decision was upheld by the Court of Appeal. *Held*, allowing the appeal and reversing the decision of the Court of Appeal, that the essential breach on which the action was founded was the failure to ship the pig-iron from Sweden: it was not a breach within the jurisdiction. Accordingly, the case did not come within the scope of (the old) O.11, r.1(1)(e). (Note: under the present RSC 1965, O.11, r.1(1)(e), leave could be granted.)

K v B (Brussels Convention) [1994] 1 FLR 267 [250]

The parties to a marriage lived in different jurisdictions. The mother and her 10-year-old daughter lived in Italy. The father, who lived in England, issued proceedings in Italy in September 1992 applying for access to his daughter to be regulated, and that once that was settled he would be prepared to pay for her (his daughter) the amount of maintenance which was decided by the court. The proceedings were served on the mother in October 1992. In the first week of December 1992, the mother instituted proceedings in England for maintenance, and the following week she made a cross-application in the Italian proceedings seeking maintenance and other relief. In April 1993, the Italian court specifically declined jurisdiction to deal with the question of maintenance, holding that it had no jurisdiction to decide on the contribution to be legally imposed on the father, this being in the competence of the English court 'before which proceedings are already tendered in this matter'. It was common ground that the Brussels Convention applied to this case and that the Italian and the English courts had jurisdiction under the Convention. Thus, the issue to be decided was that under

Article 21, where the proceedings involved the same cause of action between the same parties and brought in the courts of different Contracting States, which court was first seised of the application for maintenance? *Held*, the English court was first seised by virtue of the mother's proceedings in the first week of December 1992. The nature of the father's proceedings was for contact. WALL J was of the opinion that it was 'plain from the nature of the father's petition that he was ... saying, "I wish for contact and I am prepared to pay maintenance." The obligation to apply for maintenance from the court in any formal sense seems to me to be fair and square on the mother in those circumstances.' The judge went on to conclude that 'the English court is first in time and, therefore, has jurisdiction to entertain these proceedings'. (See also *Overseas Union Insurance Ltd* v *New Hampshire Insurance* and *Neste Chemicals SA* v *DK Line SA, The Sargasso*.)

Kahler v Midland Bank Ltd [1950] AC 24 (House of Lords) [251]

The plaintiff, a Czechoslovak living in Prague, owned Canadian bearer securities which had been bailed by him to the Z Bank, a Czechoslovakian bank, and in turn bailed by the Z Bank to the defendant, a bank in London. In order to get out of Czechoslovakia after the German invasion of 1938, he had to sign a document transferring them into the possession of the B Bank, a bank under German control. After his departure, the Z Bank wrote to the defendant instructing it thenceforth to hold the securities on behalf of the B Bank, and the plaintiff subsequently ratified this by letter. After the war, the Czechoslovakian Government decreed that it was illegal to transfer foreign securities to a 'currency foreigner' such as the plaintiff unless official consent were obtained. Without obtaining such consent, the plaintiff sued the defendant in detinue for the return of the securities. *Held*, by a majority of 3-2, the action would fail. The proper law of the contract of bailment which had arisen between the plaintiff and the B Bank by virtue of the plaintiff's ratification of the Z Bank's letter was Czechoslovakian law, being the law which the parties must be taken to have intended even though the plaintiff had by then left Czechoslovakia as a refugee. Thus, the Czechoslovakian currency decree, being neither 'penal' nor a revenue law, was effective in an English court to prevent this contract being enforced. This meant that the plaintiff could not establish a right to possession of the securities. (See also *Moulis* v *Owen, Re Helbert Wagg & Co Ltd* and *Rossano* v *Manufacturers' Life Insurance Co.*)

Kalfelis v Bankhaus Schroder, Munchmeyer, Hengst & Co (Case 189/87) [1988] ECR 5565 (European Court of Justice) [252]

A dispute based on contract and tort was litigated in the German courts between a German plaintiff and various defendants, some of whom were domiciled in Germany others being domiciled in another Contracting State. The plaintiff sought to rely upon Article 6(1) of the Brussels Convention 1968 to establish the German courts' jurisdiction over the non-Germany domiciled defendants. *Held*, if a plaintiff was to benefit from the provision of Article 6(1), then there had to be a connection between the various defendants such that if the matter was not heard in one court only there would be a risk of irreconcilable judgments. Furthermore, the Article 6(1) exception to the basic domiciliary principle of Article 2 is to be construed and applied strictly in order to ensure that there is no unwarranted derogation imported into this jurisdictional principle. It was for the national court to establish in each individual case whether that condition was satisfied. (See also *Gascoine* v *Pyrah*.)

Kaufman v Gerson [1904] 1 KB 591 (Court of Appeal) [253]

The plaintiff threatened to initiate criminal proceedings against the defendant's husband in respect of an alleged misappropriation of money. Under pressure from this threat, the defendant agreed in writing to repay the money by instalments. These events took place in France, where the parties involved were nationals and had their domicile and the agreement was legal and enforceable. *Held*, on grounds of public policy, the plaintiff could not sue on the agreement in England. It had been entered into under duress and moral coercion, and 'to enforce a contract so procured would be to contravene what by law of this country is deemed an essential moral interest' (*per* ROMER LJ). (But see *Addison v Brown*.)

Kelly v Cruise Catering Ltd and Kloster Cruise Ltd [254]
[1994] 2 ILRM 394 (Supreme Court of Ireland)

The plaintiff was employed as a waiter on board ship. The contract of employment was made with an agent incorporated in the Bahamas, signed on behalf of the agent and posted to the plaintiff from Oslo, Norway. The ship was also registered in the Bahamas and the ship's owners were incorporated under Norwegian law and its central management was located in Norway. The contract of employment was completed when it was signed by the plaintiff in Dublin and returned by post to Oslo. The plaintiff was injured in an accident on board ship on the high seas between Mexico and Texas. He claimed that his injuries were caused by a breach of the defendants' contractual duties to him. He obtained leave to serve the defendants, from whom he claimed damages for breach of contract, out of the jurisdiction. The defendants sought to have the order discharged, claiming that either Norway or the Bahamas would be a more appropriate forum, and a hearing in Ireland would result in inconvenience and expense. *Held*, when a contract was made by post the acceptance was complete when the contract was posted and the country in which it was posted was the country in which the contract was made. Moreover, it would be more expensive and inconvenient to hear the action in the Bahamas or Norway rather than in Ireland. Accordingly, the defendants' appeal would be dismissed. (See also *Albeko Schuhmaschinen AG v Kamborian Shoe Machine Co Ltd*.)

Kelly v Selwyn [1905] 2 Ch 117 [255]

The estate of an English testator was administered in England by English trustees and comprised English securities. The testator's son, who was domiciled in New York, USA, made two assignments of his interest under the will. The first was to his wife, by deed executed in New York, and no notice was given to the trustees because this was not required by New York law. The second was to mortgagees in England, who gave notice as required by English law to preserve priority. *Held*, the mortgagees were entitled to priority, as under English law. 'The fund here being an English trust fund and this being the court which would have administered that trust fund, the order in which the parties are to be held entitled to the trust fund must be regulated by the law of the court which is administering that fund' (*per* WARRINGTON J). (But see *Re Queensland Mercantile and Agency Co* and *Guatemala (Republica de) v Nunez*.)

Kendall v Kendall [1977] Fam 208 [256]

The parties to a marriage lived with their three children in Bolivia where the husband was employed under a short-term contract. It was decided that she should leave with the children and return to England in June 1974 and that the husband would leave in August when his contract expired. Before the wife left Bolivia she was told by her husband that she would have to sign some documents in order for the children to leave the country. She signed the documents without attempting to read them as they were written in Spanish, a language of which she had little knowledge. When the husband returned home more than a year later he informed the wife that they had been divorced in Bolivia and that he had remarried. It appeared that the documents the wife had signed constituted a power of attorney enabling a decree to be granted in her absence, that she was the petitioner and that the decree had been granted to her because of the husband's physical cruelty. The wife petitioned for a declaration that the divorce granted to her by the Bolivian court was invalid. *Held*, since the decree had been obtained by deception, the exception in s8(2)(b) of the Recognition of Divorces and Legal Separations Act 1971 applied as it was manifestly contrary to public policy to recognise the decree. (See also *Igra* v *Igra*.)

Kenward v Kenward [1951] P 124 (Court of Appeal) [257]

A British subject, domiciled in England and serving with the Royal Navy, met and went through a ceremony of marriage with a Russian woman in Archangel, in the former USSR, in 1945. However, the registrar failed to comply with certain formalities required by Russian law, in particular, no entry of the parties' marriage was made on their passports. Two days after the ceremony, the husband left Russia and thereafter never again saw his wife: she was refused permission to leave Russia and he was refused permission to join her there. *Held*, the marriage was void on the ground that the Russian formalities had not been observed coupled with (1) shortly after the ceremony all marriages between Russians and foreigners was forbidden by Russian legislation; and (2) the Russian authorities refusing permission for the couple to unite. The subsequent actions of the Russian authorities had given the breach of formalities an importance which they might otherwise not have possessed. Accordingly, the husband was entitled to a decree of nullity. (See also *Berthiaume* v *Dastous*.)

Kinnear v Falconfilms NV (Hospital Ruber Internacional and another, third parties) [1994] 3 All ER 42 [258]

The actor Roy Kinnear was injured when he fell from a horse whilst filming in Spain. He died of his injuries in a Madrid hospital the following day. The administrators of his estate claimed damages for breach of contract and negligence from the defendants, Falconfilms NV and the producer and director of the film on which the deceased was working at the time he sustained the fatal injuries. The defendants denied liability and claimed that the hospital and an orthopaedic surgeon (the third parties) were guilty of medical malpractice in treating the deceased and that that was the sole cause of his death. The defendants obtained leave to issue a third party notice claiming an indemnity or contribution from the hospital and the surgeon in respect of any liability that the defendants might be under to the plaintiffs. The third parties did not respond to service of the notice until judgment in default of appearance was obtained when they applied to set aside the judgment and strike out the third party proceedings. The defendants sought to rely on their claim being based on Article 6(2) of the Brussels Convention 1968, which was given the force of law in England under the Civil Jurisdiction and Judgments Act 1982. *Held*, PHILLIPS J on appeal from the decision to grant the third parties' application, that 'the nexus between the plaintiff's claim against the defendant and the defendant's claim against the third party required to satisfy [RSC] O.16, r.1(1) is likely to be sufficient to justify the special jurisdiction granted by Article 6(2) [of the Brussels Convention 1968]'. Moreover, 'Where one tortfeasor wishes to reduce his liability to reflect the fact that another tortfeasor shares responsibility for the plaintiff's damage, it may be impossible to do this unless all three parties are brought before the same tribunal. That seems to me to be the practical reality in this case and, so far as the defendants are concerned, this jurisdiction is the only one which offers that possibility. This of itself abundantly justifies the application of Article 6(2) in the present case.' Whereas England was not a more convenient jurisdiction in which to determine the issue of whether there was medical malpractice in Madrid, discretion was exercised in favour of the defendants because 'I do not believe that there is any alternative forum available to the defendants in which to seek contribution from the third parties.' (See also *Kongress Agentur Hagen GmbH* v *Zeehaghe BV*.)

Kleinwort Benson Ltd v Glasgow District Council [259]
(Case C-346/93) (1995) The Times 17 April
(European Court of Justice)

The bank had made payments to the council under a contract, the type of which the House of Lords (in another case) had ruled was beyond the powers of local authorities to enter into. Accordingly, the bank sought restitution of the sums paid by bringing an action based on unjust enrichment. The bank brought the action in England under the special jurisdiction provisions of Schedule 4 of the Civil Jurisdiction and Judgments Act 1982 (CJJA 1982), Article 5(1) matters relating to a contract or Article 5(3), matters relating to tort, delict or quasi delict, whereas the council contended that it should have been brought in Scotland, the place of its domicile. The Court of Appeal requested a preliminary ruling on the relationship between Articles 5(1) and (3) of Schedule 4 of the CJJA 1982 and Articles 5(1) and (3) of the Brussels Convention 1968, the respective wording of which was substantially the same. *Held*, the ECJ declared that it had no jurisdiction to give a preliminary ruling on the basis that any such ruling given by it would be advisory only and not binding. It was common ground that the purpose of the interpretation which the ECJ was asked to give of the Convention provisions at issue was to enable the national court to decide on the application, not of the Convention, but of national law. Although, with reference to Schedule 4, s16(3)(a) CJJA 1982 provided that 'regard shall be had to any relevant principles laid down by the European Court', s3(1) provided that 'any question as the meaning or effect of any provision of the Convention shall, if not referred to the European Court ... be determined in accordance with the principles laid down by and any relevant decision of the European Court'. Thus, in a case in which the Convention was inapplicable, such as the present one, the national court was free to decide whether the interpretation given by the ECJ was equally valid for the purposes of the application of the national law based on the Convention. As it would be contrary to the 1971 Protocol for the ECJ to render purely advisory opinions, the ECJ did not have jurisdiction to give a preliminary ruling on the question submitted by the Court of Appeal.

Kloebe, Re, Kannreuther v Gieselbrecht (1884) 28 Ch D 175 [260]

A domiciled Greek died intestate and insolvent in Greece, owing debts to English and foreign creditors and leaving assets in England. *Held*, in the administration of his estate in England, the English creditors should not be given any preference over the foreign creditors, but the assets should be shared out rateably among the whole body of creditors. This was the English rule, which was applicable because matters of collection and administration of the assets of a deceased's estate were governed by the lex fori. (See also *Re Lorillard, Griffiths* v *Catforth*.)

Kloeckner and Co AG v Gatoil Overseas Inc [261]
[1990] 1 Lloyd's Rep 177

Here the plaintiffs and defendants in contracts for the sale and purchase of oil had brought proceedings against each other in England and Germany respectively. The plaintiffs had also obtained leave to serve a writ on the defendants out of the jurisdiction. The plaintiffs' writ was issued on 25 November 1988 and their writ for service out under RSC O.11 was issued on 29 November. However, the German proceedings were served on the plaintiffs at the end of November, two months before the English proceedings were served on the defendants. The defendants claimed, inter alia, that the order granting leave to the plaintiffs to serve their writ out of the jurisdiction should be set aside and that the English court either should decline jurisdiction or stay the proceedings pursuant to Article 21 because the German court was first seised of proceedings at the end of November 1988; or that the German court was first seised of a related matter and so the English court should exercise its discretion and stay the proceedings pursuant to Article 22. *Held*, (1) all the contracts of purchase and sale stipulated English law and English jurisdiction and it was beyond doubt that the court had jurisdiction in respect of them under RSC O.11; and a contract which had not specified a jurisdiction clause was subject to the overwhelmingly strong inference that the parties to it must have intended that it should also be governed by English law; (2) Article 17 of the Brussels Convention on prorogation of jurisdiction, was not to be overridden by Article 21 requiring a stay of proceedings by a court other than the court first seised; and since the ECJ had decided that the time a court is first seised is determined by domestic law of the relevant court, and English proceedings were commenced when issued whereas German proceedings were commenced when process was served, it followed that the English court was first seised; and (3) England was clearly the more appropriate forum and the court would not decline jurisdiction. (On point (2), contrast *Dresser* v *Falcongate Freight Management* and *Neste Chemicals SA* v *DK Line SA, The Sargasso*.)

Klomps v Michel (Case 166/80) [1981] ECR 1593 [262]
(European Court of Justice)

Michel applied in summary proceedings in a German court for an order for the recovery of a debt of some DM 63,000 from Klomps. An order for payment was served, in the absence of Klomps, by depositing it at a post office and leaving a note at an address in Germany which had been cited by Michel. In due course, an enforcement order was issued. After the expiry of the period for lodging an objection, Klomps contended that when the enforcement order was served his habitual residence was in The Netherlands, not Germany. A German local court found that, according to German law, he was also habitually resident in Germany and that his objection was out of time. Consequently, an enforcement order was served on him under the provisions of the Brussels Convention 1968 by a Dutch District Court. Klomps appealed, contending that as he was habitually resident in The Netherlands, service was not duly effected and, further, that it was not effected in good time since the order for payment gave him only three days in which to arrange a defence and submit an objection to that order. Proceedings were stayed while the Dutch court sought preliminary rulings on several questions from the ECJ, including: 'If the court first seised has ruled that at the time of service of the document which instituted the proceedings the defendant had his habitual residence in the State of that court, with the result that in that respect service was duly effected, do the provisions of the opening words and point 2 of Article 27 require that a separate examination be carried out into the question whether the document was served in sufficient time to enable the defendant to arrange for his defence?' *Held*, 'Article 27, point 2, lays down two conditions, the first of which, that service should be duly effected, entails a decision based on the legislation of the State in which judgment was given and on the conventions binding on that State in regard to service whilst the second, concerning the time necessary to enable the defendant to arrange for his defence, implies appraisals of a factual nature. A decision concerning the first of those conditions made in the State in which the judgment was given accordingly does not release the court in the State in which enforcement is sought from its duty to examine the second condition, even if that decision was made in the context of separate adversary proceedings.' (See also *Debaecker* v *Bouwman*.)

Kochanski v Kochanska [1958] P 147 [263]

In 1945, a soldier in the Polish army and a Polish nurse who were living in a camp for 'displaced' Poles in occupied Germany were married by a Polish Roman Catholic priest who acted as chaplain to the camp. The people in the camp made a point of living entirely separate from the local populace. The ceremony was formally defective under German law. *Held*, it was none the less a valid marriage at common law because in the peculiar circumstances the parties could not be taken to have submitted its validity to the lex loci celebrationis. (See also *Preston (orse Putynski)* v *Preston (orse Putynska)(orse Basinska)*.)

Kohnke v Karger [1951] 2 KB 670 [264]

The plaintiff was injured in France when a car in which she was being driven by the defendant collided with a French lorry. In proceedings in France against the lorry driver, she obtained an award of damages, which were paid to her, and responsibility for the accident was apportioned between the lorry driver, who was held to be two-thirds responsible for the accident, and the defendant, who was one-third responsible. This apportionment was not binding in law on other French courts, but it would be treated as binding in practice. While the French proceedings were pending, the plaintiff sued the defendant in England, where he resided, undertaking to give credit for the damages already paid to her. The defendant contended that the plaintiff could not recover damages from him as she had already obtained a satisfied judgment of a competent court. However, under English law, though not under French law, she was entitled to compensation for damage done to her wristwatch and for the possibility of her personal injuries being later aggravated, so that an English court would award a higher sum. *Held*, the French judgment against the lorry driver did not bar her from suing the defendant in England. Although she had suffered only one set of injuries from the negligence of the two drivers, she could choose a different forum in which to sue each of them. The English court was not bound by the French court's assessment of damages, but should award the higher sum indicated by its own rules, giving credit for the amount already paid under the French judgment. (Compare *D'Almeida Araujo Lda* v *Sir Frederick Becker & Co Ltd* and *Carl Zeiss Stiftung* v *Rayner and Keeler Ltd (No 2)*.)

Kongress Agentur Hagen GmbH v Zeehage BV [265]
(Case C–365/88) [1990] ECR 1845 (European Court of Justice)

K, an undertaking with a registered office in Germany, booked a large number of rooms in an hotel, owned by Z, in The Netherlands. K booked the rooms in its own name but at the request of and on behalf of S, a third party. The reservation was cancelled and Z brought an action in The Netherlands claiming damages. K claimed that the Dutch court should declare that it did not have jurisdiction or, in the alternative, that S, as its principal, should be summoned to appear to answer a claim for indemnity. Z objected to S being joined as third party on the basis that proceedings between themselves (Z) and K would become complicated and protracted. Initially, the Dutch court agreed that Z's objections were well founded. However, K appealed to the Regional Court of Appeal contending that under Article 6(2) of the Brussels Convention 1968, the court seised of the original proceedings were bound to grant leave to bring an action as a warranty or guarantee unless the proceedings were instituted solely with the object of removing the third party from the jurisdiction of the court which would be competent in the case in issue. Z objected, contending that an action on a warranty or guarantee could be brought only if jurisdiction of the court seised of the main proceedings was based on the ordinary rule of jurisdiction as contained in Article 2 of the Convention. Here, they contended, it would be inappropriate to grant K's application under the special rule of jurisdiction contained in Article 6(2), since the original proceedings were also based on a special rule of jurisdiction, as provided for in Article 5(1). The Supreme Court of The Netherlands referred the issue to the ECJ for a preliminary ruling. *Held*, '(1) Where a defendant domiciled in a Contracting State is sued in a court of another Contracting State pursuant to Article 5(1) of the Brussels Convention, that court also has jurisdiction by virtue of Article 6(2) of the Brussels Convention to entertain an action on a warranty or guarantee brought against a person domiciled in a Contracting State other than that of the court seised of the original proceedings. (2) Article 6(2) must be interpreted as meaning that it does not require the national court to accede to the request for leave to bring an action on a warranty or guarantee and that the national court may apply the procedural rules of its national law in order to determine whether that action is admissible, provided that the effectiveness of the Convention in that regard is not impaired and, in particular, that leave to bring the action on the warranty or guarantee is not refused on the ground that the third party resides or is domiciled in a Contracting State other than that of the court seised of the original proceedings.' (See also *Kinnear* v *Falconfilms NV*.)

Korvine's Trust, Re, Levashoff v Block [1921] 1 Ch 343 [266]

Prior to undergoing a serious operation in London, a domiciled Russian made a gift of money and chattels situated in England, to a Russian lady living in Switzerland, stipulating that the gift should only take effect on his death. He died without recovering from the operation and without revoking the gift. *Held*, the gift was valid: it constituted a good donatio mortis causa by English law. Its true character was that of a dealing inter vivos with movable property, not a testamentary gift, so its validity was determined by the lex situs of the subject matter, not by the donor's lex domicilii. (See also *Cammell* v *Sewell* and *Winkworth* v *Christie, Manson & Woods*.)

Kroch v Rossell et Cie [1937] 1 All ER 725 (Court of Appeal) [267]

The plaintiff, a 'gentleman of no occupation', was living temporarily in England, where he had no connections or associations. He sued the defendants, the publishers of a Belgian newspaper and a French newspaper respectively, for damages for libel in an article which had been widely circulated in Belgium and France, but very little (no more than 50 copies) in England. He obtained leave under (what is now) RSC O.11, r.1 (1)(f) to serve the writs out of the jurisdiction. On application by the defendants, *Held*, service should be set aside. Assuming that technically the tort of defamation had been committed in England, the court should still exercise its discretion in this way, because 'the reality of the cause of action' was in Belgium and in France. In England, the libel was scarcely circulated, and the plaintiff had little or no reputation to be injured. (See also *Bata* v *Bata*; but see *Oppenheimer* v *Louis Rosenthal & Co AG*.)

Kurz v Stella Musical Veranstaltungs GmbH [268]
[1991] 3 WLR 1046

The plaintiff, who was domiciled in England, served a writ on the defendant company, seated in Germany, claiming that it owed him money. In giving notice of intention to defend the proceedings, the company claimed that the English courts had no jurisdiction under the Civil Jurisdiction and Judgments Act 1982 and Article 17 of the Brussels Convention. *Held*, dismissing the defendant's contention and upholding the jurisdiction of the English courts, the word 'exclusive' in Article 17 'does not mean "unique", that the parties are limited to choosing a single jurisdiction. It means only that their choice, whatever it is, shall ... have effect to the exclusion of the jurisdiction which would otherwise be imposed upon the parties by the earlier articles of the Convention' (*per* HOFFMAN J). (See also *Meeth* v *Glacetal Sarl*.)

Kuwait Airways Corporation v Iraqi Airways Co [269]
and Others [1995] 3 All ER 694 (House of Lords)

During the short-term annexation of Kuwait by Iraq, aircraft belonging to Kuwait Airways Corporation (KAC) were sequestered and incorporated into the fleet of the Iraqi Airways Co (IAC). However, following the cessation of hostilities between the allied forces and Iraq and Iraq's recognition of Kuwait as an independent state, a default judgment was given for KAC against IAC and Iraq for US$500 million in respect of payment for the aircraft wrongly interfered with. Under provisions of RSC O.11 and the State Immunity Act 1978, an attempt to serve a writ on Iraq had been made by sending a letter via the Foreign and Commonwealth Office to the Iraqi Embassy in London requesting them to forward the documents to the Ministry of Foreign Affairs in Baghdad. Service of the writ on IAC was by way of leaving it with a named employee of IAC at their premises in London. Four issues then arose for consideration: validity of service on (1) IAC and (2) Iraq; (3) applicability of provisions of the State Immunity Act 1978; and (4) whether the issues were justiciable in the English courts. *Held*, (1) The writ was effectively served on IAC under RSC O.65, r.3: the employee came within the scope of 'other similar officer' within rule 3; accordingly, it was not necessary to consider whether IAC was an 'overseas company' within provisions of the Companies Act 1985. (2) The purported service of the writ on Iraq was ineffective: delivery of the writ by the Foreign and Commonwealth Office to the Iraqi Embassy was at best a request to the Embassy to forward the writ on behalf of the Foreign and Commonwealth Office to the Iraqi Ministry of Foreign Affairs. The evidence was that this was not carried out. (3) IAC could only claim state immunity provided that they could satisfy the provisions of s14(2)(a) and (b) of the State Immunity Act 1978. The central question was whether the acts performed by IAC to which the proceedings related were performed in the exercise of sovereign authority. There was unanimous agreement that taking the aircraft from Kuwait amounted to things done in the exercise of sovereign authority. However, by a majority of 3-2, the House opined that acts carried out on and relating to the performance of the aircraft *after* their incorporation into the IAC fleet under an Iraqi Governmental resolution dissolving KAC meant that IAC as a separate entity did not satisfy s14(2)(a) that 'the proceedings relate to anything done by it in the exercise of sovereign authority'; accordingly, IAC could not claim state immunity in respect of those acts. (It is submitted that the better view is that of LORD MUSTILL who dissented on this point: he argued that the provisions of sections 3 and 14(2) taken together afforded IAC state immunity and, as a consequence, the writ and all subsequent proceedings should be set aside. In essence, LORD SLYNN agreed with LORD MUSTILL.) (4) Because of the uncertainty relating to IAC's submissions on issues relating to justiciability, the matter would be referred to the commercial court. (See also *Trendtex* v *Central Bank of Nigeria* and the State Immunity Act 1978.)

Lakhta, The [1992] 2 Lloyd's Rep 269 [270]

The result of arbitration proceedings in Moscow in 1992, was that the Russian defendants in the current action, Progress, were declared to be the owners of the vessel the *Lakhta*. The Latvian plaintiffs, Kontinent, were not party to the arbitration and complained against the award. The vessel was arrested after the plaintiffs issued a writ in rem when the vessel was within the jurisdiction of the English Admiralty Court. The plaintiffs sought a declaration that they were the sole owners of the vessel and that they were entitled to possession and control of the vessel. The defendants applied for a stay of action on the grounds of forum non conveniens. *Held*, granting the stay, (1) Russia was another available forum and, prima facie, the appropriate forum, and the plaintiff was unable to show that there were special reasons by virtue of which justice required that trial should take place in England. (2) Indeed, 'the case is in every respect intimately connected with Russia and the Baltic States and it has no connection with England. The language of the documents is Russian. The language of the witnesses is Russian. ... many questions of Russian law arise and there will be nuances with which this court is not familiar. All the witnesses would have to come to this country from Russia, thereby greatly adding to the expense and causing them personally great inconvenience. For these reasons a Russian forum would clearly and distinctly be more appropriate than this court' (*per* SHEEN J). (See also *Spiliada Maritime Corporation* v *Cansulex*.)

Langley's Settlement Trusts, Re, Lloyds Bank Ltd [271]
v Langley [1962] Ch 541 (Court of Appeal)

L, a settlor domiciled in California, exercised an express power to withdraw funds from a settlement governed by English law which he himself had created. In fact, both L and his wife executed the notice of withdrawal because, owing to L's multiple sclerosis, by reason of which he had little power of movement in his limbs, though his mental capacity was unaffected, he had been declared an 'incompetent' by a Californian court and his wife had been appointed his guardian with power to execute such documents on his behalf. *Held*, (1) the court would exercise its discretion with due regard to common sense and reasonable policy and disregard any status of incapacity by Californian law because, in so far as the status operated to deprive the settlor of a valuable right, it was of a penal character which would not be recognised; and (2) the notice of withdrawal was effective because if the settlor's status as an 'incompetent' were to be recognised, it should be recognised in full, which would entail recognising as effective the wife's powers as his guardian. (See also *Re Selot's Trust*; but see *Re Macartney, Macfarlane* v *Macartney*.)

Lashley v Hog (1804) 4 Paton 581 (House of Lords) [272]

A Scotsman who had acquired an English domicile married an Englishwoman, then reverted to his Scottish domicile. Under the Scottish system of community of property between spouses, the wife was entitled to a share in his movable property on his death. She in fact died first, without leaving a will, then on her husband's death one of their children brought proceedings in Scotland claiming this share in right of the wife. *Held*, this claim must be upheld, as under Scottish law. Initially, the marital property rights of the spouses were determined by English law, but this law had been supplanted by Scottish law as a result of the change of domicile. (But see *De Nicols* v *Curlier*.)

Lawrence v Lawrence [1985] Fam 106 (Court of Appeal) [273]

Mrs L, who was domiciled in Brazil according to the English conflict rule, divorced her first husband in Nevada, USA. The following day she married H2 in Nevada. Mrs L and H2 came to live in England where, subsequently, H2 petitioned for a declaration as to the validity of this (L's second) marriage. The English conflict rules provide that the formal validity of a marriage is governed by the lex loci celebrationis (Nevada) and the essential validity (which includes capacity) is governed by the parties' ante-nuptial domicile, ie Brazil in relation to Mrs L. However, whereas Brazilian law did not recognise divorce, the Nevada divorce decree was recognised in England under (what is now) the Family Law Act 1986. In essence, then, the main question to decide was: did Mrs L have the capacity to marry? And the incidental question which arose was: was the Nevada divorce valid? *Held*, the marriage was valid and would be recognised by the English court. (Contrast *R v Brentwood Superintendent Registrar of Marriages, ex parte Arias*.)

Lazard Bros & Co v Midland Bank Ltd [1933] AC 289 [274]
(House of Lords)

In garnishee proceedings between two English banks, the court had to determine the effect of decrees of the revolutionary Soviet Government which purported to dissolve the judgment-debtor, a Russian bank. *Held*, 'What the Russian Soviet law is in that respect is a question of fact, of which the English court cannot take judicial cognizance, even though the foreign law has already been proved before it in another case. The court must act upon the evidence before it in the actual case. [Recent legislation], which provides that this question of fact must be decided by the judge alone instead of by the jury, if there be a jury, expressly treats the question as depending on the evidence given with respect to the foreign law ... The evidence it is clear must be that of qualified experts in the foreign law' (*per* LORD WRIGHT). (See also *Brailey v Rhodesia Consolidated Ltd*.)

Lazarewicz (orse Fadanelli) v Lazarewicz [1962] P 171 [275]

In 1946, a Polish soldier serving with the occupying Allied Forces in Italy married a domiciled Italian woman who was living in Italy in a Polish civilian camp. The ceremony, which was conducted in the camp by the camp chaplain, purported to comply with Italian law but was, in fact, defective in certain vital respects under that law and under Polish law. *Held*, the marriage was void. It could not be validated under the doctrine of common law marriage because the parties clearly intended to submit its validity to the lex loci celebrationis. (Compare *Berthiaume v Dastous*.)

Lecouturier v Rey [1910] AC 262 (House of Lords) [276]

Under a French statute declaring unlicensed religious associations to be illegal, the Order of Carthusian Monks in France was disbanded and its property and business, which included the distillation of the liqueur 'Chartreuse', were confiscated and sold. After re-establishing their business in Spain, the monks disputed the right of the purchaser of their French business to claim their English trade-marks for the liqueur. *Held*, the monks were entitled to retain these trade marks because the French statute was not intended to have extra-territorial effect. (Contrast *Williams and Humbert v W & H Trademarks (Jersey) Ltd*.)

Lee v Abdy (1886) 17 QBD 309 [277]

By an instrument executed in South Africa, the plaintiff's husband, being domiciled and resident in South Africa, assigned to the plaintiff his interest under an insurance policy on his own life which he had taken out with the defendant, an English insurer. The assignment was void under South African law because the husband was insolvent at the time. *Held*, the plaintiff could not sue the defendant for the policy moneys after her husband's death, because South African law, being the lex domicilii of the parties and the lex actus, governed the validity of the assignment. (See also *Colonial Bank* v *Cady*.)

Le Mesurier v Le Mesurier [1895] AC 517 (Privy Council) [278]

A married couple lived together for some years in Ceylon, but the husband never lost his English domicile of origin. *Held*, the Ceylonese courts had no jurisdiction to grant him a decree of divorce. 'According to international law, the domicile for the time being of the married pair affords the only true test of jurisdiction to dissolve their marriage.' Furthermore, a decree granted in the domicile 'ought to be respected by the tribunals of every civilised country' (*per* LORD WATSON). (See also *Bater* v *Bater (orse Lowe)*.)

Lepre v Lepre [1965] P 52 [279]

A Roman Catholic Maltese domiciled in Malta married a domiciled Englishwoman in a civil ceremony in England. They lived together in Malta until eventually he sent her back to live in England. He then obtained a decree of nullity in Malta on the ground that religious formalities had not been observed at the marriage ceremony. *Held*, even if the effect of the decree under Maltese law was to make the marriage void ab initio and the wife's domicile English, the Maltese court's jurisdiction should still be considered adequate on grounds of reciprocity, seeing that domicile of the petitioner alone was a sufficient ground of nullity jurisdiction in England. But the decree itself offended 'intolerably' against English notions of justice and on that ground would be refused recognition, in the court's discretion. (See also *Mitford* v *Mitford and Von Kuhlmann* and *Gray (otherwise Formosa)* v *Formosa*.)

Leroux v Brown (1852) 12 CB 801 [280]

By an oral agreement made in France and valid under French law, the defendant promised to take the plaintiff into his employment. When the plaintiff sued the defendant in England for damages for its breach, the defendant pleaded s4 of the Statute of Frauds, which provided that 'no action shall be brought' upon such a contract unless it was evidenced in writing. *Held*, this was a good defence. The section related not to the formalities of contracts but to the mode of procedure for enforcing them, so it was applicable as a rule of the lex fori even though the contract was governed by French law. (Compare *Van Grutten* v *Digby*.)

Libyan Arab Foreign Bank v Bankers Trust [1989] 3 WLR 314 [281]

The plaintiff bank had accounts in London and New York with the defendant American bank and an arrangement whereby a peg balance of $500,000 was maintained in the New York account: ie, funds were transferred at 2pm each day to or from the New York account so as to maintain the peg balance. At 4pm on 8 January 1986, an American Presidential decree froze all Libyan property in the USA or in the possession or control of US persons, including overseas branches of US juristic persons. However, funds of over $160 million which were available for transfer to the London account, and which should have been transferred prior to the executive order, were not transferred. The plaintiff demanded payment of the sums which should have been transferred. *Held*, giving judgment for the plaintiff, there was only one contract between the parties, and that applying the general rule that a contract between a bank and its customer was governed by the place where the account was kept the rights and obligations of the parties in respect of the London account was governed by English law; that when the plaintiff had exercised its right unilaterally to determine the management of the account, it was no longer a term of the contract that sums had to pass through the New York account and so there was no infringement of US law within the US. Accordingly, the plaintiff was entitled to cash payments. (See also *Libyan Arab Foreign Bank* v *Manufacturers Hanover Trust (No 2)*.)

Libyan Arab Foreign Bank v Manufacturers Hanover Trust Co (No 2) [1989] 1 Lloyd's Rep 608

The plaintiff bank, LAFB, commenced proceedings against the defendant bank, MHT, in connection with a dispute arising out of an automatic fund transfer arrangement (AFT) between the LAFB's accounts in New York, where a peg balance of $250,000 was maintained, and London. The AFT had been blocked by a US Executive Order (Presidential decree) and subsequent telexes between the banks confirmed that the arrangements had been terminated. LAFB claimed that a substantial debt was due to them in London. MHT admitted the debt but contended that by reason of US law they were not obliged to satisfy it and because of other contractual conditions. LAFB's application for summary judgment was dismissed on the ground that the question of the proper law of the contract raised a triable issue and MHT were entitled to leave to defend. *Held*, there were two separate contracts relating to the New York and London accounts (compare with STAUGHTON J's decision in the *Bankers Trust* case) and the proper law of the contract in relation to the London bank account was English law as was the proper law of the AFT in so far as it affected that account; that the AFT was not 'property' or an 'obligation' or a 'bank deposit' within the possession or control of US persons and that the AFT was not prohibited under regulations made under the Executive Order. The plaintiff would succeed in its claims. (See also *Libyan Arab Foreign Bank* v *Bankers Trust*.)

Lieber v Gobel, (Case C–292/93) [1994] ECR 2535
(European Court of Justice)

The result of a friendly settlement in 1978 was that the Gobels, who were domiciled in Germany, transferred the ownership of an apartment they owned in Cannes, France, to Mr Lieber, who also was domiciled in Germany. Mr Lieber was in possession of the apartment from 1978 until 1987. However, when the settlement was declared void in 1987, the Gobels sought compensation from him in the German courts. Mr Lieber contested the jurisdiction of the German courts, contending that the French courts had exclusive jurisdiction under Article 16(1) of the Brussels Convention of 1968. The German court referred the following question to the ECJ for a preliminary ruling: 'Do matters governed by Article 16(1) of the Brussels Convention also cover questions of compensation for use made of a dwelling after a failed property transfer?' *Held*, as the object of the settlement was the transfer of ownership of immovable property, it did not constitute a tenancy of immovable property within the meaning of Article 16(1); accordingly, the court had to consider whether the compensation in question was a right in rem in immovable property within the meaning of that provision. However, 'The court has consistently held ... that Article 16 must not be given a wider interpretation than is required by its objective, since it results in depriving the parties of the choice of forum which would otherwise be theirs and, in certain cases, results in their being brought before a court which is not that of any of them.' It follows from (previous cases) and from the judgment in Case C–294/92 *Webb*, 'that in order for Article 16(1) to apply, it is not sufficient that the action *concerns* a right in rem in immovable property or that the action is connected with immovable property. The action must be *based* on a right in rem and not, apart from the exception for tenancies of immovable property, on a right in personam'. Thus, the claim for compensation was not included in the matters governed by Article 16(1) and the claim could be heard in Germany. (See also *Webb* v *Webb*.)

Littauer Glove Corporation v F W Millington (1920) Ltd [284]
(1928) 44 TLR 746

The defendant company was incorporated in England and carried on business as a clothier's merchant. While its managing director was paying a brief visit to New York, USA, on company business, process of the New York court, which the plaintiff corporation had issued against the defendant, was served upon him in his official capacity whilst he was on the premises of one of the defendant's customers. The plaintiff proceeded to obtain a default judgment against the defendant, then sued to recover the amount of the judgment in England. *Held*, the judgment was not enforceable, on account of the New York court's lack of jurisdiction over the defendant. The managing director's activities as a commercial traveller for the company did not involve 'a carrying on of business at a definite and, to some reasonable extent, permanent place' in New York, so the company was not 'resident' there for the purposes of jurisdiction (*per* SALTER J). (See also *Vogel* v *Kohnstamm* and *Adams* v *Cape Industries*; compare *Carrick* v *Hancock*.)

Lloyd v Guibert (1865) LR 1 QB 115 (Exchequer Chamber) [285]

While in a Danish island in the West Indies, the plaintiff, a British subject, chartered a French ship belonging to the defendant, a French shipowner, to carry a cargo from Haiti to England. During the voyage the captain gave a bond over the cargo for the cost of repairs effected in Portugal, which in due course was enforced against the plaintiff. The plaintiff sought an indemnity from the defendant, to which he was entitled under the 'general maritime law' prevailing in Denmark, Portugal and England, but not under French law. *Held*, his claim would fail because, in respect of sea damage and its incidents, the contract of affreightment was governed by French law, the law of the ship's flag. When a ship visited many ports on a voyage, this law was in general 'not only in accordance with the probable intention of the parties, but also most consistent and intelligible, and therefore most convenient to those engaged in commerce' (*per* WILLES J). (See also *The Gaetano and Maria* and *The Assunzione*.)

Lord Advocate v Jaffrey [1921] 1 AC 146 (House of Lords) [286]

A husband domiciled in Scotland left his wife with her consent, settled and became domiciled in Queensland and contracted a bigamous marriage there. His lawful wife remained in Scotland, where she died. *Held*, in Scottish proceedings, she died domiciled in Queensland. The unity of a husband's and wife's domicile had to be maintained while the marriage subsisted, even where the wife had never been to the country of domicile and the husband by his conduct had given her grounds for divorce. (See also *Attorney-General for Alberta* v *Cook*.)

Lorillard, Re, Griffiths v Catforth [1922] 2 Ch 638 [287]
(Court of Appeal)

The estate of a testator dying domiciled in New York, USA, included assets and liabilities in New York and England and was administered in both of these jurisdictions. The assets in New York were insufficient to satisfy certain debts to American creditors which, though enforceable in New York, were statute-barred in England. For this reason, the creditors concerned did not lodge claims in the English administration, where there was a surplus after the English creditors had been paid off. *Held*, in the exercise of the court's discretion, the New York administrator would not be granted an order for transfer of the surplus into his hands to be paid out to the American creditors, even though he was the principal administrator by virtue of the testator's New York domicile. The English administration was governed by the lex fori, according to which all claims had been satisfied and the surplus was free for distribution among the beneficiaries. (See also *Re Manifold, Slater* v *Chryssafinis* and *Re Wilks, Keefer* v *Wilks*.)

LTU v Eurocontrol (Case 29/76) [1976] ECR 1541 [288]
(European Court of Justice)

LTU, a German airline corporation, disputed the validity of charges imposed by Eurocontrol, a public authority and international organisation, which provided air safety services. Eurocontrol was acting within the exercise of its powers when it sought to collect charges from LTU for the use of its services. Although the use of the services was obligatory and the rate of charge was fixed unilaterally, ie, it was non-negotiable, Eurocontrol succeeded in obtaining a judgment in Belgium, the Belgian court expressly finding the matter to be commercial in nature. However, when the German court was asked to enforce this judgment it referred the question of interpretation of 'civil and commercial matters' to the ECJ. *Held*, this was not a civil or commercial matter. Accordingly, the enforcement of the judgment fell outside the scope of the Convention. The court made it clear that the meaning of a 'civil and commercial matter' would be derived from the Convention and not from the provisions of the national laws involved in the litigation. (See also *Netherlands State* v *Ruffer*.)

Luck's Settlement Trusts, Re, Walker v Luck [289]
[1940] Ch 864 (Court of Appeal)

A domiciled Englishman left his first wife in 1905, went to California, USA, and had a son in the following year by another woman. He then acquired a Californian domicile, procured the dissolution of his first marriage and got married again, though not to the mother of his son. With his second wife's consent he signed a formal declaration in 1925 acknowledging the son as his own and receiving him into his home, thus legitimating the son under Californian law but not under English law. *Held*, the legitimation would not be recognised in England because English law, the law of the father's domicile at his birth, did not provide for legitimation by parental recognition. 'If by the law of that domicile the relationship is immutably that of putative father and illegitimate child, nothing thereafter can change it' (*per* LUXMOORE LJ). (See, however, the dissenting judgment of SCOTT LJ and the Legitimacy Act 1976.)

Luther (A M) Aksionairnoye Obschestvo [290]
v James Sagor & Co [1921] 3 KB 532 (Court of Appeal)

In 1918, the revolutionary Soviet Government passed a decree vesting the assets of sawmill businesses in Russia in the State, without any compensation being paid to the owners. Timber belonging to the plaintiff, a Russian company, was seized under the decree, sold to the defendant, an English firm, and imported into England in 1920. In 1921, the British Government recognised the Soviet Government de facto. *Held*, the plaintiff could not recover the timber from the defendant, even though the nationalisation decree conflicted with English notions of just acquisition of a property. 'I do not feel able to come to the conclusion that the legislation of a State recognised by my Sovereign as an independent sovereign State is so contrary to moral principle that the judges ought not to recognise it' (*per* SCRUTTON LJ). (See also *Anglo-Iranian Oil Co Ltd v Jaffrate, The Rose Mary*.)

Lynch v Provisional Government of Paraguay [291]
(1871) LR 2 P & D 268

After the death of a domiciled Paraguayan in Paraguay, the Government of the country passed a retrospective decree to the effect that all of his property vested in the State on his death. The 'universal legatee' named in his will applied for probate in respect of movables left by the deceased in England. *Held*, probate should be granted to him, despite opposition from the Paraguay Government. Succession to movables was regulated by the lex domicilii of the deceased as it existed at the time of his death, and subsequent changes in this law, whether or not retrospective, should be ignored. (See also *Re Maldonado, State of Spain* v *Treasury Solicitor* and *Adams* v *National Bank of Greece SA*.)

Macalpine v Macalpine [1958] P 35 [292]

A man domiciled in Wyoming, USA, obtained a divorce in that State, having induced the court to dispense with service on his wife by falsely swearing that he did not know where she was living. *Held*, the divorce was invalid in England. Prima facie, any foreign divorce granted without notice to the respondent contravened the requirements of natural justice. There was no doubt about it when the failure to notify resulted from the petitioner's fraud. (See also *Middleton* v *Middleton* and *Pemberton* v *Hughes*.)

Macartney, Re, Macfarlane v Macartney [1921] 1 Ch 522 [293]

The testator, who was domiciled in England, died in Malta leaving a fiancée who subsequently gave birth to his daughter. The daughter obtained a judgment in a Maltese court for maintenance, which under Maltese law was to be paid out of the testator's assets and was to continue all her life. *Held*, she could not enforce this judgment against the testator's assets in England, on the ground (inter alia) that an award of perpetual maintenance to an illegitimate child against the putative father and his estate contravened English public policy. (Compare *Re Langley's Settlement Trusts, Lloyds Bank Ltd* v *Langley* and *Raulin* v *Fischer*.)

M'Elroy v M'Allister [1949] SC 119 (Court of Session) [294]

The plaintiff's husband was killed in England as a result of negligent driving by the defendant. The plaintiff sued the defendant in Scotland, specifying three distinct claims based on English and/or Scottish law, and a claim in respect of funeral expenses. The distinct claims were as follows: (1) a claim in her own right for solatium (ie compensation for her grief and distress), which stemmed from Scottish law and did not exist in English law; (2) a claim in her own right for financial loss, based on Scottish law and on the English Fatal Accidents Acts, but outside the time-limit prescribed by those Acts; and (3) a claim in her capacity as executrix for damages due to the deceased, which was permitted in English law but not in

Scottish law. *Held,* the plaintiff had no remedy under any of the distinct claims. To succeed in any one claim, she had to prove that it existed in English law, the lex loci delicti commissi, and that she could sue in the same capacity under Scottish law, the lex fori. She could not do this for any one of her three principal claims. Claim (1) did not exist in English law; (2) had existed in English law but had expired; and claim (3) in which she sued as executrix, could not be maintained in the same capacity in Scottish law. The only claim which was actionable at both Scottish and English law and the only claim with which she succeeded, was her claim for £40 in respect of funeral expenses. (See also *Boys* v *Chaplin.*)

Machado v Fontes [1897] 2 QB 231 (Court of Appeal) [295]

The plaintiff sued the defendant for a libel published in Brazil. The defendant pleaded that under Brazilian law the defendant's act, although a crime, did not give rise to any civil right of action for damages. *Held,* this was a bad plea, and should be struck out. 'In order to constitute a good defence to an action [in tort] brought in this country in respect of an act done in a foreign country, the act relied on must be one which is innocent in the country where it was committed. In the present case ... the act was committed abroad, and was actionable here, and not justifiable by the law of the place where it was committed ... It then follows, directly the right of action is established in this country, that the ordinary incidents of that action and the appropriate remedies ensue' (*per* LOPES LJ). (See also *Walpole* v *Canadian Northern Railway Co*; but see *Boys* v *Chaplin* and the divergence of opinion therein as to whether *Machado* v *Fontes* should be overruled.)

Maciej Rataj, The see Tatry, The

McKee v McKee [1951] AC 352 (Privy Council) [296]

In divorce proceedings in California between an American husband and wife, custody of their infant son was awarded to the mother. The father then took the son out of the USA (despite a prior agreement with his wife not to do this) and settled with him in Ontario, Canada. In habeas corpus proceedings instituted by the wife in Ontario and heard some two years after the Californian order, the trial judge held that in his view the child was best left with the father. *Held,* on appeal, the judge had been entitled to exercise his discretion in this way. The Californian order should receive 'grave consideration' but was not binding, in view particularly of the length of time which had since elapsed. In Ontario, as in England, 'the welfare and happiness of the infant is the paramount consideration in questions of custody' (*per* LORD SIMONDS). (See also *Re H (infants)* and the Hague Convention on the Civil Aspects of Child Abduction as enacted by the Child Abduction and Custody Act 1985.)

Mackender v Feldia AG [1967] 2 QB 590 (Court of Appeal) [297]

The defendants, three diamond merchant companies incorporated and trading abroad, insured their precious stones with the plaintiffs under a block policy. This policy was negotiated and executed in England, but it provided that all disputes arising out of it should be submitted to the exclusive jurisdiction of the Belgian courts for decision according to Belgian law. The plaintiffs, alleging that the defendants were illegally smuggling diamonds into Italy, brought an action against them in England, claiming a declaration that the policy was void for illegality or voidable for non-disclosure. They served the writ after obtaining leave under (what is now) RSC O.11, r.1(1)(d)(i). *Held,* although the case fell under the rule, the court would exercise its discretion to set aside service on account of the foreign jurisdiction clause. This clause should be put into effect even though the contract which contained it might ultimately be found void or voidable under Belgian law, its proper law. (Compare *The Chaparral*.)

McMillan v Canadian Northern Railway Co [1923] AC 120 [298]
(Privy Council)

In the course of his employment by the defendant railway company, the plaintiff was injured in Ontario, Canada, owing to the negligence of the defendant's servants. Under an Ontario statute, a workman injured at work could claim compensation from his employer whether or not the injury resulted from negligence, and this right to compensation replaced any common-law rights of action. Before the statute was passed, the defence of common employment would have barred any action at common law. The plaintiff sued the defendant in Saskatchewan, where he had a simple common law right to damages in tort. *Held*, his action would fail. Before the statute, the act of the defendant would have been 'justifiable' in Ontario law, the lex loci delicti commissi, by virtue of the defence of common employment. As the right to compensation under the statute was not dependent on proof of negligence, its introduction into Ontario law did not prevent the defendant's act from still being 'justifiable'. (See also *M'Elroy v M'Allister*.)

MacShannon v Rockware Glass [1978] AC 795 [299]
(House of Lords)

The plaintiffs were four Scotsmen who lived and worked in Scotland and who suffered industrial injuries whilst working for their employers. The only connection the case had with England was that each defendant company was registered in England. The plaintiffs could equally well have sued in Scotland, but they were advised by their trade union solicitors to sue in England primarily on the grounds that they would obtain certain procedural advantages and higher damages by doing so. The defendant employers' applications for a stay were dismissed by a majority in the Court of Appeal. *Held*, by a unanimous decision, that the appeals would be allowed and stays granted. It was no longer necessary for the defendants to show that the proceedings were 'oppressive or vexatious' (as had been decided in *St Pierre v South American Stores*) in order for a stay to be granted. Nevertheless, 'In order to justify a stay two conditions must be satisfied, one positive and one negative: (a) the defendant must satisfy the court that there is another forum to whose jurisdiction he is amenable in which justice can be done between the parties at substantially less inconvenience or expense, and (b) the stay must not deprive the plaintiff of a legitimate personal or juridical advantage which would be available to him if he invoked the jurisdiction of the English court' (per LORD DIPLOCK). Thus, not only was the test in *St Pierre v South American Stores* reformulated, it required the plaintiff to discharge the burden of proof in the second condition: this contrasted with *St Pierre* where the onus of proof was on the defendant for both stages. However, this case did not introduce the doctrine of forum non conveniens into English law. (But see *The Abidin Daver* and *Spiliada Maritime Corporation v Cansulex*.)

Mahadervan v Mahadervan [1964] P 233 [300]

Domiciled Malaysians were parties to an arranged marriage in Ceylon. The Legislative Enactments of Ceylon, 1938, Marriage General Ordinance, required certain procedures to be complied with, including the marriage having to be solemnised by a registrar in his office or other authorised place and that, during the course of the ceremony, the registrar should inform the parties of the nature of the union. The parties' marriage certificate stated that their marriage had been performed at the registrar's office which, under Ceylonese law, was conclusive evidence of compliance with that formality. Proceedings were brought by the wife in England, alleging the husband's adultery. *Held,* contrary to the husband's assertion that the formalities had not been complied with because the marriage took place at the house of the wife's parents, that the parties were not addressed as to the nature of the union, and that the marriage was void for duress, the marriage was valid as to the place of celebration. The Ceylonese rule as to the effect of the certificate was a rule of substance, not procedure, and the presumption of the validity of the marriage had not been rebutted by proof beyond reasonable doubt. (See also *The Gaetano and Maria*.)

Maharanee of Baroda v Wildenstein [1972] 2 QB 283 [301]
(Court of Appeal)

Both the Maharanee, an Indian princess, and M Daniel Wildenstein, a world-famous art expert, were resident in France. It was in France that the Maharanee bought for £33,000 a painting purporting to be La Poesie by Francois Boucher, the seventeenth-century artist, from the defendant, Wildenstein. Later, the Maharanee learned from experts in England that it was probably not an original Boucher and worth only about £750. Accordingly, the Maharanee took out a writ in England claiming rescission of the contract, return of the price and damages. The writ was served on Wildenstein when he came from France to pay a fleeting visit to England to attend the Ascot races. He applied to have the action set aside on the ground that it was frivolous and vexatious and an abuse of the process of the court. Furthermore, he contended that the proper forum for trial was France and that the proceedings could be stayed without injustice to the plaintiff. *Held,* 'In this case the writ has been properly served on the defendant in this country ... [the Maharanee] has validly invoked the jurisdiction of our courts in this, the one and only action she has brought' (*per* LORD DENNING MR). This was supported by EDMUND DAVIES LJ who added that: 'Both in taking ... out [the writ] and serving it (albeit when the defendant was only fleetingly on British soil) [the Maharanee] was doing no more than our law permits ... some might regard her action as bad form; none can legitimately condemn it as an abuse of legal process.' (See *Colt Industries v Sarlie*.)

Maldonado, Re, State of Spain v Treasury Solicitor [302]
[1954] P 223 (Court of Appeal)

A domiciled Spanish woman died intestate and without heirs, leaving movables in England. The Spanish Government claimed them under a provision of the Spanish Civil Code whereby it was entitled to 'inherit' movables so left, but was bound to apply them for specified charitable purposes. The British Crown also claimed them as bona vacantia situated in England. *Held*, the Spanish provision, when classified according to Spanish law, operated as a genuine rule of succession on intestacy. It should therefore be applied, as forming part of the lex domicilii of the deceased, even though the 'heir' named was the Spanish Government itself. (Compare *In the Estate of Musurus*; see also *Lynch v Provisional Government of Paraguay*.)

Male v Roberts (1800) 3 Esp 163 [303]

The defendant, an infant, incurred a debt for 'liquors of different sorts' while the Royal Circus, in which he was a performer, was visiting Edinburgh. The plaintiff paid the debt for him to save him from being held in Scotland under legal process, then sued to recover the amount from him in England. *Held*, the question whether the defendant could plead his infancy as a defence must be determined by Scottish law, because 'the law of the country where the contract arose must govern the contract' (*per* LORD ELDON). (But see *Bank of Africa Ltd v Cohen*.)

Mamdani v Mamdani [1984] FLR 699 (Court of Appeal) [304]

Five years after their marriage in England in 1973, the husband asked the wife to commence divorce proceedings, which she did. However, the husband followed this by seeking dissolution of the marriage in Nevada, USA, and a summons sent to the wife in 1980 gave her 20 days in which to submit a defence. On legal advice, she took no part in the Nevada proceedings. She received a document headed 'Decree of Divorce' two months later, informing her that her marriage was now dissolved. She then succeeded in having her original petition for a divorce dismissed and filing a new petition. At first instance the deputy judge found that the wife, who was on low income and who would not have had the benefit of legal aid for representation in Nevada, did not have the opportunity to defend the proceedings. Accordingly, she was granted a declaration that the Nevada decree was invalid under provisions of the Recognition of Divorces and Legal Separations Act 1971. The husband appealed. *Held*, agreeing with LANE J's view in *Joyce v Joyce* that the level of a person's finances were relevant circumstances in deciding whether (s)he had the opportunity to take part in foreign proceedings and, consequently, dismissing the husband's appeal, that: 'If it is proved for sound financial reasons the respondent to the foreign proceedings could not take part in them, the English court is given a discretion to refuse to recognise the decree' (*per* CUMMING-BRUCE LJ). Moreover, 'The appellant in this appeal confines his challenge to ... the issue whether on the facts the [1971 Act] conferred a discretion to refuse to recognise the validity of the [Nevada] decree. There is no appeal against the exercise of the discretion if it existed and, indeed, there could not be on the evidence before the deputy judge.' (See also *Sabbagh v Sabbagh* and s48 of the Family Law Act 1986.)

Man (E D & F) (Sugar) Ltd v Haryanto (No 2) [305]
[1991] 1 Lloyd's Rep 429 (Court of Appeal)

The plaintiffs, Man, claimed to have contracted as sellers with Mr Yani Haryanto, an Indonesian citizen, as buyer, under contracts which were governed by English law and which provided for disputes to be referred to arbitration in London. Man referred a dispute to arbitration but Mr Haryanto sought a declaration that he was not bound by the alleged agreement. His action was dismissed as was his appeal. The issue of illegality had not been pleaded and Mr Haryanto's application to raise it was dismissed by the Court of Appeal. He then began a second English action, this time for a declaration that the contracts were unenforceable and/or void for illegality and/or for being contrary to English public policy. Man responded by seeking a declaration that Mr Haryanto was estopped from contending that that was the case. Subsequently, a settlement agreement was reached on the arbitration and legal proceedings. However, after making only the first of a specified number of payments by instalments, Mr Haryanto obtained a declaration in Indonesia that the original agreements and the settlement agreement were contrary to Indonesian public policy and that the decision of the English Court of Appeal was not binding on him. Man then commenced further English proceedings contending that the agreements were valid and binding on Mr Haryanto; that the English courts should not recognise the Indonesian judgment as it was inconsistent with prior English decisions; and they also claimed an extra-territorial injunction restraining Mr

Haryanto from repeating anywhere in the world assertions he had raised in the Indonesian court. Mr Haryanto contended, in essence, that the decision of the Indonesian court was correct and entitled to recognition. *Held,* dismissing the appeal and the cross-appeal, that the matters in question were res judicata; that the settlement was a bona fide compromise, entitling Man to the declaratory relief they sought, and that an English court would not recognise a foreign judgment if it was inconsistent with a previous decision of a competent English court. However, an injunction ought not to be granted if it was intended to take effect inside Indonesia and if it was in conflict with a decision of a competent Indonesian court, and there was no satisfactory basis for restraining Mr Haryanto from relying on the Indonesian judgment as a matter of defence in any enforcement proceedings in third countries. Accordingly, Man's appeal for extra-territorial injunctive relief was refused. (See also *Vervaeke* v *Smith*.)

Manifold, Re, Slater v Chryssafinis [1962] Ch 1 [306]

A British testatrix, whose domicile of origin was English, died domiciled in Cyprus leaving two wills covering personal property in England and Cyprus. The first will was formally valid under English and Cypriot law, but the second, which purported to revoke the first, was formally valid under English law only. Accordingly, the court in Cyprus granted probate of the first will only to its executor, but the English court, applying s2 of the Wills Act 1861, granted letters of administration with *both* wills annexed to attorneys of this executor. After paying duties and debts out of the English assets, the attorneys had a surplus remaining. *Held,* they should not transfer this surplus to the executor in Cyprus, but should distribute it among the beneficiaries under the second will, notwithstanding that this was not in accordance with Cypriot law, the lex domicilii of the testatrix at her death. (See also *Re Lorillard, Griffiths* v *Catforth*; but see *Re Trufort, Trafford* v *Blanc*.)

Maples (formerly Melamud) v Maples; Maples [307]
(formerly Melamud) v Melamud [1988] Fam 14

In 1968, W married H1 in Israel and then moved with him to London where the marriage broke down. In 1977, H1 granted and W accepted a 'gett', by which both accepted that the Israeli marriage had been dissolved according to Jewish law. An Israeli district court issued a judgment confirming the 'gett'. In 1978, W went through a ceremony of marriage in England with H2. Subsequently, however, she petitioned for a decree of nullity of marriage to H2 on the basis that she had no capacity to marry because her marriage to H1 was still subsisting; and for a dissolution of the Israeli marriage on the basis that she and H1 had lived apart for more than five years. Whereas H2 did not defend the petition relating to the 1978 marriage, H1 contended that his marriage to W in 1968 had been dissolved by the granting and acceptance of the 'gett' and that the Jewish decree should be recognised in England under s8 of the Foreign Judgments (Reciprocal Enforcement) Act 1933. *Held,* granting both petitions, that s8 was inapplicable to judgments affecting marital status since such judgments did not solely concern 'the parties thereto'; and the 'gett' was not 'the same cause of action' as the present. Furthermore, s16(1) of the Domicile and Matrimonial Proceedings Act 1973 expressly excluded from recognition a non-judicial proceeding in the UK. Thus, the gett obtained in London was not entitled to recognition. Hence, both petitions would be granted.

Marc Rich & Co v Societa Italiana Impianti PA, The Atlantic Emperor see Rich (Marc) & Co v Societa Italiana Impianti PA

Marc Rich & Co AG v Societa Italiana Impianti PA, The Atlantic Emperor (No 2) see **Rich (Marc) & Co AG v Societa Italiana Impianti PA (No 2)**

Marinari v Lloyds Bank plc and another (Case C–364/93)   [308]
(1995) The Times 19 October (European Court of Justice)

The plaintiff, who had lodged with Lloyds Bank promissory notes issued by a province of the Philippines in favour of a Beirut company, was arrested and promissory notes having an exchange value in excess of US$750,000,000 were sequestered. However, following his release, the plaintiff instituted proceedings in Italy seeking payment of the exchange value of the promissory notes and also compensation for, inter alia, the damage he claimed to have suffered as a result of his arrest and injury to his reputation. Lloyds Bank challenged the jurisdiction of the Italian courts on the basis that the alleged damage constituting the basis of the jurisdiction had occurred in England. The Italian court requested a preliminary ruling in relation to the 'place where the harmful event occurred' for the purposes of Article 5(3) of the Brussels Convention 1968. *Held*, its previous judgments in *Bier* v *Mines de Potassè* and *Shevill* v *Pressee Alliance SA* meant that the place where the damage occurred, could constitute a significant connecting factor from the point of view of jurisdiction. However, so as not to derogate too far from the general rule of jurisdiction as provided in Article 2 of the Convention, the choice of jurisdiction available to the plaintiff could not be extended beyond the particular circumstances which justified it. Accordingly, 'the term "place where the harmful event occurred" in Article 5(3) of the Convention was to be interpreted as not referring to the place where the victim claimed to have suffered financial loss consequential upon initial damage arising and suffered by him in another Contracting State'. (See also *Bier* v *Mines de Potasse d'Alsace SA* and *Shevill* v *Presse Alliance SA*.)

Marshall, Re, Barclays Bank Ltd v Marshall [1957] Ch 507   [309]
(Court of Appeal)

Under an English will, personalty was bequeathed to the 'issue' of the testator's cousin. The cousin, who was domiciled in British Columbia, had adopted a son under an order of the British Columbia Court, but under British Columbia law at the date of the testator's death an adopted could not rely on his relationship to his adoptive parents in order to claim rights of inheritance from their kindred. Later British Columbia legislation, passed before the time of distribution of the bequest, gave an adopted child full rights of succession. *Held*, the adopted son could not take under the will, because his status and capacity, as fixed by the law of his domicile when the will came into operation, were too limited to permit this. Later amendments of this law were to be ignored. (But see *Re Valentine's Settlement, Valentine* v *Valentine*.)

Martin, Re, Loustalan v Loustalan [1900] P 211   [310]
(Court of Appeal)

A domiciled Frenchwoman resident in England made a will of movables, then was married in England to a French professor who had left France to escape prosecution for offences connected with his professorship. He settled for a time in England, but ultimately resumed his French domicile when the time-limit within which he could be prosecuted in France had expired. *Held*, on the wife's death, (1) the husband had a domicile of choice in England at the time of the marriage, even though one of his reasons for staying there was to avoid prosecution; and (2) the question whether the marriage revoked the will was governed by the husband's lex domicilii at the marriage, not the wife's lex domicilii at her death. 'I think that the rule of the English law which makes a woman's will null and void on her marriage is part of the matrimonial law, and not of the testamentary law' (*per* VAUGHAN WILLIAMS LJ). It followed that the will was void, on the application of English law. (Compare *Re Groos* and *Hoskins v Matthews*.)

Martin v Stout [1925] AC 359 (Privy Council) [311]

A contract was made in England between M, a British subject resident there, and S, the owner of a concession granted by the Egyptian Government, in connection with irrigation. M had also agreed to employ S in Egypt. When M repudiated the contracts in a cable sent from England, S brought an action in the Supreme Court of Egypt claiming damages for the breach of the contracts. S also obtained an order for substituted service in Egypt. *Held*, as the breach of contract, via the despatch of the cable, took place in England, the Supreme Court of Egypt had no jurisdiction in this case. (See, now, Articles 3 and 4 of the Rome Convention 1980.)

Martin Peters v ZNAV see Peters, Martin v ZNAV

Matthews v Kuwait Bechtel Corporation [1959] 2 QB 57 [312]
(Court of Appeal)

The defendants, who were resident in Panama, employed the plaintiff to work for them in the Middle East under a contract of service which was governed by English law. The plaintiff was injured at work in Kuwait. He sued the defendants for damages, obtaining leave to serve the writ on them in Panama. *Held*, this was valid service. The action could be framed as a claim for breach of an implied term of contract governed by English law, so it fell under (what is now) RSC O.11, r.1(1)(d). As the rules in O.11 were disjunctive, it was irrelevant that, if framed in tort, the action would be outside the Order on the ground that the tort was committed out of the jurisdiction (see r.1(1)(f)).

Mary Moxham, The (1876) 1 PD 107 (Court of Appeal) [313]

The captain and crew of an English ship belonging to the defendants negligently caused it to collide with and damage a wharf in Spain owned by the plaintiffs, an English company. According to English law, but not Spanish law, the defendants were vicariously liable for this act of negligence. The parties agreed that the matter should be litigated in the English court. *Held*, the defendants were not liable to pay damages in tort because the plaintiffs could not establish that they were liable under Spanish law, the lex loci delicti commissi. (See also *Machado v Fontes*.)

May v May and Lehman [1943] 2 All ER 146 [314]

The petitioner in a 1943 divorce case had left Germany in 1939, with the intention of emigrating to the USA after first going to reside in England for the purpose of training for a job. He was permitted to enter England and reside there on condition that on completion of his training he would emigrate to the USA. However, after being released from a period of internment early in World War II, he returned to the employment in London with which he was contented. He said he experienced kindness and consideration in this country and that he was determined never to return to Germany. Nevertheless, the co-respondent in the divorce proceedings contended that the petitioner was not domiciled in England. *Held*, (PILCHER J) the petitioner has 'been resident here nearly four years at the material date, and I have come to the conclusion that by this date he had the animus manendi which, coupled with the fact of residence, is sufficient to establish domicil.' (Contrast *Winans* v *Attorney-General*.)

Mayfield v Mayfield [1969] P 119 [315]

A domiciled Englishman permanently resident in England obtained a divorce in Germany, the German court assuming jurisdiction on the ground that the wife had retained her German nationality and was permanently resident in Germany. *Held*, this divorce would be recognised in England. The principle of *Indyka* v *Indyka* could apply even though it was the respondent, and not the petitioner, who had a 'real and substantial connection' with the country where the divorce was granted. 'What is the material fact is that the German divorce operated on the status of the wife, who had such close, substantial and real connection' (*per* SIR JOCELYN SIMON P).

Medway Packaging v Meurer Maschinen GmbH & Co [316]
[1990] 2 Lloyd's Rep 112 (Court of Appeal)

The English plaintiff company, Medway, claimed to have been appointed exclusive UK distributor for the German defendant company, Meurer, who specialised in the manufacture of film packaging machines. Within two months of the agreement, however, Medway brought proceedings in the High Court alleging that, in breach of the agreement, Meurer had authorised another company to act as distributors in the UK and had purported to terminate the agreement with Medway without reasonable notice. A writ claiming damages of £270,000 was served on the defendants in West Germany and an application by the defendants to set aside the service of the writ on grounds of lack of jurisdiction was refused. *Held*, 'The repudiation consisted in (1) the failure to give reasonable notice of determination, and (2) the appointment of another distributor in the UK. The first of these relates to an obligation to give due notice of determination. ... The obligation itself is ... an obligation to give notice in England. ... Moreover, I think it can be reasonably regarded as the principal obligation in the present case' (*per* FOX LJ), who also affirmed the first instance decision that the contract for the exclusive distributorship was as much performable in England as it was in Germany. Accordingly, the appeal would be dismissed. (See also *Tesam Distribution Ltd* v *Schuh Mode Team GmbH* and *de Bloos* v *Bouyer*.)

Meeth v Glacetal Sarl (Case 23/78) [1978] ECR 2133 [317]
(European Court of Justice)

An agreement between parties who were domiciled in different Contracting States to the Convention on Jurisdiction and the Enforcement of Judgments in Civil and Commercial Matters (the Brussels Convention) provided that the parties could only be sued in the courts of the States in which they were domiciled. Whereas Article 17 of the Brussels Convention provides for the courts of *a* Contracting *State* (singular) to have exclusive jurisdiction, the effect of the agreement between the parties was to give two Contracting States exclusive jurisdiction if each party was to sue the other. *Held*, nevertheless, the agreement came within Article 17 because Article 23 would then have effect and the court seised of the matter second would defer to the court first seised. (See also *Kurz* v *Stella Musical Veranstaltungs GmbH* and *Dresser UK* v *Falcongate Freight Management*.)

Mehta (orse Kohn) v Mehta [1945] 2 All ER 690 [318]

A domiciled Englishwoman living in India agreed to go through a ceremony of conversion to the Hindu faith and betrothal to a Hindu domiciled in India. After it was over, she found that it was a ceremony of marriage. The husband's Hindu sect practised monogamy, but he could change at any time to orthodox Hinduism, which permitted polygamy. The wife petitioned in England for a decree of nullity on the ground of her mistake as to the nature of the ceremony. *Held*, (1) the court had jurisdiction because this marriage was monogamous at its inception, it being irrelevant that the husband could render it potentially polygamous by a subsequent change of sect; and (2) a decree would be granted (semble, under English law) because of the wife's mistake. (See also *Buckland v Buckland*; but see *The Sinha Peerage Claim*.)

Menten v The Federal Republic of Germany [1991] ILPr 259 [319]

As a result of a fraudulent claim made by M, the German Government had paid compensation to him and his wife amounting to DM550,000. The German Government sought restitution of this sum when the fraud was discovered. They succeeded in obtaining judgments in the German courts and then attempted to enforce them against M in The Netherlands. Enforcement was dependent on the claim for restitution being a 'civil and commercial matter' within the provisions of the Brussels Convention 1968. *Held*, (by the Dutch court), that the claim for repayment of the money, the original payment of which had been induced by fraud, was a matter 'rooted in private law': it had nothing to do with public authority powers. Accordingly, the matter was within the 'civil and commercial' category under the Brussels Convention. (Contrast *LTU v Eurocontrol*.)

Mercantile Investment and General Trust Co v River [320]
Plate Trust, Loan and Agency Co [1892] 2 Ch 303

An American company issued debentures to the plaintiffs, secured by an equitable charge on land in Mexico, then transferred the land to the defendant, an English company. The deed of transfer stated that the defendant was to hold the land subject to the charge, but a separate act of registration needed to make this particular condition binding under Mexican law was not carried out. The plaintiffs sued the defendant to enforce the charge. *Held*, the court had jurisdiction even though the charge was given over foreign land, because it would be unconscionable and 'a fraud' on the part of the defendant to ignore the plaintiffs' rights after having expressly agreed to respect them in the deed of transfer by which it obtained the land. (But see *Norris v Chambres*.)

Mercedes-Benz AG v Leiduck [1995] 3 All ER 929 [321]
(Privy Council)

In civil proceedings in Monaco, M had succeeded in gaining an order attaching L's assets in Monaco, but the court there had ruled that it had no jurisdiction to attach L's assets in Hong Kong. M appealed to the Privy Council after having had an ex parte Mareva injunction attaching the Hong Kong assets of L set aside by the Court of Appeal of Hong Kong. *Held*, the statutory enlargement of its territorial jurisdiction under RSC O.11, r.1(1) did not entitle the court to order the service of a form of process on a foreigner out of the jurisdiction when it was limited to a claim for Mareva relief to freeze assets within the jurisdiction pending the outcome of proceedings against that person in the foreign jurisdiction. Order 11 was confined to originating documents which set in motion proceedings designed to ascertain substantive rights.

Mercury Publicity v Wolfgang Loerke GmbH [322]
(1991) The Times 21 October (Court of Appeal)

Loerke, a company incorporated in Germany, had contracted in England with Mercury Publicity, a company incorporated in England, to be its sole advertising agent in Germany. The central issue in a dispute between the companies was whether the place for performance of the obligation within the meaning of Article 5(1) of the Brussels Convention 1968 was London or Germany. Mercury sought to establish that they had a good arguable case that the place for performance of the obligation was London because that was where the payment was to be made, whereas Loerke contended that it was Germany because the principle in *Ivenel* v *Schwab* had an application much wider than contracts of employment in the master and servant sense: that it extended to embrace contracts of employment of a commercial agent, notwithstanding that in this case the agent (Loerke) was an incorporated entity. *Held, per* PURCHAS LJ, the relationship between Mercury and Loerke was entirely different from that of employer and employee in *Ivenel* v *Schwab*; the principle in *Ivenel* 'was restricted to those cases of a personal nature in the relationship of master and servant where inequality of bargaining power might well become critical and in which to allow a jurisdiction in a court other than the place in which the main execution of the work was to take place might well deprive the employee or agent of the protection of restrictive agreements and of other statutory and union protections which had been negotiated for his benefit.' In the circumstances of the case, English law was the law most closely connected with the performance of the contract. (See also *Hanbridge Services Ltd* v *Aerospace Communications Ltd.*)

Merker v Merker [1963] P 283 [323]

Shortly after the end of the World War II, two domiciled Poles contracted a valid common law marriage in Germany, but it was later annulled by a German court on the ground that German formalities had not been complied with. At the time of the nullity proceedings, both spouses were resident in Germany. *Held*, the German decree would be recognised in England on grounds of reciprocity, because English courts themselves would claim jurisdiction in nullity (1) when the marriage had taken place in England (except if it was only voidable) and (2) when the spouses resided in England. (Compare *Salvesen (or Von Lorang)* v *Administrator of Austrian Property.*)

Messiniaki Tolmi, The, Astro Exito Navegacion SA [324]
v W T Hsu [1984] 1 Lloyd's Rep 266 (Court of Appeal)

In a dispute which continued after arbitration in England, the defendant sought a stay of proceedings contending that the natural and proper forum for the resolution of the dispute was the Court of Taiwan. *Held*, since the defendant had submitted to the jurisdiction of the English courts, thereafter it was not for him to contend that only the courts of some other country had jurisdiction. (Contrast *Re Dulles Settlement (No 2)* and *Williams & Glyn's Bank* v *Astro Dinamico.*)

Messina (formerly Smith orse Vervaeke) v Smith [325]
(Messina intervening) [1971] P 322

S, a domiciled Englishman, married G, a Russian woman in Hong Kong in 1937. They went to America in 1940 but S soon returned to the Far East where he was interned by the Japanese in 1941 and not released until the end of World War II. G, who had lived in the USA since 1940, moved to the State of Nevada in 1946 and after residing there for the requisite period of six weeks, she obtained a decree of divorce on the ground that she and S had lived separately and apart since 1941. S then went through another ceremony of marriage with M, a Belgian prostitute, in London in 1954. M later petitioned for divorce and contended that S's Nevada divorce from G was invalid and, therefore, her (M's) marriage to S was void for bigamy. *Held*, by ORMROD J, that recognition would be given to a divorce obtained by a wife, technically domiciled in England but resident abroad, where she had a sufficient connection with the court granting the decree. G had been resident in Nevada long enough to satisfy the jurisdictional requirements of that State and since all other US States were required to give 'full faith and credit' to the judicial decisions of other States of the Union, meaning that they would all recognise the decree, there was no justification for regarding S, who had not lived in England for many years and G, who had never had any connection with England – other than through her domicile of dependency (as it then was) – as having a subsisting marriage under English law. Accordingly, M's marriage to S in 1954 was valid and her petition would fail. (See also *Vervaeke* v *Smith*.)

Metall und Rohstoff AG v Donaldson Lufkin & Jenrette [326] Inc and another [1990] 1 QB 391 (Court of Appeal)

The plaintiffs had recovered about £7 million of the £50 million for which they had obtained judgment against brokers on the London Metal Exchange. The plaintiffs then obtained leave under RSC O.11 to serve a writ on the defendants out of the jurisdiction, the defendants being the American parent company of the brokers and the American holding company. Damages were claimed under five heads, including inducing breach of contract and conspiracy. *Held*, (1) on the assumption that one claim (for the tort of maliciously instituting legal proceedings) existed, it was rejected because the plaintiffs had neither raised nor identified that particular issue in their pleadings: the plaintiffs were bound by and limited to the specific legal basis pleaded as giving rise to a cause of action; (2) that whereas acts of inducing or procuring a breach of contract had, in the main, taken place in an American State, it was the breaches of contract by the brokers in London that had caused the plaintiffs substantial damage: accordingly, the substance of the tort of inducing or procuring the breach of contract came within RSC O.11, r.1(1)(f); however, (3) since England was the place where the substance of the alleged tort took place, then England should be regarded as the appropriate forum for the determination of that issue; and (4) the plaintiffs had no claim for conspiracy since they could not show that the defendants had the sole or predominant purpose of injuring the plaintiffs. (See also *Distillers* v *Thompson*.)

Mette v Mette (1859) 1 Sw & Tr 416 [327]

A domiciled Englishman married his deceased wife's half-sister, a domiciled German woman, in Frankfurt, Germany. Whereas the marriage was valid under German law, *Held*, it was void under English law because the parties to the marriage were within the prohibited degrees of affinity: the man had no capacity to marry his deceased wife's half-sister. (See also *Brook* v *Brook* and *Re Paine*.)

Middleton v Middleton [1967] P 62 [328]

A husband domiciled in Indiana, USA, falsely represented to an Illinois court that he had lived in Indiana for more than a year, so as to induce the court to assume jurisdiction over his petition for divorce. The wife did not defend the proceedings and the husband obtained a divorce, which became irreversible in Illinois despite his fraud and also was recognised in Indiana. *Held*, the divorce would not be recognised in England, on three alternative grounds: (1) that the court had been fraudulently induced to exercise jurisdiction; (2) that the decree offended 'substantial justice'; and (3) that the court should exercise its discretion against recognition. (See also *Abouloff* v *Oppenheimer & Co.*)

Midland Bank v Laker Airways [1986] QB 689 [329]
(Court of Appeal)

Following the liquidation of Laker Airways, the liquidator commenced several actions against various defendants in the USA. However, in the present action the liquidator, who threatened to take proceedings having extra-territorial application, was mistaken in believing that the defendant was under the direct control of the Midland Bank in England and that it had had dealings with Laker Airways. Accordingly, the Midland Bank sought a declaration that it was not liable in the USA for the collapse of Laker Airways and an injunction restraining the liquidator from commencing proceedings. *Held*, (1) the presence of the bank's subsidiary in the USA was irrelevant: it did not mean that the bank in this country had submitted to the jurisdiction; the bank had had dealings with the airline only in England and there was no connection with another forum nor with any other defendants accused of conspiring to drive Laker Airlines out of business; (2) to be able to invoke American anti-trust jurisdiction and make the bank in England liable for acts intended to be governed by English law and not giving rise to any claim in England was prima facie offensive: accordingly, the bank was entitled to the injunction. (Contrast *British Airways Board* v *Laker Airways Ltd.*)

Mighell v Sultan of Johore [1894] 1 QB 149 (Court of Appeal) [330]

The Sultan of Johore, while living in England under the assumed name of 'Albert Baker', agreed to marry the plaintiff. When he later broke off the engagement, she sued him for breach of promise. *Held*, he could plead sovereign immunity. His living in England under a false name did not amount to a waiver of the immunity which, as a foreign sovereign, he was entitled to assert in a civil proceedings against him. (See also *Compania Naviera Vascongado* v *SS Cristina*.)

Miliangos v George Frank (Textiles) Ltd [331]
[1976] AC 443 (House of Lords)

P, a Swiss national, sold polyester yarn to D, an English company. The price was payable in Swiss francs and the contract was governed by Swiss law. When D refused to pay for the yarn, P sued in the English courts for the agreed price. The sterling equivalent of the price was £42,000 in 1971 when payment was due, but by 1974 (the date of the hearing), the depreciation of the pound meant that the sterling equivalent was £60,000. *Held*, 'justice demands that the creditor should not suffer from fluctuations in the value of sterling. His contract has nothing to do with sterling; he has bargained in his own currency and only in his own currency. The substance of the debtor's obligations depends upon the proper law of the contract ... and though English law ... prevails as regards procedural matters, it must surely be wrong in principle to allow procedure to affect, detrimentally, the substance of the creditor's rights' (*per* LORD WILBERFORCE). (See also *The Despina R.*)

Miller, Re, Bailie v Miller [1914] 1 Ch 511 [332]

A testator dying domiciled in Scotland left a will in Scottish form which included a devise of English and Scottish land expressed in technical terms sufficient to create an estate tail under English law in favour of his eldest son. Under Scottish law, such a devise vested the land absolutely in the eldest son. *Held*, so far as the

English land was concerned, the son took an estate tail only. The words used were apt to create this type of estate and its 'incidents', ie, the rights conferred by it on the devisee, were determined by the lex situs, not by the law governing the will's construction. (See also *Philipson-Stow* v *IRC*.)

Minster Investments Ltd v Hyundai Precision & Industry Co Ltd and another [1988] 2 Lloyd's Rep 621

The plaintiffs, who were incorporated in England and carried on business in England, contracted with the first defendants, a South Korean company having a branch in London, for the purchase of goods. The second defendants, who were based in France and had an office in South Korea, contracted with the first defendants to inspect, test and certify the compliance of the goods with the contract specification. The second defendants certified the goods and sent the certificates to the first defendants who, in turn, delivered them to the plaintiffs. In reliance on these certificates, the plaintiffs paid US$580,000 under the principal contract to the first defendants in South Korea. However, the plaintiffs rejected the goods as not conforming to the terms of the contract and they served a writ on the first defendants at their London branch. The plaintiffs also obtained leave to serve a writ on the second defendants in France claiming loss of interest on US$580,000, loss of executive time and loss of goodwill and damage to reputation. It was common ground that the court only had jurisdiction if the plaintiffs' claim against the second defendants fell within the scope of s5(3) of Schedule 1 of the Civil Jurisdiction and Judgments Act 1982 which provides that a person domiciled in a Contracting State may, in another Contracting State, be sued: 'in matters relating to tort ... in the courts for the place where the harmful event occurred'. The second defendants sought to set aside service of the writ on the basis that they had performed their work under contract with the first defendants in France and South Korea. *Held*, 'common sense and policy considerations require one to ask where in substance the cause of action in tort arises, or what place the tort is most closely connected with. ... The event which caused harm to the plaintiffs in this case was the receipt in England of the negligently produced certificates of the second defendants, which the plaintiffs were intended to rely on and did rely on. If that view is right, it follows, on a realistic appraisal of the plaintiffs' cause of action against the second defendants, that "the place where the harmful event occurred" within the meaning of s5(3) was England. In my judgment there is jurisdiction to entertain the claim against the second defendants' (*per* STEYN J). (See also *Bier* v *Mines de Potasse d'Alsace SA*.)

Mitford v Mitford and Von Kuhlmann [1923] P 130

A domiciled Englishman married a domiciled German woman in Germany, but later, while they were both residing in Germany, she obtained a German nullity decree on the ground that she had been mistaken as to certain of his personal attributes which, if known before the marriage, would have prevented her from contracting it. This ground of nullity was unknown to English law. *Held*, the nullity decree would be recognised in England. The German court had jurisdiction because of the spouses' joint residence in Germany and the ground of the decree was sufficient because it was treated by the lex loci celebrationis (German law) as equivalent to a mistake of identity. In any event, a nullity decree by a competent foreign court which observed the requirements of natural justice 'would seem to be as conclusive as a like judgment in any other civil proceeding' and thus could not be examined on the merits (*per* SIR HENRY DUKE P). (See also *Merker* v *Merker*.)

Mohamed v Knott [1969] 1 QB 1 (Court of Appeal) [335]

A 26-year-old Nigerian Muslim married a 13-year-old Nigerian girl, also a Muslim, in Nigeria. The marriage was potentially polygamous but valid according to Nigerian law. Three months after their marriage in 1967 they moved to and cohabited in London, England. However, within three months of their arrival in London, a complaint was preferred by WPC Knott under s62 of the Children and Young Persons Act 1933 (CYPA 1933), that the girl was in need of care, protection or control in that she was not receiving such care, protection and guidance as a good parent might reasonably be expected to give and was exposed to moral danger within s2 of the Children and Young Persons Act 1963. The magistrates in the Juvenile Court found the complaint proved and ordered the girl to be committed to a local authority as a fit person under s62 of the CYPA 1933. *Held*, allowing the appeal, (1) 'the justices came to a wrong conclusion in this case, and that for the purposes of ascertaining the status of this wife, the courts here will recognise the marriage as a valid marriage giving her that status'. (2) 'If, as I think, this is a case of husband and wife validly married, recognised as validly married according to the law of this country, I certainly would not say that the wife was exposed to moral danger merely because she carried out her wifely duties' (*per* PARKER CJ). (Contrast *Pugh v Pugh*.)

Molnlycke AB v Procter & Gamble Ltd [336]
[1992] 1 WLR 1112 (Court of Appeal)

In an action over the alleged infringement of a UK patent relating to disposable nappies, the plaintiffs, being the registered proprietor of the patent and the exclusive licensee under the patent, contended that the defendants had infringed their patent by marketing in the UK nappies manufactured by a member of the defendants' multi-national group, a German company domiciled in Germany. The plaintiffs sought to rely on Articles 5(3) and 6(1) of the Brussels Convention 1968 for leave to join the German company as defendants so as to obtain discovery of documents in that company's possession. Joinder was allowed at first instance and the defendants appealed. *Held*, dismissing the appeal, in relation to Article 5(3) and applying *Tesam Distribution v Schuh Mode Team GmbH*, the plaintiffs had established a good arguable case that there was a serious question which called for a trial for its proper determination. However, DILLON LJ was of the opinion that had the plaintiffs relied solely on Article 6(1) then it would have been improper to join the German company merely to obtain discovery as this could have been achieved by other, more satisfactory, methods. (See also *Gascoine v Pyrah*.)

Monro (George) Ltd v American Cyanamid and [337]
Chemical Corporation [1944] 1 KB 432 (Court of Appeal)

The plaintiff, an English company, applied for leave under the predecessor of what is now RSC O.11, r.1(1)(f) to serve in the USA a writ claiming damages in tort against the defendant, an American corporation. The alleged cause of action was that the plaintiff had bought vermin poison from the defendant without being warned of its dangerous qualities and had had to pay damages to a farmer who, buying it from the plaintiff, had suffered injury by using it on his land. *Held*, the plaintiff's application should not be granted because, inter alia, the alleged tort was committed in the USA, the place of manufacture. To come within the predecessor of r.1(1)(f), it was not enough to prove simply that damage caused by a tortious act occurred in England. (See also *Cordova Land Co Ltd v Victor Bros Inc*.)

Motala v Attorney-General [1991] 4 All ER 682 (House of Lords) [338]

Four children had brought proceedings to establish their entitlement to the status of citizens of the United Kingdom and Colonies by descent at birth. Their parents, Mr and Mrs Ismail Motala, were born in India but were married according to Sunni Muslim law in (what was then) Northern Rhodesia in 1950. In 1953, whilst retaining his Indian domicile but residing in Northern Rhodesia, the children's father registered as a citizen of the United Kingdom and Colonies under s6(1) of the British Nationality Act 1948. The older two children were born in Northern Rhodesia before it became the independent Republic of Zambia, and the younger two were born there after the declaration of independence. When the father applied in 1967 for his wife to be registered under the 1948 Act, he was informed that his 1950 marriage was not valid. On advice, he re-married in 1968 according to the civil code of Zambia and thereafter his wife's application for registration as a citizen of the United Kingdom and Colonies was accepted. In 1978, Mrs Motala came to live in England and brought the older two children with her, the younger two remaining in Zambia, although she wanted all four included in her British passport. However, her application was refused on the grounds that the older two children had become citizens of Zambia on Independence Day, and the younger two were illegitimate as they were born before their parents' 1968 marriage. All four children sought a declaration that they were citizens of the United Kingdom and Colonies by descent at birth and it was necessary for each one to establish that (s)he was the legitimate child of Ismail Motala. The Court of Appeal upheld the first instance decision of SIR STEPHEN BROWN P who had decided that as a person's status is determined by the law of his domicile and since, according to Indian law, the parents had each had the capacity to marry and they had contracted a valid marriage in 1950, all the children born thereafter were legitimate. Moreover, the older two children would not be deprived of their status as citizens of the United Kingdom and Colonies on Zambian Independence Day as such an outcome would be contrary to justice and common sense. However, the Attorney-General obtained leave in respect of the older two children only on the ground that it was wrongly held that they had retained their citizenship of the United Kingdom and Colonies after Zambia became independent. *Held*, unanimously, that from the time of their birth in Northern Rhodesia until Zambia became an independent State, the older two children, the respondents, had the status both of citizens of the United Kingdom and Colonies by descent and British protected persons; that the one status was not inconsistent with the other; and that the combined effect of s3(1) of the Constitution of Zambia (which provides that 'Every person who, having been born in ... Northern Rhodesia [prior to independence and who is] a British protected person shall become a citizen of Zambia [on its independence]') and s3(3) of the Zambia Independence Act 1964 (which provides that 'any person who immediately before [independence] is a citizen of the United Kingdom and Colonies shall on that day cease to be such a citizen if he becomes on that day a citizen of Zambia') was that the respondents ceased to be citizens of the United Kingdom and Colonies and became citizens of Zambia as from the date of the State's independence. Accordingly, the Attorney-General's appeal would be allowed.

Mount Albert Borough Council v Australian Temperance & General Mutual Life Assurance Society Ltd [339]
[1938] AC 224 (Privy Council)

The defendant, a borough council in New Zealand, borrowed money from the plaintiff, a Victorian life insurance company, on the security of debentures charged on all the land in the borough. The loan was governed by New Zealand law, but was repayable in Victoria. Subsequently, the Victorian Government passed emergency legislation reducing the rate of interest on all debentures issued by local authorities. *Held*, this legislation did not reduce the interest payable by the defendant to the plaintiff, because (1) the rate of interest, being an aspect of the *substance* of the contractual obligation, not merely the mode of performance, was within the province of the proper law, not the lex loci solutionis; and (2) the Victorian statute was in any event not intended to affect debentures secured on land outside Victoria. (See also *Jacobs, Marcus & Co* v *Credit Lyonnais*; but see *Re Chesterman's Trusts, Mott* v *Browning*.)

Mulox IBC Ltd v Geels (Case C–125/92) [340]
[1994] IRLR 422 (European Court of Justice)

G, a Dutch national living in France, was appointed as international marketing manager for M, a company incorporated under English law with a registered office in London. Although G worked from home, French territory and French customers did not come within his responsibility until shortly before his contract of employment was terminated. G's proceedings in the local French labour court resulted in M being ordered to pay damages to him. The French labour court had declared that it had jurisdiction under Article 5(1) of the Brussels Convention 1968 and that the dispute was governed by French law. M appealed to a French Court of Appeal, arguing that French courts had no jurisdiction because the place of performance of the contract of employment covered the whole of Europe and the company's place of establishment was in the UK. In the alternative, M argued that the contract was governed by English law, which was chosen by the parties and indicated by the Rome Convention of 1980 on the Law Applicable to Contractual Obligations as the law of the employer's place of establishment. A preliminary ruling was requested. *Held*, 'Article 5(1) of the [Brussels] Convention 1968 ... must be interpreted as meaning that, where there is a contract of employment in performance of which an employee carries out activities in more than one Contracting State, the place where the obligation characterising the contract has been or should have been performed, within the meaning of that provision, is that where or from which the employee principally discharges his obligations to his employer.' (See also *Ivenel* v *Schwab*.)

Multinational Gas and Petrochemical Co v Multinational [341]
Gas and Petrochemical Services Ltd
[1983] 1 Ch 258 (Court of Appeal)

Three international oil companies collaborated in a commercial enterprise and formed two new companies, P and S, for the purchase, storage and transportation of liquefied petroleum gas and liquefied natural gas. The plaintiff company, P, was incorporated in Liberia and S was an English company formed to advise and act as an agent for P. P's shareholders were the oil companies and they appointed the directors who were all resident abroad. When P got into financial difficulties it obtained leave from the Companies Court to bring an action against S, alleging breach of duty of care in relation to the information and advice supplied under the agency agreement; against the oil companies for breaches of the duty of care in their powers of management and direction in relation to P's decision-making; and against P's directors for the negligent decision-making resulting in P's becoming insolvent. P applied to serve concurrent writs on the defendants outside the jurisdiction under (what is now) RSC O.11, r.1(1)(f) and (c). *Held*, for the purposes of r.1(1)(f), the place where in substance P's cause of action arose determined whether the tort was committed within the jurisdiction of the court; and since the substance of the cause of action related to negligent decisions made abroad, the court had no jurisdiction to grant leave to serve the defendants out of the jurisdiction; and whereas the court had jurisdiction under r.1(1)(c) to grant leave for a writ to be served on a foreign defendant when an action had already been properly brought against a defendant within the jurisdiction, it would not exercise its discretion to do so since the shareholders had acted intra vires and in good faith, and their approval of the directors' acts meant they approved the acts of the plaintiff: since the shareholders could manage the affairs of P as they wished while P was solvent and they owed no duties to future creditors or third parties, it was not for P to complain of lack of commercial judgment in relation to the directors' decision-making. Accordingly, the directors could not be a proper party to the action. (See also *Distillers* v *Thompson* and *Metall und Rohstoff AG* v *Donaldson Lufkin & Jenrette Inc.*)

Mund & Fester v Hatrex International Transport [342]
(1995) The Times 29 March (European Court of Justice)

Mund & Fester, a German company, claimed damages for the delivery of a defective consignment of hazelnuts. The consignment had been delivered by an international haulier having its registered office in The Netherlands. In an attempt to ensure that the damages were recovered, Mund & Fester (M & F) applied for a seizure order under paragraph 917(2) of the Zivilprozessordnung ('ZPO') against the lorry belonging to Hatrex which had transported the nuts and which was still in Germany. Whereas para. 917 ZPO provided that the fact that the judgment was to be enforced abroad was to be considered sufficient grounds for a seizure order, the application was refused on the basis that the judgment was to be enforced in a Contracting State which was party to the Brussels Convention 1968. M & F appealed this decision to the German Higher Regional Court in Hamburg who, in turn, sought a preliminary ruling from the ECJ. *Held*, there was no justification in associating the enforcement of a judgment in another Member State with impossibility or with being substantially more difficult than if it took place in Germany. That is: 'Article 7 of the EEC Treaty, read in conjunction with Article 220 of the Treaty and the Brussels Convention, precluded a national provision of civil procedure which, in the case of a judgment to be enforced within national territory, authorised seizure only on the ground that it was probable that enforcement would otherwise be made impossible or substantially more difficult, but, in the case of a judgment to be enforced in another Member State, authorised seizure simply on the ground that enforcement was to take place abroad.'

Musurus, deceased, In the estate of [1936] 2 All ER 1666 [343]

A domiciled Turkish woman died intestate and without heirs, leaving movables situated in England. This property was claimed by the British Crown and also by the Turkish Government, which alleged that it would be handed over to the Muslim Treasury to be applied for the relief and benefit of Muslims. *Held*, the British Crown was entitled to it, as the title to bona vacantia was determined by their lex situs. Had the Turkish Government been able to show that it was a true 'heir' or a trustee under Turkish law, it would have taken the property on the footing that succession is regulated by the lex domicilii, and the property would not have been bona vacantia. (Compare *Re Maldonado, State of Spain* v *Treasury Solicitor.*)

National Bank of Greece and Athens SA v Metliss [344]
[1958] AC 509 (House of Lords)

In 1927, sterling mortgage bonds governed by English law were issued by a Greek bank and were guaranteed by the National Bank of Greece (the 'old bank'), a bank established in Greece by a Greek law. In 1941, payments of interest on the bonds ceased to be made. In 1949, the Greek Government passed a moratorium law extinguishing the obligation to make any payments on the bonds. In 1953, a Greek decree amalgamated the business of the old bank and another bank into a newly constituted bank, the National Bank of Greece and Athens (the 'new bank') and declared it to be the 'universal successor' of the banks which it superseded. In 1955, a bondholder claimed arrears of interest from the new bank. *Held*, (1) the amalgamation decree must be recognised in its entirety, because the status of all the banks concerned in it was a matter for their lex domicilii, Greek law; (2) the moratorium law would not have affected the old bank's liability under the guarantee because the proper law of the bonds was after the amalgamation. The bondholder could therefore recover on his bonds from the new bank. (See also *Adams* v *National Bank of Greece SA*.)

National Mortgage and Agency Co of New Zealand Ltd [345] v Gosselin (1922) 38 TLR 832 (Court of Appeal)

The defendants, a Belgian firm, had an agent in London who had authority to negotiate on their behalf, but not to enter into binding contracts. The agent furnished the plaintiff with details of the defendants' terms of sale for their goods, then transmitted an offer by the plaintiff back to the defendants. A contract was formed when the defendants sent their acceptance direct to the plaintiff. The plaintiff later sued for damages for its breach, obtaining leave under (what is now) RSC O.11, r.1 (1)(d)(ii) to serve the writ on the defendants in Belgium. *Held*, this was good service. The contract was made 'through' the agent in England as a negotiator, though not 'by' him as signatory on the defendants' behalf. It was therefore within the rule. (See also *Union International Insurance* v *Jubilee Insurance Co.*)

Nelson (Earl) v Bridport (1845) 8 Beav 547 [346]

Lord Nelson held land and a dukedom in Sicily with power to appoint a successor but no power under Sicilian law to alter the subsequent devolution of the land upon the successor's issue. In his will, he sought to impose a different line of succession by testamentary trusts. *Held*, the trusts were invalid so far as they conflicted with Sicilian law. 'The incidents to real estate, the right of alienating or limiting it, and the course of succession to it, depend entirely on the law of the country where the estate is situated' (*per* LORD LANGDALE MR). (But see *Re Piercy, Whitwham* v *Piercy*.)

Neste Chemicals SA v DK Line SA, The Sargasso [347]
[1994] 3 All ER 180 (Court of Appeal)

Following the receipt of a contaminated cargo, the plaintiff owners of the cargo claimed that they had suffered economic loss as a result of the contamination. The cargo owners then commenced legal proceedings in The Netherlands and in England. In May 1992, a writ was issued in England and leave to serve a concurrent writ out of the jurisdiction was granted. This writ was served on the defendants on 17 July 1992. Meanwhile, a Dutch writ was issued and served on 4 July 1992. Proceedings were instituted to determine which court was first seised of the dispute. *Held*, the English court became definitively seised of the proceedings for the purposes of Article 21 of the Brussels Convention on the date of the service of the writ. STEYN LJ doubted that there were any exceptions to this rule. The granting of provisional measures was not an actual exercise of jurisdiction which rendered the court seised of the action. Accordingly, the Dutch court was first seised of the dispute and the English courts had to decline jurisdiction. (Contrast *Kloeckner* v *Gatoil* and *Dresser UK* v *Falcongate Freight Management*.)

Netherlands State v Ruffer (Case 814/79) [348]
[1980] ECR 3807 (European Court of Justice)

A claim was made by The Netherlands State for reimbursement of the costs of removing the wreck of a German vessel which had sunk in a public waterway following a collision. Dutch law classified the action as one in tort. *Held*, the action arose from international treaty obligations and the fact that the agent responsible for administering public waterways was seeking to recover those costs by means of a claim for redress before the civil courts, and not by administrative process, was not sufficient to bring the matter in dispute within the concept of 'civil and commercial matters' within the meaning of the first paragraph of Article 1 of the Brussels Convention 1968. (See also *LTU* v *Eurocontrol*; contrast *Netherlands State* v *Ruffer*.)

New England Reinsurance Corporation & First State [349]
Insurance Co v Messoghios Insurance Co SA
[1992] 2 Lloyd's Rep 251 (Court of Appeal)

In a claim for damages of US$450,000 for breach of a contract evidenced in writing by a telex from the defendants to the plaintiffs agent, WEBSTER J, at first instance, had held that the plaintiffs, who were incorporated in Boston, Massachussetts, USA, had established a good arguable case that a contract had been concluded between themselves and the defendants, who were incorporated in Greece. Whereas the general rule, as provided for in Article 2 of the Brussels Convention 1968, is that a defendant has to be sued in the courts of his domicile, here, the defendants could be sued in England under Article 5 which permits defendants to be sued 'in matters relating to a contract, in the courts for the place of performance of the obligation in question'. The obligation in question was for payment by the defendants to the plaintiffs which, the latter contended, had been varied so as to be paid in London instead of Massachussetts. *Held*, unanimously, applying the test in *Tesam Distribution* v *Schuh Mode Team GmbH and Commerzbank*, the plaintiffs had to establish that they had a good arguable case that there was a serious question to be tried; but the wording in the telexes on which the plaintiffs relied did not indicate a binding or concluded agreement between the parties, nor did the instructions to have a cheque available in London constitute a variation of contractual agreement. The defendants' appeal would therefore be allowed. (See also *Molnlycke* v *Procter & Gamble Ltd*.)

New Hampshire Insurance Co v Strabag Bau [350]
[1992] 1 Lloyd's Rep 361 (Court of Appeal)

Two German companies, S and B, and an Austrian company, U, formed a joint venture in 1981 so as to enter into a contract for the construction of Basrah International Airport. They were required to take out insurance with the National Insurance Co of Iraq. They also took out a collective policy with the New Hampshire Insurance Co. Whereas the latter policy contained an arbitration clause, it contained no express choice of law clause, although it was agreed that the intentions of the parties indicated that it would be English law. After settling a number of claims over a period of eight years, the plaintiffs, the New Hampshire Insurance Co, declined to accept liability for further claims and they purported to avoid the policy. Each of the companies was notified accordingly. The plaintiffs then sought a declaration that they had validly avoided the policy and they applied for leave to serve out of the jurisdiction. They informed S that action would be proceeded with if it was held that the parties were not bound to arbitrate their differences. *Held*, (1) The arbitration clause applied only to issues of quantum and not to disputes as to liability. (2) Only express choice of law clauses constituted agreements in writing for Article 35 of the 1978 Accession Convention: 'The intention of the parties to the contract, however clearly inferred ... is not an agreement in writing.' (3) 'The proceedings between the parties relate to insurance within the meaning of Article 7 of the convention, and accordingly ... [S and B must be sued] in Germany by virtue of Article 11.' (4) The proceedings against U did not constitute a proper case for service out of the jurisdiction. '[U] has already submitted to German jurisdiction by bringing proceedings in the German court against the plaintiffs. The German proceedings will raise precisely the same issues as would be raised in the proposed English proceedings. If the insurers take part in those proceedings, any judgment against [U] would be recognised by the English courts ...' (*per* LLOYD LJ).

New York Breweries Co v Attorney-General [351]
[1899] AC 62 (House of Lords)

The executors of a deceased American obtained probate of his will from the court of his domicile, New York, then persuaded an English company in which the deceased had been a registered shareholder to transfer his shares into their names. *Held*, the New York executors had become 'executors de son tort' in England, because without a grant of representation in England they had no right to deal with the English property of the deceased. They were accordingly liable to pay death duties on the estate in England. (But see *Vanquelin v Bouard*.)

New York Life Insurance Co v Public Trustee [352]
[1924] 2 Ch 101 (Court of Appeal)

An insurance company was incorporated and had its central office in New York, USA, but it had branches in London and other European cities. Certain policies issued from its London office contained a stipulation that the policy moneys should be payable in sterling in London. The policies became due for payment. *Held*, the situs of these debts was in England. A simple contract-debt was normally situated where the debtor resided and could be sued, but where, as here, the debtor was a company with two or more residences, one chose between them by looking to the contract to see where the debt was 'properly recoverable'. (See also *Jabbour v Custodian of Israeli Absentee Property*.)

Newmarch v Newmarch [1978] Fam 79 [353]

In 1969, a married couple left England to go to Australia where the husband had obtained a teaching post. However, as the wife could not settle she returned to the UK with the consent of her husband. Subsequently, the marriage broke down and the husband stopped paying a monthly allowance to the wife who then received social security. This was followed by the wife securing an order in England for financial provision under s27 of the Matrimonial Causes Act (MCA) 1973. The order was registered in Sydney, Australia. The husband petitioned for divorce in the Family Law Division of New South Wales, on the basis of the wife's alleged desertion, and a magistrates' court made a provisional order discharging the order for financial provision even though the wife's legal representatives informed the court that the allegation of desertion was denied and that the divorce would be defended. The wife's Australian solicitors then failed to respond to numerous requests for information from the English solicitors, the result being the husband obtained an undefended decree of divorce which was made absolute at the end of 1975. The wife sought a declaration from the High Court that the Australian decree of divorce was invalid under the Recognition of Divorces and Legal Separations Act 1971 as she was not given such opportunity to take part in the proceedings as should reasonably have been given. Moreover, she wanted the court to refuse to recognise the discharge of the order for financial provision and to make a new order based on her original application. *Held*, having regard to all the surrounding circumstances, including the inactivity of the wife's Australian solicitors depriving her of such opportunity to take part in the proceedings as she should reasonably have been given, the court would exercise its discretion by upholding the validity of the Australian decree; but as the court was satisfied that the wife was not in desertion it would exercise its discretion by refusing to confirm the Australian order relating to cessation of financial provision and a substantive order for periodical payments under s27 MCA 1973 would be made. (Contrast *Macalpine* v *Macalpine*.)

Newtherapeutics v Katz [1991] Ch 226 [354]

Newtherapeutics, an English registered company, did all its business outside the UK, mainly in France and, in particular, with a pharmaceutical undertaking, Debat. The company alleged that at a meeting with Debat in 1988 two of its former directors, the defendants, had signed documents without being authorised to do so by a meeting of the board and that the transaction was so detrimental to the company that no reasonable director could properly have entered into it. One of the directors was domiciled in an American State and the other was domiciled in France. The company sought leave under RSC O.11 to serve a writ on the defendants out of the jurisdiction. *Held*, both applications would be rejected. KNOX J pointed out that, with regard to the French domiciled ex-director, Article 16(2) of the Brussels Convention gave the court exclusive jurisdiction because the company's claim was in respect of the validity or otherwise of his powers not with the reasonableness of his actions, and that Article 16(2) provided for 'proceedings which have as their object the validity of ... the decisions of ... organs ... of companies'; but as the company had previously agreed with the ex-director that they would waive all claims against him in respect of any act on his part as a director, or in any other capacity, then the claim against him was bound to fail. The claim against the American ex-director failed on the seemingly irrelevant ground that his appointment as a director without a specific contract of employment did not come within the scope of RSC O.11, r.1(1)(d). (See also *BP Exploration Co (Libya) Ltd* v *Hunt*.)

Nile Rhapsody, The, Hamed El Chiaty & Co [355]
(t/a Travco Nile Cruise Lines) v Thomas Cook Group
[1992] 2 Lloyd's Rep 399

The plaintiffs sued in England for breach of a charter agreement contending that the defendants, Thomas Cook, had not supplied the agreed number of tourists following the Iraqi invasion and brief annexation of Kuwait. The defendants sought a stay of action on the ground that there was an agreement in respect of Egyptian choice of law and jurisdiction. In the alternative, they claimed that Egypt was the more appropriate forum. Whereas the written contract between the parties contained an Egyptian choice of law clause, there was no reference to Egyptian jurisdiction. *Held*, the agreement would be rectified to incorporate an oral agreement to refer disputes to the Egyptian courts and to uphold the exclusive jurisdiction of those courts. HURST J applied the *El Amria* (or *Eleftheria*) test and found that the plaintiffs had not established a good case for not upholding

Egyptian jurisdiction. In the alternative, Egypt was the natural and most appropriate forum. (See also *The Eleftheria*, *The El Amria*, *The Spiliada* and *Re Harrods (Buenos Aries) Ltd.*) (Note: HIRST J was bound by the Court of Appeal decision in *Re Harrods (Buenos Aires) Ltd* that the Brussels Convention was inapplicable in cases involving conflicts of jurisdiction between Contracting States and non-Contracting States. The House of Lords referred the point to the ECJ for a preliminary ruling. However, the case was settled prior to judgment.)

Noirholme (Thierry) v Walklate (David) [356]
[1992] 1 Lloyd's Rep 427

The plaintiff obtained a default judgment in Belgium against the English defendant for damage alleged to have been caused by the latter to rented property in Belgium of which he was the tenant at the relevant time. When the plaintiff attempted to enforce the judgment in England, the defendant tried to base a defence on Article 27 of the Brussels Convention 1968 which provides that a default judgment shall not be recognised 'if the defendant was not duly served with the document which instituted the proceedings'. The originating process had been sent to the defendant in England but he had taken no steps to defend the action. Indeed, he contended that the process had not been served in accordance with provisions of the Hague Convention on the Service Abroad of Judicial and Extra-Judicial Documents in Civil and Commercial Matters 1965. *Held*, his contention would be rejected: (1) service of process via the postal service was permissible under the Protocol to the 1968 Convention and the Hague Convention 1965; (2) failure to comply with a particular provision of the Hague Convention (which was not the case here) did not provide for a ground for non-recognition separate from and additional to that in Article 27 of the 1968 Convention; and (3) whereas a stay could be ordered under either the 1968 Convention or the Civil Jurisdiction and Judgments Act 1982, it would be refused because of the defendant's prolonged period of inactivity in raising a defence. (See also *Debaecker* v *Bouwman* and *Pendy Plastic Products* v *Pluspunkt*.)

Norris v Chambres (1861) 3 De GF & J 583 [357]

The chairman of a company entered into an agreement to buy certain mines in Prussia on the company's behalf and paid part of the purchase price to the vendor. He then committed suicide, whereupon the vendor repudiated the agreement and conveyed the mine to trustees for another company, who knew of the chairman's payments. The administrator of the chairman's estate brought proceedings in Chancery against the trustees (who were in England) claiming a lien on the mines for the amount of these payments. Neither the original company nor the vendor was joined in the action. *Held*, the court had no jurisdiction to declare a lien, because foreign land was involved and there was no contract or privity or other personal obligation between the parties to the action. The trustees' knowledge of the chairman's payments was not enough to create such an obligation. (See also *Deschamps* v *Miller*.)

Norton's Settlement, Re, Norton v Norton [358]
[1908] 1 Ch 471 (Court of Appeal)

A married couple of English domicile lived in India, where the husband practised as a barrister. Their marriage settlement had been executed in India and its trustees and the property which it contained were in India. The wife left the husband, took up residence in France and instituted proceedings in England for money due under the settlement, serving the writ on the husband and on one of the trustees while they were temporarily in England. The husband and the trustee applied for a stay of proceedings. *Held*, a stay would be granted, because the wife was making an 'oppressive' use of the court's process. She was suing away from the forum conveniens in India in order to vex and harass the husband into surrendering his legal rights and not to obtain a legitimate advantage. (See also *de Dampierre* v *de Dampierre*.)

Nouvion v Freeman (1889) 15 App Cas 1 [359]
(House of Lords)

The plaintiff obtained from a Spanish court a 'remate' judgment for a debt against the defendant. This form of judgment could be immediately executed in Spain, but it arose out of summary proceedings only, where only certain limited defences could be raised. Furthermore, either party had the right under Spanish law to have the case wholly re-tried in the same court in 'plenary' proceedings, where the 'remate' judgment was not res judicata and all defences arising out of the facts could be raised. *Held*, the plaintiff could not enforce his 'remate' judgment against the defendant in England, because it was not 'final and conclusive'. It did not settle all possible controversies between the parties, and to enforce it as a binding judgment in England would be to give it greater force than it had in Spain. (See also *Blohn* v *Desser*.)

Obikoya and others v Silvernorth (1983) The Times 6 July [360]

Held, PARKER J that the mere fact that a Mareva injunction had been sought did not of itself confer jurisdiction on the court to grant leave to serve a writ out of the jurisdiction under RSC O.11, r.1(1)(i); and with reference to the main action, a defendant was not to be taken to have submitted to the jurisdiction merely because he had later applied to discharge the Mareva injunction. To assert that a defendant had submitted to the jurisdiction by virtue of his challenging the issue of a Mareva injunction would be to deprive him of his right under RSC O.12, r.8 to contest the court's jurisdiction by applying to set aside the writ. (Contrast *Boyle* v *Sacker*.)

O'Callaghan v Thomond (1810) 3 Taunt 82 [361]

A creditor of the defendant obtained judgment against her in Ireland for his debt, then assigned the judgment to the plaintiff. Under Irish law, but not English law, the plaintiff could then sue the defendant for the debt in his own name. *Held*, he could sue in his own name in England, because this was a question of substance, not procedure. (See also *Leroux* v *Brown*, *Re Cohn* and *Trendtex Trading Corporation* v *Credit Suisse*.)

Ogden v Ogden (orse Philip) [1908] P 46 (Court of Appeal) [362]

A domiciled Frenchman aged 19 married a domiciled Englishwoman in England without obtaining the consent of his parents. Under French law this was a requirement going to the essential, not merely formal, validity of the marriage. *Held*, the marriage was valid. 'Why should ... a person who comes over to this country and validly enters into a marriage with one of its inhabitants according to English law ... be held unable to do so here because of the regulations of a foreign system of jurisprudence which places upon him a personal incapacity to contract unless he complies with formalities required by the foreign law?' (*per* SIR GORELL BARNES P). (See also *Sottomayor (orse De Barros)* v *De Barros (No 2)*; compare *Simonin (orse Mallac)* v *Mallac*.)

Ogilvie, Re, Ogilvie v Ogilvie [1918] 1 Ch 492 **[363]**

The will of a testatrix who died domiciled in England contained a devise of land in Paraguay for charitable purposes and a bequest of movables to the defendants. The devise was invalid under Paraguay law except as to one-fifth, the remaining four-fifths going compulsorily to the defendants as the testatrix's heirs. *Held*, the defendants had to elect between the four-fifths share of the land and the bequest of movables. The question whether it was a case for election was determined by English law, the lex domicilii of the testatrix at death. In exercising control over the bequest of movables, this law would insist upon election in order to carry out the 'paramount object' of effectuating the testatrix's whole intentions, because in its view the devise was wholly valid. (See also *Balfour* v *Scott*.)

Ohochuku v Ohochuku [1960] 1 WLR 183 **[364]**

Two domiciled Nigerians who were Christians married each other in Nigeria according to local custom, which permitted polygamy. In pursuance of an intention to make their marriage monogamous, they later went through a monogamous civil ceremony of marriage in England. *Held*, the court had jurisdiction to hear a divorce petition brought by the wife, but only as regards the second marriage. The first marriage, being potentially polygamous under Nigerian law and custom despite the spouses' intentions and beliefs, was outside the matrimonial jurisdiction of the English courts. (Compare *Mehta (orse Kohn)* v *Mehta*.)

O'Keefe, Re, Poingdestre v Sherman [1940] Ch 124 **[365]**

A woman of British nationality and Italian domicile died intestate, leaving movable property. Under Italian law, succession thereto was a matter for her lex nationalis. Her domicile of origin was in Southern Ireland (now Eire), but she had only ever been there once, for a short visit, and since her birth that country had left the British Commonwealth and had ceased to treat people in her position as its citizens. She had been born in India and the only country where she had ever settled was Italy. *Held*, succession to her estate should be governed by the law of Eire. The lex domicilii, the law governing succession to movables, referred the question to her lex nationalis, which should be taken to mean the law of that country within the British Commonwealth to which she 'belonged' at her death. (See also *Collier* v *Rivaz*.)

Oppenheimer v Cattermole [1976] AC 249 (House of Lords) **[366]**

A German Jew, O, who emigrated to England in 1939, became a naturalised British subject in 1948. When a pension he received from 1953 onwards from the (then) Federal German Republic was assessed as to income tax, he appealed against the decision to the special commissioners on the basis that he had dual British and German nationality. The special commissioners found that O was not entitled to relief under the double taxation relief orders though GOULDING J at first instance allowed O's appeal. On appeal by the Crown, however, the Court of Appeal decided, that whether the taxpayer had a German nationality was a question for German domestic law: and decrees of 1913 and 1941 had deprived him of his German nationality; and even if the English courts had refused to recognise the later decree during a time of war, they should not refuse to recognise it in peacetime. Accordingly, O had only a single (British) nationality and he was liable to pay English income tax. *Held*, the decision of the Court of Appeal would be affirmed as, on the facts, which were to be determined by the English courts, O was not, during the relevant years, a German national.

Oppenheimer v Louis Rosenthal & Co AG [367]
[1937] 1 All ER 23 (Court of Appeal)

The plaintiff, a German Jew, sued his employer, a German company, for damages for wrongful dismissal. The contract of employment was governed by German law, but the breach took place in England. If the plaintiff had gone to Germany to sue there, he would probably not have been allowed representation in court on account of his religion and he might have been put in a concentration camp. He obtained leave to serve the writ in Germany under the predecessor of what is now RSC O.11, r.1(1)(e) but the company challenged service. *Held*, the court should not exercise its discretion to set aside service. Despite the case's substantial contracts with Germany, the English court was the forum conveniens because it would be unjust to the plaintiff to compel him to sue in Germany. (Compare *The Hagen*.)

Overseas Union Insurance v Incorporated General Insurance [368]
[1992] 1 Lloyd's Rep 439 (Court of Appeal)

Neither company was statutorily authorised to conduct insurance business, nor was either of them domiciled in England. Nevertheless, they took steps to comply with the English law of insurance. The plaintiff sued and sought leave to serve a writ out of the jurisdiction. *Held*, the companies' active steps to comply with English law were a strong indication that they wished English law to apply to their contract. England was the appropriate forum and leave to serve the writ would be granted.

Overseas Union Insurance v New Hampshire Insurance [369]
(Case C–351/89) [1991] ECR 3317 (European Court of Justice)

In proceedings which involved insurance companies, neither of which was domiciled in a Contracting State to the Brussels Convention, but both of which were registered in England as an overseas company, and in which it was common ground that the French courts were the courts first seised of the proceedings, the Court of Appeal referred two questions to the ECJ for a preliminary ruling. *Held*, (1) 'Article 21 of the [Brussels] Convention ... must be interpreted as applying irrespective of the domicile of the parties to the ... proceedings'; and (2) 'Without prejudice to the case where the court second seised has exclusive jurisdiction under the Convention and in particular under Article 16 thereof, Article 21 of the Convention must be interpreted as meaning that, where the jurisdiction of the court first seised is contested, the court second seised may, if it does not decline jurisdiction, only stay proceedings and may not itself examine the jurisdiction of the court first seised.' (See also *Neste Chemicals SA v DK Line SA*, *The Sargasso* and *The Tatry*.)

Owens Bank Ltd v Bracco [1992] 2 AC 443 (House of Lords); [370]
Owens Bank Ltd v Bracco (No 2) (Case C–129/92)
[1994] 1 All ER 336 (European Court of Justice)

The plaintiffs succeeded at first instance and before the Court of Appeal of St Vincent in obtaining judgment for the repayment of a loan of SFr9,000,000. The defendants contested enforcement in England, maintaining, as they had done in St Vincent and before the Italian courts, that the judgment was obtained by fraud. Furthermore, the defendants relied on Articles 21 and 22 of the Brussels Convention 1968 in requesting that the English courts decline jurisdiction or stay proceedings pending the outcome of the Italian enforcement proceedings. *Held*, it was not necessary for fresh evidence to be adduced for the defence of fraud to be raised: *Abouloff* v *Oppenheimer* would be applied. However, with regard to the defence based on provisions of the Brussels Convention, the House of Lords referred three questions to the ECJ for preliminary rulings before declaring that the provisions were inapplicable to enforcement in Contracting States of judgments given in non-Contracting States. (See also *Jet Holdings Inc* v *Patel*; contrast *House of Spring Gardens* v *Waite*.)

Owners of Cargo Lately Laden on Board Tatry v Owners of Maciej Rataj see **Tatry, The**

P (GE) (an infant), Re [1965] Ch 568 (Court of Appeal) [371]

An infant son of stateless Jewish parents living apart in England stayed with his mother until, in the course of a visit to his father, he was taken off by the father to Israel. The two of them travelled under British documents issued to stateless persons, which conferred no diplomatic protection but only a right to be readmitted to the UK within three months after departure. The father acquired a domicile in Israel on arrival there. Within two months the wife instituted custody proceedings in England. *Held*, the court had jurisdiction by virtue of the child's ordinary existence in England when proceedings were instituted. Such residence existed because (1) the child did not lose his home with his mother simply by being 'kidnapped'; and (2) the document under which he travelled preserved his allegiance to the Crown, this being the ultimate basis for assuming custody jurisdiction over infants resident in England. It was not relevant to consider where he was domiciled in determining the issue of jurisdiction.

Padolecchia v Padolecchia [1968] P 314 [372]

A domiciled Italian married his first wife in Italy, then divorced her by proxy in Mexico; and during her lifetime, he married his second wife in the course of a one-day visit to England. Italian law did not recognise any dissolution of the first marriage. The husband sought a decree that the second marriage was null and void. *Held*, (1) the court had jurisdiction to declare the second marriage void ab initio because it had been celebrated in England; and (2) a decree would be granted because under Italian law, the husband's lex domicilii at the time of the marriage, he lacked capacity to marry. (Compare *Schwebel* v *Ungar* and *Ross Smith (orse Radford)* v *Ross Smith* [1963] AC 280.)

Paine, Re, Griffiths v Waterhouse [1940] Ch 46 [373]

A domiciled German married in Germany to his deceased wife's sister, who was a domiciled Englishwoman. The marriage was valid in German law but prohibited by English law on grounds of affinity. On the wife's death, certain property in her father's will devolved upon her 'child or children'. *Held*, (1) the marriage was void because the wife lacked capacity to enter into it under her lex domicilii at the time of the marriage; and (2) the children of the void marriage were therefore illegitimate and unable to inherit under the will. (See also *Shaw* v *Gould*, *Mette* v *Mette*, *Pugh* v *Pugh*, s1 of the Marriage (Enabling) Act 1960, and s15 of the Family Law Reform Act 1969.)

Papadopoulos v Papadopoulos [1930] P 55 [374]

A domiciled Cypriot married a Frenchwoman in a civil ceremony in England, but later purported to repudiate the marriage on the ground that under Cypriot law a marriage of a Cypriot was void unless celebrated by a Greek Orthodox priest. He returned to Cyprus and with the wife's consent obtained a decree of nullity on this ground, coupled with a lump sum award of maintenance to the wife. Under Cypriot law, the court had no jurisdiction in nullity. Subsequent maintenance proceedings were brought in England by the wife. *Held*, the decree and the award of maintenance were ineffective in England. The Cypriot court had no jurisdiction to make the decree under its own law and could not acquire it merely from the consent of the parties because a matter of status was involved. The maintenance award, being ancillary to the decree, could have no more force than the decree. (Compare *Pemberton v Hughes*.)

Paramount Airways Ltd, Re [1992] 3 WLR 690 [375]
(Court of appeal)

The administrators of Paramount Airways sought a declaration that money transferred to a Jersey bank by one of the Airways' directors was a tranaction at an undervalue within the meaning of Provisions of the Insolvency Act 1986 and an order for repayment. The administrators were granted leave to serve a writ on the bank which carried on business in Jersey but not in England and Wales. The administrators also commenced proceedings against the director. At first instance, however, the bank succeeded in having the writ set aside on the basis that s238 of the Insolvency Act 1986 did not have extra-territorial effect and that the reference to 'any person' in that section could not apply to the bank. The administrators appealed. *Held*, allowing the appeal, no particular limitation could be read into the expression 'any person' in s238 of the 1986 Act: the words had to be given their ordinary literal meaning, unrestricted as to persons or territory. There was no constraint preventing service of a writ on a foreigner resident abroad under the Act and rules made under that Act.

Parkasho v Singh [1968] P 233 [376]

Two Sikhs domiciled in India entered into a marriage there which under their religious law was potentially polygamous. Some years later, the Hindu Marriage Act was passed in India, converting Sikh marriages between domiciled Indians into monogamous unions. The wife subsequently claimed maintenance from the husband in England. *Held*, the court had jurisdiction because, by virtue of the Act, the marriage had become monogamous. The nature of the marriage at the time of the proceedings, not at the time of its inception, was the matter to be considered. (See also *Ali v Ali*.)

Parlement Belge, The (1880) 5 PD 197 (Court of Appeal) [377]

A Belgian tug at anchor off Dover was struck by a Belgian mail ship which belonged to the Belgian Crown, flew the royal flag, was manned by members of the Royal Navy and was carrying goods and passengers for reward as well as the Royal Mail. The owners of the tug brought an action in rem against the ship, claiming damages. *Held*, the court lacked jurisdiction, because the King of Belgium, who was being 'impleaded' as owner of the ship, and the ship itself, being public property of the State of Belgium, were entitled to sovereign immunity. This immunity stemmed from 'the absolute independence of every sovereign authority and ... the international comity which induces every sovereign State to respect the independence of every other State' (*per* BRETT LJ). (See also *The Harmattan* and the State Immunity Act 1978; contrast *Trendtex v Central Bank of Nigeria*.)

Parojcic (orse Ivetic) v Parojcic [1958] 1 WLR 1280 [378]

On her arrival in England, a Yugoslavian refugee was compelled by the threats of her father to submit to marriage with another Yugoslavian refugee, who was domiciled in England. *Held*, the marriage was voidable at the instance of the wife, because the duress to which she had been subjected prevented her consent from being effective according to English law, the lex loci celebrationis. (But see *Kenward* v *Kenward*.)

Parouth, The [1982] 2 Lloyd's Rep 351 (Court of Appeal) [379]

A German company sought the assistance of freight forwarders in Florida, USA, in obtaining the services of a vessel to transport cargo from Germany to Mexico. The freight forwarders requested the help of Dutch brokers who entered into negotiations with the Panamanian plaintiffs for the charter of their Greek vessel, Parouth. Subsequently, the plaintiffs alleged that a charterparty was concluded but that the defendants, the freight forwarders, had failed to provide a cargo. The plaintiffs provided the court with telexes which they maintained evidenced the terms of the charter-party which included a provision for arbitration in London. The defendants contended that either there was no binding contract or, if there was, then it was made without their authority by the Dutch brokers. Initially, the plaintiffs were granted leave to serve a writ out of the jurisdiction, though this was then set aside by BINGHAM J. *Held* (*per* ACKNER LJ citing Dicey & Morris's *The Conflict of Laws*, 10th ed), 'The formation of a contract is governed by the law which would be the proper law of the contract if the contract was validly concluded. ... that if this case is heard then the probabilities are that the putative law, namely English law, will be applied to resolve the issue ... What made this a case to which [what is now] RSC O.11, r.1(1)(d) applied was that it was arguably a contract which by its terms or implication was governed by English law. [And since] There is a good arguable case that there was a contract [which] by its terms or implication, governed by English law [the appeal would be allowed].' (See also *Amin Rasheed* v *Kuwait Insurance Co* and *Metall und Rohstoff* v *Donaldson Lufkin & Jenrette*.)

Partenreederei M/S Heidburg v Grosvenor Grain and Feed Co
see **Heidburg, The**

Pemberton v Hughes [1899] 1 Ch 781 (Court of Appeal) [380]

A husband domiciled in Florida obtained a divorce there on the ground of his wife's 'violent and ungovernable temper'. By mistake, the time allowed for the wife's appearance was only nine days after issue of process instead of the ten days required by the rules of the court. *Held*, even if this irregularity made the divorce void in Florida, it was still valid in England. 'If a judgment is pronounced by a foreign court over persons within its jurisdiction and in a matter with which it is competent to deal, English courts never investigate the propriety of the proceedings ... unless they offend against English views of substantial justice' (*per* LINDLEY MR). (See also *Vanquelin* v *Bouard* and *Gray (otherwise Formosa)* v *Formosa*.)

Pendy Plastic Products v Pluspunkt (Case 228/81) [381]
[1982] ECR 2723 (European Court of Justice)

Pendy, a Dutch company, had obtained judgment in default against Pluspunkt in the Dutch courts and wished to enforce it in Germany where Pluspunkt was registered. However, enforcement was refused both by a Regional Court and, on appeal, a Higher Regional Court in Germany which considered that a precondition for the issue of an order for the enforcement of the Dutch judgment by default was observance of the procedural rules laid down in Articles 27 and 34 of the Brussels Convention 1968, viz, service on the defendant of the document which instituted the proceedings. Pendy, who had not cited the defendant's correct address for service of the writ, appealed to the Federal Court, who then requested a preliminary ruling from the ECJ. *Held*, 'The court of the State in which enforcement is sought may, if it considers that the conditions laid down by Article 27(2) of the Brussels Convention are fulfilled, refuse to grant recognition and enforcement of a judgment, even though the court of the State in which the judgment was given regarded it as proven ... that the defendant, who failed to enter an appearance, had an opportunity to receive service of the document instituting the proceedings in sufficient time to enable him to make arrangements for his defence.' (See also *Debaecker* v *Bouwman* and *Noirholme* v *Walklate*.)

Penhas (Isaac) v Tan Soo Eng [1953] AC 304 (Privy Council) [382]

In Singapore in 1937, two British subjects, a Jewish man and a non-Christian Chinese woman, both of whom were domiciled and resident in Singapore, went through a ceremony of marriage conducted by a Chinese gentleman in a modified Chinese form. Thereafter they lived together as man and wife and had two children. With minor exceptions, the common law of England was in force in Singapore in 1937. In a dispute which arose after the death of the man, the principal question to be answered was, 'Whether there was in 1937 anything in the religions, manners or customs of Jews or Chinese domiciled in Singapore which prevented them from contracting a common law monogamous marriage.' *Held*, first, 'in a country such as Singapore, where priests are few and there is no true parochial system, where the vast majority are not Christians, it is neither convenient nor necessary that two persons such as the respondent and the deceased should be required to call in an episcopally ordained priest to effect a marriage. [Moreover] There was no form of marriage in the present case which was applicable to both parties to the marriage, and accordingly they seem to have adopted a composite ceremony, the wife worshipping according to her Chinese custom and the husband according to his Jewish custom. Such a ceremony ... was indubitably intended by the parties to constitute a valid marriage. [And on the evidence found, such as] The wishes expressed by the respondent and her mother for a Church marriage, ... the words spoken by the Chinese gentleman who performed the ceremony as to a life-long union, [and] the co-habitation as man and wife which followed and continued till the husband's death, ... all indicate that the spouses intended to contract a common law monogamous marriage' (*per* LORD OAKSEY). (See also *Wolfenden* v *Wolfenden* and *Hyde* v *Hyde*.)

Penn v Lord Baltimore (1750) 1 Ves Sen 444 [383]

The plaintiff sued the defendant in the Court of Chancery for specific performance of an agreement fixing the boundaries of Maryland, Pennsylvania, and three 'lower counties' in the USA. *Held*, although this claim related to foreign immovable property, the Court of Chancery had jurisdiction because it could act in personam against the defendant, treating his 'conscience' as bound by the agreement. (See also *Deschamps* v *Miller*; compare *British South Africa Co* v *Companhia de Mocambique*.)

Perrini v Perrini [1979] Fam 84 [384]

An American woman, W1, domiciled in New Jersey, married a domiciled Italian man in Italy. The marriage was not consummated so she returned to New Jersey and obtained a decree of nullity. This was not recognised in Italy. The Italian man then came to England where he married a domiciled Englishwoman, W2. Later, W2 petitioned for a decree of nullity on the basis that the man was still married to W1. *Held*, the remarriage was valid: the New Jersey decree was recognised in England so the man had the capacity to marry. (See also *Lawrence* v *Lawrence*.)

Petereit v Babcock International Holdings Ltd [385]
[1990] 1 WLR 350

The plaintiff, in his capacity as receiver for the assets of a bankrupt German firm, had obtained judgment in the sum of DM40 million against the defendant and another company in the same group in the German courts. The defendant sought, inter alia, to set aside or stay an order that the judgment be registered in England pending an appeal to the German courts. *Held*, 'looking simply at the wording of the [Brussels] Convention, I would draw three provisional conclusions as follows: (1) that the enforcing court has a general and unfettered discretion under the Convention to stay the enforcement proceedings if an appeal is pending in the State in which the judgment was obtained; (2) that a judgment obtained in a Contracting State is to be regarded as prima facie enforceable, and accordingly the enforcing court should not adopt a general practice of depriving a successful plaintiff of the fruits of the judgment by the imposition of a more or less automatic stay, merely on the ground that there is a pending appeal; (3) that the purpose of Articles 30 and 38 is to protect the position of the defendant in an appropriate case and to ensure that, if the appeal succeeds, then the defendant will be able to enforce the order of the appeal court and will not be deprived of the fruits of his success by reason of a previous unconditional enforcement of the judgment. It seems to me that the court's discretion to grant a stay should be exercised with this purpose in mind. ... It is, however, important to note that Article 38 sets out two alternative methods of protecting the position of the defendant in the interval between the time when the judgment becomes enforceable in the State in which it is given and the time when the appeal against that judgment is finally determined; one is to grant a stay; the other is to make enforcement conditional on the provision of security by the plaintiff. I do not think that the Convention expresses any preference as to which method is to be employed by the enforcing court ... [Applying these principles this was] a case where in all the circumstances the appropriate course is to order a stay of the enforcement proceedings subject to the provision by the defendant of appropriate security to protect the position of the plaintiff in the interval until the final result of the appeal is known' (*per* ANTHONY DIAMOND QC). (See also *Industrial Diamond Supplies* v *Riva*.)

Peters, Martin v ZNAV (Case 34/82) [1983] ECR 987 [386]
(European Court of Justice)

Martin Peters, a limited liability construction company having its registered office in Germany, was sued by ZNAV, an association having its registered office in The Netherlands and having legal personality, of which Peters was a member. In essence, a rule of the association which was binding on its members provided that any member who tendered for and obtained a contract should pay a sum by way of compensation and contributions to unsuccessful members who tendered for the same contract or a contribution towards the costs of the association's office. When sued in the Dutch courts for non-payment of a sum in excess of HFL110,000, Peters appeared in court solely to contest the jurisdiction of the court, contending that since it had its domicile in Germany it could not be sued in the Dutch courts by virtue of the provision of Article 2 of the Brussels Convention 1968. This contention was dismissed on the basis that it was a dispute which arose out of a contract and, accordingly, the special jurisdiction provision of Article 5(1) of the Convention enabled them to be sued in the courts for the place of performance of the obligation in question. Peters appealed and a question was referred to the ECJ for a preliminary ruling. *Held*, (1) 'Obligations in regard to the payment of a sum of money which have their basis in the relationship existing between an association and its members by virtue of membership are 'matters relating to a contract' within the meaning of Article 5(1) of the [Brussels] Convention 1968 ... [and] (2) it makes no difference in that regard whether the obligations in question arise simply from the act of becoming a member or from that act in conjunction with one or more decisions made by organs of the association.' (See also *Hanbridge Services Ltd* v *Aerospace Communications Ltd*.)

Peters (orse Petrovic) v Peters [1967] 3 All ER 318 [387]

Two domiciled Yugoslavs were married in Belgrade, but then came to England and acquired English domicile and nationality. The wife returned briefly to Yugoslavia and obtained a divorce there, jurisdiction being assumed on the ground that the marriage had taken place there. *Held*, this divorce would not be recognised in England, because the mere fact that the spouses were married in Yugoslavia did not constitute a 'real and substantial connection' with that country at the time of the divorce, even though at the time of the marriage they had Yugoslavian nationality and domicile. (Compare *Indyka* v *Indyka*.)

Philipson-Stow v Inland Revenue Commissioners [388]
[1961] AC 727 (House of Lords)

A testator dying domiciled in England left a will in English form which stipulated that it should operate according to English law. The residue of the estate included land in South Africa. Under the UK Finance Act, immovable property situated out of the UK was exempt from estate duty if 'the proper law regulating ... the disposition under or by reason of which it passes' was not English or Scottish law. *Held*, the land in South Africa was exempt from duty. Although construction of a will, even when it disposed of immovables, was in general governed by the testator's *lex domicilii* at the time of execution and was here governed by English law as stated in the will, the law under which a disposition of immovables was 'regulated' was the *lex situs*. (See also *In re Cunnington, Healing* v *Webb*.)

Phillips v Eyre (1869) LR 6 QB 1 (Exchequer Chamber) [389]

In the course of suppressing a rebellion in the Colony of Jamaica, officers acting on the orders of the defendant, who was the Governor of the Colony, arrested, flogged and imprisoned the plaintiff. The Jamaican legislature later passed a statute which indemnified the defendant and all those who acted under his authority in respect of their conduct in suppressing the rebellion and retrospectively declared such conduct to be lawful. The plaintiff sued the defendant in England for damages in tort. *Held*, his action would fail, because the statute prevented any liability arising under Jamaican law, the *lex loci delicti commissi*. 'As a general rule, in order to found a suit in England for a wrong alleged to have been committed abroad, two conditions must be fulfilled. First, the wrong must be of such character that it would have been actionable if committed in England ... Secondly, the act must not have been justifiable by the law of the place where it was done ...' (*per* WILLES J). (See also *The Halley, The Mary Moxham* and *Boys* v *Chaplin*.)

Phrantzes v Argenti [1960] 2 QB 19 [390]

Under Greek law, a father who did not grant a dowry to his daughter's husband could be compelled to do so in legal proceedings brought by the daughter. The Greek court would assess the amount of the dowry, having regard to all the relevant circumstances, and would order the father, whether in Greece or abroad, to enter into a notarial deed of agreement with the husband. The plaintiff, a Greek woman married to an Englishman, brought proceedings in England against her father, a domiciled Greek, to compel him to grant a dowry in this way. *Held*, although the plaintiff's rights under Greek law were in principle entitled to recognition in England, the court would not grant the order sought. This was because (1) the task of assessing the amount of the dowry was best left to the discretion of a Greek court; and (2) there being no remedy in the lex fori whereby a defendant could be compelled to enter into an agreement with someone who was not a party to the action (ie here, the husband), the court would have to award the dowry to the plaintiff herself, and this remedy was so different from the Greek remedy as to 'make the right sought to be enforced a different right' (*per* LORD PARKER CJ).

Piercy, Re, Whitwham v Piercy [1895] 1 Ch 83 [391]

A testator who died domiciled in England, devised and bequeathed his real and personal property to his trustees on trust for sale and conversion and to hold the same before and after conversion on trust for his children for life with remainder to their issue. The estate included land in Italy, under whose law the imposition of limited interests on land was forbidden. *Held*, although Italian law, the lex situs, struck down the limitation while the land was unsold, it did not prevent the trustees carrying out their duty to convert it, whereupon the proceeds of conversion, being funds held by trustees of an English will, would be governed by English, not Italian law, and the limitation would be valid and operative. (But see *Duncan* v *Lawson* and *Re Berchtold, Berchtold* v *Capron*.)

Plummer v Inland Revenue Commissioners [392]
[1988] 1 WLR 292

Ms P's domicile was in issue for income tax purposes. She was born in England of English parents in 1965. In 1980 her mother and younger sister had moved permanently to Guernsey. P's father, who worked in London, also spent his weekends and holidays in Guernsey. Ms P remained in London to finish her education although she, too, spent many weekends and holidays in Guernsey. She grew very fond of the island and intended to settle there permanently once her education was complete. Ms P opened a Guernsey bank account, acquired a Guernsey driver's licence and a Guernsey passport. *Held*, whereas it was possible for Ms P, or any other person, to acquire a new domicile of choice in a new country (ie Guernsey) without ceasing to be resident in her domicile of origin, that person had to establish that his/her residence in the new country was his/her chief residence. HOFFMANN J decided that Ms P had failed to establish this. (See also *IRC* v *Bullock*.)

Po, The [1991] 2 Lloyd's Rep 206 (Court of Appeal) [393]

A collision occurred in Rio de Janeiro between an American ship, *Bowditch*, and an Italian merchant ship, *Po*. A writ in rem was served on the *Po* when it was in Southampton. The defendants applied to stay the proceedings on the ground that the case could be tried in Brazil more suitably for the interests of all parties and the ends of justice; and for a declaration that the English courts had no jurisdiction because, under the Brussels Convention 1968, the action should have been brought in Italy where they were domiciled. The plaintiffs sought to rely on the 1952 Brussels Collision Convention, contending that the Brussels Convention 1968 did not apply to collisions, but the defendants argued that this could not be so as no statutory enactment had incorporated it into English law. At first instance, SHEEN J decided that many provisions of the Collision Convention were already part of English law and that as the Collision Convention gave the English courts jurisdiction, a stay would not be granted. The defendants appealed, citing England as forum non conveniens, that proceedings should have been brought in Brazil, and that the English courts should decline jurisdiction in favour of the Italian courts. *Held*, dismissing the appeal, (1) although the court had discretion to stay proceedings on the ground of forum non conveniens, even where a defendant was domiciled in a Contracting State under the Brussels Convention 1968, the defendants had failed to show that Brazil was clearly a more appropriate forum; (2) the High Court had jurisdiction under English municipal law because the writ in rem was properly served on the *Po* in Southampton, and that assumption of jurisdiction was in any event expressly authorised by the Collision Convention. (See also *The Anna H, The Tatry* and *Re Harrods (Buenos Aires) Ltd*.)

Ponticelli v Ponticelli [1958] P 204 [394]

An Italian national, domiciled and resident in England, married by proxy in Italy, a woman who, at the time of the marriage, was domiciled and resident in Italy. When the husband petitioned for a nullity of marriage on the ground that the wife had wilfully refused to consummate the marriage, the question arose as to which was the appropriate choice of law which governed the question providing the proxy marriage was recognised as being valid. *Held*, (1) the court would apply *Apt v Apt* and recognise the proxy marriage; and (2) the appropriate law was English law as the lex domicilii and the law of the intended matrimonial home. SACHS J expressed the view that 'it is surely a matter of some importance that the initial validity of a marriage should, in relation to all matters except form and ceremony ... be consistently decided according to the law of one country alone ... and that consistency cannot be attained if the test is lex fori.'

Porter v Freudenberg [1915] 1 KB 857 (Court of Appeal) [395]

In giving judgment during World War I in three cases involving the rights of alien enemies to institute appellate proceedings in England, the Court of Appeal laid down the following principles: on grounds of public policy, an alien enemy (ie one who resides voluntarily or carries on business in an enemy country) cannot sue in England unless he has Crown permission to be in England. He can, however, be sued in England in which case he can enter an appearance, defend the action and appeal against any decision, whether final or interlocutory. However, if he was the plaintiff in a case in which judgment was delivered before the war, any right of appeal which he had before the war is suspended until the conclusion of peace, ie until the was is over. (See also *Dynamit v Rio Tinto Zinc Co Ltd*.)

Potinger v Wightman (1817) 3 Mer 67 [396]

An Englishman died domiciled in Guernsey, whereupon his widow, having been appointed guardian of their infant children by a court in Guernsey, brought them with her to England and acquired a domicile of choice there. *Held*, the children thereby acquired a domicile in England. A mother who retained care of her infant children after the death of their father would change their domicile when she changed her own, provided that the change was not effected fraudulently in order to improve her own position in regard to rights of succession. (See also *Re Beaumont*.)

Preston (orse Putynski) v Preston (orse Putynska) (orse Basinska) [1963] P 411 (Court of Appeal) [397]

In 1945, two domiciled Poles living in a camp in occupied Germany were married before the camp chaplain according to Roman Catholic rites. The camp was run by the occupying forces to receive Polish soldiers, such as the husband, from the disbanded Polish army. The marriage ceremony was invalid under German law. *Held*, the marriage was none the less valid at common law. This ground of validity was not to be invoked by any foreigner wishing to bypass local formalities, but was available where either spouse was a member of or associated with a military force occupying conquered territory. (But see *Lazarewicz (orse Fadanelli) v Lazarewicz*.)

Price v Dewhurst (1837) 8 Sim 279 [398]

A married couple who had been residing in St Croix made a joint will operating according to Danish law, the prevailing law there, but later made separate wills in which they revoked the joint will. They died domiciled in England, whereupon the executors of the joint will obtained probate of it in St Croix, constituting themselves an 'Executor's Court of Dealing' and made a declaration that the spouses' property should be distributed according to the joint will. Such a declaration would normally be effective under Danish law, but not where, as here, the executors stood to gain under the will being administered. In England, the executors and beneficiaries under the separate wills applied for a declaration that these wills had revoked the joint will. *Held*, the declaration would be granted. The decision of the 'Executor's Court of Dealing' was null and void and would not be recognised because the court was made up of parties who had an interest in the matter. (Compare *Jacobson v Frachon*.)

Priest, Re, Bellfield v Duncan [1944] Ch 58 [399]

A testator died domiciled in England leaving an estate of personal property in England. He had executed a holograph will in Scotland on a Scottish printed form with attestation by two witnesses, one of whom was the husband of a beneficiary. Under English domestic rules as to the validity of wills, the gift to this beneficiary was therefore rendered invalid, but under Scottish law a holograph will of personalty was valid even when unattested. *Held*, the gift was void. Had the testator intended to make an unattested holograph will of personalty in the manner accepted by Scottish law, it would have been valid under s2 of the Wills Act 1861. But he did not so intend, so the Act did not apply and the gift was invalid on application of English law, his lex domicilii. (See also *Collier v Rivaz*.)

Prins Bernhard, The [1964] P 117 [400]

In February 1962, the plaintiffs issued a writ in rem against the defendants, alleging breach of contract and, alternatively, negligence and claiming damages for loss of, and damage to, cargo carried in the defendants' vessel, the *Prins Bernhard*. At the end of January 1963, solicitors acting for the Polish insurers applied ex parte for a renewal of the writ for a further six months. The reason given for the non-service of the writ within the preceding 12 months was that negotiations were continuing between the insurers and the defendants with a view to settling the claim. The extension was granted as it constituted a 'good reason' within (what was then) RSC O.8, r.1, and a further extension was granted at the end of July 1963. The writ was handed to the master of the *Prins Bernhard* in his cabin in September 1963. The defendants sought to set aside the writ and all subsequent proceedings on the basis that the renewal of the writ at the end of January 1963 was in breach of the prevailing RSC Order, since service of the writ could have been effected on three occasions between the date of issue and that of renewal; and to set aside service of the writ for not being made in the prescribed manner of nailing or affixing it to the mast. *Held*, the court's wish to see amicable settlements of disputes and the plaintiffs' belief that service of the writ within 12 months of its issue might prejudice the ongoing negotiations constituted good reason why discretion should be exercised in favour of extending the writ; but the plaintiffs' failure to follow the prescribed method of serving a writ against a ship vitiated the service.

Proctor v Frost (1938) 89 NH 304 [401]

M, a married woman domiciled in Massachusetts, USA, mortgaged her land in New Hampshire in order to secure her husband's debts. Under New Hampshire law, a married woman did not have the capacity to become surety for her husband. M relied on this defence when the mortgagee sought to foreclose the mortgage. *Held*, the defence would be rejected: its purpose was to protect New Hampshire married women. (See also *Bank of Africa* v *Cohen*.)

Pugh v Pugh [1951] P 482 [402]

A domiciled Hungarian girl of 15 married a domiciled Englishman in Austria, intending to return with him to live in England. This they ultimately did four years later. The marriage was valid according to Hungarian and Austrian law, but s1 of the English Age of Marriage Act 1929 provided that 'A marriage between persons, either of whom is under the age of 16 shall be void'. *Held*, the marriage was void on either of two grounds: (1) that the Act regulated the capacity to marry of all persons domiciled in the UK, even in respect of marriages abroad; or (2) that the husband's lex domicilii, being the law governing his capacity to marry, made it a marriage into which he could not lawfully enter. (Compare *Cheni (orse Rodriguez)* v *Cheni* and *Mohamed* v *Knott*.)

Quazi v Quazi [1980] AC 744 (House of Lords) [403]

Pakistani nationals divorced by khula (a signed document terminating marriage) in Thailand though they continued to live together there and, later, in Malaysia. They returned to Pakistan, where they did not live together, prior to the husband coming to live in England where he bought a house and where he was joined by his son and other members of his family who came to live with him. The following year, and against his wishes, the wife came to live in the house. In order to ensure that he had a valid divorce, the husband went to Pakistan and pronounced a talaq in accordance with the laws of Pakistan and then returned to live in England. When the wife petitioned for a divorce in England, the action was stayed to allow the husband to petition for a declaration that the marriage had been lawfully dissolved either by the khula in Thailand or talaq in Pakistan. At first instance, WOOD J held that both the khula and talaq would be recognised by the English courts as dissolving the marriage. The Court of Appeal reversed his decision and allowed the wife's appeal. *Held*, unanimously, allowing the husband's appeal, under s2(a) of the Recognition of Divorces and Legal Separations Act 1971, the words 'other proceedings' referred to any proceedings which were recognised in the country in which they were taken and the divorce obtained by talaq in Pakistan was a divorce obtained by such 'other proceedings'. The talaq was entitled to recognition under the aforementioned statutory provision and the husband was entitled to a declaration that the marriage had been dissolved thereby. (See, now, ss45 and 46 of the Family Law Act 1986.)

Queensland Mercantile and Agency Co, Re [1891] 1 Ch 536 [404]

A company incorporated in Queensland gave a charge over its uncalled share capital to an Australian bank, but did not give notice of the charge to its Scottish shareholders. The company then called in this capital, thereby creating an immediate debt from all its shareholders, but before it had been paid, a Scottish creditor of the company issued arrestment proceedings in Scotland against the amounts due from the Scottish shareholders. Under Scottish law, but not English or Australian law, this creditor could claim these amounts against the bank because it was the first to give notice of its claim to the shareholders. A winding-up of the company proceeded in England. *Held*, the Scottish creditor had priority over the bank, because the effect of the arrestment proceedings on the debts due from the Scottish shareholders to the company on their shares was a matter for Scottish law, the lex situs of those debts. (But see *The Zigurds*, *The Colorado* and *The Halcyon Isle*.)

Qureshi v Qureshi [1972] Fam 173 [405]

A 1966 English registry office marriage between Muslims was followed by a Muslim ceremony in which the husband consented to a type of dower in that he promised to pay the wife on demand at any time or on dissolution of the marriage for any reason a sum of approximately £800. The following year, the husband, who claimed to be domiciled in Pakistan, purported to divorce his wife by way of a talaq in a letter written to her and the subsequent confirmation of the breakdown of the marriage in a hearing in the London office of the High Commissioner for Pakistan. However, the wife petitioned the court for a declaration either that the marriage subsisted and for maintenance; or, if the marriage had been validly dissolved, that she was entitled to the dower in the sum of approximately £800. The husband cross-petitioned for a declaration that, inter alia, the talaq was valid. *Held*, 'Both the wife and the husband have been resident in England at the commencement of and throughout the present proceedings. [Accordingly] each party is entitled to the declaration sought under RSC O.15, r.6, as to the effect of the purported talaq' (*per* SIMON P). The husband had established a Pakistani domicile and the marriage had been validly dissolved by the talaq which would be recognised in England. Thus, the wife would be entitled to the dower. (See, now, ss44 and 45 of the Family Law Act 1986.)

R v Brentwood Superintendent Registrar of Marriages, [406]
ex parte Arias [1968] 2 QB 956

An Italian domiciled in Switzerland married a Swiss woman, but this marriage was later dissolved by a Swiss court. The wife remarried in Switzerland but the husband was unable to do the same thing because Swiss law referred the matter of his capacity to his lex nationalis, the Italian law, which did not recognise the divorce. *Held*, he could not remarry in England either, because there were no special circumstances to displace the operation of the 'normal' rule, viz, that capacity to marry was regulated by the law of the ante-nuptial domicile. (See also *Padolecchia* v *Padolecchia*; compare *Hooper* v *Hooper* and *Lawrence* v *Lawrence*. Note, now, that s50 of the Family Law Act 1986 would bring about a different decision in the *Brentwood* case.)

R v C (kidnapping: abduction) [1991] 2 FLR 252 [407]
(Court of Appeal)

A man had been charged with and convicted of (1) kidnapping his son and (2) of abducting him. The man had had his wife's permission to take the son abroad but not to taking him to the USA, hiding the son's whereabouts, and seeking a custody order in the family court of New York. The man appealed against convictions on both counts. With regard to (1) the appeal was based on, inter alia, the judge's ruling that evidence of a previous episode of the man taking his son to the USA without the mother's consent was admissible; and (2) the judge had supplied the jury with incomplete photocopies of s1 of the Child Abduction Act 1984 – subs6 was omitted – thus depriving the jury of a vital caution as to the burden of proof. Moreover, the judge's summing up had lacked the proper direction as to his good character. *Held*, (1) There was no good reason for the prosecution to have brought a charge of kidnapping against the man – the second count alone should have been relied upon; and the admission of evidence of the previous occasion when the man took his son to visit the USA had been seriously prejudicial to him (the father). Accordingly, the conviction of kidnapping was unsafe and it was quashed. (2) To the extent that since no jury, properly directed, could have failed to convict the man of abducting his child, his appeal would be dismissed.

R v International Trustee for the Protection of [408]
Bondholders AG [1937] AC 500 (House of Lords)

In 1917, the British Government borrowed a large sum of dollars in the USA, issuing convertible gold notes expressed to be payable with interest in US gold coin in New York or, at the holder's option, in sterling (converted at a stipulated rate) in London. As security, the British Government deposited bonds and stocks with a New York company under a pledge agreement in which the company's remedies were governed by New York law. In 1933, the US Congress passed a resolution that all debts due in gold or foreign currency could be discharged dollar for dollar in any currency which was legal tender. If applicable to the loan, this would entitle the British Government to repay holders of the converted notes in depreciated paper dollars. *Held*, the US resolution was applicable because, even though the British Government was a party, the proper law of the contract contained in the notes was New York law. 'The proper law of a contract ... is the law which the parties intended to apply ... If no intention be expressed the intention will be presumed by the court from the terms of the contract and the relevant surrounding circumstances' (*per* LORD ATKIN). (See also *Kahler* v *Midland Bank*; but see *Bonython* v *Commonwealth of Australia*.)

R v Sarwan Singh [1962] 3 All ER 612 (Quarter Sessions) [409]

A Sikh indicted for bigamy raised the defence that the first marriage had taken place in India under Sikh laws permitting polygamy. *Held*, this was a good defence, because the first marriage for the purposes of a bigamy charge must be a monogamous marriage.

Radwan v Radwan (No 2) [1973] Fam 35 [410]

W, a domiciled English woman, contracted a polygamous marriage in Paris with H, a domiciled Egyptian, who had a wife living in Egypt. The matrimonial home of H and W was established in Egypt and H divorced the Egyptian wife by talaq the following year. Subsequently, H and W decided to live permanently in England where H acquired a domicile of choice and where W petitioned and H cross-petitioned for a decree of divorce. Was the marriage of H and W valid and did W have the capacity to contract a polygamous marriage? *Held*, since there was an absence of clear authority concerning the validity of the marriage under French law, the lex loci contractus, there was a presumption that the ceremony of marriage was valid; and where the parties were domiciled in different countries prior to their marriage, their capacity to enter into a polygamous marriage was governed by the law of the intended matrimonial domicile. Accordingly, W's intention to settle with H in Egypt, where polygamy was a recognised form of marriage, validated H and W's marriage. (See also *Perrini* v *Perrini* and *Hussain* v *Hussain*; contrast *Re Paine, Pugh* v *Pugh, Sottomayor* v *De Barros (No 1)* and *Shaw* v *Gould*.)

Raffenel, In the Goods of (1863) 3 Sw & Torr 49 [411]

A widow whose husband died domiciled in France and who still resided there, went aboard a cross-channel ferry at Calais, intending to sail to England, her domicile of origin, and settle there. Before the ship left the harbour, she was taken ill and had to return to the mainland. She died in France without recovering sufficiently to complete the voyage. *Held*, she died domiciled in France. She had not lost her French domicile because her intention to lose it had never been put into effect by actual physical departure. (See also *Zanelli* v *Zanelli*.)

Ralli Bros v Compania Naviera Sota y Aznar [412]
[1920] 2 KB 287 (Court of Appeal)

By an agreement governed by English law, the defendants, an English firm, chartered a Spanish ship from the plaintiffs, a Spanish firm, to carry a cargo of jute from Calcutta to Barcelona. The agreement provided for payment of one-half of the freight in Barcelona on completion of the voyage. A Spanish decree, confirmed after the agreement was executed, prescribed a maximum rate for freight for jute imported into Spain and imposed penalties for exceeding it. The contract rate did, in fact, exceed it. *Held*, the defendants should pay the balance of the freight at the rate allowed by the decree, not the contract-rate, because Spain was expressly stipulated as the place of payment. 'Where a contract requires an act to be done in a foreign country, it is, in the absence of very special circumstances, an implied term of the continuing validity of such a provision that the act ... shall not be illegal by the law of that country' (*per* SCRUTTON LJ).

Ramsay-Fairfax (orse Scott-Gibson) v Ramsay-Fairfax [413]
[1956] P 115 (Court of Appeal)

A domiciled Scotsman was married in Egypt, then lived with his wife in England. She presented a nullity petition on the alternative grounds of impotence and wilful refusal to consummate, both of which would make the marriage voidable. *Held*, the court had jurisdiction despite the spouses' Scottish domicile because they were both resident in England. 'The jurisdiction in cases of nullity is, in my judgment, entirely different from the jurisdiction in cases of divorce' (*per* DENNING LJ).

Ramsay (or Bowie) v Liverpool Royal Infirmary [414]
[1930] AC 588 (House of Lords)

A Scotsman born in Glasgow and having a Scottish domicile of origin, gave up working when he was 37 years of age; and at the age of 46 went to live in Liverpool until his death at the age of 87. His reason for so doing was to live off other members of his family, who were the only people with whom he formed any attachments. He described himself in conversation and in his will as 'a

Glasgow man' but he refused to go back there for his mother's funeral and said he never wanted to go back there. *Held*, as had been decided in Scottish proceedings, he had died domiciled in Scotland. His long residence in England was insufficient evidence of a positive intention to abandon his Scottish domicile of origin because it was a 'colourless' residence, motivated only by his attachment to his family and his disinclination to work or change his residence. (See also *Bell* v *Kennedy*, *Winans* v *A-G* and *IRC* v *Bullock*; contrast *White* v *Tennant* and *Re Furse*.)

Rank Film Distributors v Lanterna Editrice SRL [415]
(1991) Financial Times 14 June

Rank purported to grant film exploitation rights to a licensee in return for a sum of $8.5 million, payable in three instalments, of which $6.5 million was payable 'by means of' a bank guarantee. The payment of the $6.5 million was not paid on the due date and this was followed by the firm holding the licensee's rights, Lanterna, obtaining a court order in Rome temporarily prohibiting the bank from making the payment on the ground that Rank had not properly performed its obligations. The following week, Rank instituted proceedings in England against the licensee and the bank for breach of contract. The licensee and the bank sought to set aside or stay the English proceedings and the licensee also commenced substantive proceedings against Rank in Rome. Rank served a defence and a counterclaim in the substantive proceedings and joined the bank as third party claiming the $6.5 million from both the licensee and the bank. *Held*, given that under Article 5(1) of the Brussels Convention 1968 a person domiciled in a Contracting State could be sued in contract in 'the place of performance of the obligation in question', and that on the *Tesam* test Rank had established a serious question which called for a trial for its proper determination, namely, whether the licensee was obliged to pay the $6.5 million in London, then English courts had jurisdiction. Article 22 did not assist the defendants as the proceedings in Italy, which were designed to provide temporary protective relief pending resolution of the merits elsewhere, and the English proceedings were not related actions for the purposes of that Article. Nor did the Italian courts have jurisdiction over Rank's defence and counterclaim since not only was Rank's appearance accompanied by a clear statement of intention to contest jurisdiction but, prior to instituting the Italian proceedings, Rank had also started proceedings on the same cause of action and between the same parties in London. (See also *Tesam Distribution Ltd* v *Schuh Mode Team GmbH and Commerzbank AG* and *Elefanten Schuh GmbH* v *Jacqmain*.)

Raulin v Fischer [1911] 2 KB 93 [416]

The defendant injured the plaintiff while galloping her horse recklessly along an avenue in Paris. French criminal proceedings were instituted against the defendant and the plaintiff intervened in them to claim compensation. The court convicted and fined the defendant and awarded damages against the defendant in England. Although the award and the conviction were the outcome of a single set of proceedings, they were severable from each other, so enforcement of the award alone would not in any way involve the execution of the penal law of France. (Compare *Huntington* v *Attrill* and *Re Macartney, Macfarlane* v *Macartney*.)

Rayner (J H) (Mincing Lane) Ltd v Department of [417]
Trade & Industry [1990] 2 AC 418 (House of Lords)

The International Tin Council (ITC), an international organisation established by treaty to which the UK was a party, had the legal capacity of a corporate body in English law and it also enjoyed certain immunities. It had its headquarters and principal office in London. After the ITC ran out of money in 1985, the appellants obtained an arbitration award against it and they issued a writ against the DTI, who represented the UK, claiming that each Member State that was a signatory to the treaty which had created the ITC was jointly and severally liable in respect of any such arbitration award which remained unsatisfied. *Held,* inter alia, since the ITC had separate legal capacity, a contract entered into by it did not subject its members to any liability: the ITC, alone, had incurred liability under its own contracts. Moreover, if the ITC was a foreign corporation that was established in the UK under the Companies Acts, then its relevant liabilities were those grounded in English law, and there was nothing in English law which made a member liable for the corporation's debts.

Red Sea Insurance Co Ltd v Bouygues SA and others [418]
[1995] 1 AC 190 (Privy Council)

Proceedings were instituted in Hong Kong against the Red Sea Insurance Co Ltd, a company incorporated in Hong Kong but having its head office in Saudi Arabia. All the plaintiffs were involved in some capacity in the design and construction work at the University of Riyadh, Saudi Arabia. In essence, for the purposes of this litigation, the plaintiffs fell into two groups, viz, (1) PCG, who supplied precast concrete prime building units required for the project, and (2) the other plaintiffs. The plaintiffs claimed under an insurance policy issued by Red Sea to be indemnified for loss and expense incurred in repairing or replacing structural damage which occurred in the buildings constructed. However, Red Sea counterclaimed that PCG was not covered by the contract of insurance, contending, inter alia, that the costs incurred by the plaintiffs were not for the purpose of rectifying structural damage, but were for work not covered by the policy such as the supply of faulty precast prime building units by PCG in breach of its duty of care to the other plaintiffs; and that if they (Red Sea) were liable under the policy to the other plaintiffs, then they were entitled to recover the costs of indemnifying those plaintiffs from PCG by way of subrogation to the rights of the other plaintiffs. In response to PCG's application to strike out their counterclaim on the basis that it showed no reasonable cause of action, Red Sea applied for leave to amend their counterclaim so as to allege that the applicable law was that of Saudi Arabia, under which they were entitled to sue PCG directly for the damage caused to the other plaintiffs. Neither the counterclaim nor the application for leave to amend succeeded at first instance, though the order striking out the counterclaim was set aside by the Court of Appeal of Hong Kong. The reason given for not permitting Red Sea to sue PCG directly for negligence relying solely on Saudi Arabian law as the lex loci delicti was because Hong Kong law, which was the same as English law, did not recognise the right of subrogation until payment had been made by the insurer and then proceedings had to be brought in the name of the insured. *Held,* Red Sea's appeal to the Privy Council would be successful and affirmed the general rule of English law with regard to foreign torts requiring the conduct to be both actionable as a tort according to English law and actionable in civil proceedings according to the lex loci delicti. With regard to the flexible application of the rule, LORD SLYNN said that of the 'many questions [which] may need to be resolved in regard to the application of the exception to the double actionability rule [,] [o]nly two ... need to be answered in the present case'. First, 'In *Boys* v *Chaplin* it is not suggested that the exception can be relied on only to exclude the lex loci delicti in favour of the lex fori. Their Lordships do not consider that the element of flexibility which exists is so limited. ... To limit the rule so as to enable an English court only to apply English law would be in conflict with the degree of flexibility envisaged by LORD WILBERFORCE [in *Boys* v *Chaplin*], though the fact that the forum is being required to apply a foreign law in a situation where its own law would give no remedy will be a factor to be taken into account when the court decides whether to apply the exception.' Secondly, 'the exception is not limited to specific isolated issues [as in *Boys* v *Chaplin*] but may apply to the whole claim, for example, where all or virtually all of the significant factors are in favour of the lex loci delicti.' On the facts of the case, 'The arguments in favour of the lex loci delicti are indeed overwhelming.' (See also *Boys* v *Chaplin* and *Johnson* v *Coventry Churchill*.)

Regazzoni v K C Sethia (1944) Ltd [1958] AC 301 [419]
(House of Lords)

In a contract governed by English law, the plaintiff, a Swiss merchant, agreed to buy jute from the defendant, an English company, to be delivered to him at Genoa. Both parties knew that the plaintiff intended to resell the jute in South Africa, that it would be coming from India (there being no other place to get it) and that an Indian statute prohibited the export of jute where it was intended to be taken directly or ultimately to South Africa. The defendant repudiated the contract before delivery. *Held*, the plaintiff's action for damages for breach of contract failed. On considerations of public policy and international comity, an English court would not enforce a contract, whatever its proper law, when the parties intended, though did not necessarily agree expressly, that the performance of it should involve committing an act in a foreign and friendly country which would violate that country's law. (See also *Re Emery's Investments Trusts, Emery* v *Emery*.)

Reichert v Dresdner Bank (Case C–115/88) [420]
[1990] ECR 27 (European Court of Justice)

German nationals resident in Germany donated the legal ownership of a property they owned in France to their son who was also a German national residing in Germany. However, the bank, as a creditor of the Reichert's and whose registered office was in Germany, challenged the donation before a French court, within whose judicial district the immovable property in question was situated, by bringing an action paulienne (a revocatory action brought by a creditor whereby transactions entered into by his debtor in fraud of the creditor's rights may be declared ineffective as against the creditor in so far only as his interests are prejudiced) under provisions of the French civil code. The bank relied on Article 16(1) (as it then was) of the Brussels Convention 1968 in that it provided that: 'in proceedings which have as their object rights in rem in immovable property or tenancies of immovable property, the courts of the Contracting State in which the property is situated' are to have exclusive jurisdiction. The court decided that it had the jurisdiction to hear the complaint, but on appeal by the Reichert's, the French Court of Appeal sought a preliminary ruling from the ECJ on the interpretation of Article 16(1). *Held*, 'An action whereby a creditor seeks to have a disposition of a right in rem of immovable property rendered ineffective as against him on the ground that it was made in fraud of his rights by his debtor does not come within the scope of Article 16(1) of the convention.' (See also *Reichert* v *Dresdner Bank (Case C–261/90)*.)

Reichert v Dresdner Bank (Case C–261/90) [421]
[1992] ECR 2149 (European Court of Justice)

Prior to the ECJ delivering its judgment in the earlier case (C–115/88) of the same name, the Dresdner Bank applied to the same French Court of Appeal to supplement the question referred to the ECJ by seeking rulings on Articles 5(3),

16(5) and 24 of the Brussels Convention 1968. The bank claimed that this was necessary because, in the event of a negative answer to the first question raised, it would not be known whether the French court of first instance had jurisdiction under the aforementioned Articles. Despite objections from the Reichert's, a supplementary question was referred to the ECJ by the French Court of Appeal. *Held*, 'An action provided for by national law, such as the action paulienne in French law, whereby a creditor seeks to obtain the revocation in regard to him of a transfer of a right in rem in immovable property by his debtor in a way which the creditor regards as being in fraud of his rights does not come within the scope of Articles 5(3), 16(5) or 24 of the [Brussels] Convention 1968 ...'. (See also *Reichert v Dresdner Bank (Case C-115/88).*)

Republic of Haiti v Duvalier see **Haiti, Republic of v Duvalier**

Republic of India and the Government of the Republic of India (Ministry of Defence) v India Steamship Co, The Indian Grace see **India, Republic of, and the Government of the Republic of India (Ministry of Defence) v India Steamship Co, The Indian Grace**

Rich (Marc) & Co v Societa Italiana Impianti PA, The Atlantic Emperor (Case C–190/89) [1992] 1 Lloyd's Rep 342 (European Court of Justice) [422]

Here a dispute had arisen between M, the Swiss purchaser, and Impianti (S), the Italian seller of a cargo of Iranian crude oil. The dispute arose because the oil was contaminated with 58,000 tons of water. M had telexed S the terms of the contract, one of which subjected the contract to English law and provided for arbitration in London. However, S did not reply to this telex. Whereas a significant part of the dispute revolved around the issue of whether the telexed terms were part of the contract, the principal issue concerned whether M's request to the English court to appoint an arbitrator came within the Brussels Convention on Jurisdiction and the Enforcement of Judgments in Civil and Commercial Matters. S alleged that it did on the basis that it was a commercial matter and, by coming within the scope of the Convention, S could only be sued in their own jurisdiction unless it could be proved that they had contracted to submit to another jurisdiction (Article 2). Otherwise, contended S, it would be possible to evade the application of the Convention simply by alleging the existence of an arbitration clause. *Held*, reference solely to the subject matter of the dispute would suffice to determine whether the dispute was within the scope of the Convention. Here, the reference was to 'arbitration'. Accordingly, it was irrelevant that the validity or otherwise of the arbitration term was to be determined as a preliminary point: once the subject matter of the dispute came within an excluded category then the litigation fell outside the scope of the Convention.

Rich (Marc) & Co AG v Societa Italiana Impianti PA, The Atlantic Emperor (No 2) [1992] 1 Lloyd's Rep 624 (Court of Appeal) [423]

Prior to the decision of the ECJ in the earlier *Atlantic Emperor* case (*Marc Rich & Co v Societa Italiana Impianti PA*), the defendants, S, had sought in Italy a declaration of non-liability in respect of the sale of the contaminated oil and, in England, to set aside an order granting M leave to serve S out of the jurisdiction because the dispute should be resolved in Italy. In Italy, the plaintiffs' contention that the Italian courts lacked jurisdiction because of the arbitration agreement and that Italian proceedings should be stayed was rejected. Moreover, the Italian court decided that there was no binding arbitration agreement and that Italy was the only relevant jurisdiction as that it was in Italy that the contract was made. M's application in England for an injunction restraining S from continuing with the Italian proceedings until the result of the arbitration was published was dismissed. Furthermore, HOBHOUSE J decided, inter alia, that M had submitted to the jurisdiction of the Italian courts by virtue of 'one further factor', which was that the plaintiffs further lodging of pleadings before the Italian courts in May 1991, could not 'be viewed other than as a submission to the jurisdiction of the Italian court to decide the substantive question'. M had not merely contested the jurisdiction of the Italian courts, but they had contested 'the claim of the opposing party to be free of liability'. M's pleading was 'a step taken in the face of the court which is neither necessary for the purpose of disputing the jurisdiction nor relevant to such a dispute. It is inconsistent with continuing to reject the jurisdiction of the [Italian] court ...'. *Held*, M's appeal against this decision would be rejected, NEIL LJ repeating part of HOBHOUSE J's judgment at first instance. Thus, M was bound by the Italian court's decision that the contract did not contain an arbitration clause.

Rosler v Hilbery [1925] 1 Ch 250 (Court of Appeal) [424]

A Belgian company, having been found to have a preponderance of enemy interest therein, had been ordered to be wound up by the Belgian court; and an English company was being wound up under the Trading With the Enemy Acts. The English company owed the Belgian company £22,500. The defendants were the sequestrator, C, in Belgium and H, a solicitor, in England. The sequestrator had asked the English court to order the £22,500 to be paid to H who gave an undertaking not to part with it until further order. However, the three plaintiffs, who were members of the Belgian company and all of whom were resident abroad, issued a writ claiming, inter alia, (1) an injunction to restrain H from parting with the £22,500 otherwise than with the consent of the plaintiffs or order of the court; (2) an inquiry as to how much of such sum was due and payable to the plaintiffs respectively; and (3) an order on H to pay such amounts to the plaintiffs respectively. The writ was served on H and leave was obtained to serve an order out of the jurisdiction on C. C applied to have the order discharged. RUSSELL J (and later the Court of Appeal) said 'the forum conveniens in this case is the Belgian, and not the British court'. Accordingly, the order for substituted service was discharged and service of the notice of the writ on C was set aside. The plaintiffs appealed. *Held*, the appeal would be dismissed on the grounds given by RUSSELL J. Further, the action against H was not part of the substantive relief sought: 'I do not think ... that an injunction of such a fleeting nature is the sort of injunction which is referred to or indeed to be included in [the then sub rule of RSC O.11]' (*per* POLLOCK MR); and as C was the primary defendant, not H, C could not be a necessary or proper party to a claim in this case: 'the terms of [the then sub-rule of RSC O.11] are precisely inverted here' (*per* SARGANT LJ).

Rosler v Rottwinkel (Case 241/83) [425]
[1986] 1 QB 33 (European Court of Justice)

The plaintiff agreed to let to the defendant a flat in his holiday villa in Italy for three weeks. The plaintiff, who stayed at the villa at the same time as the defendant, claimed that the defendant had breached terms of the agreement by, inter alia, accommodating more than four people, causing noise and damage, and spoiling the plaintiff's holiday. The plaintiff sued the defendant in Germany where they both lived. However, the judge decided that the Italian courts had exclusive jurisdiction under Article 16(1) of the Brussels Convention 1968 which (at the relevant time) provided that: 'The following courts shall have exclusive jurisdiction, regardless of domicile: (1) in proceedings which have as their object rights in rem in, or tenancies of, immovable property, the courts of the Contracting State in which the property is situated ...'. After appeals both by the plaintiff and the defendant, the German Federal Court sought a preliminary ruling from the ECJ on whether Article 16(1) applied to a short-term holiday letting and, if so, whether it applied to actions for damages for breach of the lease and for the recovery of incidental charges payable under the lease. *Held*, 'The raison d'etre of the exclusive jurisdiction conferred by Article 16(1) on the courts of the Contracting State in which the property is situated is the fact that tenancies are closely bound up with the law of immovable property and with the provisions, generally of a mandatory character, governing its use, such as legislation controlling the level of rents and protecting the rights of tenants ... Article 16(1) seeks to ensure a rational allocation of jurisdiction by opting for a solution whereby the court having jurisdiction is determined on the basis of its proximity to the property since that court is in a better position to obtain first-hand knowledge of the facts relating to the creation of tenancies and to the performance of the terms thereof. ... [Accordingly] ... The reply to the first question must therefore be that Article 16(1) of the Convention applies to all lettings of immovable property, even for a short term and even where they relate only to the use and occupation of a holiday home.' With regard to the second question, 'Disputes concerning the obligations of the landlord or of the tenant under the terms of the tenancy fall within that exclusive jurisdiction. On the other hand, disputes which are only indirectly related to the use of the property let, such as those concerning the loss of holiday enjoyment and travel expenses, do not fall within the exclusive jurisdiction conferred by that Article.' (Contrast *Hacker* v *Euro Relais* and *Lieber* v *Gobel*.)

Rose Mary, The see Anglo-Iranian Oil Co Ltd v Jaffrate, The Rose Mary

Ross v Ellison (or Ross) [1930] AC 1 (House of Lords) [426]

A Scottish nobleman, whose domicile of origin was in Scotland, lived in New York, USA, for the four years preceding divorce proceedings instituted by his wife in the Scottish courts. During his period of residence in New York, he informed business associates of his intention to settle there permanently. At other times, however, in correspondence with his wife, he said that he thought of Scotland as his home. In the divorce proceedings, he contested the jurisdiction of the Scottish courts on the basis that he had acquired a domicil in the USA. *Held*, he had failed to show that his Scottish domicile of origin had been supplanted by a domicile of choice in any state of the USA. 'Declarations as to intention are rightly regarded in determining the question of change of domicile, but they must be examined by considering the person to whom the purposes for which, and the circumstances in which they are made and they must further be fortified and carried into effect by conduct and action consistent with the declared expression' (*per* LORD BUCKMASTER). (See also *Wahl* v *Attorney General*.)

Ross, Re, Ross v Waterfield [1930] 1 Ch 377 [427]

An English testatrix died domiciled in Italy without leaving to her son any of her property, which comprised movables in England and Italy and immovables in Italy. Under Italian law, a son was entitled to a 'compulsory portion' of his parent's estate, but Italian courts referred succession to the property of aliens to their lex nationalis. *Held*, the testatrix could validly exclude her son. The succession was primarily governed by Italian law, being the law of the country of domicile and the lex situs of the immovables. But 'the English courts have generally, if not invariably, meant by 'the law of the country of domicile' the whole law of that country as administered by the courts of that country' (*per* LUXMOORE J), and 'lex situs' was to be similarly construed. Here, an Italian court would refer succession to the domestic law of England, so this was the law to apply. (See also *Re Askew, Marjoribanks* v *Askew*; but compare *Re United Railways of Havana and Regla Warehouses Ltd*.)

Rossano v Manufacturers' Life Insurance Co [428]
[1963] 2 QB 352

The plaintiff, an Egyptian national residing in Egypt, applied for three endowment policies at the Cairo office of the defendant, an insurance company incorporated in Ontario, Canada, with branches in many countries. The policies were ultimately executed at the defendant's head office in Ontario on a form prepared there and were paid for in Cairo. They stipulated for payment of the policy moneys in sterling or US dollars in London or New York. When the plaintiff claimed the policy moneys, the defendant raised two defences: (1) that Egyptian legislation forbade payments in foreign currency between two residents of Egypt; and (2) that the Egyptian revenue authorities had served garnishee orders on the defendant in Cairo in respect of a tax claim against the plaintiff. *Held*, both these defences would fail: (1) because Egyptian law did not apply, being neither the lex loci solutionis nor the proper law (Ontario law was the proper law by virtue of the imputed intention of the parties, even though the law with which the transaction had its closest and most real connection might well be Egyptian law); and (2) because an English court would not recognise or enforce directly or indirectly a foreign revenue law of claim. (See also *R* v *International Trustee for the Protection of Bondholders AG*.)

Russell (John) v Cayzer, Irvine and Co Ltd [429]
[1916] 2 AC 298 (House of Lords)

The plaintiffs had shipped goods from England to India, the intended port of destination being Calcutta. The cargo-carrying ship, *Masunda*, was owned by a Scottish company and was under charter to Clan Line Steamers of which Cayzer, Irvine, were the managers and, in due course, the defendants. They, too, were domiciled in Scotland. When the *Masunda* arrived at Madras, it was requisitioned by the Indian Government and its cargo was discharged there. The defendants, without the knowledge or consent of the cargo owners, loaded the cargo on another vessel of the same line which was bound for Calcutta. That vessel was sunk en route by a German cruiser and all its cargo was lost. The plaintiffs sued the shipowners and the defendants claiming 'damages for breach of contract or duty in and about the carriage of goods by sea and/or for trespassing against or wrongfully depriving the plaintiffs of such goods and converting the same'. The plaintiffs issued a writ that was endorsed 'Not for service out of the jurisdiction.' London solicitors accepted service of the writ on behalf of the shipowners and gave an undertaking that they would appear in due course. The plaintiffs then sought leave to serve a concurrent writ out of the jurisdiction against the managers, Cayzer, Irvine, under RSC O.11. This was granted by the Court of Appeal. The defendants sought to rescind the order of the Court of Appeal and to set aside service of the writ. *Held*, 'The root principle of the English law about jurisdiction is that ... whoever is served with the King's writ, and can be compelled consequently to submit to the decree made, is a person over whom the court's have jurisdiction' (*per* VISCOUNT HALDANE). The question to be addressed, however, was whether the action was one which was properly brought within the meaning of (what is now) RSC O.11, r.1(1)(c). That provided that where: 'any person out of the jurisdiction is a necessary or proper party to an action properly brought against some other person duly served within the jurisdiction', service out of the jurisdiction may be allowed. A unanimous House of Lords was of the opinion that the action was not 'properly brought' as the writ was 'Not for service out of the jurisdiction.' 'The words "properly brought" enure to the protection of the person out of the jurisdiction whom it is proposed to serve with process. His protection is not to be found exclusively in the words "necessary or proper party". ... the persons who are already defendants in the action, although they may submit to the jurisdiction and so preclude themselves from raising any objection, cannot by that procedure affect the rights of third parties' (per LORD SUMNER). (See also *Witted* v *Galbraith*.)

SA Consortium General Textiles v Sun and Sand Agencies [1978] 1 QB 279 (Court of Appeal) [430]

The defendant objected to the enforcement of part of a French judgment for 10,000 francs awarded on account of his 'resistance abusive', or unjustified opposition to the plaintiff's claim, on the ground that the sum was for punitive or exemplary damages and so a penalty. *Held*, 'The word "penalty" in this statute [the Foreign Judgments (Reciprocal Enforcement) Act 1933] means, I think, a sum payable to the state by way of punishment and not a sum payable to a private individual, even though it is payable by way of exemplary damages' (per LORD DENNING MR). (See also *Huntington* v *Attrill* and *Raulin* v *Fischer*.)

Sabbagh v Sabbagh [1984] FLR 29 [431]

Shortly after the marriage in Brazil of Brazilian domiciliaries in 1965, the parties to the marriage moved to England where they acquired an English domicile of choice. They lived together until 1980 when the wife petitioned for divorce and the husband left England to return permanently to Brazil. In 1983, the husband obtained a decree of judicial separation in Brazil. Whereas there was no requirement in Brazilian law for the wife to be informed of the hearing of the petition she was, in fact, informed of the first instance hearing but not of the appeal proceedings. The effect of the decree was, inter alia, to freeze the proprietary rights of the parties without dissolving the marriage. Moreover, after three years either party could apply for divorce though they could not vary the property rights or review the grounds on which the decree was granted. Thus, the two questions which fell to be answered by the English court were whether it should recognise the Brazilian decree and whether it had jurisdiction to entertain the wife's claim for ancillary relief on the grant of an English decree of divorce. *Held*, (1) since there was no basis on which it could be said that recognition of the Brazilian decree was contrary to public policy, the decree of judicial separation obtained by the husband would be recognised; and (2) with regard to the purported effect of the Brazilian decree, 'there is no basis here for the contention that the Brazilian decree of judicial separation will have the effect of excluding the English courts' powers to deal with the wife's financial application once she has been granted a decree of divorce in England ...' (per BALCOMBE J). (See also *Mamdani* v *Mamdani* and s48 of the Family Law Act 1986)

Sadler v Robins (1808) 1 Camp 253 [432]

The plaintiff obtained a decree in Jamaica ordering the defendant and various other persons to pay him £3,670, with interest, less their costs to be taxed by a Master of the Court. *Held*, the plaintiff could not enforce the judgment against the defendant in England without first having the costs taxed, because until this was done the amount payable was unascertained. (But see *Beatty* v *Beatty*.)

St Pierre v South American Stores (Gath and Chaves) Ltd [433]
[1936] 1 KB 382 (Court of Appeal)

The defendants, two English companies, took a lease of land in Chile from the plaintiffs, who were Chileans. The defendants brought an action in Chile to determine the mode of payment of rent, then the plaintiffs sued the defendants in England to recover arrears of rent. The defendants (1) contested jurisdiction and (2) sought a stay of proceedings. *Held*, (1) the English court had jurisdiction even though foreign land was involved, because the defendants' obligation to pay rent was a personal one under the contract of lease; and (2) to obtain a stay, the defendants, being plaintiffs in the Chilean proceedings, had to prove that continuance of the English action would be oppressive or vexatious or an abuse of the court's process *and* that a stay would not cause injustice to the plaintiffs. This they had failed to do. (Compare *British South Africa Co* v *Companhia de Mocambique*.)

Salvesen (or Von Lorang) v Administrator of [434]
Austrian Property [1927] AC 641 (House of Lords)

A domiciled Austrian married a British woman of Scottish domicile in Paris. Subsequently, the wife obtained a decree of nullity from a court in Germany, where she and her husband had become domiciled. The ground of the decree was that the marriage ceremony did not comply with either French or Austrian law. In Scottish proceedings by the Administrator of Austrian Property, the validity of the decree was challenged. *Held,* since the decree was pronounced in the court of the common domicile of the spouses, it was valid against all the world. It was tantamount to a judgment in rem, because it affected the spouses' status. (See also *Abate* v *Abate (orse Cauvin)* and *Chapelle* v *Chapelle*.)

SAR Schotte GmbH v Parfums Rothschild SARL [435]
(Case 218/86) [1987] ECR 4905 (European Court of Justice)

Schotte contracted with Rothschild GmbH (Germany) to produce atomiser pumps for Rothschild SARL (France). The 'French Rothschild', SARL, was a wholly owned subsidiary of the 'German Rothschild'. As agreed, invoices for the work done by Schotte were submitted to the French subsidiary. However, complaints that the atomisers did not satisfy customer requirements were sent to Schotte by the German parent company, the letters being written on Rothschild GmbH headed notepaper and signed by a director of the French subsidiary and a director of Rothschild GmbH. Schotte claimed payment for work done from the German parent company as they had not been paid by SARL. When Rothschild GmbH denied that it owed the money, Schotte brought proceedings against SARL before the German Regional Court, claiming that Rothschild GmbH was in reality an 'establishment' of SARL within the meaning of Article 5(5) of the Brussels Convention 1968. SARL contested the jurisdiction of the German courts and said that, contrary to Schotte's claims, it (SARL) was a wholly-owned subsidiary of Rothschild GmbH. Furthermore, SARL contended that there was no dispute arising out of the 'operations' (of a branch, agency or other establishment) as required by Article 5(5). A reference was made to the ECJ for a preliminary ruling. *Held*, 'Article 5(5) of the [Brussels] Convention 1968 ... must be interpreted as applying to a case in which a legal entity established in a Contracting State maintains no dependent branch, agency or other establishment in another Contracting State but nevertheless pursues its activities there through an independent company with the same name and identical management which negotiates and conducts business in its name and which it uses as an extension of itself.' (See also *de Bloos* v *Bouyer* and *Blanckaert & Willems* v *Trost*.)

Sargasso, The see Neste Chemicals SA v DK Line SA

Saxby v Fulton [1909] 2 KB 208 (Court of Appeal) [436]

The plaintiff lent money to the defendant to enable him to play roulette at Monte Carlo. This form of gambling was legal in Monte Carlo but not under the English gaming statutes. *Held*, the plaintiff could recover the loan in England, because the gaming statutes did not purport to strike down foreign contracts of loan made to enable gambling to take place in a country where it was legal, and it was not contrary to public policy for such a contract to be enforced in an English court. (See also *Addison* v *Brown*.)

Sayers v International Drilling Co NV [437]
[1971] 1 WLR 1176 (Court of Appeal)

Sayers, an English employee of a Dutch company, was engaged in England to work on an oil-rig in Nigerian territorial waters. He sued his employer when he was injured by the negligence of a fellow employee. *Held*, his claim could not succeed. An exemption clause in his contract of employment was valid by the proper law of the contract – Dutch law – although it was void by English domestic law under s1(3) of the Law Reform (Personal Injuries) Act 1948. (Contrast *Coupland* v *Arabian Gulf Petroleum Co* and *Johnson* v *Coventry Churchill*.)

Scarpetta v Lowenfield (1911) 27 TLR 509 [438]

The plaintiff was awarded damages by the Italian court for breach of contracts by the defendant. When the plaintiff sought to enforce the judgments in England, the defendant claimed that the decisions offended against English notions of substantial justice because, under Italian law, neither party in a case could give evidence on his own behalf. *Held*, the plaintiff could enforce the judgments because the Italian rule of evidence, having also been a rule of English law until 1846, did not offend against English notions of 'substantial justice'. (See also *Jacobson* v *Frachon*.)

Scherrens v Maenhout (Case 158/87) [439]
[1988] ECR 3791 (European Court of Justice)

A dispute arose out of a claim by an agricultural tenant that land in two Contracting States, Belgium and The Netherlands, was the subject of a single lease. The Dutch court observed that if the two parts of the farm had been situated in different cantons of The Netherlands, the court in the canton in which the main farm building was situated would have jurisdiction. However, in the absence of corresponding provisions in the Brussels Convention 1968, it fell to be decided whether the Belgian courts or the Dutch courts had jurisdiction in a case such as this. *Held*, 'Article 16(1) of the [Brussels] Convention 1968 ... must be interpreted as meaning that, in a dispute as to the existence of a lease relating to immovables situated in two Contracting States, exclusive jurisdiction over the immovable property situated in each Contracting State is held by the courts of that State.' (Contrast *Webb* v *Webb*.)

Schibsby v Westenholz (1870) LR 6 QB 155 [440]

Under the French Civil Code, an alien residing in France could invoke the jurisdiction of the French courts to enforce contractual obligations against non-residents. Relying on this, the plaintiff, a Dane, obtained a French default judgment for breach of a contract made in London against the defendants, who were Danes residing in England. *Held*, the plaintiff could not enforce this judgment in England, because the French court was not competent to bind the defendants. 'We think that ... the true principle on which the judgments of foreign tribunals are enforced in England is ... that the judgment of a court of competent jurisdiction over the defendant imposes a duty or obligation on the defendant to pay the sum for which judgment is given, which the courts in this country are bound to enforce; and consequently that anything which negatives that duty, or forms a legal excuse for not performing it, is a defence to the action' (*per* BLACKBURN J). (See also *Emanuel* v *Symon* and *Godard* v *Gray*.)

Schwebel v Ungar (1964) 48 DLR (2d) 644 [441]

A Hungarian Jewish married couple left Hungary, their country of domicile, and while temporarily in Italy were divorced by 'gett', an extra-judicial Jewish divorce. They then acquired a domicile of choice in Israel and the wife remarried in Ontario, Canada, her new husband being domiciled in that province. The 'gett' was entitled to recognition under Israeli law, but not Hungarian or Ontario law. *Held*, the wife's second marriage was valid, because she had capacity to enter into it under her lex domicilii at the time of celebration. The invalidity of the 'gett' under Ontario rules of recognition was irrelevant because 'the inquiry is as to her status' (*per* MACKAY JA). (But see *Warter* v *Warter*, compare *Brook* v *Brook*.)

Scott v Attorney-General (1886) 11 PD 128 [442]

A husband domiciled in South Africa obtained a divorce there on the ground of his wife's adultery. She came to England and remarried in spite of a South African law which prohibited remarriage by the guilty party after a divorce for so long as the innocent remained alive and unmarried. *Held*, her remarriage was valid. The divorce made her an 'unmarried person' despite the accompanying prohibition on remarriage, so she was free to settle in another jurisdiction and marry there. (But see *R* v *Brentwood Superintendent Registrar of Marriages, ex parte Arias* and (providing a statutory reversal of the decision in *Brentwood*) s50 of the Family Law Act 1986.)

Scullard's Estate, Re, Smith v Brock [1957] Ch 107 [443]

A wife left her husband and went to live permanently in Guernsey. She died there about six weeks after her husband's death, of which she was never told. His domicile since before the separation had been in England. *Held*, she died domiciled in Guernsey. Her residence and continuing intention to remain there established a domicile of choice as soon as her domicile of dependence ceased. She did not have to commit some 'new overt act' to acquire the new domicile. (See also *Re Cooke's Trusts*; compare *Harrison* v *Harrison*.)

Seaconsar Far East Ltd v Bank Markazi Jomhouri Islami Iran [1994] 1 AC 438 (House of Lords) [444]

The plaintiffs, international arms dealers, claimed nearly US$7,000,000 from the defendants for two shipments of artillery shells which had been delivered to the Iranian Ministry of Defence. After being twice refused payment, the plaintiffs sought leave to serve a writ out of the jurisdiction. At first instance this was granted in respect of the first presentation of the requisite documents but not the second (for the balance of US$4,000,000) because the claim was insufficiently strong on the merits. The plaintiffs appealed against the latter decision. The Court of Appeal, by a majority of 2-1, dismissed the appeal but granted the plaintiffs leave to appeal to the House of Lords. *Held*, (1) the standard of proof of good arguable case would determine whether the jurisdiction of the court was sufficiently established to grant leave to serve a writ out of the jurisdiction under RSC O.11 and there was no dispute that the plaintifs' claim came within O.11, r.1(1); and (2) in this case, the plaintiffs were able to discharge their burden of proof under rules 1(1) and 4 by demonstrating that there was a serious issue to be tried in that 'there [was] a substantial question of fact or law or both, arising on the facts disclosed by the affidavits …' (*per* LORD GOFF). Accordingly, the appeal would be allowed. (See also *Metall und Rohstoff* v *Donaldson Lufkin & Jenrette*.)

Seale's Marriage Settlement, Re [1961] Ch 574 [445]

A marriage settlement governed by English law was created when the parties to a marriage in England were living and domiciled in England. Later, they acquired a domicile in Quebec, Canada, and in order to minimise tax and estate duty and facilitate administration of the trusts, they created a settlement having Quebec law as its governing law, a Canadian company as the trustee and the same trusts as the English settlement. They then made an application under the Variation of Trusts Act 1958 for an order approving, on behalf of their two infant children, the transfer of the property in the English settlement to the Quebec settlement. *Held*, approval could and would be granted, even though this involved wholly replacing the English settlement with a settlement governed by Quebec law.

Selot's Trust, Re [1902] 1 Ch 488 [446]

A Frenchman living in Paris was declared a 'prodigal' by a French court under the Code Napoleon, on account of his extravagant habits. This meant, inter alia, that he could not receive money without the intervention of a legal adviser, judicially appointed. He applied to the Chancery Division for payment out of his share of a trust fund which the trustee had paid into court, but his official adviser opposed the application. *Held*, the money should nevertheless be paid to him, because (1) the French court's declaration did not change his status, but merely affected and modified it and 'affecting and modifying the status appears to me to be a very different thing from changing the status' (*per* FARWELL J); and (2) even if 'prodigality' was a status, it was a penal status, which would not be recognised in England. (See also *Worms* v *De Valdor*.)

Sennar (No 2), The, DSV Silo-und Verwaltungs-Gesellschaft MBH v Owners of The Sennar and 13 other ships [1985] 1 WLR 490 (House of Lords) [447]

The plaintiffs claimed against the owners of the *Sennar* and 13 sister ships an indemnity and/or damages for fraud and/or breach of duty and/or negligence in connection with the shipment of groundnut expellers loaded on the *Sennar* in Sudan in August/September 1973 for consignment to Rotterdam. The place and date of issue of the bill of lading, expressed to be signed by the master of the *Sennar*, were stated to be Port Sudan, 30 August 1973. However, it was later discovered that the loading had no been completed until 7 September 1973, by which time the price of groundnut expellers had fallen sharply. P1, the original purchasers, had taken up the shipping documents, including the bill of lading, before presenting the same documents to P2 who took them up and paid for them and then P2 presented them to P3 who, likewise, took them up and paid for them. On discovering the discrepancy in the dates of loading, P3 claimed against P2, rejecting the shipping documents, for reimbursement of the price paid by P3. An award in favour of P3 and the other claimant buyers (P2 and P1) was made by arbitrators. However, whereas P3 were reimbursed by P2, P2 failed to be reimbursed by P1 since P1 had become insolvent. Accordingly, P2 took possession of the goods and sold them to mitigate their loss. They then arrested a sister ship of the *Sennar* and brought proceedings in the Dutch courts. There, it was held that P2 could not found a claim for damages in tort, and since there was an exclusive jurisdiction clause in the bill of lading in favour of the Sudanese courts, the Dutch courts were bound to decline jurisdiction. P2 then commenced an action in rem in England, having served a writ on another sister ship of the *Sennar*, which continued as an action in personam. The defendants sought a stay on the basis that Sudan was the appropriate forum and Sudanese law should apply. This was rejected at first instance but the decision was reversed by the Court of Appeal. *Held*, the plaintiffs' claim was barred by issue estoppel: the decision of the Dutch courts that they had no jurisdiction was a decision 'on the merits' of the case; and the issues there and in the Admiralty Court had been the same, viz, whether the exclusive jurisdiction clause in the bill of lading applied to the plaintiffs' claim – which it did. Whereas the plaintiffs' were able to found jurisdiction in England in rem, the plaintiffs' claim had no other connection with England and there was no reason to interfere with the exercise by the Court of Appeal of its discretion to grant the defendants the stay they sought. (On issue estoppel, see also *House of Spring Gardens v Waite*.)

Sfeir & Co v National Insurance Co of New Zealand Ltd [448]
[1964] 1 Lloyd's Rep 330

The plaintiffs, Sfeir & Co (S), who had brought actions in respect of claims for losses of various goods insured by the defendants under policies of marine insurance, had obtained judgments in the High Court of Ghana in default of appearance by the defendants (N) for substantial sums. They appealed when their application to register the judgment in England was set aside. Provisions of the Administration of Justice Act 1920 which were relevant to the appeal included s9(2) which provided, inter alia, that 'No judgment shall be ordered to be registered under this section if ... (b) the judgment debtor, being a person who was neither carrying on business nor ordinarily resident within the jurisdiction of the original court, did not voluntarily appear or otherwise submit or agree to submit to the jurisdiction of that court.' Relying on this, N contended that they did not at any material time carry on business in Ghana and, secondly, that they did not submit or agree to submit to the jurisdiction of the Ghanaian court. Glyndova (G) acted as N's claims settling agents in Ghana although they had no authority to settle claims for losses of more than £5 without submitting the claims to N for prior approval. N was incorporated in New Zealand where its directors were resident: it did not directly carry on any business in Ghana, nor own nor possess any real or personal property in Ghana, nor had they ever issued any policy of insurance there nor had they any agents there other than G. *Held, per* MOCATTA J, 'the limited authority possessed by [G] to bind the defendants [N] by settlements of claims arising in Ghana under the defendants' policies issued elsewhere ... did not amount to a carrying on business by [N] in Ghana'. Moreover, whatever was the proper law of the contract of marine insurance, 'the inclusion in the policy of the claims payable clause does not give rise to the necessary implication that the defendants, by issuing the policy impliedly submitted or agreed to submit to the jurisdiction of the courts of Ghana.' Accordingly, the appeal would be dismissed. (See also *Vogel v Kohnstamm*.)

Shaw v Gould (1868) LR 3 HL 55 (House of Lords)

Some years after the marriage in England of a domiciled couple, the wife bribed the husband to go to Scotland for 40 days in order to confer jurisdiction in divorce on the Scottish courts. She then obtained a Scottish divorce and soon after was married in Scotland to a second husband, an Englishman of Scottish domicile. On her death, her children by the second marriage claimed to inherit under an English will which left personalty to her 'children' and realty to her sons 'lawfully begotten'. *Held*, the claim would fail. Because of the first husband's English domicile and of the collusion practised by the parties, the Scottish divorce would not be recognised in England. This meant that the claimants' parents were not lawfully married and that they themselves were illegitimate and could not take under the will. (Contrast *Re Bischoffsheim, Cassel v Grant*; see also s15 of the Family Law Reform Act 1969.)

Shenavai v Kreischer (Case 266/85)
[1987] ECR 239 (European Court of Justice)

An architect based in Germany brought proceedings in a German court for the payment of fees for plans for holiday homes he drew up on the basis of an oral commission from the defendant who was domiciled in The Netherlands. The defendant denied that a contract had been concluded. Moreover, he contested the jurisdiction of the German court on the ground that his Netherlands domicile was the place of performance of the obligation to pay any debt that had accrued. In response to a question referred to the ECJ for a preliminary ruling the ECJ *Held*, 'For the purposes of determining the place of performance within the meaning of Article 5(1) of the [Brussels] convention 1968 ... the obligation to be taken into consideration in a dispute concerning proceedings for the recovery of fees commenced by an architect commissioned to draw up plans for the building of houses is the contractual obligation which forms the actual basis of legal proceedings.' (See also *Union Transport v Continental Lines*.)

Shevill v Presse Alliance SA (Case C-68/93) [1995] AC 18
(European Court of Justice)

A French newspaper (*France Soir*) had published an article alleging that a certain firm of bureaux de change operators and some of their employees were involved in the laundering of drug money. The firm, plus an English domiciled employee of the firm, sued the French domiciled owners of the newspaper for libel in England. A question to be answered was whether the English court had jurisdiction, particularly in view of the fact that only 250 copies of the offending newspaper had been sold in England. By contrast, the newspaper had a circulation of 200,000 in France. The House of Lords sought a preliminary ruling from the ECJ. *Held*, (1) since the libel had been published in England, that publication constituted a harmful event for the purposes of special jurisdiction under article 5(3) of the Brussels Convention 1968; (2) whereas the court of the jurisdiction in which the publisher was established or domiciled could award damages for the harm irrespective of where it was suffered, the court in another jurisdiction where the plaintiff suffered harm could award damages only for the harm suffered within its jurisdiction; (3) the substantive and evidential criteria to be applied by the national court in deciding whether and to what extent harm had occurred were governed not by the Convention, but by the national conflict of laws rules, provided that the effectiveness of the convention was not impaired. (Contrast *Re the Unauthorised Publication of Approved Photographs*.)

Showlag v Mansour [1994] 2 WLR 615 (Privy Council) [452]

The personal representatives of the late Sheik Showlag believed that money had been stolen from him before his death. In order to recover this money, they began proceedings in England and in Egypt. They obtained judgment in their favour in England on 5 December 1990. However, whereas an Egyptian court gave a similar judgment on 31 December 1990, the Egyptian Appeal Court reversed this decision in May 1991. In June 1991 the personal representatives sought to enforce the English judgment in Jersey where some of the money had been found. *Held*, giving judgment for the plaintiffs, the general rule was that where there were two competing foreign judgments each pronounced by a court of competent jurisdiction and otherwise entitled to recognition and enforcement, the first judgment should be recognised and given effect to the exclusion of the later judgment. Accordingly, the English judgment could be enforced.

Simonin (orse Mallac) v Mallac (1860) Sw & Tr 67 [453]

A domiciled Frenchman aged 29 married a domiciled Frenchwoman aged 22 in England. In French law the marriage was void because neither of them had requested parental consent, although if consent were not forthcoming after several requests over a period of three months, the marriage would be valid without it. The wife petitioned in England for a decree of nullity. *Held*, (1) the court had jurisdiction to hear the petition because the marriage had been celebrated in England; and (2) the marriage was valid because the requirement of a parental consent (being little more than a delaying procedure) was a formal requirement, and formalities were regulated by the lex loci celebrationis, not the lex domicilii. (See also *Padolecchia v Padolecchia*; but see *Ogden v Ogden (orse Philip)*.)

Sinha Peerage Claim, The [1946] 1 All ER 348n [454]
(House of Lords, Committee of Privileges)

A Bengalese Hindu, whose domicile at all times was in Bengal, contracted a marriage in Bengal according to the rites of a sect which allowed him to take more wives. He never exercised this right, but instead he and his wife changed to another Hindu sect, which practised monogamy. Later, they had a son and the husband was created a Baron by English Letters Patent. *Held*, on his death, his son could succeed to the peerage. The son was the lawful son of a marriage that had never been actually polygamous and had been rendered monogamous according to the spouses' lex domicilii by a change of a religious law occurring before the peerage was bestowed. (See also *Cheni (orse Rodriguez) v Cheni*.)

Siskina (owners of cargo lately laden on board), The v [455]
Distos Compania Naviera SA [1979] AC 210 (House of Lords)

Greek shipowners chartered their only ship, the *Siskina*, to Italian charterers for the carriage of general cargo from Italy to Saudi Arabia. However, when the ship arrived at the Suez Canal, the shipowners refused to take it through, claiming that the charterers had not paid the requisite charter freight. Instead, the shipowners ordered the ship to sail to Cyprus where they issued a writ in rem against the cargo claiming a lien for the balance of the charter freight. The ship was arrested in Cyprus and the cargo unloaded. the *Siskina* left Cyprus in ballast without cargo and sank in Greek waters two weeks later. The shipowners claimed on London underwriters for the total loss of the *Siskina*. Meanwhile, some cargo owners had applied to the Cyprus courts for release of their goods and for damages against the shipowners for the arrest of the cargo. Given that the shipowners had no assets other than the insurance money in respect of the *Siskina*, the plaintiff cargo owners applied for a writ in England for service out of the jurisdiction, claiming, inter alia, an injunction restraining the shipowners from disposing of the insurance money or from removing it out of the jurisdiction. *Held*, to come within (what is now) RSC O.11, r.1(1)(b), the injunction sought had to be part of the substantive relief to which the plaintiff's cause of action entitled him. This meant that what the defendant was sought to be restrained from doing in England would have to amount to the invasion of some legal or equitable right of the plaintiff's in England which was enforceable via a final judgment for an injunction. However, as the plaintiff had no legal or equitable right or interest in the insurance moneys payable, the writ would be set aside. (See, now, ss24 and 25 of the Civil Jurisdiction and Judgments Act 1982.)

SISRO v Ampersand Software BV see Société d' Informatique Service Réalisation Organisation v Ampersand Software BV

Smith Kline & French Laboratories v Bloch [456]
[1983] 1 WLR 730 (Court of Appeal)

Under a written agreement made in England, B gave the wholly owned English subsidiary of a multinational corporation the sole right to develop and market a drug he had formulated. However, when, subsequently, the subsidiary company made the decision not to proceed with further development of the drug, B commenced proceedings in Pennsylvania (the home of the parent company) contending that discontinuation of development amounted to an actionable breach of contract on the part of the American parent and its English subsidiary. B's contention was not successful at first instance, but the subsidiary was granted an injunction restraining B from proceeding further with the American action. *Held*, dismissing B's appeal, application of the test of whether justice could be done in England at significantly less cost and inconvenience than if the Pennsylvanian proceedings were allowed to continue, without depriving B of any legitimate advantage, illustrated that England was clearly the more appropriate forum. That B was on legal aid meant that he would derive no advantage from the American contingency fee system; whereas discovery in English law differed from that in Pennsylvania it was sufficiently adequate to ensure that B would be at no disadvantage; and, if he succeeded in Pennsylvania, it was likely that the Pennsylvania court would apply English law to the quantum of damages. The Court of Appeal agreed that the judge at first instance had been correct in granting the injunction. (See also *Connelly* v *RTZ Corporation plc;* contrast *Castanho* v *Brown & Root.*)

Société d'Informatique Service Réalisation Organisation [457]
v Ampersand Software BV (1993) The Times 29 July
(Court of Appeal)

SISRO obtained judgment in France against Ampersand for breach of copyright. Ampersand had appealed in France, claiming that the judgment had been obtained by fraud. Ampersand had also appealed in England against an order that the French judgment should be registered. The appeal was brought under Article 27 of the Brussels Convention 1968 which provided that: 'A judgment shall not be recognised: (1) If such recognition is contrary to public policy in the state in which recognition is sought.' Furthermore, Ampersand sought to stay proceedings pending the outcome of the French appeal. *Held*, since the allegation of fraud had been rejected by the French court, there was no ground under Articles 27 or 28 for refusing registration. Accordingly, it would not be against public policy to do so; but with regard to the application to stay proceedings pending the result of the

French appeal, the outcome would be dependent on whether Article 38 was free standing or subordinate to Article 37. Article 38 provides that: 'The court with which the appeal under ... Article 37 is lodged may, on the application of the appellant, stay the proceedings if an ordinary appeal has been lodged against the judgment in the State in which that judgment was given.' Article 37 provides that: 'An appeal against the decision authorising enforcement shall be lodged in accordance with the rules governing procedure in contentious matters: ... in England and Wales, with the High Court of Justice ...'. It was directed that the question of whether Article 38 is free standing should be referred to the European Court. (See below.)

Société d'Informatique Service Réalisation Organisation v Ampersand Software BV (Case C–432/93)
(1995) The Times 25 September (European Court of Justice)

In 1993, the Court of Appeal (see previous case) had requested the ECJ to give a preliminary ruling on the question of whether Article 38 of the Brussels Convention 1968 was free standing or whether it was subordinate to Article 37. If it was the latter, it meant that a court could only grant a stay pending a decision on whether the judgment to be enforced should or should not be refused recognition on one or other of the grounds set out in Articles 27 and 28. Article 37 provides that: 'An appeal against the decision authorising enforcement shall be lodged in accordance with the rules governing procedure in contentious matters: ... in the United Kingdom: (1) in England and Wales, with the High Court of Justice ... The judgment given on the appeal may be contested only: ... in the United Kingdom, by a single further appeal on a point of law.' Article 38 provides that: 'The court with which the appeal under the first paragraph of Article 37 is lodged may, on the application of the appellant, stay the proceedings if an ordinary appeal has been lodged against the judgment in the State in which that judgment was given ...'. The ECJ referred to the Jenard and Schlosser Reports and noted that they required the second paragraph of Article 37 to be interpreted strictly and, indeed, the ECJ had, on previous occassions, favoured a restrictive interpretation of the phrase 'judgment given on the appeal' in Article 37: *Van Dalfsen v Van Loon* was cited as an example. *Held*, 'Articles 37 and 38 of the 1968 Convention, as amended, were to be interpreted as meaning that a decision by which a court of a Contracting State, seised of an appeal against authorisation to enforce an enforceable judgment of a court in another Contracting State, refused a stay or lifted a stay previously ordered, could not be contested by an appeal in cassation or similar form of appeal limited to the examination of points of law only.'

Société Nationale Industrielle Aerospatiale v Lee Kui Jak [1987] 1 AC 871 (Privy Council)

Y had been in a helicopter crash in Brunei. The plaintiffs (Y's widow and the administrators of the estate of Y) had instituted actions in Brunei and Texas against S, the helicopter manufacturers, and M, the helicopter operators. Jurisdiction in the Texas proceedings was based on the fact that S did business in Texas – and that was sufficient to give the Texas courts jurisdiction. The dispute had nothing to do with Texas other than the 'business connection' and Texas having product liability laws favourable to the plaintiffs. *Held*, an injunction would be granted restraining the plaintiffs from pursuing the Texas proceedings. The natural forum for the trial of the plaintiffs action against S was Brunei. Trial in Texas would involve serious injustice to S amounting to oppression in that the company might be unable to claim a contribution from M in the Texas proceedings: they would then have to institute proceedings against M in Brunei to try and rectify this injustice. For the plaintiffs, however, they would not be deprived of any advantages by proceeding with the trial in Brunei: S had already given an undertaking that evidence already obtained in the Texas proceedings would be unavailable in Brunei proceedings. (Contrast *Castanho v Brown & Root* and *Spiliada Maritime Corporation v Cansulex*.)

Solo Kleinmotoren v Emilio Boch (Case 414/92) [460]
[1992] ECR 2237 (European Court of Justice)

Bloch, an Italian businessman, ran a business in Milan, Italy, under the name 'SOLO' dealing with agricultural machinery supplied by a German company, Solo Kleinmorten. However, when another company began business in Italy under the name SOLO Italiana SpA and Mr Bloch's supplies were discontinued, he commenced two actions in Italy. The first action was against the German suppliers for breach of contract, and the second was against the suppliers and the new Italian company for misuse of a trade name and unfair competition. Bloch succeeded in his first claim for damages for breach of contract and the judgment was declared enforceable in Germany. However, following the German supplier's appeal to a German court, and at the suggestion of that court, the parties reached a settlement. Bloch also succeeded in his second claim when, again, he was awarded damages. The Italian court did not agree with the contention that Bloch's claims had been satisfied in their entirety in the German settlement, saying that, inter alia, that that was a judgment which had not been declared enforceable in Italy and, in any case, the settlement was unrelated to the present Italian case. Solo Kleinmorten's appeals to Italian courts on the issue of the alleged finality of the German settlement were dismissed on the basis that the issue had already been dealth with and, therefore, it was, res judicata. Finally, Solo Kleinmorten appealed to a German court against an order enforcing the judgment of the Italian court in the second, contested action, the appeal being based on Article 27(3) of the Brussels Convention 1968 which provides that: 'A judgment shall not be recognised if the judgment is irreconcilable with a judgment given in a dispute between the same parties in the State in which recognition is sought.' The German court then sought a preliminary ruling from the ECJ on whether a court settlement could be regarded as a judgment which would bar recognition under Article 27(3). *Held*, it did not. The ECJ stated: 'Article 27(3) of the [Brussels Convention] is to be interpreted as meaning that an enforceable settlement reached before a court of the State in which recognition is sought in order to settle legal proceedings which are in progress does not constitute a "judgment" within the meaning of that provision, "given in a dispute between the same parties in the State in which recognition is sought" which, under the Convention, may preclude recognition and enforcement of a judgment given in another Contracting State.' (See also *Hoffman v Krieg*.)

Sonntag v Waidmann (Case C–172/91) (1993) [461]
The Independent 24 May (European Court of Justice)

An action for damages was brought before a German criminal court against a teacher whose illegal and culpable breach of duty had injured a pupil in a school trip to another Member State. The criminal act had already been the subject of criminal proceedings. *Held*, even though insurance cover was provided for such liability by a scheme of social insurance under public law, the claim for damages was a 'civil matter' under Article 1(1) of the Brussels Convention 1968. (See also *Menten v The Federal Republic of Germany*.)

Sottomayor (orse De Barros) v De Barros (No 1) [462]
(1877) 3 PD 1 (Court of Appeal)

Two first cousins, being domiciled Portuguese subjects, were married to each other in England. Under English law this marriage was valid, but it was void for consanguinity under Portuguese law except when a Papal dispensation had been obtained, and this had not been done. *Held*, the marriage was void because, despite the provision for dispensation, the Portuguese prohibition related to capacity, not formal validity, and 'as in other contracts, so in that of marriage, personal capacity must depend on the law of the domicile' (*per* COTTON LJ). (But see *Sottomayor (orse De Barros) v De Barros (No 2)*.)

Sottomayor (orse De Barros) v De Barros (No 2) [463]
(1879) 5 PD 94

In proceedings after the judgment in *Sottomayor v De Barros (No 1)*, it emerged that the husband in that case was domiciled in England, not Portugal. *Held*, this meant that the marriage was valid after all. Where the husband in a marriage celebrated in England was domiciled in England and the marriage was valid in English law, it was not to be rendered void by the fact that the wife had a foreign domicile whose law imposed an incapacity not recognised by English law. (See also *Chetti v Chetti*; but see *Sottomayor (orse De Barros) v De Barros (No 1)*.)

South Carolina Insurance Co v Assurantie Maatschappij [464]
De Zeven Provincein NV [1987] 1 AC 24 (House of Lords)

The plaintiffs, an American insurance company, brought an action in England against the defendants, a number of other insurance companies of different domiciles, under a contract of reinsurance. The defendants had commenced proceedings in the USA for pre-trial discovery of documents relevant to the claim against persons resident there who were not parties to the English action. The plaintiffs sought an injunction restraining the defendants from continuing with the American proceedings. *Held*, unanimoulsy, no injunction would be granted if: (1) a party to an action had invaded or threatened to invade a legal or equitable right of another; or (2) where one party had behaved or threatened to behave in a manner which was unconscionable. On the facts of the case, no injunction was necessary. (Applied: *Castanho v Brown & Root* and *British Airways Board v Laker Airways Ltd*.)

South India Shipping Corp Ltd v Export-Import [465]
Bank of Korea [1985] 1 WLR 585 (Court of Appeal)

The plaintiffs, who were incorporated in India, served a writ on the defendant bank in London, although the bank did not carry on in London the recognised banking practices of accepting deposits and making loans. However, within the jurisdiction the bank had premises and staff; it conducted external relations with other banks; it carried out the necessary line of enquiries prior to obtaining loans for clients; it sought to publicise its activities; and it encouraged trade between the UK. Had the bank established a place of business in England? *Held*, 'a company established a place of business within Great Britain if it carried on part of its business activities within the jurisdiction and it was not necessary for those activities to be either a substantial part of or more than incidental to the main objects of the company' (*per* ACKNER LJ). (See, now, ss691 and 695 of the Companies Act 1985, as amended.)

Spiliada Maritime Corporation v Cansulex [466]
[1987] AC 460 (House of Lords)

A cargo of sulphur was shipped from British Columbia, Canada, to India on board the *Spiliada*. Severe corrosion was caused to the vessel, allegedly because the cargo was wet when loaded. The shipowners, Spiliada Maritime Corporation, a Liberian company, decided to sue the shippers, Cansulex Ltd, a British firm, in England and thus sought leave to serve Cansulex outside the jurisdiction. The bills of lading contained an express choice of English law, so the case plainly fell within RSC O.11, (r1)(d)(iii); but the question to answer was whether the court would exercise its discretion and allow service outside the jurisdiction. At the same time, a very similar action for sulphur damage (involving the same shippers but a different vessel, the *Cambridgeshire*) was being litigated in England, and the *Cambridgeshire* action involved many of the same solicitors, counsel and expert witnesses as were involved in the *Spiliada* action. (This suggested that trial in England of the *Spiliada* action might be more convenient.) If the shipowners were forced to sue in British Columbia, they would be faced with a defence of limitation in the British Columbian courts but were in time in England. *Held*, following an extensive review of the applicable law, the court should exercise its discretion in the interests of the parties and for the ends of justice. In the circumstances, taking the '*Cambridge* factor' into account, and the fact that English law was the proper law of the contract, England was the appropriate forum for the more suitable trial of the action. Leave would, therefore, be granted. The applicable law was summarised by LORD GOFF in six propositions, viz, '(a) The basic principle is that a stay will only be granted on the ground of forum non conveniens where the court is satisfied that there is some other available forum, having competent jurisdiction, which is the appropriate forum for the trial of the action, ie in which the case may be tried more suitably for the interests of all the parties and the ends of justice. [Note that the search is for an *appropriate* rather than a convenient forum.] (b) ... In general the burden of proof rests on the defendant to persuade the court to exercise its discretion to grant a stay ... [but] if the court is satisfied that there is another available forum which is the prima facie the appropriate forum for the trial of the action, the burden will then shift to the plaintiff to show that there are special circumstances by reason of which justice requires that the trial should nevertheless take place in this country ... (c) [Contrary to the position in the USA and Canada] ... I can see no reason why the English court should not refuse to grant a stay ... [where no particular forum can be described as the natural forum]. It is significant that in all the leading English cases where a stay has been granted there has been another clearly more appropriate forum ... In my opinion, the burden resting on the defendant is not just to show that England is not the natural or appropriate forum, but to establish that there is another available forum which is clearly or distinctly more appropriate ... [If] the connection of the defendant with the English forum is a fragile one (for example, if he is served with proceedings during a short visit to this country), it should be all the easier for him to prove that there is another clearly more appropriate forum for the trial overseas. (d) Since the question is whether there exists some other forum which is clearly more appropriate for the trial of the action, the court will look first to see what factors there are which point in the direction of another forum. These are the factors LORD DIPLOCK described [in *Macshannon* v *Rockware Glass*] as indicating that justice can be done in the other forum at 'substantially less inconvenience or expense'. [But] ... it may be more desirable ... to adopt the expression used by LORD KEITH in the *Abidin Daver* ... when he referred to the 'natural forum' as being 'that with which the action has the most real and substantial connection.' So it is for connecting factors in this sense that the court must first look; and these will include not only factors affecting convenience or expense (such as the availability of witnesses), but also other factors such as the law governing the relevant transaction ... and the places where the parties respectively reside or carry on business. (e) If, however, the court concludes at that stage that there is no other available forum which is clearly more appropriate for the trial of the action, it will ordinarily refuse a stay ... It is difficult to imagine circumstances when, in such a case, a stay may be granted. (f) If, however, the court concludes at that stage that there is some other available forum which prima facie is clearly more appropriate for the trial of the action, it will ordinarily grant a stay unless there are circumstances by reason of which justice requires that a stay should nevertheless not be granted. In this inquiry, the court will consider all the circumstances of the case, including circumstances which go beyond those taken into account when considering connecting factors with the other jurisdiction. One such factor can be the fact, if established objectively by cogent evidence, that the plaintiff will not obtain justice, in the foreign jurisdiction ... [but here] the burden of proof shifts to the plaintiff.' (See also *de Dampiere* v *de Dampiere*; contrast *SNIA* v *Lee Kui Jak*.)

Standard Chartered Bank v International Tin Council [1986] 3 All ER 257 [467]

When the ITC had entered into an agreement with the UK government, it had been accorded limited immunity under the International Tin Council Immunities and Privileges Order 1972; Article 6(1)(a) of the order provided that the ITC was granted 'immunity from jurisdiction and execution except ... to the extent that it [the ITC] shall have expressly waived such immunity in a particular case'. The ITC sought to rely on this immunity when it sued in respect of a £10,000,000 loan made to it by the Standard Chartered Bank. However, a term of the loan was that in the event of a dispute, the ITC would submit irrevocably to the English courts once the dispute had arisen: it could not submit in advance. (However, this is an argument expressly rejected by ss2(2) and 17(2) of the State Immunity Act 1978, and BINGHAM J applied the same principle to this case.) *Held*, international organisations (the ITC in this case) only enjoy such immunity as is granted by legislative instrument; and a true construction of Article 6(1)(a) revealed that there could be submission via prior written agreement.

Starkowski v Attorney-General [1954] AC 155 [468]
(House of Lords)

In 1945, a couple domiciled in Poland and resident in Austria were married in Austria in a religious ceremony, which was then insufficient under Austrian law to conclude a valid marriage. Shortly after, an Austrian statute was passed retrospectively validating such marriages providing they were registered. Through an oversight, the priest failed to register the marriage until 1949, by which time the couple had acquired a domicile in England. In 1950, the wife married another man in England. *Held*, this second marriage was void, because the first marriage was valid and subsisting. It was rendered formally valid by the retrospective statute, which should be allowed to operate according to its terms as part of the lex loci celebrationis, even though the couple were neither domiciled nor resident in Austria at the time when it was complied with. It might be otherwise if the second ceremony of marriage had taken place *before* the statute was passed or was complied with. (See also *Simonin (orse Mallac)* v *Mallac* and *Apt (orse Magnus)* v *Apt*.)

Star Texas, The, Star Shipping AS v China National Foreign Trade Transportation Corporation [469]
[1993] 2 Lloyd's Rep 445 (Court of Appeal)

The plaintiffs let their vessel, *Star Texas*, to the defendants for a period of one time chartered trip. A container in a consignment of chemicals, part of a cargo loaded in China, was found to be leaking while the *Star Texas* was in Singapore. Consequently, the *Star Texas* was required to return to China. The plaintiffs claimed that the vessel remained on hire during the return journey and they claimed more than US$300,000 for, inter alia, unpaid hire. In response to the plaintiffs' issue of a writ for service out of the jurisdiction, the defendants sought to set aside the service contending that it did not fall under any of the heads of RSC O.11, r.1 and they applied for a stay under s1 of the Arbitration Act 1975. The charter contained an arbitration clause, clause 35, which provided that: 'Any dispute arising under the charter is to be referred to arbitration in Beijing or London in defendant's option.' However, the plaintiffs retorted that s1 of the 1975 Act did not apply because the arbitration agreement was null and void, inoperative or incapable of being performed within s1(1). One of their contentions was that, since under clause 35 the choice of the venue for the arbitration was to be at the defendant's option, this necessarily imported into the contract what has come to be known as a floating proper law – which is a concept English law will not countenance. *Held, per* LLOYD LJ criticising the plaintiffs' argument for attaching too much importance to clause 35 as an indication of the parties' intentions as to the proper law of the contract and saying: 'Where the arbitration clause provides for a single situs ... then [it] provides a strong, although not conclusive, indication of what the parties intended as to the proper law of the contract, including the arbitration agreement. But where the arbitration clause provides for a dual situs, the indication that they intended both laws to apply, according to where the arbitration takes place, is much less strong. Suppose clause 35 had contained no provision as to where the arbitration was to take place ... It could not be argued with any hope of success that that was an indication that the parties intended the proper law of the contract to depend upon wherever the arbitration ultimately took place. [By analogy] I would therefore reject [the plaintiffs'] argument that these parties ... intended to adopt a floating proper law. The truth is that they probably never gave their minds to the matter at all. At all events, one cannot deduce from clause 35 what they would have intended if they had.' In the alternative, even if the parties had chosen a floating curial law for their contract, there was no good reason to see why a floating curial law invalidated an arbitration clause. Clause 35 was deemed to be valid and enforceable and 'the Chinese charterers were entitled to a stay of the English legal proceedings pursuant to s1 of the Arbitration Act 1975' (*per* STEYN LJ). (See also *Amin Rasheed* v *Kuwait Insurance Co.*)

Stevens v Head (1993) 67 ALJR 343 (High Court of Australia)   [470]

Mrs Stevens, a New Zealand citizen and resident, was on holiday in New South Wales, Australia, when she was injured in a road traffic accident. The motor vehicle which struck her was registered and insured in the neighbouring State of Queensland and driven by a Queensland resident. Mrs Stevens commenced proceedings in Queensland seeking damages for personal injuries. The driver of the vehicle that injured her admitted responsibility, but contended that as the accident occurred in New South Wales damages should be assessed according to the provisions of s79 of the Motor Accidents Act 1988 (NSW). If applicable, this would operate to limit the damages otherwise available at common law in respect of Mrs Stevens' injuries. Section 79(1) prohibited the awarding of any such damages 'unless the injured person's ability to lead a normal life is significantly impaired by the injury'. However, where the injured person was not disqualified by that sub-section, the following sub-sections dealt with the amount of damages which could be awarded up to a maximum sum for 'a most extreme case'. *Held* (by a majority), s79 was not to be construed as containing a substantive provision for the purposes of conflict of laws rules governing the assessment of damages for extraterritorial but intranational torts. Section 79 was a law which applied to the quantification of damages: it was procedural and, accordingly, the NSW limitation was to be disregarded in Queensland. The choice of law rule for intra-Australian torts is that of double actionability as propounded by the House of Lords in *Boys* v *Chaplin*.

Stone v Stone [1958] 1 WLR 1287 [471]

An American soldier domiciled in an American State was posted to England for a while, then to Korea, Japan and finally France. While stationed in France, he paid another visit to England and decided to settle there, so he took a lease of a room and spent all his subsequent leave there. *Held,* he thereby acquired a domicile of choice in England. His obligation as a soldier to reside chiefly where he was stationed in France did not prevent him from forming the necessary intention. (Contrast *Plummer* v *IRC*.)

Swedish Central Railway Co Ltd v Thompson [472]
[1925] AC 495 (House of Lords)

The Swedish Central Railway Co Ltd was a company incorporated in England in 1870 under the Companies Acts 1862–1867. The company's registered office was in London and the object of the company was to construct and run a railway in Sweden. In 1900, the company leased its railway to a traffic company for 50 years at an annual rent of £33,500, payable to the company in England. The company's articles of association were then altered for the purpose of removing the control and management of its business from England to Sweden. Thereafter, whereas general meetings of shareholders and directors meetings were held in Sweden, merely formal administrative business within the UK was transacted by a committee appointed by the directors of the company. The company appealed against a finding that it was resident in the UK for income tax purposes. *Held*, the company might have a residence in England as well as abroad because 'the central control and management of a company may be divided' (*per* VISCOUNT CAVE LC); and the evidence suggested that it was resident in England. (Contrast *De Beers Consolidated Mines* v *Howe*.)

Swiss Bank Corporation v Boehmische [473]
Industrial Bank [1923] 1 KB 673 (Court of Appeal)

A creditor obtained a judgment for its debt in England after submission to the jurisdiction by the debtor, a Czechoslovakian bank trading in Prague. The creditor then applied for a garnishee order against two other banks which were the judgment-debtor's agents in England and owed money to it in that capacity. *Held,* the order should be granted, because there was no real risk of the agents being ordered by a foreign court, in Czechoslovakia or anywhere else, to pay their debts over again to the judgment-debtor. As the judgment-debtor had submitted to the jurisdiction and the agents' debts were 'situated' and 'properly recoverable' in England, payment of them under an English garnishee order would be recognised abroad as a valid discharge.

Syal v Heyward [1948] 2 KB 443 (Court of Appeal) [474]

The plaintiff, an Indian moneylender, obtained judgment in India against the defendants for payment of 20,000 rupees due on a promissory note. The defendants had received due notice of the proceedings but did not file a defence. The plaintiff registered his judgment in England under the Foreign Judgments (Reciprocal Enforcement) Act 1933, but the defendants applied to set this aside under s4(1)(a)(iv). They alleged that in the Indian action the plaintiff had fraudulently misrepresented the amount of his loan to them to be the full 20,000 rupees in the promissory note, whereas he had only lent 10,800 rupees, and they argued that the court might have held the loan to be unenforceable under Indian law if it had known this fact. *Held*, this constituted a sufficient ground for setting aside registration. In examining a foreign judgment for fraud, an English court could retry the merits of the case, even where the party making the allegation of fraud knew the facts on which it was based at the time of the foreign action but did not put them before the foreign court. (Compare *Macalpine* v *Macalpine*.)

Szalatnay-Stacho v Fink [1947] KB 1 (Court of Appeal) [475]

During World War II, the government and military authorities of the Czechoslovakian Republic were operating in London. The defendant, the General Prosecutor of the Military Court of Appeal, wrote a letter to the Military Office, in which he defamed the plaintiff. Under Czechoslovakian law, the defendant, being a State official, could not be sued for libel. Libel proceedings were instituted by the plaintiff after the war. *Held*, the case was governed by English law, so the defendant could not rely on the absolute defence which Czechoslovakian law afforded him. (Compare *Boys* v *Chaplin*.)

Szechter (orse Karsov) v Szechter [1971] P 286 [476]

Polish domiciliaries went through a ceremony of marriage in a Polish prison where the wife was serving a three-year sentence for 'anti-state activities'. The wife's health was seriously impaired and deteriorating. They succeeded in their object of extricating the wife from prison and they came to England where they acquired a domicile of choice and where the wife petitioned for annulment of the marriage on the grounds of duress. *Held*, on grounds of common residence and common domicile in England of the parties, the court had jurisdiction to grant the decree sought; and it was for Polish law, as the law of the domicile of the parties at the time of the marriage, to determine the validity of the marriage. The evidence was that Polish law would find the marriage void for duress. Accordingly, the decree would be granted. (Compare *Buckland* v *Buckland*.)

Taczanowska (orse Roth) v Taczanowski [1957] P 301 [477]
(Court of Appeal)

In 1946, two domiciled Poles were married to each other in Italy in a ceremony conducted by a Polish army chaplain according to Roman Catholic rites. The husband was serving as a soldier with the Allied Forces occupying Italy and the wife was a civilian refugee. The ceremony was formally defective under Italian domestic law and under Polish law (to which Italian conflicts rules referred the issue of formal validity). *Held*, the marriage was none the less valid as a common law marriage. The common law doctrine could be applied because the parties, being associated with conquering forces, could not be taken to have submitted the validity of their marriage to the lex loci celebrationis. (See also *Kochanski* v *Kochanska*.)

Tatry, The, Owners of Cargo Lately Laden on Board Tatry [478]
v Owners of Maciej Rataj (Case C–406/92) (1994)
The Times 28 December (European Court of Justice)

In a dispute relating to the contamination of a cargo of soya-bean oil by diesel oil on board ship (the *Tatry*), the shipowners brought proceedings in The

Netherlands for a declaration that they were not liable for the contamination, whereas the cargo owners later brought actions in rem in England against a sister ship (the *Maciej Rataj*) of the *Tatry*. The actions of the cargo owners were based on the Arrest Convention 1952 and the shipowners requested that these actions be stayed in favour of proceedings already brought in The Netherlands. The Court of Appeal sought a preliminary ruling on jurisdiction from the ECJ. *Held*, (1) Article 57 of the Brussels Convention 1968 would preclude the application of that Convention in cases governed by some other specialised convention. However, Article 3(3) of the Arrest Convention had no bearing on the concept of lis pendens within the meaning of Article 21 of the Brussels Convention: accordingly, Articles 21 and 22 of the Brussels Convention were applicable. (2) Article 21 of the Brussels Convention meant that where two actions involved the same cause of action and some, but not all, of the parties to the second action were the same as the parties to the action started earlier in another Contracting State, the second court seised was required to decline jurisdiction only to the extent to which the parties to the action before it were also parties to the action previously started: Article 21 did not prevent the action from continuing between the other parties. (3) An action seeking to have the defendant held liable for causing loss and ordered to pay damages has the same cause of action and the same object as earlier proceedings brought by that defendant seeking a declaration that he is not liable for that loss: a subsequent action does not cease to have the same cause of action and the same object and to be between the same parties as the previous action because one action in one Contracting State is brought in personam and the second action in the other Contracting state is brought in rem. (4) Proof of the necessary relationships between cargo owners in various jurisdictions and the defendants to warrant related actions under Article 22 would eliminate the risk of conflicting decisions in related trials and judgments. (See also *The Anna H* and *The Po*.)

Tesam Distribution Ltd v Schuh Mode Team GmbH and Commerzbank AG (1989) The Times [479]
24 October (Court of Appeal)

The plaintiffs, an English firm of shoe importers, contended that the defendants, German shoe suppliers and a German bank, were in breach of a contract for, inter alia, the sale and delivery of shoes. If there was a contract, the obligation in question was delivery of the shoes in London and the English courts would have special jurisdiction under Article 5(1) of the Brussels Convention 1968. However, it had to be determined whether the extensive correspondence between the litigants resulted in a binding contract. *Held*, 'the court's jurisdiction ... is not dependent upon the court first satisfying itself that the contract does exist. That is the subject matter of the dispute, and [it has previously been] established [that] the court has jurisdiction [to determine such a matter]. If in due course the court finds that no contract was entered into, it will dismiss the claim: but it has jurisdiction to determine that issue.' A mere assertion by the plaintiff of the existence of a contract would not suffice: he had to satisfy the court of 'evidence from which the conclusion could properly be drawn that a contract existed and that the place of performance was the country in which the action was brought'. It was for the courts of each Contracting State to determine the burden of proof of facts relevant to its jurisdiction. (See also *Effer v Kanter* and *Tessili v Dunlop*.)

Tessili v Dunlop (Case 12/76) [480]
[1976] ECR 1473 (European Court of Justice)

In a dispute over the alleged defective performance by the defendant Italian company, Tessili, of its contractual obligation, the German plaintiff, Dunlop, began an action in the German courts. The defendants contested the jurisdiction of the German courts and a German appellate court referred to the ECJ for a preliminary ruling the question of which was 'the court for the place where the obligation has been or is to be performed?' *Held*, 'The "place of performance of the obligation in question" within the meaning of Article 5(1) [of the Brussels Convention] is to be determined in accordance with the law which governs the obligations in question according to the rules of the conflict of laws of the court before which the matter is brought.' (See also *Effer* v *Kanter* and *Mulox IBC Ltd* v *Geels*.)

Texaco Melbourne, The, Attorney-General of the Republic of Ghana and Ghana National Petroleum Corporation v Texaco Overseas Tankships Ltd [481]
[1994] 1 Lloyd's Rep 473 (House of Lords)

There was no disputing that the defendants had breached a contract for which they were liable in damages. They had failed to ship a consignment of oil belonging to the plaintiffs from one Ghanaian port to another. The issue was whether damages should be in US dollars or Ghanaian cedis. In the House of Lords, LORD GOFF stated that: 'The identification of that currency is of crucial importance in the present case, because of the collapse of the Ghanaian currency, the cedi, between the date of the relevant breach of contract [1982] and the date of judgment [1994].' At the relevant date (the date of breach) the cost of obtaining a replacement cargo was approximately US$3 million which was the equivalent of about 8 million cedis; at the time of judgment, 8 million cedis was worth about US$20,000. Had the oil been delivered, it could have been sold for Gc11.5 million. The dollar equivalent of that sum at the date of trial was US$31,000. *Held, per* LORD GOFF on behalf of a unanimous House, that 'fluctuations in the relevant currency between the date of breach and the date of judgment are not taken into account. ... The proper approach is to identify, in accordance with established principle, the appropriate currency in which the award of damages is to be made, and to award an appropriate sum by way of damages in that currency, and also of interest in that currency to compensate for the delay between the date of breach and the date of judgment. ... There are a number of facts which point to the Ghanaian cedi as the currency in which the [plaintiff] felt its loss. [These included] First of all, the currency in which [the plaintiff] carried on business within Ghana was at the material time the cedi. ... In particular, had the cargo been delivered by the shipowners at [the port of destination, then the plaintiffs] could and would have sold it on the market there to Ghanaian companies, and would have recovered payment in cedis. ... Second, ... no person other than the Bank of Ghana was or is permitted to receive or own foreign currency. Accordingly, when the [plaintiff] wanted to purchase crude oil from overseas ... the bank would provide the necessary foreign currency for this purpose, debiting the [plaintiffs'] account with the amount in cedis equivalent to the sum in foreign currency required, and itself paying the foreign currency to the seller out of its own foreign currency holdings.' Thus, LORD GOFF went on to conclude that damages were payable in cedis. (See also *Miliangos* v *George Frank (Textiles)* and *The Despina R.*)

Thames and Mersey Marine Insurance Co v Societa di Navigazione a Vapore del Lloyd Austriaco [482]
(1914) 111 LT 97 (Court of Appeal)

The defendant, a foreign shipping corporation, permitted a London company with a fixed place of business to act as its general agents in this country. In return for commission and a lump sum for rent and expenses, the agency accepted bookings for passengers and their luggage and goods on the defendant's ships, and they were authorised to book a limited number of berths on a ship without consulting the defendant. The agency used the defendant's headed notepaper and maintained at its office two special clerks, a telephone number and a telegraphic address for the defendant. The plaintiff company issued a writ against the defendant and served it at the place of business of the London agents on a member of their firm. *Held,* the court had jurisdiction over the defendant because it was carrying on business in England by means of the agency. In determining whether a foreign corporation carries on business in England, 'The test in each case is to find the answer to the following question: does the agent in carrying on the foreign corporation's business make a contract for the foreign corporation, or does the agent, in carrying on the agent's own business, sell a contract with the foreign corporation? In the former case, the corporation is and in the latter it is not carrying on business at that place. [The agents in this case] do the former' (*per* BUCKLEY LJ). (Compare *Littauer Glove Corporation* v *F W Millington (1920) Ltd.*)

Tharsis Sulphur and Copper Co Ltd, The v La Société des Métaux (1889) 58 LJQB 435 [483]

A contract for delivery and acceptance of certain quantities of copper between the plaintiff, a company having its registered office in Glasgow and carrying on its business there and in the North East of England, and the defendant, a French company with no place of business in the UK, provided that for the purposes of any dispute arising out of the contract the defendant submitted to the jurisdiction of the High Court of Justice in England and they appointed a firm in London to be its agent to accept service. The plaintiff issued a writ claiming damages from the defendant for breach of contract and served it on the London agent. *Held,* the court had jurisdiction and service was valid. The defendant's submission in the contract to the High Court's jurisdiction and its appointment of an agent to accept service were effective and binding upon it. (See also *Copin* v *Adamson* and, now, RSC Ord. 11, r.1(1)(d)(iv).)

Theodohos, The [1977] 2 Lloyd's Rep 428 [484]

The plaintiff cargo owners issued a writ in personam against, inter alia, Lefka, a Panamanian company, the shippers of a cargo of resin found damaged after carriage on board the vessel *Theodohos*. They purported to serve the writ on Lefka by serving it personally on G in London. G was named as the president and director of Lefka in the register of companies in Panama. The plaintiffs contended that this amounted to good service under O.65, r.3 which provided that: 'Personal service of a document on a body corporate may in cases for which provision is not otherwise made by any enactment, be effected by serving it ... on the ... president of the body ... or other similar officer ...'. *Held* (*per* BRANDON J), 'unless a foreign company is carrying on business at a place within the jurisdiction, it cannot be served with process within the jurisdiction, either by the method employed in the present case or at all. [And] there is no evidence on which a court could possibly find that Lefka was carrying on business in England ... when service of the writ on [G] took place.' Moreover, 'From the time of the passing of the Companies Act 1929 onwards there have been in force statutory provisions relating to service of process on a foreign company having a place of business here ... [Accordingly] It follows that, from the time of the passing of the Companies Act 1929 onwards [the predecessors of and] the present O.65, r.3, have no longer applied ...'. (Contrast *Thames and Mersey Marine Insurance Co* v *Societa di Navigazione a Vapore del Lloyd Austriaco*.)

Tracomin SA v Sudan Oil Seeds Co (Nos 1 and 2) [485]
[1983] 1 WLR 1026 (Court of Appeal)

Contracts between the Sudanese sellers and Swiss buyers of ground nuts provided that they should be governed by English law, and that in the event of a dispute arising out of the contracts neither party should take legal action against the other without first referring the dispute to arbitration in London. Nevertheless, when a dispute arose, the buyers brought an action in a Swiss court claiming damages for breach of contract. The sellers sought a stay on the basis that the dispute was to be settled by arbitration but they did not bring to the attention of the court the fact that the contract was governed by English law. In the absence of the citation of English law, the court took English law to be the same as Swiss law and decided that the arbitration term was not incorporated into the contracts. When the sellers initiated arbitration proceedings in London, the buyers applied to the High Court for a declaration that the arbitrators had no jurisdiction and an injunction restraining the arbitration on the ground that the Swiss judgment created an estoppel per rem judicatam. The sellers then counterclaimed, seeking an order to restrain the buyers from continuing with the Swiss action. At first instance, the counterclaim was dismissed on the basis of the seller's negligence in failing to cite English law in the Swiss courts. *Held*, (1) since ss32 and 33 of the Civil Jurisdiction and Judgments Act 1982 [which provided a defence for the non-recognition and enforcement of foreign judgments] came into force during the course of the hearing and the Swiss judgment was not one of the judgments which was not to have retrospective effect, the principle of estoppel per rem judicatam did not apply: accordingly, the buyer's application failed; (2) the sellers were granted an injunction restraining the buyers from litigating in Switzerland: the court's jurisdiction was based on the existence of the agreement to submit disputes to arbitration in England. (See also *MacShannon v Rockware Glass* and *Spiliada Maritime Corporation v Cansulex*.)

Travers v Holley [1953] P 246 (Court of Appeal) [486]

A married couple had emigrated from England to New South Wales, Australia, where the husband acquired a domicile of choice. The husband returned to England after deserting the wife who then obtained an undefended divorce in New South Wales under a statutory provision permitting her to do so on account of her being deserted and irrespective of the husband's domicile. Both husband and wife later remarried. The husband's second marriage proved unsatisfactory and, on legal advice, he petitioned for a divorce from his first wife on the ground that the New South Wales decree of divorce was invalid because at the time it was granted neither he nor his first wife was domiciled there, and the wife, by remarrying, had committed adultery. The wife appealed against the granting of the decree. *Held*, by a majority, the husband had acquired a domicile of choice in New South Wales and the subsequent divorce there had to be recognised in England because English law provided a similar statutory jurisdiction for deserted wives. As HODSON LJ noted, 'where, as here, there is in substance reciprocity, it would be contrary to principle and inconsistent with comity if the courts of this country were to refuse to recognise a jurisdiction which mutatis mutandis they claim for themselves.'

Trendtex v Central Bank of Nigeria [487]
[1977] 2 WLR 356 (Court of Appeal)

Trendtex, the plaintiffs, had contracted to sell nearly a quarter of a million tons of cement for shipment to and use in Nigeria, the purchase price to be paid under a letter of credit issued by the Central Bank of Nigeria. The plaintiffs sued the bank for US$14 million when the latter failed to honour the letter of credit. However, the bank contended successfully at first instance that it was entitled to sovereign immunity. On appeal, allowing the plaintiffs' appeal, the Court of Appeal *Held*, inter alia, the bank was not an alter ego of the State: accordingly, it was not entitled to governmental status; and, in any event, sovereign immunity was inapplicable to commercial transactions. (See also *The Harmattan* and the State Immunity Act 1978.)

Trendtex Trading Corporation v Credit Suisse [488]
[1982] AC 679 (House of Lords)

Following the Court of Appeal decision in *Trendtex* v *Central Bank of Nigeria*, the defendants in that case, the Central Bank of Nigeria (CBN), were allowed to appeal to the House of Lords. However, as the plaintiffs, Trendtex, could not have undertaken its contractual duties without the substantial financial assistance of one of its major creditors, Credit Suisse, they (Trendtex) purported to make a conditional assignment to Credit Suisse of its cause of action against CBN for US$800,000. The agreement confirming the assignment expressly stated that it was 'governed by Swiss law' and any dispute which arose from it was to be 'judged by the Court of Geneva, exclusive of any other jurisdiction'. Credit Suisse then assigned Trendtex's cause of action to a third party for US$1.1 million. The following month the action was settled by a payment by CBN of US$8 million. Trendtex then commenced an action in England alleging that the assignment was void. At first instance ROBERT GOFF J agreed that the assignment of a bare cause of action was unenforceable for maintenance and champerty, but he held that effect should be given to the 'overwhelming strong Swiss connection' and granted a stay. The plaintiffs appeal was dismissed. *Held*, dismissing the appeal, the assignment was void but it was for the Swiss court to decide what effect the invalidity of the assignment under English law had on the agreement as a whole. The decision to stay the English proceedings had been correct. (See also *Re Trepca Mines Ltd*.)

Trepca Mines Ltd, Re [1960] 1 WLR 1273 (Court of Appeal) [489]

A creditor in the liquidation of an English company alleged that he was the owner of a mine in Yugoslavia, that the company had committed conversion of a quantity of concentrates extracted from the mine and that he was entitled to prove in the liquidation for a contingent debt depending on the outcome of an action which he had commenced in Yugoslavia for damages for this act of conversion. The liquidator disputed the jurisdiction of the Yugoslav court. *Held*, the Yugoslav court, being the court of the situs, was competent to deliver a binding judgment as to the title to the mine, which was an essential issue in the creditor's action. But its judgment on the whole claim for conversion would not be binding, even though mutatis mutandis an English court might assume jurisdiction over such a claim by virtue of RSC O.11. (See also *Castrique* v *Imrie*.)

Trufort, Re, Trafford v Blanc (1887) 36 Ch D 600 [490]

A Swiss subject died domiciled in France, thus falling within a French-Swiss treaty which provided that Swiss courts should determine succession to his property according to Swiss law. He left his property to his godson, but his son obtained a Swiss judgment awarding him the bulk of it as his 'compulsory portion' under Swiss law. *Held*, the son could enforce the judgment in England. Where the court of a deceased person's domicile assumed jurisdiction to determine the succession to his movable property, its decision was binding on the courts in England. Here, by virtue of the treaty, the lex domicilii referred the matter to the law and courts of the deceased's country of nationality, so the decision given there was binding also.

(See also *R v Brentwood Superintendent Registrar of Marriages, ex parte Arias* and *In the Estate of Yahuda* [1956] P 388.)

Tursi v Tursi [1958] P 54 [491]

The parties to a marriage in Italy in 1942 were both domiciled and resident in Italy. Shortly after the marriage the husband deserted the wife and never returned to her. The wife obtained a decree of judicial separation in the Italian courts in 1947 and then, in 1949, she went to live in England where she petitioned for a divorce in 1955, citing her husband's desertion. *Held*, as the Italian decree was a final order of the court of the domicile regulating personal rights and obligations consistent with the existence of the status of marriage, it should be recognised by the English courts on the bases of both principle and convenience; and as the husband had been in desertion for the requisite period preceding the decree, the marriage should be dissolved.

Tyburn Productions v Conan Doyle [1991] Ch 75 [492]

The plaintiffs, Tyburn Productions (TP), a UK company, were producers and distributors of television programmes. In 1984, they produced a programme which was original in all respects other than it featured the characters Sherlock Holmes and Dr Watson, created by Sir Arthur Conan Doyle who died in 1930, and the UK copyright of whose works had expired in 1980. On hearing of the plaintiffs' intentions to distribute the film in the USA, agents for the defendant, Dame Jean Conan Doyle, Sir Arthur's only surviving child, informed TP's US distributor that the defendant was the person entitled to copyright under US law and that any distribution of the film would infringe her copyright in the aforementioned characters. The US distributors agreed to pay the defendant $30,000 in consideration of her waiving her rights to sue TP and themselves. In 1989, when TP produced another original film except, again, for featuring Holmes and Watson, which they sought to distribute in the USA, they decided to seek a declaration from the UK court that the defendant held no copyright in the characters in the USA and an injunction preventing her from asserting that she did. *Held*, the statement of claim would be struck out as disclosing no cause of action. Disputes arising under foreign copyright fell exclusively within the jurisdiction of the courts of the country by the law of which those rights were created. Thus, the question of whether the defendant was entitled under US law to the copyright in the characters of Holmes and Watson was not justiciable in the English courts. Accordingly, the declaration and injunction would not be granted. (Applied *British South Africa v Companhia de Mocambique* and dictum of SIR NICHOLAS BROWNE-WILKINSON V-C in *Def Lepp Music v Stuart-Brown* [1986] RPC 273.)

Tzortzis v Monark Line A/B [1968] 1 WLR 406 [493]
(Court of Appeal)

A contract concluded in Sweden for the sale of a Swedish vessel to Greek buyers provided for delivery and payment in Sweden and any dispute in connection with the contract should be decided by arbitration in London. A dispute arose and the arbitrators requested that the court to decide whether the contract was governed by Swedish or English law. *Held*, affirming the view of DONALDSON J (as he was then), whereas the contract had its closest and most real connection with Sweden, which was the place of the contract and the place where it was to be performed both as to delivery and payment, 'by choosing the city of London as the place of arbitration, the parties have impliedly chosen English law as the proper law of the contract' (*per* DENNING MR). (Applied: dictum of LORD WRIGHT in *Vita Foods Products v Unus Shipping*.)

Udny v Udny (1869) LR 1 Sc & Div 441 (House of Lords) [494]

A Scottish colonel, whose domicile of origin was in Scotland, acquired a domicile of choice in England, but then went to live in France to evade creditors. He never actually acquired a domicile in France. In Scottish proceedings, *Held*, his Scottish domicile of origin revived when he abandoned his English domicile. 'When another domicile is put on, the domicile of origin is for that purpose relinquished, and remains in abeyance during the continuance of the domicile of choice; but ... it revives and exists whenever there is no other domicile, and it does not require to be regained or reconstituted animo et facto' (*per* LORD WESTBURY). (See also *Bell* v *Kennedy*.)

Unauthorised Publication of Approved Photographs, the, Re [1991] ILPr 468 [495]

P, a German domiciliary, sued D, a Dutch domiciled publisher of a pornographic magazine when, without his consent, his (P's) photograph appeared in the magazine which could be bought in Germany. *Held*, in the German courts, no harmful event had occurred in Germany even though the Dutch magazine could be bought there. The publication had to circulate to a significant extent or to be distributed regularly, even if only in small numbers, before the German courts would have jurisdiction. If it was regarded as the courts having jurisdiction 'simply on the ground that the publication could be bought in Germany, that would produce the result that this court would have jurisdiction over all injury caused by newspapers and periodicals anywhere in the world, since it is possible eventually to buy any newspaper appearing in the world in Germany'. (Contrast *Shevill* v *Presse Alliance SA*.)

Union International Insurance Co v Jubilee Insurance Co [1991] 1 WLR 415 [496]

The plaintiff insurance company registered in Bermuda contracted with the defendant insurance company registered in Kenya through the agency of London brokers. The contract provided for disputes involving interpretation of the agreement to go to arbitration in Bermuda and disputes concerning the validity of the agreement to be submitted to a court of competent jurisdiction. The defendants applied to set aside a writ which had been served on them claiming sums due under the agreement. They claimed that service out of the jurisdiction under RSC O.11, r.1(1)(d)(ii) only applied to an action in which the contract had been entered into by an agent acting on behalf of a foreign defendant, and not on behalf of a foreign plaintiff. *Held*, 'Careful consideration of other provisions of Ord.11, r.1(1) demonstrates ... the need to imply additional words by way of restriction in order to give sensible effect to those provisions. ... similar additional words must be implied to give sensible effect to Ord.11, r.1(1)(d).' Thus, r.1(1)(d)(ii) would read: '(ii) was made by or through an agent trading or residing within the jurisdiction on behalf of a principal trading or residing out of the jurisdiction [and the defendant to be served is that principal]' (*per* PHILLIPS J). Accordingly, service of the writ would be set aside.

Union Transport v Continental Lines SA [497]
[1992] 1 Lloyd's Rep 229 (House of Lords)

The plaintiffs contended that a contract was made in London for the charter of a vessel to be nominated by the defendants, who were domiciled in Belgium, to carry a load a cargo of telegraph poles from Florida to Bangladesh. The defendants denied the existence of a concluded contract though, in line with arbitration terms incorporated in previous contracts between the parties, they appointed an arbitrator without prejudice to their claim that they were not a party to a concluded contract. However, instead of relying on arbitration, the plaintiffs then claimed damages for breach of contract in respect of the defendants failure to nominate or provide a vessel at the loading port in accordance with the terms of the charter. They based their claim to sue in London on Article 5(1) of the Brussels Convention, ie, in matters relating to contract, the defendants could be sued 'in courts of the place of performance of the obligation in question', and the obligation was to nominate the vessel. The defendants claimed that the English courts had no jurisdiction and that any proceedings against them should be brought in Belgium. The plaintiffs succeeded at first instance and in the Court of Appeal. *Held*, unanimously, the obligation in question was to nominate a vessel and the place of performance of the obligation was London: thus, the English courts had jurisdiction under Article 5(1); the nomination of the vessel was the identification of the subject matter of the contract; and that failure to nominate led to litigation in the most appropriate forum which was England. Accordingly, the defendant's appeal would be dismissed. (See also *Shenavai* v *Kreischer*.)

United Bank of the Middle East v Clapham [498]
(1981) The Times 20 July (Court of Appeal)

The defendants had been guarantors of a loan to a United Arab Emirates company of which they were directors and shareholders. The bank, also registered in the United Arab Emirates, issued a writ against the defendants claiming in excess of £500,000 in respect of sums lent, and it sought summary judgment in England under RSC O.14. However, the defendants, who contended that the bank had earlier taken over the company's assets wrongfully and conducted the business to the exclusion of the company, wanted the company joined as counterclaimants against the bank for, inter alia, wrongful possession of company assets and to claim a sum in excess of the debt owed. At first instance, the judge thought that the company should not be allowed to join in the action as it would not get leave under RSC O.11 to sue the bank. *Held*, unanimously, by coming to England to sue, the bank submitted to the jurisdiction of the English court, which could then deal with any counterclaim connected with the bank's claim; and the court had a wide power to join a party to an action under RSC O.15, r.6, and this would include 'any person between whom and any party to the cause or matter there may exist a question or issue arising out of or relating to or connected with any relief or remedy claimed in the cause or matter which in the opinion of the court it would be just and convenient to determine as between him and that party as well as between the parties to the cause or matter ...'. DENNING MR concluded that whereas O.11 had no relevance to the present case, once the bank brought proceedings, it was proper that the company should be joined under O.15, r.6 as a counterclaimant against the bank. Accordingly, the defendants' appeal would be allowed.

United Railways of Havana and Regla Warehouses Ltd, Re [499]
[1960] Ch 52 (Court of Appeal); affirmed [1961] AC 1007
(House of Lords)

A railway company incorporated in England and operating in Cuba obtained finance for the purchase of rolling stock by issuing loan certificates to the public in the USA. This was done by means of a highly complex transaction in which the rolling stock, which was situated in Cuba, came to be held as security for the loan by a trustee company, incorporated in Pennsylvania. Some years later, when the railway company had defaulted in making payments of interest due to the trustee company, the Cuban Government compulsorily purchased the railway company's assets in Cuba, including the rolling stock. The trustee claimed arrears of interest from the railway company. *Held*, (1) the proper law of the loan agreement was the law of Pennsylvania; (2) there was no reason to consider whether a court in Pennsylvania might apply some other system of law, because it seemed that 'the principle of renvoi finds no place in the field of contract' (*per* JENKINS LJ); and (3) the question whether the Cuban Government's act operated as a novation, substituting the Government for the railway company as the debtor under the loan agreement, was one to be determined by the proper law, not the lex situs of the debt, because it involved the discharge of the railway company and questions of discharge of an agreement were always determined by the proper law. (Compare *Re Ross, Ross* v *Waterfield*; see also *Re Helbert Wagg & Co Ltd*.)

United States of America v Inkley [1988] QB 255   [500]
(Court of Appeal)

Inkley, a British subject, had been charged with various criminal offences under the laws of the USA. He was released on bail from a district court on condition that he entered into an appearance bond for US$48,000. He also obtained leave of the court to return to England for 30 days. He returned to England and remained there: he did not return to the USA. The US Government then obtained a final judgment in the US civil courts against Inkley and sought to enforce it against him in England. *Held* (*per* PURCHAS LJ): 'notwithstanding its civil clothing, the purpose of the action ... was the due execution by the USA of a public law process aimed to ensure the attendance of persons accused of crime before the criminal courts'. Accordingly, enforcement of the judgment would be refused. (See also *Huntington* v *Attrill* and *Attorney-General of New Zealand* v *Ortiz*.)

Vadala v Lawes (1890) 25 QBD 310 (Court of Appeal)   [501]

The plaintiff sued the defendant in Italy on a number of bills of exchange which had been accepted on the defendant's behalf by an agent. The defendant maintained that the bills were not ordinary commercial bills, but had been accepted by the agent without his authority in order to pay gambling debts owed by the agent to the plaintiff. The Italian court rejected this defence on its merits and gave judgment for the plaintiff. In proceedings by the plaintiff to enforce the judgment in England, the defendant pleaded that the plaintiff had fraudulently misled the Italian court by representing the bills to be commercial ones when he knew they were for gambling debts. *Held*, this was a good plea, because a foreign judgment procured by fraud of this sort would not be enforced in England. Moreover, 'if the fraud upon the foreign court consists in the fact that the plaintiff has induced that court by fraud to come to a wrong conclusion, you can reopen the whole case even although you will have in this court to go into the very facts which were investigated, and which were in issue in the foreign court' (*per* LINDLEY LJ). (See also *Syal* v *Heyward*.)

Valentine's Settlement, Re, Valentine v Valentine   [502]
[1965] Ch 831 (Court of Appeal)

Pursuant to orders of a South African court, two children domiciled and resident in South Africa were adopted by parents domiciled and resident in Southern Rhodesia. These orders were apparently not recognised in Southern Rhodesia and, although South African law at the time recognised adopted children as legitimate children of their adoptive parents, English law conferred no such rights on children adopted by court order in England. The children claimed under a settlement which was governed by English law and conferred interests in remainder on 'the children' of their adoptive father. *Held*, the claim would fail. The adoption orders would not be recognised in England because adoptive parents had to be domiciled (and perhaps also the child resident) in the country where the order was made. Even if the orders were recognised, the children's rights would be limited to those conferred by English law at the date of the orders, which were insufficient to support their claim. (See, now, provisions of the Adoption Act 1976.)

Van Dalfsen v Van Loon (Case C–183/90) [503]
[1991] ECR 4743 (European Court of Justice)

In a dispute over a tenancy agreement, Van Loon, the landlord, sought to enforce in The Netherlands, where Van Dalfsen resided, a judgment for arrears of rent he had obtained in Belgium. Van Dalfsen appealed in The Netherlands and sought a stay of action as he had appealed against the Belgian court's decision and provided a bank guarantee for the amount of rent arrears he was ordered to pay Van Loon. Furthermore, he was able to plead that a counterclaim for the reimbursement of capital expenditure had been declared to be justified and that an independent report had estimated it at about 20 per cent of the sum he had been ordered to pay Van Loon. Van Dalfesen's appeal for a stay was dismissed and his appeal was declared unfounded. Consequently, enforcement of the Belgian order was authorised, conditional upon the provision by Van Loon of a bank guarantee in the sum equal to that for reimbursement of capital expenditure. Van Dalfsen appealed, contending that the court had misinterpreted the extent of the powers conferred by Article 38 of the Brussels Convention 1968 on 'the court with which the appeal is lodged.' Questions of interpretation were referred to the ECJ for a preliminary ruling. *Held*: (1) 'The second paragraph of Article 37 of the [Brussels Convention] is to be interpreted as meaning that a decision taken under Article 38 of the Convention by which the court with which an appeal has been lodged against an order for the enforcement of a judgment given in another Contracting State has refused to stay the proceedings and has ordered the party to whom the enforcement order was granted to provide security does not constitute a "judgment given on the appeal" within the meaning of the second paragraph of Article 37 of the Convention and may not, therefore, be contested by an appeal ...'. (2) 'The first paragraph of Article 38 of the Convention is to be interpreted as meaning that a court with which an appeal is lodged against an order for the enforcement of a judgment given in another Contracting State may take into consideration, in a decision concerning an application for the proceedings to be stayed under that paragraph, only such submissions as the appellant was unable to make before the court of the State in which the judgment was given.'

Van Grutten v Digby (1862) 31 Beav 561 [504]

Prior to their marriage, a domiciled Frenchman and an Englishwoman executed a marriage settlement in France, observing formalities complying with English law, but not with French law. The governing law of the settlement was English law. *Held*, even though the formal requirements of French law, the lex loci contractus and the husband's lex domicilii, had not been complied with, the settlement was none the less valid because it was properly executed according to its governing law. (Compare *Bristow* v *Sequeville*.)

Vanquelin v Bouard (1863) 15 CB NS 341 [505]

On the death of her husband, a French merchant, the plaintiff became his 'universal heir' under French law, being personally liable to pay his debts and personally entitled to his property. She paid to an indorsee of a bill of exchange an amount for which the husband, as drawer of the bill, and the defendant, as acceptor, had been held liable in a French court, then she recovered a French judgment for the same amount against the defendant by way of indemnity. When she sought to enforce this judgment in England, the defendant raised two defences: (1) that she had not obtained representation of her husband's estate in England; and (2) that the French court lacked jurisdiction because under its own rules jurisdiction was limited to bills drawn in a particular area with traders as acceptors. *Held*, both these defences would fail: (1) because the plaintiff was suing not in her husband's right but in her own right under French law, and in respect of a debt which arose because of her own payment to the indorsee; and (2) because the French court, having jurisdiction 'over the person and over the subject matter of the action', was the proper tribunal to decide whether the limitations on jurisdiction in its own rules had been exceeded. (Compare *New York Breweries Co v Attorney-General* and *Papadopoulos v Papadopoulos*.)

Vervaeke (formerly Messina) v Smith [1983] AC 145
(House of Lords)

In 1954, V, a Belgian domiciled prostitute, went through a ceremony of marriage in England with S, a domiciled Englishman, in order to acquire British nationality and a British passport so that she could continue her trade without fear of deportation. The parties to the marriage went their separate ways immediately after the marriage. In 1970, V went through another ceremony of marriage in Italy with M who died the same day leaving in England property to the value of £100,000. V would have a claim to this property only if her marriage to M was valid. In proceedings commenced in 1970, she failed to obtain a declaration of nullity in respect of her marriage to S in 1954 when she contended that she had not realised it was a ceremony of marriage that she had gone through and so she had not validly consented to it. At first instance, ORMROD J exposed her claim as fraudulent and dismissed it (see *Messina v Smith*). However, she obtained, in the Belgian courts, a declaration that her 1954 marriage was void ab initio. V then sought a declaration from the English courts that the Belgian decree was entitled to recognition. *Held*, dismissing her appeal, (1) 'the appeal fails and must be dismissed, first on the ground of res judicata, secondly on the ground of public policy ...' (per LORD HAILSHAM); (2) the marriage of S and V was valid, notwithstanding its extraneous purpose, as upholding the status of marriage was a doctrine of English public policy: accordingly, the Belgian nullity decree was not within the rules of recognition of foreign judgments by the English courts. (See also *E D & F Man v Haryanto*.)

Viditz v O'Hagan [1900] 2 Ch 87 (Court of Appeal)

Before the marriage of a domiciled Austrian to a domiciled Irish girl aged 18, marriage articles were executed by them and other parties in Switzerland whereby they agreed to establish a marriage settlement after the marriage. About 16 years later, they executed the settlement, and the wife subsequently exercised certain powers thereunder, but they then revoked it by notarial act in Austria. Under Irish law, the wife lacked capacity to make the original agreement, though it would become binding unless revoked within a 'reasonable time' after attaining 21. Under Austrian law a marriage settlement could not be irrevocable. *Held*, the revocation was effective, because the wife's lex domicilii before marriage rendered her original agreement revocable until a 'reasonable time' after her majority, and her lex domicilii after her marriage made the settlement itself revocable. 'This lady never had, either before or after her marriage, power to make an irrevocable statement' (*per* LINDLEY MR). (See also *Re Cooke's Trusts*.)

Vishva Abha, The [1990] 2 Lloyd's Rep 312 [508]

The plaintiffs, who were owners of the cargo lately laden on board the *Dias*, claimed damages for loss and damage arising from a collision which occurred in the Red Sea between the *Dias* and the defendants' vessel, *Vishva Apurva*, which sank, the writ being served on a sister ship, *Vishva Abha*. The defendants contended that England was not the natural or appropriate forum and they applied for a stay of action on the ground that they had already commenced proceedings in South Africa where it was entirely fortuitous that they had found and arrested *Dias*. If the defendants invoked limitation in South Africa, the fund would be less than £375,000 whereas, in England, it would be more than £1,500,000. *Held* (per SHEEN J), the action was 'not between the same parties as the litigation ... being pursued in South Africa and that the plaintiffs' prima facie should not be deprived of litigating in the forum of their choice merely because others have chosen to litigate in South Africa'. The defendants 'would not be put to any more inconvenience or expense by having their witnesses attend this court than they would in attending a court in South Africa'. Moreover, since South Africa was not a distinctly more appropriate forum than the English court for the hearing of the action, the defendants' motion would be dismissed. (See also *Spiliada Maritime Corporation* v *Cansulex*.)

Vishva Prabha, The [1979] 2 Lloyd's Rep 286 [509]

A cargo of hessian cloth and hessian bags loaded on board a ship was severely damaged by oil, which leaked from a pierced fuel tank. It was contended that no reasonable inspection would have failed to have seen the rectangular-shaped horizontal hole, which must have been present prior to the cargo being loaded, because the metal that was pierced was 10 mm thick and the damage was wholly inconsistent with the loading of the hessian cargo. However, the defendants applied for a stay because bills of lading had specifically included a clause providing for contracts to be governed by Indian law in India 'to the exclusion of the jurisdiction of the courts of any other country'. *Held*, SHEEN J refusing the stay, (1) there was no defence to the claim of prior damage, hence no dispute as to liability which, therefore, 'ought to be submitted to the court in India'; (2) the stay would be refused, however, because, inter alia, (a) there was no difference in the relevant law whether the proceedings were heard in Bombay or London since 'the bills of lading were subject to the Hague rules and ... the principles to be applied would be the same in India as in this country'; (b) 'all the relevant evidence is in Europe; it is documentary evidence'; and (c) if a stay was granted 'the proceedings in India would be time barred'. (See also *The Eleftheria*.)

Vita Food Products Inc v Unus Shipping Co Ltd [510]
[1939] AC 277 (Privy Council)

Under Newfoundland law, every bill of lading issued in Newfoundland, Canada, for the carriage of goods by sea from Newfoundland to a foreign country had to have a clause subjecting it to the 'Hague Rules', a set of maritime rules laid down in an international convention to which Newfoundland was a party. For a shipment of herrings from Newfoundland to New York, USA, the shipowner's agent in Newfoundland inadvertently used a form of bill which did not have this clause and which expressly stated that the bill was 'governed by English law'. The ship and cargo were lost off the coast of Nova Scotia. In an action for damages brought in Nova Scotia, Canada, by the consignees of the herrings against the shipowner, *Held*, despite the Newfoundland provision incorporating the Hague Rules, the rights of the parties were governed by English law, because this was the proper law of the contract. 'It is now well settled that by English law ... the proper law of the contract "is the law which the parties intended to apply" ... [W]here there is an express statement by the parties of their intention to select the law of the contract, it is difficult to see what qualifications are possible, provided the intention expressed is bona fide and legal, and provided there is no reason for avoiding the choice on grounds of public policy' (*per* LORD WRIGHT). (See also *Tzortzis* v *Monark Line A/B.*)

Vogel v R A Kohnstamm [1973] 1 QB 133

The plaintiff leather merchant in Israel sued the defendant English company in Israel in respect of a breach of contract. The plaintiff contended that the Israeli court had jurisdiction because the pre-contractual negotiations had been conducted in Israel through a Mr Kornbluth (K) who described himself as 'a manufacturer's representative'. That is, K was not an agent in the legal sense since he had no power to contract. Nevertheless, the plaintiff obtained judgment in the Israeli court and sought to enforce it in England. *Held*, dismissing the plaintiff's claim, (1) K's 'intermediary' activities did not make the defendants resident in Israel. ASHWORTH J said: 'I have asked myself ... whether in any real sense of the word the defendants can be said to have been [present or resident] in Israel; and all that emerges from this case is that there was [a representative] who sought customers for them, ... [but] had no authority whatever to bind the defendants in any shape or form. I have come to the conclusion really without hesitation that the defendants were not resident in Israel at any material time.' Accordingly, the contract was made in England and the Israeli courts had no jurisdiction over the case. (2) There was no submission by the defendants to the Israeli court: they had not expressly submitted to the jurisdiction and implied submission was impossible. (See also *Sfeir & Co* v *National Insurance Co of New Zealand Ltd.*)

Volvox Hollandia, The, Saipem SpA v Dredging VO2 BV and Geosite Surveys Ltd [1988]
2 Lloyd's Rep 361 (Court of Appeal)

A dredger owned by subcontractors, VO2, a Dutch corporation, had damaged an oil pipeline belonging to an English corporation causing damage which amounted to £4.5 million. The subcontract had contained an identical clause to a clause in the head contract which provided for: 'Governing law and jurisdiction. The construction validity and performance of the contract ... shall be governed in all respects by English law. The English courts will have jurisdiction to entertain any action brought in connection with or arising out of the contract ...". However, VO2 succeeded in gaining an order from the Rotterdam District Court limiting their liability and they provided security in the amount ordered. The limitation proceedings were in accordance with the 'International Convention relating to the limitation of the liability of owners of seagoing ships' to which both The Netherlands and the UK were parties. Sapiem, contractors in the head contract, began proceedings in England claiming damages for breach of contract or duty or negligence against VO2 and for a declaration that VO2 were not entitled to limit their liability; and for damages for negligence or breach of duty against Geosite, an English company, who had supplied VO2 with 'high-tech' equipment and personnel. Sapiem were granted leave to serve VO2 out of the jurisdiction. VO2 applied for service of process to be set aside or for the actions to be stayed. At first instance, STAUGHTON J decided that both the English and Dutch courts had jurisdiction under the Brussels Convention 1968, but as England was clearly or distinctly shown to be the forum in which this case could be suitably tried for the interests of the parties and for the ends of justice, the applications to set aside service or stay the actions would be dismissed. *Held*, allowing the appeals by a majority of 2-1, 'the claims for the negative declarations in the plaintiffs' writs served in Holland cannot properly be maintained. [This was because] Properly viewed, these claims for negative declarations are a novel type of pre-emptive forum shopping with novel implications. They distort the settled law and practice governing the rights of shipowners to seek to limit their liability. They involve an exorbitant assumption of jurisdiction by the English courts under O.11 without regard for the implications of two relevant international Conventions. And they involve an attempt at forum shopping in the face of a lis alibi pendens, properly instituted by the defendants in Holland before the English proceedings, so that a race for judgment in these two jurisdictions would be likely to result. In the upshot, the inclusion of these claims in the plaintiffs' writs for service out of the jurisdiction was improper and should not be allowed to stand' (*per* KERR LJ). (See also *The Sennar* and *Spiliada Maritime Corporation* v *Cansulex*.)

Wahl v Attorney-General (1932) 147 LT 382 (House of Lords) [513]

A German citizen who had a German domicile of origin lived in various places in England for five years, then applied for and obtained naturalisation as a British subject. In his memorial he stated that he intended to reside permanently in the UK and that he had no intention of permanently leaving it (this being a stronger declaration than the law required). He spent the remaining years until his death living in England and Germany. *Held*, he did not acquire a domicile of choice in England, despite the statement in his memorial (which referred anyway to the UK, not England) and the naturalisation itself. 'A change of domicile is not a condition of naturalisation, and naturalisation does not necessarily involve a change of domicile' (*per* LORD ATKIN). (See also *Ross* v *Ellison (or Ross)*.)

Walpole v Canadian Northern Railway Co [514]
[1923] AC 113 (Privy Council)

In the course of his employment by the defendant railway company, the plaintiff was killed in British Columbia, Canada, owing to the negligence of the defendant's servants. Under British Columbia law, he would have had no common law right of action for damages against the defendant if he had lived, but merely a statutory claim against a fund contributed to by employers and used to compensate employees injured at work. The plaintiff sued the defendant for damages under the Fatal Accidents Act in Saskatchewan, where there was no such statutory fund. *Held*, the action would fail, on the ground, inter alia, that the act of negligence, although conferring a right to statutory compensation, did not involve the defendant in civil or criminal liability under British Columbia law, the lex loci delicti commissi. (See also *McMillan* v *Canadian Northern Railway Co*.)

Warter v Warter (1890) 16 PD 152 [515]

A husband obtained a divorce in India on the ground of his wife's adultery. Under Indian law, neither spouse was free to remarry until six months after the decree absolute; however, the wife remarried in England within this period. *Held*, her remarriage was invalid. The six months' prohibition was effective outside India because it formed 'an integral part of the proceedings' (*per* SIR JAMES HANNEN P) and it covered both spouses. It was distinct from a 'penal' incapacity affecting the guilty spouse only, which would be inoperative out of the jurisdiction in which it was imposed. (Compare *Re Langley's Settlement Trusts, Lloyds Bank Ltd* v *Langley* and *Scott* v *Attorney-General*.)

Watkins v North American Land and Timber Co Ltd [516]
(1904) 20 TLR 534 (House of Lords)

A dispute had arisen between a company registered in England, with the 'object of acquiring land in the United States of America and other kindred objects', and Mr Watkins (W), its general manager in the USA, who was a US citizen resident in Kansas. In addition to litigation commenced in the USA, the company had, unknown to W, issued a writ against W in which it claimed to recover moneys had and received by W for the company's use and for moneys received by W as trustee for the company and retained by him or converted to his own use, and for a declaration that the company was entitled to a lien upon all shares of the company registered in W's name. The writ was not served on W until he came into the jurisdiction at the invitation of the company. W contended that the company had no real intention of discussing the matters at issue between them as he had been led to believe was the point of his coming to England, and that he was induced to come within the jurisdiction in order for the sole purpose that he might be served with the writ. *Held*, LORD DAVEY agreeing with a dictum of KEKEWICH J at first instance, if a defendant had been induced by fraud of any kind to come within the jurisdiction for the concealed purpose of serving him with a writ in an action, then service would be set aside as being an abuse of the process of the court. Here, however, fraud had not been proved. Accordingly, W's appeal would be dismissed. (See also *Maharanee of Baroda v Wildenstein*.)

Wayland, In the Estate of [1951] 2 All ER 1041 [517]

A British subject who died domiciled in England left two unrevoked wills, of which the first dealt with all his property in Belgium and the second with all his property in England. The executors under both wills applied for probate of both of them in England, alleging that if probate was refused for the Belgian will, Belgian estate duty would be substantially increased and would exhaust the Belgian assets. *Held*, by virtue of s2(1) of the Administration of Justice Act 1932, the court had jurisdiction to grant probate of the Belgian will even though it did not dispose of property in England, and it would make a grant to obviate the 'injustice' of the Belgian estate duty law.

Waylink and Brady Maria, The, Aldington [518]
Shipping Ltd v Bradstock Shipping Corporation and
Mabanaft GmbH [1988] 1 Lloyd's Rep 475
(Gibraltar Court of Appeal)

The plaintiffs' vessel, *Brady Maria*, collided with the *Waylink* in the River Elbe, in (as it was then) West Germany. The *Brady Maria* was managed by an English company and had mainly a Yugoslav crew. The *Waylink* was a Gibraltarian vessel, also with a Yugoslav crew. The collision had caused extensive damage to both vessels, especially the *Brady Maria*, and oil pollution. Aldington, the owners of the *Waylink*, commenced proceedings for damages against Bradstock, a Liberian registered company, the owners of the *Brady Maria*, in the Regional Court of Hamburg, together with limitation proceedings in the Hamburg District Court. Bradstock then sued Aldington for damages in Gibraltar and Aldington sought a stay of those proceedings on the grounds of forum non conveniens and lis alibi pendens. DAVIS CJ refused the stay, against which Aldington appealed, and Bradstock sought a declaration that Aldington were not entitled to limit their liability in respect of the damages resulting from the collision. *Held*, allowing the appeal, 'that Germany was the natural and appropriate forum in which the dispute could be tried more suitably, in the interests of the parties and the ends of justice ...' (*per* LAW JA); and 'There was no sufficient evidence that by refusing a stay of the Gibraltar proceedings the plaintiffs would suffer any juridical disadvantage justifying a finding that they would suffer any injustice from having to pursue their claim in Germany' (*per* FIELDSEND JA). (See also *Spiliada Maritime Corporation* v *Cansulex*.)

Webb v Webb (Case C–294/92) [1994] ILP 389   [519]
(European Court of Justice)

In a dispute between father and son, the plaintiff father sought a declaration that property bought in the South of France in the son's name was held on trust for him (the plaintiff father), and that the son be ordered to execute the necessary deeds to vest the property in the father's name. The father had contended that he had provided the money to purchase the property as a holiday home for his wife and himself, and that they had used the property regularly as a holiday home over the past 20 years and that they had also paid the outgoings and maintenance costs on the property. The son contended that the French courts had exclusive jurisdiction in this case as, under Article 16(1) of the Brussels Convention 1968, in proceedings with rights in rem in immovable property as their object, exclusive jurisdiction was given to the courts of the Contracting State in which the property was situated. *Held*, dismissing the son's contention, the plaintiff's action had as its object not a right in rem but the establishment of the accountability of the defendant as trustee for the plaintiff. Thus, Article 16(1) was inapplicable. It was reported that: 'The aim of proceedings before the national court is to obtain a declaration that the son holds the flat for the exclusive benefit of the father and that in that capacity he is under a duty to execute the documents necessary to convey the ownership of the flat to the father. The father does not claim that he already enjoys rights directly relating to the property which are enforceable against the whole world, but seeks only to assert rights as against the son. Consequently, his action is not an action in rem within the meaning of Article 16(1) of the Convention but an action in personam.' (See also *Hacker* v *Euro Relais*, *Lieber* v *Gobel* and *Reichert* v *Dresdner Bank*; contrast *Rosler* v *Rottwinkel*.)

Welch v Tennent [1891] AC 639 (House of Lords)   [520]

The parties to a marriage were domiciled in Scotland. The wife, with her husband's consent, sold land in England which belonged to her at the time of their marriage, the proceeds of the sale being paid to the husband. The couple later separated by mutual consent and the wife sought to recover the proceeds of the sale, arguing either that under Scots law she was validly recalling a donation made to her husband or that the court should declare that the money paid to the husband was held as surrogata for her heritable estate. *Held*, whereas 'the rights of the spouses as regards movable property must, in the circumstances of this case be regulated by the law of Scotland ... it is equally clear that their rights in relation to heritable estate are governed by the law of the place where it is situate' (*per* LORD HERSCHELL). Accordingly, English law would be applied and the husband permitted to retain the proceeds of sale.

Wellington (Duke of), Re, Glentanar v Wellington   [521]
[1948] 1 Ch 118 (Court of Appeal)

The Duke of Wellington died domiciled in England, leaving a will in which he disposed of land which he owned in Spain. Under Spanish law, freedom of testation was restricted to one-half of the testator's property, but succession to the property of deceased aliens was regulated according to their lex nationalis. *Held*, the succession to this land should be decided as if by the Supreme Court of Spain, being the court of the situs, though 'it would be difficult to imagine a harder task' to perform because the court had never dealt with this particular situation. However, it would apparently apply the domestic law of England, ignoring its private international law, which meant that the Duke had complete freedom of testation, as under English law. (See also *Re O'Keefe, Poingdestre* v *Sherman* and *Nelson* v *Bridport*.)

Westminster City Council v Government of the Islamic Republic of Iran [1986] 1 WLR 979 [522]

Premises used as the Iranian Embassy within the area of Westminster City Council in May 1980 were stormed by the SAS to free hostages held there. A consequence of the action was that the premises were gutted by fire, leaving them in a dangerous state. In accordance with its statutory powers, the Westminster City Council then shored up and secured the structure but it was frustrated in its attempt to recover its expenses from the Iranian Government. Subsequently, it applied to have its expenses registered as five local land charges, though solicitors for the Iranian Government objected to the registration on the ground that the property formed part of the diplomatic mission of the Iranian Government and that state immunity applied. The solicitors also refused to accept service on behalf of the Iranian Government. Furthermore, service of the originating summons under s12(1) of the State Immunity Act 1978 was rendered impossible by the discontinuance of diplomatic relations between Iran and the UK. *Held*, since it had not been possible to effect service on the Iranian Government the court could not rule on the question of whether the charges should be registered.

White v Tennant 1888 31 W.Va 790 [523]
(Supreme Court of Appeals of West Virginia)

A man left his home in West Virginia, USA, and entered into occupation of what was intended to be his new home in the neighbouring State of Pennsylvania later the same evening. However, the Pennsylvania house was found to be damp and uncomfortable so, after unloading their goods and putting them in the house, the man and his wife decided to spend the night with relatives who lived nearby and to return to their new home in the morning. The wife was able to make only a brief visit because of illness, however, and she returned to stay with her relatives. Thereafter, the man made only daily visits to the new house because he spent the rest of his time attending to his wife who became very ill and this continued until he died intestate a few weeks later. When it came to distributing the man's property, it became necessary to determine where he was domiciled at the time of his death. *Held*, 'if it is shown that a person has entirely abandoned his former domicile in one State with the intention of making his home at a fixed place in another State with no intention of returning to his former domicile and then establishes a residence in the new place for any period of time, however brief, that will be in law a change of domicile, and the latter will remain his domicile until changed in a like manner' (*per* SNYDER J). (Contrast *Winans* v *Attorney-General* and *IRC* v *Bullock*.)

Whitworth Street Estates (Manchester) Ltd v James Miller & Partners Ltd [1970] AC 583 (House of Lords) [524]

By an agreement in the standard form issued by the Royal Institute of British Architects, a Scottish company agreed to carry out conversion work at an English company's factory in Scotland under the supervision of a London architect. The form of contract included terms which were only intelligible by reference to English law and it provided for arbitration of any disputes by an arbitrator nominated by the President of the Institute. A dispute was submitted to a Scottish arbitrator thus nominated, who at a hearing in Scotland refused to state a special case for the court because under Scottish law, in contrast to English law, he could not be compelled to do this. Proceedings were instituted in England by the English company. *Held,* the arbitrator was wrong in so refusing. Although the *country* with which the agreement was most closely connected was Scotland, the *system of law* with which it was most closely connected was English law, on account of the parties' use of a standard form appropriate for English but not Scottish law. Thus English law was the proper law of the agreement and the law governing the arbitration. (See also *Bonython* v *Commonwealth of Australia.*)

Wilks, Re, Keefer v Wilks [1935] Ch 645 [525]

A man died domiciled in Ontario, Canada, being intestate as to his property in England. The administrators appointed in England to deal with this property sought to postpone the sale of certain English shares, this being permissible under English law but not under Ontario law. *Held,* they could do this, because the matter was one of administration of the estate, not distribution among those beneficially entitled to it, and was therefore regulated by the lex fori. (See also *Re Kloebe, Kanreuther* v *Gieselbrecht.*)

Williams & Glyn's Bank v Astro Dinamico [526]
[1984] 1 WLR 438 (House of Lords)

The appellant bank had lent US$10 million to one of its customers, Ulysses Shipping Agency Ltd, (U) a Greek company, on the security of guarantees purported to have been given by the two respondents who were companies owned and managed in Greece. When U defaulted in repayment, the bank sought to enforce its securities against the defendants by instituting proceedings in England on the basis of a clause in the guarantees which provided that, 'The guarantor irrevocably submits to the jurisdiction of the English courts ...'. The respondents contended that the guarantees were invalid on various grounds, including that they had been obtained by fraudulent means. Furthermore, the respondents, who had commenced proceedings in Greece, made an application under RSC O.12, r.8 disputing the jurisdiction of the English courts and a stay of action 'on grounds which may be summarised in one or other or both of the brocards forum non conveniens and lis alibi pendens' (*per* LORD FRASER). At first instance, BINGHAM J (as he then was) decided that the first question to be decided was whether the English court has jurisdiction. The Court of Appeal reversed his decision and ordered that the question of whether to grant a stay should be decided first. *Held, per* LORD FRASER, speaking on behalf of their Lordships, that whereas 'logically the court must decide whether it has jurisdiction before it can go on to consider any other question in the action ... the peculiarity of this case is that a decision on jurisdiction could only be reached by deciding whether the guarantees were valid or not and thus in effect deciding the issue which is at the heart of the action'; that s49(3) of the Supreme Court Act 1981 provides for the court to stay proceedings 'of its own motion' and this would include an action where its own jurisdiction was in issue; that it would be 'quite unrealistic to say that the respondents had waived their objection to the jurisdiction by applying for a stay as an alternative ... for an order giving effect to their objection to the jurisdiction' (*per* LORD FRASER, applying a dictum of DENNING LJ in *Re Dulles' Settlement (No 2)*); and that at first instance two different kinds of jurisdiction were confused, viz, 'first is jurisdiction to decide the action on its merits, and the second is jurisdiction to decide whether the court has jurisdiction of the former kind. ... By entertaining the application for a stay in this case, the court would be assuming (rightly) that it has jurisdiction to decide whether or not it has jurisdiction to deal with the merits, but would not be making any assumption about its jurisdiction to deal with the merits.' Accordingly, the application for a stay should be considered first: the order of the Court of Appeal would be affirmed and the appeal dismissed. (See also *Re Dulles' Settlement (No 2)*.)

Williams and Humbert v W & H Trade Marks (Jersey) Ltd [1986] AC 368 (House of Lords) [527]

Whereas the Spanish State compulsorily acquired all the shares in a Spanish company, it did not make any attempt to change ownership of the shares in its wholly-owned English subsidiary. In an action over the 'Dry Sack' sherry trade mark which, initially, was owned by the plaintiff company, who then assigned it to the Jersey company which was incorporated to hold and exploit trade marks and which, in turn, licensed it back to the plaintiff English company, the plaintiffs contended that the Jersey company's grant of the licence on terms that it would be summarily terminated if, inter alia, part of the share capital of the Spanish company were expropriated was ultra vires Williams and Humbert as involving a gratuitous disposition of its assets made for the benefit not of itself but of the directors of the Jersey company; or an unauthorised reduction of its capital; and in any event, void and unenforceable. The defendants relied on the defence of the Spanish expropriation law being a foreign penal law which ought not to be recognised or enforced in England. *Held*, giving judgment for the plaintiffs, the foreign expropriatory decree was not a penal law: the English courts would recognise the acquisition of property by the foreign State when the property was in the State at the time the expropriatory decree was made with the proviso that the decree was not discriminatory or penal; and, with regard to the English company, the expropriating decree did not have the effect of obtaining assets for the State of Spain. Accordingly, the plaintiffs' application to strike out the defence on the grounds that it showed no reasonable cause of defence would be permitted. (See also *Luther* v *Sagor*, contrast *Banco de Vizcaya* v *Don Alfonso de Borbon y Austria* and *Lecouturier* v *Rey*.)

Winans v Attorney-General [1904] AC 287 (House of Lords) [528]

Winans, an American citizen, whose domicile of origin was uncertain, although either it was in New Jersey or Maryland, came to England at the age of 36 and took tenancies of two furnished houses in Brighton, which he maintained until his death 37 years later. During this period, he spent various parts of each year in Russia, Germany, Scotland and England, except that in the last four years of his life he confined himself to England. His main preoccupations were his health and a project, never actually fulfilled, for the construction of spindle-shaped vessels, commonly called cigar ships, for sale to the US for trade and military purposes. He acquired a water frontage in Baltimore, in the State of Maryland, USA, to provide a harbour for these ships and spoke of returning to Baltimore to develop the scheme. He did not like the English and never mixed with them socially. *Held*, by a majority of 2-1, he died without having acquired an English domicile of choice because there was insufficient evidence to discharge the heavy onus of proving that his domicile of origin had been supplanted by an English domicile of choice. It was not proved 'with perfect clearness and satisfaction' that Winans was 'determined [to make and had made England] his home with the intention of establishing himself and his family there, and ending his days in that country' (*per* LORD MACNAGHTEN, quoting from *Bell* v *Kennedy*). Moreover, a domicile of origin was 'more enduring, its hold stronger, and less easily shaken off' than a domicile of choice (*per* LORD MACNAGHTEN). (See also *Ramsay (or Bowie)* v *Liverpool Royal Infirmary* and *IRC* v *Bullock*; contrast *White* v *Tennant* and *Re Furse*.)

Winkworth v Christie, Manson & Woods Ltd [1980] Ch 496 [529]

Works of art were stolen from P and taken to Italy where they were sold and delivered to the second defendant who, apparently, acquired good title under Italian law. The second defendant then delivered the works of art to the first defendants, a firm of auctioneers, for sale in England. P sought a declaration that they were his property. *Held*, the declaration would be refused: the sale could proceed. SLADE J said: 'Security of title is as important to an innocent purchaser as it is to an innocent owner whose goods have been stolen from him. Commercial convenience may be said imperatively to demand that proprietary rights to movables shall generally be determined by the lex situs under the rules of private international law. Were the position otherwise, it would not suffice for the protection of a purchaser of any valuable movables to ascertain that he was acquiring title to them under the law of the country where the goods were situate at the time of the purchase; he would have to try to effect further investigations as to the past title, with a view to ensuring, so far as possible, that there was no person who might successfully claim a title to the movables by reference to some other system of law...'. (See also *Cammell* v *Sewell*.)

Witted v Galbraith [1893] 1 QB 577 (Court of Appeal) [530]

A vessel belonging to the defendants, who carried on business in Scotland, docked in Milwall, London, for unloading, as arranged by a London shipbroker. The plaintiff's husband was killed during the unloading by falling down a hatchway, which it was alleged was insufficiently protected. The plaintiff sued the shipbrokers and also served a writ under RSC O.11, on the defendants out of the jurisdiction. The defendants sought to set aside the writ. *Held*, 'there is no plausible cause of action against the brokers ... [they] have been brought into the action simply to enable the plaintiff to bring the other defendants within the jurisdiction. It is not a bona fide case of an action properly brought against a person who has been served within the jurisdiction. Consequently, there is no right to proceed under the order, and the appeal must be allowed' (*per* LINDLEY LJ). (See also *John Russell* v *Cayzer, Irvine and Co Ltd*.)

Wolfenden v Wolfenden [1946] P 61 [531]

Two Canadians were married to each other in a Chinese province in which British subjects were to be regulated according to English law 'as far as circumstances permit'. The ceremony was conducted by a minister of the Church of Scotland Mission, who was the only minister available in the district. *Held*, the marriage was valid at common law. To require that the minister should have been episcopally ordained (as in England or Ireland) would be clearly unsuitable for local conditions. (See also *Penhas (Isaac)* v *Tan Soo Eng*.)

Wood v Wood [1957] P 254 (Court of Appeal) [532]

A deserted wife domiciled in England obtained a summary order for maintenance, then her husband acquired a domicile in Nevada, USA, and was granted a divorce there on the ground of three years' separation. The wife did not know of the divorce proceedings (though they were advertised) and the question of maintenance was not raised in them. The husband applied to discharge the maintenance order. *Held*, even though the divorce was valid in England, the court still had a discretion whether or not to discharge the order. In fact, it would not discharge the order because the wife had not had a chance to contest the divorce proceedings, the question of maintenance had not been considered in them and the ground of the decree did not impute any guilt on her part. (See now provisions of the Family Law Act 1986.)

Worms v De Valdor (1880) 49 LJ Ch 261 [533]

A Frenchman who brought an action for delivery up and cancellation of certain bills of exchange was met with the defence that on account of his extravagant habits he had been declared a 'prodigal' by a French court, and that he was therefore debarred by French law from bringing action in any court except on the advice of a legal adviser specially appointed by the court in question. *Held,* this defence would fail because (1) the French court's declaration did not change his status but merely imposed a special French rule for certain types of court action; and (2) even if 'prodigality' was a status, it was a form of personal or penal disqualification which was strictly territorial. Accordingly, it would not be recognised outside France. (See also *Re Selot's Trust*; compare *Warter* v *Warter*.)

Zanelli v Zanelli (1948) 64 TLR 556 (Court of Appeal) [534]

An Italian resided for some time in England under a series of six-monthly alien's permits, which he could generally renew without difficulty. He then deserted his wife, who was also Italian, and went straight back to Italy, the country of his domicile of origin. The wife filed a petition for divorce on the ground of desertion. *Held,* the court had jurisdiction under s13 of the Matrimonial Causes Act 1937 because the husband was domiciled in England immediately before the desertion, and it would grant a decree even though the present lex domicilii, Italian law, did not permit divorce for Italians. The husband had acquired an English domicile of choice even though his stay was 'precarious in the sense that he [might] be turned out, and permissive in the sense that from time to time he [had] to ask permission to stay' (*per* LORD DU PARCQ). He had retained his English domicile of choice at the time of the desertion because, although he was intending to abandon it, he had not yet physically departed from England. (Compare *Re Flynn, Flynn* v *Flynn*.)

Zapata Off-Shore Co v The Bremen and Unterweser Reederei GmbH see **The Chaparral**

Zigurds, The (No 1) [1932] P 113 [535]

A Latvian steamship, *Zigurds*, was arrested in England and sold by court order. The question of the order of priorities of mortgagees and other necessaries men then fell to be decided by the court. The plaintiffs in this action, a German firm that had supplied bunker coal to the ship, were one of several necessaries men. They claimed that the German Commercial Code conferred a status upon them which gave them priority not only over other necessaries men, but also over a mortgagee: that, in essence, they were given a maritime lien permitting them to follow the ship or its proceeds into the hands of subsequent owners. *Held,* the rights possessed by the plaintiffs and conferred by German law were of no value unless they were able to be enforced by the German courts: the order of priorities was to be determined by the lex fori. English law gave the plaintiffs no maritime lien or special priority over mortgagees or other necessaries men. (See also *The Zigurds (Nos 2-4)* (in the same report as (No 1)) and *The Colorado*; contrast *The Halcyon Isle*.)

Statutes

WILLS ACT 1837
(7 Will 4 & 1 Vict c 26)

1 Meaning of certain words in this Act [536]

The words and expressions hereinafter mentioned, which in their ordinary signification have a more confined or a different meaning, shall in this Act, except where the nature of the provision or the context of the Act shall exclude such construction, be interpreted as follows: (that is to say,) the word 'will' shall extend to a testament, and to a codicil, and to an appointment by will or by writing in the nature of a will in exercise of a power, and also to an appointment by will of a guardian of a child, and to any other testamentary disposition; and the words 'real estate' shall extend to manors, advowsons, messuages, lands, tithes, rents, and hereditaments, whether freehold, customary freehold, tenant right, customary or copyhold, or of any other tenure, and whether corporeal, incorporeal, or personal, and to any undivided share thereof, and to any estate, right, or interest (other than a chattel interest) therein; and the words 'personal estate' shall extend to leasehold estates, and other chattels real, and also to moneys, shares of government and other funds, securities for money (being not real estates), debts, choses in action, rights, credits, goods, and all other property whatsoever, which by law devolves upon the executor or administrator, and to any share or interest therein; and every word importing the singular number only shall extend and be applied to several persons or things as well as one person or thing; and every word importing the masculine gender only shall extend and be applied to a female as well as a male.

7 No will of a person under age valid [537]

No will made by any person under the age of eighteen years shall be valid.

9 Signing and attestation of wills [538]

No will shall be valid unless –

(a) it is in writing, and signed by the testator, or by some other person in his presence and by his direction; and
(b) it appears that the testator intended by his signature to give effect to the will; and
(c) the signature is made or acknowledged by the testator in the presence of two or more witnesses present at the same time; and
(d) each witness either –
 (i) attests and signs the will; or
 (ii) acknowledges his signature,

in the presence of the testator (but not necessarily in the presence of any other witness),

but no form of attestation shall be necessary.

10 Appointments by will to be executed like other wills, [539] and to be valid, although other required solemnities are not observed

No appointment made by will, in exercise of any power, shall be valid, unless the same be executed in manner hereinbefore required; and every will executed in manner hereinbefore required shall, so far as respects the execution and attestation thereof, be a valid execution of a power of appointment by will, notwithstanding it shall have been expressly required that a will made in exercise of such power should be executed with some additional or other form of execution or solemnity.

18 Will to be revoked by marriage [540]

(1) Subject to subsections (2) to (4) below, a will shall be revoked by the testator's marriage.

(2) A disposition in a will in exercise of a power of appointment shall take effect notwithstanding the testator's subsequent marriage unless the property so appointed would in default of appointment pass to his personal representatives.

(3) Where it appears from a will that at the time it was made the testator was expecting to be married to a particular person and that he intended that the will should not be revoked by the marriage, the will shall not be revoked by his marriage to that person.

(4) Where it appears from a will that at the time it was made the testator was expecting to be married to a particular person and that he intended that a disposition in the will should not be revoked by his marriage to that person –

(a) that disposition shall take effect notwithstanding the marriage; and
(b) any other disposition in the will shall take effect also, unless it appears from the will that the testator intended the disposition to be revoked by the marriage.

18A Effect of dissolution or annulment of marriage on wills [541]

(1) Where, after a testator has made a will, a decree of a court of civil jurisdiction in England and Wales dissolves or annuls his marriage or his marriage is dissolved or annulled and the divorce or annulment is entitled to recognition in England and Wales by virtue of Part II of the Family Law Act 1986, –

(a) provisions of the will appointing executors or trustees or conferring a power of appointment, if they appoint or confer the power on the former spouse, shall take effect as if the former spouse had died on the date on which the marriage is dissolved or annulled, and
(b) any property which, or an in interest in which, is devised or bequeathed to the former spouse shall pass as if the former spouse had died on that date,

except in so far as a contrary intention appears by the will.

(2) Subsection (1)(b) above is without prejudice to any right of the former spouse to apply for financial provision under the Inheritance (Provision for Family and Dependants) Act 1975.

(3) Where –

(a) by the terms of a will an interest in remainder is subject to a life interest; and
(b) the life interest lapses by virtue of subsection (1)(b) above,

the interest in remainder shall be treated as if it had not been subject to the life interest and, if it was contingent upon the termination of the life interest, as if it had not been so contingent.

NB Section 18A(1), as amended, has effect as respects a will made by a person dying on or after 1 January 1996, regardless of the date of the will and the date of the dissolution or annulment: s3(2) of the Law Reform (Succession) Act 1995.

[As amended by the Statute Law Revision (No 2) Act 1888; Statute Law Revision Act 1893; Statute Law (Repeals) Act 1969; Family Law Reform Act 1969, s3(1)(a); Administration of Justice Act 1982, ss17, 18(1), (2); Family Law Act 1986, s53; Children Act 1989, s108(5), Schedule 13, para 1; Law Reform (Succession) Act 1995, s3(1).]

BILLS OF EXCHANGE ACT 1882
(45 & 46 Vict c 61)

PART I

PRELIMINARY

2 Interpretation of terms

In this Act, unless the context otherwise requires, –
  'Acceptance' means an acceptance completed by delivery or notification.
  'Action' includes counter claim and set off.
  'Banker' includes a body of persons whether incorporated or not who carry on the business of banking.
  'Bankrupt' includes any person whose estate is vested in a trustee or assignee under the law for the time being in force relating to bankruptcy.
  'Bearer' means the person in possession of a bill or note which is payable to bearer.
  'Bill' means bill of exchange, and 'note' means promissory note.
  'Delivery' means transfer of possession, actual or constructive, from one person to another.
  'Holder' means the payee or indorsee or a bill or note who is in possession of it, or the bearer thereof.
  'Indorsement' means an indorsement completed by delivery.
  'Issue' means the first delivery of a bill or note, complete in form to a person who takes it as a holder.
  'Person' includes a body of persons whether incorporated or note.
  'Value' means a valuable consideration.
  'Written' includes printed, and 'writing' includes print.

PART II

BILLS OF EXCHANGE

3 Bill of exchange defined

(1) A bill of exchange is an unconditional order in writing, addressed by one person to another, signed by the person giving it, requiring the person to whom it is addressed to pay on demand or at a fixed or determinable future time a sum certain in money to or to the order of a specified person, or to bearer.

(2) An instrument which does not comply with these conditions, or which orders any act to be done in addition to the payment of money, is not a bill of exchange.

(3) An order to pay out of a particular fund is not unconditional within the meaning of this section; but an unqualified order to pay, coupled with (a) an indication of a particular fund out of which the drawee is to re-imburse himself or a particular account to be debited with the amount, or (b) a statement of the transaction which gives rise to the bill is unconditional.

(4) A bill is not invalid by reason –

(a) That it is not dated;
(b) That it does not specify the value given, or that any value has been given therefor;
(c) That it does not specify the place where it is drawn or the place where it is payable.

72 Rules where laws conflict [544]

Where a bill drawn in one country is negotiated, accepted, or payable in another, the rights, duties, and liabilities of the parties thereto are determined as follows –

(1) The validity of a bill as regards requisites in form is determined by the law of the place of issue, and the validity as regards requisites in form of the supervening contracts, such as acceptance, or indorsement, or acceptance supra protest, is determined by the law of the place where such contract was made.

Provided that –

(a) Where a bill is issued out of the United Kingdom it is not invalid by reason only that it is not stamped in accordance with the law of the place of issue;
(b) Where a bill, issued out of the United Kingdom, conforms, as regards requisites in form, to the law of the United Kingdom, it may, for the purpose of enforcing payment thereof, be treated as valid as between all persons who negotiate, hold, or become parties to it in the United Kingdom.

(2) Subject to the provisions of this Act, the interpretation of the drawing, indorsement, acceptance, or acceptance supra protest of a bill, is determined by the law of the place where such contract is made. Provided that where an inland bill is indorsed in a foreign country the indorsement shall as regards the payer be interpreted according to the law of the United Kingdom.

(3) The duties of the holder with respect to presentment for acceptance or payment and the necessity for or sufficiency of a protest or notice of dishonour or otherwise, are determined by the law of the place where the act is done or the bill is dishonoured.

(5) Where a bill is drawn in one country and is payable in another, the due date thereof is determined according to the law of the place where it is payable.

PART III

CHEQUES ON A BANKER

73 Cheque defined [545]

A cheque is a bill of exchange drawn on a banker payable on demand.

Except as otherwise provided in this Part, the provisions of this Act applicable to a bill of exchange payable on demand apply to a cheque.

FOREIGN MARRIAGE ACT 1892
(55 & 56 Vict c 23)

1 Validity of marriages solemnised abroad in manner provided by Act [546]

(1) All marriages between parties of whom at least one is a United Kingdom national solemnised in the matter in this Act provided in any foreign country or place by or before a marriage officer within the meaning of this Act shall be as valid as if the same had been solemnised in the United Kingdom with a due observance of all forms required by law.

(2) In this Act 'United Kingdom national' means a person who is –

(a) a British citizen, a British Dependant Territories citizen, a British Overseas citizen or a British National (Overseas); or
(b) a British subject under the British Nationality Act 1981; or
(c) a British protected person, within the meaning of that Act.

8 Solemnisation of marriage at office in presence of marriage officer and two witnesses [547]

(1) After the expiration of fourteen days after the notice of an intended marriage has been entered under this Act, then, if no lawful impediment to the marriage is shown to the satisfaction of the marriage officer, and the marriage has not been forbidden in manner provided by this Act, the marriage may be solemnised under this Act.

(2) Every such marriage shall be solemnised –

(a) at the official house of the marriage officer, with open doors, between 8 am and 6 pm, in the presence of two or more witnesses;
(b) by the marriage officer or, if the parties so desire, by another person in his presence; and
(c) according to such form and ceremony as the parties see fit to adopt.

(3) Where (apart from this subsection) it would not be stated or otherwise indicated in the course of the ceremony adopted by the parties that neither of them knows of any lawful impediment to their marriage, then, in some part of the ceremony and in the presence of the marriage officer and witnesses, they shall each declare –

'I solemnly declare that I know not of any lawful impediment why I *AB [or CD]* may not be joined in matrimony to *CD [or AB]*.'

(4) Where (apart from this subsection) it would not be stated by each of the parties in the course of the ceremony adopted by them that he or she takes the other as wife or husband, then, in some part of the ceremony and in the presence of the marriage officer and witnesses, each of the parties shall say to the other –

'I call upon these persons here present to witness that I *AB [or CD]* take thee *CD [or AB]* to be my lawful wedded wife [*or husband*]'.

11 Marriage officers and their districts [548]

(1) For the purposes of this Act the following officers shall be marriage officers that is to say:

(a) Any officer authorised in that behalf by a Secretary of State by authority in writing under his hand (in this Act referred to as a marriage warrant); and
(b) Any officer who, under the marriage regulations hereinafter mentioned, is authorised to act as marriage officers without any marriage warrant,

and the district of the marriage officer shall be the area within which the duties of his office are exercisable, or any such less area as is assigned by the marriage warrant or any other warrant of a Secretary of State, or is fixed by the marriage regulations.

(2) Any marriage warrant of a Secretary of State may authorise to be a marriage officer –

(a) a British ambassador residing in a foreign country to the government of which he is accredited, and also any officer prescribed as an officer for solemnising marriages in the official house of such ambassador;
(b) the holder of the office of British consul in any foreign country or place specified in the warrant; and
(c) a governor, high commissioner, resident, consular or other officer, or any person appointed in pursuance of the marriage regulations to act in the place of a high commissioner or resident, and this Act shall apply with the prescribed modifications to a marriage by or before a governor, high commissioner, resident, or officer so authorised by the warrant, and such an application shall not be limited to places outside Her Majesty's dominions.

(3) If a marriage warrant refers to the office without designating the name of any particular person holding the office, then, while the warrant is in force, the person for the time being holding or acting in such office shall be a marriage officer.

(4) A Secretary of State may, by warrant under his hand, vary or revoke any marriage warrant previously issued under this Act.

(5) Where a marriage officer has no seal of his office, any reference in this Act to the official seal shall be construed to refer to any seal ordinarily used by him, if authenticated by his signature with his official name and description.

19 Power to refuse solemnisation of marriage where marriage inconsistent with international law

A marriage officer shall not be required to solemnise a marriage, or to allow a marriage to be solemnised in his presence, if in his opinion the solemnisation thereof would be inconsistent with international law or the comity of nations:

Provided that any person requiring his marriage to be solemnised shall, if the officer refuses to solemnise it or allow it to be solemnised in his presence, have the right of appeal to the Secretary of State given by this Act.

22 Validity of marriages solemnised by chaplains of HM forces serving abroad and other persons

(1) A marriage solemnised in any foreign territory by a chaplain serving with any part of the naval, military or air forces of His Majesty serving in that territory or by a person authorised, either generally or in respect of the particular marriage, by the commanding officer of any part of those forces serving in that territory shall, subject as hereinafter provided, be as valid in law as if the marriage had been solemnised in the United Kingdom with a due observance of all forms required by law.

(1A) Subsection (1) above shall not apply to a marriage unless –

(a) at least one of the parties to the marriage is a person who –

(i) is a member of the said forces serving in the foreign territory concerned or is employed in that territory in such other capacity as may be prescribed by Order in Council; or
(ii) is a child of a person falling within sub-paragraph (i) above and has his home with that person in that territory; and

(b) such other conditions as may be so prescribed are complied with.

(1B) In determining for the purposes of subsection (1A) above whether one person is the child of another –

(a) it shall be immaterial whether the person's father and mother were at any time married to each other; and
(b) a person who is or was treated by another as a child of the family in relation to any marriage to which that other is or was a party shall be regarded as his child.

(2) In this section the expression 'foreign territory' means territory other than:

(a) any part of His Majesty's dominions;
(b) any British protectorate; or
(c) any other country or territory under His Majesty's protection or suzerainty or in which His Majesty has for the time being jurisdiction:

Provided that His Majesty may by Order in Council direct that –

(i) any British protectorate or any such other country or territory as is referred to in paragraph (c) hereof; or
(ii) any part of His Majesty's dominions which has been occupied by a State at war with His Majesty and in which the facilities for marriage in accordance with the local law have not in the opinion of His Majesty been adequately restored;

shall, while the Order remains in force, be treated as foreign territory for the purposes of this section.

(3) Any reference in this section to foreign territory, to forces serving in foreign territory and to persons employed in foreign territory shall include references to ships which are for the time being in the waters of any foreign territory, to forces serving in any such ship and to persons employed in any such ship, respectively.

(4) His Majesty may by Order in Council provide for the registration of marriages solemnised under this section.

(5) Where a marriage purports to have been solemnised under this section, it shall not be necessary in any legal proceedings touching the validity of the marriage to prove the authority of the person by or before whom it was solemnised, nor shall any evidence to prove his want of authority be given in any such proceedings.

(6) Any Order in Council made under the foregoing provisions of this section may be varied or revoked by a subsequent Order in Council, and any Order in Council made under this section shall be laid forthwith before each House of Parliament.

23 Saving [551]

Nothing in this Act shall confirm or impair or in anywise affect the validity in law of any marriage solemnised beyond the seas, otherwise than as herein provided, and this Act shall not extend to the marriage of any of the Royal family.

[As amended by the Foreign Marriage Act 1947, s2; Foreign Marriage (Amendment) Act 1988, ss1(1), (2), 4, 6, 7(2), Schedule.]

EVIDENCE (COLONIAL STATUTES) ACT 1907
(7 Edw 7 c 16)

1 Proof of statutes of British possessions [552]

(1) Copies of Acts, ordinances, and statutes passed (whether before or after the passing of this Act) by the Legislature of any British possession, and of orders,

regulations, and other instruments issued or made, whether before or after the passing of this Act, under the authority of any such Act, ordinance, or statute, if purporting to be printed by the Government printer, shall be received in evidence by all courts of justice in the United Kingdom without any proof being given that the copies were so printed.

(3) In this Act –

The expression 'Government printer' means, as respects any British possession, the printer purporting to be the printer authorised to print the Acts, ordinances, or statutes of the Legislature of that possession, or otherwise to be the Government printer of that possession:

The expression 'British possession' means any part of His Majesty's dominions exclusive of the United Kingdom, and, where parts of those dominions are under both a central and a local Legislature, shall include both all parts under the central Legislature and each part under a local Legislature. ...

PERJURY ACT 1911
(1 & 2 Geo 5 c 6)

1A False unsworn statement under Evidence (Proceedings in Other Jurisdictions) Act 1975 [553]

If any person, in giving any testimony (either orally or in writing) otherwise than on oath, where required to do so by an order under section 2 of the Evidence (Proceedings in Other Jurisdictions) Act 1975, makes a statement –

(a) which he knows to be false in a material particular, or
(b) which is false in a material particular and which he does not believe to be true,

he shall be guilty of an offence and shall be liable on conviction on indictment to imprisonment for a term not exceeding two years or a fine or both.

[As inserted by the Evidence (Proceedings in Other Jurisdictions) Act 1975, s8(1), Schedule 1.]

MAINTENANCE ORDERS (FACILITIES FOR ENFORCEMENT) ACT 1920
(10 & 11 Geo 5 c 33)

1 Enforcement in England and Ireland of maintenance orders made in His Majesty's dominions outside the United Kingdom [554]

(1) Where a maintenance order has, whether before or after the passing of this Act, been made against any person by any court in any part of His Majesty's dominions outside the United Kingdom to which this Act extends, and a certified copy of the order has been transmitted by the governor of that part of His Majesty's dominions to the Lord Chancellor, the Lord Chancellor shall send a copy of the order to the prescribed officer of a court in England or Ireland for registration; and on receipt thereof the order shall be registered in the prescribed manner, and shall, from the date of such registration, be of the same force and effect, and, subject to the provisions of this Act, all proceedings may be taken on such order as if it had been an order originally obtained in the court in which it is so registered, and that court shall have power to enforce the order accordingly.

(2) The Court in which an order is to be so registered as aforesaid shall, if the court by which the order was made was a court of superior jurisdiction, be the Family Division of the High Court, or in Ireland the King's Bench Division (Matrimonial) of the High Court of Justice in Ireland, and, if the court was not a court of superior jurisdiction, be a court of summary jurisdiction.

2 Transmission of maintenance orders made in England or Ireland [555]

Where a court in England or Ireland has, whether before or after the commencement of this Act, made a maintenance order against any person, and it is proved to that court that the person against whom the order was made is resident in some part of His Majesty's dominions outside the United Kingdom to which this Act extends, the court shall send to the Lord Chancellor for transmission to the governor of that part of His Majesty's dominions a certified copy of the order.

3 Power to make provisional orders of maintenance against persons resident in His Majesty's dominions outside the United Kingdom [556]

(1) Where an application is made to a court of summary jurisdiction in England or Ireland for a maintenance order against any person, and it is proved that that person is resident in a part of His Majesty's dominions outside the United Kingdom to which this Act extends, the court may, in the absence of that person, if after hearing the evidence it is satisfied of the justice of the application, make any such order as it might have made if that person had been resident in England and Wales, had received reasonable notice of the date of the hearing of the application and had failed to appear at the hearing, but in such case the order shall be provisional only, and shall have no effect unless and until confirmed by a competent court in such part of His Majesty's dominions as aforesaid.

(2) The evidence of any witness who is examined on any such application shall be put into writing, and such deposition shall be read over to and signed by him.

(3) Where such an order is made, the court shall send to the Lord Chancellor for transmission to the governor of the part of His Majesty's dominions in which the person against whom the order is made is alleged to reside the depositions so taken and a certified copy of the order, together with a statement of the grounds on which the making of the order might have been opposed if the person against whom the order is made had been resident in England and Wales, had received reasonable notice of the date of the hearing and had appeared at the hearing, and such information as the court possesses for facilitating the identification of that person, and ascertaining his whereabouts.

(4) Where any such provisional order has come before a court in a part of His Majesty's dominions outside the United Kingdom to which this Act extends for confirmation, and the order has by that court been remitted to the court of summary jurisdiction which made the order for the purpose of taking further evidence, that court or any other court of summary jurisdiction appointed for the same commission area (within the meaning of) the Justices of the Peace Act 1979 shall, after the prescribed notice, proceed to take the evidence in like manner and subject to the like conditions as the evidence in support of the original application.

If upon the hearing of such evidence it appears to the court that the order ought not to have been made, the court may revoke the order, but in any other case the depositions shall be sent to the Secretary of State and dealt with in like manner as the original depositions.

(5) The confirmation of an order made under this section shall not affect any power of a court of summary jurisdiction to vary or revoke that order:

Provided that on the making of a varying or revoking order the court shall send a certified copy thereof to the Lord Chancellor for transmission to the governor of the part of His Majesty's dominions in which the original order was confirmed, and that in the case of an order varying the original order the order shall not have any effect unless and until confirmed in like manner as the original order.

(6) The application shall have the same right of appeal, if any, against a refusal to make a provisional order as he would have had against a refusal to make the order had the person against whom the order is sought to be made been resident in England and Wales and received reasonable notice of the date of the hearing of the application.

(7) Where subsection (1) of section 60 of the Magistrates' Courts Act 1980 (revocation, variation etc of orders for periodical payment) applies in relation to an order made under this section which has been confirmed, that subsection shall have effect as if for the words 'by order on complaint', there were substituted 'on an application being made, by order'.

(8) In this section 'revoke' includes discharge.

4 Power of court of summary jurisdiction to confirm maintenance order made out of the United Kingdom [557]

(1) Where a maintenance order has been made by a court in a part of His Majesty's dominions outside the United Kingdom to which this Act extends, and the order is provisional only and has no effect unless and until confirmed by a court of summary jurisdiction in England or Ireland, and a certified copy of the order, together with the depositions of witnesses and a statement of the grounds on which the order might have been opposed has been transmitted to the Lord Chancellor, and it appears to the Lord Chancellor that the person against whom the order was made is resident in England or Ireland, the Lord Chancellor may send the said documents to the prescribed officer of a court of summary jurisdiction, with a requisition that a notice be served on the person informing him that he may attend a hearing at the time and place specified in the notice to show cause why that order should not be confirmed, and upon receipt of such documents and requisition the court shall cause such a notice to be served upon such a person.

(2) A notice required to be served under this section may be served by post.

(3) At the hearing it shall be open to the person on whom the notice was served to oppose the confirmation of the order on any grounds on which he might have opposed the making of the order in the original proceedings had he been a party to them, but on no other grounds, and the certificate from the court which made the provisional order stating the grounds on which the making of the order might have been opposed if the person against whom the order was made had been a party to the proceedings shall be conclusive evidence that those grounds are grounds on which objection may be taken.

(4) If at the hearing the person served with the notice does not appear or, on appearing, fails to satisfy the court that the order ought not to be confirmed, the court may confirm the order either without modification or with such modifications as to the court after hearing the evidence may seem just.

(5) If the person served with the notice appears at the hearing and satisfies the court that for the purpose of establishing any grounds on which he opposes the confirmation of the order it is necessary to remit the case to the court which made the provisional order for the taking of any further evidence, the court may so remit the case and adjourn the proceedings for the purpose.

(5A) Where a magistrates' court confirms a provisional order under this section, it shall at the same time exercise one of its powers under subsection (5B).

(5B) The powers of the court are –

(a) the power to order that payments under the order be made directly to the clerk of the court or the clerk of any other magistrates' court;

(b) the power to order that payments under the order be made to the clerk of the court, or to the clerk of any other magistrates' court, by such method of payment falling within section 59(6) of the Magistrates' Courts Act 1980 (standing order, etc) as may be specified;

(c) the power to make an attachment of earnings order under the Attachment of Earnings Act 1971 to secure payments under the order.

(5C) In deciding which of the powers under subsection (5B) it is to exercise, the court shall have regard to any representations made by the person liable to make payments under the order.

(5D) Subsection (4) of section 59 of the Magistrates' Courts Act 1980 (power of court to require debtor to open account) shall apply for the purposes of subsection (5B) as it applies for the purposes of that section but as if for paragraph (a) there were substituted –

'(a) the court proposes to exercise its power under paragraph (b) of section 4(5B) of the Maintenance Orders (Facilities for Enforcement) Act 1920, and'.

(6) Subject to subsection (6A), where a provisional order has been confirmed under this section, it may be varied or revoked in like manner as if it had originally been made by the confirming court.

(6A) Where the confirming court is a magistrates' court, section 60 of the Magistrates' Courts Act 1980 (revocation, variation etc of orders for periodical payment) shall have effect in relation to a provisional order confirmed under this section –

(za) as if in subsection (1) for the words 'by order on complaint' there were substituted 'on application being made, by order';

(a) as if in subsection (3) for the words 'paragraphs (a) to (d) of section 59(3) above' there were substituted 'section 4(5B) of the Maintenance Orders (Facilities for Enforcement) Act 1920';

(b) as if in subsection (4) for paragraph (b) there were substituted –

'(b) payments under the order are required to be made to the clerk of the court, or to the clerk of any other magistrates' court, by any method of payment falling within section 59(6) above (standing order, etc)';

and as if after the words 'the court' there were inserted 'which made the order';

(c) as if in subsection (5) for the words 'to the clerk' there were substituted 'in accordance with paragraph (a) of section 4(5B) of the Maintenance Orders (Facilities for Enforcement) Act 1920';

(d) as if in subsection (7), paragraph (c) and the word 'and' immediately preceding it were omitted;

(e) as if in subsection (8) for the words 'paragraphs (a) to (d) of section 59(3) above' there were substituted 'section 4(5B) of the Maintenance Orders (Facilities for Enforcement) Act 1920';

(f) as if for subsections (9) and (10) there were substituted the following subsections –

'(9) In deciding, for the purposes of subsections (3) and (8) above, which of the powers under section 4(5B) of the Maintenance Orders (Facilities for Enforcement) Act 1920 it is to exercise, the court shall have regard to any representations made by the debtor.

(10) Subsection (4) of section 59 above (power of court to require debtor to

open account) shall apply for the purposes of subsections (3) and (8) above as it applies for the purposes of that section but as if for paragraph (a) there were substituted –

"(a) The court proposes to exercise its power under paragraph (b) of section 4(5B) of the Maintenance Orders (Facilities for Enforcement) Act 1920, and".'

(6B) Where on an application for variation or revocation the confirming court is satisfied that it is necessary to remit the case to the court which made the order for the purpose of taking any further evidence, the court may so remit the case and adjourn the proceedings for the purpose.

(7) Where an order has been so confirmed, the person bound thereby shall have the same right of appeal, if any, against the confirmation of the order as he would have had against the making of the order had the order been an order made by the court confirming the order.

4A Variation and revocation of maintenance orders [558]

(1) This section applies to –
   (a) any maintenance order made by virtue of section 3 of this Act which has been confirmed as mentioned in that section; and
   (b) any maintenance order which has been confirmed under section 4 of this Act.

(2) Where the respondent to an application for the variation or revocation of a maintenance order to which this section applies is residing in a part of Her Majesty's dominions outside the United Kingdom to which this Act extends, a magistrates' court in England and Wales shall have jurisdiction to hear the application (where it would not have such jurisdiction apart from this subsection) if that court would have had jurisdiction to hear it had the respondent been residing in England and Wales. ...

(4) Where –
   (a) the respondent to an application for the variation or revocation of a maintenance order to which this section applies does not appear at the time and place appointed for the hearing of the application by a magistrates' court in England and Wales, and
   (b) the court is satisfied that the respondent is residing in a part of Her Majesty's dominions outside the United Kingdom to which this Act extends,

the court may proceed to hear and determine the application at the time and place appointed for the hearing or for any adjourned hearing in like manner as if the respondent had appeared at that time and place. ...

(6) In this section 'revocation' includes discharge.

NB This Act is repealed by s22(2) of the Maintenance Orders (Reciprocal Enforcement) Act 1972 as from a day which has yet to be appointed.

[As amended by the Administration of Justice Act 1970, s1(6), Schedule 2, para 2; Domestic Proceedings and Magistrates' Courts Act 1978, s89(2)(a), Schedule 2, para 2; Justice of the Peace Act 1979, s71, Schedule 2, para 1; Maintenance Enforcement Act 1991, s10, Schedule 1, para 1; Transfer of Functions (Magistrates' Courts and Family Law) Order 1992, art 4; Maintenance Orders (Reciprocal Enforcement) Act 1992, s1(1); Schedule 1, Pt I, paras 1, 2, 3.]

ADMINISTRATION OF JUSTICE ACT 1920
(10 & 11 Geo 5 c 81)

PART II

RECIPROCAL ENFORCEMENT OF JUDGMENTS IN THE UNITED KINGDOM AND IN OTHER PARTS OF HIS MAJESTY'S DOMINIONS

9 Enforcement in the United Kingdom of judgments obtained in superior courts in other British dominions [559]

(1) Where a judgment has been obtained in a superior court in any part of His Majesty's dominions outside the United Kingdom to which this Part of this Act extends, the judgment creditor may apply to the High Court in England or [Northern] Ireland, or to the Court of Session in Scotland, at any time within twelve months after the date of the judgment, or such longer period as may be allowed by the court, to have the judgment registered in the court, and on any such application the court may, if in all the circumstances of the case they think it is just and convenient that the judgment should be enforced in the United Kingdom, and subject to the provisions of this section, order the judgment to be registered accordingly.

(2) No judgment shall be ordered to be registered under this section if –

(a) the original court acted without jurisdiction; or
(b) the judgment debtor, being a person who was neither carrying on business nor ordinarily resident within the jurisdiction of the original court, did not voluntarily appear or otherwise submit or agree to submit to the jurisdiction of that court; or
(c) the judgment debtor, being the defendant in the proceedings, was not duly served with the process of the original court and did not appear, notwithstanding that he was ordinarily resident or was carrying on business within the jurisdiction of that court or agreed to submit to the jurisdiction of that court; or
(d) the judgment was obtained by fraud; or
(e) the judgment debtor satisfies the registering court either that an appeal is pending, or that he is entitled and intends to appeal, against the judgment; or
(f) the judgment was in respect of a cause of action which for reasons of public policy or for some other similar reason could not have been entertained by the registering court.

(3) Where a judgment is registered under this section –

(a) the judgement shall, as from the date of registration, be of the same force and effect, and proceedings may be taken thereon, as if it had been a judgment originally obtained or entered up on the date of registration in the registering court;
(b) the registering court shall have the same control and jurisdiction over the judgment as it has over similar judgments given by itself, but in so far only as relates to execution under this section;
(c) the reasonable costs of and incidental to the registration of the judgment (including the costs of obtaining a certified copy thereof from the original court and of the application for registration) shall be recoverable in like manner as if they were sums payable under the judgment. ...

(5) In any action brought in any court in the United Kingdom on any judgment which might be ordered to be registered under this section, the plaintiff shall not be entitled to recover any costs of the action unless an application to register the

judgment under this section has previously been refused or unless the court otherwise orders.

10 Issue of certificates of judgment obtained in the United Kingdom [560]

(1) Where –

(a) a judgment has been obtained in the High Court in England or Northern Ireland, or in the Court of Session in Scotland, against any person; and
(b) the judgment creditor wishes to secure the enforcement of the judgment in a part of Her Majesty's dominions outside the United Kingdom to which this Part of this Act extends,

the court shall, on an application made by the judgment creditor, issue to him a certified copy of the judgment.

(2) The reference in the preceding subsection to Her Majesty's dominions shall be construed as if that subsection had come into force in its present form at the commencement of this Act.

12 Interpretation [561]

(1) In this Part of this Act, unless the context otherwise requires –

The expression 'judgment' means any judgment or order given or made by a court in any civil proceedings, whether before or after the passing of this Act, whereby any sum of money is made payable, and includes an award in proceedings on an arbitration if the award has, in pursuance of the law in force in the place where it was made, become enforceable in the same manner as a judgment given by a court in that place;

The expression 'original court' in relation to any judgment means the court by which the judgment was given;

The expression 'registering court' in relation to any judgment means the court by which the judgment was registered;

The expression 'judgment creditor' means the person by whom the judgment was obtained, and includes the successors and assigns of that person;

The expression 'judgment debtor' means the person against whom the judgment was given, and includes any person against whom the judgment is enforceable in the place where it was given.

(2) Subject to rules of court, any of the powers conferred by this Part of this Act on any court may be exercised by a judge of the court.

14 Extent of Part II of Act [562]

(1) Where His Majesty is satisfied that reciprocal provisions have been made by the legislature of any part of His Majesty's dominions outside the United Kingdom for the enforcement within that part of His dominions of judgment obtained in the High Court in England, the Court of Session in Scotland, and the High Court in Ireland, His Majesty may by Order in Council declare that this Part of this Act shall extend to that part of His dominions, and on any such Order being made this Part of this Act shall extend accordingly.

(2) An Order in Council under this section may be varied or revoked by a subsequent Order.

(3) Her Majesty may by Order in Council under this section consolidate any Orders in Council under this section which are in force when the consolidating Order is made.

21 Short title, repeal and application [563]

(3) This Act, except Part II thereof, applies only to England and Wales.
[As amended by the Civil Jurisdiction and Judgments Act 1982, s35(2), (3).]

ADMINISTRATION OF ESTATES ACT 1925
(15 & 16 Geo 5 c 23)

33 Trust for sale [564]

(1) On the death of a person intestate as to any real or personal estate, such estate shall be held by his personal representatives –

    (a) as to the real estate upon trust to sell the same; and
    (b) as to the personal estate upon trust to call in sell and convert into money such part thereof as may not consist of money,

with power to postpone such sale and conversion for such a period as the personal representatives, without being liable to account, may think proper, and so that any reversionary interest be not sold until it falls into possession, unless the personal representatives see special reason for sale, and so also that, unless required for purposes of administration owing to want of other assets, personal chattels be not sold except for special reason. ...

45 Abolition of descent to heir, curtesy, dower and escheat [565]

(1) With regard to the real estate and personal inheritance of every person dying after the commencement of this Act, there shall be abolished –

    (a) all existing modes rules and canons of descent, and of devolution by special occupancy or otherwise, of real estate, or of a personal inheritance, whether operating by the general law or by the custom of gavelkind or borough english or by any other custom of any county, locality, or manor, or otherwise howsoever; and
    (b) tenancy by the curtesy and every other estate and interest of a husband in real estate as to which his wife dies intestate, whether arising under the general law or by custom or otherwise; and
    (c) dower and freebench and every other estate and interest of a wife in real estate as to which her husband dies intestate, whether arising under the general law or by custom or otherwise: Provided that where a right (if any) to freebench or other like right has attached before the commencement of this Act which cannot be barred by a testamentary or other disposition made by the husband, such right shall, unless released, remain in force as an equitable interest; and
    (d) escheat to the Crown or the Duchy of Lancaster or the Duke of Cornwall or to a mesne lord for want of heirs.

(2) Nothing in this section affects the descent or devolution of an entailed interest.

46 Succession to real and personal estate on intestacy [566]

(1) The residuary estate of an intestate shall be distributed in the manner or be held on the trusts mentioned in this section, namely –

    (i) If the intestate leaves a husband or wife, then in accordance with the following Table:

TABLE

If the intestate –

(1) leaves –

    (a) no issue, and
    (b) no parent, or brother or sister of the whole blood, or issue of a brother or sister of the whole blood

    the residuary estate shall be held in trust for the surviving husband or wife absolutely.

(2) leaves issue (whether or not persons mentioned in sub-paragraph (b) above also survive)

    the surviving husband or wife shall take the personal chattels absolutely and, in addition, the residuary estate of the intestate (other than the personal chattels) shall stand charged with the payment of a fixed net sum [£125,000], free of death duties and costs, to the surviving husband or wife with interest thereon from the date of the death at such rate as the Lord Chancellor may specify by order until paid or appropriated, and, subject to providing for that sum and the interest thereon, the residuary estate (other than the personal chattels) shall be held –

    (a) as to one half upon trust for the surviving husband or wife during his or her life, and, subject to such life interest, on the statutory trusts for the issue of the intestate, and
    (b) as to the other half, on the statutory trusts for the issue of the intestate.

(3) leaves one or more of the following, that is to say, a parent, a brother or sister of the whole blood, or issue of a brother or sister of the whole blood, but leaves no issue

    the surviving husband or wife shall take the personal chattels absolutely and, in addition, the residuary estate of the intestate (other than the personal chattels) shall stand charged with the payment of a fixed net sum [£200,000], free of death duties and costs, to the surviving husband or wife with interest thereon from the date of the death at such rate as the Lord Chancellor may specify by order until paid or appropriated, and, subject to providing for that sum and the interest thereon, the residuary estate (other than the personal chattels) shall be held –

    (a) as to one half in trust for the surviving husband or wife absolutely, and

(b) as to the other half –

(i) where the intestate leaves one parent or both parents (whether or not brothers or sisters of the intestate or their issue also survive) in trust for the parent absolutely or, as the case may be, for the two parents in equal shares absolutely,

(ii) where the intestate leaves no parent, on the statutory trusts for the brothers and sisters of the whole blood of the intestate.

The fixed net sums referred to in paragraphs (2) and (3) of this Table shall be of the amounts provided by or under section 1 of the Family Provision Act 1966.

(ii) If the intestate leaves issue but no husband or wife the residuary estate of the intestate shall be held on the statutory trusts for the issue of the intestate;

(iii) If the intestate leaves no husband or wife and no issue but both parents, then the residuary estate of the intestate shall be held in trust for the father and mother in equal shares absolutely;

(iv) If the intestate leaves no husband or wife and no issue but one parent, then the residuary estate of the intestate shall be held in trust for the surviving father or mother absolutely;

(v) If the intestate leaves no husband or wife and no issue and no parent, then the residuary estate of the intestate shall be held in trust for the following persons living at the death of the intestate, and in the following order and manner, namely –

First, on the statutory trusts for the brothers and sisters of the whole blood of the intestate; but if no person takes an absolutely vested interest under such trusts; then

Secondly, on the statutory trusts for the brothers and sisters of the half blood of the intestate; but if no person takes an absolutely vested interested under such trusts; then

Thirdly, for the grandparents of the intestate and, if more than one survive the intestate, in equal shares; but if there is no member of this class; then

Fourthly, on the statutory trusts for the uncles and aunts of the intestate (being brothers or sisters of the whole blood of a parent of the intestate); but if no person takes an absolutely vested interest under such trusts; then

Fifthly, on the statutory trusts for the uncles and aunts of the intestate (being brothers or sisters of the half blood of a parent of the intestate).

(vi) In default of any person taking an absolute interest under the foregoing provisions, the residuary estate of the intestate shall belong to the Crown or to the Duchy of Lancaster or to the Duke of Cornwall for the time being, as the case may be, as bona vacantia, and in lieu of any right to escheat.

The Crown or the said Duchy or the said Duke may (without prejudice to the powers reserved by section 9 of the Civil List Act 1910, or any other powers), out of the whole or any part of the property devolving on them respectively, provide, in accordance with the existing practice, for dependants, whether kindred or not, of the intestate, and other persons for whom the intestate might reasonably have been expected to make provision.

(1A) The power to make orders under subsection (1) above shall be exercisable by statutory instrument subject to annulment in pursuance of a resolution of either House of Parliament; and any such order may be varied or revoked by a subsequent order made under the power.

(2) A husband and wife shall for all purposes of distribution or division under the foregoing provisions of this section be treated as two persons.

(2A) Where the intestate's husband or wife survived the intestate but died before the end of the period of 28 days beginning with the day on which the intestate died, this section shall have effect as respects the intestate as if the husband or wife had nor survived the intestate.

(3) Where the intestate and the intestate's husband or wife have died in circumstances rendering it uncertain which of them survived the other and the intestate's husband or wife is by virtue of section 184 of the Law of Property Act 1925 deemed to have survived the intestate, this section shall, nevertheless, have effect as respects the intestate as if the husband or wife had not survived the intestate.

(4) The interest payable on the fixed net sum payable to a surviving husband or wife shall be primarily payable out of income.

NB Section 46(2A) has effect as respects an intestate dying on or after 1 January 1996: s1(3) of the Law Reform (Succession) Act 1995.

[As amended by the Intestates Estates Act 1952, s1; Family Provision Act 1966, s1; Administration of Justice Act 1977, s28(1)(a)(i), (ii); Law Reform (Succession) Act 1995, s1(1).]

EVIDENCE (FOREIGN, DOMINION AND COLONIAL DOCUMENTS) ACT 1933
(23 & 24 Geo 5 c 4)

1 Proof and effect of foreign, dominion and colonial [567] registers and certain official certificates

(2) An Order in Council made under section 5 of the Oaths and Evidence (Overseas Authorities and Countries) Act 1963 may provide that in all parts of the United Kingdom –

(a) a register of the country to which the Order relates, being such a register as is specified in the Order, shall be deemed to be a public register kept under the authority of the law of that country and recognised by the courts thereof as an authentic record, and to be a document of such a public nature as to be admissible as evidence of the matters regularly recorded therein;

(b) such matters as may be specified in the Order shall, if recorded in such a register, be deemed, until the contrary is proved, to be regularly recorded therein;

(c) subject to any conditions specified in the Order and to any requirements of rules of court a document purporting to be issued in the country to which the Order relates as an official copy of an entry in such a register as is so specified, and purporting to be authenticated as such in the manner specified in the Order as appropriate in the case of such a register, shall, without evidence as to the custody of the register or of inability to produce it and without any further or other proof, be received as evidence that the register contains such an entry;

(d) subject as aforesaid a certificate purporting to be given in the country to which the Order relates as an official certificate of any such class as is specified in the Order, and purporting to be signed by the officer, and to be authenticated in the manner specified in the Order as appropriate in the case of a certificate of that class, shall be received as evidence of the facts stated in the certificate;

(e) no official document issued in the country to which the Order relates as proof of any matters for the proof of which provision is made by the Order shall, if otherwise admissible in evidence, be inadmissible by reason only that it is not authenticated by the process known as legislation.

(3) Official books of record preserved in a central registry and containing entries copied from original registers may, if those entries were copied by officials in the course of their duty, themselves be treated for the purposes of this section as registers. ...

[As amended by the Oaths and Evidence (Overseas Authorities and Countries) Act 1963, s5.]

FOREIGN JUDGMENTS (RECIPROCAL ENFORCEMENT) ACT 1933
(23 & 24 Geo 5 c 13)

PART I

REGISTRATION OF FOREIGN JUDGMENTS

1 Power to extend Part I of Act to foreign countries giving reciprocal treatment

(1) If, in the case of a foreign country, His Majesty is satisfied that, in the event of the benefits conferred by this Part of the Act being extended to, or to any particular class of, judgments given in the courts of that country or in any particular class of those courts, substantial reciprocity of treatment will be assured as regards the enforcement in that country of similar judgments given in similar courts of the United Kingdom, He may by Order in Council direct –

(a) that this part of this Act shall extend to that country;
(b) that such courts of that country as are specified in the Order shall be recognised courts in that country for the purposes of this Part of this Act; and
(c) that judgments of any such recognised court, or such judgments of any class so specified shall, if within subsection (2) of this section, be judgments to which this Part of this Act applies.

(2) Subject to subsection (2A) of this section, a judgment of a recognised court is within this subsection if it satisfies the following conditions, namely –

(a) it is either final and conclusive as between the judgment debtor and the judgment creditor or requires the former to make an interim payment to the latter; and
(b) there is payable under it a sum of money, not being a sum payable in respect of taxes or other charges of a like nature or in respect of a fine or other penalty; and
(c) it is given after the coming into force of the Order in Council which made that court a recognised court.

(2A) The following judgments of a recognised court are not within subsection (2) of this section –

(a) a judgment given by that court on appeal from a court which is not a recognised court;
(b) a judgment or other instrument which is regarded for the purposes of its enforcement as a judgment of that court but which was given or made in another country;

(c) a judgment given by that court in proceedings founded on a judgment of court in another country and having as their object the enforcement of that judgment.

(3) For the purposes of this section, a judgment shall be deemed to be final and conclusive notwithstanding that an appeal may be pending against it, or that it may still be subject to appeal, in the courts of the country of the original court.

(4) His Majesty may by subsequent Order in Council vary or revoke any Order previously made under this section.

(5) Any Order in Council made under this section before its amendment by the Civil Jurisdiction and Judgments Act 1982 which deems any court of a foreign country to be a superior court of that country for the purposes of this part of this Act shall (without prejudice to subsection (4) of this section) have effect from the time of that amendment as if it provided for that court to be a recognised court of that country for those purposes, and for any final and conclusive judgment of that court, if within subsection (2) of this section, to be a judgment to which this Part of the Act applies.

2 Application for, and effect of, registration of foreign judgment

(1) A person, being a judgment creditor under a judgment to which this Part of this Act applies, may apply to the High Court at any time within six years after the date of the judgment, or, where there have been proceedings by way of appeal against the judgment, after the date of the last judgment given in those proceedings, to have the judgment registered in the High Court, and on any such application the court shall, subject to proof of the prescribed matters and to the other provisions of this Act, order the judgment to be registered: Provided that a judgment shall not be registered if at the date of the application –

(a) it has been wholly satisfied; or
(b) it could not be enforced by execution in the country of the original court.

(2) Subject to the provisions of this Act with respect to the setting aside of registration –

(a) a registered judgment shall, for the purposes of execution, be of the same force and effect; and
(b) proceedings may be taken on a registered judgment; and
(c) the sum for which a judgment is registered shall carry interest; and
(d) the registering court shall have the same control over the execution of a registered judgment;

as if the judgment had been a judgment originally given in the registering court and entered on the date of registration: Provided that execution shall not issue on the judgment so long as, under this Part of the Act and the Rules of Court made thereunder, it is competent for any party to make an application to have the registration of the judgment set aside, or, where such an application is made, until after the application has been finally determined.

(4) If, at the date of the application for registration the judgment of the original court has been partly satisfied, the judgment shall not be registered in respect of the whole sum payable under the judgment of the original court, but only in respect of the balance remaining payable at that date.

(5) If, on an application for the registration of a judgment, it appears to the registering court that the judgment is in respect of different matters and that some, but not all, of the provisions of the judgment are such that if those provisions had been contained in separate judgments those judgments could properly have been

registered, the judgment may be registered in respect of the provisions aforesaid but not in respect of any other provisions contained therein.

(6) In addition to the sum of money payable under the judgment of the original court, including any interest which by the law of the country of the original court becomes due under the judgment up to the time of registration, the judgment shall be registered for the reasonable costs of and incidental to registration, including the costs of obtaining a certified copy of the judgment from the original court.

3 Rules of court [570]

(1) The power to make rules of court under section 84 of the Supreme Court Act 1981 shall, subject to the provisions of this section, include power to make rules for the following purposes –

(a) For making provision with respect to the giving of security for costs by persons applying for the registration of judgments;

(b) For prescribing the matters to be proved on an application for the registration of a judgment and for regulating the mode of proving those matters;

(c) For providing for the service on the judgment debtor of notice of the registration of a judgment;

(d) For making provision with respect to the fixing of the period within which an application may be made to have the registration of the judgment set aside and with respect to the extension of the period so fixed;

(e) For prescribing the method by which any question arising under this Act whether a foreign judgment can be enforced by execution in the country of the original court, or what interest is payable under a foreign judgment under the law of the original court, is to be determined;

(f) For prescribing any matter which under this Part of this Act is to be prescribed.

(2) Rules made for the purposes of this Part of this Act shall be expressed to have, and shall have, effect subject to any such provisions contained in Orders in Council made under section one of this Act as are declared by the said Orders to be necessary for giving effect to agreements made between His Majesty and foreign countries in relation to matters with respect to which there is power to make rules of court for the purposes of this Part of this Act.

4 Cases in which registered judgments must, or may, [571] be set aside

(1) On an application in that behalf duly made by any party against whom a registered judgment may be enforced, the registration of the judgment –

(a) shall be set aside if the registering court is satisfied –

(i) that the judgment is not a judgment to which this Part of this Act applies or was registered in contravention of the foregoing provisions of this Act; or
(ii) that the courts of the country of the original court had no jurisdiction in the circumstances of the case; or
(iii) that the judgment debtor, being the defendant in the proceedings in the original court, did not (notwithstanding that process may have been duly served on him in accordance with the law of the country of the original court) receive notice of those proceedings in sufficient time to enable him to defend the proceedings and did not appear; or
(iv) that the judgment was obtained by fraud; or

(v) that the enforcement of the judgment would be contrary to public policy in the country of the registering court; or

(vi) that the rights under the judgment are not vested in the person by whom the application for registration was made;

(b) may be set aside if the registering court is satisfied that the matter in dispute in the proceedings in the original court had previously to the date of the judgment in the original court been the subject of a final and conclusive judgment by a court having jurisdiction in the matter.

(2) For the purposes of this section the courts of the country of the original court shall, subject to the provisions of subsection (3) of this section, be deemed to have had jurisdiction –

(a) in the case of a judgment given in an action in personam –

(i) if the judgment debtor, being a defendant in the original court, submitted to the jurisdiction of that court by voluntarily appearing in the proceedings; or

(ii) if the judgment debtor was plaintiff in, or counter-claimed in, the proceedings in the original court; or

(iii) if the judgment debtor, being a defendant in the original court, had before the commencement of the proceedings agreed, in respect of the subject matter of the proceedings, to submit to the jurisdiction of that court or of the courts of the country of that court; or

(iv) if the judgment debtor, being a defendant in the original court, was at the time when the proceedings were instituted resident in, or being a body corporate had its principal place of business in, the country of that court; or

(v) if the judgment debtor, being a defendant in the original court, had an office or place of business in the country of that court and the proceedings in that court were in respect of a transaction effected through or at that office or place;

(b) in the case of a judgment given in an action of which the subject matter was immovable property or in an action in rem of which the subject matter was movable property, if the property in question was at the time of the proceedings in the original court situate in the country of that court;

(c) in the case of a judgment given in an action other than any such action as is mentioned in paragraph (a) or paragraph (b) of this subsection, if the jurisdiction of the original court is recognised by the law of the registering court.

(3) Notwithstanding anything in subsection (2) of this section, the courts of the country of the original court shall not be deemed to have had jurisdiction –

(a) if the subject matter of the proceedings was immovable property outside the country of the original court; or

(c) if the judgment debtor, being a defendant in the original proceedings, was a person who under the rules of public international law was entitled to immunity from the jurisdiction of the courts of the country of the original court and did not submit to the jurisdiction of that court.

5 Powers of registering court on application to set aside registration [572]

(1) If, on an application to set aside the registration of a judgment, the applicant satisfies the registering court either that an appeal is pending, or that he is entitled and intends to appeal, against the judgment, the court, if it thinks fit, may, on such terms as it may think just, either set aside the registration or adjourn the application to set aside the registration until after the expiration of such period as

appears to the court to be reasonably sufficient to enable the applicant to take the necessary steps to have the appeal disposed of by the competent tribunal.

(2) Where the registration of a judgment is set aside under the last foregoing subsection, or solely for the reason that the judgment was not at the date of the application for registration enforceable by execution in the country of the original court, the setting aside of the registration shall not prejudice a further application to register the judgment when the appeal has been disposed of or if and when the judgment becomes enforceable by execution in that country, as the case may be.

(3) Where the registration of a judgment is set aside solely for the reason that the judgment, notwithstanding that it had at the date of the application for registration been partly satisfied, was registered for the whole sum payable thereunder, the registering court shall, on the application of the judgment creditor, order judgment to be registered for the balance remaining payable at that date.

6 Foreign judgments which can be registered not to be enforceable otherwise [573]

No proceedings for the recovery of a sum payable under a foreign judgment, being a judgment to which this Part of this Act applies, other than proceedings by way of registration of the judgment, shall be entertained by any court in the United Kingdom.

PART II

MISCELLANEOUS AND GENERAL

8 General effect of certain foreign judgments [574]

(1) Subject to the provisions of this section, a judgment to which Part I of this Act applies or would have applied if a sum of money had been payable thereunder, whether it can be registered or not, and whether, if it can be registered, it is registered or not, shall be recognised in any court in the United Kingdom as conclusive between the parties thereto in all proceedings founded on the same cause of action and may be relied on by way of defence or counterclaim in any such proceedings.

(2) This section shall not apply in the case of any judgment –

(a) where the judgment has been registered and the registration thereof has been set aside on some ground other than –

(i) that a sum of money was not payable under the judgment; or
(ii) that the judgment had been wholly or partly satisfied; or
(iii) that at the date of the application the judgment could not be enforced by execution in the country of the original court; or

(b) where the judgment has not been registered, it is shown (whether it could have been registered or not) that if it had been registered the registration thereof would have been set aside on an application for that purpose on some ground other than one of the grounds specified in paragraph (a) of this subsection.

(3) Nothing in this section shall be taken to prevent any court in the United Kingdom recognising any judgment as conclusive of any matter of law or fact decided therein if that judgment would have been so recognised before the passing of this Act.

9 Power to make foreign judgments unenforceable in United Kingdom if no reciprocity [575]

(1) If it appears to His Majesty that the treatment in respect of recognition and enforcement accorded by the courts of any foreign country to judgments given in the courts of the United Kingdom is substantially less favourable than that accorded by the courts of the United Kingdom to judgments of the courts of that country, His Majesty may by Order in Council apply this section to that country.

(2) Except in so far as His Majesty may by Order in Council under this section otherwise direct, no proceedings shall be entertained in any court in the United Kingdom for the recovery of any sum alleged to be payable under a judgment given in a court of a country to which this section applies.

(3) His Majesty may by a subsequent Order in Council vary or revoke any Order previously made under this section.

10 Provision for issue of copies of, and certificates in connection with, United Kingdom judgments [576]

(1) Rules may make provision for enabling any judgment creditor wishing to secure the enforcement in a foreign country to which Part I of this Act extends of a judgment to which this subsection applies, to obtain, subject to any conditions specified in the rules –

(a) a copy of the judgment; and

(b) a certificate giving particulars relating to the judgment and the proceedings in which it was given.

(2) Subsection (1) applies to any judgment given by a court or tribunal in the United Kingdom under which a sum of money is payable, not being a sum payable in respect of taxes or other charges of a like nature or in respect of a fine or other penalty.

(3) In this section 'rules' –

(a) in relation to judgments given by a court, means rules of court;

(b) in relation to judgments given by any other tribunal, means rules or regulations made by the authority having power to make rules or regulations regulating the procedure of that tribunal.

10A Arbitration awards [577]

The provisions of this Act, except sections 1(5) and 6, shall apply as they apply to a judgment, in relation to an award in proceedings on an arbitration which has, in pursuance of the law in force in the place where it was made, become enforceable in the same manner as a judgment given by a court in that place.

11 Interpretation [578]

(1) In this Act, unless the context otherwise requires, the following expressions have the meanings hereby assigned to them respectively, that is to say –

'Appeal' includes any proceeding by way of discharging or setting aside a judgment or an application for a new trial or a stay of execution;

'Country of the original court' means the country in which the original court is situated;

'Court', except in section 10 of this Act includes a tribunal;

'Judgment' means a judgment or order given or made by a court in any civil proceedings, or a judgment or order given or made by a court in any criminal proceedings for the payment of a sum of money in respect of compensation or damages to an injured party;

'Judgment creditor' means the person in whose favour the judgment was given and includes any person in whom the rights under the judgment have become vested by succession or assignment or otherwise;

'Judgment debtor' means the person against whom the judgment was given, and includes any person against whom the judgment is enforceable under the law of the original court;

'Original court' in relation to any judgment means the court by which the judgment was given;

'Prescribed' means prescribed by rules of court;

'Registration' means registration under Part I of this Act, and the expressions 'register' and 'registered' shall be construed accordingly;

'Registering court' in relation to any judgment means the court to which an application to register the judgment is made.

(2) For the purposes of this Act, the expression 'action in personam' shall not be deemed to include any matrimonial cause or any proceedings in connection with any of the following matters, that is to say, matrimonial matters, administration of the estates of deceased persons, bankruptcy, winding up of companies, lunacy, or guardianship of infants.

[As amended by the Administration of Justice Act 1977, ss4, 32(4), Schedule 5; Supreme Court Act 1981, ss152(1), 153(4), Schedule 4; Civil Jurisdiction and Judgments Act 1982, ss35(1), 54, Schedule 10, paras 1–5, Schedule 14.]

NATIONAL ASSISTANCE ACT 1948
(11 & 12 Geo 6 c 29)

42 Liability to maintain wife or husband, and children [579]

(1) For the purposes of this Act –

(a) a man shall be liable to maintain his wife and his children, and
(b) a woman shall be liable to maintain her husband and her children.

(2) Any reference in subsection (1) of this section to a person's children shall be construed in accordance with section 1 of the Family Law Reform Act 1987. ...

43 Recovery of cost of assistance from persons liable [580]
for maintenance

(1) Where assistance is given or applied for by reference to the requirements of any person (in this section referred to as a person assisted), the local authority concerned may make a complaint to the court against any other person who for the purposes of this Act is liable to maintain the person assisted.

(2) On a complaint under this section the court shall have regard to all the circumstances and in particular to the resources of the defendant, and may order the defendant to pay such sum, weekly or otherwise, as the court may consider appropriate.

(3) For the purposes of the application of the last foregoing subsection to payments in respect of assistance given before the complaint was made, a person shall not be treated as having at the time when the complaint is heard any greater resources than he had at the time when the assistance was given.

(4) In this section the expression 'assistance' means the provision of accommodation under Part III of this Act (hereinafter referred to as 'assistance

under Part III of this Act'); and the expression 'the court' means a court of summary jurisdiction appointed for the commission area (within the meaning of the Justices of the Peace Act 1979) where the assistance was given or applied for.

(5) Payments under subsection (2) of this section shall be made –

(a) to the local authority concerned, in respect of the cost of assistance, whether given before or after the making of the order, or
(b) to the applicant for assistance or any other person being a person assisted, or
(c) to such other person as appears to the court expedient in the interests of the person assisted,

or as to part in one such manner and as to part in another, as may be provided by the order.

(6) An order under this section shall be enforceable as a magistrates' court maintenance order within the meaning of section 150(1) of the Magistrates' Courts Act 1980. ...

[As amended by the Domestic Proceedings and Magistrates' Courts Act 1978, s89(2)(a), Schedule 2, para 6; Justices of the Peace Act 1979, s71, Schedule 2, para 3; Family Law Reform Act 1987, s33(1), Schedule 2, para 6.]

MARRIAGE ACT 1949
(12, 13 & 14 Geo 6 c 76)

1 Marriages within prohibited degrees [581]

(1) A marriage solemnised between a man and any of the persons mentioned in the first column of Part 1 of the First Schedule to the Act, or between a woman and any of the persons mentioned in the second column of the said Part 1, shall be void.

(2) Subject to subsection (3) of this section, a marriage solemnised between a man and any of the persons mentioned in the first column of Part II of the First Schedule to this Act, or between a woman and any of the persons mentioned in the second column of the said Part II, shall be void.

(3) Any such marriage as is mentioned in subsection (2) of this section shall not be void by reason only of affinity if both the parties to the marriage have attained the age of twenty-one at the time of the marriage and the younger party has not at any time before attaining the age of eighteen been a child of the family in relation to the other party.

(4) Subject to subsection (5) of this section, a marriage solemnised between a man and any of the persons mentioned in the first column of Part III of the First Schedule to this Act or between a woman and any of the persons mentioned in the second column of the said Part III shall be void.

(5) Any such marriage as is mentioned in subsection (4) of this section shall not be void by reason only of affinity if both the parties to the marriage have attained the age of twenty-one at the time of the marriage and the marriage is solemnised –

(a) in the case of a marriage between a man and the mother of a former wife of his, after the death of both the former wife and the father of the former wife;
(b) in the case of a marriage between a man and the former wife of his son, after the death of both his son and the mother of his son;
(c) in the case of a marriage between a woman and the father of a former husband of hers, after the death of both the former husband and the mother of the former husband;

(d) in the case of a marriage between a woman and a former husband of her daughter, after the death of both her daughter and the father of her daughter.

2 Marriages of persons under sixteen [582]

A marriage solemnised between persons either of whom is under the age of sixteen shall be void.

41 Registration of buildings [583]

(1) Any proprietor or trustee of a building which has been certified as required by law as a place of religious worship may apply to the superintendent registrar of the registration district in which the building is situated for the building to be registered for the solemnisation of marriages therein.

(2) Any person making such an application as aforesaid shall deliver to the superintendent registrar a certificate, signed in duplicate by at least twenty householders and dated not earlier than one month before the making of the application, stating that the building is being used by them as their usual place of public religious worship and that they desire that the building should be registered as aforesaid, and both certificates shall be countersigned by the proprietor or trustee by whom they are delivered.

(3) The superintendent registrar shall send both certificates delivered to him under the last foregoing subsection to the Registrar General who shall register the building in a book to be kept for that purpose in the General Register Office.

(4) The Registrar General shall endorse on both certificates sent to him as aforesaid the date of the registration, and shall keep one certificate with the records of the General Register Office and shall return the other certificate to the superintendent registrar who shall keep it with the records of his office.

(5) On the return of the certificate under the last foregoing subsection, the superintendent registrar shall –

(a) enter the date of the registration of the building in a book to be provided for that purpose by the Registrar General;
(b) give a certificate of the registration signed by him, on durable materials, to the proprietor or trustee by whom the certificates delivered to him under subsection (2) of this section were countersigned; and
(c) give public notice of the registration of the building by advertisement in some newspaper circulating in the country in which the building is situated and in the London Gazette.

(6) For every entry, certificate and notice made or given under the last foregoing subsection the superintendent registrar shall be entitled to receive, at the time of the delivery of the certificates under subsection (2) of this section, the sum of £93.00.

(7) A building may be registered for the solemnisation of marriages under this section whether it is a separate building or forms part of another building.

46 Register office marriage followed by religious ceremony [584]

(1) If the parties to a marriage solemnised in the presence of a superintendent registrar desire to add the religious ceremony ordained or used by the church or persuasion of which they are members, they may present themselves, after giving notice of their intention so to do, to the clergyman or minister of the church or persuasion of which they are members, and the clergyman or minister, upon the production of a certificate of their marriage before the superintendent registrar and

upon the payment of the customary fees (if any), may, if he sees fit, read or celebrate in the church or chapel of which he is the regular minister the marriage service of the church or persuasion to which he belongs or nominate some other minister to do so.

(2) Nothing in the reading or celebration of a marriage service under this section shall supersede or invalidate any marriage previously solemnised in the presence of a superintendent registrar, and the reading or celebration shall not be entered as a marriage in any marriage register book kept under Part IV of this Act. ...

75 Offences relating to solemnisation of marriages ... [585]

(2) Any person who knowingly and wilfully –

(a) solemnises a marriage (not being a marriage by special licence, a marriage according to the usages of the Society of Friends or a marriage between two persons professing the Jewish religion according to the usages of the Jews) in any place other than –

(i) a church or other building in which marriages may be solemnised according to the rites of the Church of England, or
(ii) the registered building, office, approved premises or person's residence specified as the place where the marriage was to be solemnised in the notice of marriage and certificate required under Part III of this Act;

(aa) solemnises a marriage purporting to be in pursuance of section 26(1)(bb) of this Act on premises which are not approved premises;
(b) solemnises a marriage in any such registered building as aforesaid (not being a marriage in the presence of an authorised person) in the absence of a registrar of the district in which the registered building is situated;
(bb) solemnises a marriage in pursuance of section 26(1)(dd) of this Act, otherwise than according to the rites of the Church of England, in the absence of a registrar of the registration district in which the place where the marriage is solemnised is situated;
(c) solemnises a marriage in the office of a superintendent registrar in the absence of a registrar of the district in which the office is situated;
(cc) solemnises a marriage on approved premises in pursuance of section 26(1)(bb) of this Act in the absence of a registrar of the district in which the premises are situated;
(d) solemnises a marriage on the authority of a certificate of a superintendent registrar (not being a marriage by licence) within twenty-one days after the day on which the notice of marriage was entered in the marriage notice book; or
(e) solemnises a marriage on the authority of a certificate of a superintendent registrar after the expiration of three months from the said day on which the notice of marriage was entered as aforesaid;

shall be guilty of felony and shall be liable to imprisonment for a term not exceeding five years. ...

FIRST SCHEDULE

KINDRED AND AFFINITY

PART I

Prohibited degrees of relationship

Mother	Father
Adoptive mother or former adoptive mother	Adoptive father or former adoptive father
Daughter	Son
Adoptive daughter or former adoptive daughter	Adoptive son or former adoptive son
Father's mother	Father's father
Mother's mother	Mother's father
Son's daughter	Son's son
Daughter's daughter	Daughter's son
Sister	Brother
Father's sister	Father's brother
Mother's sister	Mother's brother
Brother's daughter	Brother's son
Sister's daughter	Sister's son

PART II

Degrees of affinity referred to in section 1(2) and (3) of this Act

Daughter of former wife	Son of former husband
Former wife of father	Former husband of mother
Former wife of father's father	Former husband of father's mother
Former wife of mother's father	Former husband of mother's mother
Daughter of son of former wife	Son of son of former husband
Daughter of daughter of former wife	Son of daughter of former husband

PART III

Degrees of affinity referred to in section 1(4) and (5) of this Act

Mother of former wife	Father of former husband
Former wife of son	Former husband of daughter

[As amended by the Marriage Acts Amendment Act 1958, s1(1); Children Act 1975, s108(1)(a); Marriage Act 1983, s1(7), Schedule 1, paras 12, 20; Marriage (Prohibited Degrees of Relationship) Act 1986, s1(6), Schedule 1, paras 2, 8; Marriage (Registration of Buildings) Act 1990, s1(1); Marriage Act 1994, s1, Schedule, para 7; Registration of Births, Deaths and Marriages (Fees) Order 1994.]

ARBITRATION ACT 1950
(14 Geo 6 c 27)

PART I

GENERAL PROVISIONS AS TO ARBITRATION

1 Authority of arbitrators and umpires to be irrevocable [587]

The authority of an arbitrator or umpire appointed by or by virtue of an arbitration agreement shall, unless a contrary intention is expressed in the agreement, be irrevocable except by leave of the High Court or a judge thereof.

2 Death of party [588]

(1) An arbitration agreement shall not be discharged by the death of any party thereto, either as respects the deceased or any other party, but shall in such an event be enforceable by or against the personal representative of the deceased.

(2) The authority of an arbitrator shall not be revoked by the death of any party by whom he was appointed.

(3) Nothing in this section shall be taken to affect the operation of any enactment or rule of law by virtue of which any right of action is extinguished by the death of a person.

3 Bankruptcy [589]

(1) Where it is provided by a term in a contract to which a bankrupt is a party that any differences arising thereout or in connection therewith shall be referred to arbitration, the said term shall, if the trustee in bankruptcy adopts the contract, be enforceable by or against him so far as relates to any such differences.

(2) Where a person who has been adjudged bankrupt had, before the commencement of the bankruptcy, become a party to an arbitration agreement, and any matter to which the agreement applies requires to be determined in connection with or for the purposes of the bankruptcy proceedings, then, if the case is one to which subsection (1) of this section does not apply, any other party to the agreement or, with the consent of the creditors' committee established under section 301 of the Insolvency Act 1986, the trustee in bankruptcy, may apply to the court having jurisdiction in the bankruptcy proceedings for an order directing that the matter in question shall be referred to arbitration in accordance with the agreement, and that court may, if it is of opinion that, having regard to all the circumstances of the case, the matter ought to be determined by arbitration, make an order accordingly.

4 Staying court proceedings where there is submission to arbitration [590]

(1) If any party to an arbitration agreement, or any person claiming through or under him, commences any legal proceedings in any court against any other party to the agreement, or any person claiming through or under him, in respect of any matter agreed to be referred, any party to those legal proceedings may at any time after appearance, and before delivering any pleadings or taking any other steps in the proceedings, apply to that court to stay the proceedings, and that court or a judge thereof, if satisfied that there is no sufficient reason why the matter should not be referred in accordance with the agreement, and that the applicant was, at

the time when the proceedings were commenced, and still remains, ready and willing to do all things necessary to the proper conduct of the arbitration, may make an order staying the proceedings.

5 Reference of interpleader issues to arbitration [591]

Where relief by way of interpleader is granted and it appears to the High Court that the claims in question are matters to which an arbitration agreement, to which the claimants are parties, applies, the High Court may direct the issue between the claimants to be determined in accordance with the agreement.

6 When reference is to a single arbitrator [592]

Unless a contrary intention is expressed therein, every arbitration agreement shall, if no other mode of reference is provided, be deemed to include a provision that the reference shall be to a single arbitrator.

7 Power of parties in certain cases to supply vacancy [593]

Where an arbitration agreement provides that the reference shall be to two arbitrators, one to be appointed by each party, then, unless a contrary intention is expressed therein –

(a) if either of the appointed arbitrators refuses to act, or is incapable of acting, or dies, the party who appointed him may appoint a new arbitrator in his place;

(b) if, on such a reference, one party fails to appoint an arbitrator, either originally, or by way of substitution as aforesaid, for seven clear days after the other party, having appointed his arbitrator, has served the party making default with notice to make the appointment, the party who has appointed an arbitrator may appoint that arbitrator to act as sole arbitrator in the reference and his award shall be binding on both parties as if he had been appointed by consent:

Provided that the High Court or a judge thereof may set aside any appointment made in pursuance of this section.

8 Umpires [594]

(1) Unless a contrary intention is expressed therein, every arbitration agreement shall, where the reference is to two arbitrators, be deemed to include a provision that the two arbitrators may appoint an umpire at any time after they are themselves appointed and shall do so forthwith if they cannot agree.

(2) Unless a contrary intention is expressed therein, every arbitration agreement shall, where such a provision is applicable to the reference, be deemed to include a provision that if the arbitrators have delivered to any party to the arbitration agreement, or to the umpire, a notice in writing stating that they cannot agree, the umpire may forthwith enter on the reference in lieu of the arbitrators.

(3) At any time after the appointment of an umpire, however appointed, the High Court may, on the application of any party to the reference and notwithstanding anything to the contrary in the arbitration agreement, order that the umpire shall enter upon the reference in lieu of the arbitrators and as if he were a sole arbitrator.

9 Majority award of three arbitrators [595]

Unless the contrary intention is expressed in the arbitration agreement, in any case where there is a reference to three arbitrators, the award of any two of the arbitrators shall be binding.

10 Power of court in certain cases to appoint an arbitrator or umpire [596]

(1) In any of the following cases –

(a) where an arbitration agreement provides that the reference shall be to a single arbitrator, and all the parties do not, after differences have arisen, concur in the appointment of an arbitrator;
(b) if an appointed arbitrator refuses to act, or is incapable of acting, or dies, and the arbitration agreement does not show that it was intended that the vacancy should not be supplied and the parties do not supply the vacancy;
(c) where the parties or two arbitrators are required or are at liberty to appoint an umpire or third arbitrator and do not appoint him;
(d) where an appointed umpire or third arbitrator refuses to act, or is incapable of acting, or dies, and the arbitration agreement does not show that it was intended that the vacancy should not be supplied, and the parties or arbitrators do not supply the vacancy;

any party may serve the other parties or the arbitrators, as the case may be, with a written notice to appoint or, as the case may be, concur in appointing, an arbitrator, umpire or third arbitrator, and if the appointment is not made within seven clear days after the service of the notice, the High Court or a judge thereof may, on application by the party who gave the notice, appoint an arbitrator, umpire or third arbitrator who shall have the like powers to act in the reference and make an award as if he had been appointed by consent of all parties.

(2) In any case where –

(a) an arbitration agreement provides for the appointment of an arbitrator or umpire by a person who is neither one of the parties nor an existing arbitrator (whether the provision applies directly or in default of agreement by the parties or otherwise), and
(b) that person refuses to make the appointment or does not make it within the time specified in the agreement or, if no time is so specified, within a reasonable time,

any party to the agreement may serve the person in question with a written notice to appoint an arbitrator or umpire and, if the appointment is not made within seven clear days after the service of the notice, the High Court or a judge thereof may, on the application of the party who gave the notice, appoint an arbitrator or umpire who shall have the like powers to act in the reference and make an award as if he had been appointed in accordance with the terms of the agreement.

(3) In any case where –

(a) an arbitration agreement provides that the reference shall be to three arbitrators, one to be appointed by each party and the third to be appointed by the two appointed by the parties or in some other manner specified in the agreement; and
(b) one of the parties ('the party in default') refuses to appoint an arbitrator or does not do so within the time specified in the agreement or, if no time is specified, within a reasonable time,

the other party to the agreement, having appointed his arbitrator, may serve the party in default with a written notice to appoint an arbitrator. ...

11 Power of official referee to take arbitrations [597]

(1) An official referee may, if in all the circumstances he thinks fit, accept appointment as sole arbitrator, or as umpire, by or by virtue of an arbitration agreement.

(2) An official referee shall not accept appointment as arbitrator or umpire unless the Lord Chief Justice has informed him that, having regard to the state of official referees' business, he can be made available to do so.

(3) The fees payable for the services of an official referee as arbitrator or umpire shall be taken in the High Court.

(4) Schedule 3 to the Administration of Justice Act 1970 (which modifies this Act in relation to arbitration by judges, in particular by substituting the Court of Appeal for the High Court in provisions whereby arbitrators and umpires, their proceedings and awards are subject to control and review by the court) shall have effect in relation to official referees appointed as arbitrators or umpires as it has effect in relation to judge-arbitrators and judge-umpires (within the meaning of that Schedule).

(5) Any jurisdiction which is exercisable by the High Court in relation to arbitrators and umpires otherwise than under this Act shall, in relation to an official referee appointed as arbitrator or umpire, be exercisable instead by the Court of Appeal.

(6) In this section 'official referee' means any person nominated under section 68(1)(a) of the Supreme Court Act 1981 to deal with official referees' business ...

12 Conduct of proceedings, witnesses, etc [598]

(1) Unless a contrary intention is expressed therein, every arbitration agreement shall, where such a provision is applicable to the reference, be deemed to contain a provision that the parties to the reference, and all persons claiming through them respectively, shall, subject to any legal objection, submit to be examined by the arbitrator or umpire, on oath or affirmation, in relation to the matters in dispute, and shall, subject as aforesaid, produce before the arbitrator or umpire all documents within their possession or power respectively which may be required or called for, and do all other things which during the proceedings on the reference the arbitrator or umpire may require.

(2) Unless a contrary intention is expressed therein, every arbitration agreement shall, where such a provision is applicable to the reference, be deemed to contain a provision that the witnesses on the reference shall, if the arbitrator or umpire thinks fit, be examined on oath or affirmation.

(3) An arbitrator or umpire shall, unless a contrary intention is expressed in the arbitration agreement, have power to administer oaths to, or take the affirmations of, the parties to and witnesses on a reference under the agreement.

(4) Any party to a reference under an arbitration agreement may sue out a writ of subpoena ad testificandum or a writ of subpoena duces tecum, but no person shall be compelled under any such writ to produce any document which he could not be compelled to produce on the trial of an action, and the High Court or a judge thereof may order that a writ of subpoena ad testificandum or of subpoena duces tecum shall issue to compel the attendance before an arbitrator or umpire of a witness wherever he may be within the United Kingdom.

(5) The High Court or a judge thereof may also order that a writ of habeas corpus ad testificandum shall issue to bring up a prisoner for examination before an arbitrator or umpire.

(6) The High Court shall have, for the purpose of and in relation to a reference, the same power of making orders in respect of –

(a) security for costs;
(c) the giving of evidence by affidavit;
(d) examination on oath of any witness before an officer of the High Court or any other person, and the issue of a commission or request for the examination of a witness out of the jurisdiction;
(e) the preservation, interim custody or sale of any goods which are the subject matter of the reference;
(f) securing the amount in dispute in the reference;
(g) the detention, preservation or inspection of any property or thing which is the subject of the reference or as to which any question may arise therein, and authorising for any of the purposes aforesaid any persons to enter upon or into any land or building in the possession of any party to the reference, or authorising any samples to be taken or any observation to be made or experiment to be tried which may be necessary or expedient for the purpose of obtaining full information or evidence; and
(h) interim injunctions or the appointment of a receiver;

as it has for the purpose of and in relation to an action or matter in the High Court: Provided that nothing in this subsection shall be taken to prejudice any power which may be vested in an arbitrator or umpire of making orders with respect to any of the matters aforesaid.

13 Time for making award

(1) Subject to the provisions of subsection (2) of section 22 of this Act, and anything to the contrary in the arbitration agreement, an arbitrator or umpire shall have power to make an award at any time.

(2) The time, if any, limited for making an award, whether under this Act or otherwise, may from time to time be enlarged by order of the High Court or a judge thereof, whether that time has expired or not.

(3) The High Court may, on the application of any party to a reference, remove an arbitrator or umpire who fails to use all reasonable dispatch in entering on and proceeding with the reference and making an award, and an arbitrator or umpire who is removed by the High Court under this subsection shall not be entitled to receive any remuneration in respect of his services.

For the purposes of this subsection, the expression 'proceeding with a reference' includes, in a case where two arbitrators are unable to agree, giving notice of that fact to the parties and to the umpire.

13A Want of prosecution

(1) Unless a contrary intention is expressed in the arbitration agreement, the arbitrator or umpire shall have power to make an award dismissing any claim in a dispute referred to him if it appears to him that the conditions mentioned in subsection (2) are satisfied.

(2) The conditions are –

(a) that there has been inordinate and inexcusable delay on the part of the claimant in pursuing the claim; and
(b) that the delay –

(i) will give rise to a substantial risk that it is not possible to have a fair resolution of the issues in that claim; or
(ii) has caused, or is likely to cause or to have caused, serious prejudice to the respondent.

(3) For the purpose of keeping the provision made by this section and the corresponding provision which applies in relation to proceedings in the High Court in step, the Secretary of State may by order made by statutory instrument amend subsection (2) above...

14 Interim awards [601]

Unless a contrary intention is expressed therein, every arbitration agreement shall, where such a provision is applicable to the reference, be deemed to contain a provision that the arbitrator or umpire may, if he thinks fit, make an interim award, and any reference in this Part of this Act to an award includes a reference to an interim award.

15 Specific performance [602]

Unless a contrary intention is expressed therein, every arbitration agreement shall, where such a provision is applicable to the reference, be deemed to contain a provision that the arbitrator or umpire shall have the same power as the High Court to order specific performance of any contract other than a contract relating to land or any interest in land.

16 Awards to be final [603]

Unless a contrary intention is expressed therein, every arbitration agreement shall, where such a provision is applicable to the reference, be deemed to contain a provision that the award to be made by the arbitrator or umpire shall be final and binding on the parties and the persons claiming under them respectively.

17 Power to correct slips [604]

Unless a contrary intention is expressed in the arbitration agreement, the arbitrator or umpire shall have power to correct in an award any clerical mistake or error arising from any accidental slip or omission.

18 Costs [605]

(1) Unless a contrary intention is expressed therein, every arbitration agreement shall be deemed to include a provision that the costs of the reference and awards shall be in the discretion of the arbitrator or umpire, who may direct to and by whom and in what manner those costs or any part thereof shall be paid, and may tax or settle the amount of costs to be so paid or any part thereof, and may award costs to be paid as between solicitor and client.

(2) Any costs directed by an award to be paid shall, unless the award otherwise directs, be taxable in the High Court.

(3) Any provision in an arbitration agreement to the effect that the parties or any party thereto shall in any event pay their or his own costs of the reference or award or any part thereof shall be void, and this Part of this Act shall, in the case of an arbitration agreement containing any such provision, have effect as if that provision were not contained therein: Provided that nothing in this subsection shall invalidate such a provision when it is a part of an agreement to submit to arbitration a dispute which has arisen before the making of that agreement.

(4) If no provision is made by an award with respect to the costs of the reference, any party to the reference may, within fourteen days of the publication of the award or such further time as the High Court or a judge thereof may direct, apply

to the arbitrator for an order directing by and to whom those costs shall be paid, and thereupon the arbitrator shall, after hearing any party who may desire to be heard, amend his award by adding thereto such directions as he may think proper with respect to the payment of the costs of the reference.

(5) Section 69 of the Solicitors Act 1932 (which empowers a court before which any proceeding is being heard or is pending to charge property recovered or preserved in the proceeding with the payment of solicitors' costs) shall apply as if an arbitration were proceeding in the High Court, and the High Court may make declarations and orders accordingly.

19 Taxation of arbitrator's or umpire's fees [606]

(1) If in any case an arbitrator or umpire refuses to deliver his award except on payment of the fees demanded by him, the High Court may, on an application for the purpose, order that the arbitrator or umpire shall deliver the award to the applicant on payment into court by the applicant of the fees demanded, and further that the fees demanded shall be taxed by the taxing officer and that out of the money paid into court there shall be paid out to the arbitrator or umpire by way of fees such sum as may be found reasonable on taxation and that the balance of the money, if any, shall be paid out to the applicant.

(2) An application for the purposes of this section may be made by any party to the reference unless the fees demanded have been fixed by a written agreement between him and the arbitrator or umpire.

(3) A taxation of fees under this section may be reviewed in the same manner as a taxation of costs.

(4) The arbitrator or umpire shall be entitled to appear and be heard on any taxation or review of taxation under this section.

19A Power of arbitrator to award interest [607]

(1) Unless a contrary intention is expressed therein, every arbitration agreement shall, where such a provision is applicable to the reference, be deemed to contain a provision that the arbitrator or umpire may, if he thinks fit, award simple interest at such rate as he thinks fit –

(a) on any sum which is the subject of the reference but which is paid before the award, for such period ending not later than the date of the payment as he thinks fit; and
(b) on any sum which he awards, for such period ending not later than the date of the payment as he thinks fit.

(2) The power to award interest conferred on an arbitrator or umpire by subsection (1) above is without prejudice to any other power of an arbitrator or umpire to award interest.

20 Interest on awards [608]

(1) A sum directed to be paid by an award shall, unless the award otherwise directs, carry interest as from the date of the award.

(2) The rate of interest shall be –

(a) the rate for judgment debts specified in section 17 of the Judgments Act 1838 at the date of the award; or
(b) if the power under subsection (3) below is exercised, the rate specified in the award.

(3) Where the sum is expressed in a currency other than sterling, the award may specify such rate as the arbitrator or umpire thinks fit instead of the rate mentioned in subsection (2)(a) above.

22 Power to remit award [609]

(1) In all cases of reference to arbitration the High Court or a judge thereof may from time to time remit the matters referred, or any of them, to the reconsideration of the arbitrator or umpire.

(2) Where an award is remitted, the arbitrator or umpire shall, unless the order otherwise directs, make his award within three months after the date of the order.

23 Removal of arbitrator and setting aside of award [610]

(1) Where an arbitrator or umpire has misconducted himself or the proceedings, the High Court may remove him.

(2) Where an arbitrator or umpire has misconducted himself or the proceedings, or an arbitration or award has been improperly procured, the High Court may set the award aside.

(3) Where an application is made to set aside an award, the High Court may order that any money made payable by the award shall be brought into court or otherwise secured pending the determination of the application.

24 Power of court to give relief where arbitrator is not [611]
impartial or the dispute involves question of fraud

(1) Where an agreement between any parties provides that disputes which may arise in the future between them shall be referred to an arbitrator named or designated in the agreement, and after a dispute has arisen any party applies, on the ground that the arbitrator so named or designated is not or may not be impartial, for leave to revoke the authority of the arbitrator or for an injunction to restrain any other party or the arbitrator from proceeding with the arbitration, it shall not be a ground for refusing the application that the said party at the time when he made the agreement knew, or ought to have known, that the arbitrator, by reason of his relation towards any other party to the agreement or of his connection with the subject referred, might not be capable of impartiality.

(2) Where an agreement between any parties provides that disputes which may arise in the future between them shall be referred to arbitration, and a dispute which so arises involves the question whether any such party has been guilty of fraud, the High Court shall, so far as may be necessary to enable that question to be determined by the High Court, have power to order that the agreement shall cease to have effect and power to give leave to revoke the authority of any arbitrator or umpire appointed by or by virtue of the agreement.

(3) In any case where by virtue of this section the High Court has power to order that an arbitration agreement shall cease to have effect or to give leave to revoke the authority of an arbitrator or umpire, the High Court may refuse to stay an action brought in breach of the agreement.

25 Power of court where arbitrator is removed or authority [612]
of arbitrator is revoked

(1) Where an arbitrator (not being a sole arbitrator), or two or more arbitrators (not being all the arbitrators) or an umpire who has not entered on the reference is or are removed by the High Court or the Court of Appeal, the High Court or the

Court of Appeal, as the case may be, may, on the application of any party to the arbitration agreement, appoint a person or persons to act as arbitrator or arbitrators or umpire in place of the person or persons so removed.

(2) Where the authority of an arbitrator or arbitrators or umpire is revoked by leave of the High Court or the Court of Appeal, or a sole arbitrator or all the arbitrators or an umpire who has entered on the reference is or are removed by the High Court or the Court of Appeal, the High Court or the Court of Appeal, as the case may be, may, on the application of any party to the arbitration agreement, either –

(a) appoint a person to act as sole arbitrator in place of the person or persons removed; or

(b) order that the arbitration agreement shall cease to have effect with respect to the dispute referred.

(3) A person appointed under this section by the High Court or the Court of Appeal as an arbitrator or umpire shall have the like power to act in the reference and to make an award as if he had been appointed in accordance with the terms of the arbitration agreement.

(4) Where it is provided (whether by means of a provision in the arbitration agreement or otherwise) that an award under an arbitration agreement shall be a condition precedent to the bringing of an action with respect to any matter to which the agreement applies, the High Court or the Court of Appeal if it orders (whether under this section or under any other enactment) that the agreement shall cease to have effect as regards any particular dispute, may further order that the provision making an award a condition precedent to the bringing of an action shall also cease to have effect as regards that dispute.

26 Enforcement of award [613]

(1) An award on an arbitration agreement may, by leave of the High Court or a judge thereof, be enforced in the same manner as a judgment or order to the same effect, and where leave is so given, judgment may be entered in terms of the award.

(2) If a county court so orders, the amount sought to be recovered shall be recoverable (by execution issued from the county court or otherwise) as if payable under an order of that court and shall not be enforceable under subsection (1) above.

(3) An application to the High Court under this section shall preclude an application to a county court and an application to a county court under this section shall preclude an application to the High Court.

27 Power of court to extend time for commencing arbitration proceedings [614]

Where the terms of an agreement to refer future disputes to arbitration provide that any claims to which the agreement applies shall be barred unless notice to appoint an arbitrator is given or an arbitrator is appointed or some other step to commence arbitration proceedings is taken within a time fixed by the agreement, and a dispute arises to which the agreement applies, the High Court, if it is of opinion that in the circumstances of the case undue hardship would otherwise be caused, and notwithstanding that the time so fixed has expired, may, on such terms, if any, as the justice of the case may require, but without prejudice to the provisions of any enactment limiting the time for the commencement of arbitration proceedings, extend the time for such period as it thinks proper.

28 Terms as to costs, etc [615]

Any order made under this Part of this Act may be made on such terms as to costs or otherwise as the authority making the order thinks just.

29 Commencement of arbitration [616]

(2) An arbitration shall be deemed to be commenced when one party to the arbitration agreement serves on the other party or parties a notice requiring him or them to appoint or concur in appointing an arbitrator, or, where the arbitration agreement provides that the reference shall be to a person named or designated in the agreement, requiring him or them to submit the dispute to the person so named or designated.

(3) Any such notice as is mentioned in subsection (2) of this section may be served either –
  (a) by delivering it to the person on whom it is to be served; or
  (b) by leaving it at the usual or last known place of abode in England of that person; or
  (c) by sending it by post in a registered letter addressed to that person at his usual or last known place of abode in England;

as well as in any other manner provided in the arbitration agreement; and where a notice is sent by post in manner prescribed by paragraph (c) of this subsection, service thereof shall, unless the contrary is proved, be deemed to have been effected at the time at which the letter would have been delivered in the ordinary course of post.

30 Crown to be bound [617]

This Part of this Act shall apply to any arbitration to which His Majesty, either in right of the Crown or of the Duchy of Lancaster or otherwise, or the Duke of Cornwall, is a party.

31 Application of Part I to statutory arbitrations [618]

(1) Subject to the provisions of section 33 of this Act, this Part of this Act, except the provisions thereof specified in subsection (2) of this section, shall apply to every arbitration under any other Act (whether passed before or after the commencement of this Act) as if the arbitration were pursuant to an arbitration agreement and as if that other Act were an arbitration agreement, except in so far as this Act is inconsistent with that other Act or with any rules or procedure authorised or recognised thereby.

(2) The provisions referred to in subsection (1) of this section are subsection (1) of section2, section 3, section 5, subsection (3) of section 18 and sections 24, 25, 27 and 29.

32 Meaning of 'arbitration agreement' [619]

In this Part of this Act, unless the context otherwise requires, the expression 'arbitration agreement' means a written agreement to submit present or future differences to arbitration, whether an arbitrator is named therein or not.

33 Operation of Part I [620]

This Part of this Act shall not affect any arbitration commenced (within the meaning of subsection (2) of section 29 of this Act) before the commencement of this Act, but shall apply to an arbitration so commenced after the commencement of this Act under an agreement made before the commencement of this Act.

34 Extent of Part I [621]

None of the provisions of this Part of this Act shall extend to Scotland or Northern Ireland.

PART II

ENFORCEMENT OF CERTAIN FOREIGN AWARDS

35 Awards to which Part II applies [622]

(1) This Part of this Act applies to any award made after the twenty-eighth day of July, nineteen hundred and twenty-four –

(a) in pursuance of an agreement for arbitration to which the protocol set out in the First Schedule to this Act applies; and
(b) between persons of whom one is subject to the jurisdiction of some one of such Powers as His Majesty, being satisfied that reciprocal provisions have been made, may by Order in Council declare each to be parties to the convention set out in the Second Schedule to this Act, and of whom the other is subject to the jurisdiction of some other of the Powers aforesaid; and
(c) in one of such territories as His Majesty, being satisfied that reciprocal provisions have been made, may by Order in Council declare to be territories to which the said convention applies;

and an award to which this Part of this Act applies is in this Part of this Act referred to as 'a foreign award'.

(2) His Majesty may by a subsequent Order in Council vary or revoke any Order previously made under this section.

(3) Any Order in Council under section 1 of the Arbitration (Foreign Awards) Act 1930, which is in force at the commencement of this Act shall have effect as if it had been made under this section.

36 Effect of foreign awards [623]

(1) A foreign award shall, subject to the provisions of this Part of this Act, be enforceable in England either by action or in the same manner as the award of an arbitrator is enforceable by virtue of section 26 of this Act.

(2) Any foreign award which would be enforceable under this Part of this Act shall be treated as binding for all purposes on the persons as between whom it was made, and may accordingly be relied on by any of those persons by way of defence, set off or otherwise in any legal proceedings in England, and any references in this Part of this Act to enforcing a foreign award shall be construed as including references to relying on an award.

37 Conditions for enforcement of foreign awards [624]

(1) In order that a foreign award may be enforceable under this Part of this Act it must have –

(a) been made in pursuance of an agreement for arbitration which was valid under the law by which it was governed;

(b) been made by the tribunal provided for in the agreement or constituted in manner agreed upon by the parties;
(c) been made in conformity with the law governing the arbitration procedure;
(d) become final in the country in which it was made;
(e) been in respect of a matter which may lawfully be referred to arbitration under the law of England;

and the enforcement thereof must not be contrary to the public policy or the law of England.

(2) Subject to the provisions of this subsection, a foreign award shall not be enforceable under this Part of this Act if the court dealing with the case is satisfied that –

(a) the award has been annulled in the country in which it was made; or
(b) the party against whom it is sought to enforce the award was not given notice of the arbitration proceedings in sufficient time to enable him to present his case, or was under some legal incapacity and was not properly represented; or
(c) the award does not deal with all the questions referred or contains decisions on matters beyond the scope of the agreement for arbitration: Provided that, if the award does not deal with all the questions referred, the court may, if it thinks fit, either postpone the enforcement of the award or order its enforcement subject to the giving of such security by the person seeking to enforce it as the court may think fit.

(3) If a party seeking to resist the enforcement of a foreign award proves that there is any ground other than the non-existence of the conditions specified in paragraphs (a), (b) and (c) of subsection (1) of this section, or the existence of the conditions specified in paragraphs (b) and (c) of subsection (2) of this section, entitling him to contest the validity of the award, the court may, if it thinks fit, either refuse to enforce the award or adjourn the hearing until after the expiration of such period as appears to the court to be reasonably sufficient to enable that party to take the necessary steps to have the award annulled by the competent tribunal.

38 Evidence [625]

(1) The party seeking to enforce a foreign award must produce –

(a) the original award or a copy thereof duly authenticated in manner required by the law of the country in which it was made; and
(b) evidence proving that the award has become final; and
(c) such evidence as may be necessary to prove that the award is a foreign award and that the conditions mentioned in paragraphs (a), (b) and (c) of subsection (1) of the last foregoing section are satisfied.

(2) In any case where any document required to be produced under subsection (1) of this section is in a foreign language, it shall be the duty of the party seeking to enforce the award to produce a translation certified as correct by a diplomatic or consular agent of the country to which that party belongs, or certified as correct in such other manner as may be sufficient according to the law of England.

(3) Subject to the provisions of this section, rules of court may be made under section 84 of the Supreme Court Act 1981 with respect to the evidence which must be furnished by a party seeking to enforce an award under this Part of this Act.

39 Meaning of 'final award'

For the purposes of this Part of this Act, an award shall not be deemed final if any proceedings for the purpose of contesting the validity of the award are pending in the country in which it was made.

40 Saving for other rights, etc

Nothing in this Part of this Act shall –

(a) prejudice any rights which any person would have had of enforcing in England any award or of availing himself in England of any award if neither this Part of this Act nor Part I of the Arbitration (Foreign Awards) Act 1930, had been enacted; or

(b) apply to any award made on an arbitration agreement governed by the law of England.

FIRST SCHEDULE

PROTOCOL ON ARBITRATION CLAUSES SIGNED ON BEHALF OF HIS MAJESTY AT A MEETING OF THE ASSEMBLY OF THE LEAGUE OF NATIONS HELD ON THE TWENTY-FOURTH DAY OF SEPTEMBER NINETEEN HUNDRED AND TWENTY-THREE

The undersigned, being duly authorised, declare that they accept, on behalf of the countries which they represent, the following provision:–

1. Each of the Contracting States recognises the validity of an agreement whether relating to existing or future differences between parties, subject respectively to the jurisdiction of different Contracting States by which the parties to a contract agree to submit to arbitration all or any differences that may arise in connection with such contract relating to commercial matters or to any other matter capable of settlement by arbitration, whether or not the arbitration is to take place in a country to whose jurisdiction none of the parties is subject.

Each Contracting State reserves the right to limit the obligation mentioned above to contracts which are considered as commercial under its national law. Any Contracting State which avails itself of this right will notify the Secretary-General of the League of Nations, in order that the other Contracting States may be so informed.

2. The arbitral procedure, including the constitution of the arbitral tribunal, shall be governed by the will of the parties and by the law of the country in whose territory the arbitration takes place.

The Contracting States agree to facilitate all steps in the procedure which require to be taken in their own territories, in accordance with the provisions of their law governing arbitral procedure applicable to existing differences.

3. Each Contracting State undertakes to ensure the execution by its authorities and in accordance with the provisions of its national laws of arbitral awards made in its own territory under the preceding articles.

4. The tribunals of the Contracting Parties, on being seized of a dispute regarding a contract made between persons to whom Article 1 applies and including an arbitration agreement whether referring to present or future differences which is valid in virtue of the said article and capable of being carried into effect, shall refer the parties on the application of either of them to the decision of the arbitrators.

Such reference shall not prejudice the competence of the judicial tribunals in case the agreement or the arbitration cannot proceed or becomes inoperative.

5. The present Protocol, which shall remain open for signature by all States, shall be ratified. The ratifications shall be deposited as soon as possible with the Secretary-General of the League of Nations, who shall notify such deposit to all the signatory States.

6. The present Protocol shall come into force as soon as two ratifications have been deposited. Thereafter it will take effect, in the case of each Contracting State, one month after the notification by the Secretary-General of the deposit of its ratification.

7. The present Protocol may be denounced by any Contracting State on giving one year's notice. Denunciation shall be effected by a notification addressed to the Secretary-General of the League, who will immediately transmit copies of such notification to all the other signatory States and inform them of the date on which it was received. The denunciation shall take effect one year after the date on which it was notified to the Secretary General, and shall operate only in respect of the notifying State.

8. The Contracting States may declare that their acceptance of the present Protocol does not include any or all of the under-mentioned territories: that is to say, their colonies, overseas possessions or territories, protectorates or the territories over which they exercise a mandate.

The said States may subsequently adhere separately on behalf of any territory thus excluded. The Secretary General of the League of Nations shall be informed as soon as possible of such adhesions. He shall notify such adhesions to all signatory States. They will take effect one month after the notification by the Secretary General to all signatory States.

The Contracting States may also denounce the Protocol separately on behalf of any of the territories referred to above. Article 7 applies to such denunciation.

SECOND SCHEDULE [629]

CONVENTION ON THE EXECUTION OF FOREIGN ARBITRAL AWARDS SIGNED AT GENEVA ON BEHALF OF HIS MAJESTY ON THE TWENTY-SIXTH DAY OF SEPTEMBER, NINETEEN HUNDRED AND TWENTY-SEVEN

Article 1

In the territories of any High Contracting Party to which the present Convention applies, an arbitral award made in pursuance of an agreement, whether relating to existing or future differences (hereinafter called 'a submission to arbitration') covered by the Protocol on Arbitration Clauses, opened at Geneva on September 24, 1923, shall be recognised as being and shall be enforced in accordance with the rules of the procedure of the territory where the award is relied upon, provided that the said award has been made in a territory of one of the High Contracting Parties to which the present Convention applies and between persons who are subject to the jurisdiction of one of the High Contracting Parties.

To obtain such recognition or enforcement, it shall, further, be necessary –

(a) That the award has been made in pursuance of a submission to arbitration which is valid under the law applicable thereto;
(b) That the subject-matter of the award is capable of settlement by arbitration under the law of the country in which the award is sought to be relied upon;
(c) That the award has been made by the arbitral tribunal provided for in the submission to arbitration or constituted in the manner agreed upon by the parties and in conformity with the law governing the arbitration procedure;

(d) That the award has become final in the country in which it has been made, in the sense that it will not be considered as such if it is open to opposition, appel or pourvoi en cassation (in the countries where such forms of procedure exist) or if it is proved that any proceedings for the purpose of contesting the validity of the award are pending;

(e) That the recognition or enforcement of the award is not contrary to the public policy or to the principles of the law of the country in which it is sought to be relied upon.

Article 2

Even if the conditions laid down in Article 1 hereof are fulfilled, recognition and enforcement of the award shall be refused if the Court is satisfied:–

(a) That the award has been annulled in the country in which it was made;

(b) That the party against whom it is sought to use the award was not given notice of the arbitration proceedings in sufficient time to enable him to present his case; or that, being under a legal incapacity, he was not properly represented;

(c) That the award does not deal with the differences contemplated by or falling within the terms of the submission to arbitration or that it contains decisions on matters beyond the scope of the submission to arbitration.

If the award has not covered all the questions submitted to the arbitral tribunal, the competent authority of the country where recognition or enforcement of the award is sought can, if it think fit, postpone such recognition or enforcement or grant it subject to such guarantee as that authority may decide.

Article 3

If the party against whom the award has been made proves that, under the law governing the arbitration procedure, there is a ground, other than the grounds referred to in Article 1 (a) and (c), and Article 2 (b) and (c), entitling him to contest the validity of the award in a Court of Law, the Court may, if it thinks fit, either refuse recognition or enforcement of the award or adjourn the consideration thereof, giving such party a reasonable time within which to have the award annulled by the competent tribunal.

Article 4

The party relying upon an award or claiming its enforcement must supply, in particular:–

(1) The original award or a copy thereof duly authenticated, according to the requirements of the law of the country in which it was made;

(2) Documentary or other evidence to prove that the award has become final, in the sense defined in Article 1 (d), in the country in which it was made;

(3) When necessary, documentary or other evidence to prove that the conditions laid down in Article 1, paragraph 1 and paragraph 2 (a) and (c), have been fulfilled.

A translation of the award and of the other documents mentioned in this Article into the official language of the country where the award is sought to be relied upon may be demanded. Such translation must be certified correct by a diplomatic or consular agent of the country to which the party who seeks to rely upon the award belongs or by a sworn translator of the country where the award is sought to be relied upon.

Article 5

The provisions of the above Articles shall not deprive any interested party of the right of availing himself of an arbitral award in the manner and to the extent allowed by the law or the treaties of the country where such award is sought to be relied upon.

Article 6

The present Convention applies only to arbitral awards made after the coming into force of the Protocol on Arbitration Clauses, opened at Geneva on September 24th, 1923.

Article 7

The present Convention, which will remain open to the signature of all the signatories of the Protocol of 1923 on Arbitration Clauses, shall be ratified.

It may be ratified only on behalf of those Members of the League of Nations and non-Member States on whose behalf the Protocol of 1923 shall have been ratified.

Ratifications shall be deposited as soon as possible with the Secretary General of the League of Nations, who will notify such deposit to all the signatories.

Article 8

The present Convention shall come into force three months after it shall have been ratified on behalf of two High Contracting Parties. Thereafter, it shall take effect, in the case of each High Contracting Party, three months after the deposit of the ratification on its behalf with the Secretary General of the League of Nations.

Article 9

The present Convention may be denounced on behalf of any Member of the League or non-Member State. Denunciation shall be notified in writing to the Secretary General of the League of Nations, who will immediately send a copy thereof, certified to be in conformity with the notification, to all the other Contracting Parties, at the same time informing them of the date on which he received it.

The denunciation shall come into force only in respect of the High Contracting Party which shall have notified it and one year after such notification shall have reached the Secretary General of the League of Nations.

The denunciation of the Protocol on Arbitration Clauses shall entail, ipso facto, the denunciation of the present Convention.

Article 10

The present Convention does not apply to the Colonies, Protectorates or territories under suzerainty or mandate of any High Contracting Party unless they are specially mentioned.

The application of this Convention to one or more of such Colonies, Protectorates or territories to which the Protocol on Arbitration Clauses, opened at Geneva on September 24th, 1923, applies, can be effected at any time by means of a declaration addressed to the Secretary General of the League of Nations by one of the High Contracting Parties.

Such declaration shall take effect three months after the deposit thereof.

The High Contracting Parties can at any time denounce the Convention for all or any of the Colonies, Protectorates or territories referred to above. Article 9 hereof applies to such denunciation.

Article 11

A certified copy of the present Convention shall be transmitted by the Secretary-General of the League of Nations to every Member of the League of Nations and to every non-Member State which signs the same.

[As amended by the Administration of Justice Act 1970, s4(4), Schedule 3, para 11; Arbitration Act 1975, s8(2); Administration of Justice Act 1977, s17(2); Arbitration Act 1979, s6(2), (3), (4), 8(3); Administration of Justice Act 1982, s15(6), Schedule 1, Pt IV; Insolvency Act 1986, s439(2), Schedule 14; Courts and Legal Services Act 1990, ss99, 101(1), 102, 103, 125(7), Schedule 20; High Court and County Courts Jurisdiction Order 1991, art 2(8), Schedule, Pt I; Statute Law (Repeals) Act 1993, Schedule 1, Pt XV; Private International Law (Miscellaneous Provisions) Act 1995, s3(1).]

MARRIAGE (ENABLING) ACT 1960
(8 & 9 Eliz c 29)

1 Certain marriages not to be void [630]

(1) No marriage hereafter contracted (whether in or out of Great Britain) between a man or a woman who is the sister, aunt or niece of a former wife of his (whether living or not), or was formerly the wife of his brother, uncle or nephew (whether living or not), shall by reason of that relationship be void or voidable under any enactment or rule of law applying in Great Britain as a marriage between persons within the prohibited degrees of affinity.

(2) In the foregoing subsection words of kinship apply equally to kin of the whole and of the half blood.

(3) This section does not validate a marriage, if either party to it is at the time of the marriage domiciled in a country outside Great Britain, and under the law of that country there cannot be a valid marriage between the parties.

OATHS AND EVIDENCE (OVERSEAS AUTHORITIES AND COUNTRIES) ACT 1963
(1963 c 27)

1 Taking of evidence for foreign civil proceedings [631]

Any person appointed by a court or other judicial authority of any foreign country shall have power in the United Kingdom to administer oaths for the purpose of taking evidence for use in proceedings, not being criminal proceedings, carried on under the law of that country.

5 Amendment of 23 & 24 Geo 5 c 4 [632]

(1) If Her Majesty in Council is satisfied as respects any country that –

(a) there exist in that country public registers kept under the authority of the law of that country and recognised by the courts of that country as authentic records, and
(b) that the registers are regularly and properly kept,

Her Majesty may by Order in Council make in respect of that country and all or any of those registers such provision as is specified in subsection (2) of section 1 of the Evidence (Foreign, Dominion and Colonial Documents) Act 1933. ...

WILLS ACT 1963
(1963 c 44)

1 General rule as to formal validity [633]

A will shall be treated as properly executed if its execution conformed to the internal law in force in the territory where it was executed, or in the territory where, at the time of its execution or of the testator's death, he was domiciled or had his habitual residence, or in a state of which, at either of those times, he was a national.

2 Additional rules [634]

(1) Without prejudice to the preceding section, the following shall be treated as properly executed –

(a) a will executed on board a vessel or aircraft of any description, if the execution of the will conformed to the internal law in force in the territory with which, having regard to its registration (if any) and other relevant circumstances, the vessel or aircraft may be taken to have been most closely connected;

(b) a will so far as it disposes of immovable property, if its execution conformed to the internal law in force in the territory where the property was situated;

(c) a will so far as it revokes a will which under this Act would be treated as properly executed or revokes a provision which under this Act would be treated as comprised in a properly executed will, if the execution of the later will conformed to any law by reference to which the revoked will or provision would be so treated;

(d) a will so far as it exercises a power of appointment, if the execution of the will conformed to the law governing the essential validity of the power.

(2) A will so far as it exercises a power of appointment shall not be treated as improperly executed by reason only that its execution was not in accordance with any formal requirements contained in the instrument creating the power.

3 Certain requirements to be treated as formal [635]

Where (whether in pursuance of this Act or not) a law in force outside the United Kingdom falls to be applied in relation to a will, any requirement of that law whereby special formalities are to be observed by testators answering a particular description, or witnesses to the execution of a will are to possess certain qualifications, shall be treated, notwithstanding any rule of that law to the contrary, as a formal requirement only.

4 Construction of wills [636]

The construction of a will shall not be altered by reason of any change in the testator's domicile after the execution of the will.

6 Interpretation [637]

(1) In this Act –

'internal law' in relation to any territory or state means the law which would apply in a case where no question of the law in force in any other territory or state arose;

'state' means a territory or group of territories having its own law of nationality;

'will' includes any testamentary instrument or act, and 'testator' shall be construed accordingly.

(2) Where under this Act the internal law in force in any territory or state is to be applied in the case of a will, but there are in force in that territory or state two or more systems of internal law relating to the formal validity of wills, the system to be applied shall be ascertained as follows –

(a) if there is in force throughout the territory or state a rule indicating which of those systems can properly be applied in the case in question, that rule shall be followed; or
(b) if there is no such rule, the system shall be that with which the testator was most closely connected at the relevant time, and for this purpose the relevant time is the time of the testator's death where the matter is to be determined by reference to circumstances prevailing at his death, and the time of execution of the will in any other case.

(3) In determining for the purposes of this Act whether or not the execution of a will conformed to a particular law, regard shall be had to the formal requirements of that law at the time of execution, but this shall not prevent account being taken of an alteration of law affecting wills executed at that time if the alteration enables the will to be treated as properly executed.

7 Short title, commencement, repeal and extent [638]

(2) This Act shall come into operation on 1 January 1964.

(4) This Act shall not apply to a will of a testator who died before the time of the commencement of this Act and shall apply to a will of a testator who dies after that time whether the will was executed before or after that time ...

DIPLOMATIC PRIVILEGES ACT 1964
(1964 c 81)

1 Replacement of existing law [639]

The following provisions of this Act shall, with respect to the matters dealt with therein, have effect in substitution for any previous enactment or rule of law.

2 Application of Vienna Convention [640]

(1) Subject to section 3 of this Act, the Articles set out in Schedule 1 to this Act (being Articles of the Vienna Convention on Diplomatic Relations signed in 1961) shall have the force of law in the United Kingdom and shall for that purpose be construed in accordance with the following provisions of this section.

(2) In those Articles –

'agents of the receiving State' shall be construed as including any constable and any person exercising a power of entry to any premises under any enactment (including any enactment of the Parliament of Northern Ireland);
'national of the receiving State' shall be construed as meaning citizen of the United Kingdom and Colonies;
'Ministry for Foreign Affairs or such other ministry as may be agreed' shall be construed as meaning the department of the Secretary of State concerned;

and, in the application of those Articles to Scotland, any reference to attachment or execution shall be construed as a reference to the execution of diligence, and any reference to the execution of diligence, and any reference to the execution of a judgment as a reference to the enforcement of a decree by diligence.

(3) For the purposes of Article 32 a waiver by the head of the mission of any State or any person for the time being performing his functions shall be deemed to be a waiver by that State.

(4) The exemption granted by Article 33 with respect to any services shall be deemed to except those services from any class of employment in respect of which contributions are payable under the enactments relating to social security..., but not so as to render any person liable to any contribution which he would not be required to pay if those services were not so excepted.

(5) Articles 35, 36 and 40 shall be construed as granting any privilege or immunity which they require to be granted.

(5A) The reference in Article 36 to customs duties shall be construed as including a reference to excise duties chargeable on goods imported into the United Kingdom and to value added tax charged in accordance with section 10 or 15 of the Value Added Tax Act 1994 (acquisitions from other member States and importations from outside the European Community).

(6) The references in Articles 37 and 38 to the extent to which any privileges and immunities are admitted by the receiving State and to additional privileges and immunities that may be granted by the receiving State shall be construed as referring respectively to the extent to which any privileges and immunities may be specified by Her Majesty by Order in Council and to any additional privileges and immunities that may be so specified.

3 Restriction of privileges and immunities [641]

(1) If it appears to Her Majesty that the privileges and immunities accorded to a mission of Her Majesty in the territory of any State, or to persons connected with that mission, are less than those conferred by this Act on the mission of that State or on persons connected with that mission, Her Majesty may by an Order in Council withdraw such of the privileges and immunities so conferred from the mission of that State or from such persons connected with it as appears to Her Majesty to be proper.

(2) An Order in Council under this section shall be disregarded for the purposes of section 50(4) of the British Nationality Act 1981 (circumstances in which certain persons entitled to exemption under section 8(3) of the Immigration Act 1971 are to be regarded for the purposes of section 1(1) of the said Act of 1981 as settled in the United Kingdom).

4 Evidence [642]

If in any proceedings any question arises whether or not any person is entitled to any privilege or immunity under this Act a certificate issued by or under the authority of the Secretary of State stating any fact relating to that question shall be conclusive evidence of that fact.

6 Orders in Council [643]

(1) No recommendation shall be made to Her Majesty in Council to make an Order under section 2 of this Act unless a draft thereof has been laid before Parliament and approved by resolution of each House of Parliament; and any statutory instrument containing an Order under section 3 of this Act shall be subject to annulment in pursuance of a resolution of either House of Parliament.

(2) Any power to make an Order conferred by the foregoing provisions of this Act includes power to vary or revoke an Order by a subsequent Order.

7 Saving for certain bilateral arrangements [644]

(1) Where any special agreement or arrangement between the Government of any State and the Government of the United Kingdom in force at the commencement of this Act provides for extending –
    (a) such immunity from jurisdiction and from arrest or detention, and such inviolability of residence, as are conferred by this Act on a diplomatic agent; or
    (b) such exemption from duties (whether of customs or excise) chargeable on imported goods, taxes and related charges as is conferred by this Act in respect of articles for the personal use of a diplomatic agent;
to any class of person, or to articles for the personal use of any class of person, connected with the mission of that State, that immunity and inviolability or exemption shall so extend, so long as that agreement or arrangement continues in force.

(2) The Secretary of State shall publish in the London, Edinburgh and Belfast Gazettes a notice specifying the States with which and the classes of person with respect to which such an agreement or arrangement as is mentioned in subsection (1) of this section is in force and whether its effect is as mentioned in paragraph (a) or paragraph (b) of that subsection, and shall whenever necessary amend the notice by a further such notice; and the notice shall be conclusive evidence of the agreement or arrangement and the classes of person with respect to which it is in force.

8 Short title, interpretation, commencement, repeal and saving [645]

(1) This Act may be cited as the Diplomatic Privileges Act 1964.

(3) This Act shall come into force on such day as Her Majesty may by Order in Council appoint.

(5) Any Order in Council under the Diplomatic Immunities Restriction Act 1955 which is in force immediately before the commencement of this Act shall, so far as it could have been made under section 3 of this Act, have effect as if so made.

SCHEDULE 1 [646]

ARTICLES OF VIENNA CONVENTION HAVING THE FORCE OF LAW IN THE UNITED KINGDOM

Article 1

For the purpose of the present Convention, the following expressions shall have the meanings hereunder assigned to them:
    (a) the 'head of the mission' is the person charged by the sending State with the duty of acting in that capacity;
    (b) the 'members of the mission' are the head of the mission and the members of the staff of the mission;
    (c) the 'members of the staff of the mission; are the members of the diplomatic staff, of the administrative and technical staff and of the service staff of the mission;

(d) the 'members of the diplomatic staff' are the members of the staff of the mission having diplomatic rank;
(e) a 'diplomatic agent' is the head of the mission or a member of the diplomatic staff of the mission;
(f) the 'members of the administrative and technical staff' are the members of the staff of the mission employed in the administrative and technical service of the mission;
(g) the 'members of the service staff' are the members of the staff of the mission in the domestic service of the mission;
(h) a 'private servant' is a person who is in the domestic service of a member of the mission and who is not an employee of the sending State;
(i) the 'premises of the mission' are the buildings or parts of buildings and the land ancillary thereto, irrespective of ownership used for the purposes of the mission including the residence of the head of the mission.

Article 22

1. The premises of the mission shall be inviolable. The agents of the receiving State may not enter them, except with the consent of the head of the mission.

2. The receiving State is under a special duty to take all appropriate steps to protect the premises of the mission against any intrusion or damage and to prevent any disturbance of the peace of the mission or impairment of its dignity.

3. The premises of the mission, their furnishings and other property thereon and the means of transport of the mission shall be immune from search, requisition, attachment or execution.

Article 23

1. The sending State and the head of the mission shall be exempt from all national, regional or municipal dues and taxes in respect of the premises of the mission, whether owned or leased, other than such as represent payment for specific services rendered.

2. The exemption from taxation referred to in this Article shall not apply to such dues and taxes payable under the law of the receiving State by persons contracting with the sending State or the head of the mission.

Arrticle 24

The archives and documents of the mission shall be inviolable at any time and wherever they may be.

Article 27

1. The receiving State shall permit and protect free communication on the part of the mission for all official purposes. In communicating with the Government and other missions and consulates of the sending State, wherever situated, the mission may employ all appropriate means, including diplomatic couriers and messages in code or cipher However, the mission may install and use a wireless transmitter only with the consent of the receiving State.

2. The official correspondence of the mission shall be inviolable. Official correspondence means all correspondence relating to the mission and its functions.

3. The diplomatic bag shall not be opened or detained.

4. The packages constituting the diplomatic bag must bear visible external marks of their character and may contain only diplomatic documents or articles intended for official use.

5. The diplomatic courier, who shall be provided with an official document indicating his status and the number of packages constituting the diplomatic bag, shall be protected by the receiving State in the performance of his functions. He shall enjoy personal inviolability and shall not be liable to any form of arrest or detention.

6. The sending State or the mission may designate diplomatic couriers ad hoc. In such cases the provisions of paragraph 5 of this Article shall also apply, except that the immunities therein mentioned shall cease to apply when such a courier has delivered to the consignee the diplomatic bag in his charge.

7. A diplomatic bag may be entrusted to the captain of a commercial aircraft scheduled to land at an authorised port of entry. He shall be provided with an official document indicating the number of packages constituting the bag but he shall not be considered to be a diplomatic courier. The mission may send one of its members to take possession of the diplomatic bag directly and freely from the captain of the aircraft.

Article 28

The fees and charges levied by the mission in the course of its official duties shall be exempt from all dues and taxes.

Article 29

The person of a diplomatic agent shall be inviolable. He shall not be liable to any form of arrest or detention. The receiving State shall treat him with due respect and shall take all appropriate steps to prevent any attack on his person, freedom or dignity.

Article 30

1. The private residence of a diplomatic agent shall enjoy the same inviolability and protection as the premises of the mission.

2. His papers, correspondence and, except as provided in paragraph 3 of Article 31, his property, shall likewise enjoy inviolability.

Article 31

1. A diplomatic agent shall enjoy immunity from the criminal jurisdiction of the receiving State. He shall also enjoy immunity from its civil and administrative jurisdiction, except in the case of:

> (a) a real action relating to private immovable property situated in the territory of the receiving State, unless he holds it on behalf of the sending State for the purposes of the mission;
> (b) an action relating to succession in which the diplomatic agent is involved as executor, administrator, heir or legatee as a private person and not on behalf of the sending State;
> (c) an action relating to any professional or commercial activity exercised by the diplomatic agent in the receiving State outside his official functions.

2. A diplomatic agent is not obliged to give evidence as a witness.

3. No measures of execution may be taken in respect of a diplomatic agent except in the cases coming under sub-paragraphs (a), (b) and (c) of paragraph 1 of this Article, and provided that the measures concerned can be taken without infringing the inviolability of his person or of his residence.

4. The immunity of a diplomatic agent from the jurisdiction of the receiving State does not exempt him from the jurisdiction of the sending State.

Article 32

1. The immunity from jurisdiction of diplomatic agents and of persons enjoying immunity under Article 37 may be waived by the sending State.

2. The waiver must always be express.

3. The initiation of proceedings by a diplomatic agent or by a person enjoying immunity from jurisdiction under Article 37 shall preclude him from invoking immunity from jurisdiction in respect of any counter-claim directly connected with the principal claim.

4. Waiver of immunity from jurisdiction in respect of civil or administrative proceedings shall not be held to imply waiver of immunity in respect of the execution of the judgment, for which a separate waiver shall be necessary.

Article 33

1. Subject to the provisions of paragraph 3 of this Article, a diplomatic agent shall with respect to services rendered for the sending State be exempt from social security provisions which may be in force in the receiving State.

2. The exemption provided for in paragraph 1 of this Article shall also apply to private servants who are in the sole employ of a diplomatic agent, on condition:

(a) that they are not nationals of or permanently resident in the receiving State; and

(b) that they are covered by the social security provisions which may be in force in the sending State or a third State.

3. A diplomatic agent who employs persons to whom the exemption provided for in paragraph 2 of this Article does not apply shall observe the obligations which the social security provisions of the receiving State impose upon employers.

4. The exemption provided for in paragraphs 1 and 2 of this Article shall not preclude voluntary participation in the social security system of the receiving State provided that such participation is permitted by that State.

5. The provisions of this Article shall not affect bilateral or multilateral agreements concerning social security concluded previously and shall not prevent the conclusion of such agreements in the future.

Article 34

A diplomatic agent shall be exempt from all dues and taxes, personal or real, national, regional or municipal except:

(a) indirect taxes of a kind which are normally incorporated in the price of goods or services;

(b) dues and taxes on private immovable property situated in the territory of the receiving State, unless he holds it on behalf of the sending State for the purposes of the mission;

(c) estate, succession or inheritance duties levied by the receiving State, subject to the provisions of paragraph 4 of Article 39;

(d) dues and taxes on private income having its source in the receiving State and capital taxes on investments made in commercial undertakings in the receiving State;

(e) charges levied for specific services rendered;

(f) registration, court or record fees, mortgage dues and stamp duty, with respect to immovable property, subject to the provisions of Article 23.

Article 35

The receiving State shall exempt diplomatic agents from all personal services, from all public service of any kind whatsoever, and from military obligations such as those connected with requisitioning, military contributions and billeting.

Article 36

1. The receiving State shall, in accordance with such laws and regulations as it may adopt, permit entry of and grant exemption from all customs duties, taxes, and related charges other than charges for storage, cartage and similar services, on:

(a) articles for the official use of the mission;
(b) articles for the personal use of a diplomatic agent or members of his family forming part of his household, including articles intended for his establishment.

2. The personal baggage of a diplomatic agent shall be exempt from inspection, unless there are serious grounds for presuming that it contains articles not covered by the exemptions mentioned in paragraph 1 of this Article, or articles the import or export of which is prohibited by the law or controlled by the quarantine regulations of the receiving State. Such inspection shall be conducted only in the presence of the diplomatic agent or of his authorised representative.

Article 37

1. The members of the family of a diplomatic agent forming part of his household shall, if they are not nationals of the receiving State, enjoy the privileges and immunities specified in Articles 29 to 36.

2. Members of the administrative and technical staff of the mission, together with members of their families forming part of their respective households, shall, if they are not nationals of or permanently resident in the receiving State, enjoy the privileges and immunities specified in Articles 29 to 35, except that the immunity from civil and administrative jurisdiction of the receiving State specified in paragraph 1 of Article 31 shall not extend to acts performed outside the course of their duties. They shall also enjoy the privileges specified in Article 36, paragraph 1, in respect of articles imported at the time of first installation.

3. Members of the service staff of the mission who are not nationals of or permanently resident in the receiving State shall enjoy immunity in respect of acts performed in the course of their duties, exemption from dues and taxes on the emoluments they receive by reason of their employment and the exemption contained in Article 33.

4. Private servants of members of the mission shall, if they are not nationals of or permanently resident in the receiving State, be exempt from dues and taxes on the emoluments they receive by reason of their employment. In other respects, they may enjoy privileges and immunities only to the extent admitted by the receiving State. However, the receiving State must exercise its jurisdiction over those persons in such a manner as not to interfere unduly with the performance of the functions of the mission.

Article 38

1. Except in so far as additional privileges and immunities may be granted by the receiving State, a diplomatic agent who is a national of or permanently resident in that State shall enjoy only immunity from jurisdiction and inviolability, in respect of official acts performed in the exercise of his functions.

2. Other members of the staff of the mission and private servants who are nationals of or permanently resident in the receiving State shall enjoy privileges

and immunities only to the extent admitted by the receiving State. However, the receiving State must exercise its jurisdiction over those persons in such a manner as not to interfere unduly with the performance of the functions of the mission.

Article 39

1. Every person entitled to privileges and immunities shall enjoy them from the moment he enters the territory of the receiving State on proceeding to take up his post or, if already in its territory, from the moment when his appointment is notified to the Ministry for Foreign Affairs or such other ministry as may be agreed.

2. When the functions of a person enjoying privileges and immunities have come to an end, such privileges and immunities shall normally cease at the moment when he leaves the country, or on expiry of a reasonable period in which to do so, but shall subsist until that time, even in case of armed conflict. However, with respect to acts performed by such a person in the exercise of his functions as a member of the mission, immunity shall continue to subsist.

3. In case of the death of a member of the mission, the members of his family shall continue to enjoy the privileges and immunities to which they are entitled until the expiry of a reasonable period in which to leave the country.

4. In the event of the death of a member of the mission not a national of or permanently resident in the receiving State or a member of his family forming part of his household, the receiving State shall permit the withdrawal of the movable property of the deceased, with the exception of any property acquired in the country the export of which was prohibited at the time of his death. Estate, succession and inheritance duties shall not be levied on movable property the presence of which in the receiving State was due solely to the presence there of the deceased as a member of the mission or as a member of the family of a member of the mission.

Article 40

1. If a diplomatic agent passes through or is in the territory of a third State, which has granted him a passport visa if such visa was necessary, while proceeding to take up or to return to his post, or when returning to his own country, the third State shall accord him inviolability and such other immunities as may be required to ensure his transit or return. The same shall apply in the case of any members of his family enjoying privileges or immunities who are accompanying the diplomatic agent, or travelling separately to join him or to return to their country.

2. In circumstances similar to those specified in paragraph 1 of this Article, third States shall not hinder the passage of members of the administrative and technical or service staff of a mission, and of members of their families, through their territories.

3. Third States shall accord to official correspondence and other official communications in transit, including messages in code or cipher, the same freedom and protection as is accorded by the receiving State. They shall accord to diplomatic couriers, who have been granted a passport visa if such visa was necessary, and diplomatic bags in transit the same violability and protection as the receiving State is bound to accord.

4. The obligations of third States under paragraphs 1, 2 and 3 of this Article shall also apply to the persons mentioned respectively in those paragraphs, and to official communications and diplomatic bags, whose presence in the territory of the third State is due to force majeure.

Article 45

If diplomatic relations are broken off between two States, or if a mission is permanently or temporarily recalled:

(a) the receiving State must, even in case of armed conflict, respect and protect the premises of the mission, together with its property and archives;
(b) the sending State may entrust the custody of the premises of the mission, together with its property and archives, to a third State acceptable to the receiving State;
(c) the sending State may entrust the protection of its interests and those of its nationals to a third State acceptable to the receiving State.

[As amended by: the Social Security Act 1973, ss100, 101, Schedule 27, para 24; Social Security (Consequential Provisions) Act 1975, ss1(2), 5, Schedule 1, Pt I; Customs and Excise Management Act 1979, s177(1), Schedule 4, paras 3, 12; British Nationality Act 1981, s52(6), Schedule 7; Diplomatic and Consular Premises Act 1987, s6, Schedule 2, para 1; Finance (No 2) Act 1992, s14, Schedule 3, Pt III, para 87; Value Added Tax Act 1994, s100(1), Schedule 14, para 1.]

CARRIAGE OF GOODS BY ROAD ACT 1965
(1965 c 37)

1 Convention to have force of law [647]

Subjects to the following provisions of this Act, the provisions of the Convention on the Contract for the International Carriage of Goods by Road (in this Act referred to as 'the Convention'), as set out in the Schedule to this Act, shall have the force of law in the United Kingdom so far as they relate to the rights and liabilities of persons concerned in the carriage of goods by road under a contract to which the Convention applies.

4 Registration of foreign judgments [648]

(1) Subject to the next following subsection, Part I of the Foreign Judgments (Reciprocal Enforcement) Act 1933 (in this section referred to as 'the Act of 1933') shall apply, whether or not it would otherwise have so applied, to any judgment which –
(a) has been given in any such action as is referred to in paragraph 1 of article 31 in the Schedule to this Act, and
(b) has been so given by any court or tribunal of a territory in respect of which one of the High Contracting Parties, other than the United Kingdom, is a party to the Convention, and
(c) has become enforceable in that territory.

(2) In the application of Part I of the Act of 1933 in relation to any such judgment as is referred to in the preceding subsection, section 4 of that Act shall have effect with the omission of subsections (2) and (3).

(3) The registration, in accordance with Part I of the Act of 1933, of any such judgment as is referred to in subsection (1) of this section shall constitute, in relation to that judgment, compliance with the formalities for the purposes of paragraph 3 of article 31 in the Schedule to this Act.

7 Arbitrations [649]

(1) Any reference in the preceding provisions of this Act to a court includes a reference to an arbitration tribunal acting by virtue of article 33 in the Schedule to this Act. ...

8 Resolution of conflicts between Conventions [650]
on carriage of goods

(1) If it appears to Her Majesty in Council that there is any conflict between the provisions of this Act (including the provisions of the Convention as set out in the Schedule to this Act) and any provisions relating to the carriage of goods for reward by land, sea or air contained in –

(a) any other Convention which has been signed or ratified by or on behalf of Her Majesty's Government in the United Kingdom before the passing of this Act, or

(b) any enactment of the Parliament of the United Kingdom giving effect to such a Convention,

Her Majesty may by Order in Council make such provision as may seem to Her to be appropriate for resolving that conflict by amending or modifying this Act or any such enactment.

(2) Any statutory instrument made by virtue of this section shall be subject to annulment in pursuance of a resolution of either House of Parliament.

8A Amendments consequential on revision of Convention [651]

(1) If at any time it appears to Her Majesty in Council that Her Majesty's Government in the United Kingdom have agreed to any revision of the Convention, Her Majesty may by Order in Council make such amendment of –

(a) this Act; and

(c) section 5(1) of the Carriage by Air and Road Act 1979,

as appear to Her to be appropriate in consequence of the revision.

(2) In the preceding subsection 'revision' means an omission from, addition to or alteration of the Convention and includes replacement of the Convention or part of it by another convention.

(3) An Order in Council under this section shall not be made unless a draft of the Order has been laid before Parliament and approved by a resolution of each House of Parliament.

[As amended by the Carriage by Air and Road Act 1979, s3(3); International Transport Convention Act 1983, s9, Schedule 2, para 2.]

CONSULAR RELATIONS ACT 1968
(1968 c 18)

1 Application of Vienna Convention [652]

(1) Subject to sections 2 and 3(2) of this Act, the provisions set out in Schedule 1 to this Act (being Articles or parts of Articles of the Vienna Convention on Consular Relations signed in 1963) shall have the force of law in the United Kingdom and shall for that purpose be construed in accordance with subsections (2) to (11) of this section.

(2) In those provisions –

'authorities of the receiving State' shall be construed as including any constable and any person exercising a power of entry to any premises under any enactment (including any enactment of the Parliament of Northern Ireland);

'grave crime' shall be construed as meaning any offence punishable (on a first conviction) with imprisonment for a term that may extend to five years or with a more severe sentence;

'Ministry for Foreign Affairs' shall be construed as meaning the Department of the Secretary of State concerned;

'national of the receiving State' shall be construed as meaning –

(a) a British citizen, a British Dependent Territories citizen, a British National (Overseas) or a British Overseas citizen; or

(b) a person who under the British Nationality Act 1981 is a British subject; or

(c) a British protected person (within the meaning of that Act).

(3) The reference in paragraph 2 of Article 17 to any privileges and immunities accorded by customary international law or by international agreements shall be construed as a reference to any privileges and immunities conferred under the International Organisations (Immunities and Privileges) Act 1950 or the International Organisations Act 1968.

(4) The references in Article 44 to matters connected with the exercise of the functions of members of a consular post shall be construed as references to matters connected with the exercise of consular functions by consular officers or consular employees.

(5) For the purposes of Article 45 and that Article as applied by Article 58 a waiver shall be deemed to have been expressed by a State if it had been expressed by the head, or any person for the time being performing the functions of head, of the diplomatic mission of that State or, if there is no such mission, of the consular post concerned.

(6) The exemption granted by Article 48 with respect to any services shall be deemed to except those services from any class of employment in respect of which contributions are payable under the enactments relating to social security ... but not so as to render any person liable to any contribution which he would not be required to pay if those services were not so excepted.

(7) Article 48 shall not affect any agreement made between the United Kingdom and any other State before the commencement of this Act and shall not be taken to prevent the making of any such agreement after the commencement of this Act.

(8) Articles 50, 51, 52, 54, 62 and 67 shall be construed as granting any privilege or immunity which they require to be granted.

(8A) The references in Articles 50 and 62 to customs duties shall be construed as including references to excise duties chargeable on goods imported into the United Kingdom and to value added tax charged in accordance with section 10 or 15 of the Value Added Tax Act 1994.

(9) The reference in Article 57 to the privileges and immunities provided in Chapter 11 shall be construed as referring to those provided in Section II of that Chapter.

(10) The reference in Article 70 to the rules of international law concerning diplomatic relations shall be construed as a reference to the provisions of the Diplomatic Privileges Act 1964.

(11) The references in Article 71 to additional privileges and immunities that may be granted by the receiving State or to privileges and immunities so far as these are granted by the receiving State shall be construed as referring to such privileges and immunities as may be specified by Her Majesty by Order in Council.

2 Restriction of privileges and immunities [653]

If it appears to Her Majesty that the privileges and immunities accorded to a consular post of the United Kingdom in a territory of any State, or to persons connected with such a consular post, are less than those conferred by this Act on a consular post of that State or on persons connected with such a consular post, Her Majesty may by Order in Council withdraw such of the privileges and immunities so conferred from all or any of the consular posts of that State or from such persons connected therewith as appears to Her Majesty to be proper.

3 Agreements providing for additional or reduced privileges and immunities [654]

(1) Where any agreement made, whether before or after the passing of this Act, between the United Kingdom and any other State provides for according to consular posts and persons connected with them privileges and immunities not accorded to them by the other provisions of this Act, Her Majesty may by Order in Council exercise, with respect to the consular posts of that State and persons connected with them, the powers specified in Schedule 2 to this Act so far as may be necessary to give effect to that agreement.

(2) Where any agreement made, whether before or after the passing of this Act, between the United Kingdom and any other State provides for according to consular posts and persons connected with them some but not all of the privileges and immunities accorded to them by the other provisions of this Act, Her Majesty may by Order in Council provide for excluding, with respect to consular posts of that State and persons connected with them, any of those privileges and immunities which are not provided for by the agreement.

4 Civil jurisdiction concerning service on board ship or aircraft [655]

Her Majesty may by Order in Council make provision for excluding or limiting the jurisdiction of any court in the United Kingdom to entertain proceedings relating to the remuneration or any contract of service of the master or commander or a member of the crew of any ship or aircraft belonging to a State specified in the Order, except where a consular officer of that State has been notified of the intention to invoke the jurisdiction of that court and has not objected within such time as may be specified by or under the Order.

5 Jurisdiction over offences committed on board ship [656]

(1) Her Majesty may by Order in Council make provision for securing that, where an offence is alleged to have been committed on board any ship by the master or a member of the crew and the ship belongs to a State specified in the Order, proceedings for the offence instituted otherwise than at the request or with the consent of a consular officer of that State are not entertained by any court in the United Kingdom, unless –

(a) the offence is alleged to have been committed by or against a person who is a citizen of the United Kingdom and Colonies or is otherwise comprised in the definition of 'national of the receiving State' in section 1(2) of this Act, or against a person other than the master or a member of the crew; or
(b) the offence is one involving the tranquillity or safety of a port, or the law relating to safety of life at sea, public health, oil pollution, wireless telegraphy, immigration or customs or is of any other description specified in the Order; or
(c) the offence is one comprised in the definition of 'grave crime' in section 1(2) of this Act.

(1A) In subsection (1)(b) of this section the expression 'the law relating to customs', to the extent that it refers to the law relating to duties on goods, refers to the law relating to duties (whether of customs or excise) for the time being chargeable on goods imported into the United Kingdom.

(2) For the purposes of this section, an offence which affects the property of any person shall be deemed to have been committed against him.

(3) For the purposes of this section, any document purporting to be signed by or on behalf of a consular officer and stating that he has requested or consented to the institution of any proceedings shall be sufficient proof of that fact unless the contrary is shown.

6 Detention on board ship for disciplinary offences [657]

Her Majesty may by Order in Council designate any State for the purposes of this section; and where a State is so designated, a member of the crew of a ship belonging to that State who is detained in custody on board for a disciplinary offence shall not be deemed to be unlawfully detained unless –

    (a) his detention is unlawful under the laws of that State or the conditions of detention are inhumane or unjustifiably severe; or
    (b) there is reasonable cause for believing that his life or liberty will be endangered for reasons of race, nationality, political opinion or religion, in any country to which the ship is likely to go.

10 Right of diplomatic agents and consular officers [658]
to administer oaths and do notarial acts in certain cases

(1) A diplomatic agent or consular officer of any State may, if authorised to do so under the laws of that State, administer oaths, take affidavits and do notarial acts –

    (a) required by a person for use in that State or under the laws thereof; or
    (b) otherwise required by a national of that State but not for use in the United Kingdom except under the laws of some other country.

(2) Her Majesty may by Order in Council exclude or restrict the provisions of the preceding subsection in relation to the diplomatic agents or consular officers of any State if it appears to Her that in any territory of that State diplomatic agents or consular officers of the United Kingdom are not permitted to perform functions corresponding in nature and extent to those authorised by that subsection.

(3) Her Majesty may by Order in Council make provision for applying section 6 of the Commissioners for Oaths Act 1889 (powers as to oaths and notarial acts abroad) to countries within the Commonwealth or the Republic of Ireland by requiring the section to be construed as if –

    (a) the references therein to a foreign country or place included such country or place as may be specified in the Order; and
    (b) the diplomatic ranks specified in that section, included such ranks of any United Kingdom mission in a country specified in the Order as may be so specified in relation to that country.

(4) In this section 'diplomatic agent' has the same meaning as in the Diplomatic Privileges Act 1964.

11 Evidence [659]

If in any proceedings any question arises whether or not any person is entitled to any privilege or immunity under this Act, a certificate issued by or under the authority of the Secretary of State stating any fact relating to that question shall be conclusive evidence of that fact.

12 Privileges and immunities in connection with Commonwealth and Irish establishments [660]

(1) Her Majesty may, in relation to any such Commonwealth representatives as are described in subsection (2) below, provide by Order in Council for conferring all or any of the privileges and immunities which are conferred by or may be conferred under this Act on consular posts or persons connected with consular posts…

(2) The Commonwealth representatives in relation to whom this section applies are:

> (a) persons in the service of the Government of any country within the Commonwealth (other than the United Kingdom) who hold offices appearing to Her Majesty to involve the performance of duties substantially corresponding to duties which, in the case of a foreign sovereign power, would be performed by a consular officer; and
> (b) any person for the time being recognised by Her Majesty's Government in the United Kingdom as the chief representative in the United Kingdom of a state or province of a country within the Commonwealth.

(3) The privileges and immunities which may be conferred under this section shall include those which in other cases may, if an agreement so requires, be conferred by virtue of Schedule 2 of this Act.

(4) The provisions of this section shall have effect in relation to persons in the service of the Government of the Republic of Ireland as they have effect in relation to persons in the service of the Government of a country within the Commonwealth.

14 Orders in Council [661]

(1) No recommendation shall be made to Her Majesty in Council to make an Order containing such provision as is mentioned in section 1(11) o section 3(1) of this Act unless a draft thereof has been laid before and approved by resolution of each House of Parliament.

(2) Any other statutory instrument made under the foregoing provisions of this Act shall be subject to annulment in pursuance of a resolution of either House of Parliament.

(3) Any power to make an Order conferred by this Act includes power to vary or revoke such an Order by a subsequent Order.

16 Short title, interpretation, commencement and repeal [662]

(1) This Act may be cited as the Consular Relations Act 1968.

(2) For the purposes of section 4, 5 or 6 of this Act a ship, and for the purposes of section 4 an aircraft, shall be treated as belonging to a State in such circumstances as may be so specified by an Order in Council under that section; and different circumstances may be so specified with respect to different States and different classes of ship or aircraft …

SCHEDULE 1

PROVISONS OF VIENNA CONVENTION HAVING THE FORCE OF LAW IN THE UNITED KINGDOM

Article 1

1. For the purposes of the present Convention, the following expressions shall have the meanings hereunder assigned to them:

(a) 'consular post' means any consulate-general, consulate, vice-consulate or consular agency;

(b) 'consular district' means the area assigned to a consular post for the exercise of consular functions;

(c) 'head of consular post' means the person charged with the duty of acting in that capacity;

(d) 'consular officer' means any person, including the head of a consular post, entrusted in that capacity with the exercise of consular functions;

(e) 'consular employee' means any person employed in the administrative or technical service of a consular post;

(f) 'member of the service staff' means any person employed in the domestic service of a consular post;

(g) 'member of the consular post' means consular officers, consular employees and members of the service staff;

(h) 'members of the consular staff' means consular officers, other than the head of a consular post, consular employees and members of the service staff;

(i) 'member of the private staff' means a person who is employed exclusively in the private service of a member of the consular post;

(f) 'consular premises' means the buildings or parts of buildings and the land ancillary thereto, irrespective of ownership, used exclusively for the purposes of the consular post;

(k) 'consular archives' includes all the papers, documents, correspondence, books, films, tapes and registers of the consular post, together with the ciphers and codes, the card-indexers and any article of furniture intended for their protection or safekeeping.

2. Consular officers are of two categories, namely career consular officers and honorary consular officers. The provisions of Chapter II of the present Convention apply to consular posts headed by career consular officers; the provisions of Chapter III governs consular posts headed by honorary consular officers.

3. The particular status of members of the consular posts who are nationals or permanent residents of the receiving State is governed by Article 71 of the present Convention.

CHAPTER I – CONSULAR RELATIONS IN GENERAL

SECTION I – ESTABLISHMENT AND CONDUCT OF CONSULAR RELATIONS

Article 5

Consular functions consist in:

(a) protecting in the receiving State the interests of the sending State and of its nationals, both individuals and bodies corporate, within the limits permitted by international law;

(b) furthering the development of commercial, economic, cultural and scientific relations between the sending State and the receiving State and otherwise promoting friendly relations between them in accordance with the provisions of the present Convention;

(c) ascertaining by all lawful means conditions and developments in the commercial, economic, cultural and scientific life of the receiving State, reporting thereon to the Government of the sending State and giving information to persons interested;

(d) issuing passports and travel documents to nationals of the sending State and visas or appropriate documents to persons wishing to travel to the sending State;

(e) helping and assisting nationals, both individuals and bodies corporate, of the sending State;

(f) acting as notary and civil registrar and in capacities of a similar kind, and performing certain functions of an administrative nature, provided that there is nothing contrary thereto in the laws and regulations of the receiving State;

(g) safeguarding the interests of nationals, both individuals and bodies corporate, of the sending State in cases of succession mortis causa in the territory of the receiving State, in accordance with the laws and regulations of the receiving State;

(h) safeguarding, within the limits imposed by the laws and regulations of the receiving State, the interests of minors and other persons lacking full capacity who are nationals of the sending State, particularly where any guardianship or trusteeship is required with respect to such persons;

(i) subject to the practices and procedures obtaining in the receiving State, representing or arranging appropriate representation for nationals of the sending State before the tribunals and other authorities of the receiving State, for the purpose of obtaining, in accordance with the laws and regulations of the receiving State, provisional measures for the preservation of the rights and interests of these nationals, where, because of absence or any other reason, such nationals are unable at the proper time to assume the defence of their rights and interests;

(j) transmitting judicial and extra-judicial documents or executing letters rogatory or commissions to take evidence for the courts of the sending State in accordance with international agreements in force or, in the absence of such international agreements, in any other manner compatible with the laws and regulations of the receiving State;

(k) exercising rights of supervision and inspection provided for in the laws and regulations of the sending State in respect of vessels having the nationality of the sending State, and of aircraft registered in that State, and in respect of their crews;

(l) extending assistance to vessels and aircraft mentioned in sub-paragraph (k) of this Article and to their crews, taking statements regarding the voyage of a vessel, examining and stamping the ship's papers, and, without prejudice to the powers of the authorities of the receiving State, conducting investigations into any incidents which occurred during the voyage, and settling disputes of any kind between the master, the officers and the seamen in so far as this may be authorised by the laws and regulations of the sending State;

(m) performing any other functions entrusted to a consular post by the sending State which are not prohibited by the laws and regulations of the receiving State or to which no objection is taken by the receiving State or which are referred to in the international agreements in force between the sending State and the receiving State.

Article 15

1. If the head of a consular post is unable to carry out his functions or the position of head of consular post is vacant, an acting head of post may act provisionally as head of the consular post.

2. The full name of the acting head of post shall be notified either by the diplomatic mission of the sending State or, if that State has no such mission in the receiving State, by the head of the consular post, or, if he is unable to do so, by any competent authority of the sending State, to the Ministry for Foreign Affairs of the receiving State or to the authority designated by that Ministry. As a general rule, this notification shall be given in advance. The receiving State may make the admission as acting head of post of a person who is neither a diplomatic agent nor a consular officer of the sending State in the receiving State conditional on its consent.

3. The competent authorities of the receiving State shall afford assistance and protection to the acting head of post. While he is in charge of the post, the provisions of the present Convention shall apply to him on the same basis as to the head of the consular post concerned. The receiving State shall not, however, be obliged to grant to an acting head of post any facility, privilege or immunity which the head of the consular post enjoys only subject to conditions not fulfilled by the acting head of post.

4. When, in the circumstances referred to in paragraph 1 of this Article, a member of the diplomatic staff of the diplomatic mission of the sending State in the receiving State is designated by the sending State as an acting head of post, he shall, if the receiving State does not object thereto, continue to enjoy diplomatic privileges and immunities.

Article 17

1. In a State where the sending State has no diplomatic mission and is not represented by a diplomatic mission of a third State, a consular officer may, with the consent of the receiving State, and without affecting his consular status, be authorised to perform diplomatic acts. The performance of such acts by a consular officer shall not confer upon him any right to claim diplomatic privileges and immunities.

2. A consular officer may, after notification addressed to the receiving State, act as representative of the sending State to any inter-governmental organisation. When so acting, he shall be entitled to enjoy any privileges and immunities accorded to such a representative by customary international law or by international agreements; however, in respect of the performance by him of any consular function, he shall not be entitled to any greater immunity from jurisdiction than that to which a consular officer is entitled under the present Convention.

SECTION II – END OF CONSULAR FUNCTIONS

Article 27

1. In the event of the severance of consular relations between two States:

(a) the receiving State shall, even in case of armed conflict, respect and protect the consular premises, together with the property of the consular post and the consular archives;
(b) the sending State may entrust the custody of the consular premises, together with the property contained therein and the consular archives, to a third State acceptable to the receiving State;
(c) the sending State may entrust the protection of its interests and those of its nationals to a third State acceptable to the receiving State.

2. In the event of the temporary or permanent closure of a consular post, the provisions of sub-paragraph (a) of paragraph 1 of this Article shall apply. In addition,

(a) if the sending State, although not represented in the receiving State by a diplomatic mission, has another consular post in the territory of that State, that consular post may be entrusted with the custody of the premises of the consular post which has been closed, together with the property contained therein and the consular archives, and, with the consent of the receiving State, with the exercise of consular functions in the district of that consular post; or
(b) if the sending State has no diplomatic mission and no other consular post in the receiving State, the provisions of sub-paragraphs (b) and (c) of paragraph 1 of this Article shall apply.

CHAPTER II – FACILITIES; PRIVILEGES AND IMMUNITIES RELATING TO CONSULAR POSTS, CAREER CONSULAR OFFICERS AND OTHER MEMBERS OF A CONSULAR POST

SECTION I – FACILITIES, PRIVILEGES AND IMMUNITIES RELATING TO A CONSULAR POST

Article 31

1. Consular premises shall be inviolable to the extent provided in this Article.

2. The authorities of the receiving State shall not enter that part of the consular premises which is used exclusively for the purpose of the work of the consular post except with the consent of the head of the consular post or of his designee or of the head of the diplomatic mission of the sending State. The consent of the head of the consular post may, however, be assumed in case of fire or other disaster requiring prompt protective action.

3. Subject to the provisions of paragraph 2 of this Article, the receiving State is under a special duty to take all appropriate steps to protect the consular premises against any intrusion or damage and to prevent any disturbance of the peace of the consular post or impairment of its dignity.

4. The consular premises, their furnishings, the property of the consular post and its means of transport shall be immune from any form of requisition for purposes of national defence or public utility. If expropriation is necessary for such purposes, all possible steps shall be taken to avoid impeding the performance of consular functions, and prompt, adequate and effective compensation shall be paid to the sending State.

Article 32

1. Consular premises and the residence of the career head of consular post of which the sending State or any person acting on its behalf is the owner or lessee shall be exempt from all national, regional or municipal dues and taxes whatsoever, other than such as represent payment for specific services rendered.

2. The exemption from taxation referred to in paragraph 1 of this Article shall not apply to such dues and taxes if, under the law of the receiving State, they are payable by the person who contracted with the sending State or with the person acting on its behalf.

Article 33

The consular archives and documents shall be inviolable at all times and wherever they may be.

Article 35

1. The receiving State shall permit and protect freedom of communication on the part of the consular post for all official purposes. In communicating with the Government, the diplomatic missions and other consular posts, wherever situated, of the sending State, the consular post may employ all appropriate means, including diplomatic or consular couriers, diplomatic or consular bags and messages in code or cipher. However, the consular post may install and use a wireless transmitter only with the consent of the receiving State.

2. The official correspondence of the consular post shall be inviolable. Official correspondence means all correspondence relating to the consular post and its functions.

3. The consular bag shall be neither opened nor detained. Nevertheless, if the competent authorities of the receiving State have serious reason to believe that the bag contains something other than the correspondence, documents or articles referred to in paragraph 4 of this Article, they may request that the bag be opened in their presence by an authorised representative of the sending State. If this request is refused by the authorities of the sending State, the bag shall be returned to its place of origin.

4. The packages constituting the consular bag shall bear visible external marks of their character and may contain only official correspondence and documents or articles intended exclusively for official use.

5. The consular courier shall be provided with an official document indicating his status and the number of packages constituting the consular bag. Except with the consent of the receiving State, he shall be neither a national of the receiving State, nor, unless he is a national of the sending State, a permanent resident of the receiving State. In the performance of his functions he shall be protected by the receiving State. He shall enjoy personal inviolability and shall not be liable to any form of arrest or detention.

6. The sending State, its diplomatic missions and its consular posts may designate consular couriers ad hoc. In such cases the provisions of paragraph 5 of this Article shall also apply except that the immunities therein mentioned shall cease to apply when such a courier has delivered to the consignee the consular bag in his charge.

7. A consular bag may be entrusted to the captain of a ship or of a commercial aircraft scheduled to land at an authorised port of entry. He shall be provided with an official document indicating the number of packages constituting the bag, but he shall not be considered to be a consular courier. By arrangement with the appropriate local authorities, the consular post may send one of its members to take possession of the bag directly and freely from the captain of the ship or of the aircraft.

Article 39

1. The consular post may levy in the territory of the receiving State the fees and charges provided by the laws and regulations of the sending State for consular acts.

2. The sums collected in the form of the fees and charges referred to in paragraph 1 of this Article, and the receipts for such fees and charges, shall be exempt from all dues and taxes in the receiving State.

SECTION II – FACILITIES, PRIVILEGES AND IMMUNITIES RELATING TO CAREER CONSULAR OFFICERS AND OTHER MEMBERS OF A CONSULAR POST

Article 41

1. Consular officers shall not be liable to arrest or detention pending trial, except in the case of a grave crime and pursuant to a decision by the competent judicial authority.

2. Except in the case specified in paragraph 1 of this Article, consular officers shall not be committed to prison or liable to any other form of restriction on their personal freedom save in execution of a judicial decision of final effect.

Article 43

1. Consular officers and consular employees shall not be amenable to the jurisdiction of the judicial or administrative authorities of the receiving State in respect of acts performed in the exercise of consular functions.

2. The provisions of paragraph 1 of this Article shall not, however, apply in respect of a civil action either:

> (a) arising out of a contract concluded by a consular officer or a consular employee in which he did not contract expressly or impliedly as an agent of the sending State; or
> (b) by a third party for damage arising from an accident in the receiving State caused by a vehicle, vessel or aircraft.

Article 44

1. Members of a consular post may be called upon to attend as witnesses in the course of judicial or administrative proceedings. A consular employee or a member of the service staff shall not, except in the cases mentioned in paragraph 3 of this Article, decline to give evidence. If a consular officer should decline to do so, no coercive measure or penalty may be applied to him.

2. The authority requiring the evidence of a consular officer shall avoid interference with the performance of his functions. It may, when possible, take such evidence at his residence or at the consular post or accept a statement from him in writing.

3. Members of a consular post are under no obligation to give evidence concerning matters connected with the exercise of their functions or to produce official correspondence and documents relating thereto. They are also entitled to decline to give evidence as expert witnesses with regard to the law of the sending State.

Article 45

1. The sending State may waive, with regard to a member of the consular post, any of the privileges and immunities provided for in Articles 41, 43 and 44.

2. The waiver shall in all cases be express, except as provided in paragraph 3 of this Article, and shall be communicated to the receiving State in writing.

3. The initiation of proceedings by a consular officer or a consular employee in a matter where he might enjoy immunity from jurisdiction under Article 43 shall preclude him from invoking immunity from jurisdiction in respect of any counter-claim directly connected with the principal claim.

4. The waiver of immunity from jurisdiction for the purposes of civil or administrative proceedings shall not be deemed to imply the waiver of immunity

from the measures of execution resulting from the judicial decision; in respect of such measures, a separate waiver shall be necessary.

Article 48

1. Subject to the provisions of paragraph 3 of this Article, members of the consular post with respect to services rendered by them for the sending State, and members of their families forming part of their households, shall be exempt from social security provisions which may be in force in the receiving State.

2. The exemption provided for in paragraph 1 of this Article shall apply also to members of the private staff who are in the sole employ of members of the consular post, on condition:

   (a) that they are not nationals of or permanently resident in the receiving State; and
   (b) that they are covered by the social security provisions which are in force in the sending State or a third State.

3. Members of the consular post who employ persons to whom the exemption provided for in paragraph 2 of this Article does not apply shall observe the obligations which the social security provisions of the receiving State impose upon employers.

4. The exemption provided for in paragraphs 1 and 2 of this Article shall not preclude voluntary participation in the social security system of the receiving State, provided that such participation is permitted by that State.

Article 49

1. Consular officers and consular employees and members of their families forming part of their households shall be exempt from all dues and taxes, personal or real, national, regional or municipal, except:

   (a) indirect taxes of a kind which are normally incorporated in the price of goods or services;
   (b) dues or taxes on private immovable property situated in the territory of the receiving State, subject to the provisions of Article 32;
   (c) estate, succession or inheritance duties, and duties on transfers, levied by the receiving State, subject to the provisions of paragraph (b) of Article 51;
   (d) dues and taxes on private income, including capital gains, having its source in the receiving State and capital taxes relating to investments made in commercial or financial undertakings in the receiving State;
   (e) charges levied for specific services rendered;
   (f) registration, court or record fees, mortgage dues and stamp duties, subject to the provisions of Article 32.

2. Members of the service staff shall be exempt from dues and taxes on the wages which they receive for their services.

3. Members of the consular post who employ persons whose wages or salaries are not exempt from income tax in the receiving State shall observe the obligations which the laws and regulations of that State impose upon employers concerning the levying of income tax.

Article 50

1. The receiving State shall, in accordance with such laws and regulations as it may adopt, permit entry of and grant exemption from all customs duties, taxes, and related charges other than charges for storage, cartage and similar services, on:

   (a) articles for the official use of the consular post;

(b) articles for the personal use of a consular officer or members of his family forming part of his household, including articles intended for his establishment. The articles intended for consumption shall not exceed the quantities necessary for direct utilisation by the persons concerned.

2. Consular employees shall enjoy the privileges and exemptions specified in paragraph 1 of this Article in respect of articles imported at the time of first installation.

3. Personal baggage accompanying consular officers and members of their families forming part of their households shall be exempt from inspection. It may be inspected only if there is serious reason to believe that it contains articles other than those referred to in sub-paragraph (b) of paragraph 1 of this Article, or articles the import or export of which is prohibited by the laws and regulations of the receiving State or which are subject to its quarantine laws and regulations. Such inspection shall be carried out in the presence of the consular officer or member of his family concerned.

Article 51

In the event of the death of a member of the consular post or of a member of his family forming part of his household, the receiving State:

(a) shall permit the export of the movable property of the deceased, with the exception of any such property acquired in the receiving State the export of which was prohibited at the time of his death;
(b) shall not levy national, regional or municipal estate, succession or inheritance duties, and duties on transfers, on movable property the presence of which in the receiving State was due solely to the presence in that State of the deceased as a member of the consular post or as a member of the family of a member of the consular post.

Article 52

The receiving State shall exempt members of the consular post and members of their families forming part of their households from all personal services, from all public service of any kind whatsoever, and from military obligations such as those connected with requisitioning, military contributions and billeting.

Article 53

1. Every member of the consular post shall enjoy the privileges and immunities provided in the present Convention from the moment he enters the territory of the receiving State on proceeding to take up his post or, if already in its territory, from the moment when he enters on his duties with the consular post.

2. Members of the family of a member of the consular post forming part of his household and members of his private staff shall receive the privileges and immunities provided in the present Convention from the date from which he enjoys privileges and immunities in accordance with paragraph 1 of this Article or from the date of their entry into the territory of the receiving State or from the date of their becoming a member of such family or private staff, whichever is the latest.

3. When the functions of a member of the consular post have come to an end, his privileges and immunities and those of a member of his family forming part of his household or a member of his private staff shall normally cease at the moment when the person concerned leaves the receiving State or on the expiry of a reasonable period in which to do so, whichever is the sooner, but shall subsist until that time, even in case of armed conflict. In the case of the persons referred to in paragraph 2 of this Article, their privileges and immunities shall come to an end when they cease to belong to the household or to be in the service of a

member of the consular post provided, however, that if such persons intend leaving the receiving State within a reasonable period thereafter, their privileges and immunities shall subsist until the time of their departure.

4. However, with respect to acts performed by a consular officer or a consular employee in the exercise of his functions, immunity from jurisdiction shall continue to subsist without limitation of time.

5. In the event of the death of a member of the consular post, the members of his family forming part of his household shall continue to enjoy the privileges and immunities accorded to them until they leave the receiving State or until the expiry of a reasonable period enabling them to do so, whichever is the sooner.

Article 54

1. If a consular officer passes through or is in the territory of a third State, which has granted him a visa if a visa was necessary, while proceeding to take up or return to his post or when returning to the sending State, the third State shall accord to him all immunities provided for by the other Articles of the present Convention as may be required to ensure his transit or return. The same shall apply in the case of any member of his family forming part of his household enjoying such privileges and immunities who are accompanying the consular officer or travelling separately to join him or to return to the sending State.

2. In circumstances similar to those specified in paragraph 1 of this Article, third States shall not hinder the transit through their territory of other members of the consular post or of members of their families forming part of their households.

3. Third States shall accord to official correspondence and to other official communications in transit, including messages in code or cipher, the same freedom and protection as the receiving State is bound to accord under the present Convention. They shall accord to consular couriers who have been granted a visa, if a visa was necessary, and to consular bags in transit, the same inviolability and protection as the receiving State is bound to accord under the present Convention.

4. The obligations of third States under paragraphs 1, 2 and 3 of this Article shall also apply to the persons mentioned respectively in those paragraphs, and to official communications and to consular bags, whose presence in the territory of the third State is due to force majeure.

Article 55

2. The consular premises shall not be used in any manner incompatible with the exercise of consular functions.

3. The provisions of paragraph 2 of this Article shall not exclude the possibility of offices of other institutions or agencies being installed in part of the building in which the consular premises are situated, provided that the premises assigned to them are separate from those used by the consular post. In that event, the said offices shall not, for the purposes of the present convention, be considered to form part of the consular premises.

Article 57

2. Privileges and immunities provided in this Chapter shall not be accorded:

    (a) to consular employees or to members of the service staff who carry on any private gainful occupation in the receiving State;
    (b) to members of the family of a person referred to in sub-paragraph (a) of this paragraph or to members of his private staff;
    (c) to members of the family of a member of a consular post who themselves carry on any private gainful occupation in the receiving State.

CHAPTER III – REGIME RELATING TO HONORARY CONSULAR OFFICERS AND CONSULAR POSTS HEADED BY SUCH OFFICERS

Article 58

1. Articles 35 and 39, paragraph 3 of Article 54 and paragraphs 2 and 3 of Article 55 shall apply to consular posts headed by an honorary consular officer. In addition, the facilities, privileges and immunities of such consular posts shall be governed by Articles 60, 61 and 62.

2. Articles 43, paragraph 3 of Article 44, Articles 45 and 53 shall apply to honorary consular officers. In addition, the facilities, privileges and immunities of such consular officers shall be governed by Articles 66 and 67.

3. Privileges and immunities provided in the present Convention shall not be accorded to members of the family of an honorary consular officer or of a consular employee employed at a consular post headed by an honorary consular officer.

Article 59

The receiving State shall take such steps as may be necessary to protect the consular premises of a consular post headed by an honorary consular officer against any intrusion or damage and to prevent any disturbance of the peace of the consular post or impairment of its dignity.

Article 60

1. Consular premises of a consular post headed by an honorary consular officer of which the sending State is the owner or lessee shall be exempt from all national, regional or municipal dues and taxes whatsoever, other than such as represent payment for specific services rendered.

2. The exemption from taxation referred to in paragraph 1 of this Article shall not apply to such dues and taxes if, under the laws and regulations of the receiving State, they are payable by the person who contracted with the sending State.

Article 61

The consular archives and documents of a consular post headed by an honorary consular officer shall be inviolable at all times and wherever they may be, provided that they are kept separate from other papers and documents and, in particular, from the private correspondence of the head of a consular post and of any person working with him, and from the materials, books or documents relating to their profession or trade.

Article 62

The receiving State shall, in accordance with such laws and regulations as it may adopt, permit entry of, and grant exemption from all customs duties, taxes, and related charges other than charges for storage, cartage and similar services on the following articles, provided that they are for the official use of a consular post headed by an honorary consular officer: coats-of-arms, flags, signboards, seals and stamps, books, official printed matter, office furniture, office equipment and similar articles supplied by or at the instance of the sending State to the consular post.

Article 66

An honorary consular officer shall be exempt from all dues and taxes on the remuneration and emoluments which he receives from the sending State in respect of the exercise of consular functions.

Article 67

The receiving State shall exempt honorary consular officers from all personal services and from all public services of any kind whatsoever and from military obligations such as those connected with requisitioning, military contributions and billeting.

CHAPTER IV – GENERAL PROVISIONS

Article 70

1. The provisions of the present Convention apply also, so far as the context permits, to the exercise of consular functions by a diplomatic mission.

2. The names of members of a diplomatic mission assigned to the consular section or otherwise charged with the exercise of the consular functions of the mission shall be notified to the Ministry for Foreign Affairs of the receiving State or to the authority designated by that Ministry....

4. The privileges and immunities of the members of a diplomatic mission referred to in paragraph 2 of this Article shall continue to be governed by the rules of international law concerning diplomatic relations.

Article 71

1. Except in so far as additional facilities, privileges and immunities may be granted by the receiving State, consular officers who are nationals of or permanently resident in the receiving State shall enjoy only immunity from jurisdiction and personal inviolability in respect of official acts performed in the exercise of their functions, and the privilege provided in paragraph 3 of Article 44.

2. Other members of the consular post who are nationals of or permanently resident in the receiving State and members of their families, as well as members of the families of consular officers referred to in paragraph 1 of this Article, shall enjoy facilities, privileges and immunities only in so far as these are granted to them by the receiving State. Those members of the families of members of the consular post and those members of the private staff who are themselves nationals of or permanently resident in the receiving State shall likewise enjoy facilities, privileges and immunities only in so far as these are granted to them by the receiving State.

SCHEDULE 2

PROVISIONS FOR GIVING EFFECT TO OTHER AGREEMENTS

1. The like exemption from dues and taxes may be extended to the residence of any member of a consular post as is accorded under Article 32 in Schedule 1 to this Act to the residence of the career head of a consular post.

2. Paragraph 1 of Article 49 in that Schedule may be extended to members of the service staff.

3. Paragraph 2 of Article 50 in that Schedule may be applied as if it were among the Articles mentioned in paragraph 2 of Article 58 in that Schedule, as if the reference to consular employees included members of the service staff and also such members of the families of consular employees or of members of the service staff as form part of their households, and as if the words 'in respect of articles imported at the time of first installation' were omitted.

4. Articles 29 and 31 in Schedule 1 to the Diplomatic Privileges Act 1964 (inviolability and immunity from jurisdiction and arrest of diplomatic agents and

exemption from duty to give evidence) may be extended to members of a consular post and members of their families forming part of their households.

5. Article 22 in Schedule 1 to the Diplomatic Privileges Act 1964 (inviolability and protection of mission) may be extended to consular premises and paragraph 1 of Article 30 in that Schedule (inviolability of private residence) may be extended to the residences of consular officers.

6. Article 27 in Schedule 1 to the Diplomatic Privileges Act 1964 (freedom of communications) may be extended to the communications of a consular post.

[As amended by the International Organisations Act 1968, s12(2); Diplomatic and other Privileges Act 1971, s4, Schedule; Social Security Act 1973, ss100, 101, Schedule 27, para 78; Social Security (Consequential Provisions) Act 1975, ss1(2), 5, Schedule 1, Pt I; Customs and Excise Management Act 1979, s177(1), Schedule 4, paras 6, 7; British Nationality Act 1981, s52(6), Schedule 7; Hong Kong (British Nationality) Order 1986, art 8, Schedule 1; Diplomatic and Consular Premises Act 1987, s6, Schedule 2, paras 3–6; Finance (No 2) Act 1992, s14, Schedule 3, Pt III, para 89(1); Value Added Tax Act 1994, s100(1), Schedule 14, para 3.]

INTERNATIONAL ORGANISATIONS ACT 1968
(1968 c 48)

1 Organisations of which United Kingdom is a member [665]

(1) This section shall apply to any organisation declared by Order in Council to be an organisation of which –

(a) the United Kingdom, or Her Majesty's Government in the United Kingdom, and

(b) any other sovereign Power or the Government of any other sovereign Power,

are members.

(2) Subject to subsection (6) of this section, Her Majesty may by Order in Council made under this subsection specify an organisation to which this section applies and make any one or more of the following provisions in respect of the organisation so specified (in the following provisions of this section referred to as 'the organisation'), that is to say –

(a) confer on the organisation the legal capacities of a body corporate;

(b) provide that the organisation shall, to such extent as may be specified in the Order, have the privileges and immunities set out in Part I of Schedule 1 to this Act;

(c) confer the privileges and immunities set out in Part II of Schedule 1 to this Act, to such extent as may be specified in the Order, on persons of any such class as is mentioned in the next following subsection;

(d) confer the privileges and immunities set out in Part III of Schedule 1 to this Act, to such extent as may be specified in the Order, on such classes of officers and servants of the organisation (not being classes mentioned in the next following subsection) as may be so specified.

(3) The classes of persons referred to in subsection (2)(c) of this section are –

(a) persons who (whether they represent Governments or not) are representatives to the organisation or representatives on, or members of, any organ, committee or other subordinate body of the organisation (including any sub-committee or other subordinate body of a subordinate body of the organisation);

(b) such number of officers of the organisation as may be specified in the Order, being the holders (whether permanent, temporary or acting) of such high offices in the organisation as may be so specified; and
(c) persons employed by or serving under the organisation as experts or as persons engaged on missions for the organisation.

(4) Where an Order in Council is made under subsection (2) of this section, the provisions of Part IV of Schedule 1 to this Act shall have effect by virtue of that Order (in those provisions, as they so have effect, referred to as 'the relevant Order'), except in so far as that Order otherwise provides.

(5) Where an Order in Council is made under subsection (2) of this section, then for the purpose of giving effect to any agreement made in that behalf between the United Kingdom or Her Majesty's Government in the United Kingdom and the organisation Her Majesty may by the same or any subsequent Order in Council make either or both of the following provisions, that is to say –

(a) confer the exemptions set out in paragraph 13 of Schedule 1 to this Act, to such extent as may be specified in the Order, in respect of officers and servants of the organisation of any class specified in the Order in accordance with subsection (2)(d) of this section and in respect of members of the family of any such officer or servant who form part of his household;
(b) confer the exemptions set out in Part V of that Schedule in respect of –

(i) members of the staff of the organisation recognised by Her Majesty's Government in the United Kingdom as holding a rank equivalent to that of a diplomatic agent, and
(ii) members of the family of any such member of the staff of the organisation who form part of his household.

(6) Any Order in Council made under subsection (2) or subsection (5) of this section shall be so framed as to secure –

(a) that the privileges and immunities conferred by the Order are not greater in extent than those which, at the time when the Order takes effect, are required to be conferred in accordance with any agreement to which the United Kingdom or Her Majesty's Government in the United Kingdom is then a party (whether made with any other sovereign Power or Government or made with one or more organisations such as are mentioned in subsection (1) of this section), and
(b) that no privilege or immunity is conferred on any person as the representative of the United Kingdom, or of Her Majesty's Government in the United Kingdom, or as a member of the staff of such a representative.

2 Specialised agencies of United Nations

(1) Where an Order in Council under section 1(2) of this Act is made in respect of an organisation which is a specialised agency of the United Nations having its headquarters or principal office in the United Kingdom, then for the purpose of giving effect to any agreement between the United Kingdom or Her Majesty's Government in the United Kingdom and that organisation Her Majesty may by the same or any other Order in Council confer the exemptions, privileges and reliefs specified in the next following subsection, to such extent as may be specified in the Order, on officers of the organisation who are recognised by Her Majesty's Government in the United Kingdom as holding a rank equivalent to that of a diplomatic agent.

(2) The exemptions, privileges and reliefs referred to in the preceding subsection are –

(a) the like exemption or relief from income tax, capital gains tax and rates as, in accordance with Article 34 of the 1961 Convention Articles, is accorded to a diplomatic agent, and
(aa) the like exemption or relief from being liable to pay anything in respect of council tax as in accordance with that Article is accorded to a diplomatic agent, and
(b) the exemptions, privileges and reliefs specified in paragraphs 10 to 12 of Schedule 1 to this Act and the exemption comprised in paragraph 9 of that Schedule from vehicle excise duty (that is to say, duty under section 1 of the Vehicles (Excise) Act 1971, whether chargeable by virtue of that section or otherwise, or any corresponding duty under an enactment of the Parliament of Northern Ireland).

(3) Where by virtue of subsection (1) of this section any of the exemptions, privileges and reliefs referred to in subsection (2)(b) of this section are conferred on persons as being officers of the organisation, Her Majesty may by the same or any other Order in Council confer the like exemptions, privileges and reliefs on persons who are members of the families of those persons and form part of their households.

(4) The powers conferred by the preceding provisions of this section shall be exercisable in addition to any power exercisable by virtue of subsection (2) or subsection (5) of section 1 of this Act; and any exercise of the powers conferred by those provisions shall have effect without prejudice to the operation of subsection (4) of that section.

(5) Subsection (6) of section 1 of this Act shall have effect in relation to the preceding provisions of this section as it has effect in relation to subsections (2) and (5) of that section.

(6) In this section 'specialised agency' has the meaning assigned to it by Article 57 of the Charter of the United Nations.

4 Other organisations of which United Kingdom is not a member [667]

Where an organisation of which two or more sovereign Powers, or the Governments of two or more such Powers, are members but of which neither the United Kingdom nor Her Majesty's Government in the United Kingdom is a member, maintains or proposes to maintain an establishment in the United Kingdom, then for the purpose of giving effect to any agreement made in that behalf between the United Kingdom or Her Majesty's Government in the United Kingdom and that organisation, Her Majesty may by Order in Council specifying the organisation make either or both of the following provisions in respect of the organisation, that is to say –

(a) confer on the organisation the legal capacities of a body corporate, and
(b) provide that the organisation shall, to such extent as may be specified in the Order, be entitled to the like exemption or relief from taxes on income and capital gains as is accorded to a foreign sovereign Power.

4A International commodity organisations [668]

(1) In this section, 'international commodity organisation' means any such organisation as is mentioned in section 4 of this Act (international organisations of which the United Kingdom is not a member) which appears to Her Majesty to satisfy each of the following conditions –

(a) that the members of the organisation are States or the Governments of States in which a particular commodity is produced or consumed;
(b) that the exports or imports of that commodity from or to those States account (when taken together) for a significant volume of the total exports or imports of that commodity throughout the world; and
(c) that the purpose or principal purpose of the organisation is –

(i) to regulate trade in that commodity (whether as an import or an export or both) or to promote or study that trade; or
(ii) to promote research into that commodity or its uses or further development.

(2) Subject to the following provisions of this section, an Order made under section 4 of this Act with respect to an international commodity organisation may, for the purpose there mentioned and to such extent as may be specified in the Order –

(a) provide that the organisation shall have the privileges and immunities set out in paragraphs 2, 3, 4, 6 and 7 of Schedule 1 to this Act;
(b) confer on persons of any such class as is mentioned in sub-section (3) of this section the privileges and immunities set out in paragraphs 11 and 14 of that Schedule;
(c) provide that the official papers of such persons shall be inviolable; and
(d) confer on officers and servants of the organisation of any such class as may be specified in the Order the privileges and immunities set out in paragraphs 13, 15 and 16 of that Schedule.

(3) The classes of persons referred to in subsection (2)(b) of this section are –

(a) persons who (whether they represent Governments or not) are representatives to the organisation or representatives on, or members of, any organ, committee or other subordinate body of the organisation (including any sub-committee or other subordinate body of a subordinate body of the organisation);
(b) persons who are members of the staff of any such representative and who are recognised by Her Majesty's Government in the United Kingdom as holding a rank equivalent to that of a diplomatic agent.

(4) An Order in Council made under section 4 of this Act shall not confer on any person of such class as is mentioned in sub-section (3) of this section any immunity in respect of a civil action arising out of an accident caused by a motor vehicle or other means of transport belonging to or driven by such a person, or in respect of a traffic offence involving such a vehicle and committed by such a person.

(5) In this section 'commodity' means any produce of agriculture, forestry or fisheries, or any mineral, either in its natural state or having undergone only such processes as are necessary or customary to prepare the produce or mineral for the international market.

5 International judicial and other proceedings [669]

(1) Her Majesty may by Order in Council confer on any class of persons to whom this section applies such privileges, immunities and facilities as in the opinion of Her Majesty in Council are or will be required for giving effect –

(a) to any agreement to which, at the time when the Order takes effect, the United Kingdom or Her Majesty's Government in the United Kingdom is or will be a party, or
(b) to any resolution of the General Assembly of the United Nations.

(2) This section applies to any persons who are for the time being –

(a) judges or members of any international tribunal, or persons exercising or performing, or appointed (whether permanently or temporarily) to exercise or perform, any jurisdiction or functions of such a tribunal;
(b) registrars or other officers of any international tribunal;
(c) parties to any proceedings before any international tribunal;
(d) agents, advisers or advocates (by whatever name called) for any such parties;
(e) witnesses in, or assessors for the purposes of, any proceedings before any international tribunal.

(3) For the purposes of this section any petition, complaint or other communication which, with a view to action to be taken by or before an international tribunal, –

(a) is made to the tribunal, or
(b) is made to a person through whom, in accordance with the constitution, rules or practice of the tribunal, such a communication can be received by the tribunal,

shall be deemed to be proceedings before the tribunal, and the person making any such communication shall be deemed to be a party to such proceedings.

(4) Without prejudice to subsection (3) of this section, any reference in this section to a party to proceedings before an international tribunal shall be construed as including a reference to –

(a) any person who, for the purposes of any such proceedings, acts as next friend, guardian or other representative (by whatever name called) of a party to the proceedings, and
(b) any person who (not being a person to whom this section applies apart from this paragraph) is entitled or permitted, in accordance with the constitution, rules or practice of an international tribunal, to participate in proceedings before the tribunal by way of advising or assisting the tribunal in the proceedings.

(5) In this section 'international tribunal' means any court (including the International Court of Justice), tribunal, commission or other body which, in pursuance of any such agreement or resolution as is mentioned in subsection (1) of this section, –

(a) exercises, or is appointed (whether permanently or temporarily) for the purpose of exercising, any jurisdiction, or
(b) performs, or is appointed (whether permanently or temporarily) for the purpose of performing, any functions of a judicial nature or by way of arbitration, conciliation or inquiry,

and includes any individual who, in pursuance of any such agreement or resolution, exercises or performs, or is appointed (whether permanently or temporarily) for the purpose of exercising or performing, any jurisdiction or any such functions.

5A Orders under ss1 and 4 extending to United Kingdom conferences [670]

(1) An Order in Council made under section 1 of this Act in respect of any organisation, or under section 4 of this Act in respect of an international commodity organisation, may to such extent as may be specified in the Order, and subject to the following provisions of this section –

(a) confer on persons of any such class as may be specified in the Order, being persons who are or are to be representatives (whether of Government or not) at any conference which the organisation may convene in the United Kingdom –

(i) in the case of an Order under section 1, the privileges and immunities set out in Part II of Schedule 1 to this Act;
(ii) in the case of an Order under section 4, the privileges and immunities set out in paragraphs 11 and 14 of that Schedule; and

(b) in the case of an Order under section 4, provide that the official papers of such persons shall be inviolable.

(2) Where in the exercise of the power conferred by subsection (1)(a) of this section an Order confers privileges and immunities on persons of any such class as is mentioned in that paragraph, the provisions of paragraphs 19 to 22 of Schedule 1 to this Act shall have effect in relation to the members of the official staffs of such persons as if in paragraph 29 of that Schedule 'representative' were defined as a person of such a class.

(3) The powers exercisable by virtue of this section may be exercised notwithstanding the provisions of any such agreement as is mentioned in section 1(6)(a) or 4 of this Act, but no privilege or immunity may thereby be conferred on any such representative, or member of his staff, as is mentioned in section 1(6)(b) of this Act.

(4) In this section 'international commodity organisation' has the meaning given by section 4A(1) of this Act.

(5) This section is without prejudice to section 6 of this Act.

6 Representatives at international conferences in United Kingdom [671]

(1) This section applies to any conference which is, or is to be, held in the United Kingdom and is, or is to be, attended by representatives –

(a) of the United Kingdom, or of Her Majesty's Government in the United Kingdom, and
(b) of any other sovereign Power or the Government of any other sovereign Power.

(2) Her Majesty may by Order in Council specify one or more classes of persons who are, or are to be, representatives of a sovereign Power (other than the United Kingdom) or of the Government of such a Power, at a conference to which this section applies, and confer on persons of the class or classes in question, to such extent as may be specified in the Order, the privileges and immunities set out in Part II of Schedule 1 to this Act.

(3) Where an Order in Council is made under subsection (2) of this section in relation to a particular conference, then, except in so far as that Order otherwise provides, the provisions of paragraphs 19 to 22 of Schedule 1 to this Act shall have effect in relation to members of the official staffs of persons of a class specified in the Order in accordance with that subsection as if in paragraph 19 of that Schedule 'representative' were defined as a person of a class so specified in the Order.

7 Priority of telecommunications [672]

So far as may be necessary for the purpose of giving effect to the International Telecommunication Convention done at Montreux on 12 November 1965 or any subsequent treaty or agreement whereby that Convention is amended or

superseded, priority shall, wherever practicable, be given to messages from, and to replies to messages from, any of the following, that is to say –
- (a) the Secretary General of the United Nations;
- (b) the heads of principal organs of the United Nations; and
- (c) the International Court of Justice.

8 Evidence [673]

If in any proceedings a question arises whether a person is or is not entitled to any privilege or immunity by virtue of this Act or any Order in Council made thereunder, a certificate issued by or under the authority of the Secretary of State stating any fact relating to that question shall be conclusive evidence of that fact.

9 Financial provisions [674]

Any amount refunded under any arrangement made in accordance with any provisions of Schedule 1 to this Act relating to refund of customs duty, value added tax or car tax –
- (a) if the arrangements were made by the Secretary of State, shall be paid out of moneys provided by Parliament, or
- (b) if the arrangements were made by the Commissioners of Customs and Excise, shall be paid out of the moneys standing to the credit of the General Account of those Commissioners.

10 Orders in Council [675]

(1) No recommendation shall be made to Her Majesty in Council to make an Order under any provision (other than section 6) of this Act unless a draft of the Order has been laid before Parliament and approved by a resolution of each House of Parliament.

(2) Any Order in Council made under section 6 of this Act shall be subject to annulment in pursuance of a resolution of either House of Parliament.

(3) Any power conferred by any provision of this Act to make an Order in Council shall include power to revoke or vary the Order by a subsequent Order in Council made under that provision.

11 Interpretation [676]

(1) In this Act 'the 1961 Convention Articles' means the Articles (being certain Articles of the Vienna Convention on Diplomatic Relations signed in 1961) which are set out in Schedule 1 to the Diplomatic Privileges Act 1964, and 'the International Court of Justice' means the court set up by that name under the Charter of the United Nations.

(2) Expressions used in this Act to which a meaning is assigned by Article 1 of the 1961 Convention Articles, and other expressions which are used both in this Act and in those Articles, shall, except in so far as the context otherwise requires, be construed as having the same meanings in this Act as in those Articles.

(3) For the purpose of giving effect to any arrangements made in that behalf between Her Majesty's Government in the United Kingdom and any organisation, premises which are not premises of the organisation but are recognised by that Government as being temporarily occupied by the organisation for its official purposes shall, in respect of such period as may be determined in accordance with the arrangements, be treated for the purposes of this Act as if they were premises of the organisation.

(4) Except in so far as the context otherwise requires, any reference in this Act to an enactment is a reference to that enactment as amended or extended by or under any other enactment.

12 Consequential amendments, repeals and transitional provisions

(3) References in any enactment to the powers conferred by the International Organisations (Immunities and Privileges) Act 1950 shall be construed as including references to the powers conferred by this Act.

(5) Any Order in Council which has been made, or has effect as if made, under an enactment repealed by subsection (4) of this section and is in force immediately before the passing of this Act shall continue to have effect notwithstanding the repeal of that enactment and, while any such Order in Council continues to have effect in relation to an organisation –

(a) the enactment in question shall continue to have effect in relation to that organisation as if that enactment had not been repealed, and
(b) section 8 of this Act shall have effect as if in that section any reference to this Act or an Order in Council made thereunder included a reference to that enactment or that Order in Council.

(6) Any such Order in Council as is mentioned in subsection (5) of this section –

(a) if made, or having effect as if made, under section 1 of the International Organisations (Immunities and Privileges) Act 1950, may be revoked or varied as if it had been made under section 1 of this Act;
(b) if made, or having effect as if made, under section 3 of that Act, may be revoked or varied as if it had been made under section 5 of this Act.

SCHEDULE 1

PRIVILEGES AND IMMUNITIES

PART I

1. Immunity from suit and legal process.

2. The like inviolability of official archives and premises of the organisation as, in accordance with the 1961 Convention Articles, is accorded in respect of the official archives and premises of a diplomatic mission.

3. (1) Exemption or relief from taxes, other than duties (whether of customs or excise) and taxes on the importation of goods.

(2) The like relief from rates as in accordance with Article 23 of the 1961 Convention Articles is accorded in respect of the premises of a diplomatic mission.

4. Exemption from duties (whether of customs or excise) and taxes on the importation of goods imported by or on behalf of the organisation for its official use in the United Kingdom, or on the importation of any publications of the organisation imported by it or on its behalf, such exemption to be subject to compliance with such conditions as the Commissioners of Customs and Excise may prescribe for the protection of the Revenue.

5. Exemption from prohibitions and restrictions on importation or exportation in the case of goods imported or exported by the organisation for its official use and in the case of any publication of the organisation imported or exported by it.

6. Relief, under arrangements made either by the Secretary of State or by the Commissioners of Customs and Excise, by way of refund of duty (whether of

customs or excise) paid on imported hydrocarbon oil (within the meaning of the Hydrocarbon Oil Duties Act 1979) or value added tax paid on the importation of such oil which is brought in the United Kingdom and used for the official purposes of the organisation, such relief to be subject to compliance with such conditions as may be imposed in accordance with the arrangements.

7. Relief, under arrangements made by the Secretary of State, by way of refund of car tax paid on any vehicles and value added tax paid on the supply of any goods or services which are used for the official purposes of the organisation, such relief to be subject to compliance with such conditions as may be imposed in accordance with the arrangements.

PART II

8. For the purpose of conferring on any person any such exemption, privilege or Schedule, any reference in that paragraph to the representative or officer shall be construed as a reference to that person.

9. The like immunity from suit and legal process, the like inviolability of residence, and the like exemption or relief from taxes and rates, other than customs duties and taxes on the importation of goods, as are accorded to or in respect of the head of a diplomatic mission.

9A. The like inviolability of official premises as is accorded in respect of the premises of a diplomatic mission.

9B. The like exemption or relief from being liable to pay anything in respect of council tax, as is accorded to or in respect of the head of a diplomatic mission.

10. The like exemption from duties (whether of customs or excise) and taxes on the importation of articles imported for the personal use of the representative or officer or of members of his family forming part of his household, including articles intended for his establishment and the like privilege as to the importation of such articles, as in accordance with paragraph 1 of Article 36 of the 1961 Convention Articles is accorded to a diplomatic agent.

11. The like exemption and privileges in respect of the personal baggage of the representative or officer as in accordance with paragraph 2 of Article 36 of those Articles are accorded to a diplomatic agent, as if in that paragraph the reference to paragraph 1 of that Article were a reference to paragraph 10 of this Schedule.

12. Relief, under arrangements made either by the Secretary of State or by the Commissioners of Customs and Excise, by way of refund of duty (whether of customs or excise) paid on imported hydrocarbon oil (within the meaning of the Hydrocarbon Oil Duties Act 1979) or value added tax paid on the importation of such oil which is bought in the United Kingdom by or on behalf of the representative or officer, such relief to be subject to compliance with such conditions as may be imposed in accordance with the arrangements.

13. Exemptions whereby, for the purposes of the enactments relating to social security ... –

(a) services rendered for the organisation by the representative or officer shall be deemed to be excepted from any class of employment in respect of which contributions under those enactments are payable, but
(b) no person shall be rendered liable to pay any contribution which he would not be required to pay if those services were not deemed to be so excepted.

PART III

14. Immunity from suit and legal process in respect of things done or omitted to be done in the course of the performance of official duties.

15. Exemption from income tax in respect of emoluments received as an officer or servant of the organisation.

16. The like exemption from duties (whether of customs or excise) and taxes on the importation of articles which –

(a) at or about the time when an officer or servant of the organisation first enters the United Kingdom as such an officer or servant are imported for his personal use or that of members of his family forming part of his household, including articles intended for his establishment, and

(b) are articles which were in his ownership or possession or that of such a member of his family, or which he or such a member of his family was under contract to purchase, immediately before he so entered the United Kingdom,

and the like privilege as to the importation of such articles as in accordance with paragraph 1 of Article 36 of the 1961 Convention Articles is accorded to a diplomatic agent.

17. Exemption from duties (whether of customs or excise) and taxes on the importation of any motor vehicle imported by way of replacement of a motor vehicle in respect of which the conditions specified in sub-paragraphs (a) and (b) of paragraph 16 of this Schedule were fulfilled, such exemption to be subject to compliance with such conditions as the Commissioners of Customs and Excise may prescribe for the protection of the Revenue.

18. The like exemption and privileges in respect of the personal baggage of an officer or servant of the organisation as in accordance with paragraph 2 of Article 36 of the 1961 Convention Articles are accorded to a diplomatic agent, as if in that paragraph the reference to paragraph 1 of that Article were a reference to paragraph 16 of this Schedule.

19. In this Part of this Schedule –

(a) 'representative' means a person who is such a representative to the organisation specified in the relevant Order or such a representative on, or member of, an organ, committee or other subordinate body of that organisation as is mentioned in section 1(3)(a) of this Act;

(b) 'member of the official staff' means a person who accompanies a representative as part of his official staff in his capacity as a representative;

(c) references to the importation, in relation to value added tax, shall include references to anything charged with tax in accordance with section 10 or 15 of the Value Added Tax Act 1994 (acquisitions from other member States and importations from outside the European Community), and 'imported' shall be construed accordingly.

20. A member of the official staff who is recognised by Her Majesty's Government in the United Kingdom as holding a rank equivalent to that of a diplomatic agent shall be entitled to the privileges and immunities set out in Part II of this Schedule to the like extent as, by virtue of the relevant Order, the representative whom he accompanies is entitled to them.

21 (1) Subject to sub-paragraph (2) of this paragraph, a member of the official staff who is not so recognised, and who is employed in the administrative or technical service of the representative whom he accompanies, shall be entitled to the privileges and immunities set out in paragraphs 9 and 13 of this Schedule to the like extent as, by virtue of the relevant Order, that representative is entitled to them.

(2) Such a member of the official staff shall not by virtue of the preceding sub-paragraph be entitled to immunity from any civil proceedings in respect of any cause of action arising otherwise than in the course of his official duties.

(3) Such a member of the official staff shall also be entitled to the exemption set out in paragraph 16 of this Schedule as if he were an officer of the organisation specified in the relevant Order.

22. A member of the official staff who is employed in the domestic service of the representative whom he accompanies shall be entitled to the following privileges and immunities, that is to say –

(a) immunity from suit and legal process in respect of things done or omitted to be done in the course of the performance of official duties, and
(b) the exemptions set out in paragraph 13 of this Schedule,

to the like extent as, by virtue of the relevant Order, that representative is entitled to them, and shall be entitled to exemption from taxes on his emoluments in respect of that employment to the like extent as, by virtue of the relevant Order, that representative is entitled to exemption from taxes on his emoluments as a representative.

23 (1) Persons who are members of the family of a representative and form part of his household shall be entitled to the privileges and immunities set out in Part II of this Schedule to the like extent as, by virtue of the relevant Order, that representative is entitled to them.

(2) Persons who are members of the family and form part of the household of an officer of the organisation specified in the relevant Order, where that officer is the holder (whether permanent, temporary or acting) of an office specified in that Order in accordance with section 1(3)(b) of this Act, shall be entitled to the privileges and immunities set out in Part II of this Schedule to the like extent as, by virtue of the relevant Order, that officer is entitled to them.

(3) Persons who are members of the family and form part of the household of such a member of the official staff as is mentioned in paragraph 20 of this Schedule shall be entitled to the privileges and immunities set out in Part II of this Schedule to the like extent as, by virtue of that paragraph, that member of the official staff is entitled to them.

(4) Persons who are members of the family and form part of the household of such a member of the official staff as is mentioned in paragraph 21 of this Schedule shall be entitled to the privileges and immunities set out in paragraphs 9 and 13 of this Schedule to the like extent as, by virtue of paragraph 21 of this Schedule, that member of the official staff is entitled to them.

PART V

24. In the event of the death of the person in respect of whom the exemptions under this paragraph are conferred, exemptions from –

(a) estate duty leviable on his death under the law of any part of the United Kingdom in respect of movable property which is in the United Kingdom immediately before his death and whose presence in the United Kingdom at that time is due solely to his presence there in the capacity by reference to which the exemptions are conferred.

[As amended by the Diplomatic and other Privileges Act 1971, s3; European Communities Act 1972, s4, Schedule 3, Pt IV; Finance Act 1972, s55(5), (7); Social Security Act 1973, ss100, 101, Schedule 27, para 80(a); Customs and Excise Management Act 1979, s177(1), Schedule 4, para 12; International Organisations Act 1981, ss1(1), (2), (3), 2, 3, 5(1), (2), (3), 6(4), Schedule; Local Government Finance Act 1988, s137, Schedule 12, Pt III, para 40; Local Government and Housing Act 1989, s194(1), Schedule II, para 14; Local Government Finance Act 1992, s117(1), Schedule 13, paras 27, 28; Taxation of Chargeable Gains Act 1992, s290(3), Schedule 12; Finance (No 2) Act 1992, s14, Schedule 3, Pt III, para 90; Value Added Tax Act 1994, s100(1), Schedule 14, para 4.]

FAMILY LAW REFORM ACT 1969
(1969 c 46)

1 Reduction of age of majority from 21 to 18 [679]

(1) As from [1 January 1970] a person shall attain full age on attaining the age of eighteen instead of on attaining the age of twenty-one; and a person shall attain full age on that date if he has then already attained the age of eighteen but not the age of twenty-one.

(2) The foregoing subsection applies for the purposes of any rule of law, and, in the absence of a definition or of any indication of a contrary intention, for the construction of 'full age', 'infant', 'infancy', 'minor', 'minority' and similar expressions in –

(a) any statutory provision, whether passed or made before, on or after the date on which this section comes into force; and
(b) any deed, will or other instrument of whatever nature (not being a statutory provision) made on or after that date.

(3) In the statutory provisions specified in Schedule 1 to this Act for any reference to the age of twenty-one years there shall be substituted a reference to the age of eighteen years; but the amendment by this subsection of the provisions specified in Part II of that Schedule shall be without prejudice to any power of amending or revoking those provisions. ...

ADMINISTRATION OF JUSTICE ACT 1970
(1970 c 31)

44A Interest on judgment debts expressed in currencies other than sterling [680]

(1) Where a judgment is given for a sum expressed in a currency other than sterling and the judgment debt is one to which section 17 of the Judgments Act 1838 applies, the court may order that the interest rate applicable to the debt shall be such a rate as the court thinks fit.

(2) Where the court makes such an order, section 17 of the Judgments Act 1838 shall have effect in relation to the judgment debt as if the rate specified in the order were substituted for the rate specified in that section.

[As inserted by the Private International Law (Miscellaneous Provisions) Act 1995, s1(1).]

ADMINISTRATION OF ESTATES ACT 1971
(1971 c 25)

1 Recognition in England and Wales of Scottish confirmations and Northern Irish grants of representation [681]

(1) Where a person dies domiciled in Scotland –

(a) a confirmation granted in respect of all or part of his estate and noting his Scottish domicile, and

(b) a certificate of confirmation noting his Scottish domicile and relating to one or more items of his estate,

shall, without being resealed, be treated for the purposes of the law of England and Wales as a grant of representation (in accordance with subsection (2) below) to the executors named in the confirmation or certificate in respect of the property of the deceased of which according to the terms of the confirmation they are executors or, as the case may be, in respect of the item or items of property specified in the certificate of confirmation.

(2) Where by virtue of subsection (1) above a confirmation or certificate of confirmation is treated for the purposes of the law of England and Wales as a grant of representation to the executors named therein then, subject to subsections (3) and (5) below, the grant shall be treated –

(a) as a grant of probate where it appears from the confirmation or certificate that the executors so named are executors nominate; and
(b) in any other case, as a grant of letters of administration.

(3) Section 7 of the Administration of Estates Act 1925 (executor of executor represents original testator) shall not, by virtue of subsection (2)(a) above, apply on the death of an executor named in a confirmation or certificate of confirmation.

(4) Subject to subsection (5) below, where a person dies domiciled in Northern Ireland a grant of probate of his will or letters of administration in respect of his estate (or any part of it) made by the High Court in Northern Ireland and noting his domicile there shall, without being resealed, be treated for the purposes of the law of England and Wales as if it had been originally made by the High Court in England and Wales.

(5) Notwithstanding anything in the preceding provisions of this section, a person who is a personal representative according to the law of England and Wales by virtue only of those provisions may not be required, under section 25 of the Administration of Estates Act 1925, to deliver up his grant to the High Court.

(6) This section applies in relation to confirmations, probates and letters of administration granted before as well as after the commencement of this Act, and in relation to a confirmation, probate or letters of administration granted before the commencement of this Act, this section shall have effect as if it had come into force immediately before the grant was made.

(7) In this section 'confirmation' includes an additional confirmation, and the term 'executors', where used in relation to a confirmation or certificate of confirmation, shall be construed according to the law of Scotland.

2 Recognition in Northern Ireland of English grants of representation and Scottish confirmations [682]

(1) Where a person dies domiciled in England and Wales a grant of probate of his will or letters of administration in respect of his estate (or any part of it) made by the High Court in England and Wales and noting his domicile there shall, without being resealed, be treated for the purposes of the law of Northern Ireland as if it had been originally made by the High Court in Northern Ireland.

(2) Where a person dies domiciled in Scotland –

(a) a confirmation granted in respect of all or part of his estate and noting his Scottish domicile, and
(b) a certificate of confirmation noting his Scottish domicile and relating to one or more items of his estate,

shall, without being resealed, be treated for the purposes of the law of Northern

Ireland as a grant of representation (in accordance with subsection (3) below) to the executors named in the confirmation or certificate in respect of the property of the deceased of which according to the terms of the confirmation they are executors or, as the case may be, in respect of the item or items of property specified in the certificate of confirmation.

(3) Where by virtue of subsection (2) above a confirmation or certificate of confirmation is treated for the purposes of the law of Northern Ireland as a grant of representation to the executors named therein then, subject to subsection (4) below, the grant shall be treated –

(a) as a grant of probate where it appears from the confirmation or certificate that the executors so named are executors nominate; and
(b) in any other case, a grant of letters of administration.

(4) Notwithstanding anything in any enactment or rule of law, subsection (3)(a) above shall not operate to entitle an executor of a sole or last surviving executor of a testator, whose will has been proved in Scotland only, to act as the executor of that testator.

(5) This section applies in relation to probates, letters of administration and confirmations granted before as well as after the commencement of this Act, and –

(a) in relation to a probate, letters of administration or confirmation granted, and resealed in Northern Ireland, before the commencement of this Act, this section shall have effect as if it had come into force immediately before the grant was so resealed; and
(b) a probate, letters of administration or confirmation granted but not resealed in Northern Ireland before the commencement of this Act shall, for the purposes of this section, be treated as having been granted at the commencement of this Act.

(6) In this section 'confirmation' includes an additional confirmation, and the term 'executors', where used in relation to a confirmation or certificate of confirmation shall be construed according to the law of Scotland.

3 Recognition in Scotland of English and Northern Irish grants of representation [683]

(1) Where a person dies domiciled in England and Wales or in Northern Ireland a grant of probate or letters of administration

(a) from the High Court in England and Wales and noting his domicile there, or
(b) from the High Court in Northern Ireland and noting his domicile there

shall, without being resealed, be of the like force and effect and have the same operation in relation to property in Scotland as a confirmation given under the seal of office of the Commissariat of Edinburgh to the executor or administrator named in the probate or letters of administration.

(2) This section applies in relation to probate and letters of administration granted before as well as after the commencement of this Act, and in relation to a probate or letters of administration granted before the commencement of this Act, this section shall have effect as if it had come into force immediately before the grant was made.

MAINTENANCE ORDERS (RECIPROCAL ENFORCEMENT) ACT 1972
(1972 c 18)

PART I

RECIPROCAL ENFORCEMENT OF MAINTENANCE ORDERS MADE IN UNITED KINGDOM OR RECIPROCATING COUNTRY

1 Orders in Council designating reciprocating countries

(1) Her Majesty, if satisfied that, in the event of the benefits conferred by this Part of this Act being applied to, or to particular classes of, maintenance orders made by the courts of any country or territory outside the United Kingdom, similar benefits will in that country or territory be applied to, or to those classes of, maintenance orders made by the courts of the United Kingdom, may by Order in Council designate that country or territory as a reciprocating country for the purposes of this Part of this Act; and, subject to subsection (2) below, in this Part of this Act 'reciprocating country' means a country or territory that is for the time being so designated.

(2) A country or territory may be designated under subsection (1) above as a reciprocating country either as regards maintenance orders generally, or as regards maintenance orders other than those of any specified class, or as regards maintenance orders of one or more specified classes only; and a country or territory which is for the time being so designated otherwise than as regards maintenance orders generally shall for the purposes of this Part of this Act be taken to be a reciprocating country only as regards maintenance orders of the class to which the designation extends.

2 Transmission of maintenance order made in United Kingdom for enforcement in reciprocating country

(1) Subject to subsection (2) below, where the payer under a maintenance order made, whether before or after the commencement of this Part of this Act, by a court in the United Kingdom is residing or has assets in a reciprocating country, the payee under the order may apply for the order to be sent to that country for enforcement.

(2) Subsection (1) above shall not have effect in relation to a provisional order or to an order made by virtue of a provision of Part II of this Act.

(3) Every application under this section shall be made in the prescribed manner to the prescribed officer of the court which made the maintenance order to which the application relates.

(4) If, on an application duly made under this section to the prescribed officer of a court in the United Kingdom, that officer is satisfied that the payer under the maintenance order to which the application relates is residing or has assets in a reciprocating country, the following documents, that is to say –

(a) a certified copy of the maintenance order;
(b) a certificate signed by that officer certifying that the order is enforceable in the United Kingdom;
(c) a certificate of arrears so signed;
(d) a statement giving such information as the officer possesses as to the whereabouts of the payer and the nature and location of his assets in that country;
(e) a statement giving such information as the officer possesses for facilitating the identification of the payer; and

(f) where available, a photograph of the payer;

shall be sent by that officer to the Lord Chancellor with a view to their being transmitted by the Lord Chancellor to the responsible authority in the reciprocating country if he is satisfied that the statement relating to the whereabouts of the payer and the nature and location of his assets in that country gives sufficient information to justify that being done.

(5) Nothing in this section shall be taken as affecting any jurisdiction of a court in the United Kingdom with respect to a maintenance order to which this section applies, and any such order may be enforced, varied or revoked accordingly.

3 Power of magistrates' court to make provisional maintenance order against person residing in reciprocating country [686]

(1) Where an application is made to a magistrates' court for a maintenance order against a person residing in a reciprocating country and the court would have jurisdiction to determine the application under the Domestic Proceedings and Magistrates' Courts Act 1978 or the Children Act 1989 if that person –

(a) were residing in England and Wales, and
(b) received reasonable notice of the date of the hearing of the application,

the court shall (subject to subsection (2) below) have jurisdiction to determine the application.

(2) A maintenance order made by virtue of this section shall be a provisional order.

(4) No enactment (or provision made under an enactment) requiring or enabling –

(a) a court to transfer proceedings from a magistrates' court to a county court or the High Court, or
(b) a magistrates' court to refuse to make an order on an application on the ground that any matter in question is one that would be more conveniently dealt with by the High Court.

(5) Where a court makes a maintenance order which is by virtue of this section a provisional order, the following documents, that is to say –

(a) a certified copy of the maintenance order;
(b) a document, authenticated in the prescribed manner, setting out or summarising the evidence given in the proceedings;
(c) a certificate signed by the prescribed officer of the court certifying that the grounds stated in the certificate are the grounds on which the making of the order might have been opposed by the payer under the order;
(d) a statement giving such information as was available to the court as to the whereabouts of the payer;
(e) a statement giving such information as the officer possesses for facilitating the identification of the payer; and
(f) where available, a photograph of the payer;

shall be sent by that officer to the Lord Chancellor with a view to their being transmitted by the Lord Chancellor to the responsible authority in the reciprocating country in which the payer is residing if he is satisfied that the statement relating to the whereabouts of the payer gives sufficient information to justify that being done.

(6) A maintenance order made by virtue of this section which has been confirmed by a competent court in a reciprocating country shall be treated for all purposes as if the magistrates' court which made the order had made it in the form in which it

was confirmed and as if the order had never been a provisional order, and subject to section 5 of this Act, any such order may be enforced, varied or revoked accordingly. ...

5 Variation and revocation of maintenance order made in United Kingdom [687]

(1) This section applies to a maintenance order a certified copy of which has been sent to a reciprocating country in pursuance of section 2 of this Act and to a maintenance order made by virtue of section 3 or 4 thereof which has been confirmed by a competent court in such a country.

(2) A court in the United Kingdom having power to vary a maintenance order to which this section applies shall have power to vary that order by a provisional order.

(3) Where the court hearing an application for the variation of a maintenance order to which this section applies proposes to vary it by increasing the rate of the payments under the order then, unless either –

(a) both the payer and the payee under the order appear in the proceedings, or
(b) the applicant appears and the appropriate process has been duly served on the other party,

the order varying the order shall be a provisional order.

(3A) Where subsection (1) of section 60 of the Magistrates' Courts Act 1980 (revocation, variation etc of orders for periodical payment) applies in relation to a maintenance order to which this section applies, that subsection shall have effect as if for the words 'by order on complaint', there were substituted 'on an application being made, by order'.

(4) Where a court in the United Kingdom makes a provisional order varying a maintenance order to which this section applies, the prescribed officer of the court shall send in the prescribed manner to the court in a reciprocating country having power to confirm the provisional order a certified copy of the provisional order together with a document, authenticated in the prescribed manner, setting out or summarising the evidence given in the proceedings.

(5) Where a certified copy of a provisional order made by a court in a reciprocating country, being an order varying or revoking a maintenance order to which this section applies, together with a document, duly authenticated, setting out or summarising the evidence given in the proceedings in which the provisional order was made, is received by the court in the United Kingdom which made the maintenance order, that court may confirm or refuse to confirm the provisional order and, if that order is an order varying the maintenance order, confirm it either without alteration or with such alterations as it thinks reasonable.

(6) For the purpose of determining whether a provisional order should be confirmed under subsection (5) above, the court shall proceed as if an application for the variation or revocation, as the case may be, of the maintenance order in question had been made to it.

(7) Where a maintenance order to which this section applies has been varied by an order (including a provisional order which has been confirmed) made by a court in the United Kingdom or by a competent court in a reciprocating country, the maintenance order shall, as from the date on which under the provisions of the order the variation is to take effect, have effect as varied by that order and, where that order was a provisional order, as if that order had been made in the form in which it was confirmed and as if it had never been a provisional order.

(8) Where a maintenance order to which this section applies has been revoked by

an order made by a court in the United Kingdom or by a competent court in a reciprocating country, including a provisional order made by the last-mentioned court which has been confirmed by a court in the United Kingdom, the maintenance order shall, as from the date on which under the provisions of the order the revocation is to take effect, be deemed to have ceased to have effect except as respects any arrears due under the maintenance order at that date.

(9) Where before a maintenance order made by virtue of section 3 or 4 of this Act is confirmed a document, duly authenticated, setting out or summarising evidence taken in a reciprocating country for the purpose of proceedings relating to the confirmation of the order is received by the court in the United Kingdom which made the order, or that court, in compliance with a request made to it by a court in such a country, takes the evidence of a person residing in the United Kingdom for the purpose of such proceedings, the court in the United Kingdom which made the order shall consider that evidence and if, having done so, it appears to it that the order ought not to have been made –

(a) it shall, in such manner as may be prescribed, give to the person on whose application the maintenance order was made an opportunity to consider that evidence, to make representations with respect to it and to adduce further evidence; and

(b) after considering all the evidence and any representations made by that person, it may revoke the maintenance order. ...

6 Registration in United Kingdom court of maintenance order made in reciprocating country [688]

(1) This section applies to a maintenance order made, whether before or after the commencement of this Part of this Act, by a court in a reciprocating country, including such an order made by such a court which has been confirmed by a court in another reciprocating country but excluding a provisional order which has not been confirmed.

(2) Where a certified copy of an order to which this section applies is received by the Lord Chancellor from the responsible authority in a reciprocating country, and it appears to the Lord Chancellor that the payer under the order is residing or has assets in the United Kingdom, he shall send a copy of the order to the prescribed officer of the appropriate court.

(3) Where the prescribed officer of the appropriate court receives from the Lord Chancellor a certified copy of an order to which this section applies, he shall, subject to subsection (4) below, register the order in the prescribed manner in that court.

(4) Before registering an order under this section an officer of a court shall take such steps as he thinks fit for the purpose of ascertaining whether the payer under the order is residing or has assets within the jurisdiction of the court, and if after taking those steps he is satisfied that the payer is not residing and has no assets within the jurisdiction of the court he shall return the certified copy of the order to the Lord Chancellor with a statement giving such information as he possesses as to the whereabouts of the payer and the nature and location of his assets.

7 Confirmation by United Kingdom court of provisional maintenance order made in reciprocating country [689]

(1) This section applies to a maintenance order made, whether before or after the commencement of this Part of this Act, by a court in a reciprocating country being a provisional order.

(2) Where a certified copy of an order to which this section applies together with –

(a) a document, duly authenticated, setting out or summarising the evidence given in the proceedings in which the order was made; and
(b) a statement of the grounds on which the making of the order might have been opposed by the payer under the order,

is received by the Lord Chancellor from the responsible authority in a reciprocating country, and it appears to the Lord Chancellor that the payer under the order is residing in the United Kingdom, he shall send the copy of the order and documents which accompanied it to the prescribed officer of the appropriate court, and that court shall –

(i) if the payer under the order establishes any grounds on which he might have opposed the making of the order in the proceedings in which the order was made, refuse to confirm the order; and
(ii) in any other case, confirm the order either without alteration or with such alteration as it thinks reasonable.

(3) In any proceedings for the confirmation under this section of a provisional order, the statement received from the court which made the order of the grounds on which the making of the order might have been opposed by the payer under the order shall be conclusive evidence that the payer might have opposed the making of the order on any of those grounds. ...

(5) The prescribed officer of a court having power under this section to confirm a provisional order shall, if the court confirms the order, register the order in the prescribed manner in that court, and shall, if the court refuses to confirm the order, return the certified copy of the order and the documents which accompanied it to the Secretary of State.

(5A) Where a magistrates' court in England and Wales confirms a provisional order under this section, it shall at the same time exercise one of its powers under subsection (5B) below.

(5B) The powers of the court are –

(a) the power to order that payments under the order be made directly to the clerk of the court or the clerk of any other magistrates' court in England and Wales;
(b) the power to order that payments under the order be made to the clerk of the court, or to the clerk of any other magistrates' court in England and Wales, by such method of payment falling within section 59(6) of the Magistrates' Courts Act 1980 (standing order, etc) as may be specified;
(c) the power to make an attachment of earnings order under the Attachment of Earnings Act 1971 to secure payments under the order.

(5C) In deciding which of the powers under subsection (5B) above it is to exercise, the court shall have regard to any representations made by the payer under the order.

(5D) Subsection (4) of section 59 of the Magistrates' Courts Act 1980 (power of court to require debtor to open account) shall apply for the purposes of subsection (5B) above as it applies for the purposes of that section but as if for paragraph (a) there were substituted –

'(a) the court proposes to exercise its power under paragraph (b) of section 7(5B) of the Maintenance Orders (Reciprocal Enforcement) Act 1972, and'

(6) If notice of the proceedings for the confirmation of the provisional order cannot be duly served on the payer under that order the officer by whom the certified copy of the order was received shall return that copy and the documents which accompanied it to the Secretary of State with a statement giving such information as he possesses as to the whereabouts of the payer. ...

8 Enforcement of maintenance order registered in the United Kingdom court

(1) Subject to subsection (2) below, a registered order may be enforced in the United Kingdom as if it had been made by the registering court and as if that court had had jurisdiction to make it; and proceedings for or with respect to the enforcement of any such order may be taken accordingly.

(2) Subsection (1) above does not apply to an order which is for the time being registered in the High Court under Part I of the Maintenance Orders Act 1958...

(3) Any person for the time being under an obligation to make payments in pursuance of a registered order shall give notice of any change of address to the clerk of the registering court, and any person failing without reasonable excuse to give such a notice shall be liable on summary conviction to a fine not exceeding level 2 on the standard scale.

(4) An order which by virtue of this section is enforceable by a magistrates' court shall, subject to the modifications of sections 76 and 93 of the Magistrates' Courts Act 1980 specified in subsections (4A) and (4B) below, be enforceable as if it were a magistrates' court maintenance order made by that court.

In this subsection 'magistrates' court maintenance order' has the same meaning as in section 150(1) of the Magistrates' Courts Act 1980. ...

(5) The magistrates' court by which an order is enforceable by virtue of this section, and the officers thereof, shall take all such steps for enforcing or facilitating the enforcement of the order as may be prescribed.

(6) In any proceedings for or with respect to the enforcement of an order which is for the time being registered in any court under this Part of this Act a certificate of arrears sent to the prescribed officer of the court shall be evidence of the facts stated therein.

(7) Subject to subsection (8) below, sums of money payable under a registered order shall be payable in accordance with the order as from the date on which they are required to be paid under the provisions of the order.

(8) The court having power under section 7 of this Act to confirm a provisional order may, if it decides to confirm the order, direct that the sums of money payable under it shall be deemed to have been payable in accordance with the order as from such date, being a date later than the date on which the order was made, as it may specify; and subject to any such direction, a maintenance order registered under the said section 7 shall be treated as if it had been made in the form in which it was confirmed and as if it had never been a provisional order. ...

9 Variation and revocation of maintenance order registered in United Kingdom court

(1) Subject to the provisions of this section, the registering court –

(a) shall have the like power, on an application made by the payer or payee under a registered order, to vary or revoke the order as if it had been made by the registering court and as if that court had had jurisdiction to make it; and
(b) shall have power to vary or revoke a registered order by a provisional order. ...

(1A) The powers conferred by subsection (1) above are not exercisable in relation to so much of a registered order as provides for the payment of a lump sum.

(1B) The registering court shall not vary or revoke a registered order if neither the payer nor the payee under the order is resident in the United Kingdom.

(2) The registering court shall not vary a registered order otherwise than by a provisional order unless –

(a) both the payer and the payee under the registered order are for the time being residing in the United Kingdom; or
(b) the application is made by the payee under the registered order; or
(c) the variation consists of a reduction in the rate of the payments under the registered order and is made solely on the ground that there has been a change in the financial circumstances of the payer since the registered order was made or, in the case of an order registered under section 7 of this Act, since the registered order was confirmed, and the courts in the reciprocating country in which the maintenance order in question was made do not have power, according to the law in force in that country, to confirm provisional orders varying maintenance orders.

(3) The registering court shall not revoke a registered order otherwise than by a provisional order unless both the payer and the payee under the registered order are for the time being residing in the United Kingdom.

(4) On an application for the revocation of a registered order the registering court shall, unless both the payer and the payee under the registered order are for the time being residing in the United Kingdom, apply the law applied by the reciprocating country in which the registered order was made; but where by virtue of this subsection the registering court is required to apply that law, that court may make a provisional order if it has reason to believe that the ground on which the application is made is a ground on which the order could be revoked according to the law applied by the reciprocating country, notwithstanding that it has not been established that it is such a ground.

(5) Where the registering court makes a provisional order varying or revoking a registered order the prescribed officer of the court shall send in the prescribed manner to the court in the reciprocating country which made the registered order a certified copy of the provisional order together with a document, authenticated in the prescribed manner, setting out or summarising the evidence given in the proceedings.

(6) Where a certified copy of a provisional order made by a court in a reciprocating country, being an order varying a registered order, together with a document, duly authenticated, setting out or summarising the evidence given in the proceedings in which the provisional order was made, is received by the registering court, that court may confirm the order either without alteration or with such alterations as it thinks reasonable or refuse to confirm the order.

(7) For the purpose of determining whether a provisional order should be confirmed under subsection (6) above the court shall proceed as if an application for the variation of the registered order had been made to it.

(8) Where a registered order has been varied by an order (including a provisional order which has been confirmed) made by a court in the United Kingdom or by a competent court in a reciprocating country, the registered order shall, as from the date on which under the provisions of the order the variation is to take effect, have effect as varied by that order and, where that order was a provisional order, as if that order had been made in the form in which it was confirmed and as if it had never been a provisional order.

(9) Where a registered order has been revoked by an order made by a court in the United Kingdom or by a competent court in a reciprocating country, including a provisional order made by the first-mentioned court which has been confirmed by a competent court in a reciprocating country, the registered order shall, as from the date on which under the provisions of the order the revocation is to take effect, be deemed to have ceased to have effect except as respects any arrears due under the registered order at that date.

(10) The prescribed officer of the registering court shall register in the prescribed manner any order varying a registered order other than a provisional order which is not confirmed. ...

12 Appeals [692]

(1) No appeal shall lie from a provisional order made in pursuance of any provision of this Part of this Act by a court in the United Kingdom.

(2) Where in pursuance of any such provision any such court confirms or refuses to confirm a provisional order made by a court in a reciprocating country, whether a maintenance order or an order varying or revoking a maintenance order, the payer or payee under the maintenance order shall have the like right of appeal (if any) from the confirmation of, or refusal to confirm, the provisional order as he would have if that order were not a provisional order and the court which confirmed or refused to confirm it had made or, as the case may be, refused to make it.

(3) Where in pursuance of any such provision any such court makes, or refuses to make, an order varying or revoking a maintenance order made by a court in a reciprocating country, then, subject to subsection (1) above, the payer or payee under the maintenance order shall have the like right of appeal (if any) from that order or from the refusal to make it as he would have if the maintenance order had been made b y the first-mentioned court.

(4) Nothing in this section (except subsection (1)) shall be construed as affecting any right of appeal conferred by any other enactment.

13 Admissibility of evidence given in reciprocating country [693]

(1) A statement contained in –
    (a) a document, duly authenticated, which purports to set out or summarise evidence given in proceedings in a court in a reciprocating country; or
    (b) a document, duly authenticated, which purports to set out or summarise evidence taken in such a country for the purpose of proceedings in court in the United Kingdom under this Part of this Act, whether in response to a request made by such a court or otherwise; or
    (c) a document, duly authenticated, which purports to have been received in evidence in proceedings in a court in such a country or to be a copy of a document so received,

shall in any proceedings in a court in the United Kingdom relating to a maintenance order to which this Part of this Act applies be admissible as evidence of any fact stated therein to the same extent as oral evidence of that fact is admissible in those proceedings.

(2) A document purporting to set out or summarise evidence given as mentioned in subsection (1)(a) above, or taken as mentioned in subsection (1)(b) above, shall be deemed to be duly authenticated for the purposes of that subsection if the document purports to be certified by the judge, magistrate or other person before whom the evidence was given, or, as the case may be, by whom it was taken, to be the original document containing or recording, or, as the case may be, summarising, that evidence or a true copy of that document.

(3) A document purporting to have been received in evidence as mentioned in subsection (1)(c) above, or to be a copy of a document so received, shall be deemed to be duly authenticated for the purposes of that subsection if the document purports to be certified by a judge, magistrate or officer of the court in question to have been, or to be a true copy of a document which has been, so received.

(4) It shall not be necessary in any such proceedings to prove the signature or official position of the person appearing to have given such a certificate.

(5) Nothing in this section shall prejudice the admission in evidence of any document which is admissible in evidence apart from this section.

14 Obtaining of evidence needed for purpose of certain proceedings [694]

(1) Where for the purpose of any proceedings in a court in a reciprocating country relating to a maintenance order to which this Part of this Act applies a request is made by or on behalf of that court for the taking in the United Kingdom of the evidence of a person residing therein relating to matters specified in the request, such court in the United Kingdom as may be prescribed shall have power to take that evidence and, after giving notice of the time and place at which the evidence is to be taken to such persons and in such manner as it thinks fit, shall take the evidence in such manner as may be prescribed.

Evidence taken in compliance with such a request shall be sent in the prescribed manner by the prescribed officer of the court to the court in the reciprocating country by or on behalf of which the request was made.

(2) Where any person, not being the payer or the payee under the maintenance order to which the proceedings in question relate, is required by virtue of this section to give evidence before a court in the United Kingdom the court may order that there shall be paid –

(a) if the court is a court in England, Wales or Scotland, out of moneys provided by Parliament; ...

such sums as appear to the court reasonably sufficient to compensate that person for the expense, trouble or loss of time properly incurred in or incidental to his attendance.

(3) Section 97(1), (3) and (4) of the Magistrates' Courts Act 1980 (which provide for compelling the attendance of witnesses etc) shall apply in relation to a magistrates' court having power under subsection (1) above to take the evidence of any person as if the proceedings in the court in a reciprocating country for the purpose of which a request for the taking of the evidence has been made were proceedings in the magistrates' court and had been begun by complaint. ...

(5) A court in the United Kingdom may for the purpose of any proceedings in that court under this Part of this Act relating to a maintenance order to which this Part of this Act applies request a court in a reciprocating country to take or provide evidence relating to such matters as may be specified in the request and may remit the case to that court for that purpose. ...

15 Order, etc made abroad need not be proved [695]

For the purposes of this Part of this Act, unless the contrary is shown –

(a) any order made by a court in a reciprocating country purporting to bear the seal of that court or to be signed by any person in his capacity as a judge, magistrate or officer of the court, shall be deemed without further proof to have been duly sealed or, as the case may be, to have been signed by that person;

(b) the person by whom the order was signed shall be deemed without further proof to have been a judge, magistrate or officer, as the case may be, of that court when he signed it and, in the case of an officer, to have been authorised to sign it; and

(c) a document purporting to be a certified copy of an order made by a court in a reciprocating country shall be deemed without further proof to be such a copy.

16 Payment of sums under orders made abroad: conversion of currency [696]

(1) Payment of sums due under a registered order shall, while the order is registered in a court in England, Wales or Northern Ireland, be made in such manner and to such person as may be prescribed.

(2) Where the sums required to be paid under a registered order are expressed in a currency other than the currency of the United Kingdom, then, as from the relevant date, the order shall be treated as if it were an order requiring the payment of such sums in the currency of the United Kingdom as, on the basis of the rate of exchange prevailing at that date, are equivalent to the sums so required to be paid.

(3) Where the sum specified in any statement, being a statement of the amount of any arrears due under a maintenance order made by a court in a reciprocating country, is expressed in a currency other than the currency of the United Kingdom, that sum shall be deemed to be such sum in the currency of the United Kingdom as, on the basis of the rate of exchange prevailing at the relevant date, is equivalent to the sum so specified.

(4) For the purposes of this section a written certificate purporting to be signed by an officer of any bank in the United Kingdom certifying that a specified rate of exchange prevailed between currencies at a specified date and that at such rate a specified sum in the currency of the United Kingdom is equivalent to a specified sum in another specified currency shall be evidence of the rate of exchange so prevailing on that date and of the equivalent sums in terms of the respective currencies.

(5) In this section 'the relevant date' means –

(a) in relation to a registered order or to a statement of arrears due under a maintenance order made by a court in a reciprocating country, the date on which the order first becomes a registered order or (if earlier) the date on which it is confirmed by a court in the United Kingdom;
(b) in relation to a registered order which has been varied, the date on which the last order varying that order is registered in a court in the United Kingdom or (if earlier) the date on which the last order varying that order is confirmed by such a court. ...

21 Interpretation of Part I [697]

(1) In this Part of this Act –

'affiliation order' means an order (however described) adjudging, finding or declaring a person to be the father of a child, whether or not it also provides for the maintenance of the child;
'the appropriate court' in relation to a person residing or having assets in England and Wales or in Northern Ireland means a magistrates' court, and in relation to a person residing or having assets in Scotland means a sheriff court within the jurisdiction of which that person is residing or has assets;
'certificate of arrears', in relation to a maintenance order, means a certificate certifying that the sum specified in the certificate is to the best of the information or belief of the officer giving the certificate the amount of the arrears due under the order at the date of the certificate or, as the case may be, that to the best of his information or belief there are no arrears due thereunder at that date;

'certified copy', in relation to an order of a court, means a copy of the order certified by the proper officer of the court to be a true copy;

'court' includes any tribunal or person having power to make, confirm, enforce, vary or revoke a maintenance order; ...

'maintenance order' means an order (however described) of any of the following descriptions, that is to say –

(a) an order (including an affiliation order or order consequent upon an affiliation order) which provides for the payment of a lump sum or the making of periodical payments towards the maintenance of any person, being a person whom the person liable to make payments under the order is, according to the law applied in the place where the order was made, liable to maintain; and

(b) an affiliation order or order consequent upon an affiliation order, being an order which provides for the payment by a person adjudged, found or declared to be a child's father of expenses incidental to the child's birth or, where the child has died, of his funeral expenses,

and, in the case of a maintenance order which has been varied, means that order as varied; ...

'payee', in relation to a maintenance order, means the person entitled to the payments for which the order provides;

'payer', in relation to a maintenance order, means the person liable to make payments under the order;

'prescribed', in relation to a magistrates' court in England and Wales or in Northern Ireland, means prescribed by rules made under section 144 of the Magistrates' Courts Act 1980 and in relation to any other court means prescribed by rules of court;

'provisional order' means (according to the context) –

(a) an order made by a court in the United Kingdom which is provisional only and has no effect unless and until confirmed, with or without alteration, by a competent court in a reciprocating country; or

(b) an order made by a court in a reciprocating country which is provisional only and has no effect unless and until confirmed, with or without alteration, by a court in the United Kingdom having power under this Part of this Act to confirm it;

'reciprocating country' has the meaning assigned to it by section 1 of this Act;

'registered order' means a maintenance order which is for the time being registered in a court in the United Kingdom under this Part of this Act;

'registering court', in relation to a registered order, means the court in which that order is for the time being registered under this Part of this Act;

'the responsible authority', in relation to a reciprocating country, means any person who in that country has functions similar to those of the Lord Chancellor under this Part of this Act;

'revoke' and 'revocation' include discharge.

(2) For the purposes of this Part of this Act an order shall be taken to be a maintenance order so far (but only so far) as it relates to the payment of a lump sum or the making of periodical payments as mentioned in paragraph (a) of the definition of 'maintenance order' in subsection (1) above or to the payment by a person adjudged, found or declared to be a child's father of any such expenses as are mentioned in paragraph (b) of that definition.

(3) Any reference in this Part of this Act to the payment of money for the maintenance of a child shall be construed as including a reference to the payment of money for the child's education.

23 Maintenance order registered in High Court under the Maintenance Orders, etc Act 1920

(1) Where a country or territory, being a country or territory to which at the commencement of section 1 of this Act the Maintenance Orders (Facilities for Enforcement) Act 1920 extended, becomes a reciprocating country, then, if immediately before the order in Council made under section 12 of that Act extending that Act to that country or territory was revoked any maintenance order made by a court in that country or territory was registered in the High Court under section 1 of that Act, the High Court may, on an application by the payer or the payee under the order or of its own motion, transfer the order to such magistrates' court as having regard to the place where the payee is residing and to all the circumstances it thinks most appropriate, with a view to the order being registered in that court under this Part of this Act.

(2) Where the High Court transfers an order to magistrates' court under this section it shall –

(a) cause a certified copy of the order to be sent to the clerk of that court, and
(b) cancel the registration of the order in the High Court.

(3) The clerk of the court who receives a certified copy of an order sent to him under this section shall register the order in the prescribed manner in that court.

(4) On registering a maintenance order in a magistrates' court by virtue of this section the clerk of the court shall, if the order is registered in that court under Part I of the Maintenance Orders Act 1958, cancel that registration. ...

24 Application of Part I to certain orders and proceedings under the Maintenance Orders, etc Act 1920

Where Her Majesty proposes by an Order in Council under section 1 of this Act to designate as a reciprocating country a country or territory to which at the commencement of that section the Maintenance Orders (Facilities for Enforcement) Act 1920 extended, that Order in Council may contain such provisions as Her Majesty considers expedient for the purpose of securing –

(a) that the provisions of this Part of this Act apply, subject to such modifications as may be specified in the Order, to maintenance orders, or maintenance orders of a specified class –

(i) made by a court in England, Wales or Northern Ireland against a person residing or having assets in that country or territory, or
(ii) made by court in that country or territory against a person residing or having assets in England, Wales or Northern Ireland,

being orders to which immediately before the date of the coming into operation of the Order in Council the said Act of 1920 applied, except any order which immediately before that date is registered in the High Court or the High Court of Justice in Northern Ireland under section 1 of that Act;

(b) that any maintenance order, or maintenance order of a specified class, made by a court in that country or territory which has been confirmed by a court in England, Wales or Northern Ireland under section 4 of the said Act of 1920 and is in force immediately before that date is registered under section 7 of this Act;

(c) that any proceedings brought under or by virtue of a provision of the said Act of 1920 in a court in England, Wales or Northern Ireland which are pending at that date, being proceedings affecting a person resident in that country or territory, are continued as if they had been brought under or by virtue of the corresponding provision of this Part of this Act.

PART II

RECIPROCAL ENFORCEMENT OF CLAIMS FOR THE RECOVERY OF MAINTENANCE

25 Convention countries [700]

(1) Her Majesty may by Order in Council declare that any country or territory specified in the Order, being a country or territory outside the United Kingdom to which the Maintenance Convention extends, is a convention country for the purposes of this Part of this Act.

(2) In this section 'the Maintenance Convention' means the United Nations Convention on the Recovery Abroad of Maintenance done at New York on 20 June 1956.

26 Application by person in United Kingdom for recovery, [701] etc of maintenance in convention country

(1) Where a person in the United Kingdom ('the applicant') claims to be entitled to recover in a convention country maintenance from another person, and that other person is for the time being subject to the jurisdiction of that country, the applicant may apply to the Lord Chancellor, in accordance with the provisions of this section, to have his claim for the recovery of maintenance from that other person transmitted to that country.

(2) Where the applicant seeks to vary any provision made in a convention country for the payment by any other person of maintenance to the applicant, and that other person is for the time being subject to the jurisdiction of that country, the applicant may apply to the Lord Chancellor, in accordance with the provisions of this section, to have his application for the variation of that provision transmitted to that country.

(3) An application to the Lord Chancellor under subsection (1) or (2) above shall be made through the appropriate officer, and that officer shall assist the applicant in completing an application which will comply with the requirements of the law applied by the convention country and shall send the application to the Lord Chancellor, together with such other documents, if any, as are required by that law.

(3A) An application under subsection (1) or (2) above, for the purpose of recovering maintenance from a person in a specified State within the meaning of the Recovery of Maintenance (United States of America) Order 1993, and a certificate signed by a justice of the peace or, where the applicant is residing in Scotland, the sheriff, to the effect that the application sets forth facts from which it may be determined that the respondent owes a duty to maintain the applicant and any other person named in the application and that court in the specified State may obtain jurisdiction of the respondent or his property, shall be registered in the court in the prescribed manner by the appropriate officer or, in Scotland, by the sheriff clerk in the Maintenance Orders (Reciprocal Enforcement) Act 1972 register.

(4) On receiving an application from the appropriate officer the Lord Chancellor shall transmit it, together with any accompanying documents, to the appropriate authority in the convention country, unless he is satisfied that the application is not made in good faith or that it does not comply with the requirements of the law applied by that country.

(5) The Lord Chancellor may request the appropriate officer to obtain from the court of which he is an officer such information relating to the application as may

be specified in the request, and it shall be the duty of the court to furnish the Lord Chancellor with the information he requires.

(6) Where the applicant is residing in England and Wales or in Northern Ireland the appropriate officer for the purposes of this section is the clerk of a magistrates' court acting for the petty sessions area or petty sessions district, as the case may be, in which the applicant is residing. ...

27A Applications for recovery of maintenance in England and Wales

(1) This section applies to any application which –

(a) is received by the Lord Chancellor from the appropriate authority in a convention country, and
(b) is an application by a person in that country for the recovery of maintenance from another person who is for the time being residing in England and Wales.

(2) Subject to sections 27B to 28B of this Act, an application to which this section applies shall be treated for the purposes of any enactment as if it were an application for a maintenance order under the relevant Act, made at the time when the application was received by the Lord Chancellor.

(3) In the case of an application for maintenance for a child (or children) alone, the relevant Act is the Children Act 1989.

(4) In any other case, the relevant Act is the Domestic Proceedings and Magistrates' Courts Act 1978.

(5) In subsection (3) above, 'child' means the same as in Schedule 1 to the Children Act 1989.

27B Sending application to the appropriate magistrates' court

(1) On receipt of an application to which section 27A of this Act applies, the Lord Chancellor shall send it, together with any accompanying documents, to the clerk of a magistrates' court acting for the petty sessions area in which the respondent is residing.

(2) Subject to subsection (4) below, if notice of the hearing of the application by a magistrates' court having jurisdiction to hear it cannot be duly served on the respondent, the clerk of the court shall return the application and the accompanying documents to the Lord Chancellor with a statement giving such information as he possesses as to the whereabouts of the respondent.

(3) If the application is returned to the Lord Chancellor under subsection (2) above, then, unless he is satisfied that the respondent is not residing in the United Kingdom, he shall deal with it in accordance with subsection (1) above or section 28C of this Act or send it to the Secretary of State to be dealt with in accordance with section 31 of this Act (as the circumstances of the case require).

(4) If the clerk of a court to whom the application is sent under this section is satisfied that the respondent is residing within the petty sessions area for which another magistrates' court acts, he shall send the application and accompanying documents to the clerk of that other court and shall inform the Lord Chancellor that he has done so.

(5) If the application is sent to the clerk of a court under subsection (4) above, he shall proceed as if it had been sent to him under subsection (1) above.

27C Applications to which section 27A applies: general [704]

(1) This section applies where a magistrates' court makes an order on an application to which section 27A of this Act applies.

(2) Section 59 of the Magistrates' Courts Act 1980 (orders for periodical payment: means of payment) shall not apply.

(3) The court shall, at the same time that it makes the order, exercise one of its powers under subsection (4) below.

(4) Those powers are –

(a) the power to order that payments under the order be made directly to the clerk of the court as the clerk of any other magistrates' court in England and Wales;
(b) the power to order that payments under the order be made to the clerk of the court, or to the clerk of any other magistrates' court in England and Wales, by such method of payment falling within section 59(6) of the Magistrates' Courts Act 1980 (standing order, etc) as may be specified;
(c) the power to make an attachment of earnings order under the Attachment of Earnings Act 1971 to secure payments under the order.

(5) In deciding which of the powers under subsection (4) above it is to exercise, the court shall have regard to any representations made by the person liable to make payments under the order.

(6) Subsection (4) of section 59 of the Magistrates' Courts Act 1980 (power of court to require debtor to open account) shall apply for the purposes of subsection (4) above as it applies for the purposes of that section, but as if for paragraph (a) there were substituted –

'(a) the court proposes to exercise its power under paragraph (b) of section 27C(4) of the Maintenance Orders (Reciprocal Enforcement) Act 1972, and'.

(7) The clerk of the court shall register the order in the prescribed manner in the court.

28 Application by spouses under the Domestic Proceedings and Magistrates' Courts Act 1978 [705]

(1) The magistrates' court hearing an application which by virtue of section 27A of this Act is to be treated as if it were an application for a maintenance order under the Domestic Proceedings and Magistrates' Courts Act 1978 may make any order on the application which it has power to make under section 2 or 19(1) of that Act.

(2) Part I of that Act shall apply in relation to such an application, and to any order made on such an application, with the following modifications –

(a) sections 6 to 8, 16 to 18, 20ZA, 25 to 27 and 28(2) shall be omitted,
(b) in section 30(1), for the words 'either the applicant or the respondent ordinarily resides' there shall be substituted 'the respondent resides', and
(c) section 32(2) shall be omitted.

(3) Subsections (1) and (2) above do not apply where section 28A of this Act applies.

28A Applications by former spouses under the Domestic Proceedings and Magistrates' Courts Act 1978 [706]

(1) This section applies where in the case of any application which by virtue of section 27A of this Act is to be treated as if it were an application for a

maintenance order under the Domestic Proceedings and Magistrates' Courts Act 1978 ('the 1978 Act') –

(a) the applicant and respondent were formerly married,
(b) their marriage was dissolved or annulled in a country or territory outside the United Kingdom by a divorce or annulment which is recognised as valid by the law of England and Wales,
(c) an order for the payment of maintenance for the benefit of the applicant or a child of the family has, by reason of the divorce or annulment, been made by a court in a convention country, and
(d) where the order for the payment of maintenance was made by a court of a different country from that in which the divorce or annulment was obtained, either the applicant or the respondent was resident in the convention country whose court made that order at the time that order was applied for.

(2) Any magistrates' court that would have jurisdiction to hear the application under section 30 of the 1978 Act (as modified in accordance with subsection (6) below) if the applicant and the respondent were still married shall have jurisdiction to hear it notwithstanding the dissolution or annulment of the marriage.

(3) If the magistrates' court hearing the application is satisfied that the respondent has failed to comply with the provisions of any order such as is mentioned in subsection (1)(c) above, it may (subject to subsections (4) and (5) below) make any order which it has power to make under section 2 or 19(1) of the 1978 Act.

(4) The court shall not make an order for the making of periodical payments for the benefit of the applicant or any child of the family unless the order made in the convention country provides for the making of periodical payments for the benefit of the applicant or as the case may be, that child.

(5) The court shall not make an order for the payment of a lump sum for the benefit of the applicant or any child of the family unless the order made in the convention country provides for the payment of a lump sum to the applicant or, as the case may be, to that child.

(6) Part I of the 1978 Act shall apply in relation to the application, and to any order made on the application with the following modifications –

(a) section 1 shall be omitted,
(b) for the reference in section 2(1) to any ground mentioned in section 1 of that Act there shall be substituted a reference to non-compliance with any such order as is mentioned in subsection (1)(c) of this section,
(c) for the references in section 3(2) and (3) to the occurrence of the conduct which is alleged as the ground of the application there shall be substituted references to the breakdown of the marriage,
(d) the reference in section 4(2) to the subsequent dissolution or annulment of the marriage of the parties affected by the order shall be omitted,
(e) sections 6 to 8, 16 to 18, 20ZA and 25 to 28 shall be omitted,
(f) in section 30(1), for the words 'either the applicant or the respondent ordinarily resides' there shall be substituted 'the respondent resides', and
(g) section 32(2) shall be omitted.

(7) A divorce or annulment obtained in a country or territory outside the United Kingdom shall be presumed for the purposes of this section to be one the validity of which is recognised by the law of England and Wales, unless the contrary is proved by the respondent.

(8) In this section, 'child of the family' has the meaning given in section 88 of the 1978 Act.

28B Applications under the Children Act 1989 [707]

No provision of an order made under Schedule 11 to the Children Act 1989 requiring or enabling a court to transfer proceedings from a magistrates' court to a county court or the High Court shall apply in relation to an application which by virtue of section 27A of this Act is to be treated as if it were an application for a maintenance order under that Act.

33 Enforcement of orders [708]

(1) Subject to subsection (2) below, a registered order which is registered in a court other than the court by which the order was made may be enforced as if it had been made by the registering court and as if that court had had jurisdiction to make it; and proceedings for or with respect to the enforcement of any such order may be taken in accordance with this subsection but not otherwise.

(2) Subsection (1) above does not apply to an order which is for the time being registered in the High Court under Part I of the Maintenance Orders Act 1958 ...

(3) An order which by virtue of subsection (1) above is enforceable by a magistrates' court shall, subject to the modifications of sections 76 and 93 of the Magistrates' Courts Act 1980 (enforcement of sums adjudged to be paid and complaint for arrears) specified in subsection (4A) and (4B) of section 8 of this Act, be enforceable as if it were a magistrates' court maintenance order made by that court.

In this subsection 'magistrates' court maintenance order' has the same meaning as in section 150(1) of the Magistrates' Courts Act 1980.

(3A) Where, by virtue of being registered in the magistrates' court in which it was made, a registered order is enforceable as a magistrates' court maintenance order, sections 76 and 93 of the Magistrates' Courts Act 1980 shall have effect subject to the modifications specified in subsection (4A) and (4B) of section 8 of this Act.

(4) A magistrates' court in which an order is registered under this Part of this Act, and the officers thereof, shall take all such steps for enforcing the order as may be prescribed.

(5) In any proceedings for or with respect to the enforcement of an order which is for the time being registered in any court under this Part of this Act a certificate of arrears sent under section 32 of this Act to the prescribed officer of the court shall be evidence of the facts stated therein.

(6) Part II of the Maintenance Orders Act 1950 (enforcement of certain orders throughout the United Kingdom) shall not apply to a registered order. ...

36 Admissibility of evidence given in convention country [709]

(1) A statement contained in –
   (a) a document, duly authenticated, which purports to set out or summarise evidence given in proceedings in a court in a convention country; or
   (b) a document, duly authenticated, which purports to set out or summarise evidence taken in such a country for the purpose of proceedings in a court in the United Kingdom under this Part of this Act, whether in response to a request made on behalf of such a court or otherwise; or
   (c) a document, duly authenticated, which purports to have been received in evidence in proceedings in a court in such a country, or to be a copy of a document so received,

shall, in any proceedings in a magistrates' court or in, or remitted from, a sheriff court arising out of an application to which section 27A(1) of this Act applies, an application received by the Lord Chancellor as mentioned in section 28C(1) of this Act, an application received by the Secretary of State as mentioned in section 31(1) of this Act or an application made by any person for the variation or revocation of a registered order or in proceedings on appeal from any such proceedings, be admissible as evidence of any fact stated therein to the same extent as oral evidence of that fact is admissible in those proceedings.

(2) A document purporting to set out or summarise evidence given as mentioned in subsection (1)(a) above, or taken as mentioned in subsection (1)(b) above, shall be deemed to be duly authenticated for the purposes of that subsection if the document purports to be certified by the judge, magistrate or other person before whom the evidence was given or, as the case may be, by whom it was taken, to be the original document containing or recording, or, as the case may be, summarising, that evidence or a true copy of that document.

(3) A document purporting to have been received in evidence as mentioned in subsection (1)(c) above, or to be a copy of a document so received, shall be deemed to be duly authenticated for the purposes of that subsection if the document purports to be certified by a judge, magistrate or officer of the court in question to have been, or to be a true copy of a document which has been, so received.

(4) It shall not be necessary in any such proceedings to prove the signature or official position of the person appearing to have given such a certificate.

(5) Nothing in this section shall prejudice the admission in evidence of any document which is admissible in evidence apart from this section.

37 Obtaining of evidence for purpose of proceedings in United Kingdom court [710]

(1) A court in the United Kingdom may for the purpose of any proceedings in that court under this Part of this Act arising out of an application received by the Secretary of State from a convention country request the Secretary of State to make to the appropriate authority or court in the convention country a request for the taking in that country of the evidence of a person residing therein relating to matters connected with the application. ...

38 Taking of evidence at request of court in convention country [711]

(1) Where a request is made to the Secretary of State by or on behalf of a court in a convention country to obtain the evidence of a person residing in the United Kingdom relating to matters connected with an application to which section 26 of this Act applies, the Secretary of State shall request such court, or such officer of a court, as he may determine to take the evidence of that person relating to such matters connected with that application as may be specified in the request. ...

39 Interpretation of Part II [712]

In this Part of this Act – ...

'maintenance order' has the same meaning as in Part I of this Act;
'prescribed' has the same meaning as in Part I of this Act;
'registered order' means an order which is for the time being registered in a court in the United Kingdom under this Part of this Act;
'registering court', in relation to a registered order, means the court in which that order is for the time being registered under this Part of this Act;
'revoke' and 'revocation' include discharge.

PART III

MISCELLANEOUS AND SUPPLEMENTAL

40 Power to apply Act to maintenance orders and applications for recovery of maintenance made in certain countries [713]

Where Her Majesty is satisfied –

(a) that arrangements have been or will be made in a country or territory outside the United Kingdom to ensure that maintenance orders made by courts in the United Kingdom can be enforced in that country or territory or that applications by persons in the United Kingdom for the recovery of maintenance from persons in that country or territory can be entertained by courts in that country or territory; and

(b) that in the interest of reciprocity it is desirable to ensure that maintenance orders made by courts in that country or territory can be enforced in the United Kingdom or, as the case may be, that applications by persons in that country or territory for the recovery of maintenance from persons in the United Kingdom can be entertained by courts in the United Kingdom,

Her Majesty may by Order in Council make provision for applying the provisions of this Act, with such exceptions, adaptations and modifications as may be specified in the Order, to such orders or applications as are referred to in paragraphs (a) and (b) above and to maintenance and other orders made in connection with such applications by courts in the United Kingdom or in that country or territory.

42 Provisional order for maintenance of party to marriage made by magistrates' court to cease to have effect on remarriage of party [714]

(1) Where a magistrates' court has, by virtue of section 3 of this Act, made a provisional maintenance order consisting of, or including, a provision such as is mentioned in section 2(1)(a) of the Domestic Proceedings and Magistrates' Courts Act 1978 (making of periodical payments by husband or wife)... and the order has been confirmed by a competent court in a reciprocating country, then, if after the making of that order the marriage of the parties to the proceedings in which the order was made is dissolved or annulled but the order continues in force, that order or, as the case may be, that provision thereof shall cease to have effect on the remarriage of the party in whose favour it was made, except in relation to any arrears due under it on the date of such remarriage and shall not be capable of being revived.

(2) For the avoidance of doubt it is hereby declared that references in this section to remarriage include references to a marriage which is by law void or voidable. ...

44 Exclusion of certain enactments relating to evidence [715]

(1) Section 20 of the Family Law Reform Act 1969 (power of court hearing certain proceedings to require use of blood tests to determine paternity) and any corresponding enactment of the Parliament of Northern Ireland shall not apply to any proceedings under this Act, but the foregoing provision is without prejudice to the power of a court to allow the report of any person who has carried out such tests to be given in evidence in those proceedings.

(2) The Evidence (Proceedings in Other Jurisdictions) Act 1975 shall not apply to

the taking of evidence in the United Kingdom for the taking of which section 14 or section 38 of this Act provides.

47 Interpretation general [716]

(1) In this Act –

'enactment' includes an enactment of the Parliament of Northern Ireland; ...

(2) References in this Act to a part of the United Kingdom are references to England and Wales, to Scotland, or to Northern Ireland.

(3) Any reference in this Act to the jurisdiction of a court, where the reference is to assets being located or to a person residing within the jurisdiction of a court, shall be construed in relation to a magistrates' court in England and Wales as a reference to the petty sessions area, and in relation to a magistrates' court in Northern Ireland as a reference to the petty sessions district, for which the court acts.

(4) Any reference in this Act to any other enactment is a reference thereto as amended, and includes a reference thereto as extended or applied, by or under any other enactment.

[As amended by the Evidence (Proceedings in Other Jurisdictions) Act 1975, s8(1), Schedule 1; Domestic Proceedings and Magistrates' Courts Act 1978, ss54(a)–(f), 60(3), Schedule 2, para 37; Magistrates' Courts Act 1980, s154, Schedule 7, paras 105, 107; Civil Jurisdiction and Judgements Act 1982, s37(1), Schedule 11, Pt III, paras 9–12, 15–18, Schedule 14; Criminal Justice Act 1982, s46; Family Law Reform Act 1987, s33(1), Schedule 2, paras 45, 50; Maintenance Enforcement Act 1991, s10, Schedule 1, paras 12-14, 18; Maintenance Orders (Reciprocal Enforcement) Act 1992, s1(2), Schedule 1, Pt II, paras 6–8, 12, 13, 17, 19; Transfer of Functions (Magistrates' Courts and Family Law Order 1992, art 4(3), (5); Recovery of Maintenance (United States of America) Order 1993, art 3(2).]

CIVIL EVIDENCE ACT 1972
(1972 c 30)

4 Evidence of foreign law [717]

(1) It is hereby declared that in civil proceedings a person who is suitably qualified to do so on account of his knowledge or experience is competent to give expert evidence as to the law of any country or territory outside the United Kingdom, or of any part of the United Kingdom other than England and Wales, irrespective of whether he has acted or is entitled to act as a legal practitioner there.

(2) Where any question as to the law of any country or territory outside the United Kingdom, or of any part of the United Kingdom other than England and Wales, with respect to any matter has been determined (whether before or after the passing of this Act) in any such proceedings as are mentioned in subsection (4) below, then in any civil proceedings (not being proceedings before a court which can take judicial notice of the law of that country, territory or part with respect to that matter) –

> (a) any finding made or decision given on that question in the first-mentioned proceedings shall, if reported or recorded in citable form, be admissible in evidence for the purpose of proving the law of that country, territory or part with respect to that matter; and
> (b) if that finding or decision, as so reported or recorded, is adduced for that purpose, the law of that country, territory or part with respect to that matter

shall be taken to be in accordance with that finding or decision unless the contrary is proved:

Provided that paragraph (b) above shall not apply in the case of a finding or decision which conflicts with another finding or decision on the same question adduced by virtue of this subsection in the same proceedings.

(3) Except with the leave of the court, a party to any civil proceedings shall not be permitted to adduce any such finding or decision as is mentioned in subsection (2) above by virtue of that subsection unless he has in accordance with rules of court given to every other party to the proceedings notice that he intends to do so.

(4) The proceedings referred to in subsection (2) above are the following, whether civil or criminal, namely –

(a) proceedings at first instance in any of the following courts, namely the High Court, the Crown Court, a court of quarter sessions, the Court of Chancery of the county palatine of Lancaster and the Court of Chancery of the county palatine of Durham;
(b) appeals arising out of any such proceedings as are mentioned in paragraph (a) above;
(c) proceedings before the Judicial Committee of the Privy Council on appeal (whether to Her Majesty in Council or to the Judicial Committee as such) from any decision of any court outside the United Kingdom.

(5) For the purposes of this section a finding or decision on any such question as is mentioned in subsection (2) above shall be taken to be reported or recorded in citable form if, but only if, it is reported or recorded in writing in a report, transcript or other document which, if that question had been a question as to the law of England and Wales, could be cited as an authority in legal proceedings in England and Wales.

EUROPEAN COMMUNITIES ACT 1972
(1972 c 68)

2 General implementation of Treaties [718]

(1) All such rights, powers, liabilities, obligations and restrictions from time to time created or arising by or under the Treaties, and all such remedies and procedures from time to time provided for by or under the Treaties, as in accordance with the Treaties are without further enactment to be given legal effect or used in the United Kingdom shall be recognised and available in law, and be enforced, allowed and followed accordingly; and the expression 'enforceable Community right' and similar expressions shall be read as referring to one to which this subsection applies.

(2) Subject to Schedule 2 to this Act, at any time after its passing Her Majesty may by Order in Council, and any designated Minister or department may by regulations, make provision –

(a) for the purpose of implementing any Community obligation of the United Kingdom, or enabling any such obligation to be implemented, or of enabling any rights enjoyed or to be enjoyed by the United Kingdom under or by virtue of the Treaties to be exercised;
(b) for the purpose of dealing with matters arising out of or related to any such obligation or rights or the coming into force, or the operation from time to time, of subsection (1) above;

and in the exercise of any statutory power or duty, including any power to give directions or legislate by means of orders, rules, regulations or other subordinate instrument, the person entrusted with the power or duty may have regard to the objects of the Communities and to any such obligation or rights as aforesaid.

In this subsection 'designated Minister or department' means such Minister of the Crown or government department as may from time to time be designated by Order in Council in relation to any matter or for any purpose, but subject to such restrictions or conditions (if any) as may be specified by the Order in Council. ...

(4) The provision that may be made under subsection (2) above includes, subject to Schedule 2 to this Act, any such provision (of any such extent) as might be made by Act of Parliament, and any enactment passed or to be passed, other than one contained in this Part of this Act, shall be construed and have effect subject to the foregoing provisions of this section; but, except as may be provided by any Act passed after this Act, Schedule 2 shall have effect in connection with the powers conferred by this and the following sections of this Act to make Orders in Council and regulations.

3 Decisions on, and proof of, Treaties and Community Instruments, etc [719]

(1) For the purposes of all legal proceedings any question as to the meaning or effect of any of the Treaties, or as to the validity, meaning or effect of any Community instrument, shall be treated as a question of law and, if not referred to the European Court, be for determination as such in accordance with the principles laid down by and any relevant decision of the European Court or any court attached thereto.

(2) Judicial notice shall be taken of the Treaties, of the Official Journal of the Communities and of any decision of, or expression of opinion by, the European Court or any court attached thereto on any such question as aforesaid; and the Official Journal shall be admissible as evidence of any instrument or other act thereby communicated of any of the Communities or of any Community institution.

(3) Evidence of any instrument issued by a Community institution, including any judgment or order of the European Court or any court attached thereto, or of any document in the custody of a Community institution, or any entry in or extract from such a document, may be given in any legal proceedings by production of a copy certified as a true copy by an official of that institution; and any document purporting to be such a copy shall be received in evidence without proof of the official position or handwriting of the person signing the certificate.

(4) Evidence of any Community instrument may also be given in any legal proceedings –

(a) by production of a copy purporting to be printed by the Queen's Printer;
(b) where the instrument is in the custody of a government department (including a department of the Government of Northern Ireland), by production of a copy certified on behalf of the department to be a true copy by an officer of the department generally or specially authorised so to do;

and any document purporting to be such a copy as is mentioned in paragraph (b) above of an instrument in the custody of a department shall be received in evidence without proof of the official position or handwriting of the person signing the certificate, or of his authority to do so, or of the document being in the custody of the department. ...

SCHEDULE 2

PROVISIONS AS TO SUBORDINATE LEGISLATION

1 – (1) The powers conferred by section 2(2) of this Act to make provision for the purposes mentioned in section 2(2)(a) and (b) shall not include power –

(a) to make any provision imposing or increasing taxation; or
(b) to make any provision taking effect from a date earlier than that of the making of the instrument containing the provision; or
(c) to confer any power to legislate by means of orders, rules, regulations or other subordinate instrument, other than rules of procedure for any court or tribunal; or
(d) to create any new criminal offence punishable with imprisonment for more than two years or punishable on summary conviction with imprisonment for more than three months or with a fine of more than level 5 on the standard scale (if not calculated on a daily basis) or with a fine of more than £100 a day.

(2) Sub-paragraph (1)(c) above shall not be taken to preclude the modification of a power to legislate conferred otherwise than under section 2(2), or the extension of any such power to purposes of the like nature as those for which it was conferred; and a power to give directions as to matters of administration is not to be regarded as a power to legislate within the meaning of sub-paragraph (1)(c).

2 – (1) Subject to paragraph 3 below, where a provision contained in any section of this Act confers power to make regulations (otherwise than by modification or extension of an existing power), the power shall be exercisable by statutory instrument.

(2) Any statutory instrument containing an Order in Council or regulations made in the exercise of a power so conferred, if made without a draft having been approved by resolution of each House of Parliament, shall be subject to annulment in pursuance of a resolution of either House.

3 Nothing in paragraph 2 above shall apply to any Order in Council made by the Governor of Northern Ireland or to any regulations made by a Minister or department of the Government of Northern Ireland; but where a provision contained in any section of this Act confers power to make such an Order in Council or regulations, then any Order in Council or regulations made in the exercise of that power, if made without a draft having been approved by resolution of each House of the Parliament of Northern Ireland, shall be subject to negative resolution within the meaning of section 41(6) of the Interpretation Act (Northern Ireland) 1954 as if the Order or regulations were a statutory instrument within the meaning of that Act. ...

[As amended by the Criminal Justice Act 1982, ss40, 46; European Communities (Amendment) Act 1986, s2.]

MATRIMONIAL CAUSES ACT 1973
(1973 c 18)

1 Divorce on breakdown of marriage

(1) Subject to section 3 below, a petition for divorce may be presented to the court by either party to a marriage on the ground that the marriage has broken down irretrievably.

(2) The court hearing a petition for divorce shall not hold the marriage to have broken down irretrievably unless the petitioner satisfies the court of one or more of the following facts, that is to say –

(a) that the respondent has committed adultery and the petitioner finds it intolerable to live with the respondent;
(b) that the respondent has behaved in such a way that the petitioner cannot reasonably be expected to live with the respondent;
(c) that the respondent has deserted the petitioner for a continuous period of at least two years immediately preceding the presentation of the petition;
(d) that the parties to the marriage have lived apart for a continuous period of at least two years immediately preceding the presentation of the petition (hereafter in this Act referred to as 'two years' separation') and the respondent consents to a decree being granted;
(e) that the parties to the marriage have lived apart for a continuous period of at least five years immediately preceding the presentation of the petition (hereafter in this Act referred to as 'five years' separation').

(3) On a petition for divorce it shall be the duty of the court to inquire, so far as it reasonably can, into the facts alleged by the petitioner and into any facts alleged by the respondent.

(4) If the court is satisfied on the evidence of any such fact as is mentioned in subsection (2) above, then, unless it is satisfied on all the evidence that the marriage has not broken down irretrievably, it shall, subject to section 5 below, grant a decree of divorce.

(5) Every decree of divorce shall in the first instance be a decree nisi and shall not be made absolute before the expiration of six months from its grant unless the High Court by general order from time to time fixes a shorter period, or unless in any particular case the court in which the proceedings are for the time being pending from time to time by special order fixes a shorter period than the period otherwise applicable for the time being by virtue of this subsection.

11 Grounds on which a marriage is void

A marriage celebrated after 31 July 1971 shall be void on the following grounds only, that is to say –

(a) that it is not a valid marriage under the provisions of the Marriage Acts 1949 to 1986 (that is to say where –
(i) the parties are within the prohibited degrees of relationship;
(ii) either party is under the age of sixteen; or
(iii) the parties have intermarried in disregard of certain requirements as to the formation of marriage);
(b) that at the time of the marriage either party was already lawfully married;
(c) that the parties are not respectively male and female;
(d) in the case of a polygamous marriage entered into outside England and Wales, that either party was at the time of the marriage domiciled in England and Wales.

For the purposes of paragraph (d) of this subsection a marriage is not polygamous if at its inception neither party has any spouse additional to the other.

12 Grounds on which a marriage is voidable

A marriage celebrated after 31 July 1971 shall be voidable on the following grounds only, that is to say –

(a) that the marriage has not been consummated owing to the incapacity of either party to consummate it;
(b) that the marriage has not been consummated owing to the wilful refusal of the respondent to consummate it;

(c) that either party to the marriage did not validly consent to it, whether in consequence of duress, mistake, unsoundness of mind or otherwise;
(d) that at the time of the marriage either party, though capable of giving a valid consent, was suffering (whether continuously or intermittently) from mental disorder within the meaning of the Mental Health Act 1983 of such kind or to such an extent as to be unfitted for marriage;
(e) that at the time of the marriage the respondent was suffering from venereal disease in a communicable form;
(f) that at the time of the marriage the respondent was pregnant by some person other than the petitioner.

13 Bars to relief where marriage is voidable [724]

(1) The court shall not, in proceedings instituted after 31 July 1971, grant a decree of nullity on the ground that a marriage is voidable if the respondent satisfies the court –

(a) that the petitioner, with knowledge that it was open to him to have the marriage avoided, so conducted himself in relation to the respondent as to lead the respondent reasonably to believe that he would not seek to do so; and
(b) that it would be unjust to the respondent to grant the decree.

(2) Without prejudice to subsection (1) above, the court shall not grant a decree of nullity by virtue of section 12 above on the grounds mentioned in paragraph (c), (d), (e) or (f) of that section unless –

(a) it is satisfied that proceedings were instituted within the period of three years from the date of the marriage, or
(b) leave for the institution of proceedings after the expiration of that period has been granted under subsection (4) below.

(3) Without prejudice to subsections (1) and (2) above, the court shall not grant a decree of nullity by virtue of section 12 above on the grounds mentioned in paragraph (e) or (f) of that section unless it is satisfied that the petitioner was at the time of the marriage ignorant of the facts alleged.

(4) In the case of proceedings for the grant of a decree of nullity by virtue of section 12 above on the grounds mentioned in paragraph (c), (d), (e) or (f) of that section, a judge of the court may, on an application made to him, grant leave for the institution of proceedings after the expiration of the period of three years from the date of the marriage if –

(a) he is satisfied that the petitioner has at some time during that period suffered from mental disorder within the meaning of the Mental Health Act 1983, and
(b) he considers that in all the circumstances of the case it would be just to grant leave for the institution of proceedings.

(5) An application for leave under subsection (4) above may be made after the expiration of the period of three years from the date of the marriage.

14 Marriages governed by foreign law or celebrated abroad under English law [725]

(1) Where, apart from this Act, any matters affecting the validity of a marriage would fall to be determined (in accordance with the rules of private international law) by reference to the law of a country outside England and Wales, nothing in section 11, 12 or 13(1) above shall –

(a) preclude the determination of that matter as aforesaid; or

(b) require the application to the marriage of the grounds or bar there mentioned except so far as applicable in accordance with those rules.

(2) In the case of a marriage which purports to have been celebrated under the Foreign Marriage Acts 1892 to 1947 or has taken place outside England and Wales and purports to be a marriage under common law, section 11 above is without prejudice to any ground on which the marriage may be void under those Acts or, as the case may be, by virtue of the rules governing the celebration of marriages outside England and Wales under common law.

16 Effect of decree of nullity in case of voidable marriage [726]

A decree of nullity granted after 31 July 1971 in respect of a voidable marriage shall operate to annul the marriage only as respects any time after the decree has been made absolute, and the marriage shall, notwithstanding the decree, be treated as if it had existed up to that time.

24 Property adjustment orders in connection with divorce proceedings, etc [727]

(1) On granting a decree of divorce, a decree of nullity of marriage or a decree of judicial separation or at any time thereafter (whether, in the case of a decree of divorce, or of nullity of marriage, before or after the decree is made absolute), the court may make any one or more of the following orders, that is to say –

(a) an order that a party to the marriage shall transfer to the other party, to any child of the family or to such person as may be specified in the order for the benefit of such a child such property as may be so specified, being property to which the first-mentioned party is entitled, either in possession or reversion;
(b) an order that a settlement of such property as may be so specified, being property to which a party to the marriage is so entitled, be made to the satisfaction of the court for the benefit of the other party to the marriage and of the children of the family or either or any of them;
(c) an order varying for the benefit of the parties to the marriage and of the children of the family or either or any of them any ante-nuptial or post-nuptial settlement (including such a settlement made by will or codicil) made on the parties to the marriage;
(d) an order extinguishing or reducing the interest of either of the parties to the marriage under any such settlement;

subject, however, in the case of an order under paragraph (a) above, to the restrictions imposed by section 29(1) and (3) below on the making of orders for a transfer of property in favour of children who have attained the age of eighteen.

(2) The court may make an order under subsection (1)(c) above notwithstanding that there are no children of the family.

(3) Without prejudice to the power to give a direction under section 30 below for the settlement of an instrument by conveyancing counsel, where an order is made under this section on or after granting a decree of divorce or nullity of marriage, neither the order nor any settlement made in pursuance of the order shall take effect unless the decree has been made absolute.

47 Matrimonial relief and declarations of validity in respect of polygamous marriages [728]

(1) A court in England and Wales shall not be precluded from granting matrimonial relief or making a declaration concerning the validity of a marriage by

reason only that either party to the marriage is, or has during the substance of the marriage been, married to more than one person.

(2) In this section 'matrimonial relief' means –

(a) any decree under Part I of this Act;
(b) a financial provision order under section 27 above;
(c) an order under section 35 above altering a maintenance agreement;
(d) an order under any provision of this Act which confers a power exercisable in connection with, or in connection with proceedings for, any such decree or order as is mentioned in paragraphs (a) to (c) above;
(dd) an order under Part III of the Matrimonial and Family Proceedings Act 1984;
(e) an order under Part I of the Domestic Proceedings and Magistrates' Courts Act 1978.

(3) In this section 'a declaration concerning the validity of a marriage' means any declaration under Part III of the Family Law Act 1986 involving a determination as to the validity of a marriage.

(4) Provision may be made by rules of court –

(a) for requiring notice of proceedings brought by virtue of this section to be served on any additional spouse of a party to the marriage in question; and
(b) for conferring on any such additional spouse the right to be heard in the proceedings,

in such cases as may be specified in the rules.

[As amended by the Domestic Proceedings and Magistrates' Courts Act 1978, s89(2)(a), Schedule 2, para 39; Mental Health Act 1983, s148, Schedule 4, para 34; Matrimonial and Family Proceedings Act 1984, ss2, 46(1), Schedule 1, paras 10, 15; Marriage (Prohibited Degrees of Relationship) Act 1986, s6(4); Family Law Act 1986, s68(1), Schedule 1, para 14; Private International Law (Miscellaneous Provisions) Act 1995, s8(2), Schedule, para 2.]

DOMICILE AND MATRIMONIAL PROCEEDINGS ACT 1973
(1973 c 45)

1 Abolition of wife's dependent domicile [729]

(1) Subject to subsection (2) below, the domicile of a married woman as at any time after the coming into force of this section shall, instead of being the same as her husband's by virtue only of marriage, be ascertained by reference to the same factors as in the case of any other individual capable of having an independent domicile.

(2) Where immediately before this section came into force a woman was married and then had her husband's domicile by dependence, she is to be treated as retaining that domicile (as a domicile of choice, if it is not also her domicile of origin) unless and until it is changed by acquisition or revival of another domicile either on or after the coming into force of this section. ...

3 Age at which independent domicile can be acquired [730]

(1) The time at which a person first becomes capable of having an independent domicile shall be when he attains the age of sixteen or marries under that age; and in the case of a person who immediately before 1 January 1974 was incapable of having an independent domicile, but has then attained the age of sixteen or been married, it shall be that date. ...

4 Dependent domicile of child not living with his father [731]

(1) Subsection (2) of this section shall have effect with respect to the dependent domicile of a child as at any time after the coming into force of this section when his father and mother are alive but living apart.

(2) The child's domicile as at that time shall be that of his mother if –

    (a) he then has his home with her and has no home with his father; or
    (b) he has at any time had her domicile by virtue of paragraph (a) above and has not since had a home with his father.

(3) As at any time after the coming into force of this section, the domicile of a child whose mother is dead shall be that which she last had before she died if at her death he had her domicile by virtue of subsection (2) above and he has not since had a home with his father.

(4) Nothing in this section prejudices any existing rule of law as to the cases in which a child's domicile is regarded as being, by dependence, that of his mother.

(5) In this section, 'child' means a person incapable of having an independent domicile. ...

[As amended by the Children Act 1975, s108(1)(b), Schedule 4, Pt I.]

ARBITRATION ACT 1975
(1975 c 8)

1 Staying court proceedings where party proves arbitration agreement [732]

(1) If any party to an arbitration agreement to which this section applies, or any person claiming through or under him, commences any legal proceedings in any court against any other party to the agreement, or any person claiming through or under him, in respect of any matter agreed to be referred, any party to the proceedings may at any time after appearance, and before delivering any pleadings or taking any other steps in the proceedings, apply to the court to stay the proceedings; and the court, unless satisfied that the arbitration agreement is null and void, inoperative or incapable of being performed or that there is not in fact any dispute between the parties with regard to the matter agreed to be referred, shall make an order staying the proceedings.

(2) This section applies to any arbitration agreement which is not a domestic arbitration agreement; and neither section 4(1) of the Arbitration Act 1950 nor section 4 of the Arbitration Act (Northern Ireland) 1937 shall apply to an arbitration agreement to which this section applies. ...

(4) In this section 'domestic arbitration agreement' means an arbitration agreement which does not provide, expressly or by implication, for arbitration in a State other than the United Kingdom and to which neither –

    (a) an individual who is a national of, or habitually resident in, any State other than the United Kingdom; nor
    (b) a body corporate which is incorporated in, or whose central management and control is exercised in, any State other than the United Kingdom;

is a party at the time the proceedings are commenced.

2 Replacement of former provisions [733]

Sections 3 to 6 of this Act shall have effect with respect to the enforcement of Convention awards; and where a Convention award would, but for this section, be also a foreign award within the meaning of Part II of the Arbitration Act 1950, that Part shall not apply to it.

3 Effect of Convention awards

(1) A Convention award shall, subject to the following provisions of this Act, be enforceable –

(a) in England and Wales, either by action or in the same manner as the award of an arbitrator is enforceable by virtue of section 26 of the Arbitration Act 1950;...

(2) Any Convention award which would be enforceable under this Act shall be treated as binding for all purposes on the persons as between whom it was made, and may accordingly be relied on by any of those persons by way of defence, set off or otherwise in any legal proceedings in the United Kingdom; and any reference in this Act to enforcing a Convention award shall be construed as including references to relying on such an award.

4 Evidence

The party seeking to enforce a Convention award must produce –

(a) the duly authenticated original award or a duly certified copy of it; and
(b) the original arbitration agreement or a duly certified copy of it; and
(c) where the award or agreement is in a foreign language, a translation of it certified by an official or sworn translator or by a diplomatic or consular agent.

5 Refusal of enforcement

(1) Enforcement of a Convention award shall not be refused except in the cases mentioned in this section.

(2) Enforcement of a Convention award may be refused if the person against whom it is invoked proves –

(a) that a party to the arbitration agreement was (under the law applicable to him) under some incapacity; or
(b) that the arbitration agreement was not valid under the law to which the parties subjected it or, failing any indication thereon, under the law of the country where the award was made; or
(c) that he was not given proper notice of the appointment of the arbitrator or of the arbitration proceedings or was otherwise unable to present his case; or
(d) (subject to subsection (4) of this section) that the award deals with a difference not contemplated by or not falling within the terms of the submission to arbitration or contains decisions on matters beyond the scope of the submission to arbitration; or
(e) that the composition of the arbitral authority or the arbitral procedure was not in accordance with the agreement of the parties or, failing such agreement, with the law of the country where the arbitration took place; or
(f) that the award has not yet become binding on the parties, or has been set aside or suspended by a competent authority of the country in which, or under the law of which, it was made.

(3) Enforcement of a Convention award may also be refused if the award is in respect of a matter which is not capable of settlement by arbitration, or if it would be contrary to public policy to enforce the award.

(4) A Convention award which contains decisions on matters not submitted to arbitration may be enforced to the extent that it contains decisions on matters

submitted to arbitration which can be separated from those on matters not so submitted.

(5) Where an application for the setting aside or suspension of a Convention award has been made to such a competent authority as is mentioned in subsection (2)(f) of this section, the court before which enforcement of the award is sought may, if it thinks fit, adjourn the proceedings and may, on the application of the party seeking to enforce the award, order the other party to give security.

6 Saving [737]

Nothing in this Act shall prejudice any right to enforce or rely on an award otherwise than under this Act or Part II of the Arbitration Act 1950.

7 Interpretation [738]

(1) In this Act –

'arbitration agreement' means an agreement in writing (including an agreement contained in an exchange of letters or telegrams) to submit to arbitration present or future differences capable of settlement by arbitration;
'Convention award' means an award made in pursuance of an arbitration agreement in the territory of a State, other than the United Kingdom, which is a party to the New York Convention; and
'the New York Convention' means the Convention on the Recognition and Enforcement of Foreign Arbitral Awards adopted by the United Nations Conference on International Commercial Arbitration on 10 June 1958.

(2) If Her Majesty by Order in Council declares that any State specified in the Order is a party to the New York Convention the Order shall, while in force, be conclusive evidence that that State is a party to that Convention.

(3) An Order in Council under this section may be varied or revoked by a subsequent Order in Council.

EVIDENCE (PROCEEDINGS IN OTHER JURISDICTIONS) ACT 1975
(1975 c 84)

1 Application to United Kingdom court for assistance in obtaining evidence for civil proceedings in other court [739]

Where an application is made to the High Court, the Court of Session or the High Court of Justice in Northern Ireland for an order for evidence to be obtained in the part of the United Kingdom in which it exercises jurisdiction, and the court is satisfied –

(a) that the application is made in pursuance of a request issued by or on behalf of a court or tribunal ('the requesting court') exercising jurisdiction in any other part of the United Kingdom or in a country or territory outside the United Kingdom; and
(b) that the evidence to which the application relates is to be obtained for the purposes of civil proceedings which either have been instituted before the requesting court or whose institutions before that court is contemplated,

the High Court, Court of Session or High Court of Justice in Northern Ireland, as the case may be, shall have the powers conferred on it by the following provisions of this Act.

2 Power of United Kingdom court to give effect to application for assistance [740]

(1) Subject to the provisions of this section, the High Court, the Court of Session and the High Court of Justice in Northern Ireland shall each have power, on any such application as is mentioned in section 1 above, by order to make such provision for obtaining evidence in the part of the United Kingdom in which it exercises jurisdiction as may appear to the court to be appropriate for the purpose of giving effect to the request in pursuance of which the application is made; and any such order may require a person specified therein to take such steps as the court consider appropriate for that purpose.

(2) Without prejudice to the generality of subsection (1) above but subject to the provisions of this section, an order under this section may, in particular, make provision –

> (a) for the examination of witnesses, either orally or in writing;
> (b) for the production of documents;
> (c) for the inspection, photographing, preservation, custody or detention of any property;
> (d) for the taking of samples of any property and the carrying out of any experiments on or with any property;
> (e) for the medical examination of any person;
> (f) without prejudice to paragraph (e) above, for the taking and testing of samples of blood from any person.

(3) An order under this section shall not require any particular steps to be taken unless they are steps which can be required to be taken by way of obtaining evidence for the purposes of civil proceedings in the court making the order (whether or not proceedings of the same description as those to which the application for the order relates); but this subsection shall not preclude the making of an order requiring a person to give testimony (either orally or in writing) otherwise than on oath where this is asked for by the requesting court.

(4) An order under this section shall not require a person –

> (a) to state what documents relevant to the proceedings to which the application for the order relates are or have been in his possession, custody or power; or
> (b) to produce any documents other than particular documents specified in the order as being documents appearing to the court making the order to be, or to be likely to be, in his possession, custody or power.

(5) A person who, by virtue of an order under this section, is required to attend at any place shall be entitled to the like conduct money and payment for expenses and loss of time as on attendance as a witness in civil proceedings before the court making the order.

3 Privilege of witnesses [741]

(1) A person shall not be compelled by virtue of an order under section 2 above to give any evidence which he could not be compelled to give –

> (a) in civil proceedings in the part of the United Kingdom in which the court that made the order exercises jurisdiction; or
> (b) subject to subsection (2) below, in civil proceedings in the country or territory in which the requesting court exercises jurisdiction.

(2) Subsection (1)(b) above shall not apply unless the claim of the person in question to be exempt from giving the evidence is either –

(a) supported by a statement contained in the request (whether it is so supported unconditionally or subject to conditions that are fulfilled); or

(b) conceded by the applicant for the orders;

and where such a claim made by any person is not supported or conceded as aforesaid he may (subject to the other provisions of this section) be required to give the evidence to which the claim relates but that evidence shall not be transmitted to the requesting court if that court, on the matter being referred to it, upholds the claim.

(3) Without prejudice to subsection (1) above, a person shall not be compelled by virtue of an order under section 2 above to give any evidence if his doing so would be prejudicial to the security of the United Kingdom; and a certificate signed by or on behalf of the Secretary of State to the effect that it would be so prejudicial for that person to do so shall be conclusive evidence of that fact.

(4) In this section references to giving evidence include references to answering any question and to producing any document and the reference in subsection (2) above to the transmission of evidence given by a person shall be construed accordingly.

6 Power of United Kingdom court to assist in obtaining evidence for international proceedings

(1) Her Majesty may by Order in Council direct that, subject to such exceptions, adaptations or modifications as may be specified in the Order, the provisions of sections 1 to 3 above shall have effect in relation to international proceedings of any description specified in the order.

(2) An Order in Council under this section may direct that section 1(4) of the Perjury Act 1911 ... shall have effect in relation to international proceedings to which the Order applies as it has effect in relation to a judicial proceeding in a tribunal of a foreign state.

(3) In this section 'international proceedings' means proceedings before the International Court of Justice or any other court, tribunal, commission, body or authority (whether consisting of one or more persons) which, in pursuance of any international agreement or any resolution of the General Assembly of the United Nations, exercises any jurisdiction or performs any functions of a judicial nature or by way of arbitration, conciliation or inquiry or is appointed (whether permanently or temporarily) for the purpose of exercising any jurisdiction or performing any such functions.

7 Rules of court

The power to make rules of court under section 84 of the Supreme Court Act 1981 ... shall include power to make rules of court –

(a) as to the manner in which any such application as is mentioned in section 1 above is to be made;

(b) subject to the provisions of this Act, as to the circumstances in which an order can be made under section 2 above; and

(c) as to the manner in which any such reference as it mentioned in section 8(2) above is to be made;

and any such rules may include such incidental, supplementary and consequential provision as the authority making the rules may consider necessary or expedient.

9 Interpretation [744]

(1) In this Act –

'civil proceedings', in relation to the requesting court, means proceedings in any civil or commercial matter;
'requesting court' has the meaning given in section 1 above;
'property' includes any land, chattel or other corporeal property of any description;
'request' includes any commission, order or other process issued by or on behalf of the requesting court. ...

[As amended by the Supreme Court Act 1981, s152(1), Schedule 5.]

LEGITIMACY ACT 1976
(1976 c 31)

1 Legitimacy of children of certain void marriages [745]

(1) The child of a void marriage, whenever born, shall, subject to subsection (2) below and Schedule 1 to this Act, be treated as the legitimate child of his parents if at the time of the insemination resulting in the birth or, where there was no such insemination, the child's conception (or at the time of the celebration of the marriage if later) both or either of the parties reasonably believed that the marriage was valid.

(2) This section only applies where the father of the child was domiciled in England and Wales at the time of the birth or, if he died before the birth, was so domiciled immediately before his death.

(3) It is hereby declared for the avoidance of doubt that subsection (1) above applies notwithstanding that the belief that the marriage was valid was due to a mistake as to law.

(4) In relation to a child born after the coming into force of section 28 of the Family Law Reform Act 1987, it shall be presumed for the purposes of subsection (1) above, unless the contrary is shown, that one of the parties to the void marriage reasonably believed at the time of the insemination resulting in the birth or, where there was no such insemination, the child's conception (or at the time of the celebration of the marriage if later) that the marriage was valid.

2 Legitimation by subsequent marriage of parents [746]

Subject to the following provisions of this Act, where the parents of an illegitimate person marry one another, the marriage shall, if the father of the illegitimate person is at the date of marriage domiciled in England and Wales, render that person, if living, legitimate from the date of the marriage.

3 Legitimation by extraneous law [747]

Subject to the following provisions of this Act, where the parents of an illegitimate person marry one another and the father of the illegitimate person is not at the time of the marriage domiciled in England and Wales but is domiciled in a country by the law of which the illegitimate person becomes legitimated by virtue of such subsequent marriage, that person, if living, shall in England and Wales be recognised as having been so legitimated from the date of the marriage notwithstanding that, at the time of his birth, his father was domiciled in a country the law of which did not permit legitimation by subsequent marriage.

4 Legitimation of adopted child

(1) Section 39 of the Adoption Act 1976 does not prevent an adopted child being legitimated under section 2 or 3 above if either natural parent is the sole adoptive parent.

(2) Where an adopted child (with a sole adoptive parent) is legitimated –

(a) subsection (2) of the said section 39 shall not apply after the legitimation to the natural relationship with the other natural parent, and

(b) revocation of the adoption order in consequence of the legitimation shall not affect sections 39, 41 or 42 of the Adoption Act 1976 as it applies to any instrument made before the date of legitimation.

5 Rights of legitimated persons and others to take interests in property

(1) Subject to any contrary indication, the rules of construction contained in this section apply to any instrument other than an existing instrument, so far as the instrument contains a disposition of property.

(2) For the purposes of this section, provisions of the law of intestate succession applicable to the estate of a deceased person shall be treated as if contained in an instrument executed by him (while in full capacity) immediately before his death.

(3) A legitimated person, and any other person, shall be entitled to take any interest as if the legitimated person had been born legitimate.

(4) A disposition which depends on the date of birth of a child or children of the parent or parents shall be construed as if –

(a) a legitimated child had been born on the date of legitimation,

(b) two or more legitimated children legitimated on the same date had been born on that date in the order of their actual births,

but this does not affect any reference to the age of a child.

(5) Examples of phrases in wills on which subsection (4) above can operate are –

1. Children of A 'living at my death or born afterwards'.
2. Children of A 'living at my death or born afterwards before any one of such children for the time being in existence attains a vested interest, and who attain the age of 21 years'.
3. As in example 1 or 2, but referring to grandchildren of A, instead of children of A.
4. A for life 'until he has a child' and then to his child or children.

Note. Subsection (4) above will not affect the reference to the age of 21 years in example 2.

(6) If an illegitimate person or a person adopted by one of his natural parents dies, or has died before the commencement of this Act, and –

(a) after his death his parents marry or have married; and

(b) the deceased would, if living at the time of the marriage, have become a legitimated person,

this section shall apply for the construction of the instrument so far as it relates to the taking of interests by, or in succession to, his spouse, children and remoter issue as if he had been legitimated by virtue of the marriage.

(7) In this section 'instrument' includes a private Act settling property, but not any other enactment.

8 Personal rights and obligations [750]

A legitimated person shall have the same rights, and shall be under the same obligations in respect of the maintenance and support of himself or of any other person, as if he had been born legitimate, and, subject to the provisions of this Act, the provisions of any Act relating to claims for damages, compensation, allowance, benefit or otherwise by or in respect of a legitimate child shall apply in like manner in the case of a legitimated person.

9 Re-registration of birth of legitimated person [751]

(1) It shall be the duty of the parents of a legitimated person or, in cases where re-registration can be effected on information furnished by one parent and one of the parents is dead, of the surviving parent to furnish to the Registrar General information with a view to obtaining the re-registration of the birth of that person within three months after the date of the marriage by virtue of which he was legitimated.

(2) The failure of the parents or either of them to furnish information as required by subsection (1) above in respect of any legitimated person shall not affect the legitimation of that person.

(3) This section does not apply in relation to a person who was legitimated otherwise than by virtue of the subsequent marriage of his parents.

(4) Any parent who fails to give information as required by this section shall be liable on summary conviction to a fine not exceeding level 1 on the standard scale.

[As amended by the Adoption Act 1976, s73(2), Schedule 3, para 23; Criminal Justice Act 1982, ss38, 46; Family Law Reform Act 1987, s28.]

ADOPTION ACT 1976
(1976 c 36)

6 Duty to promote welfare of child [752]

In reaching any decision relating to the adoption of a child a court or adoption agency shall have regard to all the circumstances, first consideration being given to the need to safeguard and promote the welfare of the child throughout his childhood; and shall so far as practicable ascertain the wishes and feelings of the child regarding the decision and give due consideration to them, having regard to his age and understanding.

12 Adoption orders [753]

(1) An adoption order is an order giving parental responsibility for a child to the adopters, made on their application by an authorised court.

(2) The order does not affect parental responsibility so far as it relates to any period before the making of the order.

(3) The making of an adoption order operates to extinguish –

(a) the parental responsibility which any person has for the child immediately before the making of the order;
(aa) any order under the Children Act 1989;
(b) any duty arising by virtue of an agreement or the order of a court to make payments, so far as the payments are in respect of the child's maintenance or upbringing for any period after the making of the order.

(4) Subsection (3)(b) does not apply to a duty arising by virtue of an agreement –
   (a) which constitutes a trust, or
   (b) which expressly provides that the duty is not to be extinguished by the making of an adoption order.

(5) An adoption order may not be made in relation to a child who is or has been married.

(6) An adoption order may contain such terms and conditions as the court thinks fit.

(7) An adoption order may be made notwithstanding that the child is already an adopted child.

14 Adoption by married couple [754]

(1) An adoption order shall not be made on the application of more than one person except in the circumstances specified in subsections (1A) and (1B).

(1A) An adoption order may be made on the application of a married couple where both the husband and the wife have attained the age of 21 years.

(1B) An adoption order may be made on the application of a married couple where –
   (a) the husband or the wife –
      (i) is the father or mother of the child; and
      (ii) has attained the age of 18 years; and
   (b) his or her spouse has attained the age of 21 years.

(2) An adoption order shall not be made on the application of a married couple unless –
   (a) at least one of them is domiciled in a part of the United Kingdom, or in the Channel Islands or the Isle of Man, or
   (b) the application is for a Convention adoption order and section 17 is complied with.

15 Adoption by one person [755]

(1) An adoption order may be made on the application of one person where he has attained the age of 21 years and –
   (a) is not married, or
   (b) is married and the court is satisfied that –
      (i) his spouse cannot be found, or
      (ii) the spouses have separated and are living apart, and the separation is likely to be permanent, or
      (iii) his spouse is by reason of ill-health, whether physical or mental, incapable of making an application for an adoption order.

(2) An adoption order shall not be made on the application of one person unless –
   (a) he is domiciled in a part of the United Kingdom, or in the Channel Islands or the Isle of Man, or
   (b) the application is for a Convention adoption order and section 17 is complied with.

(3) An adoption order shall not be made on the application of the mother or father of the child alone unless the court is satisfied that –
   (a) the other natural parent is dead or cannot be found or, by virtue of section

28 of the Human Fertilisation and Embryology Act 1990, there is no other parent, or

(b) there is some other reason justifying the exclusion of the other natural parent,

and where such an order is made the reason justifying the exclusion of the other natural parent shall be recorded by the court.

16 Parental agreement [756]

(1) An adoption order shall not be made unless –

    (a) the child is free for adoption by virtue of an order made –

        (i) in England and Wales, under section 18; or ...

    (b) in the case of each parent or guardian of the child the court is satisfied that –

        (i) he freely, and with full understanding of what is involved, agrees unconditionally to the making of an adoption order (whether or not he knows the identity of the applicants); or

        (ii) his agreement to the making of the adoption order should be dispensed with on a ground specified in subsection (2).

(2) The grounds mentioned in subsection (1)(b)(ii) are that the parent or guardian –

    (a) cannot be found or is incapable of giving agreement;
    (b) is withholding his agreement unreasonably;
    (c) has persistently failed without reasonable cause to discharge his parental responsibility for the child;
    (d) has abandoned or neglected the child;
    (e) has persistently ill-treated the child;
    (f) has seriously ill-treated the child (subject to subsection (5)).

(3) Subsection (1) does not apply in any case where the child is not a United Kingdom national and the application for the adoption order is for a Convention adoption order.

(4) Agreement is ineffective for the purposes of subsection (1)(b)(i) if given by the mother less than six weeks after the child's birth.

(5) Subsection (2)(f) does not apply unless (because of the ill-treatment or for other reasons) the rehabilitation of the child within the household of the parent or guardian is unlikely.

17 Convention adoption orders [757]

(1) An adoption order shall be made as a Convention adoption order if the application is for a Convention adoption order and the following conditions are satisfied both at the time of the application and when the order is made.

(2) The child –

    (a) must be a United Kingdom national or a national of a Convention country, and
    (b) must habitually reside in British territory or a Convention country.

(3) The applicant or applicants and the child must not all be United Kingdom nationals living in British territory.

(4) If the application is by a married couple, either –

    (a) each must be a United Kingdom national or a national of a Convention country, and both must habitually reside in Great Britain, or

(b) both must be United Kingdom nationals, and each must habitually reside in British territory or a Convention country,

and if the applicants are nationals of the same Convention country the adoption must not be prohibited by a specified provision (as defined in subsection (8)) of the internal law of that country.

(5) If the application is by one person, either –

(a) he must be a national of a Convention country, and must habitually reside in Great Britain, or
(b) he must be a United Kingdom national and must habitually reside in British territory or a Convention country,

and if he is a national of a Convention country the adoption must not be prohibited by a specified provision (as defined in subsection (8)) of the internal law of that country.

(6) If the child is not a United Kingdom national the order shall not be made. –

(a) except in accordance with the provisions, if any, relating to consents and consultations of the internal law relating to adoption of the Convention country of which the child is a national, and
(b) unless the court is satisfied that each person who consents to the order in accordance with that internal law does so with full understanding of what is involved.

(7) The reference to consents and consultations in subsection (6) does not include a reference to consent by and consultation with the applicant and members of the applicant's family (including his or her spouse), and for the purposes of subsection (6) consents may be proved in the manner prescribed by rules and the court shall be treated as the authority by whom, under the law mentioned in subsection (6), consents may be dispensed with and the adoption in question may be effected; and where the provisions there mentioned require the attendance before that authority of any person who does not reside in Great Britain, that requirement shall be treated as satisfied for the purposes of subsection (6) if –

(a) that person has been given a reasonable opportunity of communicating his opinion on the adoption in question to the proper officer or clerk of the court, or to an appropriate authority of the country in question, for transmission to the court; and
(b) where he has availed himself of that opportunity, his opinion has been transmitted to the court.

(8) In subsections (4) and (5) 'specified provision' means a provision specified in an order of the Secretary of State as one notified to the Government of the United Kingdom in pursuance of the provisions of the Convention which relate to prohibitions on an adoption contained in the national law of the Convention country in question.

38 Meaning of 'adoption' in Part IV [ss38–49] [758]

(1) In this part 'adoption' means adoption –

(a) by an adoption order;
(b) by an order made under the Children Act 1975, the Adoption Act 1958, the Adoption Act 1950 or any enactment repealed by the Adoption Act 1950;
(c) by an order made in Scotland, Northern Ireland, the Isle of Man or in any of the Channel Islands;
(d) which is an overseas adoption; or

(e) which is an adoption recognised by the law of England and Wales and effected under the law of any other country,

and cognate expressions shall be construed accordingly.

(2) The definition of adoption includes, where the context admits, an adoption effected before the passing of the Children Act 1975, and the date of an adoption effected by an order is the date of the making of the order.

39 Status conferred by adoption [759]

(1) An adopted child shall be treated in law –

(a) where the adopters are a married couple, as if he had been born as a child of the marriage (whether or not he was in fact born after the marriage was solemnised);
(b) in any other case, as if he had been born to the adopter in wedlock (but not as a child of any actual marriage of the adopter).

(2) An adopted child shall, subject to subsection (3), be treated in law as if he were not the child of any person other than the adopters or adopter.

(3) In the case of a child adopted by one of its natural parents as sole adoptive parent, subsection (2) has no effect as respects entitlement to property depending on relationship to that parent, or as respects anything else depending on that relationship.

(4) It is hereby declared that this section prevents an adopted child from being illegitimate.

(5) This section has effect –

(a) in the case of an adoption before 1 January 1976, from that date, and
(b) in the case of any other adoption, from the date of the adoption.

(6) Subject to the provisions of this Part, this section –

(a) applies for the construction of enactments or instruments passed or made before the adoption or later, and so applies subject to any contrary indication; and
(b) has effect as respects things done, or events occurring, after the adoption, or after 31 December 1975, whichever is the later.

42 Rules of construction for instruments concerning property [760]

(1) Subject to any contrary indication, the rules of construction contained in this section apply to any instrument, other than an existing instrument, so far as it contains a disposition of property.

(2) In applying section 39(1) to a disposition which depends on the date of birth of a child or children of the adoptive parent or parents, the disposition shall be construed as if –

(a) the adopted child had been born on the date of adoption,
(b) two or more children adopted on the same date had been born on that date in the order of their actual births,

but this does not affect any reference to the age of a child.

(3) Examples of phrases in wills on which subsection (2) can operate are –

1. Children of A 'living at my death or born afterwards'.
2. Children of A 'living at my death or born afterwards before any one of such children for the time being in existence attains a vested interest and who attain the age of 21 years'.

3. As in example 1 or 2, but referring to grandchildren of A instead of children of A.
4. A for life 'until he has a child', and then to his child or children.

Note. Subsection (2) will not affect the reference to the age of 21 years in example 2.

(4) Section 39(2) does not prejudice any interest vested in possession in the adopted child before the adoption, or any interest expectant (whether immediately or not) upon an interest so vested.

(5) Where it is necessary to determine for the purposes of a disposition of property effected by an instrument whether a woman can have a child, it shall be presumed that once a woman has attained the age of 55 years she will not adopt a child after execution of the instrument, and, notwithstanding section 39, if she does so that child shall not be treated as her child or as the child of her spouse (if any) for the purposes of the instrument.

(6) In this section, 'instrument' includes a private Act settling property, but not any other enactment.

46 Meaning of 'disposition' [761]

(1) In this Part, unless the context otherwise requires –

'disposition' includes the conferring of a power of appointment and any other disposition of an interest in or right over property;
'power of appointment' includes any discretionary power to transfer a beneficial interest in property without the furnishing of valuable consideration.

(2) This Part applies to an oral disposition as if contained in an instrument made when the disposition was made.

(3) For the purposes of this Part, the death of the testator is the date at which a will or codicil is to be regarded as made.

(4) For the purposes of this Part, provisions of the law of intestate succession applicable to the estate of a deceased person shall be treated as if contained in an instrument executed by him (while of full capacity) immediately before his death.

(5) It is hereby declared that references in this Part to dispositions of property include references to a disposition by the creation of an entailed interest.

47 Miscellaneous enactments [762]

(1) Section 39 does not apply for the purposes of the table of kindred and affinity in Schedule 1 to the Marriage Act 1949 or sections 10 and 11 (incest) of the Sexual Offences Act 1956.

(2) Section 39 does not apply for the purposes of any provision of –

(a) the British Nationality Act 1981,
(b) the Immigration Act 1971,
(c) any instrument having effect under an enactment within paragraph (a) or (b), or
(d) any other provision of the law for the time being in force which determines British citizenship, British Dependent Territories citizenship, the status of a British National (Overseas) or British Overseas citizenship.

52 Revocation of adoptions on legitimation [763]

(1) Where any person adopted by his father or mother alone has subsequently become a legitimated person on the marriage of his father and mother, the court

by which the adoption order was made may, on the application of any of the parties concerned, revoke that order.

(2) Where any person legitimated by virtue of section 1 of the Legitimacy Act 1959 had been adopted by his father and mother before the commencement of that Act, the court by which the adoption order was made may, on the application of any of the parties concerned, revoke that order.

(3) Where a person adopted by his father or mother alone by virtue of a regulated adoption has subsequently become a legitimated person on the marriage of his father and mother, the High Court may, upon an application under this subsection by the parties concerned, by order revoke the adoption.

(4) In relation to an adoption order made by a magistrates' court, the reference in subsections (1) and (2) to the court by which the order was made includes a reference to a court acting for the same petty sessions area.

53 Annulment, etc of overseas adoptions [764]

(1) The High Court may, upon an application under this subsection, by order annul a regulated adoption, or an adoption effected by a Convention adoption order –

(a) on the ground that at the relevant time the adoption was prohibited by a notified provision, if under the internal law then in force in the country of which the adopter was then a national or the adopters were then nationals the adoption could have been impugned on that ground;

(b) on the ground that at the relevant time the adoption contravened provisions relating to consents of the internal law relating to adoption of the country of which the adopted person was then a national, if under that law the adoption could then have been impugned on that ground;

(c) on any other ground on which the adoption can be impugned under the law for the time being in force in the country in which the adoption was effected.

(2) The High Court may, upon an application under this subsection –

(a) order that an overseas adoption or a determination shall cease to be valid in Great Britain on the ground that the adoption or determination is contrary to public policy or that the authority which purported to authorise the adoption or make the determination was not competent to entertain the case;

(b) decide the extent, if any, to which a determination has been affected by a subsequent determination.

(3) Any court in Great Britain may, in any proceedings in that court, decide that an overseas adoption or a determination shall, for the purposes of those proceedings, be treated as invalid in Great Britain on either of the grounds mentioned in subsection (2).

(4) An order or decision of the Court of Session on an application under subsection (3) of section 6 of the Adoption Act 1968 shall be recognised and have effect as if it were an order or decision of the High Court on an application under subsection (3) of this section.

(5) Except as provided by this section and section 52(3) the validity of an overseas adoption or a determination shall not be impugned in England and Wales in proceedings in any court.

54 Provisions supplementary to ss52(3) and 53

(1) Any application for an order under section 52(3) or 53 or a decision under section 53(3) shall be made in the prescribed manner and within such period, if any, as may be prescribed.

(2) No application shall be made under section 52(3) or section 53(1) in respect of an adoption unless immediately before the application is made the person adopted or the adopter habitually resides in England and Wales or, as the case may be, both adopters habitually reside there.

(3) In deciding in pursuance of section 53 whether such an authority as is mentioned in section 59 was competent to entertain a particular case, a court shall be bound by any finding of fact made by the authority and stated by the authority to be so made for the purpose of determining whether the authority was competent to entertain the case.

(4) In section 53 –

'determination' means such a determination as is mentioned in section 59 of this Act;
'notified provision' means a provision specified in an order of the Secretary of State as one in respect of which a notification to or by the Government of the United Kingdom was in force at the relevant time in pursuance of the provisions of the Convention relating to prohibitions contained in the national law of the adopter; and
'relevant time' means the time when the adoption in question purported to take effect under the law of the country in which it purports to have been effected.

55 Adoption of children abroad

(1) Where on an application made in relation to a child by a person who is not domiciled in England and Wales or Scotland or Northern Ireland an authorised court is satisfied that he intends to adopt the child under the law of or within the country in which the applicant is domiciled, the court may, subject to the following provisions of this section, make an order giving him parental responsibility for the child.

(2) The provisions of Part II relating to adoption orders, except sections 12(1), 14((2), 15(2), 17 to 21 and 25, shall apply in relation to orders under this section as they apply in relation to adoption orders subject to the modification that in section 13(1) for '19' and '13' there are substituted '32' and '26' respectively.

(3) Sections 50 and 51 and paragraphs 1 and 2(1) of Schedule 1 shall apply in relation to an order under this section as they apply in relation to an adoption order except that any entry in the Registers of Births, or the Adopted Children Register which is required to be marked in consequence of the making of an order under this section shall, in lieu of being marked with the word 'Adopted' or 'Re-adopted' (with or without the addition of the words '(Scotland)' or '(Northern Ireland)'), be marked with the words 'Proposed foreign adoption' or 'Proposed foreign re-adoption', as the case may require.

62 Courts

(1) In this Act, 'authorised court', as respects an application for an order relating to a child, shall be construed as follows.

(2) Subject to subsections (4) to (6), if the child is in England and Wales when the application is made, the following are authorised courts –

(a) the High Court;

(b) the county court within whose district the child is, and, in the case of an application for an order freeing a child for adoption, any county court within whose district a parent or guardian of the child is;
(c) any other county court prescribed by rules made under section 75 of the County Courts Act 1984;
(d) a magistrates' court within whose area the child is, and, in the case of an application for an order freeing the child for adoption, a magistrates' court within whose area a parent or guardian of the child is.

(3) If, in the case of an application for an adoption order or for an order freeing a child for adoption, the child is not in Great Britain when the application is made, the High Court is the authorised court.

(4) In the case of an application for a Convention adoption order, paragraphs (b), (c) and (d) of subsection (2) do not apply.

(6) In the case of an order under section 55, paragraph (d) of subsection (2) does not apply.

(7) Any court to which the proceedings on an application are transferred under any enactment is, as regards the transferred proceedings, an authorised court if it is not an authorised court under the preceding provisions of this section.

70 Nationality [768]

(1) If the Secretary of State by order declares that a description of persons specified in the order has, in pursuance of the Convention, been notified to the Government of the United Kingdom as the description of persons who are deemed to possess the nationality of a particular Convention country, persons of that description shall, subject to the following provisions of this section, be treated for the purposes of this Act as nationals of that country.

(2) Subject to section 54(3) and subsection (3) of this section, where it appears to the court in any proceedings under this Act, or to any court by which a decision in pursuance of section 53(3) falls to be given, that a person is or was at a particular time a national of two or more countries, then –

(a) if it appears to the said court that he is or was then a United Kingdom national, he shall be treated for the purposes of those proceedings or that decision as if he were or had then been a United Kingdom national only;
(b) if, in a case not falling within paragraph (a), it appears to the said court that one only of those countries is or was then a Convention country, he shall be treated for those purposes as if he were or had then been a national of that country only;
(c) if, in a case not falling within paragraph (a), it appears to the said court that two or more of those countries are or were then Convention countries, he shall be treated for those purposes as if he were or had then been a national of such one only of those Convention countries as the said court considers is the country with which he is or was then most closely connected;
(d) in any other case, he shall be treated for those purposes as if he were or had then been a national of such one only of those countries as the said court considers is the country with which he is or was then most closely connected.

(3) A court in which proceedings are brought in pursuance of section 17, 52(3) or 53 shall be entitled to disregard the provisions of subsection (2) in so far as it appears to that court appropriate to do so for the purposes of those proceedings; but nothing in this subsection shall be construed as prejudicing the provisions of section 54(3).

(4) Where, after such inquiries as the court in question considers appropriate, it appears to the court in any proceedings under this Act, or to any court by which

such a decision as aforesaid falls to be given, that a person has no nationality or no ascertainable nationality, he shall be treated for the purposes of those proceedings or that decision as a national of the country in which he resides or, where that country is one of two or more countries having the same law of nationality, as a national of those countries.

71 Internal law of a country

(1) In this Act 'internal law' in relation to any country means the law applicable in a case where no question arises as to the law in force in any other country.

(2) In any case where the internal law of a country falls to be ascertained for the purposes of this Act by any court and there are in force in that country two or more systems of internal law, the relevant system shall be ascertained in accordance with any rule in force throughout that country indicating which of the systems is relevant in the case in question or, if there is no such rule, shall be the system appearing to that court to be most closely connected with the case.

72 Interpretation

(1) In this Act, unless the context otherwise requires – ...

'authorised court' shall be construed in accordance with section 62; ...
'British territory' means, for the purposes of any provision of this Act, any of the following countries, that is to say, Great Britain, Northern Ireland, the Channel Islands, the Isle of Man and a colony, being a country designated for the purposes of that provision by order of the Secretary of State or, if no country is so designated, any of those countries;
'child', except where used to express a relationship, means a person who has not attained the age of 18 years;
'the Convention' means the Convention relating to the adoption of children concluded at the Hague on 15 November 1965 and signed on behalf of the United Kingdom on that date;
'Convention adoption order' means an adoption order made in accordance with section 17(1);
'Convention country' means any country outside British territory, being a country for the time being designated by an order of the Secretary of State as a country in which, in his opinion, the Convention is in force; ...
'overseas adoption' has the meaning assigned by subsection (2); ...
'regulated adoption' means an overseas adoption of a description designated by an order under subsection (2) as that of an adoption regulated by the Convention;
'United Kingdom national' means, for the purposes of any provision of this Act, a citizen of the United Kingdom and colonies satisfying such conditions, if any, as the Secretary of State may by order specify for the purposes of that provision; ...

(2) In this Act 'overseas adoption' means an adoption of such a description as the Secretary of State may by order specify, being a description of adoptions of children appearing to him to be effected under the law of any country outside Great Britain; and an order under this subsection may contain provision as to the manner in which evidence of an overseas adoption may be given. ...

[As amended by the Domestic Proceedings and Magistrates' Courts Act 1978, s74(2); British Nationality Act 1981, s52(6), (8), Schedules 7, 9; Matrimonial and Family Proceedings Act 1984, s46(1), Schedule 1, para 20(a)(b); Hong Kong (British Nationality) Order 1986, art 8, Schedule; Children Act 1989, ss88(1), 108(7), Schedule 10, Pt I, paras 3, 5, 22, Schedule 15; Human Fertilisation and Embryology Act 1990, s49(5), Schedule 4, para 4.]

UNFAIR CONTRACT TERMS ACT 1977
(1977 c 50)

26 International supply contracts

(1) The limits imposed by this Act on the extent to which a person may exclude or restrict liability by reference to a contract term do not apply to liability arising under such a contract as is described in sub-section (3) below.

(2) The terms of such a contract are not subject to any requirement of reasonableness under section 3 or 4 ...

(3) Subject to sub-section (4), that description of contract is one whose characteristics are the following –

(a) either it is a contract of sale of goods or it is one under or in pursuance of which the possession or ownership of goods passes; and
(b) it is made by parties whose places of business (or, if they have none, habitual residences) are in the territories of different States (the Channel Islands and the Isle of Man being treated for this purpose as different States from the United Kingdom).

(4) A contract falls within sub-section (3) above only if either –

(a) the goods in question are, at the time of the conclusion of the contract, in the course of carriage, or will be carried, from the territory of one State to the territory of another; or
(b) the acts constituting the offer and acceptance have been done in the territories of different States; or
(c) the contract provides for the goods to be delivered to the territory of a State other than that within whose territory those acts were done.

27 Choice of law clauses

(1) Where the law applicable to a contract is the law of any part of the United Kingdom only by choice of the parties (and apart from that choice would be the law of some country outside the United Kingdom) sections 2 to 7 [avoidance of liability for negligence, breach of contract, etc; liability arising from sale or supply of goods] ... of this Act do not operate as part of the law applicable to the contract.

(2) This Act has effect notwithstanding any contract term which applies or purports to apply the law of some country outside the United Kingdom, where (either or both) –

(a) the term appears to the court, or arbitrator or arbiter to have been imposed wholly or mainly for the purpose of enabling the party imposing it to evade the operation of this Act; or
(b) in the making of the contract one of the parties dealt as consumer, and he was then habitually resident in the United Kingdom, and the essential steps necessary for the making of the contract were taken there, whether by him or by others on his behalf ...

[As amended by the Contracts (Applicable Law) Act 1990, s5, Schedule 4, para 4.]

EMPLOYMENT PROTECTION (CONSOLIDATION) ACT 1978
(1978 c 44)

141 Employment outside Great Britain

(1) Sections 1 to 4 and 49 to 51 do not apply in relation to employment during any period when the employee is engaged in work wholly or mainly outside Great Britain unless –

(a) the employee ordinarily works in Great Britain and the work outside Great Britain is for the same employer, or
(b) the law which governs his contract of employment is the law of England and Wales or of Scotland.

(2) Sections 8 and 53 and Parts II, III and V do not apply to employment where under his contract of employment the employee ordinarily works outside Great Britain.

(2A) Part VII does not apply to employment where under his contract of employment the employee ordinarily works outside the territory of the Member States of the European Communities and of Austria, Finland, Iceland, Norway and Sweden.

(3) An employee shall not be entitled to a redundnacy payment if on the relevant date he is outside Great Britain, unless under his contract of employment he ordinarily worked in Great Britain.

(4) An employee who under his contract of employment ordinarily works outside Great Britain shall not be entitled to a redundancy payment unless on the relevant date he is in Great Britain in accordance with instructions given to him by his employer.

(5) For the purposes of subsection (2), a person employed to work on board a ship registered in the United Kingdom (not being a ship registered at a port outside Great Britain) shall, unless –

(a) the employment is wholly outside Great Britain, or
(b) he is not ordinarily resident in Great Britain.

be regarded as a person who under his contract ordinarily works in Great Britain.

153 Interpretation

(5) For the purposes of this Act it is immaterial whether the law which (apart from this Act) governs any person's employment is the law of the United Kingdom, or of a part of the United Kingdom, or not.

[As amended by the Employer (Excluded Classes) Regulations 1983; Trade Union Reform and Employment Rights Act 1993, s49(2), Schedule 8, para 22; Insolvency of Employer (Excluded Classes) Regulations 1995, regs 3, 5.]

DOMESTIC PROCEEDINGS AND MAGISTRATES' COURTS ACT 1978
(1978 c 22)

1 Grounds of application for financial provision

Either party to a marriage may apply to a magistrates' court for an order under section 2 of this Act on the ground that the other party to the marriage –

(a) has failed to provide reasonable maintenance for the applicant; or

(b) has failed to provide, or to make a proper contribution towards, reasonable maintenance for any child of the family; or
(c) has behaved in such a way that the applicant cannot reasonably be expected to live with the respondent; or
(d) has deserted the applicant.

2 Powers of court to make orders for financial provision [776]

(1) Where on an application for an order under this section the applicant satisfies the court of any ground mentioned in section 1 of this Act, the court may, subject to the provisions of this Part of this Act, make any one or more of the following orders, that is to say –
   (a) an order that the respondent shall make to the applicant such periodical payments, and for such term, as may be specified in the order;
   (b) an order that the respondent shall pay to the applicant such lump sum as may be so specified;
   (c) an order that the respondent shall make to the applicant for the benefit of a child of the family to whom the application relates, or to such a child, such periodical payments, and for such term, as may be so specified;
   (d) an order that the respondent shall pay to the applicant for the benefit of a child of the family to whom the application relates, or to such a child, such lump sum as may be so specified.

(2) Without prejudice to the generality of subsection (1)(b) or (d) above, an order under this section for the payment of a lump sum may be made for the purpose of enabling any liability or expenses reasonably incurred in maintaining the applicant, or any child of the family to whom the application relates, before the making of the order to be met.

(3) The amount of any lump sum required to be paid by an order under this section shall not exceed £1,000 or such larger amount as the Lord Chancellor may from time to time by order fix for the purposes of this subsection. Any order made by the Lord Chancellor under this subsection shall be made by statutory instrument and shall be subject to annulment in pursuance of a resolution of either House of Parliament.

3 Matters to which court is to have regard in exercising its powers under s2 [777]

(1) Where an application is made for an order under section 2 of this Act, it shall be the duty of the court, in deciding whether to exercise its powers under that section and, if so, in what manner, to have regard to all the circumstances of the case, first consideration being given to the welfare while a minor of any child of the family who has not attained the age of eighteen.

(2) As regards the exercise of its powers under subsection (1)(a) or (b) of section 2, the court shall in particular have regard to the following matters –
   (a) the income, earning capacity, property and other financial resources which each of the parties to the marriage has or is likely to have in the foreseeable future, including in the case of earning capacity any increase in that capacity which it would in the opinion of the court be reasonable to expect a party to the marriage to take steps to acquire;
   (b) the financial needs, obligations and responsibilities which each of the parties to the marriage has or is likely to have in the foreseeable future;
   (c) the standard of living enjoyed by the parties to the marriage before the occurrence of the conduct which is alleged as the ground of the application;
   (d) the age of each party to the marriage and the duration of the marriage;

(e) any physical or mental disability of either of the parties to the marriage;
(f) the contributions which each of the parties has made or is likely in the foreseeable future to make to the welfare of the family, including any contribution by looking after the home or caring for the family;
(g) the conduct of each of the parties, if that conduct is such that it would in the opinion of the court be inequitable to disregard it.

(3) As regards the exercise of its powers under subsection (1)(c) or (d) of section 2, the court shall in particular have regard to the following matters –
(a) the financial needs of the child;
(b) the income, earning capacity (if any), property and other financial resources of the child;
(c) any physical or mental disability of the child;
(d) the standard of living enjoyed by the family before the occurrence of the conduct which is alleged as the ground of the application;
(e) the manner in which the child was being and in which the parties to the marriage expected him to be educated or trained;
(f) the matters mentioned in relation to the parties to the marriage in paragraphs (a) and (b) of subsection (2) above.

(4) As regards the exercise of its powers under section 2 in favour of a child of the family who is not the child of the respondent, the court shall also have regard –
(a) to whether the respondent had assumed any responsibility for the child's maintenance and, if he did, to the extent to which, and the basis on which, he assumed that responsibility and to the length of time during which he discharged that responsibility;
(b) to whether in assuming and discharging that responsibility the respondent did so knowing that the child was not his own child;
(c) to the liability of any other person to maintain the child.

4 Duration of orders for financial provisions for a party to a marriage

(1) The term to be specified in any order made under section 2(1)(a) of this Act shall be such term as the court thinks fit except that the term shall not begin earlier than the date of the making of the application for the order and shall not extend beyond the death of either of the parties to the marriage.

(2) Where an order is made under the said section 2(1)(a) and the marriage of the parties affected by the order is subsequently dissolved or annulled but the order continues in force, the order shall, notwithstanding anything in it, cease to have effect on the remarriage of the party in whose favour it was made, except in relation to any arrears due under the order on the date of the remarriage.

[As amended by the Matrimonial and Family Proceedings Act 1984, ss9, 46(1), Schedule 1, para 21; Transfer of Functions (Magistrates' Courts and Family Law) Order 1992, art 3(2), Schedule 2.]

STATE IMMUNITY ACT 1978
(1978 c 33)

PART I

PROCEEDINGS IN UNITED KINGDOM BY OR AGAINST OTHER STATES

1 General immunity from jurisdiction

(1) A State is immune from the jurisdiction of the courts of the United Kingdom except as provided in the following provisions of this Part of this Act.

(2) A court shall give effect to the immunity conferred by this section even though the State does not appear in the proceedings in question.

2 Submission to jurisdiction

(1) A State is not immune as respects proceedings in respect of which it has submitted to the jurisdiction of the courts of the United Kingdom.

(2) A State may submit after the dispute giving rise to the proceedings has arisen or by a prior written agreement; but a provision in any agreement that it is to be governed by the law of the United Kingdom is not to be regarded as a submission.

(3) A State is deemed to have submitted –

(a) if it has instituted the proceedings; or
(b) subject to subsection (4) and (5) below, if it has intervened or taken any step in the proceedings.

(4) Subsection (3)(b) above does not apply to intervention or for any step taken for the purpose only of –

(a) claiming immunity; or
(b) asserting an interest in property in circumstances such that the State would have been entitled to immunity if the proceedings had been brought against it.

(5) Subsection (3)(b) above does not apply to any step taken by the State in ignorance of the facts entitling it to immunity if those facts could not reasonably have been ascertained and immunity is claimed as soon as reasonably practicable.

(6) A submission in respect of any proceedings extends to any appeal but not to any counter-claim unless it arises out of the same legal relationship or facts as the claim.

(7) The head of a State's diplomatic mission in the United Kingdom, or the person for the time being performing his functions, shall be deemed to have authority to submit on behalf of the State in respect of any proceedings; and any person who has entered into a contract on behalf of and with the authority of a State shall be deemed to have authority to submit on its behalf in respect of proceedings arising out of the contract.

3 Commercial transactions and contracts to be performed in United Kingdom

(1) A State is not immune as respects proceedings relating to –

(a) a commercial transaction entered into by the State; or
(b) an obligation of the State which by virtue of a contract (whether a commercial transaction or not) falls to be performed wholly or partly in the United Kingdom.

(2) This section does not apply if the parties to the dispute are States or have

otherwise agreed in writing; and subsection (1)(b) above does not apply if the contract (not being a commercial transaction) was made in the territory of the State concerned and the obligation in question is governed by its administrative law.

(3) In this section 'commercial transaction' means –

(a) any contract for the supply of goods or services;
(b) any loan or other transaction for the provision of finance and any guarantee or indemnity in respect of any such transaction or of any other financial obligation; and
(c) any other transaction or activity (whether of a commercial, industrial, financial, professional or other similar character) into which a State enters or in which it engages otherwise than in the exercise of sovereign authority;

but neither paragraph of subsection (1) above applies to a contract of employment between a State and an individual.

4 Contracts of employment [782]

(1) A State is not immune as respects proceedings relating to a contract of employment between the State and an individual where the contract was made in the United Kingdom or the work is to be wholly or partly performed there.

(2) Subject to subsections (3) and (4) below, this section does not apply if –

(a) at the time when the proceedings are brought the individual is a national of the State concerned; or
(b) at the time when the contract was made the individual was neither a national of the United Kingdom nor habitually resident there; or
(c) the parties to the contract have otherwise agreed in writing.

(3) Where the work is for an office, agency or establishment maintained by the State in the United Kingdom for commercial purposes, subsection (2)(a) and (b) above do not exclude the application of this section unless the individual was, at the time when the contract was made, habitually resident in that State.

(4) Subsection (2)(c) above does not exclude the application of this section where the law of the United Kingdom requires the proceedings to be brought before a court of the United Kingdom.

(5) In subsection (2)(b) above 'national of the United Kingdom' means:

(a) a British citizen, a British Dependent Territories citizen, a British National (Overseas) or a British Overseas citizen; or
(b) a person who under the British Nationality Act 1981 is a British subject; or
(c) a British protected person (within the meaning of that Act).

(6) In this section 'proceedings relating to a contract of employment' includes proceedings between the parties to such a contract in respect of any statutory rights or duties to which they are entitled or subject as employer or employee.

5 Personal injuries and damage to property [783]

A State is not immune as respects proceedings in respect of –

(a) death or personal injury; or
(b) damage to or loss of tangible property,

caused by an act or omission in the United Kingdom.

6 Ownership, possession and use of property [784]

(1) A State is not immune as respects proceedings relating to –

(a) any interest of the State in, or its possession or use of, immovable property in the United Kingdom; or

(b) any obligation of the State arising out of its interest in, or its possession or use of, any such property.

(2) A State is not immune as respects proceedings relating to any interest of the State in movable or immovable property, being an interest arising by way of succession, gift or bona vacantia.

(3) The fact that a State has or claims an interest in any property shall not preclude any court from exercising in respect of it any jurisdiction relating to the estates of deceased persons or persons of unsound mind or to insolvency, the winding up of companies or the administration of trusts.

(4) A court may entertain proceedings against a person other than a State notwithstanding that the proceedings relate to property –

(a) which is in the possession of a State; or

(b) in which a State claims an interest,

if the State would not have been immune had the proceedings been brought against it or, in a case within paragraph (b) above, if the claim is neither admitted nor supported by prima facie evidence.

7 Patents, trade-marks, etc

A State is not immune as respects proceedings relating to –

(a) any patent, trade-mark, design or plant breeders' rights belonging to the State and registered or protected in the United Kingdom or for which the State has applied in the United Kingdom;

(b) an alleged infringement by the State in the United Kingdom of any patent, trade-mark, design, plant breeders' rights or copyright; or

(c) the right to use a trade or business name in the United Kingdom.

8 Membership of bodies corporate, etc

(1) A State is not immune as respects proceedings relating to its membership of a body corporate, an unincorporated body or a partnership which –

(a) has members other than States; and

(b) is incorporated or constituted under the law of the United Kingdom or is controlled from or has its principal place of business in the United Kingdom,

being proceedings arising between the State and the body or its other members or, as the case may be, between the State and the other partners.

(2) This section does not apply if provision to the contrary has been made by an agreement in writing between the parties to the dispute or by the constitution or other instrument establishing or regulating the body or partnership in question.

9 Arbitrations

(1) Where a State has agreed in writing to submit a dispute which has arisen, or may arise, to arbitration, the State is not immune as respects proceedings in the courts of the United Kingdom which relate to the arbitration.

(2) This section has the effect subject to any contrary provision in the arbitration agreement and does not apply to any arbitration agreement between States.

10 Ships used for commercial purposes [788]

(1) This section applies to –

(a) Admiralty proceedings; and
(b) proceedings on any claim which could be made the subject of Admiralty proceedings.

(2) A State is not immune as respects –

(a) an action in rem against a ship belonging to that State; or
(b) an action in personam for enforcing a claim in connection with such a ship,

if, at the time when the cause of action arose, the ship was in use or intended for use for commercial purposes.

(3) Where an action in rem is brought against a ship belonging to a State for enforcing a claim in connection with another ship belonging to that State, subsection (2)(a) above does not apply as respects the first-mentioned ship unless, at the time when the cause of action relating to the other ship arose, both ships were in use or intended for use for commercial purposes.

(4) A State is not immune as respects –

(a) an action in rem against a cargo belonging to that State if both the cargo and the ship carrying it were, at the time when the cause of action arose, in use or intended for use for commercial purposes; or
(b) an action in personam for enforcing a claim in connection with such a cargo if the ship carrying it was then in use or intended for use as aforesaid.

(5) In the foregoing provisions references to a ship or cargo belonging to a State include references to a ship or cargo in its possession or control or in which it claims an interest; and, subject to subsection (4) above, subsection (2) above applies to property other than a ship as it applies to a ship.

(6) Sections 3 to 5 above do not apply to proceedings of the kind described in subsection (1) above if the State in question is a party to the Brussels Convention and the claim relates to the operation of a ship owned or operated by that State, the carriage of cargo or passengers on any such ship or the carriage of cargo owned by that State on any other ship.

14 States entitled to immunities and privileges [789]

(1) The immunities and privileges conferred by this Part of this Act apply to any foreign or commonwealth State other than the United Kingdom; and references to a State include references to –

(a) the sovereign or other head of that State in his public capacity;
(b) the government of that State; and
(c) any department of that government,

but not to any entity (hereafter referred to as a 'separate entity') which is distinct from the executive organs of the government of the State and capable of suing or being sued.

(2) A separate entity is immune from the jurisdiction of the courts of the United Kingdom if, and only if –

(a) the proceedings relate to anything done by it in the exercise of sovereign authority; and
(b) the circumstances are such that a State (or, in the case of proceedings to which section 10 above applies, a State which is not a party to the Brussels Convention) would have been so immune.

(3) If a separate entity (not being a State's central bank or other monetary authority) submits to the jurisdiction in respect of proceedings in the case of which it is entitled to immunity by virtue of subsection (2) above, subsections (1) to (4) of section 13 above shall apply to it in respect of those proceedings as if references to a State were references to that entity.

(4) Property of a State's central bank or their monetary authority shall not be regarded for the purposes of subsection (4) of section 13 above as in use or intended for use for commercial purposes; and where any such bank or authority is a separate entity subsections (1) to (3) of that section shall apply to it as if references to a State were references to the bank or authority.

(5) Section 12 above applies to proceedings against the constituent territories of a federal State; and Her Majesty may by Order in Council provide for the other provisions of this Part of this Act to apply to any such constituent territory specified in the Order as they apply to a State.

(6) Where the provisions of this Part of this Act do not apply to a constituent territory by virtue of any such Order subsections (2) and (3) above shall apply to it as if it were a separate entity.

15 Restriction and extension of immunities and privileges [790]

(1) If it appears to Her Majesty that the immunities and privileges conferred by this Part of this Act in relation to any State –

(a) exceed those accorded by the law of that State in relation to the United Kingdom; or
(b) are less than those required by any treaty, convention or other international agreement to which that State and the United Kingdom are parties,

Her Majesty may by Order in Council provide for restricting or, as the case may be, extending those immunities and privileges to such extent as appears to Her Majesty to be appropriate.

(2) Any statutory instrument containing an Order under this section shall be subject to annulment in pursuance of a resolution of either House of Parliament.

16 Excluded matters [791]

(1) This Part of this Act does not affect any immunity or privilege conferred by the Diplomatic Privileges Act 1964 or the Consular Regulations Act 1968; and –

(a) section 4 above does not apply to proceedings concerning the employment of the members of a mission within the meaning of the Convention scheduled to the said Act of 1964 or of the members of a consular post within the meaning of the Convention scheduled to the said Act of 1968;
(b) section 6(1) above does not apply to proceedings concerning a State's title to or its possession of property used for the purposes of a diplomatic mission.

(2) This Part of this Act does not apply to proceedings relating to anything done by or in relation to the armed forces of a State while present in the United Kingdom and, in particular, has effect subject to the Visiting Forces Act 1952.

(3) This Part of this Act does not apply to proceedings to which section 17(6) of the Nuclear Installations Act 1965 applies.

(4) This Part of this Act does not apply to criminal proceedings.

(5) This Part of this Act does not apply to any proceedings relating to taxation other than those mentioned in section 11 above.

17 Interpretation of Part I [792]

(1) In this Part of this Act –

'the Brussels Convention' means the International Convention for the Unification of Certain Rules Concerning the Immunity of State-owned Ships signed in Brussels on 10 April 1926;
'commercial purposes' means purposes of such transactions or activities as are mentioned in section 3(3) above;
'ship' includes hovercraft.

(2) In sections 2(2) and 13(3) above references to an agreement include references to a treaty, convention or other international agreement.

(3) For the purposes of sections 3 to 8 above the territory of the United Kingdom shall be deemed to include any dependent territory in respect of which the United Kingdom is a party to the European Convention on State Immunity.

(4) In sections 3(1), 4(1), 5 and 16(2) above references to the United Kingdom include references to its territorial waters and any area designated under section 1(7) of the Continental Shelf Act 1964. ...

PART II

JUDGMENTS AGAINST UNITED KINGDOM IN CONVENTION STATES

18 Recognition of judgments against United Kingdom [793]

(1) This section applies to any judgment given against the United Kingdom by a court in another State party to the European Convention on State Immunity, being a judgment –

(a) given in proceedings in which the United Kingdom was not entitled to immunity by virtue of provisions corresponding to those of sections 2 to 11 above; and
(b) which is final, that is to say, which is not or is no longer subject to appeal or, if given in default of appearance, liable to be set aside.

(2) Subject to section 19 below, a judgment to which this section applies shall be recognised in any court in the United Kingdom as conclusive between the parties thereto in all proceedings founded on the same cause of action and may be relied on by way of defence or counterclaim in such proceedings.

(3) Subsection (2) above (but not section 19 below) shall have effect also in relation to any settlement entered into by the United Kingdom before a court in another State party to the Convention which under the law of that State is treated as equivalent to a judgment.

(4) In this section references to a court in a State party to the Convention include references to a court in any territory in respect of which it is a party.

19 Exceptions to recognition [794]

(1) A court need not give effect to section 18 above in the case of a judgment –

(a) if to do so would be manifestly contrary to public policy or if any party to the proceedings in which the judgment was given had no adequate opportunity to present his case; or
(b) if the judgment was given without provisions corresponding to those of section 12 above having been complied with and the United Kingdom has not entered an appearance or applied to have the judgment set aside.

(2) A court need not give effect to section 18 above in the case of a judgment –

(a) if proceedings between the same parties, based on the same facts and having the same purpose –

(i) are pending before a court in the United Kingdom and were the first to be instituted; or

(ii) are pending before a court in another State party to the Convention, were the first to be instituted and may result in a judgment to which that section will apply; or

(b) if the result of the judgment is inconsistent with the result of another judgment given in proceedings between the same parties and –

(i) the other judgment is by a court in the United Kingdom and either those proceedings were the first to be instituted or the judgment of that court was given before the first-mentioned judgment became final within the meaning of subsection (1)(b) of section 18 above; or

(ii) the other judgment is by a court in another State party to the Convention and that section has already become applicable to it.

(3) Where the judgment was given against the United Kingdom in proceedings in respect of which the United Kingdom was not entitled to immunity by virtue of a provision corresponding to section 6(2) above, a court need not give effect to section 18 above in respect of the judgment if the court that gave the judgment –

(a) would not have had jurisdiction in the matter if it had applied rules of jurisdiction corresponding to those applicable to such matters in the United Kingdom; or

(b) applied a law other than that indicated by the United Kingdom rules of private international law and would have reached a different conclusion if it had applied the law so indicated.

(4) In subsection (2) above references to a court in the United kingdom include references to a court in any dependent territory in respect of which the United Kingdom is a party to the Convention, and references to a court in another State party to the Convention include references to a court in any territory in respect of which it is a party.

PART III

MISCELLANEOUS AND SUPPLEMENTARY

20 Heads of State

(1) Subject to the provisions of this section and to any necessary modifications, the Diplomatic Privileges Act 1964 shall apply to –

(a) a sovereign or other head of State;
(b) members of his family forming part of his household; and
(c) his private servants,

as it applies to the head of a diplomatic mission, to members of his family forming part of his household and to his private servants.

(2) The immunities and privileges conferred by virtue of subsection (1)(a) and (b) above shall not be subject to the restrictions by reference to nationality or residence mentioned in Article 37(1) or 38 in Schedule 1 to the said Act of 1964.

(3) Subject to any direction to the contrary by the Secretary of State, a person on whom immunities and privileges are conferred by virtue of subsection (1) above

shall be entitled to the exemption conferred by section 8(3) of the Immigration Act 1971.

(4) Except as respects value added tax and duties of customs or excise, this section does not affect any question whether a person is exempt from, or immune as respects proceedings relating to, taxation.

(5) This section applies to the sovereign or other head of any State on which immunities and privileges are conferred by Part I of this Act and is without prejudice to the application of that Part to any such sovereign or head of State in his public capacity.

21 Evidence by certificate [796]

A certificate by or on behalf of the Secretary of State shall be conclusive evidence on any question –

(a) whether any country is a State for the purposes of Part I of this Act, whether any territory is a constituent territory of a federal State for those purposes or as to the person or persons to be regarded for those purposes as the head or government of a State;
(b) whether a State is a party to the Brussels Convention mentioned in Part I of this Act;
(c) whether a State is a party to the European Convention on State Immunity, whether it has made a declaration under Article 24 of that Convention or as to the territories in respect of which the United Kingdom or any other State is a party;
(d) whether, and if so when, a document has been served or received as mentioned in section 12(1) or (5) above.

22 General interpretation [797]

(1) In this Act 'court' includes any tribunal or body exercising judicial functions; and references to the courts or law of the United Kingdom include references to the courts or law of any part of the United Kingdom.

(2) In this Act references to entry of appearance and judgments in default of appearance include references to any corresponding procedures.

(3) In this Act 'the European Convention on State Immunity' means the Convention of that name signed in Basle on 16 May 1972.

(4) In this Act 'dependent territory' means –

(a) any of the Channel Islands;
(b) the Isle of Man;
(c) any colony other than one for whose external relations a country other than the United Kingdom is responsible; or
(d) any country or territory outside Her Majesty's dominions in which Her Majesty has jurisdiction in right of the government of the United Kingdom.

(5) Any powers conferred by this Act to make an Order in Council includes power to vary or revoke a previous order.

[As amended by the British Nationality Act 1981, s52(6), Schedule 7; Hong Kong (British Nationality) Order 1986, art 8, Schedule 1.]

ARBITRATION ACT 1979
(1979 c 42)

1 Judicial review of arbitration awards

(1) In the Arbitration Act 1950 (in this Act referred to as 'the principal Act') section 21 (statement of case for a decision of the High Court) shall cease to have effect and, without prejudice to the right of appeal conferred by subsection (2) below, the High Court shall not have jurisdiction to set aside or remit an award on an arbitration agreement on the ground of errors of fact or law on the face of the award.

(2) Subject to subsection (3) below, an appeal shall lie to the High Court on any question of law arising out of an award made on an arbitration agreement; and on the determination of such an appeal the High Court may by order –

(a) confirm, vary or set aside the award; or
(b) remit the award to the reconsideration of the arbitrator or umpire together with the court's opinion on the question of law which was the subject of the appeal;

and where the award is remitted under paragraph (b) above the arbitrator or umpire shall, unless the order otherwise directs, make his award within three months after the date of the order.

(3) An appeal under this section may be brought by any of the parties to the reference –

(a) with the consent of all the other parties to the reference; or
(b) subject to section 3 below, with the leave of the court.

(4) The High Court shall not grant leave under subsection (3)(b) above unless it considers that, having regard to all the circumstances, the determination of the question of law concerned could substantially affect the rights of one or more of the parties to the arbitration agreement; and the court may make any leave which it gives conditional upon the applicant complying with such conditions as it considers appropriate.

(5) Subject to subsection (6) below, if an award is made and, on an application made by any of the parties to the reference, –

(a) with the consent of all the other parties to the reference, or
(b) subject to section 3 below, with the leave of the court,

it appears to the High Court that the award does not or does not sufficiently set out the reasons for the award, the court may order the arbitrator or umpire concerned to state the reasons for his award in sufficient detail to enable the court, should an appeal be brought under this section, to consider any question of law arising out of the award.

(6) In any case where an award is made without any reason being given, the High Court shall not make an order under subsection (5) above unless it is satisfied –

(a) that before the award was made one of the parties to the reference gave notice to the arbitrator or umpire concerned that a reasoned award would be required; or
(b) that there is some special reason why such a notice was not given.

(6A) Unless the High Court gives leave, no appeal shall lie to the Court of Appeal from a decision of the High Court:

(a) to grant or refuse leave under subsection (3)(b) or (5)(b) above; or
(b) to make or not to make an order under subsection (5) above.

(7) No appeal shall lie to the Court of Appeal from a decision of the High Court on an appeal under this section unless –

(a) the High Court or the Court of Appeal gives leave; and
(b) it is certified by the High Court that the question of law to which its decision relates either is one of general public importance or is one which for some other special reason should be considered by the Court of Appeal.

(8) Where the award of an arbiter or umpire is varied on appeal, the award as varied shall have effect (except for the purposes of this section) as if it were the award of the arbitrator or umpire.

2 Determination of preliminary point of law by court [799]

(1) Subject to subsection (2) and section 3 below, on an application to the High Court made by any of the parties to a reference –

(a) with the consent of an arbitrator who has entered on the reference or, if an umpire has entered on the reference, with his consent, or
(b) with the consent of all the other parties,

the High Court shall have jurisdiction to determine any question of law arising in the course of the reference.

(2) The High Court shall not entertain an application under subsection (1)(a) above with respect to any question of law unless it is satisfied that –

(a) the determination of the application might produce substantial savings in costs to the parties; and
(b) the question of law is one in respect of which leave to appeal would be likely to be given under section 1(3)(b) above.

(2A) Unless the High Court gives leave, no appeal shall lie to the Court of Appeal from a decision of the High Court to entertain or not to entertain an application under subsection (1)(a) above.

(3) A decision of the High Court under subsection (1) above shall be deemed to be a judgment of the court within the meaning of section 16 of the Supreme Court Act 1981 (appeals to the Court of Appeal), but no appeal shall lie from such a decision unless –

(a) the High Court or the Court of Appeal gives leave; and
(b) it is certified by the High Court that the question of law to which its decision relates either is one of general public importance or is one which for some other special reason should be considered by the Court of Appeal.

3 Exclusion agreements affecting rights under ss1 and 2 [800]

(1) Subject to the following provisions of this section and section 4 below –

(a) the High Court shall not, under section 1(3)(b) above, grant leave to appeal with respect to a question of law arising out of an award, and
(b) the High Court shall not, under section 1(5)(b) above, grant leave to make an application with respect to an award, and
(c) no application may be made under section 2(1)(a) above with respect to a question of law,

if the parties to the reference in question have entered into an agreement in writing (in this section referred to as an 'exclusion agreement') which excludes the right of appeal under section 1 above in relation to that award or, in a case falling within paragraph (c) above, in relation to an award to which the determination of the question of law is material.

(2) An exclusion agreement may be expressed so as to relate to a particular award, to awards under a particular reference or to any other description of awards, whether arising out of the same reference or not; and an agreement may be an exclusion agreement for the purposes of this section whether it is entered into before or after the passing of this Act and whether or not it forms part of an arbitration agreement.

(3) In any case where –

(a) an arbitration agreement, other than a domestic arbitration agreement, provides for disputes between the parties to be referred to arbitration, and
(b) a dispute to which the agreement relates involves the question whether a party has been guilty of fraud, and
(c) the parties have entered into an exclusion agreement which is applicable to any award made on the reference of that dispute,

then, except in so far as the exclusion agreement otherwise provides, the High Court shall not exercise its powers under section 24(2) of the principal Act (to take steps necessary to enable the question to be determined by the High Court) in relation to that dispute.

(4) Except as provided by subsection (1) above, sections 1 and 2 above shall have effect notwithstanding anything in any agreement purporting –

(a) to prohibit or restrict access to the High Court; or
(b) to restrict the jurisdiction of that court; or
(c) to prohibit or restrict the making of a reasoned award.

(5) An exclusion agreement shall be of no effect in relation to an award made on, or a question of law arising in the course of a reference under, a statutory arbitration, that is to say, such an arbitration as is referred to in subsection (1) of section 31 of the principal Act.

(6) An exclusion agreement shall be of no effect in relation to an award made on, or a question of law arising in the course of a reference under, an arbitration agreement which is a domestic arbitration agreement unless the exclusion agreement is entered into after the commencement of the arbitration in which the award is made or, as the case may be, in which the question of law arises.

(7) In this section 'domestic arbitration agreement' means an arbitration agreement which does not provide, expressly or by implication, for arbitration in a State other than the United Kingdom and to which neither –

(a) an individual who is a national of, or habitually resident in, any State other than the United Kingdom, nor
(b) a body corporate which is incorporated in, or whose central management and control is exercised in, any State other than the United Kingdom,

is a party at the time the arbitration agreement is entered into.

4 Exclusion agreements not to apply in certain cases [801]

(1) Subject to subsection (3) below, if an arbitration award or a question of law arising in the course of a reference relates, in whole or in part, to –

(a) a question or claim falling within the Admiralty jurisdiction of the High Court, or
(b) a dispute arising out of a contract of insurance, or
(c) a dispute arising out of a commodity contract,

an exclusion agreement shall have no effect in relation to the award or question unless either –

(i) the exclusion agreement is entered into after the commencement of the arbitration in which the award is made or, as the case may be, in which the question of law arises, or

(ii) the award or question relates to a contract which is expressed to be governed by a law other than the law of England and Wales.

(2) In subsection (1)(c) above 'commodity contract' means a contract –

(a) for the sale of goods regularly dealt with on a commodity market or exchange in England or Wales which is specified for the purposes of this section by an order made by the Secretary of State; and
(b) of a description so specified.

(3) The Secretary of State may by order provide that subsection (1) above –

(a) shall cease to have effect; or
(b) subject to such conditions as may be specified in the order, shall not apply to any exclusion agreement made in relation to an arbitration award of a description so specified;

and an order under this subsection may contain such supplementary, incidental and transitional provisions as appear to the Secretary of State to be necessary or expedient.

(4) The power to make an order under subsection (2) or subsection (3) above shall be exercisable by statutory instrument which shall be subject to annulment in pursuance of a resolution of either House of Parliament.

(5) In this section 'exclusion agreement' has the same meaning as in section 3 above.

5 Interlocutory orders [802]

(1) If any party to a reference under an arbitration agreement fails within the time specified in the order or, if no time is so specified, within a reasonable time to comply with an order made by the arbitrator or umpire in the course of the reference, then, on the application of the arbitrator or umpire or of any party to the reference, the High Court may make an order extending the powers of the arbitrator or umpire as mentioned in subsection (2) below.

(2) If an order is made by the High Court under this section, the arbitrator or umpire shall have power, to the extent and subject to any conditions specified in that order, to continue with the reference in default of appearance or of any other act by one of the parties in like manner as a judge of the High Court might continue with proceedings in that court where a party fails to comply with an order of that court or a requirement of rules of court.

(3) Section 4(5) of the Administration of Justice Act 1970 (jurisdiction of the High Court to be exercisable by the Court of Appeal in relation to judge-arbitrators and judge-umpires) shall not apply in relation to the power of the High Court to make an order under this section, but in the case of a reference to a judge-arbitrator or judge-umpire that power shall be exercisable as in the case of other reference to arbitration and also by the judge-arbitrator or judge-umpire himself.

(4) Anything done by a judge-arbitrator or judge-umpire in the exercise of the power conferred by subsection (3) above shall be done by him in his capacity as judge of the High Court and have effect as if done by that court.

(5) The preceding provisions of this section have effect notwithstanding anything in any agreement but do not derogate from any powers conferred on an arbitrator or umpire, whether by an arbitration agreement or otherwise.

(6) In this section 'judge-arbitrator' and 'judge-umpire' have the same meaning as in Schedule 3 to the Administration of Justice Act 1970.

7 Application and interpretation of certain provisions of Part I of principal Act

(1) References in the following provisions of Part I of the principal Act to that Part of that Act shall have effect as if the preceding provisions of this Act were included in that Part, namely –

(a) section 14 (interim awards);
(b) section 28 (terms as to costs of orders);
(c) section 30 (Crown to be bound);
(d) section 31 (application to statutory arbitration); and
(e) section 32 (meaning of 'arbitration agreement').

(2) Subsections (2) and (3) of section 29 of the principal Act shall apply to determine when an arbitration is deemed to be commenced for the purposes of this Act.

(3) For the avoidance of doubt, it is hereby declared that the reference in subsection (1) of section 31 of the principal Act (statutory arbitrations) to arbitration under any other Act does not extend to arbitration under section 64 of the County Courts Act 1984 (cases in which proceedings are to be or may be referred to arbitration) and accordingly nothing in this Act or in Part I of the principal Act applies to arbitration under the said section 64.

[As amended by the Supreme Court Act 1981, s148(2), (3), (4), 152(1), Schedule 5; County Courts Act 1984, s148(1), Schedule 2, para 70.]

PROTECTION OF TRADING INTERESTS ACT 1980
(1980 c 11)

1 Overseas measures affecting United Kingdom trading interests

(1) If it appears to the Secretary of State –

(a) that measures have been or are proposed to be taken by or under the law of any overseas country for regulating or controlling international trade; and
(b) that those measures, in so far as they apply or would apply to things done or to be done outside the territorial jurisdiction of that country by persons carrying on business in the United Kingdom, are damaging or threaten to damage the trading interests of the United Kingdom,

the Secretary of State may by order direct that this section shall apply to those measures either generally or in their applications to such cases as may be specified in the order.

(2) The Secretary of State may by order make provision for requiring, or enabling the Secretary of State to require, a person in the United Kingdom who carries on business there to give notice to the Secretary of State of any requirement or prohibition imposed or threatened to be imposed on that person pursuant to any measures in so far as this section applies to them by virtue of an order under subsection (1) above.

(3) The Secretary of State may give to any person in the United Kingdom who carries on business there such directions for prohibiting compliance with any such requirement or prohibition as aforesaid as he considers appropriate for avoiding damage to the trading interests of the United Kingdom.

(4) The power of the Secretary of State to make orders under subsection (1) or (2) above shall be exercisable by statutory instrument subject to annulment in pursuance of a resolution of either House of Parliament.

(5) Directions under subsection (3) above may be either general or special and may prohibit compliance with any requirement or prohibition either absolutely or in such cases or subject to such conditions as to consent or otherwise as may be specified in the directions; and general directions under that subsection shall be published in such manner as appears to the Secretary of State to be appropriate.

(6) In this section 'trade' includes any activity carried on in the course of a business of any description and 'trading interests' shall be construed accordingly.

2 Documents and information required by overseas courts and authorities [805]

(1) If it appears to the Secretary of State –

(a) that a requirement has been or may be imposed on a person or persons in the United Kingdom to produce to any court, tribunal or authority of an overseas country any commercial document which is not within the territorial jurisdiction of that country or to furnish any commercial information to any such court, tribunal or authority; or

(b) that any such authority has imposed or may impose a requirement on a person or persons in the United Kingdom to publish any such document or information,

the Secretary of State may, if it appears to him that the requirement is inadmissible by virtue of subsection (2) or (3) below, give directions for prohibiting compliance with the requirement.

(2) A requirement such as is mentioned in subsection (1)(a) or (b) above is inadmissible –

(a) if it infringes the jurisdiction of the United Kingdom or is otherwise prejudicial to the sovereignty of the United Kingdom; or

(b) if compliance with the requirement would be prejudicial to the security of the United Kingdom or to the relations of the government of the United Kingdom with the government of any other country.

(3) A requirement such as is mentioned in subsection (1)(a) above is also inadmissible –

(a) if it is made otherwise than for the purposes of civil or criminal proceedings which have been instituted in the overseas country; or

(b) if it requires a person to state what documents relevant to any such proceedings are or have been in his possession, custody or power or to produce for the purposes of any such proceedings any documents other than particular documents specified in the requirement.

(4) Directions under subsection (1) above may be either general or special and may prohibit compliance with any requirement either absolutely or in such cases or subject to such conditions as to consent or otherwise as may be specified in the directions; and general directions under that subsection shall be published in such manner as appears to the Secretary of State to be appropriate.

(5) For the purposes of this section the making of a request or demand shall be treated as the imposition of a requirement if it is made in circumstances in which a requirement to the same effect could be or could have been imposed; and

(a) any request or demand for the supply of a document or information which, pursuant to the requirement of any court, tribunal or authority of an overseas country, is addressed to a person in the United Kingdom; or

(b) any requirement imposed by such a court, tribunal or authority to produce or furnish any document or information to a person specified in the requirement, shall be treated as a requirement to produce or furnish that document or information to that court, tribunal or authority.

(6) In this section 'commercial document' and 'commercial information' mean respectively a document or information relating to a business of any description and 'document' includes any record or device by means of which material is recorded or stored.

3 Offences under ss1 and 2 [806]

(1) Subject to subsection (2) below, any person who without reasonable excuse fails to comply with any requirement imposed under subsection (2) of section 1 above or knowingly contravenes any directions given under subsection (3) of that section or section 2(1) above shall be guilty of an offence and liable –

    (a) on conviction on indictment, to a fine;
    (b) on summary conviction, to a fine not exceeding the statutory maximum.

(2) A person who is neither a citizen of the United Kingdom and Colonies nor a body corporate incorporated in the United Kingdom shall not be guilty of an offence under subsection (1) above by reason of anything done or omitted outside the United Kingdom in contravention of directions under section 1(3) or 2(1) above.

(3) No proceedings for an offence under subsection (1) above shall be instituted in England, Wales or Northern Ireland except by the Secretary of State or with the consent of the Attorney General or, as the case may be, the Attorney General for Northern Ireland.

(4) Proceedings against any person for an offence under this section may be taken before the appropriate court in the United Kingdom having jurisdiction in the place where that person is for the time being.

4 Restriction of Evidence (Proceedings in Other [807] Jurisdictions) Act 1975

A court in the United Kingdom shall not make an order under section 2 of the Evidence (Proceedings in Other Jurisdictions) Act 1975 for giving effect to a request issued by or on behalf of a court or tribunal of an overseas country if it is shown that the request infringes the jurisdiction of the United Kingdom or is otherwise prejudicial to the sovereignty of the United Kingdom; and a certificate signed by or on behalf of the Secretary of State to the effect that it infringes that jurisdiction or is so prejudicial shall be conclusive evidence of that fact.

5 Restriction on enforcement of certain overseas judgments [808]

(1) A judgment to which this section applies shall not be registered under Part II of the Administration of Justice Act 1920 or Part I of the Foreign Judgments (Reciprocal Enforcement) Act 1933 and no court in the United Kingdom shall entertain proceedings at common law for the recovery of any sum payable under such a judgment.

(2) This section applies to any judgment given by a court of an overseas country, being –

    (a) a judgment for multiple damages within the meaning of subsection (3) below;
    (b) a judgment based on a provision or rule of law specified or described in an order under subsection (4) below and given after the coming into force of the order; or

(c) a judgment on a claim for contribution in respect of damages awarded by a judgment falling within paragraph (a) or (b) above.

(3) In subsection (2)(a) above a judgment for multiple damages means a judgment for an amount arrived at by doubling, trebling or otherwise multiplying a sum assessed as compensation for the loss or damage sustained by the person in whose favour the judgment is given.

(4) The Secretary of State may for the purposes of subsection (2)(b) above make an order in respect of any provision or rule of law which appears to him to be concerned with the prohibition or regulation of agreements, arrangements or practices designed to restrain, distort or restrict competition in the carrying on of business of any description or to be otherwise concerned with the promotion of such competition as aforesaid.

(5) The power of the Secretary of State to make orders under subsection (4) above shall be exercisable by statutory instrument subject to annulment in pursuance of a resolution of either House of Parliament.

(6) Subsection (2)(a) above applies to a judgment given before the date of the passing of this Act as well as to a judgment given on or after that date but this section does not affect any judgment which has been registered before that date under the provisions mentioned in subsection (1) above or in respect of which such proceedings as are there mentioned have been finally determined before that date.

6 Recovery of awards of multiple damages [809]

(1) This section applies where a court of an overseas country has given a judgment for multiple damages within the meaning of section 5(3) above against –

(a) a citizen of the United Kingdom and Colonies; or
(b) a body corporate incorporated in the United Kingdom or in a territory outside the United Kingdom for whose international relations Her Majesty's Government in the United Kingdom are responsible; or
(c) a person carrying on business in the United Kingdom (in this section referred to as a 'qualifying defendant') and an amount on account of the damages has been paid by the qualifying defendant either to the party in whose favour the judgment was given or to another party who is entitled as against the qualifying defendant to contribution in respect of the damages.

(2) Subject to subsection (3) and (4) below, the qualifying defendant shall be entitled to recover from the party in whose favour the judgment was given so much of the amount referred to in subsection (1) above as exceeds the part attributable to compensation; and that part shall be taken to be such part of the amount as bears to the whole of it the same proportion as the sum assessed by the court that gave the judgment as compensation for the loss or damage sustained by that party bears to the whole of the damages awarded to that party.

(3) Subsection (2) above does not apply where the qualifying defendant is an individual who was ordinarily resident in the overseas country at the time when the proceedings in which the judgment was given were instituted or a body corporate which had its principal place of business there at that time.

(4) Subsection (2) above does not apply where the qualifying defendant carried on business in the overseas country and the proceedings in which the judgment was given were concerned with activities exclusively carried on in that country.

(5) A court in the United Kingdom may entertain proceedings on a claim under this section notwithstanding that the person against whom the proceedings are brought is not within the jurisdiction of the court.

(6) The reference in subsection (1) above to an amount paid by the qualifying defendant includes a reference to an amount obtained by execution against his property or against the property of a company which (directly or indirectly) is wholly owned by him; and references in that subsection and subsection (2) above to the party in whose favour the judgment was given or to a party entitled to contribution include references to any person in whom the rights of any such party have become vested by succession or assignment or otherwise.

(7) This section shall, with the necessary modifications, apply also in relation to any order which is made by a tribunal or authority of an overseas country and would, if that tribunal or authority were a court, be a judgment for multiple damages within the meaning of section 5(3) above.

(8) This section does not apply to any judgment given or order made before the passing of this Act.

7 Enforcement of overseas judgment under provision corresponding to s6 [810]

(1) If it appears to Her Majesty that the law of an overseas country provides or will provide for the enforcement in that country of judgments given under section 6 above, Her Majesty may by Order in Council provide for the enforcement in the United Kingdom of judgments of any description specified in the Order which are given under any provision of the law of that country relating to the recovery of sums paid or obtained pursuant to a judgment for multiple damages within the meaning of section 5(3) above, whether or not that provision corresponds to section 6 above.

(1A) Such an Order in Council may, as respects judgments to which it relates –

(a) make different provisions for different descriptions of judgment; and
(b) impose conditions or restrictions on the enforcement of judgments of any description.

(2) An Order under this section may apply, with or without modification, any of the provisions of the Foreign Judgments (Reciprocal Enforcement) Act 1933.

8 Short title, interpretation, repeals and extent ... [811]

(2) In this Act 'overseas country' means any country or territory outside the United Kingdom other than one for whose international relations Her Majesty's Government in the United Kingdom are responsible.

(3) References in this Act to the law or a court, tribunal or authority of an overseas country include, in the case of a federal state, references to the law or a court, tribunal or authority of any constituent part of that country.

(4) References in this Act to a claim for, or to entitlement to, contribution are references to a claim or entitlement based on an enactment or rule of law. ...

(8) Her Majesty may by Order in Council direct that this Act shall extend with such exceptions, adaptations and modifications, if any, as may be specified in the Order to any territory outside the United Kingdom, being a territory for the international relations of which Her Majesty's Government in the United Kingdom are responsible.

[As amended by the Shipping Contracts and Commercial Documents Act 1964; Magistrates' Courts Act 1980, s154(3), Schedule 9; Civil Jurisdiction and Judgments Act 1982, s38; Statute Law (Repeals) Act 1993, s1(1), Schedule 1, Pt XIV.]

MAGISTRATES' COURTS ACT 1980
(1980 c 43)

59 Orders for periodical payment: means of payment [812]

(1) In any case where a magistrates' court orders money to be paid periodically by one person (in this section referred to as 'the debtor') to another (in this section referred to as 'the creditor'), then –

(a) if the order is a qualifying maintenance order, the court shall at the same time exercise one of its powers under paragraphs (a) to (d) of subsection (3) below;
(b) if the order is not a maintenance order, the court shall at the same time exercise one of its powers under paragraphs (a) and (b) of that subsection.

(2) For the purposes of this section a maintenance order is a 'qualifying maintenance order' if, at the time it is made, the debtor is ordinarily resident in England and Wales.

(3) The powers of the court are –

(a) the power to order that payments under the order be made directly by the debtor to the creditor;
(b) the power to order that payments under the order be made to the clerk of the court or to the clerk of any other magistrates' court;
(c) the power to order that payments under the order be made by the debtor to the creditor by such method of payment falling within subsection (6) below as may be specified;
(cc) the power to order that payments under the order be made in accordance with arrangements made by the Secretary of State for their collection;
(d) the power to make an attachment of earnings order under the Attachment of Earnings Act 1971 to secure payments under the order.

(3A) No order made by a magistrates' court under paragraphs (a) to (d) of subsection (3) above (other than one made under paragraph (cc)) shall have effect at any time when the Secretary of State is arranging for the collection of payments under the qualifying maintenance order concerned.

(4) In any case where –

(a) the court proposes to exercise its power under paragraph (c) of subsection (3) above, and
(b) having given the debtor an opportunity of opening an account from which payment under the order may be made in accordance with the method of payment proposed to be ordered under that paragraph, the court is satisfied that the debtor has failed, without reasonable excuse, to open such an account,

the court in exercising its power under that paragraph may order that the debtor open such an account.

(5) In deciding, in the case of a maintenance order, which of the powers under paragraphs (a) to (d) of subsection (3) above (other than paragraph (cc)) it is to exercise, the court having (if practicable) given them an opportunity to make representations shall have regard to any representations made –

(a) by the debtor,
(b) by the creditor, and
(c) if the person who applied for the maintenance order is a person other than the creditor, by that other person.

(6) The methods of payment referred to in subsection (3)(c) above are the following, that is to say –

(a) payment by standing order; or

(b) payment by any other method which requires one person to give his authority for payments of a specific amount to be made from an account of his to an account of another's on specific dates during the period for which the authority is in force and without the need for any further authority from him.

(7) Where the maintenance order is an order –

(a) under the Guardianship of Minors Act 1971 and 1973,

(b) under Part I of the Domestic Proceedings and Magistrates' Courts Act 1978, or

(c) under, or having effect as if made under, Schedule 1 to the Children Act 1989,

and the court does not propose to exercise its power under paragraph (c), (cc) or (d) of subsection (3) above, the court shall, unless upon representations expressly made in that behalf by the person who applied for the maintenance order it is satisfied that it is undesirable to do so, exercise its power under paragraph (b) of that subsection.

(8) The Lord Chancellor may by regulations confer on magistrates' courts, in addition to their powers under paragraphs (a) to (d) of subsection (3) above, the power (the 'additional power') to order that payments under a qualifying maintenance order be made by the debtor to the creditor or the clerk of the magistrates' court (as the regulations may provide) by such method of payment as may be specified in the regulations.

(9) Any reference in any enactment to paragraphs (a) to (d) of subsection (3) above (but not a reference to any specific paragraph of that subsection) shall be taken to include a reference to the additional power, and the reference in subsection (10) below to the additional power shall be construed accordingly.

(10) Regulations under subsection (8) above may make provisions for any enactment concerning, or connected with, payments under maintenance orders to apply, with or without modifications, in relation to the additional power.

(11) The power of the Lord Chancellor to make regulations under subsection (8) above shall be exercisable by statutory instrument and any such statutory instrument shall be subject to annulment in pursuance of a resolution of either House of Parliament.

(12) For the purposes of this section –

(a) the reference in subsection (1) above to money paid periodically by one person to another includes, in the case of a maintenance order, a reference to a lump sum paid by instalments by one person to another; and

(b) references to arrangements made by the Secretary of State for the collection of payments are to arrangements made by him under section 30 of the Child Support Act 1991 and regulations made under that section.

60 Revocation, variation, etc of orders for periodical payment [813]

(1) Where a magistrates' court has made an order for money to be paid periodically by one person to another, the court may, by order on complaint, revoke, revive or vary the order.

(2) The power under subsection (1) above to vary an order shall include power to suspend the operation of any provision of the order temporarily and to revive the operation of any provision so suspended.

(3) Where the order mentioned in subsection (1) above is a maintenance order, the power under that subsection to vary the order shall include power, if the court

is satisfied that payment has not been made in accordance with the order, to exercise one of its powers under paragraphs (a) to (d) of section 59(3) above.

(4) In any case where –

(a) a magistrates' court has made a maintenance order, and
(b) payments under the order are required to be made by any method of payment falling within section 59(6) above,

an interested party may apply in writing to the clerk of the court for the order to be varied as mentioned in subsection (5) below.

(5) Subject to subsection (8) below, where an application has been made under subsection (4) above, the clerk, after giving written notice (by post or otherwise) of the application to any other interested party and allowing that party, within the period of 14 days beginning with the date of the giving of that notice, an opportunity to make written representations, may vary the order to provide that payments under the order shall be made to the clerk.

(6) The clerk may proceed with an application under subsection (4) above notwithstanding that any such interested party as is referred to in subsection (5) above has not received written notice of the application.

(7) In subsections (4) to (6) above 'interested party', in relation to a maintenance order, means –

(a) the debtor;
(b) the creditor; and
(c) if the person who applied for the maintenance order is a person other than the creditor, that other person.

(8) Where an application has been made under subsection (4) above, the clerk may, if he considers it inappropriate to exercise his power under subsection (5) above, refer the matter to the court which may vary the order by exercising one of its powers under paragraphs (a) to (d) of section 59(3) above.

(9) Subsections (4), (5) and (7) of section 59 above shall apply for the purposes of subsections (3) and (8) above as they apply for the purpose of that section.

(10) None of the powers of the court, or of the clerk of the court, conferred by subsections (3) to (9) above shall be exercisable in relation to a maintenance order which is not a qualifying maintenance order (within the meaning of section 59 above).

(11) For the purposes of this section –

(a) 'creditor' and 'debtor' have the same meaning as they have in section 59 above; and
(b) the reference in subsection (1) above to money paid periodically by one person to another includes, in the case of a maintenance order, a reference to a lump sum paid by instalments by one person to another.

[As amended by the Maintenance Enforcement Act 1991, ss2, 4; Transfer of Functions (Magistrates' Courts and Family Law) Order 1992, art 3(2), Schedule 2; Child Support Act 1991 (Consequential Amendments) Order 1994, art 3(1)–(6).]

LIMITATION ACT 1980
(1980 c 58)

PART I

ORDINARY TIME LIMITS FOR DIFFERENT CLASSES OF ACTION

1 Time limits under Part I subject to extension or exclusion under Part II

(1) This Part of this Act gives the ordinary time limits for bringing actions of the various classes mentioned in the following provisions of this Part.

(2) The ordinary time limits given in this Part of this Act are subject to extension or exclusion in accordance with the provisions of Part II of this Act.

2 Time limit for actions founded on tort

An action founded on tort shall not be brought after the expiration of six years from the date on which the cause of action accrued.

3 Time limit in case of successive conversions and extinction of title of owner of converted goods

(1) Where any cause of action in respect of the conversion of a chattel has accrued to any person and, before he recovers possession of the chattel, a further conversion takes place, no action shall be brought in respect of the further conversion after the expiration of six years from the accrual of the cause of action in respect of the original conversion.

(2) Where any such cause of action has accrued to any person and the period prescribed for bringing that action has expired and he has not during that period recovered possession of the chattel, the title of that person to the chattel shall be extinguished.

4 Special time limit in case of theft

(1) The right of any person from whom a chattel is stolen to bring an action in respect of the theft shall not be subject to the time limits under sections 2 and 3(1) of this Act, but if his title to the chattel is extinguished under section 3(2) of this Act he may not bring an action in respect of a theft preceding the loss of his title, unless the theft in question preceded the conversion from which time began to run for the purposes of section 3(2).

(2) Subsection (1) above shall apply to any conversion related to the theft of a chattel as it applies to the theft of a chattel; and, except as provided below, every conversion following the theft of a chattel before the person from whom it is stolen recovers possession of it shall be regarded for the purposes of this section as related to the theft. If anyone purchases the stolen chattel in good faith neither the purchase nor any conversion following it shall be regarded as related to the theft.

(3) Any cause of action accruing in respect of the theft or any conversion related to the theft of a chattel to any person from whom the chattel is stolen shall be disregarded for the purpose of applying section 3(1) or (2) of this Act to his case.

(4) Where in any action brought in respect of the conversion of a chattel it is proved that the chattel was stolen from the plaintiff or anyone through whom he claims it shall be presumed that any conversion following the theft is related to the theft unless the contrary is shown.

(5) In this section 'theft' includes –

(a) any conduct outside England and Wales which would be theft if committed in England and Wales; and
(b) obtaining any chattel (in England and Wales or elsewhere) in the circumstances described in section 15(1) of the Theft Act 1968 (obtaining by deception) or by blackmail within the meaning of section 21 of that Act;

and references in this section to a chattel being 'stolen' shall be construed accordingly.

CIVIL JURISDICTION AND JUDGMENTS ACT 1982
(1982 c 27)

PART I

IMPLEMENTATION OF THE CONVENTIONS

1 Interpretation of references to the Conventions and Contracting States [818]

(1) In this Act –

'the 1968 Convention' means the Convention on jurisdiction and the enforcement of judgments in civil and commercial matters (including the Protocol annexed to that Convention), signed at Brussels in 27 September 1968;
'the 1971 Protocol' means the Protocol on the interpretation of the 1968 Convention by the European Court, signed at Luxembourg on 3 June 1971;
'the Accession Convention' means the Convention on the accession to the 1968 Convention and the 1971 Protocol of Denmark, the Republic of Ireland and the United Kingdom, signed at Luxembourg on 9 October 1978;
'the 1982 Accession Convention' means the Convention on the accession of the Hellenic Republic to the 1968 Convention and the 1971 Protocol, with the adjustments made to them by the Accession Convention, signed at Luxembourg on 25 October 1982;
'the 1989 Accession Convention' means the Convention on the accession of the Kingdom of Spain and the Portuguese Republic to the 1968 Convention and the 1971 Protocol, with the adjustments made to them by the Accession Convention and the 1982 Accession Convention, signed at Donostia – San Sebastian on 26 May 1989;
'the Brussels Conventions' means the 1968 Convention, the 1971 Protocol, the Accession Convention, the 1982 Accession Convention and the 1989 Accession Convention;
'the Lugano Convention' means the Convention on jurisdiction and the enforcement of judgments in civil and commercial matters (including the Protocols annexed to that Convention) opened for signature at Lugano on 16 September 1988 and signed by the United Kingdom on 18 September 1989.

(2) In this Act, unless the context otherwise requires –

(a) references to, or to any provision of, the 1968 Convention or the 1971 Protocol are references to that Convention, Protocol or provision as amended by the Accession Convention, the 1982 Accession Convention and the 1989 Accession Convention;
(b) any reference in any provision to a numbered Article without more is a reference –

(i) to the Article so numbered of the 1968 Convention, in so far as the provision applies in relation to that Convention; and

(ii) to the Article so numbered of the Lugano Convention, in so far as the provision applies in relation to that Convention,

and any reference to a sub-division of a numbered Article shall be construed accordingly.

(3) In this Act:

'Contracting State', without more, in any provision means:

(a) in the application of the provision in relation to the Brussels Conventions, a Brussels Contracting State; and
(b) in the application of the provision in relation to the Lugano Convention, a Lugano Contracting State;

'Brussels Contracting State' means

(a) one of the original parties to the 1968 Convention (Belgium, the Federal Republic of Germany, France, Italy, Luxembourg and the Netherlands); or
(b) one of the parties acceding to that Convention under the Accession Convention (Denmark, the Republic of Ireland and the United Kingdom), or under the 1982 Accession Convention (the Hellenic Republic), or under the 1989 Accession Convention (Spain and Portugal), being a state in respect of which the Accession Convention has entered into force in accordance with Article 39 of that Convention, or being a state in respect of which the 1982 Accession Convention has entered into force in accordance with Article 15 of that convention, or being a state in respect of which the 1989 Accession Convention has entered into force in accordance with Article 32 of that Convention, as the case might be;

'Lugano Contracting State' means one of the original parties to the Lugano Convention, that is to say –

Austria, Belgium, Denmark, Finland, France, the Federal Republic of Germany, the Hellenic Republic, Iceland, the Republic of Ireland, Italy, Luxembourg, the Netherlands, Norway, Portugal, Spain, Sweden, Switzerland and the United Kingdom,

being a State in relation to which that Convention has taken effect in accordance with paragraph 3 or 4 of Article 61.

2 The Brussels Conventions to have the force of law [819]

(1) The Brussels Conventions shall have the force of law in the United Kingdom, and judicial notice shall be taken of them.

(2) For convenience of reference there are set out in Schedules 1, 2, 3, 3A and 3B respectively the English texts of –

(a) the 1968 Convention as amended by Titles II and III of the Accession Convention, by Titles II and III of the 1982 Accession Convention and by Titles II and III of, and Annex I(d) to, the 1989 Accession Convention;
(b) the 1971 Protocol as amended by Title IV of the Accession Convention, by Title IV of the 1982 Accession Convention and by Title IV of the 1989 Accession Convention;
(c) Titles V and VI of the Accession Convention (transitional and final provisions) as amended by Title V of the 1989 Accession Convention;
(d) Titles V and VI of the 1982 Accession Convention (transitional and final provisions); and
(e) Titles VI and VII of the 1989 Accession Convention (transitional and final provisions),

being texts prepared from the authentic English texts referred to in Articles 37 and 41 of the Accession Convention, in Article 17 of the 1982 Accession Convention and in Article 34 of the 1989 Accession Convention.

3 Interpretation of the Brussels Conventions [820]

(1) Any question as to the meaning or effect of any provision of the Brussels Conventions shall, if not referred to the European Court in accordance with the 1971 Protocol, be determined in accordance with the principles laid down by any relevant decision of the European Court.

(2) Judicial notice shall be taken of any decision of, or expression of opinion by, the European Court on any such question.

(3) Without prejudice to the generality of subsection (1), the following reports (which are reproduced in the Official Journal of the Communities), namely –

    (a) the reports by Mr P Jenard on the 1968 Convention and the 1971 Protocol;
    (b) the report by Professor Peter Schlosser on the Accession Convention;
    (c) the report by Professor Demetrios I Evrigenis and Professor KD Kerameus on the 1982 Accession Convention; and
    (d) the report by Mr Martinho de Almeida Cruz, Mr Manuel Desantes Real and Mr P Jenard on the 1989 Accession Convention,

may be considered in ascertaining the meaning or effect of any provision of the Brussels Conventions and shall be given such weight as is appropriate in the circumstances.

3A The Lugano Convention to have the force of law [821]

(1) The Lugano Convention shall have the force of law in the United Kingdom, and judicial notice shall be taken of it.

(2) For convenience of reference there is set out in Schedule 3C the English text of the Lugano Convention.

3B Interpretation of the Lugano Convention [822]

(1) In determining any question as to the meaning or effect of a provision of the Lugano Convention, a court in the United Kingdom shall, in accordance with Protocol No 2 to that Convention, take account of any principles laid down in any relevant decision delivered by a court of any other Lugano Contracting State concerning provisions of the Convention.

(2) Without prejudice to any practice of the courts as to the matters which may be considered apart from this section the report on the Lugano Convention by Mr P Jenard and Mr G Moller (which is reproduced in the Official Journal of the Communities of 28 July 1990) may be considered in ascertaining the meaning or effect of any provision of the Convention and shall be given such weight as is appropriate in the circumstances.

4 Enforcement of judgments other than maintenance orders [823]

(1) A judgment other than a maintenance order, which is the subject of an application under Article 31 of the 1968 Convention or of the Lugano Convention for its enforcement in any part of the United Kingdom shall, to the extent that its enforcement is authorised by the appropriate court, be registered in the prescribed manner in that court.

In this subsection 'the appropriate court' means the court to which the application is made in pursuance of Article 32 (that is to say, the High Court or the Court of Session).

(2) Where a judgment is registered under this section, the reasonable costs or

expenses of and incidental to its registration shall be recoverable as if they were sums recoverable under the judgment.

(3) A judgment registered under this section shall, for the purposes of its enforcement, be of the same force and effect, the registering court shall have in relation to its enforcement the same powers, and proceedings for or with respect to its enforcement may be taken, as if the judgment had been originally given by the registering court and had (where relevant) been entered.

(4) Subsection (3) is subject to Article 39 (restriction on enforcement where appeal pending or time for appeal unexpired), to section 7 and to any provision made by rules of court as to the manner in which and conditions subject to which a judgment registered under this section may be enforced.

5 Recognition and enforcement of maintenance orders [824]

(1) The function of transmitting to the appropriate court an application under Article 31 of the 1968 Convention or of the Lugano Convention for the recognition or enforcement in the United Kingdom of a maintenance order shall be discharged –

(a) as respects England and Wales and Northern Ireland, by the Lord Chancellor;
(b) as respects Scotland, by the Secretary of State.

In this subsection 'the appropriate court' means the magistrates' court or sheriff court having jurisdiction in the matter in accordance with the second paragraph of Article 32.

(2) Such an application shall be determined in the first instance by the prescribed officer of that court.

(3) Where on such an application the enforcement of the order is authorised to any extent, the order shall to that extent be registered in the prescribed manner in that court.

(4) A maintenance order registered under this section shall for the purposes of its enforcement be of the same force and effect, the registering court shall have in relation to its enforcement the same powers, and proceedings for or with respect to its enforcement may be taken, as if the order had been originally made by the registering court.

(5) Subsection (4) is subject to Article 39 (restriction on enforcement where appeal pending or time for appeal unexpired), to section 7 and to any provision made by rules of court as to the manner in which and conditions subject to which an order registered under this section may be enforced.

(5A) A maintenance order which by virtue of this section is enforceable by a magistrates' court in England and Wales shall, subject to the modifications of sections 76 and 93 of the Magistrates' Courts Act 1980 specified in subsections (5B) and (5C) below, be enforceable in the same manner as a magistrates' court maintenance order made by that court.

In this subsection 'magistrates' court maintenance order' has the same meaning as in section 150(1) of the Magistrates' Courts Act 1980.

(5B) Section 76 (enforcement of sums adjudged to be paid) shall have effect as if for subsections (4) to (6) there were substituted the following subsections –

'(4) Where proceedings are brought for the enforcement of a magistrates' court maintenance order under this section, the court may vary the order by exercising one of its powers under subsection (5) below.
(5) The powers of the court are –

(a) the power to order that payments under the order be made directly to the clerk of the court or the clerk of any other magistrates' court;

(b) the power to order that payments under the order be made to the clerk of the court, or to the clerk of any other magistrates' court, by such method of payment falling within section 59(6) above (standing order, etc) as may be specified;

(c) the power to make an attachment of earnings order under the Attachment of Earnings Act 1971 to secure payments under the order.

(6) In deciding which of the powers under subsection (5) above it is to exercise, the court shall have regard to any representations made by the debtor (within the meaning of section 59 above).

(7) Subsection (4) of section 59 above (power of court to require debtor to open account) shall apply for the purposes of subsection (5) above as it applies for the purposes of that section but as if for paragraph (a) there were substituted –

'(a) the court proposes to exercise its power under paragraph (b) of section 76(5) below, and'

(5C) In section 93 (complaint for arrears), subsection (6) (court not to impose imprisonment in certain circumstances) shall have effect as if for paragraph (b) there were substituted –

'(b) if the court is of the opinion that it is appropriate –

(i) to make an attachment of earnings order; or

(ii) to exercise its power under paragraph (b) of section 76(5) above.'...

(7) The payer under a maintenance order registered under this section in a magistrates' court in England and Wales or Northern Ireland shall give notice of any change of address to the clerk of that court.

A person who without reasonable excuse fails to comply with this subsection shall be guilty of an offence and liable on summary conviction to a fine not exceeding level 2 on the standard scale.

6 Appeals under Article 37, second paragraph, and Article 41   [825]

(1) The single further appeal on a point of law referred to in the 1968 Convention and the Lugano Convention in Article 37, second paragraph and Article 41 in relation to the recognition or enforcement of a judgment other than a maintenance order lies –

(a) in England and Wales or Northern Ireland, to the Court of Appeal or to the House of Lords in accordance with Part II of the Administration of Justice Act 1969 (appeals direct from the High Court to the House of Lords);

(b) in Scotland, to the Inner House of the Court of Session.

(2) Paragraph (a) of subsection (1) has effect notwithstanding section 15(2) of the Administration of Justice Act 1969 (exclusion of direct appeal to the House of Lords in cases where no appeal to that House lies from a decision of the Court of Appeal).

(3) The single further appeal on a point of law referred to in each of those Conventions in Article 37, second paragraph and Article 41 in relation to the recognition or enforcement of a maintenance order lies –

(a) in England and Wales, to the High Court by way of case stated in accordance with section 111 of the Magistrates' Courts Act 1980; ...

7 Interest on registered judgments [826]

(1) Subject to subsection (4), where in connection with an application for registration of a judgment under section 4 or 5 the applicant shows –

(a) that the judgment provides for the payment of a sum of money; and
(b) that in accordance with the law of the Contracting State in which the judgment was given interest on that sum is recoverable under the judgment from a particular date or time,

the rate of interest and the date or time from which it is so recoverable shall be registered with the judgment and, subject to any provisions made under subsection (2), the debt resulting, apart from section 4(2), from the registration of the judgment shall carry interest in accordance with the registered particulars.

(2) Provision may be made by rules of court as to the manner in which and the periods of reference to which any interest payable by virtue of subsection (1) is to be calculated and paid, including provision for such interest to cease to accrue as from a prescribed date.

(3) Costs or expenses recoverable by virtue of section 4(2) shall carry interest as if they were the subject of an order for the payment of costs or expenses made by the registering court on the date of registration.

(4) Interest or arrears of sums payable under a maintenance order registered under section 5 in a magistrates' court in England and Wales or Northern Ireland shall not be recoverable in that court, but without prejudice to the operation in relation to any such order of section 2A of the Maintenance Orders Act 1958 or section 11A of the Maintenance and Affiliation Orders Act (Northern Ireland) 1966 (which enable interest to be recovered if the order is re-registered for enforcement in the High Court).

(5) Except as mentioned in subsection (4), debts under judgments registered under section 4 or 5 shall carry interest only as provided by this section.

8 Currency of payment under registered maintenance orders [827]

(1) Sums payable in the United Kingdom under a maintenance order by virtue of its registration under section 5, including any arrears so payable, shall be paid in the currency of the United Kingdom.

(2) Where the order is expressed in any other currency, the amounts shall be converted on the basis of the exchange rate prevailing on the date of registration of the order.

(3) For the purposes of this section, a written certificate purporting to be signed by an officer of any bank in the United Kingdom and stating the exchange rate prevailing on a specified date shall be evidence, and in Scotland sufficient evidence, of the facts stated.

9 Provisions supplementary to Title VII of 1968 Convention [828]

(1) The provisions of Title VII of the 1968 Convention and, apart from Article 54B, of Title VII of the Lugano Convention (relationship between the Convention in question and other conventions to which Contracting States are or may become parties) shall have effect in relation to –

(a) any statutory provision, whenever passed or made, implementing any such other convention in the United Kingdom; and
(b) any rule of law so far as it has the effect of so implementing any such other convention,

as they have effect in relation to that other convention itself.

(1A) Any question arising as to whether it is the Lugano Convention or any of the Brussels Conventions which applies in the circumstances of a particular case falls to be determined in accordance with the provisions of Article 54B of the Lugano Convention.

(2) Her Majesty may by Order in Council declare a provision of a convention entered into by the United Kingdom to be a provision whereby the United Kingdom assumed an obligation of a kind provided for in Article 59 (which allows a Contracting State to agree with a third State to withhold recognition in certain cases from a judgment given by a court in another Contracting State which took jurisdiction on one of the grounds mentioned in the second paragraph of Article 3).

10 Allocation within United Kingdom of jurisdiction with respect to trusts and consumer contracts [829]

(1) The provisions of this section have effect for the purpose of allocating within the United Kingdom jurisdiction in certain proceedings in respect of which the 1968 Convention or the Lugano Convention confers jurisdiction on the courts of the United Kingdom generally and to which section 16 does not apply.

(2) Any proceedings which by virtue of Article 5(6) (trusts) are brought in the United Kingdom shall be brought in the courts of the part of the United Kingdom in which the trust is domiciled.

(3) Any proceedings which by virtue of the first paragraph of Article 14 (consumer contracts) are brought in the United Kingdom by a consumer on the ground that he is himself domiciled there shall be brought in the courts of the part of the United Kingdom in which he is domiciled.

11 Proof and admissibility of certain judgments and related documents [830]

(1) For the purposes of the 1968 Convention or the Lugano Convention –

(a) a document, duly authenticated, which purports to be a copy of a judgment given by a court of a Contracting State other than the United Kingdom shall without further proof be deemed to be a true copy, unless the contrary is shown; and
(b) the original or a copy of any such document as is mentioned in Article 46(2) or 47 (supporting documents to be produced by a party seeking recognition or enforcement of a judgment) shall be evidence, and in Scotland sufficient evidence, of any matter to which it relates.

(2) A document purporting to be a copy of a judgment given by any such court as is mentioned in subsection (1)(a) is duly authenticated for the purposes of this section if it purports –

(a) to bear the seal of that court; or
(b) to be certified by any person in his capacity as a judge or officer of that court to be a true copy of a judgment given by that court.

(3) Nothing in this section shall prejudice the admission in evidence of any document which is admissible apart from this section.

12 Provision for issue of copies of, and certificates in connection with, United Kingdom judgments [831]

Rules of court may make provision for enabling any interested party wishing to secure under the 1968 Convention or the Lugano Convention the recognition or enforcement in another Contracting State of a judgment given by a court in the United Kingdom to obtain, subject to any conditions specified in the rules –

(a) a copy of the judgment; and
(b) a certificate giving particulars relating to the judgment and the proceedings in which it was given.

13 Modifications to cover authentic instruments and court settlements [832]

(1) Her Majesty may by Order in Council provide that –

(a) any provision of this Act relating to the recognition or enforcement in the United Kingdom or elsewhere of judgments to which the 1968 Convention or the Lugano Convention applies; and
(b) any other statutory provision, whenever passed or made, so relating, shall apply, with such modifications as may be specified in the Order, in relation to documents and settlements within Title IV of the 1968 Convention or, as the case may be, Title IV of the Lugano Convention (authentic instruments and court settlements enforceable in the same manner as judgments) as if they were judgments to which the Convention in question applies.

(2) An Order in Council under this section may make different provision in relation to different descriptions of documents and settlements.

(3) Any Order in Council under this section shall be subject to annulment in pursuance of a resolution of either House of Parliament.

14 Modifications consequential on revision of the Convention [833]

(1) If at any time it appears to Her Majesty in Council that Her Majesty's Government in the United Kingdom have agreed to a revision of the Lugano Convention or any of the Brussels Conventions, including in particular any revision connected with the accession of the Lugano Convention or the 1968 Convention of one or more further states, Her Majesty may by order in Council make such modifications of this Act or any other statutory provision, whenever passed or made, as Her Majesty considers appropriate in consequence of the revision.

(2) An Order in Council under this section shall not be made unless a draft of the Order has been laid before Parliament and approved by a resolution of each House of Parliament.

(3) In this section 'revision' means an omission from, addition to or alteration of the Lugano Convention or any of the Brussels Conventions and includes replacement of the Lugano Convention or any of the Brussels Conventions to any extent by another convention, protocol or other description of international agreement.

15 Interpretation of Part I and consequential amendments [834]

(1) In this Part, unless the context otherwise requires –

'judgment' has the meaning given by Article 25;
'maintenance order' means a maintenance judgment within the meaning of the 1968 Convention or, as the case may be, Title IV of the Lugano Convention;
'payer', in relation to a maintenance order, means the person liable to make the payments for which the order provides;
'prescribed' means prescribed by rules of court.

(2) References in this Part to a judgment registered under section 4 or 5 include, to the extent of its registration, references to a judgment so registered to a limited extent only.

(3) Anything authorised or required by the 1968 Convention, the Lugano Convention or this Part to be done by, to or before a particular magistrates' court may be done by, to or before any magistrates' court acting for the same petty sessions area ... as that court.

(4) The enactments specified in Part 1 of Schedule 12 shall have effect with the amendments specified there, being amendments consequential on this Part.

PART II

JURISDICTION, AND RECOGNITION AND ENFORCEMENT OF JUDGMENTS, WITHIN UNITED KINGDOM

16 Allocation within United Kingdom of jurisdiction in certain civil proceedings [835]

(1) The provisions set out in Schedule 4 (which contains a modified version of Title II of the 1968 Convention) shall have effect for determining, for each part of the United Kingdom, whether the courts of law of that part, or any particular court of law in that part, have or has jurisdiction in proceedings where –

(a) the subject-matter of the proceedings is within the scope of the 1968 Convention as determined by Article 1 (whether or not that or any other Convention has effect in relation to the proceedings); and
(b) the defendants or defender is domiciled in the United Kingdom or the proceedings are of a kind mentioned in Article 16 of the 1968 Convention (exclusive jurisdiction regardless of domicile).

(2) In Schedule 4 modification of Title II of the 1968 Convention are indicated as follows –

(a) modifications by way of omission are indicated by dots; and
(b) within each Article words resulting from modifications by way of addition or substitution are printed in heavy type.

(3) In determining any question as to the meaning or effect of any provision contained in Schedule 4 –

(a) regard shall be had to any relevant principles laid down by the European Court in connection with Title II of the 1968 Convention and to any relevant decision of that court as to the meaning or effect of any provision of that Title; and
(b) without prejudice to the generality of paragraph (a), the reports mentioned in section 3(3) may be considered and shall, so far as relevant, be given such weight as is appropriate in the circumstances.

(4) The provisions of this section and Schedule 4 shall have effect subject to the 1968 Convention and the Lugano Convention and to the provisions of section 17.

(5) In section 15(1)(a) of the Maintenance Orders Act 1950 (domestic proceedings in which initial process may be served in another part of the United Kingdom), after sub-paragraph (v) there shall be added –

'(vi) Article 5(2) of Schedule 4 to the Civil Jurisdiction and Judgments Act 1982; or'.

17 Exclusion of certain proceedings from Schedule 4 [836]

(1) Schedule 4 shall not apply to proceedings of any description listed in Schedule 5 or to proceedings in Scotland under any enactment which confers jurisdiction on a Scottish court in respect of a specific subject-matter on specific grounds.

(2) Her Majesty may by Order in Council –

(a) add to the list in Schedule 5 any description of proceedings in any part of the United Kingdom; and
(b) remove from that list any description of proceedings in any part of the United Kingdom (whether included in the list as originally enacted or added by virtue of this subsection).

(3) An Order in Council under subsection (2) –

(a) may make different provisions for different descriptions of proceedings, for the same description of proceedings in different courts or for different parts of the United Kingdom; and
(b) may contain such transitional and other incidental provisions as appear to Her Majesty to be appropriate.

(4) An Order in Council under subsection (2) shall not be made unless a draft of the Order has been laid before Parliament and approved by a resolution of each House of Parliament.

18 Enforcement of United Kingdom judgments in other parts of United Kingdom [837]

(1) In relation to any judgment to which this section applies –

(a) Schedule 6 shall have effect for the purpose of enabling any money provisions contained in the judgment to be enforced in a part of the United Kingdom other than the part in which the judgment was given; and
(b) Schedule 7 shall have effect for the purpose of enabling any non-money provisions so contained to be enforced.

(2) In this section 'judgment' means any of the following (references to the giving of a judgment being construed accordingly) –

(a) any judgment or order (by whatever named called) given or made by a court of law in the United Kingdom;
(b) any judgment or order not within paragraph (a) which has been entered in England and Wales or Northern Ireland in the High Court or county court;
(c) any document which in Scotland has been registered for execution in the Books of Council and Session or in the sheriff court books kept for any sheriffdom;
(d) any award or order made by a tribunal in any part of the United Kingdom which is enforceable in that part without an order of a court of law;
(e) an arbitration award which has become enforceable in the part of the United Kingdom in which it was given in the same manner as a judgment given by a court of law in that part;

and, subject to the following provisions of this section, this section applies to all such judgments.

(3) Subject to subsection (4), this section does not apply to –

(a) a judgment given in proceedings in a magistrates' court in England and Wales or Northern Ireland;
(b) a judgment given in proceedings other than civil proceedings;
(ba) a judgment given in the exercise of jurisdiction in relation to insolvency law, within the meaning of section 426 of the Insolvency Act 1986;

(c) a judgment given in proceedings relating to – ...
    (iii) the obtaining of title to administer the estate of a deceased person.

(4) This section applies, whatever the nature of the proceedings in which it is made, to –

(a) a decree issued under section 13 of the Court of Exchequer (Scotland) Act 1856 (recovery of certain rent-charges and penalties by process of the Court of Session);
(b) an order which is enforceable in the same manner as a judgment of the High Court in England and Wales by virtue of section 16 of the Contempt of Court Act 1981 or section 140 of the Supreme Court Act 1981 (which relate to fines for contempt of court and forfeiture of recognisances).

(4A) This section does not apply as respects ... the enforcement in England and Wales of orders made by the Court of Session under or for the purposes of Part I of the Criminal Justice (Scotland) Act 1987.

(5) This section does not apply to so much of any judgment as –

(a) is an order to which section 16 of the Maintenance Orders Act 1950 applies (and is therefore an order for whose enforcement in another part of the United Kingdom provision is made by Part II of that Act);
(b) concerns that status or legal capacity of an individual;
(c) relates to the management of the affairs of a person not capable of managing his own affairs;
(d) is a provisional (including protective) measure other than an order for the making of an interim payment;

and except where otherwise stated references to a judgment to which this section applies are to such a judgment exclusive of any such provisions.

(6) The following are within subsection (5)(b), but without prejudice to the generality of that provision –

(a) a decree of judicial separation or of separation;
(b) any order which is a Part I order for the purposes of the Family Law Act 1986.

(7) This section does not apply to a judgment of a court outside the United Kingdom which falls to be treated for the purposes of its enforcement as a judgment of a court of law in the United Kingdom by virtue of registration under Part II of the Administration of Justice Act 1920, Part I of the Foreign Judgments (Reciprocal Enforcement) Act 1933, Part I of the Maintenance Orders (Reciprocal Enforcement) Act 1972 or section 4 or 5 of this Act.

(8) A judgment to which this section applies, other than a judgment within paragraph (e) of subsection (2), shall not be enforced in another part of the United Kingdom except by way of registration under Schedule 6 or 7.

19 Recognition of United Kingdom judgments in other parts of United Kingdom

(1) A judgment to which this section applies given in one part of the United Kingdom shall not be refused recognition in another part of the United Kingdom solely on the ground that, in relation to that judgment, the court which gave it was not a court of competent jurisdiction according to the rules of private international law in force in that other part.

(2) Subject to subsection (3), this section applies to any judgment to which section 18 applies.

(3) This section does not apply to –

(a) the documents mentioned in paragraph (c) of the definition of 'judgment' in section 18(2);
(b) the awards and orders mentioned in paragraphs (d) and (e) of that definition;
(c) the decrees and orders referred to in section 18(4).

PART IV

MISCELLANEOUS PROVISIONS

24 Interim relief and protective measures in cases of doubtful jurisdiction [839]

(1) Any power of a court in England and Wales or Northern Ireland to grant interim relief pending trial or pending the determination of an appeal shall extend to a case where –

(a) the issue to be tried, or which is the subject of the appeal, relates to the jurisdiction of the court to entertain the proceedings; or
(b) the proceedings involve the reference of any matter to the European Court under the 1971 Protocol. ...

(3) Subsections (1) and (2) shall not be construed as restricting any power to grant relief of protective measures which a court may have apart from this section.

25 Interim relief in England and Wales and Northern Ireland in the absence of substantive proceedings [840]

(1) The High Court in England and Wales or Northern Ireland shall have power to grant interim relief where –

(a) proceedings have been or are to be commenced in a Brussels or Lugano Contracting State other than the United Kingdom or in a part of the United Kingdom other than that in which the High Court in question exercises jurisdiction; and
(b) they are or will be proceedings whose subject-matter is within the scope of the 1968 Convention as determined by Article 1 (whether or not that or any other Convention has effect in relation to the proceedings).

(2) On an application for any interim relief under subsection (1) the court may refuse to grant that relief if, in the opinion of the court, the fact that the court has no jurisdiction apart from this section in relation to the subject-matter of the proceedings in question makes it inexpedient for the court to grant it.

(3) Her Majesty may by Order in Council extend the power to grant interim relief conferred by subsection (1) so as to make it exercisable in relation to proceedings of any of the following descriptions, namely –

(a) proceedings commenced or to be commended otherwise than in a Brussels or Lugano Contracting State;
(b) proceedings whose subject-matter is not within the scope of the 1968 Convention as determined by Article 1;
(c) arbitration proceedings.

(4) An Order in Council under subsection (3) –

(a) may confer power to grant only specified descriptions of interim relief;
(b) may make different provision for different classes of proceedings, for proceedings pending in different countries or courts outside the United Kingdom or in different parts of the United Kingdom, and for other different circumstances; and

(c) may impose conditions or restrictions on the exercise of any power conferred by the Order.

(5) An Order in Council under subsection (3) which confers power to grant interim relief in relation to arbitration proceedings may provide for the repeal of any provision of section 12(6) of the Arbitration Act 1950 or section 21(1) of the Arbitration Act (Northern Ireland) 1937 to the extent that it is superseded by the provisions of the Order.

(6) Any Order in Council under subsection (3) shall be subject to annulment in pursuance of a resolution of either House of Parliament.

(7) In this section 'interim relief', in relation to the High Court in England and Wales or Northern Ireland, means interim relief of any kind which that court has power to grant in proceedings relating to matters within its jurisdiction, other than –

    (a) a warrant for the arrest of property; or
    (b) provision for obtaining evidence.

26 Security in Admiralty proceedings in England and Wales or Northern Ireland in case of stay, etc [841]

(1) Where in England and Wales or Northern Ireland a court stays or dismisses Admiralty proceedings on the ground that the dispute in question should be submitted to arbitration or to the determination of the courts of another part of the United Kingdom or of an overseas country, the court may, if in those proceedings property has been arrested or bail or other security has been given to prevent or obtain release from arrest –

    (a) order that the property arrested be retained as security for the satisfaction of any award or judgment which –

        (i) is given in respect of the dispute in the arbitration or legal proceedings in favour of which those proceedings are stayed or dismissed; and
        (ii) is enforceable in England and Wales or, as the case may be, in Northern Ireland; or

    (b) order that the stay or dismissal of those proceedings be conditional on the provision of equivalent security for the satisfaction of any such award or judgment.

(2) Where a court makes an order under subsection (1), it may attach such conditions to the order as it thinks fit, in particular conditions with respect to the institution or prosecution of the relevant arbitration or legal proceedings.

(3) Subject to any provision made by rules of court and to any necessary modifications, the same law and practice shall apply in relation to property retained in pursuance of an order made by a court under subsection (1) as would apply if it were held for the purposes of proceedings in that court.

30 Proceedings in England and Wales or Northern Ireland for torts to immovable property [842]

(1) The jurisdiction of any court in England and Wales or Northern Ireland to entertain proceedings for trespass to, or any other tort affecting, immovable property shall extend to cases in which the property in question is situated outside that part of the United Kingdom unless the proceedings are principally concerned with a question of the title to, or the right to possession of, that property.

(2) Subsection (1) has effect subject to the 1968 Convention and the Lugano Convention and to the provisions set out in Schedule 4.

31 Overseas judgments given against states, etc [843]

(1) A judgment given by a court of an overseas country against a state other than the United Kingdom or the state to which that court belongs shall be recognised and enforced in the United Kingdom if, and only if –

(a) it would be so recognised and enforced if it had not been given against a state; and
(b) that court would have had jurisdiction in the matter if it had applied rules corresponding to those applicable to such matters in the United Kingdom in accordance with sections 2 to 11 of the State Immunity Act 1978.

(2) References in subsection (1) to a judgment given against a state include references to judgments of any of the following descriptions given in relation to a state –

(a) judgments against the government, or a department of the government, of the state but not (except as mentioned in paragraph (c)) judgments against an entity which is distinct from the executive organs of government;
(b) judgments against the sovereign or head of state in his public capacity;
(c) judgments against any such separate entity as is mentioned in paragraph (a) given in proceedings relating to anything done by it in the exercise of the sovereign authority of the state.

(3) Nothing in subsection (1) shall affect the recognition or enforcement in the United Kingdom of a judgment to which Part I of the Foreign Judgments (Reciprocal Enforcement) Act 1933 applies by virtue of section 4 of the Carriage of Goods by Road Act 1965, section 17(4) of the Nuclear Installations Act 1965, section 13(3) of the Merchant Shipping (Oil Pollution) Act 1971, section 6 of the International Transport Conventions Act 1983 or section 5 of the Carriage of Passengers by Road Act 1974.

(4) Sections 12, 13 and 14(3) and (4) of the State Immunity Act 1978 (service of process and procedural privileges) shall apply to proceedings for the recognition or enforcement in the United Kingdom of a judgment given by a court of an overseas country (whether or not that judgment is within subsection (1) of this section) as they apply to other proceedings.

(5) In this section 'state', in the case of a federal state, includes any of its constituent territories.

32 Overseas judgments given in proceedings brought in breach of agreement for settlement of disputes [844]

(1) Subject to the following provisions of this section, a judgment given by a court of an overseas country in any proceedings shall not be recognised or enforced in the United Kingdom if –

(a) the bringing of those proceedings in that court was contrary to an agreement under which the dispute in question was to be settled otherwise than by proceedings in the courts of that country; and
(b) those proceedings were not brought in that court by, or with the agreement of, the person against whom the judgment was given; and
(c) that person did not counterclaim in the proceedings or otherwise submit to the jurisdiction of that court.

(2) Subsection (1) does not apply where the agreement referred to in paragraph (a) of that subsection was illegal, void or unenforceable or was incapable of being performed for reasons not attributable to the fault of the party bringing the proceedings in which the judgment was given.

(3) In determining whether a judgment given by a court of an overseas country should be recognised or enforced in the United Kingdom, a court in the United Kingdom shall not be bound by any decision of the overseas court relating to any of the matters mentioned in subsection (1) or (2).

(4) Nothing in subsection (1) shall affect the recognition or enforcement in the United Kingdom of –

(a) a judgment which is required to be recognised or enforced there under the 1968 Convention or the Lugano Convention;
(b) a judgment to which Part I of the Foreign Judgments (Reciprocal Enforcement) Act 1933 applies by virtue of section 4 of the Carriage of Goods by Road Act 1965, section 17(4) of the Nuclear Installations Act 1965, section 13(3) of the Merchant Shipping (Oil Pollution) Act 1971, section 6 of the International Transport Conventions Act 1983, section 5 of the Carriage of Passengers by Road Act 1974 or section 6(4) of the Merchant Shipping Act 1974.

33 Certain steps not to amount to submission to jurisdiction of overseas court [845]

(1) For the purposes of determining whether a judgment given by a court of an overseas country should be recognised or enforced in England and Wales or Northern Ireland, the person against whom the judgment was given shall not be regarded as having submitted to the jurisdiction of the court by reason only of the fact that he appeared (conditionally or otherwise) in the proceedings for all or any one or more of the following purposes, namely –

(a) to contest the jurisdiction of the court;
(b) to ask the court to dismiss or stay the proceedings on the ground that the dispute in question should be submitted to arbitration or to the determination of the courts of another country;
(c) to protect, or obtain the release of, property seized or threatened with seizure in the proceedings.

(2) Nothing in this section shall affect the recognition or enforcement in England and Wales or Northern Ireland of a judgment which is required to be recognised or enforced there under the 1968 Convention or the Lugano Convention.

34 Certain judgments a bar to further proceedings on the same cause of action [846]

No proceedings may be brought by a person in England and Wales or Northern Ireland on a cause of action in respect of which a judgment has been given in his favour in proceedings between the same parties, or their privies, in a court in another part of the United Kingdom or in a court of an overseas country, unless that judgment is not enforceable or entitled to recognition in England and Wales or, as the case may be, in Northern Ireland.

35 Minor amendments relating to overseas judgments [847]

(1) The Foreign Judgments (Reciprocal Enforcement) Act 1933 shall have effect with the amendments specified in Schedule 10, being amendments whose main purpose is to enable Part I of that Act to be applied to judgments of courts other than superior courts, to judgments providing for interim payments and to certain arbitration awards. ...

37 Minor amendments relating to maintenance orders [848]

(1) The enactments specified in Schedule II shall have effect with the amendments specified there, being amendments whose main purpose is as follows –

Part I – to extend certain enforcement provisions to lump sum maintenance orders;

Part II – to provide for the recovery of interest according to the law of the country of origin in the case of maintenance orders made in other jurisdictions and registered in the High Court.

Part III – to extend the Maintenance Orders (Reciprocal Enforcement) Act 1972 to cases where the payer under a maintenance order is not resident within the jurisdiction but has assets there.

39 Application of provisions corresponding to 1968 Convention in relation to certain territories [849]

(1) Her Majesty may by Order in Council make provision corresponding to the provision made by the 1968 Convention as between the Contracting States to that Convention, with such modifications as appear to Her Majesty to be appropriate, for regulating, as between the United Kingdom and any of the territories mentioned in subsection (2), the jurisdiction of courts and the recognition and enforcement of judgments.

(2) The territories referred to in subsection (1) are –

(a) the Isle of Man;
(b) any of the Channel Islands;
(c) any colony.

(3) An Order in Council under this section may contain such supplementary and incidental provisions as appear to Her Majesty to be necessary or expedient, including in particular provisions corresponding to or applying any of the provisions of Part I with such modifications as may be specified in the Order.

(4) Any Order in Council under this section shall be subject to annulment in pursuance of a resolution of either House of Parliament.

PART V

SUPPLEMENTARY AND GENERAL PROVISIONS

41 Domicile of individuals [850]

(1) Subject to Article 52 (which contains provisions for determining whether a party is domiciled in a Contracting State), the following provisions of this section determine, for the purposes of the 1968 Convention, the Lugano Convention and this Act, whether an individual is domiciled in the United Kingdom or in a particular part of, or place in, the United Kingdom or in a state other than a Contracting State.

(2) An individual is domiciled in the United Kingdom if and only if –

(a) he is resident in the United Kingdom; and
(b) the nature and circumstances of his residence indicate that he has a substantial connection with the United Kingdom.

(3) Subject to subsection (5), an individual is domiciled in a particular part of the United Kingdom if and only if –

(a) he is resident in that part; and

(b) the nature and circumstances of his residence indicate that he has a substantial connection with that part.

(4) An individual is domiciled in a particular place in the United Kingdom if and only if he –

(a) is domiciled in the part of the United Kingdom in which that part is situated; and
(b) is resident in that place.

(5) An individual who is domiciled in the United Kingdom but in whose case the requirements of subsection (3)(b) are not satisfied in relation to any particular part of the United Kingdom shall be treated as domiciled in the part of the United Kingdom in which he is resident.

(6) In the case of an individual who –

(a) is resident in the United Kingdom, or in a particular part of the United Kingdom; and
(b) has been so resident for the last three months or more,

the requirements of subsection (2)(b) or, as the case may be, subsection (3)(b) shall be presumed to be fulfilled unless the contrary is proved.

(7) An individual is domiciled in a state other than a Contracting State if and only if –

(a) he is resident in that state; and
(b) the nature and circumstances of his residence indicate that he has a substantial connection with that state.

42 Domicile and seat of corporation or association [851]

(1) For the purposes of this Act the seat of a corporation or association (as determined by this section) shall be treated as its domicile.

(2) The following provisions of this section determine where a corporation or association has its seat –

(a) for the purpose of Article 53 (which for the purposes of the 1968 Convention or, as the case may be, the Lugano Convention equates the domicile of such a body with its seat); and
(b) for the purposes of this Act other than the provisions mentioned in section 43(1)(b) and (c).

(3) A corporation or association has its seat in the United Kingdom if and only if –

(a) it was incorporated or formed under the law of a part of the United Kingdom and has its registered office or some other official address in the United Kingdom; or
(b) its central management and control is exercised in the United Kingdom.

(4) A corporation or association has its seat in a particular part of the United Kingdom if and only if it has its seat in the United Kingdom and –

(a) it has its registered office or some other official address in that part; or
(b) its central management and control is exercised in that part; or
(c) it has a place of business in that part.

(5) A corporation or association has its seat in a particular place in the United Kingdom if and only if it has its seat in the part of the United Kingdom in which that place is situated and –

(a) it has its registered office or some other official address in that place; or
(b) its central management and control is exercised in that place; or

(c) it has a place of business in that place.

(6) Subject to subsection (7), a corporation or association has its seat in a state other than the United Kingdom if and only if –

(a) it was incorporated or formed under the law of that state and has its registered office or some other official address there; or
(b) its central management and control is exercised in that state.

(7) A corporation or association shall not be regarded as having its seat in a Contracting State other than the United Kingdom if it is shown that the courts of that state would not regard it as having its seat there.

(8) In this section –

'business' includes any activity carried on by a corporation or association, and 'place of business' shall be construed accordingly;
'official address', in relation to a corporation or association, means an address which it is required by law to register, notify or maintain for the purpose of receiving notices or other communications.

43 Seat of corporation or association for purposes of Article 16(2) and related provisions [852]

(1) The following provisions of this section determine where a corporation or association has its seat for the purposes of –

(a) Article 16(2) of the 1968 Convention or of the Lugano Convention (which confers exclusive jurisdiction over proceedings relating to the formation or dissolution of such bodies, or to the decisions of their organs);
(b) Articles 5A and 16(2) in Schedule 4; and
(c) Rules 2(12) and 4(1)(b) in Schedule 8.

(2) A corporation or association has its seat in the United Kingdom if and only if –

(a) it was incorporated or formed under the law of a part of the United Kingdom; or
(b) its central management and control is exercised in the United Kingdom.

(3) A corporation or association has its seat in a particular part of the United Kingdom if and only if it has its seat in the United Kingdom and –

(a) subject to subsection (5), it was incorporated or formed under the law of that part; or
(b) being incorporated or formed under the laws of a state other than the United Kingdom, its central management and control is exercised in that part.

(4) A corporation or association has its seat in a particular place in Scotland if and only if it has its seat in Scotland and –

(a) it has its registered office or some other official address in that place; or
(b) it has no registered office or other official address in Scotland, but its central management and control is exercised in that place.

(5) A corporation or association incorporated or formed under –

(a) an enactment forming part of the law or more than one part of the United Kingdom; or
(b) an instrument having effect in the domestic law of more than one part of the United Kingdom,

shall, if it has a registered office, be taken to have its seat in the part of the United Kingdom in which that office is situated, and not in any other part of the United Kingdom.

(6) Subject to subsection (7), a corporation or association has its seat in a Contracting State other than the United Kingdom if and only if –

   (a) it was incorporated or formed under the law of that State; or
   (b) its central management and control is exercised in that state.

(7) A corporation or association shall not be regarded as having its seat in a Contracting State other than the United Kingdom if –

   (a) it has its seat in the United Kingdom by virtue of subsection (2)(a); or
   (b) it is shown that the courts of that other state would not regard it for the purposes of Article 16(2) as having its seat there.

(8) In this section 'official address' has the same meaning as in section 42.

44 Persons deemed to be domiciled in the United Kingdom for certain purposes [853]

(1) This section applies to –

   (a) proceedings within Section 3 of Title II of the 1968 Convention or Section 3 of Title II of the Lugano Convention (insurance contracts), and
   (b) proceedings within Section 4 of Title II of either of those Conventions (consumer contracts).

(2) A person who, for the purposes of proceedings to which this section applies arising out of the operations of a branch, agency or other establishment in the United Kingdom, is deemed for the purposes of the 1968 Convention or, as the case may be, of the Lugano Convention to be domiciled in the United Kingdom by virtue of –

   (a) Article 8, second paragraph (insurers); or
   (b) Article 13, second paragraph (suppliers of goods, services or credit to consumers),

shall, for the purposes of those proceedings, be treated for the purposes of this Act as so domiciled and as domiciled in the part of the United Kingdom in which the branch, agency or establishment in question is situated.

45 Domicile of trusts [854]

(1) The following provisions of this section determine, for the purposes of the 1968 Convention, the Lugano Convention and this Act, where a trust is domiciled.

(2) A trust is domiciled in the United Kingdom if and only if it is by virtue of subsection (3) domiciled in a part of the United Kingdom.

(3) A trust is domiciled in a part of the United Kingdom if and only if the system of law of that part is the system of law with which the trust has its closest and most real connection.

46 Domicile and seat of the Crown [855]

(1) For the purposes of this Act the seat of the Crown (as determined by this section) shall be treated as its domicile.

(2) The following provisions of this section determine where the Crown has its seat –

   (a) for the purposes of the 1968 Convention and the Lugano Convention (in each of which Article 53 equates the domicile of a legal person with its seat); and
   (b) for the purposes of this Act.

(3) Subject to the provisions of any Order in Council for the time being in force under subsection (4) –
  (a) the Crown in right of Her Majesty's government in the United Kingdom has its seat in every part of, and every place in, the United Kingdom; and
  (b) the Crown in right of Her Majesty's government in Northern Ireland has its seat in, and in every place in, Northern Ireland.

(4) Her Majesty may by Order in Council provide that, in the case of proceedings of any specified description against the Crown in right of Her Majesty's government in the United Kingdom, the Crown shall be treated for the purposes of the 1968 Convention, the Lugano Convention and this Act as having its seat in, and in every place in, a specified part of the United Kingdom and not in any other part of the United Kingdom.

(5) An Order in Council under subsection (4) may frame a description of proceedings in any way, and in particular may do so by reference to the government department or officer of the Crown against which or against whom they fall to be instituted.

(6) Any Order in Council made under this section shall be subject to annulment in pursuance of a resolution of either House of Parliament.

(7) Nothing in this section applies to the Crown otherwise than in right of Her Majesty's government in the United Kingdom or Her Majesty's government in Northern Ireland.

47 Modifications occasioned by decisions of European Court [856] as to meaning or effect of Conventions

(1) Her Majesty may by Order in Council –
  (a) make such provision as Her Majesty considers appropriate for the purpose of bringing the law of any part of the United Kingdom into accord with the Brussels Conventions as affected by any principle laid down by the European Court in connection with the Brussels Conventions or by any decision of that court as to the meaning or effect of any provision of the Brussels Conventions; or
  (b) make such modifications of Schedule 4 or Schedule 8, or of any other statutory provision affected by any provision of either of those Schedules, as Her Majesty considers appropriate in view of any principle laid down by the European Court in connection with Title II of the 1968 Convention or of any decision of that court as to the meaning or effect of any provision of that Title.

(2) The provision which may be made by virtue of paragraph (a) of subsection (1) includes such modifications of this Act or any other statutory provision, whenever passed or made, as Her Majesty considers appropriate for the purpose mentioned in that paragraph.

(3) The modifications which may be made by virtue of paragraph (b) of subsection (1) include modifications designed to produce divergence between any provision of Schedule 4 or Schedule 8 and a corresponding provision of Title II of the 1968 Convention as affected by any such principle or decision as is mentioned in that paragraph.

(4) An Order in Council under this section shall not be made unless a draft of the Order has been laid before Parliament and approved by a resolution of each House of Parliament.

48 Matters for which rules of court may provide [857]

(1) Rules of court may make provisions for regulating the procedure to be followed in any court in connection with any provision of this Act, the Lugano Convention or the Brussels Conventions.

(2) Rules of court may make provision as to the manner in which and the conditions subject to which a certificate or judgment registered in any court under any provision of this Act may be enforced, including provision for enabling the court or, in Northern Ireland the Enforcement of Judgments Office, subject to any conditions specified in the rules, to give directions about such matters.

(3) Without prejudice to the generality of subsections (1) and (2), the power to make rules of court for magistrates' courts, and in Northern Ireland the power to make Judgment Enforcement Rules, shall include power to make such provision as the rule-making authority considers necessary or expedient for the purposes of the provisions of the Lugano Convention, the Brussels Convention and this Act relating to maintenance proceedings and the recognition and enforcement of maintenance orders, and shall in particular include power to make provisions as to any of the following matters –

(a) authorising the service in another Contracting State of process issued by or for the purposes of a magistrates' court and the service and execution in England and Wales or Northern Ireland of process issued in another Contracting State;
(b) requesting courts in other parts of the United Kingdom or in other Contracting States to take evidence there for the purposes of proceedings in England and Wales or Northern Ireland;
(c) the taking of evidence in England and Wales or Northern Ireland in response to similar requests received from such courts;
(d) the circumstances in which and the conditions subject to which any powers conferred under paragraphs (a) to (c) are to be exercised;
(e) the admission in evidence, subject to such conditions as may be prescribed in the rules, of statements contained in documents purporting to be made or authenticated by a court in another part of the United Kingdom or in another Contracting State, or by a judge or official of such a court, which purport –

(i) to set out or summarise evidence given in proceedings in that court or to be documents received in evidence in such proceedings or copies of such documents; or
(ii) to set out or summarise evidence taken for the purposes of proceedings in England and Wales or Northern Ireland, whether or not in response to any such request as is mentioned in paragraph (b); or
(iii) to record information relating to the payments made under an order of that court;

(f) the circumstances and manner in which a magistrates' court may or must vary or revoke a maintenance order registered in that court, cancel the registration of, or refrain from enforcing, such an order or transmit such an order for enforcement in another part of the United Kingdom;
(g) the cases and manner in which courts in other parts of the United Kingdom or in other Contracting States are to be informed of orders made, or other things done, by or for the purposes of a magistrates' court;
(h) the circumstances and manner in which a magistrates' court may communicate for other purposes with such courts;
(i) the giving of notice of such matters as may be prescribed in the rules to such persons as may be so prescribed and the manner in which such notice is to be given.

(4) Nothing in this section shall be taken as derogating from the generality of any power to make rules of court conferred by any other enactment.

49 Saving for powers to stay, sist, strike out or dismiss proceedings [858]

Nothing in this Act shall prevent any court in the United Kingdom from staying, sisting, striking out or dismissing any proceedings before it, on the ground of forum non conveniens or otherwise, where to do so is not inconsistent with the 1968 Convention or, as the case may be, the Lugano Convention.

50 Interpretation: general [859]

In this Act, unless the context otherwise requires –

'the Accession Convention', 'the 1982 Accession Convention' and 'the 1989 Accession Convention' have the meaning given by section 1(1);
'Article' and references to sub-divisions of numbered Articles are to be construed in accordance with section 1(2)(b);
'association' means an unincorporated body of persons;
'Brussels Contracting State' has the meaning given by section 1(3);
'Brussels Conventions' has the meaning given by section 1(1);
'Contracting State' has the meaning given by section 1(3);
'the 1968 Convention' has the meaning given by section 1(1), and references to that Convention and to provisions of it are to be construed in accordance with section 1(2)(a);
'corporation' means a body corporate, and includes a partnership subsisting under the law of Scotland;
'court', without more, includes a tribunal;
'court of law', in relation to the United Kingdom, means any of the following courts, namely –

(a) the House of Lords,
(b) in England and Wales or Northern Ireland, the Court of Appeal, the High Court, the Crown Court, a county court and a magistrates' court,
(c) in Scotland, the Court of Session and a sheriff court;

'the Crown' is to be construed in accordance with section 51(2);
'enactment' includes an enactment comprised in Northern Ireland legislation;
'judgment', subject to sections 15(1) and 18(2) and to paragraph 1 of Schedules 6 and 7, means any judgment or order (by whatever name called) given or made by a court in any civil proceedings;
'Lugano Contracting State' has the meaning given by section 1(3);
'the Lugano Convention' has the meaning given by section 1(1);
'magistrates' court', in relation to Northern Ireland, means a court of summary jurisdiction;
'modifications' includes additions, omissions and alterations;
'overseas country' means any country or territory outside the United Kingdom;
'part of the United Kingdom' means England and Wales, Scotland or Northern Ireland;
'the 1971 Protocol' has the meaning given by section 1(1), and references to that Protocol and to provisions of it are to be construed in accordance with section 1(2)(a);
'rules of court', in relation to any court, means rules, orders or regulations made by the authority having power to make rules, orders or regulations regulating the procedure of that court, and includes –

(a) in Scotland, Acts of Sederunt;
(b) in Northern Ireland, Judgment Enforcement Rules;

'statutory provision' means any provision contained in an Act, or in any Northern Ireland legislation, or in –

(a) subordinate legislation (as defined in section 21(1) of the Interpretation Act 1978); or

(b) any instrument of a legislative character made under any Northern Ireland legislation;

'tribunal' –

(a) means a tribunal of any description other than a court of law;

(b) in relation to an overseas country, includes, as regards matters relating to maintenance within the meaning of the 1968 Convention, any authority having power to give, enforce, vary or revoke a maintenance order.

51 Application to Crown

(1) This Act binds the Crown.

(2) In this section and elsewhere in this Act references to the Crown do not include references to Her Majesty in Her private capacity or to Her Majesty in right to Her Duchy of Lancaster or to the Duke of Cornwall.

52 Extent

(1) This Act extends to Northern Ireland.

(2) Without prejudice to the power conferred by section 39, Her Majesty may by Order in Council direct that all or any of the provisions of this Act apart from that section shall extend, subject to such modifications as may be specified in the Order, to any of the following territories, that is to say –

(a) the Isle of Man;
(b) any of the Channel Islands;
(c) any colony.

SCHEDULE 1

CONVENTION ON JURISDICTION AND THE ENFORCEMENT OF JUDGMENTS IN CIVIL AND COMMERCIAL MATTERS

PREAMBLE

The High Contracting Parties to the Treaty establishing the European Economic Community.

Desiring to implement the provisions of Article 220 of that Treaty by virtue of which they undertook to secure the simplification of formalities governing the reciprocal recognition and enforcement of judgments of courts or tribunals;

Anxious to strengthen in the Community the legal protection of persons therein established;

Considering that it is necessary for this purpose to determine the international jurisdiction of their courts, to facilitate recognition and to introduce an expeditious procedure for securing the enforcement of judgments, authentic instruments and court settlements;

Have decided to conclude this Convention and to this end have designated as their Plenipotentiaries: ...

Who, meeting within the Council, having exchanged their Full Powers, found in good and due form.

Have agreed as follows:

TITLE I
SCOPE

Article 1

This Convention shall apply in civil and commercial matters whatever the nature of the court or tribunal. It shall not extend, in particular, to revenue, customs or administrative matters.

The Convention shall not apply to:

> (1) the status or legal capacity of natural persons, rights in property arising out of a matrimonial relationship, wills and succession;
> (2) bankruptcy, proceedings relating to the winding-up of insolvent companies or other legal persons, judicial arrangements, compositions and analogous proceedings;
> (3) social security;
> (4) arbitration.

TITLE II
JURISDICTION
SECTION 1

Article 2

Subject to the provisions of this Convention, persons domiciled in a Contracting State shall, whatever their nationality, be sued in the courts of that State.

Persons who are not nationals of the State in which they are domiciled shall be governed by the rules of jurisdiction applicable to nationals of that State.

Article 3

Persons domiciled in a Contracting State may be sued in the courts of another Contracting State only by virtue of the rules set out in Sections 2 to 6 of this Title.

In particular the following provisions shall not be applicable as against them: ...

– in the United Kingdom the rules which enable jurisdiction to be founded on:

> (a) the document instituting the proceedings having been served on the defendant during his temporary presence in the United Kingdom; or
> (b) the presence within the United Kingdom of property belonging to the defendant; or
> (c) the seizure by the plaintiff of property situated in the United Kingdom.

Article 4

If the defendant is not domiciled in a Contracting State, the jurisdiction of the courts of each Contracting State shall, subject to the provisions of Article 16, be determined by the law of that State.

As against such a defendant, any person domiciled in a Contracting State may, whatever his nationality, avail himself in that State of the rules of jurisdiction there in force, and in particular those specified in the second paragraph of Article 3, in the same way as the nationals of that State.

SECTION 2

Article 5

A person domiciled in a Contracting State may, in another Contracting State, be sued:

(1) in matters relating to a contract, in the courts for the place of performance of the obligation in question; in matters relating to individual contracts of employment, this place is that where the employee habitually carried out his work, or if the employee does not habitually carry out his work in any one country, the employer may also be sued in the courts for the place where the business which engaged the employee was or is now situated;

(2) in matters relating to maintenance, in the courts for the place where the maintenance creditor is domiciled or habitually resident or, if the matter is ancillary to proceedings concerning the status of a person, in the court which, according to its own law, has jurisdiction to entertain those proceedings, unless that jurisdiction is based solely on the nationality of one of the parties;

(3) in matters relating to tort, delict or quasi-delict, in the courts for the place where the harmful event occurred;

(4) as regards a civil claim for damages or restitution which is based on an act giving rise to criminal proceedings, in the court seised of those proceedings, to the extent that that court has jurisdiction under its own law to entertain civil proceedings;

(5) as regards a dispute arising out of the operations of a branch, agency or other establishment, in the courts for the place in which the branch, agency or other establishment is situated;

(6) as settlor, trustee or beneficiary of a trust created by the operation of a statute, or by a written instrument, or created orally and evidenced in writing, in the courts of the Contracting State in which the trust is domiciled;

(7) as regards a dispute concerning the payment of remuneration claimed in respect of the salvage of a cargo or freight, in the court under the authority of which the cargo or freight in question:

    (a) has been arrested to secure such payment, or
    (b) could have been so arrested, but bail or other security has been given;

provided that his provision shall apply only if it is claimed that the defendant has an interest in the cargo or freight or had such an interest at the time of salvage.

Article 6

A person domiciled in a Contracting State may also be sued:

(1) where he is one of a number of defendants, in the courts for the place where any one of them is domiciled;

(2) as a third party in an action on a warranty or guarantee or in any other third party proceedings, in the court seised of the original proceedings, unless these were instituted solely with the object of removing him from the jurisdiction of the court which would be competent in his case;

(3) on a counterclaim arising from the same contract or facts on which the original claim was based, in the court in which the original claim is pending;

(4) in matters relating to a contract, if the action may be combined with an action against the same defendant in matters relating to rights in rem in immovable property, in the court of the Contracting State in which the property is situated.

Article 6A

Where by virtue of this convention a court of a Contracting State has jurisdiction in actions relating to liability arising from the use or operation of a ship, that a court, or any other court substituted for this purpose by the internal law of that State, shall also have jurisdiction over claims for limitation of such liability.

SECTION 3

Article 7

In matters relating to insurance, jurisdiction shall be determined by this Section, without prejudice to the provisions of Articles 4 and 5(5).

Article 8

An insurer domiciled in a Contracting State may be sued:

(1) in the courts of the State where he is domiciled, or
(2) in another Contracting State, in the courts for the place where the policy-holder is domiciled, or
(3) if he is a co-insurer, in the courts of a Contracting State in which proceedings are brought against the leading insurer.

An insurer who is not domiciled in a Contracting State but has a branch, agency or other establishment in one of the Contracting States shall, in disputes arising out of the operations of the branch, agency or establishment, be deemed to be domiciled in that State.

Article 9

In respect of liability insurance or insurance of immovable property, the insurer may in addition be sued in the courts for the place where the harmful event occurred. The same applies if movable and immovable property are covered by the same insurance policy and both are adversely affected by the same contingency.

Article 10

In respect of liability insurance, the insurer may also, if the law of the court permits it, be joined in proceedings which the injured party has brought against the insured.

The provisions of Articles 7, 8 and 9 shall apply to actions brought by the injured party directly against the insurer, where such direct actions are permitted.

If the law governing such direct actions provides that the policy-holder or the insured may be joined as a party to the action, the same court shall have jurisdiction over them.

Article 11

Without prejudice to the provisions of the third paragraph of Article 10, an insurer may bring proceedings only in the courts of the Contracting State in which the defendant is domiciled, irrespective of whether he is the policy-holder, the insured or a beneficiary.

The provisions of this Section shall not affect the right to bring a counterclaim in the court in which, in accordance with this Section, the original claim is pending.

Article 12

The provisions of this Section may be departed from only by an agreement on jurisdiction:

(1) which is entered into after the dispute has arisen, or
(2) which allows the policy-holder, the insured or a beneficiary to bring proceedings in courts other than those indicated in this Section, or
(3) which is concluded between a policy-holder and an insurer, both of whom are at the time of conclusion of the contract domiciled or habitually resident in the same Contracting State, and which has the effect of conferring jurisdiction on the courts of that State even if the harmful event were to occur abroad, provided that such an agreement is not contrary to the law of that State, or
(4) which is concluded with a policy-holder who is not domiciled in a Contracting State, except in so far as the insurance is compulsory or relates to immovable property in a Contracting State, or
(5) which relates to a contract of insurance in so far as it covers one or more of the risks set out in Article 12A.

Article 12A

The following are the risks referred to in Article 12(5):

(1) Any loss of or damage to

(a) seagoing ships, installations situated offshore or on the high seas, or aircraft, arising from perils which relate to their use for commercial purposes,

(b) goods in transit other than passengers' baggage where the transit consists of or includes carriage by such ships or aircraft;

(2) Any liability, other than for bodily injury to passengers or loss of or damage to their baggage,

(a) arising out of the use or operation of ships, installations or aircraft as referred to in (1)(a) above in so far as the law of the Contracting State in which such aircraft are registered does not prohibit agreements on jurisdiction regarding insurance of such risks,

(b) for loss or damage caused by goods in transit as described in (1)(b) above;

(3) Any financial loss connected with the use or operation of ships, installations or aircraft as referred to in (1)(a) above, in particular loss of freight or charter hire;

(4) Any risk or interest connected with any of those referred to in (1) to (3) above.

SECTION 4

Article 13

In proceedings concerning a contract concluded by a person for a purpose which can be regarded as being outside his trade or profession, hereinafter called the 'consumer', jurisdiction shall be determined by this Section, without prejudice to the provisions of Articles 4 and 5(5), if it is:

(1) a contract for the sale of goods on instalment credit terms, or
(2) a contract for a loan repayable by instalments, or for any other form of credit, made to finance the sale of goods, or
(3) any other contract for the supply of goods or a contract for the supply of services and

(a) in the State of the consumer's domicile the conclusion of the contract was preceded by a specific invitation addressed to him or by advertising, and

(b) the consumer took in that State the steps necessary for the conclusion of the contract.

Where a consumer enters into a contract with a party who is not domiciled in a Contracting State but has a branch, agency or other establishment in one of the Contracting States, that party shall, in disputes arising out of the operations of the branch, agency or establishment, be deemed to be domiciled in that State.

This Section shall not apply to contracts of transport.

Article 14

A consumer may bring proceedings against the other party to a contract either in the courts of the Contracting State in which that party is domiciled or in the courts of the Contracting State in which he is himself domiciled.

Proceedings may be brought against a consumer by the other party to the contract only in the courts of the Contracting State in which the consumer is domiciled.

These provisions shall not affect the right to bring a counter-claim in the court in which, in accordance with this Section, the original claim is pending.

Article 15

The provisions of this Section may be departed from only by an agreement:
  (1) which is entered into after the dispute has arisen, or
  (2) which allows the consumer to bring proceedings in courts other than those indicated in this Section, or
  (3) which is entered into by the consumer and the other party to the contract, both of whom are at the time of conclusion of the contract domiciled or habitually resident in the same Contracting State, and which confers jurisdiction on the courts of that State, provided that such an agreement is not contrary to the law of that State.

SECTION 5

Article 16

The following courts shall have exclusive jurisdiction, regardless of domicile:

(1)(a) in proceedings which have as their object rights in rem in immovable property or tenancies of immovable property, the court of the Contracting State in which the property is situated;

  (b) however, in proceedings which have as their object tenancies of immovable property concluded for temporary private use for a maximum period of six consecutive months, the courts of the Contracting State in which the defendant is domiciled shall also have jurisdiction, provided that the landlord and the tenant are natural persons and are domiciled in the same Contracting State;

(2) in proceedings which have as their object the validity of the constitution, the nullity of the dissolution of companies or other legal persons or associations of natural or legal persons, or the decisions of their organs, the courts of the Contracting State in which the company, legal person or association has its seat;

(3) in proceedings which have as their object the validity of entries in public registers, the courts of the Contracting State in which the register is kept;

(4) in proceedings concerned with the registration or validity of patents, trademarks, designs, or other similar rights required to be deposited or registered, the courts of the Contracting State in which the deposit or registration has been applied for, has taken place or is under the terms of an international convention deemed to have taken place;

(5) in proceedings concerned with the enforcement of judgments, the courts of the Contracting State in which the judgment has been or is to be enforced.

SECTION 6

Article 17

If the parties, one or more of whom is domiciled in a Contracting State, have agreed that a court or the courts of a Contracting State are to have jurisdiction to settle any disputes which have arisen or which may arise in connection with a particular legal relationship, that court or those courts shall have exclusive jurisdiction. Such an agreement conferring jurisdiction shall be either –

(a) in writing or evidenced in writing, or
(b) in a form which accords with practices which the parties have established between themselves, or
(c) in international trade or commerce, in a form which accords with a usage of which the parties are or ought to have been aware and which in such trade or commerce is widely known to, and regularly observed by, parties to contracts of the type involved in the particular trade or commerce concerned.

Where such an agreement is concluded by parties, none of whom is domiciled in a Contracting State, the courts of other Contracting States shall have no jurisdiction over their disputes unless the court or courts chosen have declined jurisdiction.

The court or courts of a Contracting State on which a trust instrument has conferred jurisdiction shall have exclusive jurisdiction in any proceedings brought against a settlor, trustee or beneficiary, if relations between these persons or their rights or obligations under the trust are involved.

Agreements or provisions of a trust instrument conferring jurisdiction shall have no legal force if they are contrary to the provisions of Articles 12 or 15, of if the courts whose jurisdiction they purport to exclude have exclusive jurisdiction by virtue of Article 16.

If an agreement conferring jurisdiction was concluded for the benefit of only one of the parties, that party shall retain the right to bring proceedings in any other court which has jurisdiction by virtue of the Convention.

In matters relating to individual contracts of employment an agreement conferring jurisdiction shall have legal force only if it is entered into after the dispute has arisen or if the employee invokes it to seise courts other than those for the defendant's domicile or those specified in Article 5(1).

Article 18

Apart from jurisdiction derived from other provisions of this Convention, a court of a Contracting State before whom a defendant enters an appearance shall have jurisdiction. This rule shall not apply where appearance was entered solely to contest the jurisdiction, or where another court has exclusive jurisdiction by virtue of Article 16.

SECTION 7

Article 19

Where a court of a Contracting State is seised of a claim which is principally concerned with a matter over which the courts of another Contracting State have exclusive jurisdiction by virtue of Article 16, it shall declare of its own motion that it has no jurisdiction.

Article 20

Where a defendant domiciled in one Contracting State is sued in a court of another Contracting State and does not enter an appearance, the court shall declare of its own motion that it has no jurisdiction unless its jurisdiction is derived from the provision of this Convention.

The court shall stay the proceedings so long as it is not shown that the defendant has been able to receive the document instituting the proceedings or an equivalent document in sufficient time to enable him to arrange for his defence, or that all necessary steps have been taken to this end.

The provisions of the foregoing paragraph shall be replaced by those of Article 15 of the Hague Convention of 15 November 1965 on the Service Abroad of Judicial and Extrajudicial Documents in Civil or Commercial Matters, if the document instituting the proceedings or notice thereof had to be transmitted abroad in accordance with that Convention.

SECTION 8

Article 21

Where proceedings involving the same cause of action and between the same parties are brought in the courts of different Contracting States, any court other than the court first seised shall of its own motion stay its proceedings until such time as the jurisdiction of the court first seised is established.

Where the jurisdiction of the court first seised is established, any court other than the court first seised shall decline jurisdiction in favour of that court.

Article 22

Where related actions are brought in the courts of different Contracting States, any court other than the court first seised may, while the actions are pending at first instance, stay its proceedings.

A court other than the court first seised may also, on the application of one of the parties, decline jurisdiction if the law of that court permits the consolidation of related actions and the court first seised has jurisdiction over both actions.

For the purposes of this Article, actions are deemed to be related where they are so closely connected that it is expedient to hear and determine them together to avoid the risk of irreconcilable judgments resulting from separate proceedings.

Article 23

Where actions come within the exclusive jurisdiction of several courts, any court other than the court first seised shall decline jurisdiction in favour of that court.

SECTION 9

Article 24

Application may be made to the courts of a Contracting State for such provisional, including protective, measures as may be available under the law of that State, even if, under this Convention, the courts of another Contracting State have jurisdiction as to the substance of the matter.

TITLE III

RECOGNITION AND ENFORCEMENT

Article 25

For the purposes of this Convention, 'judgment' means any judgment given by a court or tribunal of a Contracting State, whatever the judgment may be called, including a decree, order, decision or writ of execution, as well as the determination of costs or expenses by an officer of the court.

SECTION 1

Article 26

A judgment given in a Contracting State shall be recognised in the other Contracting States without any special procedure being required.

Any interested party who raises the recognition of a judgment as the principal issue in a dispute may, in accordance with the procedures provided for in Sections 2 and 3 of this Title, apply for a decision that the judgment be recognised.

If the outcome of proceedings in a court of a Contracting State depends on the determination of an incidental question of recognition that court shall have jurisdiction over that question.

Article 27

A judgment shall not be recognised:

(1) if such recognition is contrary to public policy in the State in which recognition is sought;
(2) where it was given in default of appearance, if the defendant was not duly served with the document which instituted the proceedings or with an equivalent document in sufficient time to enable him to arrange for his defence;
(3) if the judgment is irreconcilable with a judgment given in a dispute between the same parties in the State in which recognition is sought;
(4) if the court of the State in which the judgment was given, in order to arrive at its judgment, has decided a preliminary question concerning the status or legal capacity of natural persons, rights in property arising out of a matrimonial relationship, wills or succession in a way that conflicts with a rule of the private international law of the State in which the recognition is sought, unless the same result would have been reached by the application of the rules of private international law of that State;
(5) if the judgment is irreconcilable with an earlier judgment given in a non-Contracting State involving the same cause of action and between the same parties, provided that this latter judgment fulfils the conditions necessary for its recognition in the State addressed.

Article 28

Moreover, a judgment shall not be recognised if it conflicts with the provisions of Sections 3, 4 or 5 of Title II, or in a case provided for in Article 59.

In its examination of the grounds of jurisdiction referred to in the foregoing paragraph, the court or authority applied to shall be bound by the findings of fact on which the court of the State in which the judgment was given based its jurisdiction.

Subject to the provisions of the first paragraph, the jurisdiction of the court of the State in which the judgment was given may not be reviewed; the test of public policy referred to in Article 27(1) may not be applied to the rules relating to jurisdiction.

Article 29

Under no circumstances may a foreign judgment be reviewed as to its substance.

Article 30

A court of a Contracting State in which recognition is sought of a judgment given in another Contracting State may stay the proceedings if an ordinary appeal against the judgment has been lodged.

A court of a Contracting State in which recognition is sought of a judgment given in Ireland or the United Kingdom may stay the proceedings if enforcement is suspended in the State of origin, by reason of an appeal.

SECTION 2

Article 31

A judgment given in a Contracting State and enforceable in that State shall be enforced in another Contracting State when, on the application of any interested party, it has been declared enforceable there.

However, in the United Kingdom, such a judgment shall be enforced in England and Wales, in Scotland, or in Northern Ireland when, on the application of any interested party, it has been registered for enforcement in that part of the United Kingdom.

Article 32

(1) The application shall be submitted: ...

— in the United Kingdom —

(a) in England and Wales, to the High Court of Justice, or in the case of a maintenance judgment to the Magistrates' Court on transmission by the Secretary of State; ...

(2) The jurisdiction of local courts shall be determined by reference to the place of domicile of the party against whom enforcement is sought. If he is not domiciled in the State in which enforcement is sought, it shall be determined by reference to the place of enforcement.

Article 33

The procedure for making the application shall be governed by the law of the State in which enforcement is sought.

The applicant must give an address for service of process within the area of jurisdiction of the court applied to. However, if the law of the State in which enforcement is sought does not provide for the furnishing of such an address, the applicant shall appoint a representative ad litem.

The documents referred to in Articles 46 and 47 shall be attached to the application.

Article 34

The court applied to shall give its decision without delay; the party against whom enforcement is sought shall not at this stage of the proceedings be entitled to make any submissions on the application.

The application may be refused only for one of the reasons specified in Articles 27 and 28.

Under no circumstances may the foreign judgment be reviewed as to its substance.

Article 35

The appropriate officer of the court shall without delay bring the decision given on the application to the notice of the applicant in accordance with the procedure laid down by the law of the State in which enforcement is sought.

Article 36

If enforcement is authorised, the party against whom enforcement is sought may appeal against the decision within one month of service thereof.

If that party is domiciled in a Contracting State other than that in which the decision authorising enforcement was given, the time for appealing shall be two months and shall run from the date of service, either on him in person or at his residence. No extension of time may be granted on account of distance.

Article 37

(1) An appeal against the decision authorising enforcement shall be lodged in accordance with the rules governing procedure in contentious matters: ...
    (1) in England and Wales, with the High Court of Justice, or in the case of a maintenance judgment with the Magistrates' Court; ...

(2) The judgment given on the appeal may be contested only: ...
– in the United Kingdom, by a single further appeal on a point of law.

Article 38

The court with which the appeal under the first paragraph of Article 37(1) is lodged may, on the application of the appellant, stay the proceedings if an ordinary appeal has been lodged against the judgment in the State or origin or if the time for such an appeal has not yet expired; in the latter case, the court may specify the time within which such an appeal is to be lodged.

Where the judgment was given in Ireland or the United Kingdom any form of appeal available in the State of origin shall be treated as an ordinary appeal for the purposes of the first paragraph.

The court may also make enforcement conditional on the provision of such security as it shall determine.

Article 39

During the time specified for an appeal pursuant to Article 36 and until any such appeal has been determined, no measures of enforcement may be take other than protective measures taken against the property of the party against whom enforcement is sought.

The decision authorising enforcement shall carry with it the power to proceed to any such protective measures.

Article 40

(1) If the application for enforcement is refused, the applicant may appeal – ...
– in the United Kingdom –
    (a) in England and Wales, to the High Court of Justice, or in the case of a maintenance judgment to the Magistrates' Court; ...

(2) The party against whom enforcement is sought shall be summoned to appear before the appellate court. If he fails to appear, the provisions of the second and third paragraphs of Article 20 shall apply even where he is not domiciled in any of the Contracting States.

Article 41

A judgment given on an appeal provided for in Article 40 may be contested only: ...
– in the United Kingdom, by a single further appeal on a point of law.

Article 42

Where a foreign judgment has been given in respect of several matters and enforcement cannot be authorised for all of them, the court shall authorise enforcement for one or more of them.

An applicant may request partial enforcement of a judgment.

Article 43

A foreign judgment which orders a periodic payment by way of a penalty shall be enforceable in the State in which enforcement is sought only if the amount of the payment has been finally determined by the courts of the State of origin.

Article 44

An applicant who, in the State in which the judgment was given, has benefited from complete or partial legal aid or exemption from costs or expenses, shall be entitled, in the procedures provided for in Articles 32 to 35, to benefit from the most favourable legal aid or the most extensive exemption from costs or expenses provided for by the law of the State addressed.

An applicant who requests the enforcement of a decision given by an administrative authority in Denmark in respect of a maintenance order may, in the State addressed, claim the benefits referred to in the first paragraph if he presents a statement from the Danish Ministry of Justice to the effect that he fulfils the economic requirements to qualify for the grant of complete or partial legal aid or exemption from costs or expenses.

Article 45

No security, bond or deposit, however described, shall be required of a party who in one Contracting State applies for enforcement of a judgment given in another Contracting State on the ground that he is a foreign national or that he is not domiciled or resident in the State in which enforcement is sought.

SECTION 3

Article 46

A party seeking recognition or applying for enforcement of a judgment shall produce:

(1) a copy of the judgment which satisfies the conditions necessary to establish its authenticity;
(2) in the case of a judgment given in default, the original or a certified true copy of the document which establishes that the party in default was served with the document instituting the proceedings or with an equivalent document.

Article 47

A party applying for enforcement shall also produce:

(1) documents which establish that, according to the law of the State of origin the judgment is enforceable and has been served;
(2) where appropriate, a document showing that the applicant is in receipt of legal aid in the State of origin.

Article 48

If the documents specified in Article 46(2) and Article 47(2) are not produced, the court may specify a time for their production, accept equivalent documents or, if it considers that it has sufficient information before it, dispense with their production.

If the court so requires, a translation of the documents shall be produced; the translation shall be certified by a person qualified to do so in one of the Contracting States.

Article 49

No legalisation or other similar formality shall be required in respect of the documents referred to in Articles 46 or 47 or the second paragraph of Article 48, or in respect of a document appointing a representative ad litem.

TITLE IV

AUTHENTIC INSTRUMENTS AND COURT SETTLEMENTS

Article 50

A document which has been formally drawn up or registered as an authentic instrument and is enforceable in one Contracting State shall, in another Contracting State, be declared enforceable there, on application made in accordance with the procedures provided for in Article 31 et seq. The application may be refused only if enforcement of the instrument is contrary to public policy in the State addressed.

The instrument produced must satisfy the conditions necessary to establish its authenticity in the State of origin.

The provisions of Section 3 of Title III shall apply as appropriate.

Article 51

A settlement which has been approved by a court in the course of proceedings and is enforceable in the State in which it was concluded shall be enforceable in the State addressed under the same conditions as authentic instruments.

TITLE V

GENERAL PROVISIONS

Article 52

In order to determine whether a party is domiciled in the Contracting State whose courts are seised of the matter, the court shall apply its internal law.

If a party is not domiciled in the State whose courts are seised of the matter, then, in order to determine whether the party is domiciled in another Contracting State, the court shall apply the law of that State.

Article 53

For the purposes of this Convention, the seat of a company or other legal person or association of natural or legal persons shall be treated as its domicile. However, in order to determine that seat, the court shall apply its rules of private international law.

In order to determine whether a trust is domiciled in the Contracting State whose courts are seised of the matter, the court shall apply its rules of private international law.

TITLE VI

TRANSITIONAL PROVISIONS

Article 54

The provisions of this Convention shall apply only to legal proceedings instituted and to documents formally drawn up or registered as authentic instruments after its entry into force in the State of origin and, where recognition or enforcement of a judgment or authentic instruments is sought, in the State addressed.

However, judgments given after the date of entry into force of this Convention between the State of origin and the State addressed in proceedings instituted before that date shall be recognised and enforced in accordance with the provisions of Title III if jurisdiction was founded upon rules which accorded with those provided for either in Title II of this Convention or in a convention concluded between the State of origin and the State addressed which was in force when the proceedings were instituted.

If the parties to a dispute concerning a contract had agreed in writing before 1 June 1988 for Ireland or before 1 January 1987 for the United Kingdom that the contract was to be governed by the law of Ireland or of a part of the United Kingdom, the courts of Ireland or of that part of the United Kingdom shall retain the right to exercise jurisdiction in the dispute...

TITLE VII

RELATIONSHIP TO OTHER CONVENTIONS

Article 55

Subject to the provisions of the second paragraph of Article 54, and of Article 56, this Convention shall, for the States which are parties to it, supersede the following conventions concluded between two or more of them: ...

– the Convention between the United Kingdom and the French Republic providing for the Reciprocal Enforcement of Judgments in Civil and Commercial Matters, with Protocol, signed at Paris on 18 January 1934;

– the Convention between the United Kingdom and the Kingdom of Belgium providing for the Reciprocal Enforcement of Judgments in Civil and Commercial Matters, with Protocol, signed at Brussels on 2 May 1934; ...

– the Convention between the United Kingdom and the Federal Republic of Germany for the Reciprocal Recognition and Enforcement of Judgments in Civil and Commercial Matters, signed at Bonn on 14 July 1960; ...

– the Convention between the United Kingdom and the Republic of Italy for the Reciprocal Recognition and Enforcement of Judgments in Civil and Commercial Matters, signed at Rome on 7 February 1964, with amending Protocol signed at Rome on 14 July 1970;

– the Convention between the United Kingdom and the Kingdom of the Netherlands providing for the Reciprocal Recognition and Enforcement of Judgments in Civil Matters, signed at The Hague on 17 November 1967. ...

Article 56

The Treaty and the conventions referred to in Article 55 shall continue to have effect in relation to matters to which this Convention does not apply.

They shall continue to have effect in respect of judgments given and documents formally drawn up or registered as authentic instruments before the entry into force of this Convention.

Article 57

(1) This Convention shall not affect any conventions to which the Contracting States are or will be parties and which in relation to particular matters, govern jurisdiction or the recognition or enforcement of judgments.

(2) With a view to its uniform interpretation, paragraph 1 shall be applied in the following manner –

(a) this Convention shall not prevent a court of a Contracting State which is a party to a convention on a particular matter from assuming jurisdiction in accordance with that Convention, even where the defendant is domiciled in another Contracting State which is not a party to that Convention. The court hearing the action shall, in any event, apply Article 20 of this Convention;
(b) judgments given in a Contracting State by a court in the exercise of jurisdiction provided for in a convention on a particular matter shall be recognised and enforced in the other Contracting State in accordance with this Convention.

Where a convention on a particular matter to which both the State of origin and the State addressed are parties lays down conditions for the recognition or enforcement of judgments, those conditions shall apply. In any event, the provisions of this Convention which concern the procedure for recognition and enforcement of judgments may be applied.

(3) This Convention shall not affect the application of provisions which, in relation to particular matters, govern jurisdiction or the recognition or enforcement of judgments and which are or will be contained in acts of the institutions of the European Communities or in national laws harmonised in implementation of such acts.

Article 58

Until such time as the Convention on jurisdiction and the enforcement of judgments in civil and commercial matters, signed at Lugano on 16 September 1988, takes effect with regard to France and the Swiss Confederation, this convention shall not affect the rights granted to Swiss nationals by the Convention between France and the Swiss Confederation on Jurisdiction and the Enforcement of Judgments in Civil Matters, signed at Paris on 15 June 1869.

Article 59

This Convention shall not prevent a Contracting State from assuming, in a convention on the recognition and enforcement of judgments, an obligation towards a third State not to recognise judgments given in other Contracting States against defendants domiciled or habitually resident in the third State where, in cases provided for in Article 4, the judgment could only be founded on a ground of jurisdiction specified in the second paragraph of Article 3.

However, a Contracting State may not assume an obligation towards a third State not to recognise a judgment given in another Contracting State by a court basing its jurisdiction on the presence within that State of property belonging to the defendant, or the seizure by the plaintiff of property situated there:

(1) if the action is brought to assert or declare proprietary or possessory rights in that property, seeks to obtain authority to dispose of it, or arises from another issue relating to such property, or,
(2) if the property constitutes the security for a debt which is the subject-matter of the action.

TITLE VIII

FINAL PROVISIONS

Article 61

This Convention shall be ratified by the signatory States. The instruments of ratification shall be deposited with the Secretary-General of the Council of the European Communities.

Article 62

This convention shall enter into force on the first day of the third month following the deposit of the instrument of ratification by the last signatory State to take this step.

Article 63

The Contracting States recognise that any State which becomes a member of the European Economic Community shall be required to accept this Convention as a basis for the negotiations between the Contracting States and that State necessary to ensure the implementation of the last paragraph of Article 220 of the Treaty establishing the European Economic Community.

The necessary adjustments may be the subject of a special convention between the Contracting States of the one part and the new Member State of the other part.

Article 64

The Secretary-General of the Council of the European Communities shall notify the signatory States of:

(a) the deposit of each instrument of ratification;
(b) the date of entry into force of this Convention;
(d) any declaration received pursuant to Article IV of the Protocol;
(e) any communication made pursuant to Article VI of the Protocol.

Article 65

The Protocol annexed to this Convention by common accord of the Contracting States shall form an integral part thereof.

Article 66

This convention is concluded for an unlimited period.

Article 67

Any Contracting State may request the revision of this Convention. In this event, a revision conference shall be convened by the President of the Council of the European Communities.

Article 68

This convention, drawn up in a single original in the Dutch, French, German and Italian languages, all four texts being equally authentic, shall be deposited in the archives of the Secretariat of the Council of the European Communities. The Secretary-General shall transmit a certified copy to the Government of each signatory State. ...

SCHEDULE 2

TEXT OF 1971 PROTOCOL, AS AMENDED

Article 1

The Court of Justice of the European Communities shall have jurisdiction to give rulings on the interpretation of the Convention on Jurisdiction and the Enforcement of Judgments in Civil and Commercial Matters and of the Protocol annexed to that Convention signed at Brussels on 27 September 1968, and also on the interpretation of the present Protocol.

The Court of Justice of the European Communities shall also have jurisdiction to give rulings on the interpretation of the Convention on the Accession of the Kingdom of Denmark, Ireland and the United Kingdom of Great Britain and Northern Ireland to the Convention of 27 September 1968 and to this Protocol.

The Court of Justice of the European Communities shall also have jurisdiction to give rulings on the interpretation of the Convention on the accession of the Kingdom of Spain and the Portuguese Republic to the Convention of 27 September 1968 and to this Protocol, as adjusted by the 1978 Convention and the 1982 Convention.

Article 2

The following courts may request the Court of Justice to give preliminary rulings on questions of interpretation: ...

– in the United Kingdom: the House of Lords and courts to which application has been made under the second paragraph of Article 37 or under Article 41 of the Convention;

(2) the courts of the contracting States when they are sitting in an appellate capacity;

(3) in the cases provided for in Article 37 of the Convention, the courts referred to in that Article.

Article 3

(1) Where a question of interpretation of the Convention or of one of the other instruments referred to in Article 1 is raised in a case pending before one of the courts listed in Article 2(1) that court shall, if it considers that a decision on the question is necessary to enable it to give judgment, request the Court of Justice to give a ruling thereon.

(2) Where such a question is raised before any court referred to in Article 2(2) or (3), that court may, under the conditions laid down in paragraph (1), request the Court of Justice to give a ruling thereon.

Article 4

(1) The competent authority of a Contracting State may request the Court of Justice to give a ruling on a question of interpretation of the Convention or of one of the other instruments referred to in Article 1 if judgments given by courts of that State conflict with the interpretation given either by the Court of Justice or in a judgment of one of the courts of another Contracting State referred to in article 2(1) or (2). The provisions of this paragraph shall apply only to judgments which have become res judicata.

(2) The interpretation given by the Court of Justice in response to such a request shall not affect the judgments which gave rise to the request for interpretation.

(3) The Procurators-General of the Courts of Cassation of the Contracting States, or

any other authority designated by a Contracting State, shall be entitled to request the Court of Justice for a ruling on interpretation in accordance with paragraph (1).

(4) The Registrar of the Court of Justice shall give notice of the request to the Contracting States, to the Commission and to the Council of the European Communities; they shall then be entitled within two months of the notification to submit statements of case or written observations to the Court.

(5) No fees shall be levied or any costs or expenses awarded in respect of the proceedings provided for in this Article.

Article 5

(1) Except where this Protocol otherwise provides, the provisions of the Treaty establishing the European Economic Community and those of the Protocol on the Statute of the Court of Justice annexed thereto, which are applicable when the Court is requested to give a preliminary ruling, shall also apply to any proceedings for the interpretation of the Convention and the other instruments referred to in Article 1.

(2) The Rules of Procedure of the Court of Justice shall, if necessary, be adjusted and supplemented in accordance with Article 188 of the Treaty establishing the European Economic Community.

Article 7

This Protocol shall be ratified by the signatory States. The instruments of ratification shall be deposited with the Secretary-General of the Council of the European Communities.

Article 8

This Protocol shall enter into force on the first day of the third month following the deposit of the instrument of ratification by the last signatory State to take this step; provided that it shall at the earliest enter into force at the same time as the Convention of 27 September 1968 on Jurisdiction and the Enforcement of Judgments in Civil and Commercial Matters.

Article 9

The Contracting States recognise that any State which becomes a member of the European Economic Community, and to which Article 63 of the Convention on Jurisdiction and the Enforcement of Judgments in Civil and Commercial Matters applies, must accept the provisions of this Protocol, subject to such adjustments as may be required.

Article 10

The Secretary-General of the Council of the European Communities shall notify the signatory States of:

(a) the deposit of each instrument of ratification;

(b) the date of entry into force of this Protocol;

(c) any designation received pursuant to Article 4(3).

Article 11

The Contracting States shall communicate to the Secretary-General of the Council of the European Communities the texts of any provisions of their laws which necessitate an amendment to the list of courts in Article 2(1).

Article 12

This Protocol is concluded for an unlimited period.

Article 13

Any Contracting State may request the revision of this Protocol. In this event, a revision conference shall be convened by the President of the Council of the European Communities.

Article 14

This Protocol, drawn up in a single original in the Dutch, French, German and Italian languages, all four texts being equally authentic, shall be deposited in the archives of the Secretariat of the Council of the European Communities. The Secretary-General shall transmit a certified copy to the Government of each signatory State.

SCHEDULE 3C

TEXT OF THE LUGANO CONVENTION …

CONVENTION ON JURISDICTION AND THE ENFORCEMENT OF JUDGMENTS IN CIVIL AND COMMERCIAL MATTERS

PREAMBLE

The High Contracting Parties to this Convention,

Anxious to strengthen in their territories the legal protection of persons therein established,

Considering that it is necessary for this purpose to determine the international jurisdiction of their courts, to facilitate recognition and to introduce an expeditious procedure for securing the enforcement of judgments, authentic instruments and court settlements,

Aware of the links between them, which have been sanctioned in the economic field by the free trade agreements concluded between the European Economic Community and the States members of the European Free Trade Association,

Taking into account the Brussels Convention of 27 September 1968 on jurisdiction and the enforcement of judgments in civil and commercial matters, as amended by the Accession Conventions under the successive enlargements of the European Communities,

Persuaded that the extension of the principles of that Convention to the States parties to this instrument will strengthen legal and economic cooperation in Europe.

Desiring to ensure as uniform an interpretation as possible of this instrument,

Have in this spirit decided to conclude this Convention and

Have agreed as follows:

TITLE I

SCOPE

Article 1

This Convention shall apply in civil and commercial matters whatever the nature of the court or tribunal. It shall not extend, in particular, to revenue, customs or administrative matters.

The Convention shall not apply to

1. the status or legal capacity of natural persons, rights in property arising out of matrimonial relationship, wills and succession;

2. bankruptcy, proceedings relating to the winding-up of insolvent companies or other legal persons, judicial arrangements, compositions and analogous proceedings;

3. social security;

4. arbitration.

TITLE II

JURISDICTION

SECTION 1

Article 2

Subject to the provisions of this Convention, persons domiciled in a Contracting State shall, whatever their nationality, be sued in the courts of that State.

Persons who are not nationals of the State in which they are domiciled shall be governed by the rules of jurisdiction applicable to nationals of that State.

Article 3

Persons domiciled in a Contracting State may be sued in the courts of another Contracting State only by virtue of the rules set out in Sections 2 to 6 of this Title.

In particular the following provisions shall not be applicable as against them: ...

– in the United Kingdom: the rules which enable jurisdiction to be founded on:

(a) the document instituting the proceedings having been served on the defendant during his temporary presence in the United Kingdom; or

(b) the presence within the United Kingdom of property belonging to the defendant; or

(c) the seizure by the plaintiff of property situated in the United Kingdom.

Article 4

If the defendant is not domiciled in a Contracting State, the jurisdiction of the courts of each Contracting State shall, subject to the provisions of Article 16, be determined by the law of that State.

As against such a defendant, any person domiciled in a Contracting State may, whatever his nationality, avail himself in that State of the rules of jurisdiction there in force, and in particular those specified in the second paragraph of Article 3, in the same way as the nationals of that State.

SECTION 2

Article 5

A person domiciled in a Contracting State may, in another Contracting State, be sued:

1. in matters relating to a contract, in the courts for the place of performance of the obligation in question; in matters relating to individual contracts of employment, this place is that where the employee habitually carries out his work,

or if the employee does not habitually carry out his work in any one country, this place shall be the place of business through which he was engaged;

2. in matters relating to maintenance, in the courts for the place where the maintenance creditor is domiciled or habitually resident or, if the matter is ancillary to proceedings concerning the status of a person, in the court which, according to its own law, has jurisdiction to entertain those proceedings, unless that jurisdiction is based solely on the nationality of one of the parties;

3. in matters relating to tort, delict or quasi-delict, in the courts for the place where the harmful event occurred;

4. as regards a civil claim for damages or restitution which is based on an act giving rise to criminal proceedings, in the court seised of those proceedings, to the extent that that court has jurisdiction under its own law to entertain civil proceedings;

5. as regards a dispute arising out of the operations of a branch, agency or other establishment, in the courts for the place in which the branch, agency or other establishment is situated;

6. in his capacity as settlor, trustee or beneficiary of a trust created by the operation of a statute, or by a written instrument, or created orally and evidenced in writing, in the courts of the Contracting State in which the trust is domiciled;

7. as regards a dispute concerning the payment of remuneration claimed in respect of the salvage of a cargo or freight, in the court under the authority of which the cargo or freight in question:

(a) has been arrested to secure such payment, or

(b) could have been so arrested, but bail or other security has been given;

provided that this provision shall apply only if it is claimed that the defendant has an interest in the cargo or freight or had such an interest at the time of salvage.

Article 6

A person domiciled in a Contracting State may also be sued:

1. where he is one of a number of defendants, in the courts for the place where any one of them is domiciled;

2. as a third party in an action on a warranty or guarantee or in any other third party proceedings, in the court seised of the original proceedings, unless these were instituted solely with the object of removing him from the jurisdiction of the court which would be competent in his case;

3. on a counterclaim arising from the same contract or facts on which the original claim was based, in the court in which the original claim is pending;

4. in matters relating to a contract, if the action may be combined with an action against the same defendant in matters relating to rights in rem in immovable property, in the court of the Contracting State in which the property is situated.

Article 6A

Where by virtue of this Convention a court of a Contracting State has jurisdiction in actions relating to liability arising from the use or operation of a ship, that court, or any other court substituted for this purpose by the internal law of that State, shall also have jurisdiction over claims for limitation of such liability.

SECTION 3

Article 7

In matters relating to insurance, jurisdiction shall be determined by this Section, without prejudice to the provisions of Articles 4 and 5(5).

Article 8

An insurer domiciled in a Contracting State may be sued:

1. in the courts of the State where he is domiciled; or

2. in another Contracting State, in the courts for the place where the policy-holder is domiciled; or

3. if he is a co-insurer, in the courts of a Contracting State in which proceedings are brought against the leading insurer.

An insurer who is not domiciled in a Contracting State but has a branch, agency or other establishment in one of the Contracting States shall, in disputes arising out of the operations of the branch, agency or establishment, be deemed to be domiciled in that State.

Article 9

In respect of liability insurance or insurance of immovable property, the insurer may in addition be sued in the courts for the place where the harmful event occurred. The same applies if movable and immovable property are covered by the same insurance policy and both are adversely affected by the same contingency.

Article 10

In respect of liability insurance, the insurer may also, if the law of the court permits it, be joined in proceedings which the injured party has brought against the insured.

The provisions of Articles 7, 8 and 9 shall apply to actions brought by the injured party directly against the insurer, where such direct actions are permitted.

If the law governing such direct actions provides that the policy-holder or the insured may be joined as a party to the action, the same court shall have jurisdiction over them.

Article 11

Without prejudice to the provisions of the third paragraph of Article 10, an insurer may bring proceedings only in the courts of the Contracting State in which the defendant is domiciled, irrespective of whether he is the policy-holder, the insured or a beneficiary.

The provisions of this Section shall not affect the right to bring a counterclaim in the courts in which, in accordance with this Section, the original claim is pending.

Article 12

The provisions of this Section may be departed from only by an agreement on jurisdiction:

1. which is entered into after the dispute has arisen; or

2. which allows the policy-holder, the insured or a beneficiary to bring proceedings in courts other than those indicated in this Section; or

3. which is concluded between a policy-holder and an insurer, both of whom are

at the time of conclusion of the contract domiciled or habitually resident in the same Contracting State, and which has the effect of conferring jurisdiction on the courts of that State even if the harmful event were to occur abroad, provided that such an agreement is not contrary to the law of the State; or

4. which is concluded with a policy-holder who is not domiciled in a Contracting State, except in so far as the insurance is compulsory or relates to immovable property in a Contracting State; or

5. which relates to a contract of insurance in so far as it covers one or more of the risks set out in Article 12A.

Article 12A

The following are the risks referred to in Article 12(5):

1. any loss of or damage to:

    (a) sea-going ships, installations situated offshore or on the high seas, or aircraft, arising from perils which relate to their use for commercial purposes;
    (b) goods in transit other than passengers' baggage where the transit consists of or includes carriage by such ships or aircraft;

2. any liability, other than for bodily injury to passengers or loss of or damage to their baggage;

    (a) arising out of the use or operation of ships, installations or aircraft as referred to in (1)(a) above in so far as the law of the Contracting State in which such aircraft are registered does not prohibit agreements on jurisdiction regarding insurance of such risks;
    (b) for loss or damage caused by goods in transit as described in (1)(b) above;

3. any financial loss connected with the use or operation of ships, installations or aircraft as referred to in (1)(a) above, in particular loss of freight or charter-hire;

4. any risk or interest connected with any of those referred to in (1) to (3) above.

SECTION 4

Article 13

In proceedings concerning a contract concluded by a person for a purpose which can be regarded as being outside his trade or profession, hereinafter called 'the consumer', jurisdiction shall be determined by this Section, without prejudice to the provisions of Articles 4 and 5(5), if it is:

1. a contract for the sale of goods on instalment credit terms; or

2. a contract for a loan repayable by instalments, or for any other form of credit, made to finance the sale of goods; or

3. any other contract for the supply of goods or a contract for the supply of services, and

    (a) in the State of the consumer's domicile the conclusion of the contract was preceded by a specific invitation addressed to him or by advertising, and
    (b) the consumer took in that State the steps necessary for the conclusion of the contract.

Where a consumer enters into a contract with a party who is not domiciled in a Contracting State but has a branch, agency or other establishment in one of the Contracting States, that party shall, in disputes arising out of the operations of the branch, agency or establishment, be deemed to be domiciled in that State.

This Section shall not apply to contracts of transport.

Article 14

A consumer may bring proceedings against the other party to a contract either in the courts of the Contracting State in which that party is domiciled or in the courts of the Contracting State in which he is himself domiciled.

Proceedings may be brought against a consumer by the other party to the contract only in the courts of the Contracting State in which the consumer is domiciled.

These provisions shall not affect the right to bring a counterclaim in the court in which, in accordance with this Section, the original claim is pending.

Article 15

The provisions of this Section may be departed from only by an agreement:

1. which is entered into after the dispute has arisen; or

2. which allows the consumer to bring proceedings in courts other than those indicated in this Section; or

3. which is entered into by the consumer and the other party to the contract, both of whom are at the time of conclusion of the contract domiciled or habitually resident in the same Contracting State, and which confers jurisdiction on the courts of that State, provided that such an agreement is not contrary to the law of that State.

SECTION 5

Article 16

The following courts shall have exclusive jurisdiction, regardless of domicile:

1. (a) in proceedings which have as their object rights in rem in immovable property or tenancies of immovable property, the courts of the Contracting State in which the property is situated;

    (b) however, in proceedings which have as their object tenancies of immovable property concluded for temporary private use for a maximum period of six consecutive months, the courts of the Contracting State in which the defendant is domiciled shall also have jurisdiction, provided that the tenant is a natural person and neither party is domiciled in the Contracting State in which the property is situated;

2. in proceedings which have as their object the validity of the constitution, the nullity or the dissolution of companies or other legal persons or associations of natural or legal persons, or the decision of their organs, the courts of the Contracting State in which the company, legal persons or association has its seat;

3. in proceedings which have as their object the validity of entries in public registers, the courts of the Contracting State in which the register is kept;

4. in proceedings concerned with the registration or validity of patents, trade marks, designs, or other similar rights required to be deposited or registered, the courts of the Contracting State in which the deposit or registration has been applied for, has taken place or is under the terms of an international convention deemed to have taken place;

5. in proceedings concerned with the enforcement of judgments, the courts of the Contracting State in which the judgment has been or is to be enforced.

SECTION 6

Article 17

1. If the parties, one or more of whom is domiciled in a Contracting State, have agreed that a court or the courts of a Contracting State are to have jurisdiction to settle any disputes which have arisen or which may arise in connection with a particular legal relationship, that court or those courts shall have exclusive jurisdiction. Such an agreement conferring jurisdiction shall be either:

(a) in writing or evidenced in writing, or
(b) in a form which accords with practices which the parties have established between themselves, or
(c) in international trade or commerce, in a form which accords with a usage of which the parties are or ought to have been aware and which in such trade or commerce is widely known to, and regularly observed by, parties to contracts of the type involved in the particular trade or commerce concerned.

Where such an agreement is concluded by parties, none of whom is domiciled in a Contracting State, the courts of other Contracting States shall have no jurisdiction over their disputes unless the court or courts chosen have declined jurisdiction.

2. The court or courts of a Contracting State on which a trust instrument has conferred jurisdiction shall have exclusive jurisdiction in any proceedings brought against a settlor, trustee or beneficiary, if relations between these persons or their rights or obligations under the trust are involved.

3. Agreements or provisions of a trust instrument conferring jurisdiction shall have no legal force if they are contrary to the provisions of Article 12 or 15, or if the courts whose jurisdiction they purport to exclude have exclusive jurisdiction by virtue of Article 16.

4. If an agreement conferring jurisdiction was concluded for the benefit of only one of the parties, that party shall retain the right to bring proceedings in any other court which has jurisdiction by virtue of this Convention.

5. In matters relating to individual contracts of employment an agreement conferring jurisdiction shall have legal force only if it is entered into after the dispute has arisen.

Article 18

Apart from jurisdiction derived from other provisions of this Convention, a court of a Contracting State before whom a defendant enters an appearance shall have jurisdiction.. This rule shall not apply where appearance was entered solely to contest the jurisdiction, or where another court has exclusive jurisdiction by virtue of Article 16.

SECTION 7

Article 19

Where a court of a Contracting State is seised of a claim which is principally concerned with a matter over which the courts of another Contracting State have exclusive jurisdiction by virtue of Article 16, it shall declare of its own motion that it has no jurisdiction.

Article 20

Where a defendant domiciled in one Contracting State is sued in a court of another Contracting State and does not enter an appearance, the court shall declare of its own motion that it has no jurisdiction unless its jurisdiction is derived from the provisions of this Convention.

The court shall stay the proceedings so long as it is not shown that the defendant has been able to receive the document instituting the proceedings or an equivalent document in sufficient time to enable him to arrange for his defence, or that all necessary steps have been taken to this end.

The provisions of the foregoing paragraph shall be replaced by those of Article 15 of the Hague Convention of 15 November 1965 on the service abroad of judicial and extrajudicial documents in civil or commercial matters, if the document instituting the proceedings or notice thereof had to be transmitted abroad in accordance with that Convention.

SECTION 8

Article 21

Where proceedings involving the same cause of action and between the same parties are brought in the courts of different Contracting States any court other than the court first seised shall of its own motion stay its proceedings until such time as the jurisdiction of the court first seised is established.

Where the jurisdiction of the court first seised is established, any court other than the court first seised shall decline jurisdiction in favour of that court.

Article 22

Where related actions are brought in the courts of different Contracting States, any court other than the court first seised may, while the actions are pending at first instance, stay its proceedings.

A court other than the court first seised may also, on the application of one of the parties, decline jurisdiction if the law of that court permits the consolidation of related actions and the court first seised has jurisdiction over both actions.

For the purposes of this Article, actions are deemed to be related where they are so closely connected that it is expedient to hear and determine them together to avoid the risk of irreconcilable judgments resulting from separate proceedings.

Article 23

Where actions come within the exclusive jurisdiction of several courts, any court other than the court first seised shall decline jurisdiction in favour of that court.

SECTION 9

Article 24

Application may be made to the courts of a Contracting State for such provisional, including protective, measures as may be available under the law of that State, even if, under this Convention, the courts of another Contracting State have jurisdiction as to the substance of the matter.

TITLE III

RECOGNITION AND ENFORCEMENT

Article 25

For the purposes of this Convention, 'judgment' means any judgment given by a court or tribunal of a Contracting State, whatever the judgment may be called, including a decree, order, decision or writ of execution, as well as the determination of costs or expenses by an officer of the court.

SECTION 1

Article 26

A judgment given in a Contracting State shall be recognised in the other Contracting States without any special procedure being required.

Any interested party who raises the recognition of a judgment as the principal issue in the dispute may, in accordance with the procedures provided for in Sections 2 and 3 of this Title, apply for a decision that the judgment be recognised.

If the outcome of proceedings in a court of a Contracting State depends on the determination of an incidental question of recognition that court shall have jurisdiction over that question.

Article 27

A judgment shall not be recognised:

1. if such recognition is contrary to public policy in the State in which recognition is sought;

2. where it was given in default of appearance, if the defendant was not duly served with the document which instituted the proceedings or with an equivalent documents in sufficient time to enable him to arrange for his defence;

3. if the judgment is irreconcilable with a judgment given in a dispute between the same parties in the State in which recognition is sought;

4. if the court of the State of origin, in order to arrive at its judgment, has decided a preliminary question concerning the status or legal capacity of natural persons, rights in property arising out of a matrimonial relationship, wills or succession in a way that conflicts with a rule of the private international law of the State in which the recognition is sought, unless the same result would have been reached by the application of the rules of private international law of that State;

5. if the judgment is irreconcilable with an earlier judgment given in a non-contracting State involving the same cause of action and between the same parties, provided that this latter judgment fulfils the conditions necessary for its recognition in the State addressed.

Article 28

Moreover, a judgment shall not be recognised if it conflicts with the provisions of Section 3, 4 or 5 of Title II or in a case provided for in Article 59.

A judgment may furthermore be refused recognition in any case provided for in Article 54B(3) or 57(4).

In its examination of the grounds of jurisdiction referred to in the foregoing paragraphs, the court or authority applied to shall be bound by the findings of fact on which the court of the State of origin based its jurisdiction.

Subject to the provisions of the first and second paragraphs, the jurisdiction of the court of the State of origin may not be reviewed; the test of public policy referred to in Article 27(1) may not be applied to the rules relating to jurisdiction.

Article 29

Under no circumstances may a foreign judgment be reviewed as to its substance.

Article 30

A court of a Contracting State in which recognition is sought of a judgment given in another Contracting State may stay the proceedings if an ordinary appeal against the judgment has been lodged.

A court of a Contracting State in which recognition is sought of a judgment given in Ireland or the United Kingdom may stay the proceedings if enforcement is suspended in the State of origin by reason of an appeal.

SECTION 2

Article 31

A judgment given in a Contracting State and enforceable in that State shall be enforced in another Contracting State when, on the application of any interested party, it has been declared enforceable there.

However, in the United Kingdom, such a judgment shall be enforced in England and Wales, in Scotland, or in Northern Ireland when, on the application of any interested party, it has been registered for enforcement in that part of the United Kingdom.

Article 32

1. The application shall be submitted: ...
– in the United Kingdom:
   (a) in England and Wales, to the High Court of Justice, or in the case of a maintenance judgment to the Magistrates' Court on transmission by the Secretary of State; ...

2. The jurisdiction of local courts shall be determined by reference to the place of domicile of the party against whom enforcement is sought. If he is not domiciled in the State in which enforcement is sought, it shall be determined by reference to the place of enforcement.

Article 33

The procedure for making the application shall be governed by the law of the State in which enforcement is sought.

The applicant must give an address for service of process within the area of jurisdiction of the court applied to. However, if the law of the State in which enforcement is sought does not provide for the furnishing of such an address, the applicant shall appoint a representative ad litem.

The documents referred to in Articles 46 and 47 shall be attached to the application.

Article 34

The court applied to shall give its decision without delay; the party against whom enforcement is sought shall not at this stage of the proceedings be entitled to make any submissions on the application.

The application may be refused only for one of the reasons specified in Articles 27 and 28.

Under no circumstances may the foreign judgment be reviewed as to its substance.

Article 35

The appropriate officer of the court shall without delay bring the decision given on the application to the notice of the applicant in accordance with the procedure laid down by the law of the State in which enforcement is sought.

Article 36

If enforcement is authorised, the party against whom enforcement is sought may appeal against the decision within one month of service thereof.

If that party is domiciled in a Contracting State other than that in which the decision authorising enforcement was given, the time for appealing shall be two months and shall run from the date of service, either on him in person or at his residence. No extension of time may be granted on account of distance.

Article 37

1. An appeal against the decision authorising enforcement shall be lodged in accordance with the rules governing procedure in contentious matters: ...

– in the United Kingdom:

> (a) in England and Wales, with the High Court of Justice, or in the case of a maintenance judgment with the Magistrates' Court: ...

2. The judgment given on the appeal may be contested only: ...

– in the United Kingdom, by a single further appeal on a point of law.

Article 38

The court with which the appeal under the first paragraph of Article 37 is lodged may, on the application of the appellant, stay the proceedings if an ordinary appeal has been lodged against the judgment in the State of origin or if the time for such an appeal has not yet expired; in the latter case, the court may specify the time within which such an appeal is to be lodged.

Where the judgment was given in Ireland or the United Kingdom, any form of appeal available in the State of origin shall be treated as an ordinary appeal for the purposes of the first paragraph.

The court may also make enforcement conditional on the provision of such security as it shall determine.

Article 39

During the time specified for an appeal pursuant to Article 36 and until any such appeal has been determined, no measures of enforcement may be taken other than protective measures taken against the property of the party against whom enforcement is sought.

The decision authorising enforcement shall carry with it the power to proceed to any such protective measures.

Article 40

1. If the application for enforcement is refused, the applicant may appeal: ...

– in the United Kingdom

> (a) in England and Wales, to the High Court of Justice, or in the case of a maintenance judgment to the Magistrates' Court; ...

2. The party against whom enforcement is sought shall be summoned to appear before the appellate court. If he fails to appear, the provisions of the second and third paragraphs of Article 20 shall apply even where he is not domiciled in any of the Contracting States.

Article 41

A judgment given on an appeal provided for in Article 40 may be contested only: ...
– in the United Kingdom, by a single further appeal on a point of law.

Article 42

Where a foreign judgment has been given in respect of several matters and enforcement cannot be authorised for all of them, the court shall authorise enforcement for one or more of them.

An applicant may request partial enforcement of a judgment.

Article 43

A foreign judgment which orders a periodic payment by way of a penalty shall be enforceable in the State in which enforcement is sought only if the amount of the payment has been finally determined by the courts of the State of origin.

Article 44

An applicant who, in the state of origin, has benefited from complete or partial legal aid or exemption from costs or expenses, shall be entitled, in the procedures provided for in Articles 32 to 35, to benefit from the most favourable legal aid or the most extensive exemption from costs or expenses provided for by the law of the State addressed.

However, an applicant who requests the enforcement of a decision given by an administrative authority in Denmark or in Iceland in respect of a maintenance order may, in the State addressed, claim the benefits referred to in the first paragraph if he presents a statement from, respectively, the Danish Ministry of Justice or the Icelandic Ministry of Justice to the effect that he fulfils the economic requirements to qualify for the grant of complete or partial legal aid or exemption from costs or expenses.

Article 45

No security, bond or deposit, however described, shall be required of a party who in one Contracting State applies for enforcement of a judgment given in another Contracting State on the ground that he is a foreign national or that he is not domiciled or resident in the State in which enforcement is sought.

SECTION 3

Article 46

A party seeking recognition or applying for enforcement of a judgment shall produce:

1. a copy of the judgment which satisfies the conditions necessary to establish its authenticity;

2. in the case of a judgment given in default, the original or a certified true copy of the document which establishes that the party in default was served with the document instituting the proceedings or with an equivalent document.

Article 47

A party applying for enforcement shall also produce:

1. documents which establish that, according to the law of the State of origin, the judgment is enforceable and has been served;

2. where appropriate, a document showing that the applicant is in receipt of legal aid in the State of origin.

Article 48

If the documents specified in Article 46(2) and Article 47(2) are not produced, the court may specify a time for their production, accept equivalent documents or, if it considers that it has sufficient information before it, dispense with their production.

If the court so requires, a translation of the documents shall be produced; the translation shall be certified by a person qualified to do so in one of the Contracting States.

Article 49

No legislation or other similar formality shall be required in respect of the documents referred to in Article 46 or 47 or the second paragraph of Article 48, or in respect of a document appointing a representative ad litem.

TITLE IV

AUTHENTIC INSTRUMENTS AND COURT SETTLEMENTS

Article 50

A document which has been formally drawn up or registered as an authentic instrument and is enforceable in one Contracting State shall, in another Contracting State, be declared enforceable there, on application made in accordance with the procedures provided for in Articles 31 et seq. The application may be refused only if enforcement of the instrument is contrary to public policy in the State addressed.

The instrument produced must satisfy the conditions necessary to establish its authenticity in the State of origin.

The provisions of Section 3 of Title III shall apply as appropriate.

Article 51

A settlement which has been approved by a court in the course of proceedings and is enforceable in the State in which it was concluded shall be enforceable in the State addressed under the same conditions as authentic instruments.

TITLE V

GENERAL PROVISIONS

Article 52

In order to determine whether a party is domiciled in the Contracting State whose courts are seised of a matter, the court shall apply its internal law.

If a party is not domiciled in the State whose courts are seised of the matter, then, in order to determine whether the party is domiciled in another Contracting State, the court shall apply the law of that State.

Article 53

For the purposes of this Convention, the seat of a company or other legal person or association of natural or legal persons shall be treated as its domicile. However, in order to determine that seat, the court shall apply its rules of private international law.

In order to determine whether a trust is domiciled in the Contracting State whose courts are seised of the matter, the court shall apply its rules of private international law.

TITLE VI

TRANSITIONAL PROVISIONS

Article 54

The provisions of this Convention shall apply only to legal proceedings instituted and to documents formally drawn up or registered as authentic instruments after its entry into force in the State of origin and, where recognition or enforcement of a judgment or authentic instrument is sought, in the State addressed.

However, judgments given after the date of entry into force of this Convention between the State of origin and the State addressed in proceedings instituted before that date shall be recognised and enforced in accordance with the provisions of Title III if jurisdiction was founded upon rules which accorded with those provided for either in Title II of this Convention or in a convention concluded between the State of origin and the State addressed which was in force when the proceedings were instituted.

If the parties to a dispute concerning a contract had agreed in writing before the entry into force of this Convention that the contract was to be governed by the law of Ireland or of a part of the United Kingdom, the courts of Ireland or of that part of the United Kingdom shall retain the right to exercise jurisdiction in the dispute.

...

TITLE VII

RELATIONSHIP TO THE BRUSSELS CONVENTION AND TO OTHER CONVENTIONS

Article 54B

1. This Convention shall not prejudice the application by the Member States of the European Communities of the Convention on Jurisdiction and the Enforcement of Judgments in Civil and Commercial Matters, signed at Brussels on 27 September 1968 and of the Protocol on interpretation of that Convention by the Court of Justice, signed at Luxembourg on 3 June 1971, as amended by the Convention of Accession to the said Convention and the said Protocol by the States acceding to the European Communities, all of these Conventions and the Protocol being hereinafter referred to as the 'Brussels Convention'.

2. However, this Convention shall in any event be applied:

(a) in matters of jurisdiction, where the defendant is domiciled in the territory of a Contracting State which is not a member of the European Communities, or where Article 16 or 17 of this Convention confers a jurisdiction on the courts of such a Contracting State;

(b) in relation to a lis pendens or to related actions as provided for in Articles 21 and 22, when proceedings are instituted in a Contracting State which is not a member of the European Communities and in a Contracting State which is a member of the European Communities;

(c) in matters of recognition and enforcement, where either the State of origin or the State addressed is not a member of the European Communities.

3. In addition to the grounds provided for in Title III recognition or enforcement may be refused if the ground of jurisdiction on which the judgment has been based differs from that resulting from this Convention and recognition or enforcement is sought against a party who is domiciled in a Contracting State which is not a member of the European Communities, unless the judgment may otherwise be recognised or enforced under any rule of law in the State addressed.

Article 55

Subject to the provisions of the second paragraph of Article 54 and of Article 56, this Convention shall, for the States which are parties to it, supersede the following conventions concluded between two or more of them: ...

– the Convention between Norway and the United Kingdom providing for the reciprocal recognition and enforcement of judgments in civil matters, signed at London on 12 June 1961.

– the Convention between the United Kingdom and Austria providing for the reciprocal recognition and enforcement of judgments in civil and commercial matters, signed at Vienna on 14 July 1961, with amending Protocol signed at London on 6 March 1970.

Article 56

The Treaty and the conventions referred to in Article 55 shall continue to have effect in relation to matters to which this Convention does not apply.

They shall continue to have effect in respect of judgments given and documents formally drawn up or registered as authentic instruments before the entry into force of this Convention.

Article 57

1. This Convention shall not affect any conventions to which the Contracting States are or will be parties and which, in relation to particular matters, govern jurisdiction or the recognition or enforcement of judgments.

2. This Convention shall not prevent a court of a Contracting State which is party to a convention referred to in the first paragraph from assuming jurisdiction in accordance with that convention, even where the defendant is domiciled in a Contracting State which is not a party to that convention. The court hearing the act in shall, in any event, apply Article 20 of this Convention.

3. Judgments given in a Contracting State by a court in the exercise of jurisdiction provided for in a convention referred to in the first paragraph shall be recognised and enforced in the other Contracting States in accordance with Title III of this Convention.

4. In addition to the grounds provided for in Title III, recognition or enforcement may be refused if the State addressed is not a contracting party to a convention referred to in the first paragraph and the person against whom recognition or enforcement is sought is domiciled in that State, unless the judgment may otherwise be recognised or enforced under any rule of law in the State addressed.

5. Where a convention referred to in the first paragraph to which both the State of origin and the State addressed are parties lays down conditions for the recognition or enforcement of judgments, those conditions shall apply. In any event, the

provisions of this Convention which concern the procedures for recognition and enforcement of judgments may be applied.

Article 59

This Convention shall not prevent a Contracting State from assuming, in a convention on the recognition and enforcement of judgments, an obligation towards a third State not to recognise judgments given in other Contracting States against defendants domiciled or habitually resident in the third State where, in cases provided for in Article 4, the judgment could only be founded on a ground of jurisdiction specified in the second paragraph of Article 3.

However, a Contracting State may not assume an obligation towards a third State not to recognise a judgment given in another Contracting State by a court basing its jurisdiction on the presence within that State of property belonging to the defendant, or the seizure by the plaintiff of property situated there:

1. if the action is brought to assert or declare proprietary or possessory rights in that property, seeks to obtain authority to dispose of it, or arises from another issue relating to such property, or

2. if the property constitutes the security for a debt which is the subject-matter of the action.

TITLE VIII

FINAL PROVISIONS

Article 60

The following may be parties to this Convention:

(a) States which, at the time of the opening of this Convention for signature, are members of the European Communities or of the European Free Trade Association;

(b) States which, after the opening of this Convention for signature, become members of the European Communities or of the European Free Trade Association;

(c) States invited to accede in accordance with Article 62(1)(b).

Article 61

1. This Convention shall be opened for signature by the States members of the European Communities or the European Free Trade Association.

2. The Convention shall be submitted for ratification by the signatory States. The instruments of ratification shall be deposited with the Swiss Federal Council.

3. The Convention shall enter into force on the first day of the third month following the date on which two States, of which one is a member of the European Communities and the other a member of the European Free Trade Association, deposit their instruments of ratification.

4. The Convention shall take effect in relation to any other signatory State on the first day of the third month following the deposit of its instrument of ratification.

Article 62

1. After entering into force this Convention shall be open to accession by:
   (a) the States referred to in Article 60(b);
   (b) other States which have been invited to accede upon a request made by one of the Contracting States to the depository State. The depository State shall

invite the State concerned to accede only if, after having communicated the contents of the communications that this State intends to make in accordance with Article 63, it has obtained the unanimous agreement of the signatory States and the Contracting States referred to in Article 60(a) and (b).

2. If an acceding State wishes to furnish details for the purposes of Protocol No 1, negotiations shall be entered into to that end. A negotiating conference shall be convened by the Swiss Federal Council.

3. In respect of an acceding State, the Convention shall take effect on the first day of the third month following the deposit of its instrument of accession.

4. However, in respect of an acceding State referred to in paragraph 1(a) or (b), the Convention shall take effect only in relations between the acceding State and the Contracting States which have not made any objections to the accession before the first day of the third month following the deposit of the instrument of accession.

Article 63

Each acceding State shall, when depositing its instrument of accession, communicate the information required for the application of Articles 3, 32, 37, 40, 41 and 55 of this Convention and furnish, if need be, the details prescribed during the negotiations for the purposes of Protocol No 1.

Article 64

1. This Convention is concluded for an initial period of five years from the date of its entry into force in accordance with Article 61(3), even in the case of States which ratify it or accede to it after that date.

2. At the end of the initial five-year period, the Convention shall be automatically renewed from year to year.

3. Upon the expiry of the initial five-year period, any Contracting State may, at any time, denounce the Convention by sending a notification to the Swiss Federal Council.

4. The denunciation shall take effect at the end of the calendar year following the expiry of a period of six months from the date of receipt by the Swiss Federal Council of the notification of denunciation.

Article 65

The following are annexed to this Convention:
– a Protocol No 1, on certain questions of jurisdiction, procedure and enforcement,
– a Protocol No 2, on the uniform interpretation of the Convention,
– a Protocol No 3, on the application of Article 57.

These Protocols shall form an integral part of the Convention.

Article 66

Any Contracting State may request the revision of this Convention. To that end, the Swiss Federal Council shall issue invitations to a revision conference within a period of six months from the date of the request for revision.

Article 67

The Swiss Federal Council shall notify the States represented at the Diplomatic Conference of Lugano and the States who have later acceded to the Convention of:

(a) the deposit of each instrument of ratification or accession;

(b) the dates of entry into force of this Convention in respect of the Contracting States;

(c) any denunciation received pursuant to Article 64;

(d) any declaration received pursuant to Article 1a of Protocol No 1;

(e) any declaration received pursuant to Article 1b of Protocol No 1;

(f) any declaration received pursuant to Article IV of Protocol No 1;

(g) any communication made pursuant to Article VI of Protocol No 1.

Article 68

This Convention, drawn up in a single original in the Danish, Dutch, English, Finnish, French, German, Greek, Icelandic, Irish, Italian, Norwegian, Portuguese, Spanish and Swedish languages, all fourteen texts being equally authentic, shall be deposited in the archives of the Swiss Federal Council. The Swiss Federal Council shall transmit a certified copy to the Government of each State represented at the Diplomatic Conference of Lugano and to the Government of each acceding State.

PROTOCOL NO 2 ON THE UNIFORM INTERPRETATION [865] OF THE CONVENTION

PREAMBLE

The High Contracting Parties,

Having regard to Article 65 of this Convention,

Considering the substantial link between this Convention and the Brussels Convention,

Considering that the Court of Justice of the European Communities by virtue of the Protocol of 3 June 1971 has jurisdiction to give rulings on the interpretation of the provisions of the Brussels Convention,

Being aware of the rulings delivered by the Court of Justice of the European Communities on the interpretation of the Brussels Convention up to the time of signature of this Convention,

Considering that the negotiations which led to the conclusion of the Convention were based on the Brussels Convention in the light of these rulings,

Desiring to prevent, in full deference to the independence of the courts, divergent interpretations and to arrive at as uniform an interpretation as possible of the provisions of the Convention, and of these provisions and those of the Brussels Convention which are substantially reproduced in this Convention,

Have agreed as follows:

Article 1

The courts of each Contracting State shall, when applying and interpreting the provisions of the Convention, pay due account to the principles laid down by any relevant decision delivered by courts of the other Contracting States concerning provisions of this Convention.

Article 2

1. The Contracting Parties agree to set up a system of exchange of information concerning judgments delivered pursuant to this Convention as well as relevant judgments under the Brussels Convention. This system shall comprise:

– transmission to a central body by the competent authorities of judgments delivered by courts of last instance and the Court of Justice of the European Communities as well as judgments of particular importance which have become final and have been delivered pursuant to this Convention or the Brussels Convention,

– classification of these judgments by the central body including, as far as necessary, the drawing-up and publication of translations and abstracts,

– communication by the central body of the relevant documents to the competent national authorities of all signatories and acceding States to the Convention and to the Commission of the European Communities.

2. The central body is the Registrar of the Court of Justice of the European Communities.

Article 3

1. A Standing Committee shall be set up for the purposes of this Protocol.

2. The Committee shall be composed of representatives appointed by each signatory and acceding State.

3. The European Communities (Commission, Court of Justice and General Secretariat of the Council) and the European Free Trade Association may attend the meetings as observers.

Article 4

1. At the request of a Contracting Party, the depository of the Convention shall convene meetings of the Committee for the purpose of exchanging views on the functioning of the Convention and in particular on:

– the development of the case-law as communicated under the first paragraph first indent of Article 2,

– the application of Article 57 of the Convention.

2. The Committee, in the light of these exchanges, may also examine the appropriateness of starting on particular topics a revision of the Convention and make recommendations.

SCHEDULE 4

TITLE II OF 1968 CONVENTION AS MODIFIED FOR ALLOCATION OF JURISDICTION WITHIN UK

TITLE II

JURISDICTION

[As to the use of the dots and heavy type, see s16(2) of the Act, above]

SECTION 1

Article 2

Subject to the provisions of this **Title**, persons domiciled in a **part of the United Kingdom** shall be sued in the courts of that **part**.

Article 3

Persons domiciled in a **part of the United Kingdom** may be sued in the courts of another **part of the United Kingdom** only by virtue of the rules set out in Sections **2, 4, 5 and 6** of this Title.

SECTION 2

Article 5

A person domiciled in a **part of the United Kingdom** may, in another **part of the United Kingdom**, be sued:

(1) in matters relating to a contract, in the courts for the place of performance of the obligation in question; in matters relating to individual contracts of employment, this place is that where the employee habitually carries out his work or if the employee does not habitually carry out his work in any one country, the employer may also be sued in the courts for the place where the business which engaged the employee was or is now situated;

(2) in matters relating to maintenance, in the courts for the place where the maintenance creditor is domiciled or habitually resident or, if the matter is ancillary to proceedings concerning the status of a person, in the court which, according to its own law, has jurisdiction to entertain those proceedings, unless that jurisdiction is based solely on the nationality of one of the parties;

(3) in matters relating to tort, delict or quasi-delict, in the courts for the place where the harmful event occurred **or in the case of a threatened wrong is likely to occur**;

(4) as regards a civil claim for damages or restitution which is based on an act giving rise to criminal proceedings, in the court seised of those proceedings, to the extent that that court has jurisdiction under its own law to entertain civil proceedings;

(5) as regards a dispute arising out of the operations of a branch, agency or other establishment, in the courts for the place in which the branch, agency or other establishment is situated;

(6) in his capacity as a settlor, trustee or beneficiary of a trust created by the operation of a statute, or by a written instrument, or created orally and evidenced in writing, in the courts of the **part of the United Kingdom** in which the trust is domiciled;

(7) as regards a dispute concerning the payment of remuneration claimed in respect of the salvage of a cargo or freight, in the court under the authority of which the cargo or freight in question

    (a) has been arrested to secure such payment, or
    (b) could have been so arrested, but bail or other security has been given;

provided that this provisions shall apply only if it is claimed that the defendant has an interest in the cargo or freight or had such an interest at the time of salvage;

(8) in proceedings –

    (a) concerning a debt secured on immovable property; or
    (b) which are brought to assert, declare or determine proprietary or possessory rights, or rights of security, in or over movable property, or to obtain authority to dispose of movable property,

in the courts of the part of the United Kingdom in which the property is situated.

Article 5A

Proceedings which have as their object a decision of an organ of a company or other legal person or of an association of natural or legal persons may, without prejudice to the other provisions of this Title, be brought in the courts of the part of the United Kingdom in which that company, legal person or association has its seat.

Article 6

A person domiciled in a **part of the United Kingdom** may, **in another part of the United Kingdom**, also be sued:

(1) where he is one of a number of defendants, in the courts for the place where any one of them is domiciled;

(2) as a third party in an action on a warranty or guarantee or in any other third party proceedings, in the court seised of the original proceedings, unless these were instituted solely with the object of removing him from the jurisdiction of the court which would be competent in his case;

(3) on a counterclaim arising from the same contract or facts on which the original claim was based, in the court in which the original claim is pending.

(4) in matters relating to a contract, if the action may be combined with an action against the same defendant in matters relating to rights in rem in immovable property, in the court of the **part of the United Kingdom** in which the property is situated.

Article 6A

Where by virtue of this **Title** a court of a **part of the United Kingdom** has jurisdiction in actions relating to liability arising from the use or operation of a ship, that court, or any other court substituted for this purpose by the internal law of that **part**, shall also have jurisdiction over claims for limitation of such liability.

SECTION 4

Article 13

In proceedings concerning a contract concluded by a person for a purpose which can be regarded as being outside his trade or profession, hereinafter called 'the consumer', jurisdiction shall be determined by this Section, without prejudice to the provisions of Articles 5(5) **and (8)(b)**, if it is:

(1) a contract for the sale of goods on instalment credit terms, or

(2) a contract for a loan repayable by instalments, or for any other form of credit, made to finance the sale of goods, or

(3) any other contract for the supply of goods or a contract for the supply of services and the consumer took in **the part of the United Kingdom in which he is domiciled** the steps necessary for the conclusion of the contract.

This Section shall not apply to contracts of transport **or insurance.**

Article 14

A consumer may bring proceedings against the other party to a contract either in the courts of the **part of the United Kingdom** in which that party is domiciled or in the courts of the **part of the United Kingdom** in which he is himself domiciled.

Proceedings may be brought against a consumer by the other party to the contract only in the courts of the **part of the United Kingdom** in which the consumer is domiciled.

These provisions shall not affect the right to bring a counterclaim in the court in which, in accordance with this Section, the original claim is pending.

Article 15

The provisions of this Section may be departed from only by an agreement:

(1) which is entered into after the dispute has arisen, or

(2) which allows the consumer to bring proceedings in courts other than those indicated in this Section, or

(3) which is entered into by the consumer and the other party to the contract, both of whom are at the time of conclusion of the contract domiciled or habitually resident in the same **part of the United Kingdom,** and which confers jurisdiction on the courts of that **part**, provided that such an agreement is not contrary to the law of that **part.**

SECTION 5

Article 16

The following courts shall have exclusive jurisdiction, regardless of domicile:

(1) (a) in proceedings which have as their object rights in rem in immovable property or tenancies of immovable property, the courts of the **part of the United Kingdom** in which the property is situated;

(b) however, in proceedings which have as their object tenancies of immovable property concluded for temporary private use for a maximum period of six consecutive months, the courts of the **part of the United Kingdom** in which the defendant is domiciled shall also have jurisdiction, provided that the landlord and the tenant are natural persons and are domiciled in the same part of the United Kingdom.

(2) in proceedings which have as their object the validity of the constitution, the nullity or the dissolution of companies or other legal persons or associations of natural or legal persons, the courts of the **part of the United Kingdom** in which the company, legal person or association has its seat;

(3) in proceedings which have as their object the validity of entries in public registers, the courts of the **part of the United Kingdom** in which the register is kept;

(5) in proceedings concerned with the enforcement of judgments, the courts of the **part of the United Kingdom** in which the judgments has been or is to be enforced.

SECTION 6

Article 17

If the parties have agreed that a court or the courts of a **part of the United Kingdom** are to have jurisdiction to settle any disputes which have arisen or which may arise in connection with a particular legal relationship, **and, apart from this Schedule, the agreement would be effective to confer jurisdiction under the law of that part**, that court or those courts shall have jurisdiction.

The court or courts of a **part of the United Kingdom** on which a trust instrument has conferred jurisdiction shall have jurisdiction in any proceedings brought against a settlor, trustee or beneficiary, if relations between these persons or their rights or obligations under the trust are involved.

Agreements or provisions of a trust instrument conferring jurisdiction shall have no legal force if they are contrary to the provisions of Article 15, or if the courts whose jurisdiction they purport to exclude have exclusive jurisdiction by virtue of Article 16.

In matters relating to individual contracts of employment an agreement conferring jurisdiction shall have legal force only if it is entered into after the dispute has arisen or if the employee invokes it to seise courts other than those for the defendant's domicile or those specified in Article 5(1).

Article 18

Apart from jurisdiction derived from other provisions of this **Title**, a court of a **part of the United Kingdom** before whom a defendant enters an appearance shall have jurisdiction. This rule shall not apply where appearance was entered solely to contest the jurisdiction, or where another court has exclusive jurisdiction by virtue of Article 16.

SECTION 7

Article 19

Where a court of a **part of the United Kingdom** is seised of a claim which is principally concerned with a matter over which the courts of another **part of the United Kingdom** have exclusive jurisdiction by virtue of Article 16, it shall declare of its own motion that it has no jurisdiction.

Article 20

Where a defendant domiciled in one **part of the United Kingdom** is sued in a court of another **part of the United Kingdom** and does not enter an appearance, the court shall declare of its own motion that it has no jurisdiction unless its jurisdiction is derived from the provisions of this **Title.**

The court shall stay the proceedings so long as it is not shown that the defendant has been able to receive the document instituting the proceedings or an equivalent document in sufficient time to enable him to arrange for his defence, or that all necessary steps have been taken to this end.

SECTION 9

Article 24

Application may be made to the courts of a **part of the United Kingdom** for such provisional, including protective, measures as may be available under the law of that **part**, even if, under this **Title**, the courts of another **part of the United Kingdom** have jurisdiction as to the substance of the matter.

SCHEDULE 5

PROCEEDINGS EXCLUDED FROM SCHEDULE 4

1. Proceedings for the winding up of a company under the Insolvency Act 1986 or the Insolvency (Northern Ireland) Order 1989, or proceedings relating to a company as respects which jurisdiction is conferred on the court having winding up jurisdiction under either of those Acts.

2. Proceedings concerned with the registration or validity of patents, trade marks, designs or other similar rights required to be deposited or registered.

3. Proceedings under section 6 of the Protection of Trading Interests Act 1980 (recovery of sums paid or obtained pursuant to a judgment for multiple damages).

4. Proceedings on appeal from, or for review of, decisions of tribunals

5. Proceedings for, or otherwise relating to, an order under any of the following provisions –

(a) paragraph 23 of Schedule 2 to the Children Act 1989 ... (contributions in respect of children in care, etc);
(b) section 49 or 50 of the Child Care Act 1980 ... (applications for, or for variation of, affiliation orders in respect of children in care, etc);
(c) section 43 of the National Assistance Act 1948, section 18 of the Supplementary Benefits Act 1976, section 106 of the Social Security Administration Act 1992 ... (recovery of cost of assistance or benefit from person liable to maintain the assisted person);
(d) section 44 of the National Assistance Act 1948, section 19 of the Supplementary Benefits Act 1976 ... (applications for, or for variation of, affiliation orders in respect of children for whom assistance or benefit provided).

6. Proceedings brought in any court in pursuance of –

(a) any statutory provisions which, in the case of any convention to which Article 57 applies (conventions relating to specific matters which override the general rules in the 1969 Convention), implements the convention or makes provision with respect to jurisdiction in any field to which the convention relates; and
(b) any rule of law so far as it has the effect of implementing any such convention. ...

8. Proceedings for the rectification of the register of aircraft mortgages kept by the Civil Aviation Authority.

9. Proceedings brought in any court in pursuance of an order under section 23 of the Oil and Gas (Enterprise) Act 1982.

Proceedings such as are mentioned in section 188 of the Financial Services Act 1986.

SCHEDULE 6 [868]

ENFORCEMENT OF UNITED KINGDOM JUDGMENTS (MONEY PROVISIONS)

1. In this Schedule –

'judgment' means any judgment to which section 18 applies and references to the giving of a judgment shall be construed accordingly;
'money provision' means a provision for the payment of one or more sums of money;
'prescribed' means prescribed by rules of court.

2. (1) Any interested party who wishes to secure the enforcement in another part of the United Kingdom of any money provisions contained in a judgment may apply for a certificate under this Schedule.

(2) The application shall be made in the prescribed manner to the proper officer of the original court, that is to say –

(a) in relation to a judgment within paragraph (a) of the definition of 'judgment' in section 18(2), the court by which the judgment or order was given or made;
(b) in relation to a judgment within paragraph (b) of that definition, the court in which the judgment or order is entered;
(c) in relation to a judgment within paragraph (c) of that definition, the court in whose books the document is registered;
(d) in relation to a judgment within paragraph (d) of that definition, the tribunal by which the award or order was made;

(e) in relation to a judgment within paragraph (e) of that definition, the court which gave the judgment or made the order by virtue of which the award has become enforceable as mentioned in that paragraph.

3. A certificate shall not be issued under this Schedule in respect of a judgment unless under the law of the part of the United Kingdom in which the judgment was given –

(a) either –

(i) the time for bringing an appeal against the judgment has expired, no such appeal having been brought within that time; or
(ii) such an appeal having been brought within that time, that appeal has been finally disposed of; and

(b) enforcement of the judgment is not for the time being stayed or suspended, and the time available for its enforcement has not expired.

4. (1) Subject to paragraph 3, on an application under paragraph 2 the proper officer shall issue to the applicant a certificate in the prescribed form –

(a) stating the sum or aggregate of the sums (including any costs or expenses) payable under the money provision contained in the judgment, the rate of interest, if any, payable thereon and the date or time from which any such interest began to accrue;
(b) stating that the conditions specified in paragraph 3(a) and (b) are satisfied in relation to the judgment; and
(c) containing such other particulars as may be prescribed.

(2) More than one certificate may be issued under this Schedule (simultaneously or at different times) in respect of the same judgment. ...

6. (1) A certificate registered under this Schedule shall, for the purposes of its enforcement, be of the same force and effect, the registering court shall have in respect to its enforcement the same powers, and proceedings for or with respect to its enforcement may be taken, as if the certificate had been a judgment originally given in the registering court and had (where relevant) been entered.

(2) Sub-paragraph (1) is subject to the following provisions of this Schedule and to any provision made by rules of court as to the manner in which and the conditions subject to which a certificate registered under this Schedule may be enforced. ...

10. Where a certificate has been registered under this Schedule, the registering court –

(a) shall set aside the registration if, on an application made by any interested party, it is satisfied that the registration was contrary to the provisions of this Schedule;
(b) may set aside the registration if, on an application so made, it is satisfied that the matter in dispute in the proceedings in which the judgment in question was given had previously been the subject of a judgment by another court or tribunal having jurisdiction in the matter.

SCHEDULE 7

ENFORCEMENT OF UNITED KINGDOM JUDGMENTS
(NON-MONEY PROVISIONS)

1. In this Schedule –

'judgment' means any judgment to which section 18 applies and references to the giving of a judgment shall be construed accordingly;

'non-money provision' means a provision for any relief or remedy not requiring payment of a sum of money;
'prescribed' means prescribed by rules of court.

2. (1) Any interested party who wishes to secure the enforcement in another part of the United Kingdom of any non-money provisions contained in a judgment may apply for a certified copy of the judgment.

(2) The application shall be made in the prescribed manner to the proper officer of the original court, that is to say –

(a) in relation to a judgment within paragraph (a) of the definition of 'judgment' in section 18(2), the court by which the judgment or order was given or made;
(b) in relation to a judgment within paragraph (b) of that definition, the court in which the judgment or order is entered;
(c) in relation to a judgment within paragraph (c) of that definition, the court in whose books the document is registered;
(d) in relation to a judgment within paragraph (d) of that definition, the tribunal by which the award or order was made;
(e) in relation to a judgment within paragraph (e) of that definition, the court which gave the judgment or made the order by virtue of which the award has become enforceable as mentioned in that paragraph.

3. A certified copy of a judgment shall not be issued under this Schedule unless under the law of the part of the United Kingdom in which the judgment was given –

(a) either –
(i) the time for bringing an appeal against the judgment has expired, no such appeal having been brought within that time; or
(ii) such an appeal having been brought within that time, that appeal has been finally disposed of; and

(b) enforcement of the judgment is not for the time being stayed or suspended, and the time available for its enforcement has not expired.

4. (1) Subject to paragraph 3, on an application under paragraph 2 the proper officer shall issue to the applicant –

(a) a certified copy of the judgment (including any money provisions or expected provisions which it may contain); and
(b) a certificate stating that the conditions specified in paragraph 3(a) and (b) are satisfied in relation to the judgment.

(2) In sub-paragraph (1)(a) 'excepted provision' means any provision of a judgment which is excepted from the application of section 18 by subsection (5) of that section.

(3) There may be issued under this Schedule (simultaneously or at different times) –

(a) more than one certified copy of the same judgment; and
(b) more than one certificate in respect of the same judgment.

6. (1) The non-money provisions contained in a judgment registered under this Schedule shall, for the purposes of their enforcement, be of the same force and effect, the registering court shall have in relation to their enforcement the same powers, and proceedings for or with respect to their enforcement may be taken, as if the judgment containing them had been originally given in the registering court and had (where relevant) been entered.

(2) Sub-paragraph (1) is subject to the following provisions of this Schedule and to any provision made by rules of court as to the manner in which and conditions

subject to which the non-money provisions contained in a judgment registered under this Schedule may be enforced.

9. Where a judgment has been registered under this Schedule, the registering court –

(a) shall set aside the registration if, on an application made by an interested party, it is satisfied that the registration was contrary to the provisions of this Schedule;

(b) may set aside the registration if, on an application so made, it is satisfied that the matter in dispute in the proceedings in which the judgment was given had previously been the subject of a judgment by another court or tribunal having jurisdiction in the matter.

[As amended by the Criminal Justice Act 1982, s46; Oil and Gas (Enterprise) Act 1982, s37(1), Schedule 3, para 42; International Transport Conventions Act 1983, s11(2); Insolvency Act 1986, s439(2), Schedule 14; Family Law Reform Act 1987, s33(1), Schedule 2, para 89; Criminal Justice (Scotland) Act 1987, s45(3); Children Act 1989, s108(5), Schedule 13, para 47; Civil Jurisdiction and Judgments Act 1982 (Amendment) Order 1989, arts 3–8; Insolvency (Northern Ireland) Order 1989; Companies Act 1989, s200(2); Courts and Legal Services Act 1990, s116, Schedule 16, para 41; Civil Jurisdiction and Judgments Act 1982 (Amendment) Order 1990, arts 3–7, 9, 10, 11, 12(1)–(4), Schedules 2, 3; Civil Jurisdiction and Judgments Act 1991, ss1(1), (2), (3), 2, 3, Schedules 1, 2, paras 1–25; Maintenance Enforcement Act 1991, s10, Schedule 1, para 21; Social Security (Consequential Provisions) Act 1992, s4, Schedule 2, para 62; Transfer of Functions (Magistrates' Courts and Family Law) Order 1992, art 4(6), (7); Civil Jurisdiction and Judgments Act 1982 (Amendment) Order 1993, art 2.]

FOREIGN LIMITATION PERIODS ACT 1984
(1984 c 16)

1 Application of foreign limitation law [870]

(1) Subject to the following provisions of this Act, where in any action or proceedings in a court in England and Wales the law of any other country falls (in accordance with rules of private international law applicable by any such court) to be taken into account in the determination of any matter –

(a) the law of that other country relating to limitation shall apply in respect of that matter for the purposes of the action or proceedings; and

(b) except where that matter falls within subsection (2) below, the law of England and Wales relating to limitation shall not so apply.

(2) A matter falls within this subsection if it is a matter in the determination of which both the law of England and Wales and the law of some other country fall to be taken into account.

(3) The law of England and Wales shall determine for the purposes of any law applicable by virtue of subsection (1)(a) above whether, and the time at which, proceedings have been commenced in respect of any matter; and, accordingly, section 35 of the Limitation Act 1980 (new claims in pending proceedings) shall apply in relation to time limits applicable by virtue of subsection (1)(a) above as it applies in relation to time limits under that Act.

(4) A court in England and Wales, in exercising in pursuance of subsection (1)(a) above any discretion conferred by the law of any other country, shall so far as practicable exercise that discretion in the manner in which it is exercised in comparable cases by the courts of that other country.

(5) In this section 'law', in relation to any country, shall not include rules of private

international law applicable by the courts of that country or, in the case of England and Wales, this Act.

2 Exceptions to s1

(1) In any case in which the application of section 1 above would to any extent conflict (whether under subsection (2) below or otherwise) with public policy, that section shall not apply to the extent that its application would so conflict.

(2) The application of section 1 above in relation to any action or proceedings shall conflict with public policy to the extent that its application would cause undue hardship to a person who is, or might be made, a party to the action or proceedings.

(3) Where, under a law applicable by virtue of section 1(1)(a) above for the purposes of any action or proceedings, a limitation period is or may be extended or interrupted in respect of the absence of a party to the action or proceedings from any specified jurisdiction or country, so much of that law as provides for the extension or interruption shall be disregarded for those purposes.

3 Foreign judgments on limitation points

Where a court in any country outside England and Wales has determined any matter wholly or partly by reference to the law of that or any other country (including England and Wales) relating to limitation, then, for the purposes of the law relating to the effect to be given n England and Wales to that determination, that court shall, to the extent that it has so determined the matter, be deemed to have determined it on its merits.

4 Meaning of law relating to limitation

(1) Subject to subsection (3) below, references in this Act to the law of any country (including England and Wales) relating to limitation shall, in relation to any matter, be construed as references to so much of the relevant law of that country as (in any manner) makes provision with respect to a limitation period applicable to the bringing of proceedings in respect to that matter in the courts of that country and shall include –

(a) references to so much of that law as relates to, and to the effect of, the application, extension, reduction or interruption of that period; and
(b) a reference, where under that law there is no limitation period which is so applicable, to the rule that such proceedings may be brought within an indefinite period.

(2) In subsection (1) above 'relevant law', in relation to any country, means the procedural and substantive law applicable, apart from any rules of private international law, by the courts of that country.

(3) References in this Act to the law of England and Wales relating to limitation shall not include the rules by virtue of which a court may, in the exercise of any discretion, refuse equitable relief on the grounds of acquiescence or otherwise; but, in applying those rules to a case in relation to which the law of any country outside England and Wales is applicable by virtue of section 1(1)(a) above (not being a law that provides for a limitation period that has expired), a court in England and Wales shall have regard, in particular, to the provisions of the law that is so applicable.

5 Application of Act to arbitrations [874]

The references to any other limitation enactment in section 34 of the Limitation Act 1980 (application of limitation enactments to arbitration) include references to sections 1, 2 and 4 of this Act; and, accordingly, in subsection (5) of the said section 34, the reference to the time prescribed by a limitation enactment has effect for the purposes of any case to which section 1 above applies as a reference to the limitation period (if any) applicable by virtue of section 1 above.

6 Application to Crown [875]

(1) This Act applies in relation to any action or proceedings by or against the Crown as it applies in relation to actions and proceedings to which the Crown is not a party.

(2) For the purposes of this section references to an action or proceedings by or against the Crown include references to –

(a) any action or proceedings by or against Her Majesty in right of the Duchy of Lancaster;
(b) any action or proceedings by or against any Government department or any officer of the Crown as such or any person acting on behalf of the Crown;
(c) any action or proceedings by or against the Duke of Cornwall.

COUNTY COURTS ACT 1984
(1984 c 28)

74 Interest on judgment debts, etc [876]

(1) The Lord Chancellor may by order made with the concurrence of the Treasury provide that any sums to which this subsection applies shall carry interest at such rate and between such times as may be prescribed by the order.

(2) The sums to which subsection (1) applies are –

(a) sums payable under judgments or orders given or made in a county court, including sums payable by instalments; and
(b) sums which by virtue of any enactment are, if the county court so orders, recoverable as if payable under an order of that court, and in respect of which the county court has so ordered. ...

(5A) The power conferred by subsection (1) includes power to make provision enabling a county court to order that the rate of interest applicable to a sum expressed in a currency other than sterling shall be such rate as the court thinks fit (instead of the rate otherwise applicable).

[As amended by the Private International Law (Miscellaneous Provisions) Act 1995, s2.]

MATRIMONIAL AND FAMILY PROCEEDINGS ACT 1984
(1984 c 42)

12 Applications for financial relief after overseas divorce, etc [877]

(1) Where –

(a) a marriage has been dissolved or annulled, or the parties to a marriage have been legally separated, by means of judicial or other proceedings in an overseas country, and

(b) the divorce, annulment or legal separation is entitled to be recognised as valid in England and Wales,

either party to the marriage may apply to the court in the manner prescribed by rules of court for an order for financial relief under this Part of this Act.

(2) If after a marriage has been dissolved or annulled in an overseas country one of the parties to the marriage remarries that party shall not be entitled to make an application in relation to that marriage.

(3) For the avoidance of doubt it is hereby declared that the reference in subsection (2) above to remarriage includes a reference to a marriage which is by law void or voidable. ...

13 Leave of the court required for applications for financial relief [878]

(1) No application for an order for financial relief shall be made under this Part of this Act unless the leave of the court has been obtained in accordance with rules of court; and the court shall not grant leave unless it considers that there is substantial ground for the making of an application for such an order.

(2) The court may grant leave under this section notwithstanding that an order has been made by a court in a country outside England and Wales requiring the other party to the marriage to make any payment or transfer any property to the applicant or a child of the family.

(3) Leave under this section may be granted subject to such conditions as the court thinks fit.

14 Interim orders for maintenance [879]

(1) Where leave is granted under section 13 above for the making of an application for an order for financial relief and it appears to the court that the applicant or any child of the family is in immediate need of financial assistance, the court may make an interim order for maintenance, that is to say, an order requiring the other party to the marriage to make to the applicant or to the child such periodical payments, and for such term, being a term beginning not earlier than the date of the grant of leave and ending with the date of the determination of the application for an order for financial relief, as the court thinks reasonable.

(2) If it appears to the court that the court has jurisdiction to entertain the application for an order for financial relief by reason only of paragraph (c) of section 15(1) below the court shall not make an interim order under this section.

(3) An interim order under subsection (1) above may be made subject to such conditions as the court thinks fit.

15 Jurisdiction of the court [880]

(1) Subject to subsection (2) below, the court shall have jurisdiction to entertain an application for an order for financial relief if any of the following jurisdictional requirements are satisfied, that is to say –

(a) either of the parties to the marriage was domiciled in England and Wales on the date of the application for leave under section 13 above or was so domiciled on the date on which the divorce annulment or legal separation obtained in the overseas country took effect in that country; or
(b) either of the parties to the marriage was habitually resident in England and Wales throughout the period of one year ending with the date of the application for leave or was so resident throughout the period of one year

ending with the date on which the divorce, annulment or legal separation obtained in the overseas country took effect in that country; or

(c) either or both of the parties to the marriage had at the date of the application for leave a beneficial interest in possession in a dwelling-house situated in England or Wales which was at some time during the marriage a matrimonial home of the parties to the marriage.

(2) Where the jurisdiction of the court to entertain proceedings under this Part of this Act would fall to be determined by reference to the jurisdictional requirements imposed by virtue of Part I of the Civil Jurisdiction and Judgment Act 1982 (implementation of certain European conventions) then –

(a) satisfaction of the requirements of subsection (1) above shall not obviate the need to satisfy the requirements imposed by virtue of Part I of that Act; and
(b) satisfaction of the requirements imposed by virtue of Part I of that Act shall obviate the need to satisfy the requirements of subsection (1) above;

and the court shall entertain or not entertain the proceedings accordingly.

16 Duty of the court to consider whether England and Wales is appropriate venue for application [881]

(1) Before making an order for financial relief the court shall consider whether in all the circumstances of the case it would be appropriate for such an order to be made by a court in England and Wales, and if the court is not satisfied that it would be appropriate, the court shall dismiss the application.

(2) The court shall in particular have regard to the following matters –

(a) the connection which the parties to the marriage have with England and Wales;
(b) the connection which those parties have with the country in which the marriage was dissolved or annulled or in which they were legally separated;
(c) the connection which those parties have with any other country outside England and Wales;
(d) any financial benefit which the applicant or a child of the family has received, or is likely to receive, in consequence of the divorce, annulment or legal separation, by virtue of any agreement or the operation of the law of a country outside England and Wales;
(e) in a case where an order has been made by a court in a country outside England and Wales requiring the other party to the marriage to make any payment or transfer any property for the benefit of the applicant or a child of the family, the financial relief given by the order and the extent to which the order has been complied with or is likely to be complied with;
(f) any right which the applicant has, or has had, to apply for financial relief from the other party to the marriage under the law of any country outside England and Wales and if the applicant has omitted to exercise that right the reason for that omission;
(g) the availability in England and Wales of any property in respect of which an order under this Part of this Act in favour of the applicant could be made;
(h) the extent to which any order made under this Part of this Act is likely to be enforceable;
(i) the length of time which has elapsed since the date of the divorce, annulment or legal separation.

COMPANIES ACT 1985
(1985 c 6)

PART XXIII

OVERSEAS COMPANIES

CHAPTER I

REGISTRATION, ETC

690A Branch registration under the Eleventh Company Law Directive (89/666/EEC) [882]

(1) This section applies to any limited company which –

(a) is incorporated outside the United Kingdom and Gibraltar, and
(b) has a branch in Great Britain.

(2) Schedule 21A to this Act (Branch registration under the Eleventh Company Law Directive (89/666/EEC)) shall have effect in relation to any company to which this section applies.

690B Scope of ss691 and 692 [883]

Sections 691 and 692 shall not apply to any limited company which –

(a) is incorporated outside the United Kingdom and Gibraltar, and
(b) has a branch in the United Kingdom.

691 Documents to be delivered to registrar

(1) When a company incorporated outside Great Britain establishes a place of business in Great Britain, it shall within one month of doing so deliver to the registrar of companies for registration –

(a) a certified copy of the charter, statutes or memorandum and articles of the company or other instrument constituting or defining the company's constitution, and, if the instrument is not written in the English language, a certified translation of it; and
(b) a return in the prescribed form containing –

(i) a list of the company's directors and secretary, containing the particulars specified in the next subsection,
(ii) a list of the names and addresses of some one or more persons resident in Great Britain authorised to accept on the company's behalf service of process and any notices required to be served on it,
(iii) a list of the documents delivered in compliance with paragraph (a) of this subsection, and
(iv) a statutory declaration (made by a director or secretary of the company or by any person whose name and address are given in the list required by sub-paragraph (ii)), stating the date on which the company's place of business in Great Britain was established. ...

692 Registration of altered particulars [884]

(1) If any alteration is made in –

(a) the charter, statutes, or memorandum and articles of an oversea company or any such instrument as is mentioned above, or

(b) the directors or secretary of an oversea company or the particulars contained in the list of the directors and secretary, or
(c) the names or addresses of the persons authorised to accept service on behalf of an oversea company,

the company shall, within the time specified below, deliver to the registrar of companies for registration a return containing the prescribed particulars of the alteration.

(2) If any change is made in the corporate name of an oversea company, the company shall, within the time specified below, deliver to the registrar of companies for registration a return containing the prescribed particulars of the change.

(3) The time for delivery of the returns required by subsections (1) and (2) is –

(a) in the case of an alteration to which subsection (1)(c) applies, 21 days after the making of the alteration, and
(b) otherwise, 21 days after the date on which notice of the alteration or change in question could have been received in Great Britain in due course of post (if despatched with due diligence).

692A Change in registration regime

(1) Where a company ceases to be a company to which section 690A applies, and, immediately after ceasing to be such a company –

(a) continues to have in Great Britain a place of business which it had immediately before ceasing to be such a company, and
(b) does not have a branch in Northern Ireland,

it shall be treated for the purposes of section 691 as having established the place of business on the date when it ceased to be a company to which section 690A applies.

(2) Where a limited company incorporated outside the United Kingdom and Gibraltar –

(a) ceases to have a branch in Northern Ireland, and
(b) both immediately before and immediately after ceasing to do so, has a place of business, but not a branch, in Great Britain,

it shall be treated for the purposes of section 691 as having established the place of business on the date when it ceased to have a branch in Northern Ireland.

(3) Where a company –

(a) becomes a company to which section 690A applies,
(b) immediately after becoming such a company, has in a part of Great Britain an established place of business but no branch, and
(c) immediately before becoming such a company, had an established place of business in that part,

sections 691 and 692 shall, in relation to that part, continue to apply to the company (notwithstanding section 690B) until such time as it gives notice to the registrar for that part that it is a company to which that section applies. ...

693 Obligation to state name and other particulars

(1) Every oversea company shall –

(a) in every prospectus inviting subscriptions for its shares or debentures in Great Britain, state the country in which the company is incorporated,

(b) conspicuously exhibit on every place where it carries on business in Great Britain the company's name and the country in which it is incorporated,

(c) cause the company's name and the country in which it is incorporated to be stated in legible characters in all bill-heads and letter paper, and in all notices and other official publications of the company, and

(d) if the liability of the members of the company is limited, cause notice of that fact to be stated in legible characters in every such prospectus as above mentioned and in all bill-heads, letter paper, notices and other official publications of the company in Great Britain, and to be affixed on every place where it carries on its business.

(2) Every company to which section 690A applies shall, in the case of each branch of the company registered under paragraph 1 of Schedule 21A, cause the following particulars to be stated in legible characters in all letter paper and order forms used in carrying on the business of the branch –

(a) the place of registration of the branch, and
(b) the registered number of the branch.

(3) Every company to which section 690A applies, which is not incorporated in a Member State and which is required by the law of the country in which it is incorporated to be registered shall, in the case of each branch of the company registered under paragraph 1 of Schedule 21A, cause the following particulars to be stated in legible characters in all letter paper and order forms used in carrying on the business of the branch –

(a) the identity of the registry in which the company is registered in its country of incorporation, and
(b) the number with which it is registered.

(4) Every company to which section 690A applies and which is not incorporated in a Member State shall, in the case of each branch of the company registered under paragraph 1 of Schedule 21A, cause the following particulars to be stated in legible characters in all letter paper and order forms used in carrying on the business of the branch –

(a) the legal form of the company,
(b) the location of its head office, and
(c) if applicable, the fact that it is being wound up.

694 Regulation of oversea companies in respect of their names [887]

(1) If it appears to the Secretary of State that the corporate name of an oversea company is a name by which the company, had it been formed under this Act, would on the relevant date (determined in accordance with subsection (3A) and (3B)) have been precluded from being registered by section 26 either –

(a) because it falls within subsection (1) of that section, or
(b) if it falls within subsection (2) of that section, because the Secretary of State would not approve the company's being registered with that name;

the Secretary of State may serve a notice on the company, stating why the name would not have been registered.

(2) If the corporate name of an oversea company is in the Secretary of State's opinion too like a name appearing on the relevant date in the index of names kept by the registrar of companies under section 714 or which should have appeared in that index on that date, or is the same as a name which should have so appeared, the Secretary of State may serve a notice on the company specifying the name in the index which the company's name is too like or which is the same as the company's name.

(3) No notice shall be served on a company under subsection (1) or (2) later than 12 months after the relevant date.

(3A) For the purposes of subsections (1) to (3), the relevant date, in relation to a company, is the date on which it has complied with paragraph 1 of Schedule 21A or section 691(1) or, if there is more than one such date, the first date on which it has complied with that paragraph or that subsection since becoming an oversea company.

(3B) But where the company's corporate name has changed since that date ascertained in accordance with subsection (3A), the relevant date is the date on which the company has, in respect of the change or, if more than one, the latest change, complied with paragraph 7(1) of Schedule 21A or section 692(2), as the case may be.

(4) An oversea company on which a notice is served under subsection (1) or (2) –

(a) may deliver to the registrar of companies for registration a statement in the prescribed form specifying a name approved by the Secretary of State other than its corporate name under which it proposes to carry on business in Great Britain, and

(b) may, after that name has been registered, at any time deliver to the registrar for registration a statement in the prescribed form specifying a name approved by the Secretary of State (other than its corporate name) in substitution for the name previously registered.

(5) The name by which an oversea company is for the time being registered under subsection (4) is, for all purposes of the law applying in Great Britain (including this Act and the Business Names Act 1985), deemed to be the company's corporate name; but –

(a) this does not affect references to the corporate name in this section, or any rights or obligations of the company, or render defective any legal proceedings by or against the company, and

(b) any legal proceedings that might have been continued or commenced against the company by its corporate name or its name previously registered under this section may be continued or commenced against it by its name for the time being so registered.

(6) An oversea company on which a notice is served under subsection (1) or (2) shall not at any time after the expiration of 2 months from the service of that notice (or such longer period as may be specified in that notice) carry on business in Great Britain under its corporate name.

Nothing in this subsection, or in section 697(2) (which imposes penalties for its contravention) invalidates any transaction entered into by the company.

(7) The Secretary of State may withdraw a notice served under subsection (1) or (2) at any time before the end of the period mentioned in subsection (6); and that subsection does not apply to a company served with a notice which has been withdrawn.

694A Service of documents: companies to which s690A applies [888]

(1) This section applies to any company to which section 690A applies.

(2) Any process or notice required to be served on a company to which this section applies in respect of the carrying on of the business of a branch registered by it under paragraph 1 of Schedule 21A is sufficiently served if –

(a) addressed to any person whose name has, in respect of the branch, been delivered to the registrar as a person falling within paragraph 3(e) of that Schedule, and
(b) left at or sent by post to the address for that person which has been so delivered.

(3) Where –
(a) a company to which this section applies makes default, in respect of a branch, in delivering to the registrar the particulars mentioned in paragraph 3(e) of Schedule 21A, or
(b) all the persons whose names have, in respect of a branch, been delivered to the registrar as persons falling within paragraph 3(e) of that Schedule are dead or have ceased to reside in Great Britain, or refuse to accept service on the company's behalf, or for any reason cannot be served,

a document may be served on the company in respect of the carrying on of the business of the branch by leaving it at, or sending it by post to, any place of business established by the company in Great Britain.

(4) Where a company to which this section applies has more than one branch in Great Britain, any notice or process required to be served on the company which is not required to be served in respect of the carrying on of the business of one branch rather than another shall be treated for the purposes of this section as required to be served in respect of the carrying on of the business of each of its branches.

695 Service of documents on oversea company [889]

(1) Any process or notice required to be served on an oversea company to which section 691 applies is sufficiently served if addressed to any person whose name has been delivered to the registrar under preceding sections of this Part and left at or sent by post to the address which has been so delivered.

(2) However –
(a) where such a company makes default in delivering to the registrar the name and address of a person resident in Great Britain who is authorised to accept on behalf of the company service of process or notices, or
(b) if at any time all the persons whose names and addresses have been so delivered are dead or have ceased so to reside, or refuse to accept service on the company's behalf, or for any reason cannot be served,

a document may be served on the company by leaving it at, or sending it by post to, any place of business established by the company in Great Britain.

695A Registrar to whom documents to be delivered: [890] companies to which s690A applies

(1) References to the registrar, in relation to a company to which section 690A applies (except references to Schedule 21C) shall be construed in accordance with the following provisions.

(2) The documents which a company is required to deliver to the registrar shall be delivered –
(a) to the registrar for England and Wales, if required to be delivered in respect of a branch in England and Wales, and
(b) to the registrar for Scotland, if required to be delivered in respect of a branch in Scotland.

(3) If a company closes a branch in a part of Great Britain, it shall forthwith give notice of that fact to the registrar for that part; and from the date on which notice is so given it is no longer obliged to deliver documents to that registrar in respect of that branch.

(4) In subsection (3) above, the reference to closing a branch in either part of Great Britain includes a reference to a branch ceasing to be situated in that part on becoming situated elsewhere.

696 Office where documents to be filed [891]

(1) Any document which an oversea company to which section 691 applies is required to deliver to the registrar of companies shall be delivered to the registrar at the registration office in England and Wales or Scotland, according to where the company has established a place of business.

(2) If the company has established a place of business both in England and Wales and in Scotland, the document shall be delivered at the registration office both in England and Wales and in Scotland.

(3) References in this Part (except references to Schedule 21C) to the registrar of companies, in relation to a company to which section 691 applies, are to be construed in accordance with the above subsections.

(4) If an oversea company to which section 691 applies ceased to have a place of business in either part of Great Britain, it shall forthwith give notice of that fact to the registrar of companies for that part; and as from the date on which notice is so given the obligation of the company to deliver any document to the registrar ceases.

697 Penalties for non-compliance [892]

(1) If an oversea company fails to comply with any of sections 691 to 693 and 696, the company, and every officer or agent of the company who knowingly and wilfully authorises or permits the default, is liable to a fine and, in the case of a continuing offence, to a daily default fine for continued contravention.

(2) If an oversea company contravenes section 694(6), the company and every officer or agent of it who knowingly and wilfully authorises or permits the contravention is guilty of an offence and liable to a fine and, for continued contravention, to a daily default fine.

(3) If an oversea company fails to comply with section 695A or Schedule 21A, the company, and every officer or agent of the company who knowingly and wilfully authorises or permits the default, is liable to a fine and, in the case of a continuing offence, to a daily default fine for continued contravention.

698 Definitions [893]

(1) For purposes of this Chapter –

'certified' means certified in the prescribed manner to be a true copy or a correct translation;
'director', in relation to an oversea company, includes shadow director; and
'secretary' includes any person occupying the position of secretary by whatever name called.

(2) For the purposes of this Part (except section 699A and Schedule 21C):

(a) where a branch comprises places of business in more than one part of the United Kingdom, the branch shall be treated as being situated in that part of the United Kingdom where its principal place of business is situated; and

(b) 'branch' means a branch within the meaning of the Council Directive concerning disclosure requirements in respect of branches opened in a Member State by certain types of company governed by the law of another State (the Eleventh Company Law Directive, 89/666/EEC).

725 Service of documents [894]

(1) A document may be served on a company by leaving it at, or sending it by post to, the company's registered office.

(2) Where a company registered in Scotland carried on business in England and Wales, the process of any court in England and Wales may be served on the company by leaving it at, or sending it by post to, the company's principal place of business in England and Wales, addressed to the manager or other head officer in England and Wales of the company.

(3) Where process is served on a company under subsection (2), the person issuing out the process shall send a copy of it by post to the company's registered office.

NB For the partial repeal of s693(1) in certain circumstances, see the Financial Services Act 1986, s212(3), Schedule 17, Pt I.

[As amended by the Overseas Companies and Credit and Financial Institutions (Branch Disclosure) Regulations 1992, regs 3(1), 4, 5, Schedule 2, Pt I, paras 1, 2, 4, 6–13, Schedule 4, paras 1–3.]

CHILD ABDUCTION AND CUSTODY ACT 1985
(1985 c 60)

PART I

INTERNATIONAL CHILD ABDUCTION

1 The Hague Convention [895]

(1) In this Part of this Act 'the Convention' means the Convention on the Civil Aspects of International Child Abduction which was signed at The Hague on 25 October 1980.

(2) Subject to the provisions of this Part of this Act, the provisions of that Convention set out in Schedule 1 to this Act shall have the force of law in the United Kingdom.

2 Contracting States [896]

(1) For the purposes of the Convention as it has effect under this Part of this Act the Contracting States other than the United Kingdom shall be those for the time being specified by an Order in Council under this section.

(2) An Order in Council under this section shall specify the date of the coming into force of the Convention as between the United Kingdom and any State specified in the Order; and, except where the Order otherwise provides, the Convention shall apply as between the United Kingdom and that State only in relation to wrongful removals or retentions occurring on or after that date.

(3) Where the Convention applies, or applies only, to a particular territory or particular territories specified in a declaration made by a Contracting State under Article 39 or 40 of the Convention references to that State in subsections (1) and (2) above shall be construed as references to that territory or those territories.

3 Central Authorities [897]

(1) Subject to subsection (2) below, the functions under the Convention of a Central Authority shall be discharged –

(a) in England and Wales and in Northern Ireland by the Lord Chancellor; and
(b) in Scotland by the Secretary of State.

(2) Any application made under the Convention by or on behalf of a person outside the United Kingdom may be addressed to the Lord Chancellor as the Central Authority in the United Kingdom.

(3) Where any such application relates to a function to be discharged under subsection (1) above by the Secretary of State it shall be transmitted by the Lord Chancellor to the Secretary of State and where such an application is addressed to the Secretary of State but relates to a function to be discharged under subsection (1) above by the Lord Chancellor the Secretary of State shall transmit it to the Lord Chancellor.

4 Judicial authorities [898]

The courts having jurisdiction to entertain applications under the Convention shall be –

(a) in England and Wales or in Northern Ireland the High Court;
(b) in Scotland the Court of Session.

5 Interim powers [899]

Where an application has been made to a court in the United Kingdom under the Convention, the court may, at any time before the application is determined, give such interim directions as it thinks fit for the purpose of securing the welfare of the child concerned or of preventing changes in the circumstances relevant to the determination of the application.

6 Reports [900]

Where the Lord Chancellor or the Secretary of State is requested to provide information relating to a child under Article 7(d) of the Convention he may –

(a) request a local authority or a probation officer to make a report to him in writing with respect to any matter which appears to him to be relevant;
(b) request the Department of Health and Social Services for Northern Ireland to arrange for a suitably qualified person to make such a report to him;
(c) request any court to which a written report relating to the child has been made to send him a copy of the report;

and such a request shall be duly complied with.

7 Proof of documents and evidence [901]

(1) For the purposes of Article 14 of the Convention a decision or determination of a judicial or administrative authority outside the United Kingdom may be proved by a duly authenticated copy of the decision or determination; and any document purporting to be such a copy shall be deemed to be a true copy unless the contrary is shown.

(2) For the purposes of subsection (1) above a copy is duly authenticated if it bears the seal, or is signed by a judge or officer, of the authority in question.

(3) For the purposes of Articles 14 and 30 of the Convention any such document

as is mentioned in Article 8 of the Convention, or a certified copy of any such document, shall be sufficient evidence of anything stated in it.

8 Declarations by United Kingdom courts [902]

The High Court or Court of Session may, on an application made for the purposes of Article 15 of the Convention by any person appearing to the court to have an interest in the matter, make a declaration or declarator that the removal of any child from, or his retention outside, the United Kingdom was wrongful within the meaning of Article 3 of the Convention.

9 Suspension of court's powers in cases of wrongful removal [903]

The reference in Article 16 of the Convention to deciding on the merits of rights of custody shall be construed as a reference to –

(a) making, varying or revoking a custody order, or a supervision order under section 31 of the Children Act 1989 ...
(aa) enforcing under section 29 of the Family Law Act 1986 a custody order within the meaning of Chapter V of Part I of that Act.
(b) registering or enforcing a decision under Part II of this Act; ...

11 Cost of applications [904]

The United Kingdom having made such a reservation as is mentioned in the third paragraph of Article 26 of the Convention, the costs mentioned in that paragraph shall not be borne by any Minister or other authority in the United Kingdom except so far as they fall to be so borne by virtue of the grant of legal aid or legal advice and assistance under Part III or IV of the Legal Aid Act 1988...

PART II

RECOGNITION AND ENFORCEMENT OF CUSTODY DECISIONS

12 The European Convention [905]

(1) In this Part of this Act 'the Convention' means the European Convention on Recognition and Enforcement of Decisions concerning Custody of Children and on the Restoration of Custody of Children which was signed in Luxembourg on 20 May 1980.

(2) Subject to the provisions of this Part of this Act, the provisions of that Convention set out in Schedule 2 to this Act (which include Articles 9 and 10 as they have effect in consequence of a reservation made by the United Kingdom under Article 17) shall have the force of law in the United Kingdom.

13 Contracting States [906]

(1) For the purposes of the Convention as it has effect under this Part of this Act the Contracting States other than the United Kingdom shall be those for the time being specified by an Order in Council under this section.

(2) An Order in Council under this section shall specify the date of the coming into force of the Convention as between the United Kingdom and any State specified in the Order.

(3) Where the Convention applies, or applies only, to a particular territory or particular territories specified by a Contracting State under Article 24 or 25 of the Convention references to that State in subsections (1) and (2) above shall be construed as references to that territory or those territories.

14 Central Authorities [907]

(1) Subject to subsection (2) below, the functions under the Convention of a Central Authority shall be discharged –

(a) in England and Wales and in Northern Ireland by the Lord Chancellor; and
(b) in Scotland by the Secretary of State.

(2) Any application made under the Convention by or on behalf of a person outside the United Kingdom may be addressed to the Lord Chancellor as the Central Authority in the United Kingdom.

(3) Where any such application relates to a function to be discharged under subsection (1) above by the Secretary of State it shall be transmitted by the Lord Chancellor to the Secretary of State and where such an application is addressed to the Secretary of State but relates to a function to be discharged under subsection (1) above by the Lord Chancellor the Secretary of State shall transmit it to the Lord Chancellor.

15 Recognition of decisions [908]

(1) Articles 7 and 12 of the Convention shall have effect in accordance with this section.

(2) A decision to which either of those Articles applies which was made in a Contracting State other than the United Kingdom shall be recognised in each part of the United Kingdom as if made by a court having jurisdiction to make it in that part but –

(a) the appropriate court in any part of the United Kingdom may, on the application of any person appearing to it to have an interest in the matter, declare on any of the grounds specified in Article 9 or 10 of the Convention that the decision is not to be recognised in any part of the United Kingdom; and
(b) the decision shall not be enforceable in any part of the United Kingdom unless registered in the appropriate court under section 16 below.

(3) The references in Article 9(1)(c) of the Convention to the removal of the child are to his improper removal within the meaning of the Convention.

16 Registration of decisions [909]

(1) A person on whom any rights are conferred by a decision relating to custody made by an authority in a Contracting State other than the United Kingdom may make an application for the registration of the decision in an appropriate court in the United Kingdom.

(2) The Central Authority in the United Kingdom shall assist such a person in making such an application if a request for such assistance is made by him or on his behalf by the Central Authority of the Contracting State in question.

(3) An application under subsection (1) above or a request under subsection (2) above shall be treated as a request for enforcement for the purposes of Articles 10 and 13 of the Convention.

(4) The High Court or Court of Session shall refuse to register a decision if –

(a) the court is of the opinion that on any of the grounds specified in Article 9 or 10 of the Convention the decision should not be recognised in any part of the United Kingdom;
(b) the court is of the opinion that the decision is not enforceable in the Contracting State where it was made and is not a decision to which Article 12 of the Convention applies; or
(c) an application in respect of the child under Part I of this Act is pending.

(5) Where the Lord Chancellor is requested to assist in making an application under this section to the Court of Session he shall transmit the request to the Secretary of State and the Secretary of State shall transmit to the Lord Chancellor any such request to assist in making an application to the High Court.

(6) In this section 'decision relating to custody' has the same meaning as in the Convention.

17 Variation and revocation of registered decisions [910]

(1) Where a decision which has been registered under section 16 above is varied or revoked by an authority in the Contracting State in which it was made, the person on whose behalf the application for registration of the decision was made shall notify the court in which the decision is registered of the variation or revocation.

(2) Where a court is notified under subsection (1) above of the revocation of a decision, it shall –
(a) cancel the registration, and
(b) notify such persons as may be prescribed by rules of court of the cancellation.

(3) Where a court is notified under subsection (1) above of the variation of a decision, it shall –
(a) notify such persons as may be prescribed by rules of court of the variation; and
(b) subject to any conditions which may be so prescribed, vary the registration.

(4) The court in which the decision is registered under section 16 above may also, on the application of any person appearing to the court to have an interest in the matter, cancel or vary the registration if it is satisfied that the decision has been revoked or, as the case may be, varied by an authority in the Contracting State in which it was made.

18 Enforcement of decisions [911]

Where a decision relating to custody has been registered under section 16 above, the court in which it is registered shall have the same powers for the purpose of enforcing the decision as if it had been made by that court; and proceedings for or with respect to enforcement may be taken accordingly.

19 Interim powers [912]

Where an application has been made to a court for the registration of a decision under section 16 above or for the enforcement of such a decision, the court may, at any time before the application is determined, give such interim directions as it thinks fit for the purpose of securing the welfare of the child concerned or of preventing changes in the circumstances relevant to the determination of the application or, in the case of an application for registration, to the determination of any subsequent application for the enforcement of the decision.

20 Suspension of court's powers [913]

(1) Where it appears to any court in which such proceedings as are mentioned in subsection (2) below are pending in respect of a child that –

(a) an application has been made for the registration of a decision in respect of the child under section 16 above (other than a decision mentioned in subsection (3) below) or that such a decision is registered; and
(b) the decision was made in proceedings commenced before the proceedings which are pending,

the powers of the court with respect to the child in those proceedings shall be restricted as mentioned in subsection (2) below unless, in the case of an application for registration, the application is refused.

(2) Where subsection (1) above applies the court shall not –

(a) in the case of custody proceedings, make, vary or revoke any custody order, or a supervision order under section 31 of the Children Act 1989 ...
(aa) in the case of proceedings under section 29 of the Family Law Act 1986 for the enforcement of a custody order within the meaning of Chapter V of Part I of that Act, enforce that order.

(2A) Where it appears to the Secretary of State:

(a) that an application has been made for the registration of a decision in respect of a child under section 16 above (other than a decision mentioned in subsection (3) below); or
(b) that such a decision is registered,

the Secretary of State shall not make, vary or revoke any custody order in respect of the child unless, in the case of an application for registration, the application is refused.

(3) The decision referred to in subsection (1) or (2A) above is a decision which is only a decision relating to custody within the meaning of section 16 of this Act by virtue of being a decision relating to rights of access.

(4) Paragraph (b) of Article 10(2) of the Convention shall be construed as referring to custody proceedings within the meaning of this Act...

21 Reports [914]

Where the Lord Chancellor or the Secretary of State is requested to make enquiries about a child under Article 15(1)(b) of the Convention he may –

(a) request a local authority or a probation officer to make a report to him in writing with respect to any matter relating to the child concerned which appears to him to be relevant;
(b) request the Department of Health and Social Services for Northern Ireland to arrange for a suitably qualified person to make such a report to him;
(c) request any court to which a written report relating to the child has been made to send him a copy of the report;

and any such request shall be duly complied with.

22 Proof of documents and evidence [915]

(1) In any proceedings under this Part of this Act a decision of an authority outside the United Kingdom may be proved by a duly authenticated copy of the decision; and any document purporting to be such a copy shall be deemed to be a true copy unless the contrary is shown.

(2) for the purposes of subsection (1) above a copy is duly authenticated if it bears the seal, or is signed by a judge or officer, of the authority in question.

(3) In any proceedings under this Part of this Act any such document as is mentioned in Article 13 of the Convention, or a certified copy of any such document, shall be sufficient evidence of anything stated in it.

23 Decisions of United Kingdom courts [916]

(1) Where a person on whom any rights are conferred by a decision relating to custody made by a court in the United Kingdom makes an application to the Lord Chancellor or the Secretary of State under Article 4 of the Convention with a view to securing its recognition or enforcement in another Contracting State, the Lord Chancellor or the Secretary of State may require the court which made the decision to furnish him with all or any of the documents referred to in Article 13(1)(b), (c) and (d) of the Convention.

(2) Where in any custody proceedings a court in the United Kingdom makes a decision relating to a child who has been removed from the United Kingdom, the court may also, on an application made by any person for the purposes of Article 12 of the Convention, declare the removal to have been unlawful if it is satisfied that the applicant has an interest in the matter and that the child has been taken from or sent or kept out of the United Kingdom without the consent of the person (or, if more than one, all the persons) having the right to determine the child's place of residence under the law of the part of the United Kingdom in which the child was habitually resident.

(3) In this section 'decision relating to custody' has the same meaning as in the Convention.

PART III

SUPPLEMENTARY

24A Power to order disclosure of child's whereabouts [917]

(1) Where –

(a) in proceedings for the return of a child under Part I of this Act; or
(b) on an application for the recognition, registration or enforcement of a decision in respect of a child under Part II of this Act,

there is not available to the court adequate information as to where the child is, the court may order any person who it has reason to believe may have relevant information to disclose it to the court.

(2) A person shall not be excused from complying with an order under subsection (1) above by reason that to do so may incriminate him or his spouse of an offence; but a statement or admission made in compliance with such an order shall not be admissible in evidence against either of them in proceedings for any offence other than perjury.

25 Termination of existing custody orders, etc [918]

(1) Where –

(a) an order is made for the return of a child under Part I of this Act; or
(b) a decision with respect to a child (other than a decision mentioned in subsection (2) below) is recognised under section 16 of this Act,

any custody order relating to him shall cease to have effect.

(2) The decision referred to in subsection (1)(b) above is a decision which is only a decision relating to custody within the meaning of section 16 of this Act by virtue of being a decision relating to rights of access. ...

27 Interpretation

(1) In this Act 'custody order' means (unless the contrary intention appears) any such order or authorisation as is mentioned in Schedule 3 to this Act and 'custody proceedings' means proceedings in which an order within paragraphs 1, 2, 5, 6, 8 or 9 of that Schedule may be made, varied or revoked.

(2) For the purposes of this Act 'part of the United Kingdom' means England and Wales, Scotland or Northern Ireland and 'the appropriate court', in relation to England and Wales or Northern Ireland means the High Court and, in relation to Scotland, the Court of Session.

(3) In this Act 'local authority' means –

(a) in relation to England and Wales, the council of a non-metropolitan county, a metropolitan district, a London borough or the Common Council of the City of London; ...

(4) In this Act a decision relating to rights of access in England and Wales means a decision as to the contact which a child may, or may not have, with any person.

28 Application as respects British Islands and colonies

(1) Her Majesty may by Order in Council direct that any of the provisions of this Act specified in the Order shall extend, subject to such modifications as may be specified in the Order, to –

(a) the Isle of Man,
(b) any of the Channel Islands, and
(c) any colony.

(2) Her Majesty may by Order in Council direct that this Act shall have effect in the United Kingdom as if any reference in this Act, or in any amendment made by this Act, to any order which may be made, or any proceedings which may be brought or any other thing which may be done in, or in any part of, the United Kingdom included a reference to any corresponding order which may be made or, as the case may be, proceedings which may be brought or other thing which may be done in any of the territories mentioned in subsection (1) above.

(3) An Order in Council under this section may make such consequential incidental and supplementary provision as Her Majesty considers appropriate.

(4) An Order in Council under this section shall be subject to annulment in pursuance of a resolution of either House of Parliament.

SCHEDULE 1

CONVENTION ON THE CIVIL ASPECTS OF INTERNATIONAL CHILD ABDUCTION

CHAPTER I – SCOPE OF THE CONVENTION

Article 3

The removal or the retention of a child is to be considered wrongful where –

(a) it is in breach of rights of custody attributed to a person, an institution or any other body, either jointly or alone, under the law of the State in which the child was habitually resident immediately before the removal or retention; and

(b) at the time of removal or retention those rights were actually exercised, either jointly or alone, or would have been so exercised but for the removal or retention.

The rights of custody mentioned in sub-paragraph (a) above may arise in particular by operation of law or by reason of a judicial or administrative decision, or by reason of an agreement having legal effect under the law of that State.

Article 4

The Convention shall apply to any child who was habitually resident in a Contracting State immediately before any breach of custody or access rights. The Convention shall cease to apply when the child attains the age of sixteen years.

Article 5

For the purposes of this Convention –

(a) 'rights of custody' shall include rights relating to the care of the person of the child and, in particular, the right to determine the child's place of residence;

(b) 'rights of access' shall include the right to take a child for a limited period of time to a place other than the child's habitual residence.

CHAPTER II – CENTRAL AUTHORITIES

Article 7

Central Authorities shall cooperate with each other and promote cooperation amongst the competent authorities in their respective States to secure the prompt return of children and to achieve the other objects of this Convention.

In particular, either directly or through any intermediary, they shall take all appropriate measures –

(a) to discover the whereabouts of a child who has been wrongfully removed or retained;

(b) to prevent further harm to the child or prejudice to interested parties by taking or causing to be taken provisional measures;

(c) to secure the voluntary return of the child or to bring about an amicable resolution of the issues;

(d) to exchange, where desirable, information relating to the social background of the child;

(e) to provide information of a general character as to the law of their State in connection with the application of the Convention;

(f) to initiate or facilitate the institution of judicial or administrative proceedings with a view to obtaining the return of the child and in a proper case, to make arrangements for organising or securing the effective exercise of rights of access;

(g) where the circumstances so require, to provide or facilitate the provision of legal aid and advice, including the participation of legal counsel and advisers;

(h) to provide such administrative arrangements as may be necessary and appropriate to secure the safe return of the child;

(i) to keep each other informed with respect to the operation of this Convention and, as far as possible, to eliminate any obstacles to its application.

CHAPTER III – RETURN OF CHILDREN

Article 8

Any person, institution, or other body claiming that a child has been removed or retained in breach of custody rights may apply either to the Central Authority of the child's habitual residence or to the Central Authority of any other Contracting State for assistance in securing the return of the child.

The application shall contain –

(a) information concerning the identity of the applicant, of the child and of the person alleged to have removed or retained the child;
(b) where available, the date of birth of the child;
(c) the grounds on which the applicant's claim for return of the child is based;
(d) all available information relating to the whereabouts of the child and the identity of the person with whom the child is presumed to be.

The application may be accompanied or supplemented by –

(e) an authenticated copy of any relevant decision or agreement;
(f) a certificate or an affidavit emanating from a Central Authority, or other competent authority of the State of the child's habitual residence, or from a qualified person, concerning the relevant law of that State;
(g) any other relevant document.

Article 9

If the Central Authority which receives an application referred to in Article 8 has reason to believe that the child is in another Contracting State, it shall directly and without delay transmit the application to the Central Authority of that Contracting State and inform the requesting Central Authority, or the applicant, as the case may be.

Article 10

The Central Authority of the State where the child is shall take or cause to be taken all appropriate measures in order to obtain the voluntary return of the child.

Article 11

The judicial or administrative authorities of Contracting States shall act expeditiously in proceedings for the return of children.

If the judicial or administrative authority concerned has not reached a decision within six weeks from the date of commencement of the proceedings, the applicant or the Central Authority of the requested State, on its own initiative or if asked by the Central Authority of the requesting State, shall have the right to request a statement of the reasons for the delay. If a reply is received by the Central Authority of the requested State, that Authority shall transmit the reply to the Central Authority of the requesting State, or to the applicant, as the case may be.

Article 12

Where a child has been wrongfully removed or retained in terms of Article 3 and, at the date of the commencement of the proceedings before the judicial or administrative authority of the Contracting State where the child is, a period of less than one year has elapsed from the date of the wrongful removal or retention, the authority concerned shall order the return of the child forthwith.

The judicial or administrative authority, even where the proceedings have been commenced after the expiration of the period of one year referred to in the preceding paragraph, shall also order the return of the child, unless it is demonstrated that the child is now settled in its new environment.

Where the judicial or administrative authority in the requested state has reason to believe that the child has been taken to another State, it may stay the proceedings or dismiss the application for the return of the child.

Article 13

Notwithstanding the provisions of the preceding Article, the judicial or administrative authority of the requested State is not bound to order the return of the child if the person, institution or other body which opposes its return establishes that –

> (a) the person, institution or other body having the care of the person of the child was not actually exercising the custody rights at the time of removal or retention, or had consented to or subsequently acquiesced in the removal or retention; or
> (b) there is a grave risk that his or her return would expose the child to physical or psychological harm or otherwise place the child in an intolerable situation.

The judicial or administrative authority may also refuse to order the return of the child if it finds that the child objects to being returned and has attained an age and degree of maturity at which it is appropriate to take account of its views.

In considering the circumstances referred to in this Article, the judicial and administrative authorities shall take into account the information relating to the social background of the child provided by the Central Authority or other competent authority of the child's habitual residence.

Article 14

In ascertaining whether there has been a wrongful removal or retention within the meaning of Article 3, the judicial or administrative authorities of the requested State may take notice directly of the law of, and of judicial or administrative decisions, formally recognised or not in the State of the habitual residence of the child, without recourse to the specific procedures for the proof of that law or for the recognition of foreign decisions which would otherwise be applicable.

Article 15

The judicial or administrative authorities of a Contracting State may, prior to the making of an order for the return of the child, request that the applicant obtain from the authorities of the State of the habitual residence of the child a decision or other determination that the removal or retention was wrongful within the meaning of Article 3 of the Convention, where such a decision or determination may be obtained in that State. The Central Authorities of the Contracting States shall so far as practicable assist applicants to obtain such a decision or determination.

Article 16

After receiving notice of a wrongful removal or retention of a child in the sense of Article 3, the judicial or administrative authorities of the Contracting State to which the child has been removed or in which it has been retained shall not decide on the merits of rights of custody until it has been determined that the child is not to be returned under this Convention or unless an application under this Convention is not lodged within a reasonable time following receipt of the notice.

Article 17

The sole fact that a decision relating to custody has been given in or is entitled to recognition in the requested State shall not be a ground for refusing to return a child under this Convention, but the judicial or administrative authorities of the requested State may take account of the reasons for that decision in applying this Convention.

Article 18

The provisions of this Chapter do not limit the power of a judicial or administrative authority to order the return of the child at any time.

Article 19

A decision under this Convention concerning the return of the child shall not be taken to be a determination on the merits of any custody issue.

CHAPTER IV – RIGHTS OF ACCESS

Article 21

An application to make arrangements for organising or securing the effective exercise of rights of access may be presented to the Central Authorities of the Contracting States in the same way as an application for the return of a child.

The Central Authorities are bound by the obligations of cooperation which are set forth in Article 7 to promote the peaceful enjoyment of access rights and the fulfilment of any conditions to which the exercise of those rights may be subject. The Central Authorities shall take steps to remove, as far as possible, all obstacles to the exercise of such rights. The Central Authorities, either directly or through intermediaries, may initiate or assist in the institution of proceedings with a view to organising or protecting these rights and securing respect for the conditions to which the exercise of these rights may be subject.

CHAPTER V – GENERAL PROVISIONS

Article 22

No security, bond or deposit, however described, shall be required to guarantee the payment of costs and expenses in the judicial or administrative proceedings falling within the scope of this Convention.

Article 24

Any application, communication or other document sent to the Central Authority of the requested State shall be in the original language, and shall be accompanied by a translation into the official language or one of the official languages of the requested State or, where that is not feasible, a translation into French or English.

Article 26

Each Central Authority shall bear its own costs in applying this Convention.

Central Authorities and other public services of Contracting States shall not impose any charges in relation to applications submitted under this Convention. In particular, they may not require any payment from the applicant towards the costs and expenses of the proceedings or, where applicable, those arising from the participation of legal counsel or advisers. However, they may require the payment of the expenses incurred or to be incurred in implementing the return of the child.

However, a Contracting State may, by making a reservation in accordance with Article 42, declare that it shall not be bound to assume any costs referred to in the preceding paragraph resulting from the participation of legal counsel or advisers or from court proceedings, except insofar as those costs may be covered by its system of legal aid and advice.

Upon ordering the return of a child or issuing an order concerning rights of access under this Convention, the judicial or administrative authorities may, where appropriate, direct the person who removed or retained the child, or who prevented the exercise of rights of access, to pay necessary expenses incurred by or on behalf of the applicant, including travel expenses, any costs incurred or payments made for locating the child, the costs of legal representation of the applicant, and those of returning the child.

Article 27

When it is manifest that the requirements of this Convention are not fulfilled or that the application is otherwise not well founded, a Central Authority is not bound to accept the application. In that case, the Central Authority shall forthwith inform the applicant or the Central Authority through which the application was submitted, as the case may be, of its reasons.

Article 28

A Central Authority may require that the application be accompanied by a written authorisation empowering it to act on behalf of the applicant, or to designate a representative so to act.

Article 29

This Convention shall not preclude any person, institution or body who claims that there has been a breach of custody or access rights within the meaning of Article 3 or 21 from applying directly to the judicial or administrative authorities of a Contracting State, whether or not under the provisions of this Convention.

Article 30

Any application submitted to the Central Authorities or directly to the judicial or administrative authorities of a Contracting State in accordance with the terms of this Convention, together with documents and any other information appended thereto or provided by a Central Authority, shall be admissible in the courts or administrative authorities of the Contracting States.

Article 31

In relation to a State which in matters of custody of children has two or more systems of law applicable in different territorial units –
   (a) any reference to habitual residence in that State shall be construed as referring to habitual residence in a territorial unit of that State;
   (b) any reference to the law of the State of habitual residence shall be construed as referring to the law of the territorial unit in that State where the child habitually resides.

Article 32

In relation to a State which in matters of custody of children has two or more systems of law applicable to different categories of persons, any reference to the law of that State shall be construed as referring to the legal system specified by the law of that State.

SCHEDULE 2

EUROPEAN CONVENTION ON RECOGNITION AND ENFORCEMENT OF DECISIONS CONCERNING CUSTODY OF CHILDREN

Article 1

For the purposes of this Convention:

(a) 'child' means a person of any nationality, so long as he is under 16 years of age and has not the right to decide on his own place of residence under the law of his habitual residence, the law of his nationality or the internal law of the State addressed;

(b) 'authority' means a judicial or administrative authority;

(c) 'decision relating to custody' means a decision of an authority in so far as it relates to the care of the person of the child, including the right to decide on the place of his residence, or to the right of access to him.

(d) 'improper removal' means the removal of a child across an international frontier in breach of a decision relating to his custody which has been given in a Contracting State and which is enforceable in such a State; 'improper removal' also includes:

(i) the failure to return a child across an international frontier at the end of a period of the exercise of the right of access to this child or at the end of any other temporary stay in a territory other than that where the custody is exercised;

(ii) a removal which is subsequently declared unlawful within the meaning of Article 12.

Article 4

(1) Any person who has obtained in a Contracting State a decision relating to the custody of a child and who wishes to have that decision recognised or enforced in another Contracting State may submit an application for this purpose to the central authority in any Contracting State.

(2) The application shall be accompanied by the documents mentioned in Article 13.

(3) The central authority receiving the application, if it is not the central authority in the State addressed, shall send the documents directly and without delay to that central authority.

(4) The central authority receiving the application may refuse to intervene where it is manifestly clear that the conditions laid down in this Convention are not satisfied.

(5) The central authority receiving the application shall keep the applicant informed without delay of the progress of his application.

Article 5

(1) The central authority in the State addressed shall take or cause to be taken without delay all steps which it considers to be appropriate, if necessary by instituting proceedings before its competent authorities, in order:

(a) to discover the whereabouts of the child;

(b) to avoid, in particular by any necessary provisional measures, prejudice to the interests of the child or of the applicant;

(c) to secure the recognition or enforcement of the decision;

(d) to secure the delivery of the child to the applicant where enforcement is granted;
(e) to inform the requesting authority of the measures taken and their results.

(2) Where the central authority in the State addressed has reason to believe that the child is in the territory of another Contracting State it shall send the documents directly and without delay to the central authority of that State.

(3) With the exception of the cost of repatriation, each Contracting State undertakes not to claim any payment from an applicant in respect of any measures taken under paragraph (1) of this Article by the central authority of that State on the applicant's behalf, including the costs of proceedings and, where applicable, the costs incurred by the assistance of a lawyer.

(4) If recognition or enforcement is refused, and if the central authority of the State addressed considers that it should comply with a request by the applicant to bring in that State proceedings concerning the substance of the case, that authority shall use its best endeavours to secure the representation of the applicant in the proceedings under conditions no less favourable than those available to a person who is resident in and a national of that State and for this purpose it may, in particular, institute proceedings before its competent authorities.

Article 7

A decision relating to custody given in a Contracting State shall be recognised and, where it is enforceable in the State of origin, made enforceable in every other Contracting State.

Article 9

(1) Recognition and enforcement may be refused if:

(a) in the case of a decision given in the absence of the defendant or his legal representative, the defendant was not duly served with the documents which instituted the proceedings or an equivalent document in sufficient time to enable him to arrange his defence; but such a failure to effect service cannot constitute a ground for refusing recognition or enforcement where service was not effected because the defendant had concealed his whereabouts from the person who instituted the proceedings in the State of origin;

(b) in the case of a decision given in the absence of the defendant or his legal representative, the competence of the authority giving the decision was not founded:

(i) on the habitual residence of the defendant; or
(ii) on the last common habitual residence of the child's parents, at least one parent being still habitually there, or
(iii) on the habitual residence of the child;

(c) the decision is incompatible with a decision relating to custody which became enforceable in the State addressed before the removal of the child, unless the child has had his habitual residence in the territory of the requesting State for one year before his removal.

(3) In no circumstances may the foreign decision be reviewed as to its substance.

Article 10

(1) Recognition and enforcement may also be refused on any of the following grounds:

(a) if it is found that the effects of the decision are manifestly incompatible with the fundamental principles of the law relating to the family and children in the State addressed;

(b) if it is found that by reason of a change in the circumstances including the passage of time but not including a mere change in the residence of the child after an improper removal, the effects of the original decision are manifestly no longer in accordance with the welfare of the child;
(c) if at the time when the proceedings were instituted in the State of origin:

> (i) the child was a national of the State addressed or was habitually resident there and no such connection existed with the State of origin;
> (ii) the child was a national both of the State of origin and of the State addressed and was habitually resident in the State addressed;

(d) if the decision is incompatible with a decision given in the State addressed or enforceable in that State after being given in a third State, pursuant to proceedings begun before the submission of the request for recognition or enforcement, and if the refusal is in accordance with the welfare of the child.

(2) Proceedings for recognition or enforcement may be adjourned on any of the following grounds:

(a) if an ordinary form of review of the original decision has been commenced;
(b) if proceedings relating to the custody of the child, commenced before the proceedings in the State of origin were instituted, are pending in the State addressed;
(c) if another decision concerning the custody of the child is the subject of proceedings for enforcement or of any other proceedings concerning the recognition of the decision.

Article 11

(1) Decisions on rights of access and provisions of decision relating to custody which deal with the rights of access shall be recognised and enforced subject to the same conditions as other decisions relating to custody.

(2) However, the competent authority of the State addressed may fix the conditions for the implementation and exercise of the right of access taking into account, in particular, undertakings given by the parties on this matter.

(3) Where no decision on the right of access has been taken or where recognition or enforcement of the decision relating to custody is refused, the central authority of the State addressed may apply to its competent authorities for a decision on the right of access if the person claiming a right of access so requests.

Article 12

Where, at the time of the removal of a child across an international frontier, there is no enforceable decision given in a Contracting State relating to his custody, the provisions of this Convention shall apply to any subsequent decision, relating to the custody of that child and declaring the removal to be unlawful, given in a Contracting State at the request of any interested person.

Article 13

(1) A request for recognition or enforcement in another Contracting State of a decision relating to custody shall be accompanied by:

(a) a document authorising the central authority of the State addressed to act on behalf of the applicant or to designate another representative for that purpose;
(b) a copy of the decision which satisfies the necessary conditions of authenticity;
(c) in the case of a decision given in the absence of the defendant or his legal representative, a document which establishes that the defendant was duly

served with the document which instituted the proceedings or an equivalent document;

(d) if applicable, any document which establishes that, in accordance with the law of the State of origin, the decision is enforceable;

(e) if possible, a statement indicating the whereabouts or likely whereabouts of the child in the State addressed;

(f) proposals as to how the custody of the child should be restored.

Article 15

(1) Before reaching a decision under paragraph (1)(b) of Article 10, the authority concerned in the State addressed:

(a) shall ascertain the child's views unless this is impracticable having regard in particular to his age and understanding; and

(b) may request that any appropriate enquiries be carried out.

(2) The cost of enquiries in any Contracting State shall be met by the authorities of the State where they are carried out.

Requests for enquiries and the results of enquiries may be sent to the authority concerned through the central authorities.

Article 26

(1) In relation to a State which has in matters of custody two or more systems of law of territorial application:

(a) reference to the law of a person's habitual residence or to the law of a person's nationality shall be construed as referring to the system of law determined by the rules in force in that State or, if there are no such rules, to the system of law with which the person concerned is most closely connected.

(b) reference to the State of origin or to the State addressed shall be construed as referring, as the case may be, to the territorial unit where the decision was given or to the territorial unit where recognition or enforcement of the decision or restoration of custody is requested.

(2) Paragraph (1)(a) of this Article also applies mutatis mutandis to States which have in matters of custody two or more systems of law of personal application.

SCHEDULE 3

CUSTODY ORDERS

PART I

ENGLAND AND WALES

1. The following are the orders referred to in section 27(1) of this Act –

(a) a care order under the Children Act 1989 (as defined by section 31(11) of that Act, read with section 105(1) and Schedule 14);

(b) a residence order (as defined by section 8 of the Act of 1989); and

(c) any order made by a court in England and Wales under any of the following enactments:

(i) section 9(1), 10(1)(a) or 11(a) of the Guardianship of Minors Act 1971;

(ii) section 42(1) or (2) or 43(1) of the Matrimonial Causes Act 1973;

(iii) section 2(2)(b), (4)(b) or (5) of the Guardianship Act 1973 as applied by section 34(5) of the Children Act 1975;

(iv) section 8(2)(a), 10(1) or 19(1)(ii) of the Domestic Proceedings and Magistrates' Courts Act 1978;
(v) section 26(1)(b) of the Adoption Act 1976.

2. An order made by the High Court in the exercise of its jurisdiction relating to wardship so far as it gives the care and control of a child to any person.

3. An order made by the Secretary of State under section 25(1) of the Children and Young Persons Act 1969 (except where the order superseded was made under section 74(1)(a) or (b) or 78(1) of the Children and Young Persons Act (Northern Ireland) 1968 or was made under section 97(2)(a) of that Act on a complaint by a person under whose supervision the child had been placed by an order under section 74(1)(c) of that Act).

4. An authorisation given by the Secretary of State under section 26(2) of the Children and Young Persons Act 1969 (except where the relevant order, within the meaning of that section, was made by virtue of the court which made it being satisfied that the child was guilty of an offence).

[As amended by the Family Law Act 1986, ss67(1)–(5), 68(1), Schedule 1, paras 29, 30; Children Act 1989, s108(5), (7), Schedule 13, para 57(1)–(3), Schedule 15.]

FAMILY LAW ACT 1986
(1986 c 55)

PART I

CHILD CUSTODY

CHAPTER I

PRELIMINARY

1 Orders to which Part I applies [924]

(1) Subject to the following provisions of this section, in this Part 'Part I order' means –

(a) a section 8 order made by a court in England and Wales under the Children Act 1989, other than an order varying or discharging such an order; ...
(d) an order made by a court in England and Wales in the exercise of the inherent jurisdiction of the High Court with respect to children –

(i) so far as it gives care of a child to any person or provides for contact with, or the education of, a child; but
(ii) excluding an order varying or revoking such an order. ...

(3) In this Part, 'Part I order' –

(a) includes any order which would have been a custody order by virtue of this section in any form in which it was in force at any time before its amendment by the Children Act 1989 ...; and
(b) (subject to section 32 and 40 of this Act) excludes any order which would have been excluded from being a custody order by virtue of this section in any such form. ...

CHAPTER II

JURISDICTION OF COURTS IN ENGLAND AND WALES

2 Jurisdiction: general

(1) A court in England and Wales shall not have jurisdiction to make a section 1(1)(a) order with respect to a child in or in connection with matrimonial proceedings in England and Wales unless the condition in section 2A of this Act is satisfied.

(2) A court in England and Wales shall not have jurisdiction to make a section 1(1)(a) order in a non-matrimonial case (that is to say, where the condition in section 2A of this Act is not satisfied) unless the condition in section 3 of this Act is satisfied.

(3) A court in England and Wales shall not have jurisdiction to make a section 1(1)(d) order unless –

(a) the condition in section 3 of this Act is satisfied, or
(b) the child concerned is present in England and Wales on the relevant date and the court considers that the immediate exercise of its powers is necessary for his protection.

2A Jurisdiction in or in connection with matrimonial proceedings

(1) The condition referred to in section 2(1) of this Act is that the matrimonial proceedings are proceedings in respect of the marriage of the parents of the child concerned and –

(a) the proceedings –

(i) are proceedings for divorce or nullity of marriage, and
(ii) are continuing;

(b) the proceedings –

(i) are proceedings for judicial separation,
(ii) are continuing,

and the jurisdiction of the court is not excluded by subsection (2) below; or

(c) the proceedings have been dismissed after the beginning of the trial but –

(i) the section 1(1)(a) order is being made forthwith, or
(ii) the application for the order was made on or before the dismissal. ...

(4) Where a court –

(a) has jurisdiction to make a section 1(1)(a) order in or in connection with matrimonial proceedings, but
(b) considers that it would be more appropriate for Part I matters relating to the child to be determined outside England and Wales,

the court may by order direct that, while the order under this subsection is in force, no section 1(1)(a) order shall be made by any court in or in connection with those proceedings.

3 Habitual residence or presence of child

(1) The condition referred to in section 2(2) of this Act is that on the relevant date the child concerned –

(a) is habitually resident in England and Wales, or

(b) is present in England and Wales and is not habitually resident in any part of the United Kingdom or a specified dependent territory,

and, in either case, the jurisdiction of the court is not excluded by subsection (2) below.

(2) For the purposes of subsection (1) above, the jurisdiction of the court is excluded if, on the relevant date, matrimonial proceedings are continuing in a court in Scotland, Northern Ireland or a specified dependent territory in respect of the marriage of the parents of the child concerned. ...

5 Power of court to refuse application or stay proceedings [928]

(1) A court in England and Wales which has jurisdiction to make a Part I order may refuse an application for the order in any case where the matter in question has already been determined in proceedings outside England and Wales.

(2) Where, at any stage of the proceedings on an application made to a court in England and Wales for a Part I order, or for the variation of a Part I order, it appears to the court –

(a) that proceedings with respect to the matters to which the application relates are continuing outside England and Wales, or
(b) that it would be more appropriate for those matters to be determined in proceedings to be taken outside England and Wales,

the court may stay the proceedings on the application.

(3) The court may remove a stay granted in accordance with subsection (2) above if it appears to the court that there has been unreasonable delay in the taking or prosecution of the other proceedings referred to in that subsection, or that those proceedings are stayed, sisted or concluded.

(4) Nothing in this section shall affect any power exercisable apart from this section to refuse an application or to grant or remove a stay.

6 Duration and variation of Part I orders [929]

(1) If a Part I order made by a court in Scotland, Northern Ireland or a specified dependent territory (or a variation of such an order) comes into force with respect to a child at a time when a Part I order made by a court in England and Wales has effect with respect to him, the latter order shall cease to have effect so far as it makes provision for any matter for which the same or different provision is made by (or by the variation of) the order made by the court in Scotland, Northern Ireland or the territory.

(2) Where by virtue of subsection (1) above a Part I order has ceased to have effect so far as it makes provision for any matter, a court in England or Wales shall not have jurisdiction to vary that order so as to make provision for that matter.

(3) A court in England and Wales shall not have jurisdiction to vary a Part I order if, on the relevant date, matrimonial proceedings are continuing in Scotland, Northern Ireland or a specified dependent territory in respect of the marriage of the parents of the child concerned.

(3A) Subsection (3) above shall not apply if –

(a) the Part I order was made in or in connection with proceedings for divorce or nullity in England and Wales in respect of the marriage of the parents of the child concerned; and
(b) those proceedings are continuing.

(3B) Subsection (3) above shall not apply if –

(a) the Part I order was made in or in connection with proceedings for judicial separation in England and Wales;
(b) those proceedings are continuing; and
(c) the decree of judicial separation has not yet been granted. ...

(6) Subsection (7) below applies where a Part I order which is –

(a) a residence order (within the meaning of the Children Act 1989) in favour of a person with respect to a child,
(b) an order made in the exercise of the High Court's inherent jurisdiction with respect to children by virtue of which a person has care of a child, or
(c) an order –

(ii) under which a person is entitled to the actual possession of a child,

ceases to have effect in relation to that person by virtue of subsection (1) above.

(7) Where this subsection applies, any family assistance order made under section 16 of the Children Act 1989 with respect to the child shall also cease to have effect.

(8) For the purposes of subsection (7) above the reference to a family assistance order under section 16 of the Children Act 1989 shall be deemed to include a reference to an order for the supervision of a child made under –

(a) section 7(4) of the Family Law Reform Act 1969,
(b) section 44 of the Matrimonial Causes Act 1973,
(c) section 2(2)(a) of the Guardianship Act 1973,
(d) section 34(5) or 36(3)(b) of the Children Act 1975, or
(e) section 9 of the Domestic Proceedings and Magistrates' Courts Act 1978;

but this subsection shall cease to have effect once all such orders for the supervision of children have ceased to have effect in accordance with Schedule 14 to the Children Act 1989.

7 Interpretation of Chapter II [930]

In this Chapter –

(a) 'child' means a person who has not attained the age of eighteen;
(b) 'matrimonial proceedings' means proceedings for divorce, nullity or marriage or judicial separation;
(c) 'the relevant date' means, in relation to the making or variation of an order –

(i) where an application is made for an order to be made or varied, the date of the application (or first application, if two or more are determined together), and
(ii) where no such application is made, the date on which the court is considering whether to make or, as the case may be, vary the order; and

(d) 'section 1(1)(a) order' and 'section 1(1)(d) order' means orders falling within section 1(1)(a) and (d) of this Act respectively.

CHAPTER V

RECOGNITION AND ENFORCEMENT

25 Recognition of Part I orders: general [931]

(1) Where a Part I order made by a court in any part of the United Kingdom or in

a specified dependent territory is in force with respect to a child who has not attained the age of sixteen, then, subject to subsection (2) below, the order shall be recognised in any other part or, in the case of a dependent territory order, any part of the United Kingdom as having the same effect in that part as if it had been made by the appropriate court in that part and as if that court had had jurisdiction to make it.

(2) Where a Part I order includes provision as to the means by which rights conferred by the order are to be enforced, subsection (1) above shall not apply to that provision.

(3) A court in a part of the United Kingdom in which a Part I order is recognised in accordance with subsection (1) above shall not enforce the order unless it has been registered in that part of the United Kingdom under section 27 of this Act and proceedings for enforcement are taken in accordance with section 29 of this Act.

27 Registration [932]

(1) Any person on whom any rights are conferred by a Part I order may apply to the court which made it for the order to be registered in another part of the United Kingdom under this section, or in a specified dependent territory under a corresponding provision.

(2) An application under this section shall be made in the prescribed manner and shall contain the prescribed information and be accompanied by such documents as may be prescribed.

(3) On receiving an application under this section the court which made the Part I order shall, unless it appears to the court that the order is no longer in force, cause the following documents to be sent to the appropriate court in the part of the United Kingdom or dependent territory specified in the application, namely –

    (a) a certified copy of the order, and
    (b) where the order has been varied, prescribed particulars of any variation which is in force, and
    (c) a copy of the application and of any accompanying documents.

(4) Where the prescribed officer of the appropriate court in any part of the United Kingdom receives a certified copy of a Part I order under subsection (3) above or under a corresponding dependent territory provision, he shall forthwith cause the order, together with particulars of any variation, to be registered in that court in the prescribed manner.

(5) An order shall not be registered under this section in respect of a child who has attained the age of sixteen, and the registration of an order in respect of a child who has not attained the age of sixteen shall cease to have effect on the attainment by the child of that age.

28 Cancellation and variation of registration [933]

(1) A court which revokes, recalls or varies an order registered under section 27 of this Act shall cause notice of the revocation, recall or variation to be given in the prescribed manner to the prescribed officer of the court in which it is registered and, on receiving the notice, the prescribed officer –

    (a) in the case of the revocation or recall of the order, shall cancel the registration, and
    (b) in the case of the variation of the order, shall cause particulars of the variation to be registered in the prescribed manner.

(2) Where –

(a) an order registered under section 27 of this Act ceases (in whole or in part) to have effect in the part of the United Kingdom or in a specified dependent territory in which it was made, otherwise than because of its revocation, recall or variation, or

(b) an order registered under section 27 of this Act in Scotland ceases (in whole or in part) to have effect there as a result of the making of an order in proceedings outside the United Kingdom and any specified dependent territory,

the court in which the order is registered may, of its own motion or on the application of any person who appears to the court to have an interest in the matter, cancel the registration (or, if the order has ceased to have effect in part, cancel the registration so far as it relates to the provisions which have ceased to have effect).

29 Enforcement [934]

(1) Where a Part I order has been registered under section 27 of this Act, the court in which it is registered shall have the same powers for the purpose of enforcing the order as it would have if it had itself made the order and had jurisdiction to make it; and proceedings for or with respect to enforcement may be taken accordingly.

(2) Where an application has been made to any court for the enforcement of an order registered in that court under section 27 of this Act, the court may, at any time before the application is determined, give such interim directions as it thinks fit for the purpose of securing the welfare of the child concerned or of preventing changes in the circumstances relevant to the determination of the application.

(3) The references in subsection (1) above to a Part I order do not include references to any provision of the order as to the means by which rights conferred by the order are to be enforced.

30 Staying or sisting of enforcement proceedings [935]

(1) Where in accordance with section 29 of this Act proceedings are taken in any court for the enforcement of an order registered in that court, any person who appears to the court to have an interest in the matter may apply for the proceedings to be stayed or sisted on the ground that he has taken or intends to take other proceedings (in the United Kingdom or elsewhere) as a result of which the order may cease to have effect, or may have a different effect, in the part of the United Kingdom in which it is registered.

(2) If after considering an application under subsection (1) above the court considers that the proceedings for enforcement should be stayed or sisted in order that other proceedings may be taken or concluded, it shall stay or sist the proceedings for enforcement accordingly.

(3) The court may remove a stay or recall of sist granted in accordance with subsection (2) above if it appears to the court –

(a) that there has been unreasonable delay in the taking or prosecution of the other proceedings referred to in that subsection, or

(b) that those other proceedings are concluded and that the registered order, or a relevant part of it, is still in force.

(4) Nothing in this section shall affect any power exercisable apart from this section to grant, remove or recall a stay or sist.

31 Dismissal of enforcement proceedings [936]

(1) Where in accordance with section 29 of this Act proceedings are taken in any court for the enforcement of an order registered in that court, any person who appears to the court to have an interest in the matter may apply for those proceedings to be dismissed on the ground that the order has (in whole or in part) ceased to have effect in the part of the United Kingdom or specified dependent territory in which it was made.

(2) Where in accordance with section 29 of this Act proceedings are taken in the Court of Session for the enforcement of an order registered in that court, any person who appears to the court to have an interest in the matter may apply for those proceedings to be dismissed on the ground that the order has (in whole or in part) ceased to have effect in Scotland as a result of the making of an order in proceedings outside the United Kingdom and any specified dependent territory.

(3) If, after considering an application under subsection (1) or (2) above, the court is satisfied that the registered order has ceased to have effect, it shall dismiss the proceedings for enforcement (or, if it is satisfied that the order has ceased to have effect in part, it shall dismiss the proceedings so far as they relate to the enforcement of provisions which have ceased to have effect).

32 Interpretation of Chapter V [937]

(1) In this Chapter –

'the appropriate court', in relation to England and Wales or Northern Ireland, means the High Court and, in relation to Scotland, means the Court of Session and, in relation to a specified dependent territory, means the corresponding court in that territory;

'Part I order' includes (except where the context otherwise requires) any order within section 1(3) of this Act which, on the assumptions mentioned in subsection (3) below –

>   (a) could have been made notwithstanding the provisions of this Part or the corresponding dependent territory provisions;
>   (b) would have been a Part I order for the purposes of this Part; and
>   (c) would not have ceased to have effect by virtue of section 6, 15 or 23 of this Act.

(2) In the application of this Chapter to Scotland, 'Part I order' also includes (except where the context otherwise requires) any order within section 1(3) of this Act which, on the assumptions mentioned in subsection (3) below –

>   (a) would have been a Part I order for the purposes of this Part; and
>   (b) would not have ceased to have effect by virtue of section 6 or 23 of this Act,

and which, but for the provisions of this Part, would be recognised in Scotland under any rule of law.

(3) The said assumptions are –

>   (a) that this Part or the corresponding dependent territory provisions, as the case may be, had been in force at all material times; and
>   (b) that any reference in section 1 of this Act to any enactment included a reference to any corresponding enactment previously in force.

CHAPTER VI

MISCELLANEOUS AND SUPPLEMENTAL

33 Power to order disclosure of child's whereabouts [938]

(1) Where in proceedings for or relating to a Part I order in respect of a child there is not available to the court adequate information as to where the child is, the court may order any person who it has reason to believe may have relevant information to disclose it to the court.

(2) A person shall not be excused from complying with an order under subsection (1) above by reason that to do so may incriminate him or his spouse of an offence; but a statement or admission made in compliance with such an order shall not be admissible in evidence against either of them in proceedings for any offence other than perjury.

(3) A court in Scotland before which proceedings are pending for the enforcement of an order for the custody of a child made outside the United Kingdom and any specified dependent territory which is recognised in Scotland shall have the same powers as it would have under subsection (1) above if the order were its own.

34 Power to order recovery of child [939]

(1) Where –

(a) a person is required by a Part I order, or an order for the enforcement of a Part I order, to give up a child to another person ('the person concerned'), and
(b) the court which made the order imposing the requirement is satisfied that the child has not been given up in accordance with the order,

the court may make an order authorising an officer of the court or a constable to take charge of the child and deliver him to the person concerned.

(2) The authority conferred by subsection (1) above includes authority –

(a) to enter and search any premises where the person acting in pursuance of the order has reason to believe the child may be found, and
(b) to use such force as may be necessary to give effect to the purpose of the order.

(3) Where by virtue of –

(a) section 14 of the Children Act 1989, ...

a Part I order (or a provision of a Part I order) may be enforced as if it were an order requiring a person to give up a child to another person, subsection (1) above shall apply as if the Part I order had included such a requirement.

(4) This section is without prejudice to any power conferred on a court by or under any other enactment or rule of law.

36 Effect of orders restricting removal [940]

(1) This section applies to any order made by a court in the United Kingdom or any specified dependent territory prohibiting the removal of a child from the United Kingdom or from any specified part of it or from any such territory.

(2) An order to which this section applies, made by a court in one part of the United Kingdom or in a specified dependent territory, shall have effect in each other part, or, in the case of an order made in a dependent territory, each part of the United Kingdom –

(a) as if it had been made by the appropriate court in that part, and
(b) in the case of an order which has the effect of prohibiting the child's removal to that part, as if it had included a prohibition on his further removal to any place except one to which he could be removed consistently with the order.

(3) The references in subsections (1) and (2) above to prohibitions on a child's removal include references to prohibitions subject to exceptions; and in a case where removal is prohibited except with the consent of the court, nothing in subsection (2) above shall be construed as affecting the identity of the court whose consent is required.

(4) In this section 'child' means a person who has not attained the age of sixteen; and this section shall cease to apply to an order relating to a child when he attains the age of sixteen.

37 Surrender of passports [941]

(1) Where there is in force an order prohibiting or otherwise restricting the removal of a child from the United Kingdom or from any specified part of it or from a specified dependent territory, the court by which the order was in fact made, or by which it is treated under section 36 of this Act as having been made, may require any person to surrender any United Kingdom passport which has been issued to, or contains particulars of, the child.

(2) In this section 'United Kingdom passport' means a current passport issued by the Government of the United Kingdom.

38 Automatic restriction on removal of wards of court [942]

(1) The rule of law which (without any order of the court) restricts the removal of a ward of court from the jurisdiction of the court shall, in a case to which this section applies, have effect subject to the modifications in subsection (3) below.

(2) This section applies in relation to a ward of court if –

(a) proceedings for divorce, nullity or judicial separation in respect of the marriage of his parents are continuing in a court in another part of the United Kingdom (that is to say, in a part of the United Kingdom) outside the jurisdiction of the court of which he is a ward), or in a specified dependent territory, or
(b) he is habitually resident in another part of the United Kingdom or in a specified dependent territory,

except where that other part is Scotland and he has attained the age of sixteen.

(3) Where this section applies, the rule referred to in subsection (1) above shall not prevent –

(a) the removal of the ward of court, without the consent of any court, to the other part of the United Kingdom or the specified dependent territory mentioned in subsection (2) above, or
(b) his removal to any other place with the consent of either the appropriate court in that other part of the United Kingdom or the specified dependent territory or the court mentioned in subsection (2)(a) above.

39 Duty to furnish particulars of other proceedings [943]

Parties to proceedings for or relating to a Part I order shall, to such extent and in such manner as may be prescribed, give particulars of other proceedings known to them which relate to the child concerned (including proceedings instituted abroad and proceedings which are no longer continuing).

40 Interpretation of Chapter VI [944]

(1) In this Chapter –

'the appropriate court' has the same meaning as in Chapter V;

'Part I order' includes (except where the context otherwise requires) any such order as is mentioned in section 32(1) of this Act. ...

41 Habitual residence after removal without consent, etc [945]

(1) Where a child who –
    (a) has not attained the age of sixteen, and
    (b) is habitually resident in a part of the United Kingdom or in a specified dependent territory,

becomes habitually resident outside that part of the United Kingdom or that territory in consequence of circumstances of the kind specified in subsection (2) below, he shall be treated for the purposes of this Part as continuing to be habitually resident in that part of the United Kingdom or that territory for the period of one year beginning with the date on which those circumstances arise.

(2) The circumstances referred to in subsection (1) above exist where the child is removed from or retained outside, or himself leaves or remains outside, the part of the United Kingdom or the territory in which he was habitually resident before his change of residence –
    (a) without the agreement of the person or all the persons having, under the law of that part of the United Kingdom or that territory, the right to determine where he is to reside, or
    (b) in contravention of an order made by a court in any part of the United Kingdom or in a specified dependent territory.

(3) A child shall cease to be treated by virtue of subsection (1) above as habitually resident in a part of the United Kingdom or a specified dependent territory if, during the period there mentioned –
    (a) he attains the age of sixteen, or
    (b) he becomes habitually resident outside that part of the United Kingdom or that territory with the agreement of the person or persons mentioned in subsection (2)(a) above and not in contravention of an order made by a court in any part of the United Kingdom or in any specified dependent territory.

42 General interpretation of Part I [946]

(1) In this Part –

'certified copy', in relation to an order of any court, means a copy certified by the prescribed officer of the court to be a true copy of the order or of the official record of the order;

'corresponding dependent territory order', 'corresponding dependent territory provision' and similar expressions, in relation to a specified dependent territory, shall be construed in accordance with Schedule 3 to the Family Law Act 1986 (Dependent Territories) Order 1991 as from time to time in force; 'dependent territory' has the meaning given by section 43(2) of this Act.

'part of the United Kingdom' means England and Wales, Scotland or Northern Ireland;

'prescribed' means prescribed by rules of court or act of sederunt;

'specified dependent territory' means a dependent territory for the time being specified in Schedule 1 to the said order of 1991.

(2) For the purposes of this Part proceedings in England and Wales, Northern Ireland or a specified dependent territory for divorce, nullity or judicial separation in respect of the marriage of the parents of a child shall, unless they have been dismissed, be treated as continuing until the child concerned attains the age of eighteen (whether or not a decree has been granted and whether or not, in the case of a decree of divorce or nullity of marriage, that decree has been made absolute).

(3) For the purposes of this Part, matrimonial proceedings in a court in Scotland which has jurisdiction in those proceedings to make a Part I order with respect to a child shall, unless they have been dismissed or decree of absolvitor has been granted therein, be treated as continuing until the child concerned attains the age of sixteen.

(4) Any reference in this Part to proceedings in respect of the marriage of the parents of a child shall, in relation to a child who, although not a child of both parties to the marriage, is a child of the family of those parties, be construed as a reference to proceedings in respect of that marriage; and for this purpose 'child of the family' –

(a) if the proceedings are in England and Wales, means any child who has been treated by both parties as a child of their family, except a child who is placed with those parties as foster parents by a local authority or a voluntary organisation; ...

(5) References in this Part to Part I orders include (except where the context otherwise requires) references to Part I orders as varied.

(6) For the purposes of this Part each of the following orders shall be treated as varying the Part I order to which it relates –

(a) an order which provides for a person to be allowed contact with or to be given access to a child who is the subject of a Part I order, or which makes provision for the education of such a child, ...

and for the purposes of chapter V of this Part and this Chapter, this subsection shall have effect as if any reference to any enactment included a reference to any corresponding enactment previously in force.

(7) In this Part –

(a) references to Part I proceedings in respect of a child are references to any proceedings for a Part I order or an order corresponding to a Part I order and include, in relation to proceedings outside the United Kingdom and any specified dependent territory, references to proceedings before a tribunal or other authority having power under the law having effect there to determine Part I matters; and

(b) references to Part I matters are references to matters that might be determined by a Part I order or an order corresponding to a Part I order.

PART II

RECOGNITION OF DIVORCES, ANNULMENTS AND LEGAL SEPARATIONS

44 Recognition in United Kingdom of divorces, annulments and judicial separations granted in the British Islands

(1) Subject to section 52(4) and (5)(a) of this Act, no divorce or annulment obtained in any part of the British Islands shall be regarded as effective in any part of the United Kingdom unless granted by a court of civil jurisdiction.

(2) Subject to section 51 of this Act, the validity of any divorce, annulment or judicial separation granted by a court of civil jurisdiction in any part of the British Islands shall be recognised throughout the United Kingdom.

45 Recognition in the United Kingdom of overseas divorces, annulments and legal separations

Subject to sections 51 and 52 of this Act, the validity of a divorce, annulment or legal separation obtained in a country outside the British Islands (in this Part referred to as an overseas divorce, annulment or legal separation) shall be recognised in the United Kingdom if, and only if, it is entitled to recognition –

(a) by virtue of sections 46 to 49 of this Act, or
(b) by virtue of any enactment other than this Part.

46 Grounds for recognition

(1) The validity of an overseas divorce, annulment or legal separation obtained by means of proceedings shall be recognised if –

(a) the divorce, annulment or legal separation is effective under the law of the country in which it was obtained; and
(b) at the relevant date either party to the marriage –

(i) was habitually resident in the country in which the divorce, annulment or legal separation was obtained; or
(ii) was domiciled in that country; or
(iii) was a national of that country.

(2) The validity of an overseas divorce, annulment or legal separation obtained otherwise than by means of proceedings shall be recognised if –

(a) the divorce, annulment or legal separation is effective under the law of the country in which it was obtained;
(b) at the relevant date –

(i) each party to the marriage was domiciled in that country; or
(ii) either party to the marriage was domiciled in that country and the other party was domiciled in a country under whose law the divorce, annulment or legal separation is recognised as valid; and

(c) neither party to the marriage was habitually resident in the United Kingdom throughout the period of one year immediately preceding that date.

(3) In this section 'the relevant date' means –

(a) in the case of an overseas divorce, annulment or legal separation obtained by means of proceedings, the date of the commencement of the proceedings;
(b) in the case of an overseas divorce, annulment or legal separation obtained otherwise than by means of proceedings, the date on which it was obtained.

(4) Where in the case of an overseas annulment, the relevant date fell after the death of either party to the marriage, any reference in subsection (1) or (2) above to that date shall be construed in relation to that party as a reference to the date of death.

(5) For the purpose of this section, a party to a marriage shall be treated as domiciled in a country if he was domiciled in that country either according to the law of that country in family matters or according to the law of the part of the United Kingdom in which the question of recognition arises.

47 Cross-proceedings and divorces following legal separations [950]

(1) Where there have been cross-proceedings, the validity of an overseas divorce, annulment or legal separation obtained either in the original proceedings or in the cross-proceedings shall be recognised if –

(a) the requirements of section 46(1)(b)(i), (ii) or (iii) of this Act are satisfied in relation to the date of the commencement either of the original proceedings or of the cross-proceedings, and
(b) the validity of the divorce, annulment or legal separation is otherwise entitled to recognition by virtue of the provisions of this Part.

(2) Where a legal separation, the validity of which is entitled to recognition by virtue of the provisions of section 46 of this Act or of subsection (1) above, is converted, in the country in which it was obtained, into a divorce which is effective under the law of that country, the validity of the divorce shall be recognised whether or not it would itself be entitled to recognition by virtue of those provisions.

48 Proof of facts relevant to recognition [951]

(1) For the purpose of deciding whether an overseas divorce, annulment or legal separation obtained by means of proceedings is entitled to recognition by virtue of section 46 and 47 of this court, any finding of fact made (whether expressly or by implication) in the proceedings and on the basis of which jurisdiction was assumed in the proceedings shall –

(a) if both parties to the marriage took part in the proceedings, be conclusive evidence of the fact found; and
(b) in any other case, be sufficient proof of that fact unless the contrary be shown.

(2) In this section 'finding of fact' includes a finding that either party to the marriage –

(a) was habitually resident in the country in which the divorce, annulment or legal separation was obtained; or
(b) was under the law of that country domiciled there; or
(c) was a national of that country.

(3) For the purposes of subsection (1)(a) above, a party to the marriage who has appeared in judicial proceedings shall be treated as having taken part in them.

49 Modifications of Part II in relation to countries comprising territories having different systems of law [952]

(1) In relation to a country comprising territories in which different systems of law are in force in matters of divorce, annulment or legal separation, the provisions of

this Part mentioned in subsections (2) to (5) below shall have effect subject to the modifications there specified.

(2) In a case of a divorce, annulment or legal separation the recognition of the validity of which depends on whether the requirements of subsection (1)(b)(i) or (ii) of section 46 of this Act are satisfied, that section and, in the case of a legal separation, section 47(2) of this Act shall have effect as if each territory were a separate country.

(3) In the case of a divorce, annulment or legal separation the recognition of the validity of which depends on whether the requirements of subsection (1)(b)(iii) of section 46 of this Act are satisfied –

(a) that section shall have effect as if for paragraph (a) of subsection (1) there were substituted the following paragraph –

'(a) the divorce, annulment or legal separation is effective throughout the country in which it was obtained;'; and

(b) in the case of a legal separation, section 47(2) of this Act shall have effect as if for the words 'is effective under the law of that country' there were substituted the words 'is effective throughout that country'.

(4) In the case of a divorce, annulment or legal separation the recognition of the validity of which depends on whether the requirements of subsection (2)(b) of section 46 of this Act are satisfied, that section and section 52(3) and (4) of this Act and, in the case of a legal separation, section 47(2) of this Act shall have effect as if each territory were a separate country.

(5) Paragraphs (a) and (b) of section 48(2) of this Act shall each have effect as if each territory were a separate country.

50 Non-recognition of divorce or annulment in another jurisdiction no bar to remarriage [953]

Where, in any part of the United Kingdom –

(a) a divorce or annulment has been granted by a court of civil jurisdiction, or
(b) the validity of a divorce or annulment is recognised by virtue of this Part,

the fact that the divorce or annulment would not be recognised elsewhere shall not preclude either party to the marriage from remarrying in that part of the United Kingdom or cause the remarriage of either party (wherever the remarriage takes place) to be treated as invalid in that part.

51 Refusal of recognition [954]

(1) Subject to section 52 of this Act, recognition of the validity of –

(a) a divorce, annulment or judicial separation granted by a court of civil jurisdiction in any part of the British Islands, or
(b) an overseas divorce, annulment or legal separation,

may be refused in any part of the United Kingdom if the divorce, annulment or separation was granted or obtained at a time when it was irreconcilable with a decision determining the question of the subsistence or validity of the marriage of the parties previously given (whether before or after the commencement of this Part) by a court of civil jurisdiction in that part of the United Kingdom or by a court elsewhere and recognised or entitled to be recognised in that part of the United Kingdom.

(2) Subject to section 52 of this Act, recognition of the validity of –

(a) a divorce or judicial separation granted by a court of civil jurisdiction in any part of the British Islands, or

(b) an overseas divorce or legal separation,

may be refused in any part of the United Kingdom if the divorce or separation was granted or obtained at a time when, according to the law of that part of the United Kingdom (including its rules of private international law and the provisions of this Part), there was no subsisting marriage between the parties.

(3) Subject to section 52 of this Act, recognition by virtue of section 45 of this Act of the validity of the overseas divorce, annulment or legal separation may be refused if –

(a) in the case of a divorce, annulment or legal separation obtained by means of proceedings, it was obtained –

(i) without such steps having been taken for giving notice of the proceedings to a party to the marriage as, having regard to the nature of the proceedings and all the circumstances, should reasonably have been taken; or

(ii) without a party to the marriage having been given (for any reason other than lack of notice) such opportunity to take part in the proceedings as, having regard to those matters, he should reasonably have been given; or

(b) in the case of a divorce, annulment or legal separation obtained otherwise than by means of proceedings –

(i) there is no official document certifying that the divorce, annulment or legal separation is effective under the law of the country in which it was obtained; or

(ii) where either party to the marriage was domiciled in another country at the relevant date, there is no official document certifying that the divorce, annulment or legal separation is recognised as valid under the law of that other country; or

(c) in either case, recognition of the divorce, annulment or legal separation would be manifestly contrary to public policy.

(4) In this section –

'official', in relation to a document certifying that a divorce, annulment or legal separation is effective, or is recognised as valid, under the law of any country, means issued by a person or body appointed or recognised for the purpose under that law;

'the relevant date' has the same meaning as in section 46 of this Act;

and subsection (5) of that section shall apply for the purposes of this section as it applies for the purposes of that section.

(5) Nothing in this Part shall be construed as requiring the recognition of any finding of fault made in any proceedings for divorce, annulment or separation or of any maintenance, custody or other ancillary order made in any such proceedings.

52 Provisions as to divorces, annulments, etc obtained before commencement of Part II [955]

(1) The provisions of this Part shall apply –

(a) to a divorce, annulment or judicial separation granted by a court of civil jurisdiction in the British Islands before the date of the commencement of this Part, and

(b) to an overseas divorce, annulment or legal separation obtained before that date,

as well as to one granted or obtained on or after that date.

(2) In the case of such a divorce, annulment or separation as is mentioned in subsection (1)(a) or (b) above, the provisions of this Part shall require or, as the case may be, preclude the recognition of its validity in relation to any time before that date as well as in relation to any subsequent time, but those provisions shall not –

(a) affect any property to which any person became entitled before that date, or
(b) affect the recognition of the validity of the divorce, annulment or separation if that matter has been decided by any competent court in the British Islands before that date.

(3) Subsections (1) and (2) above shall apply in relation to any divorce or judicial separation granted by a court of civil jurisdiction in the British Islands before the date of the commencement of this Part whether granted before or after the commencement of section 1 of the Recognition of Divorces and Legal Separations Act 1971.

(4) The validity of any divorce, annulment or legal separation mentioned in subsection (5) below shall be recognised in the United Kingdom whether or not it is entitled to recognition by virtue of any of the foregoing provisions of this Part.

(5) The divorces, annulments and legal separations referred to in subsection (4) above are –

(a) a divorce which was obtained in the British Islands before 1 January 1974 and was recognised as valid under rules of law applicable before that date;
(b) an overseas divorce which was recognised as valid under the Recognition of Divorces and Legal Separations Act 1971 and was not affected by section 16(2) of the Domicile and Matrimonial Proceedings Act 1973 (proceedings otherwise than in a court of law where both parties resident in the United Kingdom);
(c) a divorce of which the decree was registered under section 1 of the Indian and Colonial Divorce Jurisdiction Act 1926;
(d) a divorce or annulment which was recognised as valid under section 4 of the Matrimonial Causes (War Marriages) Act 1944; and
(e) an overseas legal separation which was recognised as valid under the Recognition of Divorces and Legal Separations Act 1971.

PART III

DECLARATIONS OF STATUS

55 Declarations as to marital status [956]

(1) Subject to the following provisions of this section, any person may apply to the court for one or more of the following declarations in relation to a marriage specified in the application, that is to say –

(a) a declaration that the marriage was at its inception a valid marriage;
(b) a declaration that the marriage subsisted on a date specified in the application;
(c) a declaration that the marriage did not subsist on a date so specified;
(d) a declaration that the validity of a divorce, annulment or legal separation obtained in any country outside England and Wales in respect of the marriage is entitled to recognition in England and Wales;

(e) a declaration that the validity of a divorce, annulment or legal separation so obtained in respect of the marriage is not entitled to recognition in England and Wales.

(2) A court shall have jurisdiction to entertain an application under subsection (1) above if, and only if, either of the parties to the marriage to which the application relates –

(a) is domiciled in England and Wales on the date of the application, or
(b) has been habitually resident in England and Wales throughout the period of one year ending with that date, or
(c) died before that date and either –

(i) was at death domiciled in England and Wales, or
(ii) had been habitually resident in England and Wales throughout the period of one year ending with the date of death.

(3) Where an application under section (1) above is made by any person other than a party to the marriage to which the application relates, the court shall refuse to hear the application if it considers that the applicant does not have a sufficient interest in the determination of that application.

56 Declarations of parentage, legitimacy or legitimation [957]

(1) Any person may apply to the court for a declaration –

(a) that a person named in the application is or was his parent; or
(b) that he is the legitimate child of his parents.

(2) Any person may apply to the court for one (or for one or, in the alternative, the other) of the following declarations, that is to say –

(a) a declaration that he has become a legitimated person;
(b) a declaration that he has not become a legitimated person.

(3) A court shall have jurisdiction to entertain an application under this section if, and only if, the applicant –

(a) is domiciled in England and Wales on the date of the application, or
(b) has been habitually resident in England and Wales throughout the period of one year ending with that date.

(4) Where a declaration is made on an application under subsection (1) above, the prescribed officer of the court shall notify the Registrar General, in such a manner and within such period as may be prescribed, of the making of that declaration.

(5) In this section 'legitimated person' means a person legitimated or recognised as legitimated –

(a) under section 2 or 3 of the Legitimacy Act 1976;
(b) under section 1 or 8 of the Legitimacy Act 1926; or
(c) by a legitimation (whether or not by virtue of the subsequent marriage of his parents) recognised by the law of England and Wales and effected under the law of another country.

57 Declarations as to adoptions effected overseas [958]

(1) Any person whose status as an adopted child of any person depends on whether he has been adopted by that person by either –

(a) an overseas adoption as defined by section 72(2) of the Adoption Act 1976, or

(b) an adoption recognised by the law of England and Wales and effected under the law of any country outside the British Islands,

may apply to the court for one (or for one or, in the alternative, the other) of the declarations mentioned in subsection (2) below.

(2) The said declarations are –

(a) a declaration that the applicant is for the purposes of section 39 of the Adoption Act 1976 the adopted child of that person;
(b) a declaration that the applicant is not for the purposes of that section the adopted child of that person.

(3) A court shall have jurisdiction to entertain an application under subsection (1) above if, and only if, the applicant –

(a) is domiciled in England and Wales on the date of the application, or
(b) has been habitually resident in England and Wales throughout the period of one year ending with that date.

58 General provisions as to the making and effect of declarations [959]

(1) Where on an application for a declaration under this Part the truth of the proposition to be declared is proved to the satisfaction of the court, the court shall make that declaration unless to do so would manifestly be contrary to public policy.

(2) Any declaration made under this Part shall be binding on Her Majesty and all other persons.

(3) The court, on the dismissal of an application for a declaration under this Part, shall not have power to make any declaration for which an application has not been made.

(4) No declaration which may be applied for under this Part may be made otherwise than under this Part by any court.

(5) No declaration may be made by any court, whether under this Part or otherwise –

(a) that a marriage was at its inception void;
(b) that any person is or was illegitimate.

(6) Nothing in this section shall affect the powers of any court to grant a decree of nullity of marriage.

59 Provisions relating to the Attorney-General [960]

(1) On an application for a declaration under this Part the court may at any stage of the proceedings, of its own motion or on the application of any party to the proceedings, direct that all necessary papers in the matter be sent to the Attorney-General.

(2) The Attorney-General, whether or not he is sent papers in relation to an application for a declaration under this Part, may –

(a) intervene in the proceedings on that application in such manner as he thinks necessary or expedient, and
(b) argue before the court any question in relation to the application which the court considers it necessary to have fully argued.

(3) Where any costs are incurred by the Attorney-General in connection with any application for a declaration under this Part, the court may make such order as it considers just as to the payment of those costs by parties to the proceedings.

60 Supplementary provisions as to declarations [961]

(1) Any declaration made under this Part, and any application for such a declaration, shall be in the form prescribed by rules of court.

(2) Rules of court may make provision –

(a) as to the information required to be given by any applicant for a declaration under this Part;
(b) as to the persons who are to be parties to proceedings on an application under this Part;
(c) requiring notice of an application under this Part to be served on the Attorney-General and on persons who may be affected by any declaration applied for.

(3) No proceedings under this Part shall affect any final judgment or decree already pronounced or made by any court of competent jurisdiction.

(4) The court hearing an application under this Part may direct that the whole or any part of the proceedings shall be heard in camera, and an application for a direction under this subsection shall be heard in camera unless the court otherwise directs.

[As amended by the Family Law Reform Act 1987, ss22, 33(1), Schedule 2, para 96; Children Act 1989, s108(5), (7), Schedule 13, paras 62(1), (2)(a), (b), (3), 63, 64, 65, 66(1), (2), (3), 70, 71, Schedule 15; Age of Legal Capacity (Scotland) Act 1991, s10(1), Schedule 10, para 47; Family Law Act 1986 (Dependent Territories) Order 1991.]

RECOGNITION OF TRUSTS ACT 1987
(1987 c 14)

1 Applicable law and recognition of trusts [962]

(1) The provisions of the Convention set out in the Schedule to this Act shall have the force of law in the United Kingdom.

(2) Those provisions shall, so far as applicable, have effect not only in relation to the trusts described in Articles 2 and 3 of the Convention but also in relation to any other trusts of property arising under the law of any part of the United Kingdom or by virtue of a judicial decision whether in the United Kingdom or elsewhere.

(3) In accordance with Articles 15 and 16 such provisions of the law as are there mentioned shall, to the extent there specified, apply to the exclusion of the other provisions of the Convention.

(4) In Article 17 the reference to a State includes a reference to any country or territory (whether or not a party to the Convention and whether or not forming part of the United Kingdom) which has its own system of law.

(5) Article 22 shall not be construed as affecting the law to be applied in relation to anything done or omitted before the coming into force of this Act.

SCHEDULE

CONVENTION ON THE LAW APPLICABLE TO TRUSTS AND ON THEIR RECOGNITION

CHAPTER 1 – SCOPE

Article 1

This Convention specifies the law applicable to trusts and governs their recognition.

Article 2

For the purposes of this Convention, the term 'trust' refers to the legal relationship created – inter vivos or on death – by a person, the settlor, when assets have been placed under the control of a trustee for the benefit of a beneficiary or for a specified purpose.

A trust has the following characteristics –

   (a) the assets constitute a separate fund and are not a part of the trustee's own estate;
   (b) title to the trust assets stands in the name of the trustee or in the name of another person on behalf of the trustee;
   (c) the trustee has the power and the duty, in respect of which he is accountable, to manage, employ or dispose of the assets in accordance with the terms of the trust and the special duties imposed upon him by law.

The reservation by the settlor of certain rights and powers, and the fact that the trustee may himself have rights as a beneficiary, are not necessarily inconsistent with the existence of a trust.

Article 3

The Convention applies only to trusts created voluntarily and evidenced in writing.

Article 4

The Convention does not apply to preliminary issues relating to the validity of wills or of other acts by virtue of which assets are transferred to the trustee.

Article 5

The Convention does not apply to the extent that the law specified by Chapter II does not provide for trusts or the category of trusts involved.

CHAPTER II – APPLICABLE LAW

Article 6

A trust shall be governed by the law chosen by the settlor. The choice must be express or be implied in the terms of the instrument creating or the writing evidencing the trust, interpreted, if necessary, in the light of the circumstances of the case.

Where the law chosen under the previous paragraph does not provide for trusts or the category of trusts involved, the choice shall not be effective and the law specified in Article 7 shall apply.

Article 7

Where no applicable law has been chosen, a trust shall be governed by the law with which it is most closely connected.

In ascertaining the law with which a trust is most closely connected reference shall be made in particular to –

(a) the place of administration of the trust designated by the settlor;
(b) the situs of the assets of the trust;
(c) the place of residence or business of the trustee;
(d) the objects of the trust and the places where they are to be fulfilled.

Article 8

The law specified by Article 6 or 7 shall govern the validity of the trust, its construction, its effects and the administration of the trust.

In particular that law shall govern –

(a) the appointment, resignation and removal of trustees, the capacity to act as a trustee, and the devolution of the office of trustee;
(b) the rights and duties of trustees among themselves;
(c) the right of trustees to delegate in whole or in part the discharge of their duties or the exercise of their powers;
(d) the power of trustees to administer or to dispose of trust assets, to create security interests in the trust assets, or to acquire new assets;
(e) the powers of investment of trustees;
(f) restrictions upon the duration of the trust, and upon the power to accumulate the income of the trust;
(g) the relationships between the trustees and the beneficiaries including the personal liability of the trustees to the beneficiaries;
(h) the variation of termination of the trust;
(i) the distribution of the trust assets;
(j) the duty of trustees to account for their administration.

Article 9

In applying this chapter a severable aspect of the trust, particularly matters of administration, may be governed by a different law.

Article 10

The law applicable to the validity of the trust shall determine whether that law or the law governing a severable aspect of the trust may be replaced by another law.

CHAPTER III – RECOGNITION

Article 11

A trust created in accordance with the law specified by the preceding chapter shall be recognised as a trust.

Such recognition shall imply, as a minimum, that the trust property constitutes a separate fund, that the trustee may sue and be sued in his capacity as trustee, and that he may appear or act in this capacity before a notary or any person acting in an official capacity.

In so far as the law applicable to the trust requires or provides, such recognition shall imply in particular –

(a) that personal creditors of the trustee shall have no recourse against the trust assets;

(b) that the trust assets shall not form part of the trustee's estate upon his insolvency or bankruptcy;
(c) that the trust assets shall not form part of the matrimonial property of the trustee or his spouse nor part of the trustee's estate upon his death;
(d) that the trust assets may be recovered when the trustee, in breach of trust, has mingled trust assets with his own property or has alienated trust assets. However, the rights and obligations of any third party holder of the assets shall remain subject to the law determined by the choice of law rules of the forum.

Article 12

Where the trustee desires to register assets, movable or immovable, or documents of title to them, he shall be entitled, in so far as this is not prohibited by or inconsistent with the law of the State where registration is sought, to do so in his capacity as trustee or in such other way that the existence of the trust is disclosed.

Article 14

The Convention shall not prevent the application of rules of law more favourable to the recognition of trusts.

CHAPTER IV – GENERAL CLAUSES

Article 15

The Convention does not prevent the application of provisions of the law designated by the conflicts rules of the forum, in so far as those provisions cannot be derogated from by voluntary act, relating in particular to the following matters –

(a) the protection of minors and incapable parties;
(b) the personal and proprietary effects of marriage;
(c) succession rights, testate and intestate, especially the indefeasible shares of spouses and relatives;
(d) the transfer of title to property and security interests in property;
(e) the protection of creditors in matters of insolvency;
(f) the protection, in other respects, of third parties acting in good faith.

If recognition of a trust is prevented by application of the preceding paragraph, the court shall try to give effect to the objects of the trust by other means.

Article 16

The Convention does not prevent the application of those provisions of the law of the forum which must be applied even to international situations, irrespective of rules of conflict of laws.

Article 17

In the Convention the word 'law' means the rules of law in force in a State other than its rules of conflict of laws.

Article 18

The provisions of the Convention may be disregarded when their application would be manifestly incompatible with public policy.

Article 22

The Convention applies to trusts regardless of the date on which they were created.

DIPLOMATIC AND CONSULAR PREMISES ACT 1987
(1987 c 46)

PART I

DIPLOMATIC AND CONSULAR PREMISES

1 Acquisition and loss by land of diplomatic or consular status

(1) Subject to subsection (2) below, where a State desires that land shall be diplomatic or consular premises, it shall apply to the Secretary of State for his consent to the land being such premises.

(2) A State need not make such an application in relation to land if the Secretary of State accepted it as diplomatic or consular premises immediately before the coming into force of this section.

(3) In no case is land to be regarded as a State's diplomatic or consular premises for the purposes of any enactment or rule of law unless it has been so accepted or the Secretary of State has given that State consent under this section in relation to it; and if –

(a) a State ceases to use land for the purposes of its mission or exclusively for the purposes of a consular post; or
(b) the Secretary of State withdraws his acceptance or consent in relation to land,

it thereupon ceases to be diplomatic or consular premises for the purposes of all enactments and rules of law.

(4) The Secretary of State shall only give or withdraw consent or withdraw acceptance if he is satisfied that to do so is permissible under international law.

(5) In determining whether to do so he shall have regard to all material considerations, and in particular, but without prejudice to the generality of this subsection –

(a) to the safety of the public;
(b) to national security; and
(c) to town and country planning.

(6) If a State intends to cease using land as premises of its mission or as consular premises, it shall give the Secretary of State notice of that intention, specifying the date on which it intends to cease so using them.

(7) In any proceedings a certificate issued by or under the authority of the Secretary of State stating any fact relevant to the question whether or not land was at any time diplomatic or consular premises shall be conclusive of that fact.

2 Vesting of former diplomatic or consular premises

(1) Where –

(a) the Secretary of State formerly accepted land as diplomatic or consular premises but did not accept it as such premises immediately before the coming into force of this section; or
(b) land has ceased to be diplomatic or consular premises after the coming into force of this section but not less than 12 months before the exercise of the power conferred on the Secretary of State by this subsection,

the Secretary of State may by order provide that this section shall apply to that land.

(2) The Secretary of State shall only exercise the power conferred by subsection (1) above if he is satisfied that to do so is permissible under international law.

(3) In determining whether to exercise it he shall have regard to all material considerations, and in particular, but without prejudice to the generality of its subsection, to any of the considerations mentioned in section 1(5) above that appears to him to be relevant.

(4) An order under subsection (1) above shall be made by statutory instrument, and a statutory instrument containing any such order shall be subject to annulment in pursuance of a resolution of either House of Parliament.

(5) The Secretary of State may by deed poll vest in himself such estate or interest in land to which this section applies as appears to him to be appropriate.

(6) A deed poll under this section may also comprise any portion of a building in which the former diplomatic or consular premises are situated.

(7) In relation to land in Scotland this section shall have effect with the substitution of references to an order for references to a deed poll, and such an order shall take effect immediately it is made.

(8) Subject to subsection (9) below, in a case falling within paragraph (a) of subsection (1) above the Secretary of State may only exercise the power conferred by that subsection before the end of the period of two months beginning with the date on which this section comes into force.

(9) In such a case the power continues to be exercisable after the end of that period if the Secretary of State within that period –

(a) certifies that he reserves the right to exercise it; and
(b) unless he considers it inappropriate or impracticable to do so, serves a copy of the certificate on the owner of any estate or interest in the land.

(10) Where –

(a) circumstances have arisen in consequence of which the power conferred by subsection (1) above is exercisable; but
(b) the Secretary of State serves on the owner of the land in relation to which it has become exercisable notice that he does not intend to exercise the power in relation to that land,

it shall cease to be exercisable in relation to it in consequence of those circumstances.

(11) If –

(a) the Secretary of State has exercised the power conferred by subsection (1) above in relation to land; but
(b) serves on the owner notice that he does not intend to execute a deed poll under this section, or if the land is in Scotland to make an order under it, relating to the land,

the power to vest conferred by this section shall cease to be exercisable.

3 Duty of sale

(1) Where an estate or interest in land has vested in the Secretary of State under section 2 above, it shall be his duty to sell it as soon as it is reasonably practicable to do so, taking all reasonable steps to ensure that the price is the best that can reasonably be obtained.

(2) The Secretary of State shall apply the purchase money –

(a) firstly in payment of expenses properly incurred by him as incidental to the sale or any attempted sale;

(b) secondly in discharge of prior incumbrances to which the sale is not made subject or in the making of any payments to mortgagees required by Schedule 1 to this Act;
(c) thirdly in payment of expenses relating to the land reasonably incurred by him on repairs or security;
(d) fourthly in discharge of such liabilities to pay rates or sums in lieu of rates on the land or on any other land as the Secretary of State thinks fit;
(e) fifthly in discharge of such judgment debts arising out of matters relating to the land or to any other land as he thinks fit,

and, subject to subsection (3) below, shall pay any residue to the person divested of the estate or interest.

(3) Where a State was divested but there is no person with whom Her Majesty's Government of the United Kingdom has dealings as the Government of that State, the Secretary of State shall hold the residue until there is such a person and then pay it.

(4) A sum held by the Secretary of State under subsection (3) above shall be placed in a bank account bearing interest at such rate as the Treasury may approve.

5 Interpretation of Part I [967]

In this Part of this Act –

'consular post' and 'consular premises' have the meanings given by the definitions in paragraph 1(a) and (j) of Article 1 of the 1963 Convention as that Article has effect in the United Kingdom by virtue of section 1 of and Schedule 1 to the Consular Relations Act 1968;
'diplomatic premises' means premises of the mission of a State;
'mortgage' includes a charge of lien for securing money or money's worth, and references to mortgagees shall be construed accordingly;
'premises of the mission' has the meaning given by the definition in Article 1(i) of the 1961 Convention as that Article has effect in the United Kingdom by virtue of section 2 of and Schedule 1 to the Diplomatic Privileges Act 1964;
'the 1961 Convention' means the Vienna Convention on Diplomatic Relations signed in 1961; and
'the 1963 Convention' means the Vienna Convention on Consular Relations signed in 1963.

FAMILY LAW REFORM ACT 1987
(1987 c 42)

1 General principle [968]

(1) In this Act and enactments passed and instruments made after the coming into force of this section, references (however expressed) to any relationship between two persons shall, unless the contrary intention appears, be construed without regard to whether or not the father and mother of either of them, or the father and mother of any person through whom the relationship is deduced, have or had been married to each other at any time.

(2) In this Act and enactments passed after the coming into force of this section, unless the contrary intention appears –

(a) references to a person whose father and mother were married to each other at the time of his birth include; and

(b) references to a person whose father and mother were not married to each other at the time of his birth do not include,

references to any person to whom subsection (3) below applies, and cognate references shall be construed accordingly.

(3) This subsection applies to any person who –
    (a) is treated as legitimate by virtue of section 1 of the Legitimacy Act 1976;
    (b) is a legitimated person within the meaning of section 10 of that Act;
    (c) is an adopted child within the meaning of Part IV of the Adoption Act 1976; or
    (d) is otherwise treated in law as legitimate.

(4) For the purpose of construing references falling within subsection (2) above, the time of a person's birth shall be taken to include any time during the period beginning with –
    (a) the insemination resulting in his birth; or
    (b) where there was no such insemination, his conception,

and (in either case) ending with his birth.

18 Succession on intestacy

(1) In Part IV of the Administration of Estates Act 1925 (which deals with the distribution of the estate of an intestate), references (however expressed) to any relationship between two persons shall be construed in accordance with section 1 above.

(2) For the purposes of subsectiopn (1) above and that Part of that Act, a person whose father and mother were not married to each other at the time of his birth shall be presumed not to have been survived by his father, or by any person related to him only through his father, unless the contrary is shown. ...

(4) This section does not affect any rights under the intestacy of a person dying before the coming into force of this section.

19 Dispositions of property

(1) In the following dispositions, namely –
    (a) dispositions inter vivos made on or after the date on which this section comes into force; and
    (b) dispositions by will or codicil where the will or codicil is made on or after that date,

references (whether expressed or implied) to any relationship between two persons shall be construed in accordance with section 1 above. ...

(5) This section is without prejudice to section 42 of the Adoption Act 1976 (construction of dispositions in cases of adoption).

(6) In this section 'disposition' means a disposition, including an oral disposition, of real or personal property whether inter vivos or by will or codicil.

(7) Notwithstanding any rule of law, a disposition made by will or codicil executed before the date on which this section comes into force shall not be treated for the purposes of this section as made on or after that date by reason only that the will or codicil is confirmed by a codicil executed on or after that date.

27 Artificial insemination

(1) Where after the coming into force of this section a child is born in England and Wales as the result of the artificial insemination of a woman who –

(a) was at the time of the insemination a party to a marriage (being a marriage which had not at that time been dissolved or annulled); and
(b) was artificially inseminated with the semen of some person other than the other party to that marriage,

then, unless it is proved to the satisfaction of any court by which the matter has to be determined that the other party to that marriage did not consent to the insemination, the child shall be treated in law as the child of the parties to that marriage and shall not be treated as the child of any person other than the parties to that marriage.

(2) Any reference in this section to a marriage includes a reference to a void marriage if at the time of the insemination resulting in the birth of the child both or either of the parties reasonably believed that the marriage was valid; and for the purposes of this section it shall be presumed, unless the contrary is shown, that one of the parties so believed at that time that the marriage was valid.

(3) Nothing in this section shall affect the succession to any dignity or title of honour or render any person capable of succeeding to or transmitting a right to succeed to any such dignity or title.

CHILDREN ACT 1989
(1989 c 41)

PART I

INTRODUCTORY

1 Welfare of the child

(1) When a court determines any question with respect to –

(a) the upbringing of a child; or
(b) the administration of a child's property or the application of any income arising from it,

the child's welfare shall be the court's paramount consideration.

(2) In any proceedings in which any question with respect to the upbringing of a child arises, the court shall have regard to the general principle that any delay in determining the question is likely to prejudice the welfare of the child.

(3) In the circumstances mentioned in subsection (4), a court shall have regard in particular to –

(a) the ascertainable wishes and feelings of the child concerned (considered in the light of his age and understanding);
(b) his physical, emotional and educational needs;
(c) the likely effect on him of any change in his circumstances;
(d) his age, sex, background and any characteristics of his which the court considers relevant;
(e) any harm which he has suffered or is at risk of suffering;
(f) how capable each of his parents, and any other person in relation to whom the court considers the question to be relevant, is of meeting his needs;
(g) the range of powers available to the court under this Act in the proceedings in question.

(4) The circumstances are that –
   (a) the court is considering whether to make, vary or discharge a section 8 order, and the making, variation or discharge of the order is opposed by any party to the proceedings; or
   (b) the court is considering whether to make, vary or discharge an order under Part IV.

(5) Where a court is considering whether or not to make one or more orders under this Act with respect to a child, it shall not make the order or any of the orders unless it considers that doing so would be better for the child than making no order at all.

2 Parental responsibility for children [973]

(1) Where a child's father and mother were married to each other at the time of his birth, they shall each have parental responsibility for the child.

(2) Where a child's father and mother were not married to each other at the time of his birth –
   (a) the mother shall have parental responsibility for the child;
   (b) the father shall not have parental responsibility for the child, unless he acquires it in accordance with the provisions of this Act.

(3) References in this Act to a child whose father and mother were, or (as the case may be) were not, married to each other at the time of his birth must be read with section 1 of the Family Law Reform Act 1987 (which extends their meaning). ...

3 Meaning of 'parental responsibility' [974]

(1) In this Act 'parental responsibility' means all the rights, duties, powers, responsibilities and authority which by law a parent of a child has in relation to the child and his property.

(2) It also includes the rights, powers and duties which a guardian of the child's estate (appointed, before the commencement of section 5, to act generally) would have had in relation to the child and his property.

(3) The rights referred to in subsection (2) include, in particular, the right of the guardian to receive or recover in his own name, for the benefit of the child, property of whatever description and wherever situated which the child is entitled to receive or recover.

(4) The fact that a person has, or does not have, parental responsibility for a child shall not affect –
   (a) any obligation which he may have in relation to the child (such as a statutory duty to maintain the child); or
   (b) any rights which, in the event of the child's death, he (or any other person) may have in relation to the child's property.

(5) A person who –
   (a) does not have parental responsibility for a particular child; but
   (b) has care of the child,

may (subject to the provisions of this Act) do what is reasonable in all the circumstances of the case for the purpose of safeguarding or promoting the child's welfare.

4 Acquisition of parental responsibility by father [975]

(1) Where a child's father and mother were not married to each other at the time of his birth –

(a) the court may, on the application of the father, order that he shall have parental responsibility for the child; or
(b) the father and mother may by agreement ('a parental responsibility agreement') provide for the father to have parental responsibility for the child.

(2) No parental responsibility agreement shall have effect for the purposes of this Act unless –

(a) it is made in the form prescribed by regulations made by the Lord Chancellor; and
(b) where regulations are made by the Lord Chancellor prescribing the manner in which such agreements must be recorded, it is recorded in the prescribed manner.

(3) Subject to section 12(4), an order under subsection (1)(a), or a parental responsibility agreement, may only be brought to an end by an order of the court made on the application –

(a) of any person who has parental responsibility for the child; or
(b) with leave of the court, of the child himself.

(4) The court may only grant leave under subsection (3)(b) if it is satisfied that the child has sufficient understanding to make the proposed application.

PART II

ORDERS WITH RESPECT TO CHILDREN IN FAMILY PROCEEDINGS

8 Residence, contact and other orders with respect to children [976]

(1) In this Act –

'a contact order' means an order requiring the person with whom a child lives, or is to live, to allow the child to visit or stay with the person named in the order, or for that person and the child otherwise to have contact with each other;

'a prohibited steps order' means an order that no step which could be taken by a parent in meeting his parental responsibility for a child, and which is of a kind specified in the order, shall be taken by any person without the consent of the court;

'a residence order' means an order settling the arrangements to be made as to the person with whom a child is to live; and

'a specific issue order' means an order giving directions for the purpose of determining a specific question which has arisen, or which may arise, in connection with any aspect of parental responsibility for a child.

(2) In this Act 'a section 8 order' means any of the orders mentioned in subsection (1) and any order varying or discharging such an order. ...

9 Restrictions on making s8 orders [977]

(1) No court shall make any section 8 order, other than a residence order, with respect to a child who is in the care of a local authority.

(2) No application may be made by a local authority for a residence order or contact order and no court shall make such an order in favour of a local authority.

(3) A person who is, or was at any time within the last six months, a local authority foster parent of a child may not apply for leave to apply for a section 8 order with respect to the child unless –
- (a) he had the consent of the authority;
- (b) he is a relative of the child; or
- (c) the child has lived with him for at least three years preceding the application.

(4) The period of three years mentioned in subsection (3)(c) need not be continuous but must have begun not more than five years before the making of the application.

(5) No court shall exercise its powers to make a specific issue order or prohibited steps order –
- (a) with a view to achieving a result which could be achieved by making a residence or contact order; or
- (b) in any way which is denied to the High Court (by section 100(2)) in the exercise of its inherent jurisdiction with respect to children.

(6) No court shall make any section 8 order which is to have effect for a period which will end after the child has reached the age of sixteen unless it is satisfied that the circumstances of the case are exceptional.

(7) No court shall make any section 8 order, other than one varying or discharging such an order, with respect to a child who has reached the age of sixteen unless it is satisfied that the circumstances of the case are exceptional.

10 Power of court to make s8 orders [978]

(1) In any family proceedings in which a question arises with respect to the welfare of any child, the court may make a section 8 order with respect to the child if –
- (a) an application for the order has been made by a person who –
  - (i) is entitled to apply for a section 8 order with respect to the child; or
  - (ii) has obtained the leave of the court to make the application; or
- (b) the court considers that the order should be made even though no such application has been made.

(2) The court may also make a section 8 order with respect to any child on the application of a person who –
- (a) is entitled to apply for a section 8 order with respect to the child; or
- (b) has obtained the leave of the court to make the application.

(3) This section is subject to the restrictions imposed by section 9.

(4) The following persons are entitled to apply to the court for any section 8 order with respect to a child –
- (a) any parent or guardian of the child;
- (b) any person in whose favour a residence order is in force with respect to the child.

(5) The following persons are entitled to apply for a residence or contact order with respect to a child –
- (a) any party to a marriage (whether or not subsisting) in relation to whom the child is a child of the family;

(b) any person with whom the child has lived for a period of at least three years;
(c) any person who –
  (i) in any case where a residence order is in force with respect to the child, has the consent of each of the persons in whose favour the order was made;
  (ii) in any case where the child is in the care of a local authority, has the consent of that authority; or
  (iii) in any other case, has the consent of each of those (if any) who have parental responsibility for the child.

(6) A person who would not otherwise be entitled (under the previous provisions of this section) to apply for the variation or discharge of a section 8 order shall be entitled to do so if –
(a) the order was made on his application; or
(b) in the case of a contact order, he is named in the order.

(7) Any person who falls within a category of person prescribed by rules of court is entitled to apply for any such section 8 order as may be prescribed in relation to that category of person.

(8) Where the person applying for leave to make an application for a section 8 order is the child concerned, the court may only grant leave if it is satisfied that he has sufficient understanding to make the proposed application for the section 8 order.

(9) Where the person applying for leave to make an application for a section 8 order is not the child concerned, the court shall, in deciding whether or not to grant leave, have particular regard to –
(a) the nature of the proposed application for the section 8 order;
(b) the applicant's connection with the child;
(c) any risk there might be of that proposed application disrupting the child's life to such an extent that he would be harmed by it; and
(d) where the child is being looked after by a local authority –
  (i) the authority's plans for the child's future; and
  (ii) the wishes and feelings of the child's parents.

(10) The period of three years mentioned in subsection (5)(b) need not be continuous but must not have begun more than five years before, or ended more than three months before, the making of the application.

CONTRACTS (APPLICABLE LAW) ACT 1990
(1990 c 36)

1 Meaning of 'the Conventions' [979]

In this Act –
(a) 'the Rome Convention' means the Convention on the law applicable to contractual obligations opened for signature in Rome on 19 June 1980 and signed by the United Kingdom on 7 December 1981;
(b) 'the Luxembourg Convention' means the Convention on the accession of the Hellenic Republic to the Rome Convention signed by the United Kingdom in Luxembourg on 10 April 1984; and
(c) 'the Brussels Protocol' means the first Protocol on the interpretation of the Rome Convention by the European Court signed by the United Kingdom in Brussels on 19 December 1988;

(d) 'the Funchal Convention' means the Convention on the accession of the Kingdom of Spain and the Portuguese Republic to the Rome Convention and the Brussels Protocol, with adjustments made to the Rome Convention by the Luxembourg Convention, signed by the United Kingdom in Funchal on 18 May 1992;

and these Conventions and this Protocol are together referred to as 'the Conventions'.

2 Conventions to have force of law

(1) Subject to sub-sections (2) and (3) below, the Conventions shall have the force of law in the United Kingdom.

(1A) The internal law for the purposes of Article 1(3) of the Rome Convention is whichever of the following are applicable, namely –

(a) the provisions of Schedule 3A to the Insurance Companies Act 1982 (law applicable to certain contracts of insurance with insurance companies), and
(b) the provisions of Schedule 20 to the Friendly Societies Act 1992 as applied by sub-sections (1)(a) and (2)(a) of section 101 of that Act (law applicable to certain contracts of insurance with friendly societies).

(2) Articles 7(1) and 10(1)(e) of the Rome Convention shall not have the force of law in the United Kingdom.

(3) Notwithstanding Article 19(2) of the Rome Convention, the Conventions shall apply in the case of conflicts between the laws of different parts of the United Kingdom.

(4) For ease of reference there are set out in Schedules 1, 2 3 and 3A to this Act respectively the English texts of –

(a) the Rome Convention;
(b) the Luxembourg Convention;
(c) the Brussels Protocol; and
(d) the Funchal Convention.

3 Interpretation of Conventions

(1) Any question as to the meaning or effect of any provision of the Conventions shall, if not referred to the European Court in accordance with the Brussels Protocol, be determined in accordance with the principles laid down by, and any relevant decision of, the European Court.

(2) Judicial notice shall be taken of any decision of, or expression of opinion by, the European Court on any such question.

(3) Without prejudice to any practice of the courts as to the matters which may be considered apart from this subsection –

(a) the report on the Rome Convention by Professor Mario Giuliano and Professor Paul Lagarde which is reproduced in the Official Journal of the Communities of 31 October 1980 may be considered in ascertaining the meaning or effect of any provision of that Convention; and
(b) any report on the Brussels Protocol which is reproduced in the Official Journal of the Communities may be considered in ascertaining the meaning or effect of any provision of that Protocol.

SCHEDULE 1

THE ROME CONVENTION ...

TITLE 1

SCOPE OF THE CONVENTION

Article 1

1. The rules of this Convention shall apply to contractual obligations in any situation involving a choice between the laws of different countries.

2. They shall not apply to:

(a) questions involving the status or legal capacity of natural persons, without prejudice to Article 11;

(b) contractual obligations relating to:

– wills and succession,
– rights in property arising out of a matrimonial relationship,
– rights and duties arising out of a family relationship, parentage, marriage or affinity, including maintenance obligations in respect of children who are not legitimate;

(c) obligations arising under bills of exchange, cheques and promissory notes and other negotiable instruments to the extent that the obligations under such other negotiable instruments arise out of their negotiable character;

(d) arbitration agreements and agreements on the choice of court;

(e) questions governed by the law of companies and other bodies corporate or unincorporate such as the creation, by registration or otherwise, legal capacity, internal organisation or winding up of companies and other bodies corporate or unincorporate and the personal liability of officers and members as such for the obligations of the company or body;

(f) the question whether an agent is able to bind a principal, or an organ to bind a company or body corporate or unincorporate, to a third party;

(g) the constitution of trusts and the relationship between settlors, trustees and beneficiaries;

(h) evidence and procedure, without prejudice to Article 14.

3. The rules of this Convention do not apply to contracts of insurance which cover risks situated in the territories of the Member States of the European Economic Community. In order to determine whether a risk is situated in these territories the court shall apply its internal law.

4. The preceding paragraph does not apply to contracts of re-insurance.

Article 2

Any law specified by this Convention shall be applied whether or not it is the law of a Contracting State.

TITLE II

UNIFORM RULES

Article 3

1. A contract shall be governed by the law chosen by the parties. The choice must be express or demonstrated with reasonable certainty by the terms of the contract or the circumstances of the case. By their choice the parties can select the law applicable to the whole or a part only of the contract.

2. The parties may at any time agree to subject the contract to a law other than that which previously governed it, whether as a result of an earlier choice under this Article or of other provisions of this Convention. Any variation by the parties of the law to be applied made after the conclusion of the contract shall not prejudice its formal validity under Article 9 or adversely affect the rights of third parties.

3. The fact that the parties have chosen a foreign law, whether or not accompanied by the choice of a foreign tribunal, shall not, where all the other elements relevant to the situation at the time of the choice are connected with one country only, prejudice the application of rules of the law of that country which cannot be derogated from by contract, hereinafter called 'mandatory rules'.

4. The existence and validity of the consent of the parties as to the choice of the applicable law shall be determined in accordance with the provisions of Articles 8, 9 and 11.

Article 4

1. To the extent that the law applicable to the contract has not been chosen in accordance with Article 3, the contract shall be governed by the law of the country with which it is most closely connected. Nevertheless, a severable part of the contract which has a closer connection with another country may by way of exception be governed by the law of that other country.

2. Subject to the provisions of paragraph 5 of this Article, it shall be presumed that the contract is most closely connected with the country where the party who is to effect the performance which is characteristic of the contract has, at the time of conclusion of the contract, his habitual residence, or, in the case of a body corporate or unincorporate, its central administration. However, if the contract is entered into in the course of that party's trade or profession, that country shall be the country in which the principal place of business is situated or, where under the terms of the contract the performance is to be effected through a place of business other than the principal place of business, the country in which that other place of business is situated.

3. Notwithstanding the provisions of paragraph 2 of this Article, to the extent that the subject matter of the contract is a right in immovable property or a right to use immovable property it shall be presumed that the contract is most closely connected with the country where the immovable property is situated.

4. A contract for the carriage of goods shall not be subject to the presumption in paragraph 2. In such a contract if the country in which, at the time the contract is concluded, the carrier has his principal place of business is also the country in which the place of loading or the place of discharge or the principal place of business of the consignor is situated, it shall be presumed that the contract is most closely connected with that country. In applying this paragraph single voyage charter-parties and other contracts the main purpose of which is the carriage of goods shall be treated as contracts for the carriage of goods.

5. Paragraph 2 shall not apply if the characteristic performance cannot be determined, and the presumptions in paragraphs 2, 3 and 4 shall be disregarded if it appears from the circumstances as a whole that the contract is more closely connected with another country.

Article 5

1. This Article applies to a contract the object of which is the supply of goods or services to a person ('the consumer') for a purpose which can be regarded as being outside his trade or profession, or a contract for the provision of credit for that object.

2. Notwithstanding the provisions of Article 3, a choice of law made by the parties shall have the result of depriving the consumer of the protection afforded to him by the mandatory rules of the law of the country in which he has habitual residence:

– if in that country the conclusion of the contract was preceded by a specific invitation addressed to him or by advertising, and he had taken in that country all the steps necessary on his part for the conclusion of the contract, or

– if the other party or his agent received the consumer's order in that country, or

– if the contract is for the sale of goods and the consumer travelled from that country to another country and there gave his order, provided that the consumer's journey was arranged by the seller for the purpose of inducing the consumer to buy.

3. Notwithstanding the provisions of Article 4, a contract to which this Article applies shall, in absence of choice in accordance with Article 3, be governed by the law of the country in which the consumer has his habital residence if it is entered into in the circumstances described in paragraph 2 of this Article.

4. This Article shall not apply to:

(a) a contract of carriage;
(b) a contract for the supply of services where the services are to be supplied to the consumer exclusively in a country other than that in which he has his habital residence.

5. Notwithstanding the provisions of paragraph 4, this Article shall apply to a contract which, for an inclusive price, provides for a combination of travel and accommodation.

Article 6

1. Notwithstanding the provisions of Article 3, in a contract of employment a choice of law made by the parties shall not have the result of depriving the employee of the protection afforded to him by the mandatory rules of the law which would be applicable under paragraph 2 in the absence of choice.

2. Notwithstanding the provisions of Article 4, a contract of employment shall, in the absence of choice in accordance with Articel 3, be governed:

(a) by the law of the country in which the employee habitually carries out his work in performance of the contract, even if he is temporarily employed in another country; or

(b) if the employee does not habitually carry out his work in any one country, by the law of the country in which the place of business through which he was engaged is situated;

unless it appears from the circumstances as a whole that the contract is more closely connected with another country, in which case the contract shall be governed by the law of that country.

Article 7

1. When applying under this Convention the law of a country, effect may be given to the mandatory rules of the law of another country with which the situation has a close connection, if and in so far as, under the law of the latter country, those rules must be applied whatever the law applicable to the contract. In considering whether to give effect to these mandatory rules, regard shall be had to their nature and purpose and to the consequences of their application or non-application.

2. Nothing in this Convention shall restrict the application of the rules of the law

of the forum in a situation where they are mandatory irrespective of the law otherwise applicable to the contract.

Article 8

1. The existence and validity of a contract, or of any term of a contract, shall be determined by the law which would govern it under this Convention if the contract or term were valid.

2. Nevertheless a party may rely upon the law of the country in which he has his habitual residence to establish that he did not consent if it appears from the circumstances that it would not be reasonable to determine the effect of his conduct in accordance with the law specified in the preceding paragraph.

Article 9

1. A contract concluded between persons who are in the same country is formally valid if it satisfies the formal requirements of the law which governs it under this Convention or of the law of the country where it is concluded.

2. A contract concluded between persons who are in different countries is formally valid if it satisfies the formal requirements of the law which governs it under this Convention or of the law of one of those countries.

3. Where a contract is concluded by an agent, the country in which the agent acts is the relevant country for the purposes of paragraphs 1 and 2.

4. An act intended to have legal effect relating to an existing or contemplated contract is formally valid if it satisfies the formal requirements of the law which under this Convention governs or would govern the contract or of the law of the country where the act was done.

5. The provisions of the preceding paragraphs shall not apply to a contract to which Article 5 applies, concluded in the circumstances described in paragraph 2 of Article 5. The formal validity of such a contract is governed by the law of the country in which the consumer has his habital residence.

6. Notwithstanding paragraphs 1 to 4 of this Article, a contract the subject matter of which is a right in immovable property or a right to use immovable property shall be subject to the mandatory requirements of form of the law of the country where the property is situated if by that law those requirements are imposed irrespective of the country where the contract is concluded and irrespective of the law governing the contract.

Article 10

1. The law applicable to a contract by virtue of Articles 3 to 6 and 12 of this Convention shall govern in particular:

    (a) interpretation;
    (b) performance;
    (c) within the limits of the powers conferred on the court by its procedural law, the consequences of breach, including the assessment of damages in so far as it is governed by rules of law;
    (d) the various ways of extinguishing obligations and prescription and limitation of actions;
    (e) the consequences of nullity of the contract.

2. In relation to the manner of performance and the steps to be taken in the event of defective performance regard shall be had to the law of the country in which performance takes place.

Article 11

In a contract concluded between persons who are in the same country, a natural person who would have capacity under the law of that country may invoke his incapacity resulting from another law only if the other party to the contract was aware of this incapacity at the time of the conclusion of the contract or was not aware thereof as a result of negligence.

Article 12

1. The mutal obligations of assignor and assignee under a voluntary assignment of a right against another person ('the debtor') shall be governed by the law which under this Convention applies to the contract between the assignor and assignee.

2. The law governing the right to which the assignment relates shall determine its assignability, the relationship between the assignee and the debtor, the conditions under which the assignment can be invoked against the debtor and any question whether the debtor's obligations have been discharged.

Article 13

1. Where a person ('the creditor') has a contractual claim upon another ('the debtor'), and a third person has a duty to satisfy the creditor, or has in fact satisfied the creditor in discharge of that duty, the law which governs the third person's duty to satisfy the creditor shall determine whether the third person is entitled to exercise against the debtor the rights which the creditor had against the debtor under the law governing their relationship and, if so, whether he may do so in full or only to a limited extent.

2. The same rule applies where several persons are subject to the same contractual claim and one of them has satisfied the creditor.

Article 14

1. The law governing the contract under this Convention applies to the extent that it contains, in the law of contract, rules which raise presumptions of law or determine the burden of proof.

2. A contract or an act intended to have legal effect may be proved by any mode of proof recognised by the law of the forum or by any of the laws referred to in Article 9 under which that contract or act is formally valid, provided that such mode of proof can be administered by the forum.

Article 15

The application of the law of any country specified by this Convention means the application of the rules of law in force in that country other than its rules of private international law.

Article 16

The application of a rule of the law of any country specified by this Convention may be refused only if such application is manifestly incompatible with the public policy ('ordre public') of the forum.

Article 17

This Convention shall apply in a Contracting State to contracts made after the date on which this Convention has entered into force with respect to that State.

Article 18

In the interpretation and application of the preceding uniform rules, regard shall be had to their international character and to the desirability of achieving uniformity in their interpretation and application.

Article 19

1. Where a State comprises several territorial units each of which has its own rules of law in respect of contractual obligations, each territorial unit shall be considered as a country for the purposes of identifying the law applicable under this Convention.

2. A State within which different territorial units have their own rules of law in respect of contractual obligations shall not be bound to apply this Convention to conflicts solely between the laws of such units.

Article 20

This Convention shall not affect the application of provisions which, in relation to particular matters, lay down choice of law rules relating to contractual obligations and which are or will be contained in acts of the institutions of the European Communities or in national laws harmonised in implementation of such acts.

Article 21

This Convention shall not prejudice the application of international conventions to which a Contracting State is, or becomes, a party.

Article 22

1. Any Contracting State may, at the time of signature, ratification, acceptance or approval, reserve the right not to apply:

(a) the provisions of Article 7(1);
(b) the provisions of Article 10(1)(e).

3. Any Contracting State may at any time withdraw a reservation which it has made; the reservation shall cease to have effect on the first day of the third calendar month after notification of the withdrawal.

TITLE III

FINAL PROVISIONS

Article 23

1. If, after the date on which this Convention has entered into force for a Contracting State, that State wishes to adopt any new choice of law rule in regard to any particular category of contract within the scope of this Convention, it shall communicate its intention to the other signatory States through the Secretary-General of the Council of the European Communities.

2. Any signatory State may, within six months from the date of the communication made to the Secretary-General, request him to arrange consultations between signatory States in order to reach agreement.

3. If no signatory State has requested consultations within this period or if within two years following the communication made to the Secretary-General no agreement is reached in the course of consultations, the Contracting State concerned may amend its law in the manner indicated. The measures taken by that State shall be brought to the knowledge of the other signatory States through the Secretary-General of the Council of the European Communities. ...

SCHEDULE 3

THE BRUSSELS PROTOCOL ...

Article 1

The Court of Justice of the European Communities shall have jurisdiction to give rulings on the interpretation of –

(a) the Convention on the law applicable to contractual obligations, opened for signature in Rome on 19 June 1980, hereinafter referred to as 'the Rome Convention';
(b) the Convention on accession to the Rome Convention by the States which have become Members of the European Communities since the date on which it was opened for signature;
(c) this Protocol.

Article 2

Any of the courts referred to below may request the Court of Justice to give a preliminary ruling on a question raised in a case pending before it and concerning interpretation of the provisions contained in the instruments referred to in Article 1 if that court considers that a decision on the question is necessary to enable it to give judgment:

(a) ... in the United Kingdom:
the House of Lords and other courts from which no further appeal is possible;
(b) the courts of the Contracting States when acting as appeal courts. ...

[As amended by the Friendly Societies (Amendment) Regulations 1993, reg 6(5); Contracts (Applicable Law) Act 1990 (Amendment) Order 1994, arts 3–7.]

FOREIGN CORPORATIONS ACT 1991
(1991 c 44)

1 Recognition of corporate status of certain foreign corporations

(1) If at any time –

(a) any question arises whether a body which purports to have or, as the case may be, which appears to have lost corporate status under the laws of a territory which is not at that time a recognised State should or should not be regarded as having legal personality as a body corporate under the law of any part of the United Kingdom, and
(b) it appears that the laws of that territory are at that time applied by a settled court system in that territory,

that question and any other material question relating to the body shall be determined (and account shall be taken of those laws) as if that territory were a recognised State.

(2) For the purposes of subsection (1) above –

(a) 'a recognised State' is a territory which is recognised by Her Majesty's Government in the United Kingdom as a State;
(b) the laws of a territory which is so recognised shall be taken to include the laws of any part of the territory which are acknowledged by the federal or other central government of the territory as a whole; and
(c) a material question is a question (whether as to capacity, constitution or

otherwise) which, in the case of a body corporate, falls to be determined by reference to the laws of the territory under which the body is incorporated.

(3) Any registration or other thing done at a time before the coming into force of this section shall be regarded as valid if it would have been valid at that time, had subsections (1) and (2) above then been in force.

SOCIAL SECURITY CONTRIBUTIONS AND BENEFITS ACT 1992
(1992 c 4)

121 Treatment of certain marriages [985]

(1) Regulations may provide –
   (a) for a voidable marriage which has been annulled, whether before or after the date when the regulations come into force, to be treated for the purposes of the provisions to which this subsection applies as if it had been a valid marriage which was terminated by divorce at the date of annulment;
   (b) as to the circumstances in which, for the purposes of the enactments to which this section applies, a marriage during the subsistence of which a party to it is at any time married to more than one person is to be treated as having, or as not having, the same consequences as any other marriage.

(2) Subsection (1) above applies –
   (a) to any enactment contained in Parts I to V or this Part of this Act; and
   (b) to regulations under any such enactment.

147 Interpretation of Part IX and supplementary provisions ... [986]

(5) Regulations may make provisions as to the circumstances in which a marriage during the subsistence of which a party to it is at any time married to more than one person is to be treated for the purposes of this Part of this Act as having, or not having, the same consequences as any other marriage.

[As amended by the Private International Law (Miscellaneous Provisions) Act 1995, s8(2), Schedule, para 4.]

MAINTENANCE ORDERS (RECIPROCAL ENFORCEMENT) ACT 1992
(1992 c 56)

1 Amendment of the 1920 and 1972 Acts [987]

(1) The Maintenance Orders (Facilities for Enforcement) Act 1920 shall have effect (until its repeal by the Maintenance Orders (Reciprocal Enforcement) Act 1972 comes into force) with the amendments set out in Part I of Schedule 1 to this Act.

(2) The Maintenance Orders (Reciprocal Enforcement) Act 1992 shall have effect with the amendments set out in Part II of Schedule 1 to this Act.

NB These amendments have been included in the texts of the 1920 and 1972 Acts, as appropriate.

EUROPEAN COMMUNITIES (AMENDMENT) ACT 1993
(1993 c 32)

1 Treaty on European Union

(2) For the purposes of section 6 of the European Parliamentary Elections Act 1978 (approval of treaties increasing the Parliament's powers) the Treaty on European Union signed at Maastricht on 7 February 1992 is approved.

2 Economic and monetary union

No notification shall be given to the Council of the European Communities that the United Kingdom intends to move to the third stage of economic and monetary union (in accordance with the Protocol on certain provisions relating to the United Kingdom adopted at Maastricht on 7 February 1992) unless a draft of the notification has first been approved by Act of Parliament and unless Her Majesty's Government has reported to Parliament on its proposals for the coordination of economic policies, its role in the European Council of Finance Ministers (ECOFIN) in pursuit of the objectives of Article 2 of the Treaty establishing the European Community as provided for in Articles 103 and 102a, and the work of the European Monetary Institute in preparation for economic and monetary union.

3 Annual report by Bank of England

In implementing Article 108 of the Treaty establishing the European Community, and ensuring compatibility of the statutes of the national central bank, Her Majesty's Government shall, by order, make provision for the Governor of the Bank of England to make an annual report to Parliament, which shall be subject to approval by a Resolution of each House of Parliament.

4 Information for Commission

In implementing the provisions of Article 103(3) of the Treaty establishing the European Community, information shall be submitted to the Commission from the United Kingdom indicating performance on economic growth, industrial investment, employment and balance of trade, together with comparisons with those items of performance from other member States.

5 Convergence criteria: assessment of deficits

Before submitting the information required in implementing Article 103(3) of the Treaty establishing the European Community, Her Majesty's Government shall report to Parliament for its approval an assessment of the medium term economic and budgetary position in relation to public investment expenditure and to the social, economic and environmental goals set out in Article 2, which report shall form the basis of any submission to the Council and Commission in pursuit of their responsibilities under Articles 103 and 104c.

6 Committee of the Regions

A person may be proposed as a member or alternative member for the United Kingdom of the Committee of the Regions constituted under Article 198a of the Treaty establishing the European Community only if, at the time of the proposal, he is an elected member of a local authority.

7 Commencement (Protocol on Social Policy) [994]

This Act shall come into force only when each House of Parliament has come to Resolution on a motion tabled by a Minister of the Crown considering the question of adopting the Protocol on Social Policy.

PRIVATE INTERNATIONAL LAW (MISCELLANEOUS PROVISIONS) ACT 1995
(1995 c 42)

PART I

INTEREST ON JUDGMENT DEBTS AND ARBITRAL AWARDS

1 Interest on judgment debts generally [995]

[Inserts s44A of the Administration of Justice Act 1970]

2 Interest on county court judgment debts [996]

[Inserts s74(5) of the County Courts Act 1984]

3 Interest on arbitral awards [997]

[Substitutes s20 of the Arbitration Act 1950]

PART II

VALIDITY OF MARRIAGES UNDER A LAW WHICH PERMITS POLYGAMY

5 Validity in English law of potentially [998]
polygamous marriages

(1) A marriage entered into outside England and Wales between parties neither of whom is already married is not void under the law of England and Wales on the ground that it is entered into under a law which permits polygamy and that either party is domiciled in England and Wales.

(2) This section does not affect the determination of the validity of a marriage by reference to the law of another country to the extent that it falls to be so determined in accordance with the rules of private international law.

6 Application of s5 to prior marriages [999]

(1) Section 5 above shall be deemed to apply, and always to have applied, to any marriage entered into before commencement which is not excluded by subsection (2) or (3) below.

(2) That section does not apply to a marriage a party to which has (before commencement) entered into a later marriage which either –

    (a) is valid apart from this section but would be void if section 5 above applied to the earlier marriage; or
    (b) is valid by virtue of this section.

(3) That section does not apply to a marriage which has been annulled before

commencement, whether by a decree granted in England and Wales or by an annulment obtained elsewhere and recognised in England and Wales at commencement.

(4) An annulment of a marriage resulting from legal proceedings begun before commencement shall be treated for the purposes of subsection (3) above as having taken effect before that time.

(5) For the purposes of subsections (3) and (4) above a marriage which has been declared to be invalid by a court of competent jurisdiction in any proceedings concerning either the validity of the marriage or any right dependent on its validity shall be treated as having been annulled.

(6) Nothing in section 5 above, in its application to marriages entered into before commencement –

(a) gives or affects any entitlement to an interest –

(i) under the will or codicil of, or on the intestacy of, a person who died before commencement; or
(ii) under a settlement or other disposition of property made before that time (otherwise than by will or codicil);

(b) gives or affects any entitlement to a benefit, allowance, pension or other payment –

(i) payable before, or in respect of a period before, commencement; or
(ii) payable in respect of the death of a person before that time;

(c) affects tax in respect of a period or event before commencement; or
(d) affects the succession to any dignity or title of honour.

(7) In this section 'commencement' means the commencement of this Part.

8 Part II: supplemental [1000]

(1) Nothing in this Part affects any law or custom relating to the marriage of members of the Royal Family. ...

PART III

CHOICE OF LAW IN TORT AND DELICT

9 Purpose of Part III [1001]

(1) The rules in this Part apply for choosing the law (in this Part referred to as 'the applicable law') to be used for determining issues relating to tort or (for the purposes of the law of Scotland) delict.

(2) The characterisation for the purposes of private international law of issues arising in a claim as issues relating to tort or delict is a matter for the courts of the forum.

(3) The rules in this Part do not apply in relation to issues arising in any claim excluded from the operation of this Part by section 13 below.

(4) The applicable law shall be used for determining the issues arising in a claim, including in particular the question whether an actionable tort or delict has occurred.

(5) The applicable law to be used for determining the issues arising in a claim shall exclude any choice of law rules forming part of the law of the country or countries concerned.

(6) For the avoidance of doubt (and without prejudice to the operation of section 14 below) this Part applies in relation to events occurring in the forum as it applies in relation to events occurring in any other country.

(7) In this Part as it extends to any country within the United Kingdom, 'the forum' means England and Wales, Scotland or Northern Ireland, as the case may be. ...

10 Abolition of certain common law rules [1002]

The rules of the common law, in so far as they –

(a) require actionability under both the law of the forum and the law of another country for the purpose of determining whether a tort or delict is actionable; or
(b) allow (as an exception from the rules falling within paragraph (a) above) for the law of a single country to be applied for the purpose of determining the issues, or any of the issues, arising in the case in question,

are hereby abolished so far as they apply to any claim in tort or delict which is not excluded from the operation of this Part by section 13 below.

11 Choice of applicable law: the general rule [1003]

(1) The general rule is that the applicable law is the law of the country in which the events constituting the tort or delict in question occur.

(2) Where elements of those events occur in different countries, the applicable law under the general rule is to be taken as being –

(a) for a cause of action in respect of personal injury caused to an individual or death resulting from personal injury, the law of the country where the individual was when he sustained the injury;
(b) for a cause of action in respect of damage to property, the law of the country where the property was when it was damaged; and
(c) in any other case, the law of the country in which the most significant element or elements of those events occurred.

(3) In this section 'personal injury' includes disease or any impairment of physical or mental condition.

12 Choice of applicable law: displacement of general rule [1004]

(1) If it appears, in all the circumstances, from a comparison of –

(a) the significance of the factors which connect a tort or delict with the country whose law would be the applicable law under the general rule; and
(b) the significance of any factors connecting the tort or delict with another country,

that it is substantially more appropriate for the applicable law for determining the issues arising in the case, or any of those issues, to be the law of the other country, the general rule is displaced and the applicable law for determining those issues or that issue (as the case may be) is the law of that other country.

(2) The factors that may be taken into account as connecting a tort or delict with a country for the purposes of this section include, in particular, factors relating to the parties, to any of the events which constitute the tort or delict in question or to any of the circumstances or consequences of those events.

13 Exclusion of defamation claims from Part III [1005]

(1) Nothing in this Part applies to affect the determination of issues arising in any defamation claim.

(2) For the purposes of this section 'defamation claim' means –

(a) any claim under the law of any part of the United Kingdom for libel or slander or for slander of title, slander of goods or other malicious falsehood and any claim under the law of Scotland for verbal injury; and
(b) any claim under the law of any other country corresponding to or otherwise in the nature of a claim mentioned in paragraph (a) above.

14 Transitional provision and savings [1006]

(1) Nothing in this Part applies to acts or omissions giving rise to a claim which occur before the commencement of this Part.

(2) Nothing in this Part affects any rules of law (including rules of private international law) except those abolished by section 10 above.

(3) Without prejudice to the generality of subsection (2) above, nothing in this Part –

(a) authorises the application of the law of a country outside the forum as the applicable law for determining issues arising in any claim in so far as to do so –

(i) would conflict with principles of public policy; or
(ii) would give effect to such a penal, revenue or other public law as would not otherwise be enforceable under the law of the forum; or

(b) affects any rules of evidence, pleading or practice or authorises questions of procedure in any proceedings to be determined otherwise than in accordance with the law of the forum.

(4) This Part has effect without prejudice to the operation of any rule of law which either has effect notwithstanding the rules of private international law applicable in the particular circumstances or modifies the rules of private international law that would otherwise be so applicable.

15 Crown application [1007]

(1) This Part applies in relation to claims by or against the Crown as it applies in relation to claims to which the Crown is not a party.

(2) In subsection (1) above a reference to the Crown does not include a reference to Her Majesty in Her private capacity or to Her Majesty in right of Her Duchy of Lancaster or to the Duke of Cornwall.

(3) Without prejudice to the generality of section 14(2) above, nothing in this section affects any rule of law as to whether proceedings of any description may be brought against the Crown.

PART IV

SUPPLEMENTAL

16 Commencement [1008]

(1) Part I shall come into force on such day as the Lord Chancellor may by order made by statutory instrument appoint; and different days may be appointed for different provisions.

(2) Part II shall come into force at the end of the period of two months beginning with the day on which this Act is passed.

(3) Part III shall come into force on such day as the Lord Chancellor and the Lord Advocate may by order made by statutory instrument appoint; and different days may be appointed for the commencement of Part III as it extends to England and Wales, Scotland or Northern Ireland.

RULES OF THE SUPREME COURT 1965
Order 11 (as amended)

1 Principal cases in which service of writ out of jurisdiction is permissible

(1) Provided that the writ does not contain any claim mentioned in Order 75, r.2(1) and is not a writ to which paragraph (2) of this rule applies, service of a writ out of the jurisdiction is permissible with the leave of the Court if in the action begun by the writ –

(a) relief is sought against a person domiciled within the jurisdiction;
(b) an injunction is sought ordering the defendant to do or refrain from doing anything within the jurisdiction (whether or not damages are also claimed in respect of a failure to do or the doing of that thing);
(c) the claim is brought against a person duly served within or out of the jurisdiction and a person out of the jurisdiction is a necessary or proper party thereto;
(d) the claim is brought to enforce, rescind, dissolve, annul or otherwise affect a contract, or to recover damages or obtain other relief in respect of the breach of a contract, being (in either case) a contract which –

(i) was made within the jurisdiction, or
(ii) was made by or through an agent trading or residing within the jurisdiction on behalf of a principal trading or residing out of the jurisdiction, or
(iii) is by its terms, or by implication, governed by English law, or
(iv) contains a term to the effect that the High Court shall have jurisdiction to hear and determine any action in respect of the contract;

(e) the claim is brought in respect of a breach committed within the jurisdiction of a contract made within or out of the jurisdiction, and irrespective of the fact, if such be the case, that the breach was preceded or accompanied by a breach committed out of the jurisdiction that rendered impossible the performance of so much of the contract as ought to have been performed within the jurisdiction;
(f) the claim is founded on a tort and the damage was sustained, or resulted from an act committed, within the jurisdiction;
(g) the whole subject-matter of the action is land situate within the jurisdiction (with or without rents of profits) or the perpetuation of testimony relating to land so situate;
(h) the claim is brought to construe, rectify, set aside or enforce an act, deed, will, contract, obligation or liability affecting land situate within the jurisdiction;
(i) the claim is made for a debt secured on immovable property or is made to assert, declare or determine proprietary or possessory rights, or rights of security, in or over movable property, or to obtain authority to dispose of movable property, situate within the jurisdiction;
(j) the claim is brought to execute the trusts of a written instrument being trusts that ought to be executed according to English law and of which the person to

be served with the writ is a trustee, or for any relief or remedy which might be obtained in any such action;

(k) the claim is made for the administration of the estate of a person who died domiciled within the jurisdiction or for any relief or remedy which might be obtained in any such action;

(l) the claim is brought in a probate action within the meaning of Order 76;

(m) the claim is brought to enforce any judgment or arbitral award;

(n) the claim is brought against a defendant not domiciled in Scotland or Northern Ireland in respect of a claim by the Commissioners of Inland Revenue for or in relation to any of the duties or taxes which have been, or are for the time being, placed under their care and management;

(o) the claim is brought under the Nuclear Installations Act 1965 or in respect of contributions under the Social Security Act 1975;

(p) the claim is made for a sum to which the Directive of the Council of the European Communities dated 15th March 1976 No.76/308/EEC applies, and service is to be effected in a country which is a member State of the European Economic Community.

(q) the claim is made under the Drug Trafficking Offences Act 1986;

(r) the claim is made under the Financial Services Act 1986 or the Banking Act 1987;

(s) the claim is made under Part VI of the Criminal Justice Act 1988;

(t) the claim is brought for money had and received or for an account or other relief against the defendant as constructive trustee, and the defendant's alleged liability arises out of acts committed, whether by him or otherwise, within the jurisdiction.

(u) the claim is made under the Immigration (Carriers' Liability) Act 1987.

(2) Service of a writ out of the jurisdiction is permissible without the leave of the Court provided that each claim made by the writ is either:–

(a) a claim which by virtue of the Civil Jurisdiction and Judgments Act 1982 the Court has power to hear and determine, made in proceedings to which the following conditions apply –

(i) no proceedings between the parties concerning the same cause of action are pending in the courts of any other part of the United Kingdom or of any other Convention territory, and

(ii) either –

the defendant is domiciled in any part of the United Kingdom or in any other Convention territory, or

the proceedings begun by the writ are proceedings to which Article 16 of Schedule 1, 3C or 4 refers, or the defendant is a party to an agreement conferring jurisdiction to which Article 17 of Schedule 1, 3C or 4 to the Act applies,

or

(b) a claim which by virtue of any other enactment the High Court has power to hear and determine notwithstanding that the person against whom the claim is made is not within the jurisdiction of the Court or that the wrongful act, neglect or default giving rise to the claim did not take place within its jurisdiction.

(3) Where a writ is to be served out of the jurisdiction under paragraph (2), the time to be inserted in the writ within which the defendant served therewith must acknowledge service shall be –

(a) 21 days where the writ is to be served out of the jurisdiction under paragraph (2)(a) in Scotland, Northern Ireland or in the European territory of another Contracting State, or

(b) 31 days where the writ is to be served under paragraph (2)(a) in any other territory of a Contracting State, or
(c) limited in accordance with the practice adopted under r.4(4) where the writ is to be served under paragraph (2)(a) in a country not referred to in sub-paragraphs (a) or (b) or under paragraph (2)(b).

(4) For the purposes of this rules, and of r.9 of this Order, domicile is to be determined in accordance with the provisions of sections 41 to 46 of the Civil Jurisdictions and Judgments Act 1982 and 'Convention territory' means the territory or territories of any Contracting State, as defined by s1(3) of that Act, to which, as defined in s1(1) of that Act, the Brussels or the Lugano Convention apply.

4 Application for, and grant of, leave to serve writ out of jurisdiction [1010]

(1) An application for the grant of leave under rule 1(1) must be supported by an affidavit stating –
   (a) the grounds on which the application is made,
   (b) that in the deponent's belief the plaintiff has a good cause of action,
   (c) in what place or country the defendant is, or probably may be found, and
   (d) where the application is made under rule 1(1)(c), the grounds for the deponent's belief that there is between the plaintiff and the person on whom a writ has been served a real issue which the plaintiff may reasonably ask the Court to try.

(2) No such leave shall be granted unless it shall be made sufficiently to appear to the Court that the case is a proper one for service out of the jurisdiction under this Order.

(3) Where the application is for the grant of leave under rule 1 to serve a writ in Scotland or Northern Ireland, if it appears to the Court that there may be a concurrent remedy there, the Court, in deciding whether to grant leave shall have regard to the comparative cost and convenience of proceeding there or in England, and (where that is relevant) to the powers and jurisdiction of the sheriff court in Scotland or the county courts or courts of summary jurisdiction in Northern Ireland.

(4) An order granting under rule 1 leave to serve a writ, out of the jurisdiction must limit a time within which the defendant to be served must acknowledge service.

5 Service of writ abroad: general [1011]

(1) Subject to the following provisions of this rule, Order 10, rule 1(1), (4), (5) and (6) and Order 65, rule 4, shall apply in relation to the service of a writ, notwithstanding that the writ is to be served out of the jurisdiction, save that the accompanying form of acknowledgement of service shall be modified in such a manner as may be appropriate.

(2) Nothing in this rule or in any order or direction of the Court made by virtue of it shall authorise or require the doing of anything in a country in which service is to be effected which is contrary to the law of that country.

(3) A writ which is to be served out of the jurisdiction –
   (a) need not be served personally on the person required to be served so long as it is served on him in accordance with the law of the country in which service is effected; and

(b) need not be served by the plaintiff or his agent if it is served by a method provided for by rule 6 or rule 7.

(5) An official certificate stating that a writ as regards which rule 6 has been complied with has been served on a person personally, or in accordance with the law of the country in which service was effected, on a specified date, being a certificate –

    (a) by a British consular authority in that country, or
    (b) by the government or judicial authorities of that country, or
    (c) by any other authority designated in respect of that country under the Hague Convention,

shall be evidence of the facts so stated.

(6) An official certificate by the Secretary of State stating that a writ has been duly served on a specified date in accordance with a request made under rule 7 shall be evidence of that fact.

(7) A document purporting to be such a certificate as is mentioned in paragraph (5) or (6) shall, until the contrary is proved, be deemed to be such a certificate.

(8) In this rule and rule 6 'the Hague Convention' means the Convention on the service abroad of judicial and extra-judicial documents in civil or commercial matters signed at the Hague on November 15, 1965.

6 Service of writ abroad through foreign governments, judicial authorities and British consuls

(1) Save where a writ is to be served pursuant to paragraph (2A) this rule does not apply to service in –

    (a) Scotland, Northern Ireland, the Isle of Man or the Channel Islands;
    (b) any independent Commonwealth country;
    (c) any associated state;
    (d) any colony;
    (e) the Republic of Ireland.

(2) Where in accordance with these rules a writ is to be served on a defendant in any country with respect to which there subsists a Civil Procedure Convention (other than the Hague Convention) providing for service in that country of process of the High Court, the writ may be served –

    (a) through the judicial authorities of that country; or
    (b) through a British consular authority in that country (subject to any provision of the convention as to the nationality of persons who may be so served).

(2A) Where in accordance with these rules, a writ is to be served on a defendant in any country which is a party to the Hague Convention, the writ may be served –

    (a) through the authority designated under the Convention in respect of that country; or
    (b) if the law of that country permits –
        (i) through the judicial authorities of that country, or
        (ii) through a British consular authority in that country.

(3) Where in accordance with these rules a writ is to be served on a defendant in any country with respect to which there does not subsist a Civil Procedure Convention providing for service in that country of process of the High Court, the writ may be served –

(a) through the government of that country, where that government is willing to effect service; or

(b) through a British consular authority in that country, except where service through such an authority is contrary to the law of that country.

(4) A person who wishes to serve a writ by a method specified in paragraph (2), (2A) or (3) must lodge in the Central Office a request for service of the writ by that method, together with a copy of the writ and an additional copy thereof for each person to be served.

(5) Every copy of a writ lodged under paragraph (4) must be accompanied by a translation of the writ in the official language of the country in which service is to be effected or, if there is more than one official language of that country, in any one of those languages which is appropriate to the place in that country where service is to be effected: Provided that this paragraph shall not apply in relation to a copy of a writ which is to be served in a country the official language of which is, or the official languages of which include, English, or is to be served in any country by a British consular authority on a British subject, unless the service is to be effected under paragraph (2) and the Civil Procedure Convention with respect to that country expressly requires the copy to be accompanied by a translation.

(6) Every translation lodged under paragraph (5) must be certified by the person making it to be a correct translation; and the certificate must contain a statement of that person's full name, of his address and of his qualifications for making the translation.

(7) Documents duly lodged under paragraph (4) shall be sent by the Senior Master to the Parliamentary Under-Secretary of State to the Foreign Office with a request that he arrange the writ to be served by the method indicated in the request lodged under paragraph (4) or, where alternative methods are so indicated, by such one of those methods as is most convenient.

7 Service of writ in certain actions under certain Acts [1013]

(1) Subject to paragraph (4) where a person to whom leave has been granted under rule 1 to serve a writ on a State, as defined in section 14 of the State Immunity Act 1978, wishes to have the writ served on that State, he must lodge in the Central Office –

(a) a request for service to be arranged by the Secretary of State; and
(b) a copy of the writ; and
(c) except where the official language of the State is, or the official languages of the State include, English, a translation of the writ in the official language or one of the official languages of that State.

(2) Rule 6(6) shall apply in relation to a translation lodged under paragraph (1) of this rule as it applies in relation to a translation lodged under paragraph (5) of that rule.

(3) Documents duly lodged under this Rule shall be sent by the Senior Master to the Secretary of State with a request that the Secretary of State arrange for the writ to be served.

(4) Where section 12(6) of the State Immunity Act 1978 applies and the State has agreed to a method of service other than that provided by the preceding paragraphs, the writ may be served either by the method agreed or in accordance with the preceding paragraphs of this rule. ...

Glossary
of Latin and other words and phrases

Ab extra. From outside.

Ab inconvenienti. *See* ARGUMENTUM

Ab initio. From the beginning.

Accessio. Addition; appendage. The combination of two chattels belonging to different persons into a single article.

Acta exteriora indicant interiora secreta. A man's outward actions are evidence of his innermost thoughts and intentions.

Actio personalis moritur cum persona. A personal right of action dies on the death of the person by or against whom it could be enforced.

Actio quanti minoris. Action for how much less.

Actor sequitur forum rei. The plaintiff follows the court of the country where the subject of the action is situated.

Actus non facit reum, nisi mens sit rea. The act itself does not make a man guilty, unless he does it with a guilty intention.

Ad colligenda bona. To collect the goods.

Ad hoc. Arranged for this purpose; special.

Ad idem. *See* CONSENSUS.

Ad infinitum. To infinity; without limit; for ever.

Ad litem. For the purpose of the law suit.

Ad opus. For the benefit of: on behalf of.

Ad valorem. Calculated in proportion to the value or price of the property.

Adversus extraneos vitiosa possessio prodesse solet. Possession, though supported only by a defective title, will prevail over the claims of strangers other than the true owner.

A fortiori (ratione). For a stronger reason; by even more convincing reasoning.

Aliter. Otherwise; the result would be different, if ...; (also, used of a judge who thinks differently from his fellow judges).

Aliud est celare; aliud est tacere; neque enim id est celare quicquid reticeas. Mere silence is one thing but active concealment is quite another thing; for it is not disguising something when you say nothing about it.

Aliunde. From elsewhere; from other sources.

A mensa et thoro. A separation from the 'table and bed' of one's spouse.

Amicus curiae. A friend of the court.

Animo contrahendi. With the intention of contracting.

Animo et facto. By act and intention.

Animo non revertendi. With the intention of not returning.

Animo revocandi. With the intention of revoking.

Animus deserendi. The intention of deserting.

Animus donandi. The intention of giving.

Animus manendi. The intention of remaining.

Animus possidendi. The intention of possessing.

Animus residendi. The intention of residing.

Animus revertendi. The intention of returning.

Animus testandi. The intention of making a will.

Ante. Before; (also used of a case referred to earlier on a page or in a book).

A posteriori. From effect to cause; inductively; from subsequent conclusions.

A priori. From cause to effect; deductively; from previous assumptions or reasoning.

Argumentum ab inconvenienti. An argument devised because of the existence of an awkward problem so as to provide an explanation for it.

Asportatio. The act of carrying away.

Assensus. *See* CONSENSUS.

Assensus ad idem. Agreement as to the same terms.

Assumpsit (super se). He undertook.

Ats. (ad sectam). At the suit of. (The opposite of VERSUS.)

Autrefois acquit. Formerly acquitted.

Autrefois convict. Formerly convicted.

A vinculo matrimonii. From the bonds of matrimony.

Bis dat qui cito dat. He gives doubly who gives swiftly; a quick gift is worth two slow ones.

Bona fide. In good faith; sincere.

Bona vacantia. Goods without an owner.

Brutum fulmen. A silent thunderbolt; an empty threat.

Cadit quaestio. The matter admits of no further argument.

Caeterorum. Of the things which are left.

Capias ad satisfaciendum. A writ commanding the sheriff to take the body of the defendant in order that he may make satisfaction for the plaintiff's claim.

Causa causans. The immediate cause of something; the last link in the chain of causation.

Causa proxima non remota spectatur. Regard is paid to the immediate, not to the remote cause.

Causa sine qua non. A cause without which an event would not happen; a preceding link in the chain of causation without which the CAUSA CAUSANS could not be operative.

Caveat emptor. The buyer must look out for himself.

Cessante ratione legis, cessat lex ipsa. When the reason for its existence ceases, the law itself ceases to exist.

Cestui(s) que trust. A person (or persons) for whose benefit property is held on trust; a beneficiary (beneficiaries).

Cestui que vie. Person for the duration of whose life an estate is granted to another person.

Chose in action. Intangible personal property or rights, which can be enjoyed or enforced only by legal action, and not by taking physical possession (eg debts).

Chose jugée. Thing it is idle to discuss.

Coitus interruptus. Interrupted sexual intercourse, i.e. withdrawal before emission.

Colore officii. Under the pretext of a person's official position.

Commorientes. Persons who die at the same time.

Confusio. A mixture; union. The mixture of things of the same nature, but belonging to different persons so that identification of the original things becomes impossible.

Consensu. By general consent; unanimously.

Consensus ad idem. Agreement as to the same thing.

Consortium. Conjugal relations with and companionship of a spouse.

Contra. To the contrary. (Used of a case in which the decision was contrary to the doctrine or cases previously cited; also of a judge who delivers a dissenting judgment.)

Contra bonos mores. Contrary to good morals.

Contra mundum. Against the world.

Contra proferentem. Against the party who puts forward a clause in a document.

Cor. (coram). In the presence of; before (a judge).

Coram non judice. Before one who is not a judge. Corpus. Body; capital.

Corpus. Body; capital.

Coverture. Marriage.

Cri de coeur. Heartfelt cry.

Cujus est solum, ejus est usque ad coelum et ad inferos. Whosoever owns the soil also owns everything above it as far as the heavens and everything below it as far as the lower regions of the earth.

Culpa. Wrongful default.

Cum onere. Together with the burden.

Cum testamento annexo. With the will annexed.

Cur. adv. vult. (curia advisari vult). The court wishes time to consider the matter.

Cy-pres. For a purpose resembling as nearly as possible the purpose originally proposed.

Damage feasant. *See* DISTRESS.

Damnosa hereditas. An insolvent inheritance.

Damnum. Loss; damage.

Damnum absque injuria. *See* DAMNUM SINE INJURIA.

Damnum emergens. A loss which arises.

Damnum fatale. Damage resulting from the workings of fate for which human negligence is not to blame.

Damnum sine (or absque) injuria. Damage which is not the result of a legally remediable wrong.

De bene esse. Evidence or action which a court allows to be given or done provisionally, subject to further consideration at a later stage.

Debitor non praesumitur donare. A debtor is presumed to give a legacy to a creditor to discharge his debt and not as a gift.

Debitum in praesenti. A debt which is due at the present time.

Debitum in futuro solvendum. A debt which will be due to be paid at a future time.

De bonis asportatis. Of goods carried away.

De bonis non administratis. Of the assets which have not been administered .

De cujus. The person about whom an issue is to be determined.

De die in diem. From day to day.

De facto. In fact.

De futuro. Regarding the future; in the future; about something which will exist in the future.

Dehors. Outside (the document or matter in question); irrelevant.

De integro. As regards the whole; entirely.

De jure. By right; rightful.

Del credere agent. An agent who for an extra commission guarantees the due performance of contracts by persons whom he introduces to his principal.

Delegatus non potest delegare. A person who is entrusted with a duty has no right to appoint another person to perform it in his place.

De minimis non curat lex. The law does not concern itself with trifles.

De momento in momentum. From moment to moment.

De novo. Anew; starting afresh.

Deodand. A chattel which caused the death of a human being and was forfeited to the Crown.

De praerogativa regis. Concerning the royal prerogative.

De son tort. Of his wrong.

Deus est procurator fatuorum. God is the protector of the simpleminded.

Devastavit. Where an executor 'has squandered' the estate.

Dictum. Saying. *See* OBITER DICTUM.

Dies non (jurisdicus). Day on which no legal business can be transacted.

Dissentiente. Delivering a dissenting judgment.

Distress damage feasant. The detention by a landowner of an animal or chattel while it is doing damage on his land.

Distringas. That you may distrain.

Doli incapax. Incapable of crime.

Dolus qui dat locum contractui. A deception which clears the way for the other party to enter into a contract.

Dominium. Ownership.

Dominus litis. The principal in a suit.

Dominus pro tempore. The master for the time being.

Donatio mortis causa. A gift made in contemplation of death and conditional thereon.

Dubitante. Doubting the correctness of the decision.

Durante absentia. During an absence abroad.

Durante minore aetate. While an infant; during minority.

Durante viduitate. During widowhood.

Ei incumbit probatio qui dicit, non qui negat. The onus of proving a fact rests upon the man who asserts its truth, not upon the man who denies it.

Ejusdem generis. General words following a list of specific things are construed as relating to things 'of the same kind' as those specifically listed.

Enceinte. Pregnant.

En ventre sa mère. Conceived but not yet born.

Eodem modo quo oritur, eodem modo dissolvitur. What has been created by a certain method may be extinguished by the same method.

Eo instanti. At that instant.

Escrow. A document delivered subject to a condition which must be fulfilled before it becomes a deed.

Estoppel. A rule of evidence which applies in certain circumstances and stops a person from denying the truth of a statement previously made by him.

Estoppel in pais. Estoppel by matter or conduct; equitable estoppel.

Et cetera (etc). And other things of that sort.

Et seq (et sequentes). And subsequent pages.

Ex. From; by virtue of.

Ex abundanti cautela. From an abundance of caution.

Ex aequo et bono. According to what is just and equitable.

Ex cathedra. From his seat of office: an authoritative statement made by someone in his official capacity.

Ex comitate et jure gentium. Out of comity (friendly recognition) and the law of nations.

Ex concessis. In view of what has already been accepted.

Ex contractu. Arising out of contract.

Ex converso. Conversely.

Ex debito justitiae. That which is due as of right; which the court has no discretion to refuse.

Ex delicto. Arising out of a wrongful act or tort.

Ex dolo malo non oritur actio. No right of action arises out of a fraud.

Executor de son tort. One who 'of his own fault' has intermeddled with an estate, purporting to act as executor.

Ex facie. On the face of it; ostensibly.

Ex gratia. Out of the kindness. Gratuitous; voluntary.

Ex hypothesi. In view of what has already been assumed.

Ex improviso. Unexpectedly, without forethought.

Ex officio. By virtue of one's official position.

Ex pacto illicito non oritur actio. No action can be brought on an unlawful contract.

Ex parte. Proceedings brought on behalf of one interested party without notice to, and in the absence of, the other.

Ex post facto. By reason of a subsequent act; acting retrospectively.

Ex relatione. An action instituted by the Attorney-General on behalf of the Crown on the information of a member of the public who is interested in the matter (the relator).

Expressio unius est exclusio alterius. When one thing is expressly specified, then it prevents anything else being implied.

Expressis verbis. In express words.

Expressum facit cessare tacitum. Where terms are expressed, no other terms can be implied.

Extra territorium. Outside the territory; extra territorial(ly).

Ex turpi causa non oritur actio. No action can be brought where the parties are guilty of illegal or immoral conduct.

Faciendum. Something which is to be done.

Factum. Deed; that which has been done; statement of facts or points in issue.

Fait accompli. An accomplished fact.

Falsa demonstratio non nocet cum de corpore constat. Where the substance of the property in question is clearly identified, the addition of an incorrect description of the property does no harm.

Falsus in ono, falsus in omnibus. False in one, false in all.

Fecundatio ab extra. Conception from outside, i.e. where there has been no penetration.

Feme covert. A married woman.

Feme sole. An unmarried woman.

Ferae naturae. Animals which are by nature dangerous to man.

Fieri facias. A writ addressed to the sheriff: 'that you cause to be made' from the defendant's goods the sum due to the plaintiff under the judgment.

Filius nullius. *See* NULLIUS FILIUS.

Force majeure. Irresistible compulsion.

Forum. Court; the court hearing the case.

Forum conveniens. The appropriate court to hear the case.

Forum domicilii. The court of the country of domicile.

Forum rei. The court of the country where the subject of the action is situated.

Fraude à la loi. Evasion of the law.

Fructus industriales. Cultivated crops.

Fructus naturales. Vegetation which grows naturally without cultivation.

Functus officio. Having discharged his duty; having exhausted its powers.

Furiosus. Frantic, mad.

Genus numquam perit. Particular goods which have been identified may be destroyed, but 'a category or type of article can never perish'.

Habeas corpus (ad subjiciendum). A writ addressed to one who detains another in custody, requiring him 'that you produce the prisoner's body to answer' to the court.

Habitue. A frequent visitor to a place.

Ibid. (ibidem). In the same place, book, or source.

Id certum est quod certum reddi potest. That which is capable of being reduced to a certainty is already a certainty.

Idem. The same thing, or person.

Ideo consideratum est per. Therefore it is considered by the court.

Ignorantia juris haud (neminem) (non) excusat, ignorantia facti excusat. A man may be excused for mistaking facts, but not for mistaking the law.

Ignorantia juris non excusat. Ignorance of the law is no excuse.

Imperitia culpae adnumeratur. Lack of skill is accounted a fault.

In aequali jure melior est conditio possidentis. Where the legal rights of the parties are equal, the party with possession is in the stronger position.

In articulo mortis. On the point of death.

In bonis. In the goods (or estate) of a deceased person.

In capite. In chief; holding as tenant directly under the Crown.

In consimili casu. In a similar case.

In custodia legis. In the keeping of the law.

Indebitatus assumpsit. A form of action in which the plaintiff alleges the defendant 'being already indebted to the plaintiff undertook' to do something.

In delicto. At fault.

Indicia. Signs; marks.

Indicium. Indication; sign; mark.

In esse. In existence.

In expeditione. On actual military service.

In extenso. At full length.

In fieri. In the course of being performed or established.

In flagrante delicto. In the act of committing the offence.

In forma pauperis. In the character of a poor person.

Infra. Below; lower down on a page; later in a book. In futuro. In the future.

In futuro. In the future.

In hac re. In this matter; in this particular aspect.

In jure non remota causa sed proxima spectatur. In law it is the immediate and not the remote cause which is considered.

Injuria. A wrongful act for which the law provides a remedy.

Injuria sine damno. A wrongful act unaccompanied by any damage yet actionable at law.

In lieu of. In place of.

In limine. On the threshold; at the outset.

In loco parentis. In the place of a parent.

In minore delicto. A person who is 'less at fault'.

In omnibus. In every respect.

Inops consilii. Lacking facilities for legal advice.

In pari delicto, potior est conditio defendentis (or possidentis). Where both parties are equally at fault, the defendant (or the party in possession) is in the stronger position.

In pari materia. In an analogous case or position.

In personam. *See* JUS IN PERSONAM.

In pleno. In full.

In praesenti. At the present time.

In propria persona. In his own capacity. In re. In the matter of. In rem. *See* JUS IN REM.

In re. In the matter of.

In rem. *See* JUS IN REM.

In situ. In its place.

In specie. In its own form; not converted into anything else.

In statu quo ante. In the condition in which it, or a person, was before.

Inter alia. Amongst other things.

Inter alios. Amongst other persons.

Interest reipublicae ut sit finis litium. It is in the interests of the community that every law suit should reach a final conclusion (and not be reopened later).

Interim. In the meanwhile; temporary.

Inter partes. Between (the) parties.

In terrorem. As a warning; as a deterrent.

Inter se. Between themselves.

Inter vivos. Between persons who are alive.

In toto. In its entirety; completely.

In transitu. In passage from one place to another.

Intra vires. Within the powers recognised by law as belonging to the person or body in question.

In utero. In the womb.

In vacuo. In the abstract; without considering the circumstances.

In vitro. In glass; in a test tube.

Ipsissima verba. 'The very words' of a speaker.

Ipso facto. By that very fact.

Jura. Rights.

Jura mariti. By virtue of the right of a husband to the goods of his wife.

Jus. A right which is recognised in law.

Jus accrescendi. The right of survivorship; the right of joint tenants to have their interests in the joint property increased by inheriting the interests of the deceased joint tenants until the last survivor inherits the entire property.

Jus actionis. Right of action.

Jus gentium. The law of nations.

Jus in personam. A right which can be enforced against a particular person only.

Jus in rem. A right which can be enforced over the property in question against all other persons.

Jus naturale. Natural justice.

Jus neque in re neque ad rem. A right which is enforceable neither over the property in question against all the world nor against specific persons only.

Jus quaesitum tertio. A right vested in a third party (who is not a party to the contract).

Jus regale. A right or privilege belonging to the Crown.

Jus tertii. *See* JUS QUAESITUM TERTIO

Laches. Slackness or delay in pursuing a legal remedy which disentitles a person from action at a later date.

Laesio fidei. Breach of faith.

Laissez faire. 'Let him do what he likes'; permissive.

Lapsus linguae. Slip of the tongue.

Lex actus. The law governing a legal act or transaction.

Lex causae. The law governing the case or a given issue therein.

Lex domicilii. The law of the country of domicile of a person.

Lex fori. The law of the court in which the case is being heard.

Lex loci actus. The law of the country where a legal act or transaction took place.

Lex loci celebrationis. The law of the place where the marriage was celebrated.

Lex loci contractus. The law of the place where the contract was made.

Lex loci delicti commissi. The law of the place where the wrong was committed.

Lex loci situs. *See* LEX SITUS.

Lex loci solutionis. The law of the place where the contract is to be performed.

Lex monetae. The law of the country in whose currency a debt or other financial obligation is expressed.

Lex nationalis. The law of the country of a person's nationality.

Lex patriae. *See* LEX NATIONALIS.

Lex pecuniae. *See* LEX MONETAE.

Lex situs. The law of the place where the thing in question is situated.

Lex successionis. The law governing the succession to a deceased's estate.

Lien. The rights to retain possession of goods, deeds or other property belonging to another as security for payment of money.

Lis alibi pendens. An action pending elsewhere.

Lis pendens. Pending action.

Loc. cit. (loco citato). In the passage previously mentioned.

Locus celebrationis. The place where the marriage was celebrated.

Locus classicus. Authoritative passage in a book or judgment; the principal authority or source for the subject.

Locus contractus. The place where the contract was made.

Locus delicti. The place where the wrong was committed.

Locus in quo. Scene of the event.

Locus poenitentiae. Scope or opportunity for repentance.

Locus regit actum. The law of the place where an act takes place governs that act.

Locus solutionis. The place where a contract is to be performed or a debt is to be paid.

Locus standi. Recognised position or standing; the right to appear in court.

Lucrum cessans. A benefit which is terminated.

Magnum opus. A great work of literature.

Mala fide(s). (In) bad faith.

Malitia supplet aetatem. Malice supplements the age of an infant wrongdoer who would (in the absence of malice) be too young to be responsible for his acts.

Malum in se. An act which in itself is morally wrong, e.g. murder.

Malum prohibitum. An act which is wrong because it is prohibited by human law but is not morally wrong.

Malus animus. Evil intent.

Mansuetae naturae. Animals which are normally of a domesticated disposition.

Mesne. Intermediate; middle; dividing.

Mesne profits. Profits of land lost by the plaintiff while the defendant remained wrongfully in possession.

Mobilia sequuntur personam. The domicile of movable property follows the owner's personal domicile.

Molliter manus imposuit. Gently laid his hand upon the other party.

Mutatis mutandis. With the necessary changes of detail being made.

Natura negotii. The nature of the transaction.

Negotiorum gestio. Handling of other people's affairs.

Nemo dat quod non habet. No one has power to transfer the ownership of that which he does not own.

Nemo debet bis vexari, si constat curiae quod sit pro una et eadem causa. No one ought to be harassed with proceedings twice, if it appears to the court that it is for one and the same cause.

Nemo est haeres viventis. No one can be the heir of a person who is still living.

Nexus. Connection; bond.

Nisi. Unless; (also used of a decree or order which will later be made absolute 'unless' good cause be shown to the contrary); provisional.

Nisi prius. Cases which were directed to be tried at Westminster only if the justices of assize should 'not' have tried them in the country 'previously'.

Nocumenta infinita sunt. There is no limit to the types of situations which constitute nuisances.

Nomen collectivum. A collective name, noun or description; a word descriptive of a class.

Non compos mentis. Not of sound mind and understanding.

Non constat. It is not certain.

Non est factum. That the document in question was not his deed.

Non haec in foedera veni. This is not the agreement which I came to sign.

Non omnibus dormio. I do not turn a blind eye on every instance of misconduct.

Non sequitur. It does not follow; an inconsistent statement.

Noscitur a sociis. The meaning of a word is known from the company it keeps (ie from its context).

Nova causa interveniens. An independent cause which intervenes between the alleged wrong and the damage in question.

Novus actus interveniens. A fresh act of someone other than the defendant which intervenes between the alleged wrong and the damage in question.

Nudum pactum. A bare agreement (unsupported by consideration).

Nullius filius. No man's son; a bastard.

Obiter dictum (dicta). Thing(s) said by the way; opinions expressed by judges in passing, on issues not essential for the decision in the case.

Obligatio quasi ex contractu. An obligation arising out of an act or event, as if from a contract, but independently of the consent of the person bound.

Omnia praesumuntur contra spoliatorem. Every presumption is raised against a wrongdoer.

Omnia praesumuntur rite et solemniter esse acta donec probetur in contrarium. All things are presumed to have been performed with all due formalities until it is proved to the contrary.

Omnis ratihabitio retrotrahitur et mandato priori aequiparatur. Every ratification of a previous act is carried back and made equivalent to a previous command to do it.

Onus probandi. The burden of proving.

Op. cit. (opere citato). In the book referred to previously.

Orse. Otherwise.

Par delictum. Equal fault.

Par in parem non habet imperium. An equal has no authority over an equal.

Parens patriae. Parent of the nation.

Pari materia. With equal substance.

Pari passu. On an equal footing; equally; in step with.

Pari ratione. By an equivalent process of reasoning.

Parol. By word of mouth, or unsealed document.

Participes criminis. Accomplices in the crime.

Passim. Everywhere; in various places.

Pater est quem nuptiae demonstrant. He is the father whom the marriage indicates to be so.

Patrimonium. Beneficial ownership.

Pendente lite. While a law suit is pending.

Per. By; through; in the opinion of a judge.

Per capita. Divided equally between all the persons filling the description.

Per curiam. In the opinion of the court.

Per formam doni. Through the form of wording of the gift or deed.

Per incuriam. Through carelessness or oversight.

Per quod. By reason of which.

Per quod consortium et servitium amisit. By reason of which he has lost the benefit of her company and services.

Per quod servitium amisit. By reason of which he has lost the benefit of his service.

Per se. By itself.

Persona(e) designata(e). A person(s) specified as an individual(s), not identified as a member(s) of a class nor as fulfilling a particular qualification.

Per stirpes. According to the stocks of descent; one share for each line of descendants; where the descendants of a deceased person (however many they may be) inherit between them only the one share which the deceased would have taken if alive.

Per subsequens matrimonium. Legitimation of a child 'by subsequent marriage' of the parents.

Plene administravit. A plea by an executor 'that he has fully administered' all the assets which have come into his hands and that no assets remain out of which the plaintiff's claim could be satisfied.

Plus quam tolerabile. More than can be endured.

Post. After; mentioned in a subsequent passage or page.

Post mortem. After death.

Post nuptial. Made after marriage.

Post obit bond. Agreement or bond by which a borrower agrees to pay the lender a sum larger than the loan on or after the death of a person on whose death he expects to inherit property.

Post obitum. After the death of a specified person.

Pour autrui. On behalf of another.

Prima facie. At first sight.

Primae impressionis. Of first impression.

Pro bono publico. For the public good.

Profit a prendre. The right to enter the land of another and take part of its produce.

Pro hac vice. For this occasion.

Propositus. The person put forward; the person about whom a legal issue is to be determined.

Pro privato commodo. For private benefit.

Pro rata. In proportion.

Pro rata itineris. At the same rate per mile as was agreed for the whole journey.

Pro tanto. So far; to that extent.

Pro tempore. For the time being.

Publici juris. Of public right.

Puisne. Inferior; lower in rank; not secured by deposit of deeds; of the High Court.

Punctum temporis. Moment, or point of time.

Pour autre vie. During the life of another person.

Q.v. (quod vide). Which see.

Qua. As; in the capacity of.

Quaere. Consider whether it is correct.

Quaeritur. The question is raised.

Quantum. Amount; how much.

Quantum meruit. As much as he has earned.

Quantum valebant. As much as they were worth.

Quare clausum fregit. Because he broke into the plaintiff's enclosure.

Quasi. As if; seemingly.

Quasi ex contractu. See OBLIGATIO.

Quatenus. How far; in so far as; since.

Quia timet. Because he fears what he will suffer in the future.

Quicquid plantatur solo solo cedit. Whatever is planted in the soil belongs to the soil.

Quid pro quo. Something for something; consideration.

Glossary

Qui elegit judicem elegit jus. He who chooses a judge chooses also the law which the judge administers.

Qui facit per alium facit per se. He who employs another person to do something does it himself.

Qui prior est tempore potior est jure. He who is earlier in point of time is in the stronger position in law.

Quoad. Until; as far as; as to.

Quoad hoc. As far as this matter is concerned.

Quo animo. With what intention.

Quot judices tot sententiae. There were as many different opinions as there were judges.

Quousque. Until the time when.

Ratio decidendi. The reason for a decision; the principle on which a decision is based.

Ratione domicilii. By reason of a person's domicile.

Re. In the matter of; by the thing or transaction.

Reductio ad absurdum. Reduction to absurdity.

Renvoi. Reference to or application of the rules of a foreign legal system in a different country's courts.

Res. Thing; affair; matter; circumstance.

Res extincta. The thing which was intended to be the subject matter of a contract but had previously been destroyed.

Res gestae. Things done; the transaction.

Res integra. A point not covered by the authority of a decided case which must therefore be decided upon principle alone.

Res inter alios acta alteri nocere non debet. A man ought not to be prejudiced by what has taken place between other persons.

Res ipsa loquitur. The thing speaks for itself, i.e. is evidence of negligence in the absence of an explanation by the defendant.

Res judicata. A matter on which a court has previously reached a binding decision; a matter which cannot be questioned.

Res nova. A matter which has not previously been decided.

Res nullius. Nobody's property.

Respondeat superior. A principal must answer for the acts of his subordinates.

Res sua. Something which a man believes to belong to another when it in faet is 'his own property'.

Restitutio in integrum. Restoration of a party to his original position; full restitution.

Res vendita. The article which was sold.

Rex est procurator fatuorum. The King is the protector of the simple minded.

Rigor aequitatis. The inflexibility of equity.

Sc. *See* SCILICET.

Sciens. Knowing.

Scienter. Knowingly; with knowledge of an animal's dangerous disposition.

Scienti non fit injuria. A man who is aware of the existence of a danger has no remedy if it materialises.

Scilicet. To wit; namely; that is to say.

Scintilla. A spark; trace; or moment.

Scire facias. A writ; that you cause to know.

Scriptum praedictum non est factum suum. A plea that the aforesaid document is not his deed.

Secundum formam doni. In accordance with the form of wording in the gift or deed.

Secus. It is otherwise; the legal position is different.

Sed. But.

Sed quaere. But inquire; look into the matter; consider whether the statement is correct.

Semble. It appears; apparently.

Sentit commodum et periculum rei. He both enjoys the benefit of the thing and bears the risk of its loss.

Seriatim. In series; one by one; point by point.

Serivitium. Service.

Sic. So; in such a manner; (also used to emphasise wording copied or quoted from another source: 'such was the expression used in the original source').

Sic utere tuo ut alienum non laedas. So use your own property as not to injure the property of your neighbour.

Similiter. Similarly; in like manner.

Simplex commendatio non obligat. Mere praise of goods by the seller imposes no liability upon him.

Simpliciter. Simply; merely; alone; without any further action; without qualification.

Sine animo revertendi. Without the intention of returning.

Sine die. Without a day being appointed; indefinitely.

Situs. The place where property is situated.

Solatium. Consolation; relief; compensation.

Sotto volce. In an undertone.

Specificatio. The making of a new article out of the chattel of one person by the labour of another.

Spes successionis. The hope of inheriting property on the death of another.

Spondes peritiam artis. If skill is inherent in your profession, you guarantee that you will display it.

Stare decisis. To stand by what has been dedided.

Status quo (ante). The previous position; the position in which things were before; unchanged position.

Stet. Let it stand; do not delete.

Stricto sensu. In the strict sense.

Sub colore officii. Under pretext of someone's official position.

Sub judice. Under judgment; being decided by the court.

Sub modo. Within limits; to a limited extent.

Sub nom. (sub nomine). Under the name of.

Sub silentio. In silence.

Sub tit. (sub titulo). Under the title of.

Suggestio falsi. The suggestion of something which is untrue.

Sui generis. Of its own special kind; unique.

Sui juris. Of his own right; possessed of full legal capacity.

Sup. *See* SUPRA.

Suppressio veri. The suppression of the truth.

Supra. (Sup.) Above; referred to higher up the page; previously.

Talis qualis. Such as it is.

Tam ... quam. As well ... as.

Tempore mortis. At the time of death.

Tempore testamenti. At the time when the will was made.

Toties quoties. As often as occasion shall require; as often as something happens.

Transit in rem judicatam. A right of action merges in the judgment recovered upon it.

Turpis causa. Immoral conduct which constitutes the subject matter of an action.

Uberrima fides. Most abundant good faith.

Ubi jus ibi remedium. Where there is a legally recognised right there is also a remedy.

Ubi supra. In the passage or reference mentioned previously.

Ultimus heres. The ultimate heir who is last in order of priority of those who may be entitled to claim the estate of an intestate.

Ultra vires. Outside the powers recognised by law as belonging to the person or body in question.

Uno flatu. With one breath; at the same moment.

Ut res magis valeat quam pereat. Words must be construed so as to support the validity of the contract rather than to destroy it.

v. (versus). Against.

Verba fortius accipiuntur contra proferentem. Ambiguous wording is construed adversely against the party who introduced it into the document.

Vera copula. True sexual unity.

Verbatim. Word by word; exactly; word for word.

Via media. Middle way; compromise.

Vice versa. The other way round; in turn.

Vide. See.

Vi et armis (et contra pacem domini regis). By force of arms (and in breach of the King's peace).

Vigilantibus et non dormientibus jura subveniunt (or jus succurrit). The law(s) assist(s) those who are vigilant, not those who doze over their rights.

Vinculum juris. Legal tie; that which binds the parties with mutual obligations.

Virgo intacta. A virgin with hymen intact.

Virtute officii. By virtue of a person's official position.

Vis-a-vis. Face to face; opposite to.

Vis major. Irresistible force.

Viva voce. Orally; oral examination.

Viz. (videlicet). Namely; that is to say.

Voir dire. Examination of a witness before he gives evidence, to ascertain whether he is competent to tell the truth on oath; trial within a trial.

Volens. Willing.

Volenti non fit injuria. In law no wrong is done to a man who consents to undergo it.

Index

The entry numbers refer to the paragraphs, not the pages.

Acceptance,
   letter of,   13, 254
   place of,   74, 345
Adoption,   502, 752 et seq. *See also* Child
   overseas, declaration as to,   958
Appointment.
   arbitrator, of,   422
   power of, validity of,   22
   will, by,   539
Arbitration. *See also* Brussels Convention; Contract
   award enforcement of,   577, 613, 733 et seq
      foreign, enforcement of,   622 et seq
      judicial review of,   798
   general provisions as to,   587 et seq
   Protocol on Arbitration Clauses,   628 et seq
   staying proceedings, where,   590, 732
Attorney, power of,   102

Bigamy,   409. *See also* Marriage
Bill of exchange,
   'cheque',   545
   conflict of laws, where,   544
   defined,   543
   title to,   14, 505, 533
Brussels Convention,   818 et seq, 862. See also England; Judgment
   'agency',   63, 435, 482
   appeals,   235, 239, 457, 458, 503
   arbitration,   422
   'civil and commercial matter',   288, 319, 348, 461
   contract within,   26, 136, 157, 161, 204, 350, 386, 415, 475, 479
   divorce,   219
   holiday home,   199
   immovable property,   420, 421, 425, 439, 519

Brussels Convention (continued)
   interpretation of,   259, 369, 420, 421, 435, 820
   judgment,
      application to,   141
      enforcement of,   342, 381, 385
      meaning of,   460
      recognition of,   167, 457
   jurisdiction under,   188, 250, 252, 261, 262, 265, 268, 284, 317, 347, 369, 370, 519, 862
   'matters relating to a contract',   386
   matrimonial proceedings,   137
   modification of,   866, 867
   place of performance,   243, 340, 349, 415, 450, 480, 487
   'place where ... event occurred',   58, 308, 333, 451, 495
   Protocol, 1971, annexed to,   863
   'related cause',   122, 240
   'same cause',   122, 478
   scope of,   862
   service under,   143, 262
   ships, arrest of,   20
   text of,   862
   third parties, claim against,   258

Chattels,
   transfer of,   165
Child. *See also* Domicile
   abduction of,   1, 2, 3, 185, 198, 407, 895 et seq, 921
   adoption, legitimation by,   748
   artificial insemination,   971
   citizenship of,   338
   custody
      of,   34, 186, 197, 223, 296, 371, 905 et seq, 922, 924 et seq
      orders,   923, 931 et seq
   legitimacy
      of,   745 et seq

Child, legitimacy (continued)
    declaration as to, 957
    majority, age of, 314, 679
    marriage of, 335
    orders with respect to, 976 et seq
    passport, surrender of, 941
    parentage, declaration as to, 957
    parental responsibility for, 973–975
    passport, surrender of, 941
    wards of court, 942
    welfare of, 972
    whereabouts of, 917, 938

Company,
  members' liability, 417
  overseas, 369, 984
    name of, 887
    registration of branch of, 882 et seq
    service on, 889, 894
  place of business of, 465, 482, 484
  presence of, 8
  recognition of, 24, 984
  residence of, 95, 135, 159, 285, 472
  seat of, 210, 852

Contract. *See also* Convention; Jurisdiction
  affreightment, of, 29, 285, 412
  applicable law, 979 et seq
  arbitration, 524
  bank account, 281, 282, 344
  bottomry bond, 187
  Brussels Convention, within, 26, 136, 157, 161, 204, 350, 386, 415, 475, 479
  capacity to, 65, 303
  carriage, of, 220, 647 et seq
  choice of law clauses, 772
  consumer, 829, 853
  damages for breach of, 245, 312
  discharge of, 499
  dowry, for, 390
  enforcement of, 67, 419
  English law, subject to, 46, 168, 311, 322, 379
  exclusive jurisdiction clause in, 76, 97, 122, 150, 297, 355, 488
  guarantee, of, 9, 41, 265, 401, 526
  illegal act, for, 226, 297, 412, 419

Contract (continued)
  insurance, of, 16, 179, 277, 297, 350, 352
  international supply, 771
  lease, of, 433
  loan, of, 106, 109, 213, 339, 436, 499
  maintenance, for, 100
  marriage, of, 81, 462
  mortgage, of, 44, 401
  proper law of, 13, 16, 29, 41, 68, 80, 87, 100, 102, 119, 245, 303, 331, 408, 437, 466, 469, 493, 510, 524
  rescision of, 54
  Rome Convention, 982, 983
  sale, of, 94, 190, 261, 345
  stolen goods, 529
  termination of rights under, 156
  undue influence, 242
  unenforceable, 251, 253, 280
  void, 148

Consular premises, 964 et seq

Convention. *See also* Brussels Convention; Hague Convention
  Custody of Children, 905 et seq, 922
  Foreign Arbitral Awards,
    Execution of, 629 et seq
    Recognition and Enforcement of, 733 et seq
  International Carriage of Goods by Road, Contract for, 647
  International Child Abduction, 921
  Lugano, 818 et seq
    interpretation of, 865
    text of, 864 et seq
  Recovery Abroad of Maintenance, 700
  Recognition of Trusts, 963
  Rome (contractual obligations), 979, 982, 983
  State Immunity, 793
  State-owned Ships, 792
  Vienna,
    Consular Relations, on, 652, 663 et seq, 967
    Diplomatic Relations, on, 640, 646 et seq, 676, 967

Conversion,
  action for, 44, 489
  doctrine of, 55

Copyright, 87. *See also* Injunction

Corporation. *See* Company

Damage,
   quantification of, 134, 264, 470
   remoteness of, 134
Debt,
   assignment of, 196
   claim to, 287, 303, 352, 361
   priority, 404
   security for, 237
   tax, of, 233, 366, 428
   transfer of, 244
Demurrage,
   claim to, 180
Diplomatic premises, 964 et seq
Diplomatic privilege. *See* Immunity
Dispute,
   seizure of, 30
Divorce. *See also* Brussels Convention
   decree of,
     deception, obtained by, 257
     recognition of, 18, 27, 50, 62, 103, 129, 133, 173, 232, 236, 315, 325, 353, 403, 405, 947 et seq
     refusal of, 278, 292, 304, 307, 328, 387, 449
     will, effect on, 541
   forum for proceedings for, 138, 318
   ground for, 721
   maintenance on, 217, 221, 353, 532
   overseas, financial relief after, 877 et seq
Domicile,
   association, of, 851
   change of, 139, 194, 272, 289, 411, 426, 523
     will, effect on construction of, 636
   child, of, 52, 396, 730, 731
   choice of, 53, 90, 103, 123, 177, 184, 215, 224, 238, 310, 314, 392, 443, 471, 486, 528, 534
   corporation, of, 851
   Crown, of, 855
   deceased, of, 39
   individuals, of, 850
   'law of the country of', 427
   matrimonial, 158, 176
   origin, of, 59, 177, 209, 414
     revival of, 494
   place of, 21
   trusts, of, 854
   wife, of, 32, 286, 729

Employment, 773
England. *See also* Foreign court; Judgment; Tort
   discovery in, 212, 336
   enforcement in, 42, 66, 67, 83, 117, 118, 203, 211, 293, 356, 359, 416, 437, 440, 500, 808, 810, 823, 835 et seq, 862, 864
     costs, 432
     exemplary damages, 430
     revenue claim, 428
   proceedings in, 60, 61, 79, 85, 151, 169, 170, 248, 269, 290, 320, 347
     alien enemies, 395
     alimony arrears, 51
     consumer contracts, 829
     defence, striking out, 527
     equity, 383
     estoppel, 88, 99, 225, 234, 305, 447, 485, 506, 846
     fraud, 474, 501, 516
     libel, 475
     lien, for, 357
     mortgagee, by, 128
     staying, 31, 41, 109, 121, 160, 162, 174, 210, 235, 270, 299, 356, 358, 370, 385, 433, 469, 488, 509, 526, 928
     tort, for, 101, 126, 127, 147, 149, 294, 295, 312, 326, 333, 337, 341, 389, 418, 437, 451, 466, 842
     trusts, 829
   service in, 89, 155, 301
Evidence. *See also* Foreign law
   false, 553
   foreign proceedings, in, 631, 739 et seq, 807
   registers, of, 567
   statutes, of, 552
Executors. *See also* Will
   de son tort, 351
   title of, 115
Export,
   illegal, 33

Foreign court. *See also* England; Jurisdiction
   jurisdiction of, 89, 518
     ouster of, 10
     submission to, 125
   proceedings in, staying, 25, 138
Foreign law,
   evidence as to, 72, 75, 717

Forum. *See also* Trial
  appropriate, 6, 41, 46, 76, 99, 121, 151, 170, 254, 261, 326, 368, 456, 466, 508
  conveniens, 6, 71, 109, 358, 367, 393, 424
  natural, 12, 91, 138, 170, 355, 459
  selection clause, 76, 97

Garnishee,
  debts, in respect of, 4, 473
  proceedings, 274, 428

Hague Convention,
  adoption of children, relating to, 757 et seq
  child, abduction of, 1, 2, 3, 185, 198, 895 et seq
  Service Abroad, on, 356

Immunity. *See also* Convention
  consular, 652 et seq, 791
  diplomatic, 218, 522, 639 et seq, 791
  international organisation, of, 467, 665 et seq
  sovereign, of, 206, 330, 377, 487
  State, 779 et seq

Injunction,
  copyright, breach of, for, 48, 492
  English court, grant by, 77, 91, 329
  grant of, 459
  Mareva, 35, 144, 175, 321, 360
  refusal of, 110, 152, 305, 424, 455, 464

Intestacy. *See also* Letters of Administration
  administration on, 525
  creditors on, 260
  partial, 131
  statutory legacy, 113
  succession on, 302, 343, 365, 564 et seq, 969

Judgment. *See also* England
  assignment of, 361
  Brussels Convention, application to, 141, 862 et seq
  currency for, 146, 331, 481, 680
  final, 163
  foreign,
    competing, 452

Judgment, foreign (continued)
  effect of, 574
  enforcement of, 7, 164, 189, 229, 247, 293, 342, 437, 559 et seq, 568 et seq
  recognition of, 167, 246, 350, 398, 460, 793, 835 et seq, 843 et seq
  registration of, 569, 648, 823
  United Kingdom, enforcement of, 868, 869

Judicial separation,
  decree of, recognition of, 431, 491, 947 et seq

Jurisdiction. *See also* Foreign court
  assumption of, 393
  Brussels Convention, under, 862
  contract, breach of, 130, 339
  equity, in, 172, 383
  ouster of, 10, 174
  'resident' in, 155
  service out of, 11, 49, 61, 71, 76, 96, 147, 168, 171, 200, 201, 241, 249, 267, 312, 316, 337, 341, 345, 354, 375, 429, 444, 496, 512, 1009 et seq
  submission to, 69, 153, 208, 324, 329, 360, 423, 429, 448, 473, 483, 498, 511, 845

Letters of administration. *See also* Intestacy
  grant of, 112
  recognition of, 681 et seq
  will, annexed with, 306

Lex situs
  application of, 154, 227, 404
  bona vacantia, 343
  devolution according to, 55, 82
  donatio mortis causa, 266
  immovables, of, 80, 132, 182, 346, 383, 388, 391, 427, 520
  personal property, of, 86
  ship, of, 93

Limitation,
  foreign law of, 870 et seq
  period of, 78, 207, 228, 814 et seq

Lugano Convention, 864 et seq
  interpretation of, 865

Maintenance,
  Convention, 700

Index

Maintenance (continued
  financial provision, application for,   775 et seq
  liability for,   217, 221, 353, 532, 579
  order,
    currency for,   827
    enforcement of,   554, 684 et seq, 812 et seq, 824, 848
    making of,   556, 686
    variation of,   558, 687, 691
Marriage. *See also* Divorce; Nullity
  buildings for,   583
  declarations as to,   957
  dissolution of,   103, 491
  foreign,   546 et seq, 725
  implied contract on,   139
  law as to,   56, 93, 406, 441
  lawful son of,   454
  legitimation by,   17, 28, 191, 193, 195, 746
    declaration as to,   957
  maintenance, claim for,   376
  offences,   585
  polygamous,   728
    potentially,   15, 37, 104, 105, 230, 231, 335, 364, 410, 998–1000
  prohibited degrees, within,   581, 586, 630
  proxy, by,   23, 394
  treatment of,   985
  'unmarried person',   442
  validity of,   105, 106, 222, 263, 273, 300, 335, 362, 364, 380, 382, 394, 397, 463, 468, 477, 486, 506, 515, 531
    solemnised abroad,   546
  void,   57, 73, 81, 84, 123, 124, 257, 275, 327, 373, 402, 462, 582, 722
  voidable,   378, 723, 724, 985
  will, revocation of, by,   310, 540

Nationalisation,
  recognition of,   19
Negligence,
  high seas, on,   101
  liability for,   36, 70, 294, 298, 313, 514
Nullity,
  decree of,
    effect of,   726
    maintenance on,   374
    petition for,   73, 84, 107, 140, 394, 413, 453, 476

Nullity, decree of (continued)
  recognition of,   5, 98, 192, 279, 323, 334, 374, 384, 434, 947 et seq

Partner,
  action against,   64
  land of,   205
  unenforceable agreement,   181
Presumption,
  advancement, of,   166
  court, as to,   110
  death, as to,   111
  marriage, as to validity of,   300, 410
  proper law, as to,   40
Probate. *See* Will

Relationships,
  general principle,   968

Settlement,
  marriage,   176, 445, 504, 507
  trustees of, claim against,   145
  validity of,   45
  withdrawal from,   271
Ships,
  arrest of,   20, 40
  claim to,   120
  collision between,   101, 506, 518
  lex citus of,   92
  lien on,   202, 535
  offences on,   656
  repairs to,   116
Statute,
  extra-territorial effect,   276
  proof of,   552
Stock,
  repayment of,   68

Tort. *See also* England
  choice of law,   1001 et seq
Trading interests,
  protection of,   804 et seq
Treaty,
  European,   718 et seq, 988 et seq
  Rome, of,   342
Trespass,
  action for,   79, 216, 842
Trial,
  place of,   6, 12
Trust,
  fund, entitlement to,   255
  payment from,   446

Trust (continued)
    proceedings, 829
    recognition of, 962

Will. *See also* Appointment; Divorce; Domicile; Executors; Marriage
    adopted son, rights under, 309
    capacity to make, 183, 537
    English, inheritance under, 59
    formal requirements, 538, 633–635
    holograph, 399
    land, gift of, by, 108, 178, 332, 346, 363, 388, 427, 521

Will (continued)
    movables, gift of, by, 291, 363, 490
    probate of, 517
        recognition of, 681 et seq
    proof of contents of, 183
    trust for sale, 391

Writ. *See also* Jurisdiction
    extension of, 400
    foreign court, issued by, 89
    probate of, 114
    service of, 47, 155, 301, 400
    setting aside, 120, 130, 516, 530